W0006136

GALILEO

IMAGES OF THE UNIVERSE FROM ANTIQUITY TO THE TELESCOPE

edited by

Paolo Galluzzi

Under the High Patronage
of the President
of the Italian Republic

GALILEO.
IMAGES OF THE UNIVERSE FROM ANTIQUITY TO THE TELESCOPE

Florence
Palazzo Strozzi
13 March-30 August
2009

with the sponsorship of the
Ministero per i Beni e le Attività Culturali
Ministero degli Affari Esteri
ESA-European Space Agency

Promoted and organised by

and

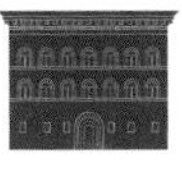

with the support of

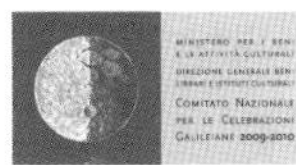

Scientific direction

Concept and direction of the exhibition
Paolo Galluzzi

Scientific Committee
Cristina Acidini (President)
Jim Bennett
Maria Giovanna Biga
Fabrizio Bònoli
Filippo Camerota
Giovanni di Pasquale
Paolo Galluzzi
Pietro Giovanni Guzzo
Hermann Hunger
David King
Eugenio Lo Sardo
Marco Ramazzotti
Alessandro Roccati
Gloria Rosati
Giorgio Strano
Albert Van Helden

Realisation of the exhibition
Fondazione Palazzo Strozzi

in collaboration with the
Istituto e Museo di Storia della Scienza
Organisational coordination and scientific secretariat
Laura Manetti, with the collaboration
of Giulia Fiorenzoli and Elisa Bonaiuti

Exhibition design
Gris Co., Padua
Studio Cupellini, Florence

Communication and exhibition graphic design
RovaiWeber design

Exhibition installation
Opera Laboratori Fiorentini S.p.A.

Electrical systems
Bagnoli srl

Security manager
Ulderigo Frusi

Preventive conservation
and climate control
Marco Ciatti, Roberto Boddi
(Opificio delle Pietre Dure di Firenze)

Exhibits, working models and copies
Concept
Filippo Camerota, Giovanni di Pasquale,
Paolo Galluzzi, Marco Ramazzotti, Giorgio Strano
Realisation
Opera Laboratori Fiorentini S.p.A.
Stella Battaglia and Gianni Miglietta with
the collaboration of Sergio Rubini and Florence
Wenig-Lynds.
Centro Studi per il Restauro e la Valorizzazione
degli Orologi Antichi e Strumentaria,
ITIS "Leonardo da Vinci", Florence (Giorgio Burzio,
Fulvio Grazzini, Andrea Palmieri, Daniele Pieri)

Facsimiles
Philobiblion di Claudius Schettino

Films and multimedia applications
Concept
Filippo Camerota, Malvina Borgherini, Natacha Fabbri,
Paolo Galluzzi, Emanuele Garbin, Eugenio Lo Sardo,
Giorgio Strano, Michael T. Wright
Realisation
Istituto e Museo di Storia della Scienza - Multimedia
department: Jacopo Tonini (coordination),
Luisa Barattin, Andrea Braghiroli, Fabio Corica, Silvia
Paoli, Monica Tassi, Daniela Vespoli
Istituto Universitario di Architettura di Venezia
Massimo Mogi Vicentini

Iconographic coordination
Istituto e Museo di Storia della Scienza:
Franca Principe, with the collaboration of Sabina
Bernacchini, Susanna Cimmino, Giovanni Volante

Exhibition texts
Paolo Galluzzi

Translation of exhibition texts
Stephen Tobin

Translation of films and multimedia
Catherine Frost

Communication and promotion
Susanna Holm
Sigma CSC

Press office
Catola&Partners (national press office)
Sue Bond Public Relations (international press office)

Reservations service
Sigma CSC

Websites
Fondazione Palazzo Strozzi - Netribe
(www.palazzostrozzi.org)
Istituto e Museo di Storia della Dcienza Web department: Iolanda Rolfo (coordination), Marco Berni, Sara Bonechi, Fabrizio Butini, Leonardo Curioni, Elena Fani, Roberta Massaini
(http://brunelleschi.imss.fi.it/galileopalazzostrozzi)

Family itinerary concept
James M. Bradburne

Illustrations for the family itinerary
Peter Sís

Texts for the family itinerary
James M. Bradburne
Ludovica Sebregondi

"Discovery trail for the Starry Messenger's Saddlebag"
L'immaginario

Consultant for the family itinerary
Lara Albanese

Workshops and educational activities
Sigma CSC

Educational programmes for families in English
Devorah Block
Elizabeth Molina

Editorial projects coordinator
Ludovica Sebregondi

Audio guides
Antennaudio

Insurance
Aon Artscope

Fine art transport
Arteria

Exhibition and ticket office
TML Service

Multi-channel ticket office
Vivaticket by Charta

Restorations
Ditta Triana Ariè associata Arianna Ariè, Rome
Silvia Bensi, conservazione e restauro dipinti e sculture lignee, Florence
Paolo Belluzzo, Conservazione e Restauro Beni Culturali, Malnate
Biblioteca Nazionale Centrale di Firenze, Laboratorio di restauro: Gisella Guasti, Alessandro Sidoti, Silvia Medagliani
Clepsydra, Catherine Oudoin-Lorenz, Klaus Lorenz, Pinsac
Loredana Gallo, Florence
Bibliothèque de l'Observatoire de Paris: Olivier Morel
Restauro Conservativo d'opere d'arte su carta di Sergio Boni, Florence
Estudio de conservación y restauración de tapices Pepa Garrido, Velilla de San Antonio
Bettina von Gilsa, Tübingen
L'Officina del Restauro Srl, Florence
Opificio delle Pietre Dure, Florence: Clarice Innocenti, Cinzia Ortolani
Andrea Palmieri, Florence
Philobiblion di Claudius Schettino, Florence
Andrea Rabbi, Florence

Lenders
Musée Boucher de Perthes, Abbeville
Museo di Fisica, Università di Bologna, Bologna
Museo della Specola, Università di Bologna, Bologna
Santa Giulia, Museo della Città, Brescia
Collezione Palazzo Foresti, Carpi
Musei Vaticani, Vatican City
Crawford Library of the Royal Observatory, Edinburgh
Biblioteca Marucelliana, Florence
Biblioteca Medicea-Laurenziana, Florence
Biblioteca Nazionale Centrale, Florence
Biblioteca Riccardiana, Florence
Comune di Firenze, Museo Bardini, Florence
Gabinetto Disegni e Stampe degli Uffizi, Florence
Galleria degli Uffizi, Florence
Istituto e Museo di Storia della Scienza, Florence
Museo Egizio, Florence
San Salvatore in Ognissanti, Florence
Soprintendenza Speciale per il Patrimonio Storico, Artistico ed Etnoantropologico e per il Polo Museale della città di Firenze, Florence
National Maritime Museum, Ministry of Defence Art Collection, Greenwich
British Library, London
British Museum, Department of Greek and Roman Antiquities, London
British Museum, Department of Middle East, London
Royal Astronomical Society, London
Science Museum, London
Michael Wright, London
Biblioteca Statale, Lucca
Museo Nacional del Prado, Madrid
Römisch-Germanisches Zentralmuseum, Mainz
Museo Civico Archeologico, Matelica
Accademia di Belle Arti di Brera, Milan
Biblioteca dell'Osservatorio Astronomico di Brera, Milan
Galleria e Museo Estense, Modena
Museo Archeologico, Naples
Museo di Capodimonte, Naples
Germanisches National Museum, Nürnberg
Biblioteca Comunale "Francesco Cini", Osimo
All Souls College, Oxford
Museum of the History of Science, Oxford
Capitolo dei Canonici della Cattedrale di Padova, Padua
Bibliothèque nationale de France, Paris
Collezione Kugel, Paris
Musée des arts et métiers - Conservatoire national des arts et métiers, Paris
Musée du Louvre, Département des Antiquités grecques, étrusques et romaines, Paris
Observatoire de Paris, Bibliothèque, Paris
Musei Civici, Pavia
Collezione Egremont, Petworth-West Sussex
Soprintendenza Speciale per i Beni Archeologici di Napoli e Pompei, Pompeii
National Technical Museum, Prague
Biblioteca Casanatense, Rome
Comune di Roma, Soprintendenza per i Beni Culturali, Museo della Civiltà Romana, Rome
Galleria Spada, Rome
Musei Capitolini, Rome
Museo Barracco, Rome
Museo Nazionale Romano, Rome
Osservatorio Astronomico, Rome
Archivio di Stato, Siena
Cabildo Catedral Primada, Toledo
Biblioteca Nazionale Universitaria di Torino, Turin
Fondazione Museo delle Antichità Egizie, Turin
Soprintendenza per i Beni Archeologici del Piemonte, Turin
Eberhard Karls-Universität, Tübingen
Fondazione Marzotto, Valdagno

Fondazione Musei Civici di Venezia, Museo Correr, Venice
Rudolf Schmidt, Vienna
Technisches Museum, Vienna
Heide Wohlschläger, Vienna

Acknowledgements

The Fondazione Palazzo Strozzi would like to express its most sincere thanks to Miel de Botton-Aynsley.

We also thank for their precious collaboration: Richard Aspin, Massimo Batoni, Dean Baylis, Laurence Bobis, Angelo Bottini, Alison Boyle, Margherita Breccia Fratadocchi, Paolo Brenni, Alberta Campitelli, Daniela Carrara, Andrea Clarke, Enrico Colle, Luciano Comacchio, Harold Cooke, Elena Corradini, Peter Damerow, Robert Davies, Stefano De Luca, Paolo Del Santo, Elisa Di Renzo, Giorgio Dragoni, Rita El Asmar, Maurizio Fallace, Silvia Ferino, Antonia Ida Fontana, Rafael García Serrano, Maurizio Ghelardi, Gianna Gheri, Owen Gingerich, Franco Giudice, Michael J. Gorman, Maria Cristina Guidotti, Alexis Kugel, Helmut Lackner, Domenico Laurenza, Giovanna Lazzi, Alessandra Lenzi, Claudio Leonardi, Michel Lerner, Jay Levenson, Luca Lombroso, Ivana Lorenzini, Agnese Mandrino, Giorgio Marini, Margherita Marrulli, Giangiacomo Martinez, Alfredo Melgar, Mons. Antonio Meneguolo, Elena Montali, Angela Napoletano, Antonio Natali, Lynne Otten, Francesco Palla, Marco Paoli, Antonio Paolucci, Anna Passavanti, Vittoria Perrone Compagni, Carla Pinzauti, Eufemia Piizzi, Emmanuel Poulle, Maria Prunai Falciani, Paulus Rainer, Giovanna Rao, Hélène Richard, Giandomenico Romanelli, Beate Salje, D. Juan Sánchez Rodríguez, Valérie Sauvestre, Alessandro Savorelli, Luciano Scala, Marisa Scarso, Marion Schikel, Francesca Spatafora, Carlo Sisi, Silvia Spinelli, Felice Stoppa, Walter Tega, Lucia Tomasi Tongiorgi, Camillo Tonini, Isabella Truci, Pasquale Tucci, Carlos Turillo Sánchez, as well as Fondazione Sistema Toscana JLT Yacht Agency and Time Concept-Custos Italia.

We thank the private collectors for their generous contributions.

We would also like to thank Ron Cordover; Martin Rees, Astronomer Royal, Presidente della Royal Society and Master of King's College, Cambridge; David King and Lara Albanese for the scientific precision with which they have examined the texts for children and families; as well as Wanny di Filippo - Il Bisonte for having furnished the knapsacks for the family itinerary, Arrigo Berni and Roberto Di Puma for the Moleskine diaries.

Sponsors

Canon

Catalogue

GIUNTI

Edited by
Paolo Galluzzi

Entries by
A.A. - Alessia Amenta
D.B. - Danilo Baldini
J.B. - Jim A. Bennett
J.Be. - Jonathan Betts
M.G.B. - Maria Giovanna Biga
L.B. - Laurence Bobis
S.B. - Sara Bonechi
A.B. - Alison Boyle
M.C. - Marinella Calisi
F.C. - Filippo Camerota
E.D.A. - Elvira D'Amicone
E.D.C. - Ernesto De Carolis
G.D.P. - Giovanni di Pasquale
G.D. - Giorgio Dragoni
N.F. - Natacha Fabbri
G.F.V. - Graziella Federici Vescovini
P.G. - Paolo Galluzzi
M.J.G. - Michael J. Gorman
A.G. - Andrea Gualandi
H.H. - Hermann Hunger
D.K. - David A. King
A.M.L. - Anna Maria Liberati
A.M. - Alexander Marr
M.Mi. - Marica Milanesi
M.M. - Mara Miniati
A.N. - Angela Napoletano
G.P. - Gabriella Pomaro
E.P. - Emmanuel Poulle
M.R. - Marco Ramazzotti
G.R. - Gloria Rosati
P.S. - Paola Salvi
A.S. - Alessandro Savorelli
R.S. - Rudolf Schmidt
G.S. - Giorgio Strano
F.T. - Federico Tognoni
A.T. - Alessandro Tosi
H.W. - Heide Wohlschläger
M.T.W. - Michael T. Wright

Managing editor
Claudio Pescio

Coordination and secretariat
Patricia Lurati

Editor
Dario Dondi

Editorial collaboration
Francesca Barberotti, Catherine Frost,
M. Lucrezia Galleschi

Iconographic research
Aurelia Nicolosi

Translation
Alicia Faraoni, Barbara Fisher, Catherine Frost,
Madeira Giacci,
NTL Traduzioni, Florence (Patrick Creagh,
Janice Loggans)

Graphic design, pagination and cover
RovaiWeber design

Technical coordination
Alessio Conticini

Photolithograph
Fotolito Toscana

Photograph credits
© 1990. Foto Opera Metropolitana Siena/Scala, Florence; © 1990. Foto Scala, Florence; © 1990. Foto Scala, Florence - with the permission of the Ministero Beni e Attività Culturali; © 2003. Foto Scala, Florence - with the permission of the Ministero Beni e Attività Culturali; © 2008. Foto Scala, Florence - with the permission of the Ministero Beni e Attività Culturali; Accademia di Belle Arti di Brera, Milano; Archivio del Museo Astronomico e Copernicano, Rome; Archivio Fotografico-Soprintendenza per i Beni Archeologici delle Marche-Ancona; Archivio Fotografico dei Musei Capitolini/photo: Maria Teresa Natale; Archivio Fotografico Fondazione Musei Civici di Venezia; Archivio fotografico Musei Vaticani/photo: Luigi Giordano, Pietro Zigrossi, Mauro Sarri; Attilio Valeri, ITIS "Leonardo da Vinci", Florence; Biblioteca Casanatense, Roma/photo: Mario Setter; Biblioteca Comunale 'F.Cini', Osimo (An); Biblioteca Medicea Laurenziana, Florence / photo: Donato Pineider; GAP S.r.l.; Biblioteca Nazionale Centrale, Florence /photo: Mario Setter/ GAP S.r.l.; Biblioteca Nazionale Universitaria di Torino; Biblioteca Riccardiana Firenze/ photo: Donato Pineider; GAP s.r.l.; Bibliothèque de l'Observatoire de Paris; BnF; © British Library Board. All Rights Reserved; Cabildo Primado, Toledo; Chiesa di San Salvatore in Ognissanti; Collezione Kugel, Parigi; Collezione Marzotto, Valdagno (Vi); Collezione Palazzo Foresti-Carpi (Mo); Comune di Roma; Crawford Library of The Royal Observatory Edinburgh; Deutsches Museum, Münich; Donato Pineider, Florence; Erwin Withaker, Tucson; © Fondazione Museo Antichità Egizie di Torino - all rights reserved; Foto Studio Bartalini, Certaldo (Fi); Fotografica Foglia S.a.s. di Alfredo e Pio Foglia, Naples; Fotostudio I Rappuzzi; Fototeca dei Musei Comunali di Firenze; Fototeca della Soprintendenza per il P.S.A.E. e del Polo Museale della città di Napoli; Fototeca Musei Civici di Pavia; GAP S.r.l.; Germanisches Nationalmuseum, Norimberga; GNM/photo: M. Runge; Istituto e Museo di Storia della Scienza, Florence; Istituto Nazionale di Astrofisica-Osservatorio astronomico di Brera, Milan; Lord Egremont; Lucca, Biblioteca Statale/photo: E. Ghilardi; Michael T. Wright, London; Michael Wright/ photo: Robert Bigio; Ministero per i Beni e le Attività Culturali-Soprintendenza per i Beni Archeologici del Piemonte e del Museo Antichità Egizie/photo: Lovera Giacomo; Musée Boucher de Perthes; Museo de Santa Cruz, Toledo; Museo della Civiltà Romana/photo: Fotografica Foglia s.a.s di Alfredo e Pio Foglia; Museo della Specola, Università di Bologna; Museo delle Antichità Egizie, Turin; Museo di Fisica, Università di Bologna; Museo Nacional del Prado, Madrid; Museum of the History of Science, Oxford; Národní Tchnické Muzeum, Prague; Osservatorio Astronomico, Padua; Photo National Technical Museum Prague; Photo: Manfred Grohe; Museo Barracco, Photo: Studio Idini; © Photoservice Electa/AISA; © Photoservice Electa/Anelli; © Photoservice Electa/Anelli - with the permission of the Ministero per i Beni e le Attività Culturali; © Photoservice Electa/Leemage Römisch-Germanisches Zentralmuseu/ photo: Sabine Steidl. The copyright is restricted to the Galileo exhibition 2009 only; © RMN/© Hervé Lewandowski; Royal Astronomical Society/SSPL; Rudolf Schmidt, Vienna; S.S.P.S.A.E. e per il Polo Museale della città di Firenze Gabinetto Fotografico; Sächsische Landesbibliothek-Staats- und Universitätsbibliothek, Dresda; Science Museum, London; Science Museum/SSPL; Siena, Archivio di Stato. Authorisation no. 770/2009; Soprintendenza per i Beni Archeologici della Toscana; Soprintendenza per i Beni Storici, Artistici ed Etnoantropologici di Modena e Reggio Emilia Galleria Estense, Archivio Fotografico; Soprintendenza Speciale per i Beni Archeologici di Napoli e Pompei/photo: Fotografica Foglia S.a.s di Alfredo e Pio Foglia; ; Soprintendenza Speciale per i Beni Archeologici di Roma; Soprintendenza Speciale per il Patrimonio Storico, Artistico ed Etnoantropologico e per il Polo Museale della città di Roma; Stefano Lampredi, Florence; The Röhsska Museum, Göteborg, Sweden/ photo: Mikael Lammgård; The Trustees of the British Museum; Villa Borghese, Rome; © Musée des arts et métiers-Cnam, Paris/photo C. Le Toquin; © Musée des arts et métiers-Cnam, Paris/photo S. Pelly; © National Maritime Museum, Greenwich, London;© The Trustees of the British Museum; © TMW- Archiv.
The works of art conserved in the Galleries, Museums and Libraries of the Italian State are reproduced with the permission of the Ministero per i Beni e le Attività Culturali.

ENTE
CASSA DI RISPARMIO
DI FIRENZE

FONDAZIONE
PALAZZO
STROZZI

Via Bolognese 165 - 50139 Firenze - Italia
Via Dante 4 - 20121 Milano - Italia

www.giunti.it

First edition: March 2009

Reprint	Year
5 4 3 2 1 0	2012 2011 2010 2009

Printed by Giunti Industrie Grafiche S.p.A. - Prato

TABLE OF CONTENTS

Presentations

13 Edoardo Speranza
14 Lorenzo Bini Smaghi
15 Cristina Acidini
16 Paolo Cocchi
17 Antonia Ida Fontana Aschero

Introduction

18 Paolo Galluzzi

I - THE ANCIENT WORLD

1 - The Dawn of Astronomy: Mesopotamia, Egypt and the Biblical Cosmos

29 *The Sources of Egyptian Astronomy*
Alessandro Roccati
35 *The Legacy of Egyptian Astronomy*
Edoardo Detoma
41 *Babylonian Astronomy*
Hermann Hunger
47 *Astrology and Divinatory Practices in the Royal Courts and among the Peoples of the Ancient Near East*
Maria Giovanna Biga
55 *A Presage of Heresy. Metaphysical Notes and Iconographic Themes for an Archaeology of the Mesopotamian Skies*
Marco Ramazzotti

2 - The Cosmos Becomes a Sphere

61 *Images of the Cosmos among the Greek philosophers*
Giovanni di Pasquale
67 *Graeco-Alexandrine Mathematical Astronomy*
Giorgio Strano
75 *Myths and Stars in Classical Greece*
Eugenio Lo Sardo

3 - The Geometry of the Cosmos

85 *Astrology, Power and Image of the Cosmos in Rome*
Giovanni di Pasquale
93 *Agriculture and the Stars*
Annamaria Ciarallo
97 *Star Myths in Vesuvian Painting*
Ernesto De Carolis

II - THE MIDDLE AGES

4 - The Skies of Islam

163 *Islamic Astronomy*
David A. King

5 - Evangelisation of the Cosmos

173 *The Christianising of Astronomy*
Stefano Caroti
181 *The Astrological Vision of Man and the Universe in the Middle Ages*
Graziella Federici Vescovini

III - FROM RENAISSANCE TO THE SCIENTIFIC REVOLUTION

6 - The Renaissance of Astronomy

219 *The Astronomical Instruments of the Renaissance*
Jim Bennett
227 *Copernicus and Tycho: the Two Faces of Reform in Astronomy*
Giorgio Strano
235 *Brief History of Celestial Cartography in the Western World*
Felice Stoppa
243 *Celestial Globes*
Rudolf Schmidt

7 - Galileo: the Cosmos through the Telescope

247 *Galileo's Telescopes and his Astronomical Discoveries*
Albert van Helden
255 *Representations and Maps of the Moon. The First Two Centuries*
Ewen A. Withaker
263 *Identification and Dating of Galileo's Observations of the Moon*
Ewen A. Withaker

8 - From Galileo to Newton

269 *The Harmony of the Spheres from Pythagoras to Kircher*
Natacha Fabbri
277 *The First Modern Observatories*
Fabrizio Bònoli
289 *Origins and Affirmation of the Universe-Machine*
Paolo Galluzzi

415 *Installation project*
417 *Bibliography*

Edoardo Speranza
Chairman
Ente Cassa di Risparmio di Firenze

Four hundred years ago Galileo aimed a telescope at the sky and opened the way to space exploration.

The Earth suddenly lost its 'centrality' in the eyes of human beings, whose thoughts turned elsewhere. Still today, the disparity between the technological means available and the sphere of the infinitely large is too great; but thanks to that gesture, which shifted the focus of observation, it is possible to think of other worlds even beyond our solar system, to formulate hypotheses, to imagine that we are not alone to enjoy the benefits bestowed by creation.

To those who may object, not without reason, that the gap between our violent world and the world of dreams almost within our reach, up there among the stars, is still today a nearly insuperable barrier, it could be answered with reasonable approximation that some solutions to difficult problems to be solved at our own latitudes might be sought in different contexts and dimensions.

Meanwhile, scientific research will inevitably take its course. The Ente Cassa di Risparmio di Firenze, also during the International Year of Astronomy declared by the United Nations, continues to support this sphere of activity, as regards both basic research conducted in the centres of excellence found in Florence and its region, and participation in projects for promoting scientific culture in its multifaceted expressions. The Galilean celebrations in particular, reaching their peak in the Tuscan capital with the great exhibition held at Palazzo Strozzi, promoted and produced by the Ente Cassa di Risparmio, have provided the occasion for implementing major projects, also financed by the Ente, such as renovation of the exhibition halls of the Museo di Storia della Scienza and those of the Museo della Specola, while the City welcomes the initiatives of the Big Little Scientific Museums that represent, as our foundation believes, the squaring of the circle in regard to what has already been done for the historic artistic and architectural heritage found throughout the territory.

And lastly, the Year of Astronomy and of Galileo, at the moment of international crisis we are now experiencing, is a stimulus for revitalizing human activity in all of its diverse manifestations.

Lorenzo Bini Smaghi
Chairman
Fondazione Palazzo Strozzi

The United Nations has declared the year 2009 'The Year of Astronomy' and its slogan is 'The Universe: yours to discover'. There has never been a more perfect time to celebrate Galileo - a universal genius who belongs both to Tuscany, and to the world.

From March 13 to August 30, 2009, the Palazzo Strozzi is hosting the exhibition *Galileo: Images of the Universe from Antiquity to the Telescope*, which represents the centrepiece of Italy's celebration of Galileo's observations of the moon through his newly perfected telescope. Although the instrument had been invented in the Netherlands in 1608, and used for the first time to observe the moon by Thomas Harriot, Galileo demonstrated a simple telescope to the Venetian Senate on August 25th, 1609, and subsequently used it to observe the moon and the 'wandering stars'. Galileo was the first to publish his observations, which appeared in a short pamphlet entitled *Sidereus nuncius* [Starry Messenger] in March 1610. There has probably been no greater revolution in the history of humankind than when Galileo turned his crude telescope towards the stars twinkling in limitless space above the dark Tuscan hills. Galileo not only stands at the end of the long tradition of positional astronomy told in the exhibition, but at the beginning of modern astronomy. Now astronomers look at the stars not only using the limited spectrum of visible light, but across the full range of wavelengths from the very smallest gamma rays to the very largest radio waves.

In addition to the curator, Professor Paolo Galluzzi, Director of the Istituto e Museo di Storia della Scienza in Florence and all the professionals who have helped create the exhibition, the Fondazione Palazzo Strozzi would especially like to thank the partners and sponsors of *Galileo: Images of the Universe from Antiquity to the Telescope*, including the Province of Florence, the City of Florence, the Florentine Chamber of Commerce, the Association of Partners of Palazzo Strozzi and the Regione Toscana, all of whom strongly supported the exhibition from the outset. The Fondazione Palazzo Strozzi would like to thank in particular the Ente Cassa di Risparmio di Firenze, the exhibition's main sponsor, which generously contributed to its success, as well as the Aeroporto di Firenze, Alitalia, APT, ATAF, Canon, Firenze Parcheggi, IKEA Family, Tuscana Promozione, Unicoop and Miel de Botto-Aynsley, without whose contributions the exhibition would have been much poorer. Lastly we would like to thank the entire Fondazione Palazzo Strozzi team - its Board of Directors, its Advisory Board, its Director and its staff - for having worked so hard to create an exhibition that gives renewed meaning to the Palazzo Strozzi's slogan 'think global, and act local'.

Cristina Acidini
Soprintendente per il Patrimonio Storico, Artistico ed Etnoantropologico e per il Polo Museale della città di Firenze

In re-reading the *Iliad* I am suddenly brought up against a 'bronze-like sky' that has always constituted a dilemma for translators and commentators. Why did Homer, whoever he was, describe the heavenly vault as bronze-like? Was it because - like the ceiling of an apartment, which is the floor of the one above it - it formed the precious metallic paving of the palace inhabited by the supernal gods? Or because it was illusorily concave, smooth, gleaming golden like a shield? Or because it let loose, at the command of Zeus, the blinding glare of lightening and the rumbling peal of thunder? Or because it was hard and inexorable, like an immense goblet enclosing all human misfortune? We could go on and on without ever circumscribing the sense of wonder and mystery in this expression, one of the many left us by the ancient world in its attempt to explain the astral and meteorological signs drawn from the uncontrollable activity of the heavens above, and even, through astrology and divination, to make use of them.

I am thus fascinated by this exhibition which, under the sign of Galileo and his perfecting of the telescope, the instrument crucial to the birth of modern astronomy, leads the visitor backwards in time through civilisations and epochs, pursuing elusive truths and impossible answers that began and ended in the most vertiginous expanse the human eye can gaze on, the sky.

The exhibition designed by Paolo Galluzzi and his collaborators (backed from its inception by the Ente Cassa di Risparmio di Firenze and its President Edoardo Speranza, with their customary clear vision of supporting Florentine and Tuscan excellence) finds admirable implementation by the Fondazione Palazzo Strozzi, and future commemoration in the beautiful catalogue produced by Giunti Arte Mostre Musei.

As can be easily seen merely by strolling through the exhibition halls or leafing through the catalogue, the exhibition is much more than a collection of images, although the judicious selection of iconographical material opens many doors in history, in the history of science, and in the lives of eminent personages. It is instead the multi-millenarian history of an elusive concept, transposed into a myriad of texts, treatises, illustrations, objects, verses of poetry and much more, destined to become a reality that is knowable and, one day, measurable. We find ourselves standing at the origins of modern science, with its burden of moral questions, ethical issues and contradictory beliefs that have lost none of their topicality, although today no one is forced by others to recite the formulas of abjuration.

The vitality of the exhibition's themes, emerging recurrently and in various forms during the stimulating debates of the International Scientific Committee which I have the honour of directing, makes of this initiative (with the many others contemporary to and correlated with it) a milestone in critical consciousness as well as a goldmine of knowledge for all those who visit or revisit it. Nothing could be better for Florence, I believe, with its younger generations to be initiated into the glory and weight of history and with its international public of visitors, than to celebrate Galileo and his invention.

Paolo Cocchi
Assessore alla Cultura, Commercio e Turismo
Regione Toscana

In 1609 Galileo Galilei built a telescope, not the first but certainly one of the most powerful of the day. He aimed it at the sky and, trusting that what appeared to his eyes 'fortified' by the instrument was not an optical illusion but a hitherto unknown reality, the Pisan scientist opened the doors to modern science. Observation, experimentation, the rationality of mathematical calculations were the cornerstones of Galileo's new scientific method.

In 2009, the year dedicated by the United Nations to astronomy (International Year of Astronomy - IYA2009), the whole world is commemorating the life and work of the great Pisan scientist. Tuscany, Galileo's homeland, is obviously one of the leaders in the Galilean celebrations. Among the many initiatives scheduled, the exhibition *Galileo. Images of the Universe from Antiquity to the Telescope*, presented by the Fondazione Palazzo Strozzi, is undoubtedly one of the most important. In this exhibition, scientific rigour joins hands with the ability to speak to the public at large, facilitating the comprehension of complex ideas also through the intelligent use of multimedia technology. Precious one-of-a-kind pieces, first among them the original telescope of Galileo, as well as archaeological exhibits, paintings, astronomical atlases, priceless manuscripts coming from museums and libraries all over the world, make his exhibition a truly unique occasion to explore and reflect on the long journey travelled by human beings in their drive to understand nature and discover her laws.

The Regione Toscana has grasped the occasion of the 'Galilean' year not only to commemorate the innovating genius of the Pisan scientist but also to encourage reflection on the prospects for scientific culture in Italy today. Unfortunately, many young people today, as we know, encounter difficulty in pursuing scientific studies. This is due to a harmful and artificial distinction between scientific studies and humanist knowledge, a separation unknown to Galileo and the men of his age, who called themselves, with good reason, 'natural philosophers' rather than 'scientists'. It is the task of the institutions, we believe, to ensure that science is no longer viewed by the young as something abstract, 'too hard', perhaps even less 'noble' than humanist studies. This is why we have strongly urged that special attention be shown to children and young people in all of the Tuscan initiatives commemorating Galileo. The exhibition *Galileo. Images of the Universe from Antiquity to the Telescope* has fully satisfied this requisite, and for this reason too the Regione Toscana has whole-heartedly supported the initiative.

In 1632 Galileo decided to publish his most famous work, the *Dialogo sopra i due massimi sistemi del mondo* [Dialogue on the two chief world systems], written not in Latin, the language of the erudite, but in the Italian vulgar tongue. His purpose was that of making known to all - to merchants, artisans, the people - the Copernican hypothesis on the structure of the universe: a great work of rigorous scientific divulging. Today as well, the best way of communicating scientific knowledge to a vast public must be found. We believe that the exhibition dedicated to Galileo by the Fondazione Palazzo Strozzi is a highly positive example of how this can and should be done.

Antonia Ida Fontana Aschero
Comitato Nazionale per le celebrazioni del IV centenario dell'invenzione del cannocchiale di Galileo Galilei
Director
Biblioteca Nazionale Centrale di Firenze

In the year that UNESCO has dedicated to astronomy in commemoration of the first astronomical observations, the Comitato Nazionale per le Celebrazioni Galileiane, instituted by the Ministero per i Beni e le Attività Culturali, has offered, within the terms of its role and its limited economic resources, support to the major initiatives and coordination among the principal institutions involved in the three Galilean cities par excellence: Florence, Pisa and Padua.

Each of these cities has chosen a particular theme, thus creating a strikingly effective overall fresco: the representation of the cosmos from antiquity to modern times in Florence, the relationship between science and art in Pisa, and the future of science in Padua.

After the exhibition curated by the Biblioteca Nazionale Centrale of Florence and the Accademia della Crusca, *Galileo and the Universe of his Books*, which, through autograph works, documents and precious annotated volumes, surveyed the library of the scientist and humanist, offering visitors a chance to trace the sources and see what kind of books he had at his disposal, the exhibition *Galileo. Images of the Universe from Antiquity to the Telescope* provides an exceptional occasion for understanding how greatly the Pisan scientist contributed to the modern world's vision of the cosmos.

Thanks to the extraordinary competence and organisational expertise of the curator Paolo Galluzzi and the Scientific Committee as a whole, the public can not only discover the heritage of a remote past, works of art, ancient scientific instruments, autograph manuscript, but will also be guided through a journey between the real and the virtual, where highly innovative digital products and models serve a crucially important educational purpose.

It is with special pleasure that I recall the collaboration offered to the exhibition by the Biblioteca Nazionale Centrale, custodian of the Galilean archive, which includes among other things the autograph manuscript of the *Sidereus Nuncius* [Starry Messenger], the true protagonist of this year's events. The activity of studying and cataloguing their respective scientific archives in which the Biblioteca has collaborated over the years with the Istituto e Museo di Storia della Scienza is basic to this exhibition, bearing witness to how the dissemination and promotion of Italy's cultural heritage must always include collaboration among the various institutions. An interdisciplinary vision of this kind can better satisfy society's demand for knowledge, a need even more urgently felt in the scientific field, which appears disregarded in our country even by the younger generations, with the risk of neglecting a primary resource of social and economic development.

Introduction

Paolo Galluzzi

It is highly probable that, in the spring of 1609, just four hundred years ago, strange objects formed of a short cardboard tube with two lenses fixed at the ends were already being sold in the narrow streets of Venice. These curious devices, through which persons, buildings and landscapes appeared enlarged, could also be bought in Paris and in some cities in Holland, Germany and England. A talented British mathematician, Thomas Harriot (1560-1621) - known among other things, for having introduced into mathematical language the symbols > < for 'greater than' and 'less than' - was probably the first to use the optical tube (as it was then called) for astronomical observations. In June 1609 Harriot, after pointing the device at the Moon, produced the earliest drawing we have of our satellite observed with a magnification power of 6x. By the gracious permission of their owner, Lord Egremont, Harriot's autograph drawings, rarely seen, are displayed in our exhibition.

A few months later, a then unknown professor of mathematics at the University of Padua, Galileo Galilei, had in his hands the curious object, almost certainly in Venice, where he often went to engage in stimulating conversations with erudite friends - among them Fra Paolo Sarpi, a combative theologian and natural scientist open to new ideas - and to enjoy the worldly pleasures of Venetian society. Galileo, immediately realising the enormous potential of the optical tube, devoted himself to perfecting it, rapidly attaining notable results. In his hands, the toy was transformed into an effective scientific instrument.

Visitors to this exhibition will have for the first time the unique chance to admire, alongside Harriot's drawings of the Moon, those made by Galileo in late November and the first weeks of December of the same year. The difference immediately strikes the eye. In addition to a natural talent for drawing, Galileo had at his disposal an instrument with a magnification power of about 20x (that is, it showed the surface of the Moon four hundred times larger), fitted with lenses of decidedly better quality as regards luminosity and transparency. This explains why the watercolours based on his observations of the Moon represent a great leap forward, providing us with the first realistic portrait of our satellite's face. Although Galileo's drawings are still far from the degree of definition to which we are accustomed, much greater is the distance separating them from the traditional iconography of the Moon in which, since the time of earliest civilisations, the imagination had seen the face of a man, with nose, eyes and mouth, or the shape of a rabbit, a dragon, a tree, etc.

The discovery of the true face of the Moon marked a sharp break, and not in the history of astronomy alone. From his telescopic observations of the Moon Galileo drew in fact revolutionary conclusions for both physics and philosophy. He immediately realised the groundlessness of the belief, at least two millenniums old, in the existence of a difference in substance between the Earth, theatre of imperfection and transmutation due to the ceaselessly changing combinations of the four elements of the sublunar world (earth, water, air and fire), and the celestial world, perfect, immutable, filled with the subtle fifth element (quintessence), and animated by the circular rotation of the crystalline celestial spheres that generated neither friction nor wear. The difference in structure between Heaven and Earth was one of the tenets of the Aristotelian concept of the universe, later assimilated into the Christian cosmological vision.

Galileo was perfectly aware of the epochal implications of the phenomena that he, first among men, had observed on those sleepless nights four centuries ago. A convinced Copernican already for many years, engaged in the battle to affirm the truth of the heliocentric system, until then ridiculed by its adversaries and accused of absurdity, he realised that the new instrument would lead not only to radical reformation in the vision of the structure of the universe and the laws governing its operation, but also to positing man's relationship with the cosmos in entirely new terms.

In the first weeks of 1610, before the astonished eyes of Galileo other undreamed of phenomena appeared. Four satellites orbited around Jupiter, showing its close kinship with the Earth, around which the Moon revolved. For Galileo, this discovery constituted convincing proof of the oneness of the universe. Observed through the telescope, the Milky Way was seen to be a mass of innumerable stars, sweeping away at one blow the fantastic mythological interpretations on the origin and nature of this part of the sky. The discovery that the surface of the Sun is marred by dark spots strengthened Galileo's belief that the celestial bodies, exactly like the Earth, were subject to corruption and change. Venus, moreover, revealed to the telescope phases similar to those of the Moon, dealing a mortal blow to the Ptolemaic hypothesis. Lastly, the strange swellings at the sides of Saturn, erroneously interpreted by Galileo as satellites, showed that even the outermost planet was similar to the Earth and to Jupiter.

Understandably cautious, Galileo checked his enthusiasm. News of the astronomical discoveries he had achieved with the telescope was entrusted, in the spring of 1610, to a little volume, published in great haste, the *Sidereus Nuncius*, the 'Messenger of celestial novelties' in which Galileo reported his series of telescopic observations and the ensuing discoveries without revealing, except through a few hints, the reflection on great philosophical issues that they had inspired in his mind.

It was the reaction to that text, which quickly ended up on the desks of the most eminent European scholars, that obliged Galileo to come out into the open. The followers of traditional natural philosophy, who saw their solidly established cultural hegemony threatened, reacted first with animosity. Soon after, representatives of the clergy began to express first subtle insinuations, then veiled threats, and lastly explicit denunciation of the menace to the faith of Galileo's discoveries. To reply to his adversaries Galileo had to throw off his mask. The Pisan scientist vigorously declared that the telescope (as it had been christened by the Accademia dei Lincei) not only revealed the true appearance of the celestial bodies, but also showed the need to proceed to a thorough-going reform of philosophy; a reform that implied full recognition of freedom of research and expression of thought, a claim firmly opposed by those who acknowledged only the authority of Aristotle and the Holy Scriptures.

Galileo's battle against the principle of authority (in its secular and religious interpretation) represents one of the salient features of the spirit of modernity. He fought with exceptional lucidity. His stabbing blows were particularly stinging to his adversaries for the subtle intelligence of his arguments, the clarity and solidity of his demonstrations and the skilful use of irony with which he derided his opponents, his words inflicting wounds deeper than those of the sword. In those industrious years Galileo lived in a ceaseless alternation of hope in the success of his efforts to renew knowledge and disappointment at the impenetrable wall of hostility he encountered. As everyone knows, the outcome of these events was dramatic: the trial of 1633, concluding with the condemnation of Galileo as being 'strongly suspected of heresy' and with the painful act of abjuration, inflicted a deep wound, not yet entirely healed, in the history of the modern conscience.

This devastating intellectual earthquake, whose shock waves reverberated well beyond the sphere of scientific research, was produced by the "toy" procured by Galileo on a certain day in 1609 which, if its exact date could be known, would merit solemn commemoration the world over. For this reason it is essential that celebration of the four-hundredth anniversary of that event should focus on the epochal transformation in the conception of the universe and the meaning of the presence in it of mankind. In a word, we must avoid the risk of emphasizing exclusively the importance of its strictly scientific implications.

Such reflections have inspired the exhibition on Galileo presented at Palazzo Strozzi. It has been conceived as a fascinating journey that starts from the remotest origins of Western civilisation. It reveals how, along with its extraordinary mathematical and instrumental dimension, astronomy has represented, more than any other branch of knowledge, a fertile terrain for the development of reflections on the nature of man, on the meaning and purpose of his presence in the cosmos, on the principles of harmony, symmetry and proportion (archetypal models of the human concepts of beauty and good) that govern the universe.

From the remotest ages, up to Galileo and beyond, astronomy has been in fact a 'universal' science, intrinsically linked to metaphysics, philosophy and religion. While it developed a direct relationship with mathematics and music, it exerted a very special attraction insofar as it promised to provide man with answers to fundamental questions of a practical nature: measuring time, carrying out agricultural activities, confronting navigation in safety, reading his destiny in the stars, recognising his natural inclinations determined by astral influence at the moment of birth, determining the most propitious positions of the stars and planets for important decisions regarding his personal life and the exercise of public functions (founding a State or a religion, declaring war, etc.); precisely predicting astronomical events of dire consequences such as eclipses and comets.

The vision of ancient, medieval, and early modern age astronomy as a global and cross boundaries science has inspired the exhibition at Palazzo Strozzi which celebrates the fourth centennial of Galileo's astronomical utilisation of the telescope. We trust that the exhibition will demonstrate that mankind's extraordinary adventure in deciphering the signs in the heavens cannot be reduced to a simple history of astronomical discoveries or of the progressive perfecting of instruments of observation and measurement.

The perspective adopted is that of clearly evincing the close connection to be observed in all epochs between the evolution of astronomical knowledge and the endeavours made to ensure that the new information gradually accumulated offered responses to the expectations and fears that accompanied the gaze of man toward the cosmos.

Starting from the ancient civilisations of Mesopotamia and the Nile delta, in which Western culture is deeply rooted, the exhibition *Galileo. Images of the Universe from Antiquity to the Telescope* illustrates, through exhibits of exceptional documentary value and remarkable beauty, the complexity of man's relationship with the heavens through the course of history. The visitor is invited on a fascinating voyage through the progressive affirmation of the image of the universe in the form of a perfect sphere accomplished by Greek culture and consolidated during the Hellenistic Age by refined geometric models. He will then have the chance to admire the great contribution made by the leading figures in Islamic culture, and the extraordinary cultural operation of Christianising the pagan cosmos carried out by the Fathers of the Church and the great medieval theologians. He will find illustrated the great season of the Renaissance, which saw the revival of the ancient gods and the pervasive suggestion of cosmological subjects on the world of art and architecture. Lastly, he will encounter Copernicus, the man who marked a dramatic change, paving the way for Galileo, a new Christopher Columbus (as he was perceived by many of his contemporaries) who had discovered not merely a continent but an immense new dimension, detonating a blast that exploded a body of knowledge whose rule had gone unchallenged for two millenniums.

It is not surprising, therefore, that the exhibition stage is often occupied by poetry and literature (means of expression that were widely used - as in Aratus' astronomical poem, or in the constant references to astronomy in Dante's *Divine Comedy* - to transmit the emotions generated by reflection on the structure and grandeur of the universe), by architecture (imposing structures such as pyramids and domes, of both the pagan and Christian worlds, monuments of striking impact, such as obelisks, evoked the obsessive influence of the cosmos on man's life), by music (the theme of the music of the spheres constantly accompanied cosmological thought), by art (the cosmos, its characteristics, the deities that inhabit it and the angelic intellects that move it greatly inspired artistic production), by politics (from ancient times rulers have sought legitimization in the stars), by religion (where the theme of cosmogony always plays a crucial part) and, of course, by astrology. The latter was one of the driving forces behind man's commitment to astronomical research, due to the enormous practical value attributed to it. Today, after much effort, we have reached a clear, yet still incomplete, distinction between astrology and astronomy, but we must not forget that for millenniums these two terms were interchangeable, and that even great figures in astronomical research whom we consider closest to our modern mentality (such as Galileo and Kepler) cast horoscopes for family members and important personages.

The decision to present on the prestigious, but not unlimited, premises of Palazzo Strozzi a voyage through the space and time of astronomical research and imagination that culminates with Galileo's extraordinary contribution has called for some selective decisions. While aware of the fact that earlier civilizations interpreted signs in the heavens, we decided to begin our story with the Mesopotamian and Egyptian civilizations. Moreover, our attention has been directed to astronomical research and cosmological visions in the civilisations of the Mediterranean basin and of Europe.

Since the core of this exhibition is devoted to the heavens we have not only distributed our items in the showcases along the walls of Palazzo Strozzi. We have also populated the "skies" of the exhibition halls with fascinating celestial signs and messages. To underline the profound interweaving of astronomy with other forms of cultural expression, we have selected exhibits that show how interpretations of the structure of the universe have been constantly translated into images by the finest representatives of the art world, thus facilitating their comprehension and diffusion. Therefore the exhibition includes a rich group of masterpieces (drawings, paintings, sculptures, miniatures on paper or parchment, objects from the minor arts, tapestries, and so on) by the most renowned artists in the classical, medieval and early modern ages (the Farnese Atlas; frescoes from Pompeii, many of which are displayed in public for the first time; splendidly illuminated medieval codices; works of great Renaissance artists such as Botticelli, Dürer, Guercino, and Rubens). The programmatic dialogue between scientific thinking and artistic activity is emblematically mirrored in the extraordinary collection of astronomical instruments presented: works combining art, science and technology, illustrating how the image of the universe as a machine or clock, which emerged in the Middle Ages and gained ground from the Renaissance, went hand in hand with the perception of the cosmos as a mechanism of harmonic proportions and spectacular beauty.

In addition to some three hundred original pieces, of unique value, the exhibition displays a number of tools destined to enhance the visit and encourage the participation of the public. A series of fascinating exhibits, some of them interactive, display the image and operational mechanisms of the world-systems conceived in antiquity (the Babylonian cosmos, that described in the Biblical *Genesis*, the homocentric spheres of Eudoxus, the intricate geometries of Ptolemy's universe, etc.). With the strictest attention to detail and respect for historical documentation, these exhibits illustrate phenomena, processes of reflection and instruments of observation and measurement (the phases of Venus, systems for projecting a sphere onto a plane, the structure and operations of the astrolabe, the optical configuration of the Galilean telescope and the subsequent evolution of the instrument, etc.) that were crucially important to the development of astronomical knowledge. The systematic use of multimedia stations, illustrating the technical aspects of astronomy in an attractive manner, facilitate comprehension of the more complex artefacts (such as the beautiful, monumental tapestry from the Cathedral of Toledo, the drawings that illustrate the inclinations generated by the influence of the planets or the rich array of astronomical instruments in an important painting from the early 17th century, on display for the first time). Some of the major implications of the relationship between microcosm and macrocosm - a theme that, in different forms, traverses the entire course of the history of reflections on the universe - are shown through fascinating exhibits, which illustrate the principles underlying the successful practice of astrological medicine (the influence of the zodiacal signs on the health of the various organs of the human body), the fascinating theme of musical resonance between man and the cosmos (monochord man) and the widespread belief in the influence of the stars and planets on the character of individuals (the theory of temperaments). Three spectacular films narrate important aspects of the history of the interpretation of the cosmos which, to be fully appreciated, call for strategies of visual communication integrating various mediums (voice, music, still and moving images, 3D modelling).

The catalogue of the exhibition, published by Giunti Publishing Group, presents contributions from scholars of recognised competence. The website, realised by the Istituto e Museo di Storia della Scienza di Firenze together with the multimedia applications and films, provides a wealth of information, useful to prepare the visit, while projecting the content of the show beyond the limited time frame of its opening to the public.

This great exhibition inaugurates the cycle of Galilean celebrations in 2009, presented under the aegis of the National Committee for the Fourth Centennial of the Celestial Discoveries of Galileo along with other initiatives organised by our colleagues in the Galilean cities of Pisa and Padua. It is hoped that it will contribute to informing the general public not only of the debt owed to Galileo by humanity, but also of the continuous dialogue between astronomical research and other forms of expression of the human mind.

An exhibition of this vast scope and ambition would have been inconceivable without the commitment of those who have supported the project since its inception, and who have accompanied it through the various stages of its realisation. My gratitude goes first of all to the authorities that have provided the conspicuous resources necessary to carry out this initiative. In a particularly difficult moment, due to the international financial crisis, the Ente Cassa di Risparmio di Firenze, with its customary generosity and interest in major cultural events, made available the resources essential for the realisation of a project that has received the decisive support of the Regione Toscana. The National Committee for the Fourth Centennial of Galileo's Celestial Discoveries, in the face of the embarrassingly inadequate means provided by government authorities for such an important event, solemnly commemorated throughout the world, has offered a contribution whose significance transcends the quantitative dimension and confers on the initiative the approval and encouragement of its prestigious members.

The final project for the exhibition grew out of intense discussions with the authoritative scholars of the International Scientific Committee coordinated by Cristina Acidini. I am especially grateful to my colleagues, internationally renowned scholars, who have offered their constant, active support, as testified by this volume to which many of them have contributed.

I would like to express my thanks to the heads of the Institutions and to the private collectors all over the world who have made it possible to offer visitors a group of original documents, works of art and scientific instruments of unprecedented number, uniqueness and beauty. The list of lenders furnishes eloquent demonstration of the widespread and generous adhesion to our project on the part of the most prestigious museums and cultural institutes.

I assumed the role of curator of this exhibition, on condition that scientific responsibility be entrusted to the Istituto e Museo di Storia della Scienza, which I have the honour to direct. I was perfectly aware that to complete this ambitious project, the full support of the staff, the collaborators, the infrastructure and the bibliographical resources of the Florentine institution, were essential. Giorgio Strano, Curator of the Institute and Museum, played a crucial role, making available his vast knowledge of the history of astronomy and astronomical instruments. Giorgio has recently curated an exhibition on Galileo's telescope - which is encountering great success in its intense and prestigious international itinerary - from which we have drawn inspiration for some of the exhibits. He gave precious assistance to the technicians of the laboratory of historical clockworks at the Istituto Tecnico Industriale "Leonardo da Vinci" (where the working models of the world systems of Eudoxus and Ptolemy were built) coordinated by Professor Andrea Palmieri and to the technicians of the scenic workshop of the Opera Laboratori Fiorentini (responsible for the realisation of the other exhibits). Filippo Camerota, Vice-Director of the Institute, designed some strikingly effective exhibits (such as the model of the astronomical ceiling of the Egyptian-Roman temple of Dendera, models that display the systems for projecting a sphere onto a plane and those that show how the astrolabe is used), and supervised their realisation by Gianni Miglietta and Stella Battaglia. Giovanni di Pasquale was the precious reference point for the set design of the sections on Graeco-Roman cosmology, and coordinator of the sections dedicated to the ancient world.

Once again, Laura Manetti has given proof of her exceptional organisational capabilities in verifying progress during all phases of preparation, in continuously updating the archival documentation, in editorial control of the texts, in maintaining contacts with the lenders, the authors, the designers, the builders of models, the suppliers of images, etc. For her intelligence and dedication in carrying out this daunting task, Laura deserves our fullest appreciation. The Secretarial staff of the Institute and Museum has provided important support, in particular Giulia Fiorenzoli, with the collaboration of Elisa Bonaiuti. The Multimedia Laboratory completed in a short time a vast range of highly effective educational tools on digital media, produced attractive films based on scripts provided by Eugenio Lo Sardo (The Challenge of the Calendar), Natacha Fabbri (The Harmony of the Spheres), and by our colleagues at the Istituto Universitario di Architettura of Venice (Astrology and the Palazzo della Ragione). Sara Bonechi provided competent assistance with bibliographical research and manuscript sources.

The Director and staff of the Fondazione Palazzo Strozzi have constantly supported this initiative, accompanying every stage of its preparation, maintaining formal relations with the lenders, developing, with Marcella Antonini of the Ente Cassa di Risparmio, the communication and promotion project and launching an ambitious program of collateral events to arouse the interest and participation of the public and to encourage families to appreciate the exhibition themes.

The design and installation of the exhibition has been carried out by the Studio Gris of Padua with the collaboration of Luigi Cupellini and, for the graphics, of the Studio Rovai/Weber. The display structures were built by Opera Laboratori Fiorentini, a firm with which we have established a long and profitable collaboration that has resulted in numerous exhibitions that have met with outstanding success all over the world.

THE ANCIENT WORLD

–

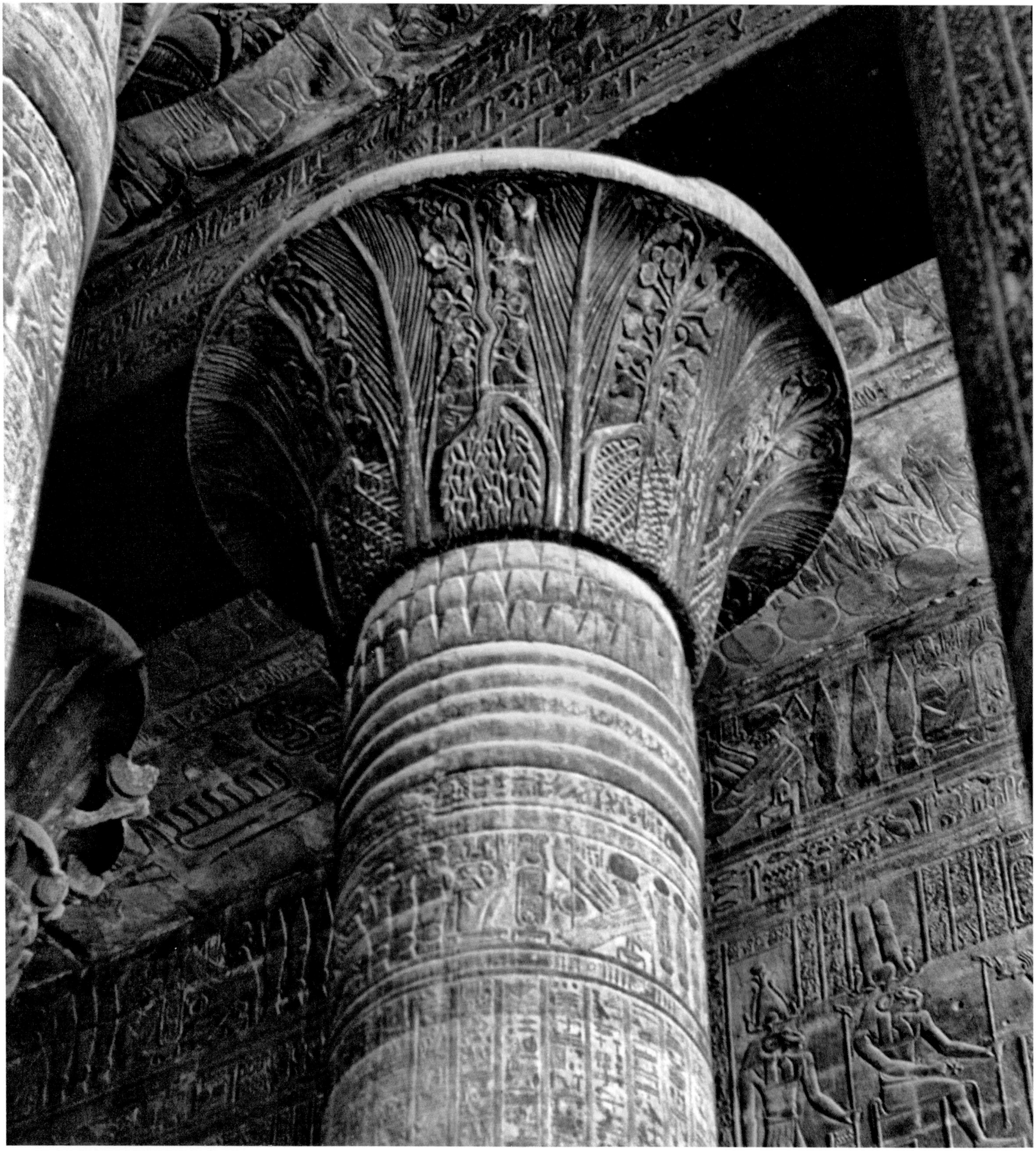

THE ANCIENT WORLD

–

1| THE DAWN OF ASTRONOMY: MESOPOTAMIA, EGYPT AND THE BIBLICAL COSMOS

–

THE SOURCES OF EGYPTIAN ASTRONOMY

–

Alessandro Roccati

–

In ancient Egypt, science was initially reproduced directly. Theory and manuals only became established after books had been created, a process that evolved during the second millennium B.C. The forms of representation were, however, developed after observations had been memorised and codified in a thought system. The forms used to express the Egyptian vision assumed the guise of mythological interpretation and their creation was closely bound to the definition of the religious structure. The cosmogonic theory remained closely tied to local experience; water was at the origin of the world and terrestrial space was thought to be enveloped in a mass of chaotic water. The sun was soon identified as the primeval god and it had given rise to creation and life in its demiurgic capacity.

In Egyptian astronomy, we must differentiate between what was the result of direct observation (e.g. the orientation of the pyramids, the largest of which were erected in the middle of the third millennium B.C.; fig. 2) and what constituted information (only from the second millennium B.C.) or a reflection (from the first millennium B.C.). The assertions in the so-called Pyramid Texts (fig. 3), inscribed in the second half of the 3rd millennium B.C., are the product of immediate utterances with a ritual/factual content. In that ancient time, the observation of the sky was combined with its interpretation, which was expressed via the elaboration of mythological formulations that also relied on religious thought. As a result, science and religion seemed to coincide but religion probably did not have the power to condition science and was an expression of scientific thought. This thought was based on a number of assumptions developed at the symbolic level. One of them was arithmetic calculation, which is a function of numerology and applied to measurement in particular, and which probably accompanied its first applications. There is reason to believe that archaic thought was fairly insensitive to the dimension of space and time, as they appear circumscribed and inscribed in a circular process based on the immediate perception of reality. As a result, number systems did not initially take the form of an *arithmetic*, or abstract science of calculation, but of sequence analysis: from the fingers on the hands to the components of a building (bricks or stone blocks) and periods of time (days, months, seasons, years). It did not so much measure length or duration but rather recurrence or proportion and produced, for instance, the calendar, which because of its precocity and perfection became a fundamental historic tool of measurement, even before writing was instituted.

In a world with no history, time was one of the first quantities measured, although this was originally in response to the needs of agriculture, the cycles of which were the basis for the transformation of human society via the Neolithic production system for some thousands of years. A relationship established between earthly and celestial phenomena led to the cyclical division of time into periods linked to the phases of the moon and river (the flow of the Nile and its regular floods). These observations, made at a certain time in prehistory, were 'rationalised' and inserted into structures governed by the decimal calculation system. The result was the creation of periods identified as 'months', then gathered into (three) seasons and 'years', with the further divisions into 'hours' of the day and night, plus that of daylight into three parts (morning, noon and evening). Some of these periods had already been defined when writing appeared, and were subsequently also transported onto other events such as the 'month of years' (thirty) after which the royal jubilee was celebrated and Manetho's codification of the 30 dynasties in the 3rd century B.C.

Certainly, the course of history provided many stepped innovations in successive phases. The experience of observations led to the concept of a 'Sothic era', which was the period required for the shifting calendar, produced by a fraction of time approximately equivalent to ¼ of a day, not calculable in a calendar made of whole numbers, to return to its point of departure (i.e. 365x4). In the dynastic period, the administrative years formed the basis for calculating the duration of each pharaoh's reign. This occurred as early as the third millennium B.C., ahead of all the other coeval cultures. The sum of the single reigns could correspond to longer cycles, in an attempt to calculate the time since the creation of the world and also operate on the basis of spatial dimensions, for instance to measure the length of the Sun's path, in terms of its journey around the Earth, regardless of the fact that this was thought to be flat.

1. Page 28, hypostyle atrium in the temple of Esna, 1st-2nd century A.D., with celestial references on the ceiling.

2. The pyramid of Cheops, c. 2500 B.C., oriented according to the cardinal points (course of the Sun and the Pole Star).

3. Text from the pyramids in the burial chamber of Pepi II, c. 2200 B.C. These ritual proclamations, concerning the destiny of the Pharaoh after death, could not be seen by anyone after the burial.

From the middle of the third millennium B.C., the position of the pyramids was based on the stars or on the Sun. The same occurred for the construction of sanctuaries until more recent times[1]. The path of the Sun, perpendicular to the flow of the Nile, provided a basis for orientation. It was also responsible for the fate of the Pharaoh after death, who was placed both in the company of the circumpolar stars, which never disappear, and on the Sun boat, the celestial body that circumnavigated the Earth on its day and night path. In this astral mythology, the sky was considered a liquid element in which the stars moved around on boats. The physicality of these beliefs was expressed in the depictions and even more so in the wooden boats that were associated with the place of worship from prehistoric times.

The theology of the Sun prevailed and dominated the ideology of the pharaonic state until its end, although considerable space was also given to the moon, with which it came to form an organic couple, reflected in elaborate myths. These were associated with vegetation and royal cycles in attempts to link the celestial mechanisms (e.g. the phases of the moon) to human destiny and the hope of survival after death. The afterlife would be dominated by Osiris, linked to the Moon and the constellation of Orion, to which was linked the star Sirius, *Sepdet*[2] to the Egyptians (*Sothis* in Greek) and identified as the goddess Isis, and hence also with the flooding of the Nile.

The surviving documentation is extensive and often of the highest, royal, level. The first graphic reproduction of the sky coincided with the writing of the early texts, works with a narrative/descriptive and educational content. It takes the form of star calendars concisely depicted inside the lids of coffins and based on a conventional model that established the hours of the night from the culmination of the characteristic star (decan): ten hours that corresponded to a 36th part of the year.

These calendars were depicted inside the wooden coffins of dignitaries in the 12th dynasty (approx. 1900-1800 B.C.) and this has permitted their conservation. Other cosmographic works probably dating from the same period are known only through copies or adaptations used as additional decoration, especially in the tombs dug in the Valley of the Kings in Thebes for the kings of the New Kingdom (c. 1500-1100 B.C.).

These grandiose tombs were supposed to replicate the universe for the everlasting life of the buried pharaoh and contained a detailed description of cosmological knowledge: from the measurement of the path of the Sun (some estimates are so accurate that they differ little from today's calculation of the circumference of the earth) to the depiction of the starry heavens in the room with the coffin (fig. 4). This more purely astronomical part is also recorded at Abydos, in the so-called Osireion, which was probably the tomb of Osiris.

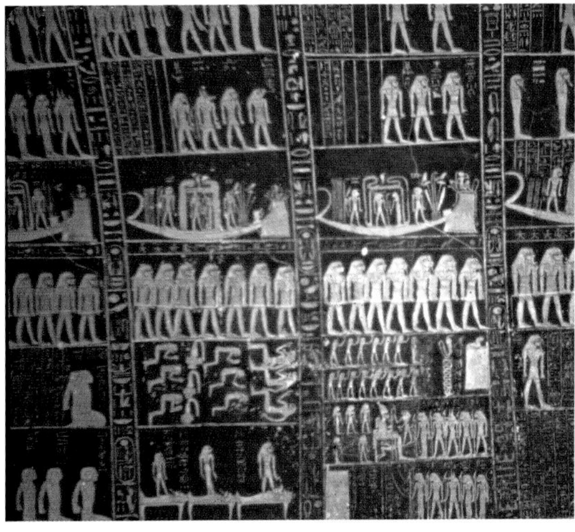

4. Part of the astronomical ceiling of the room containing the sarcophagus of Rameses VI in the Valley of the Kings at Thebes, c. 1150 B.C.

We can, however, follow the development of the forms in which scientific knowledge was recorded. The Book of the Sky (or of the goddess Nut) reproduced a map of the heavens during the New Kingdom (c. 1500-1100 B.C.) and this was transposed during the Saite period (26th dynasty: 664-525 B.C.), at the latest, in a treatise on papyrus translated into demotic in Roman times. All the portrayals seem based on a common archetype, the so-called Book of Nut (the goddess of the skies, portrayed as a woman), while the Book of the Heavenly Cow (after the portrayal of the goddess as a cow) develops its mythological aspects, narrating the destruction of humankind, which had rebelled against the Sun god, at the hand of the bovine goddess Hathor.

Moreover, the epigraphic copies of the Book of Nut, especially those at Abydos, feature sophisticated obscure graphics with cryptic hieroglyphs that would conceal this knowledge from the uninitiated.

The existence of a manual or treatise for these depictions is confirmed by the later history of the text, which was not only handed down via a longstanding handwritten tradition that spanned more than a thousand years to the times of the Roman Empire but was also translated in demotic, the popular language and script of Hellenistic-Roman Egypt. The miraculously saved library of the temple of Tebtynis, in Fayyum, contained several handwritten copies, the main parts of which are now in Copenhagen, although numerous additional fragments are to be found in Florence, Berlin, Oxford and Berkeley. This major dispersion greatly delayed hermeneutic work but a recent publication[3] shows the huge progress that can still be made in our knowledge of Egyptian astronomy. These late documents (2nd c. A.D.) are of special interest not only because the work was translated into a

5. Hypostyle atrium in the temple of the goddess Hathor at Dandara, 1st century B.C., with celestial references on the ceiling.

6. Detail of a verse in the Turin papyrus CGT 54065, containing a manual of divination, c. 1200 B.C.

more recent language (albeit not easy for us to decipher) but also because it adopted clear graphics that help decrypt the obscure epigraphic passages. This archaeoastronomy must be studied if we are to understand the complex but precise portrayals of the heavens that still cover the ceilings of more recent temples dating from the period of the Roman Empire[4] (figs. 1 and 5).

As well as these firsthand documents, which are also reflected in Greek papyri, tradition has handed down the names of scholars who are thought to have cultivated religious astronomy, mainly for astrological purposes to foretell the future such as Nechepso and Nepheros. The Egyptian Museum in Cairo has a statue of an astronomer, Harkhebi, who lived in the 2nd century B.C., with a uniquely detailed hieroglyphic inscription that describes his expertise and various duties[5]:

> Hereditary prince and count, sole companion, wise in the sacred writings, who observes everything observable in heaven and earth, clear-eyed in observing the stars, among which there is no erring,
>
> who announces rising and setting at their times, with the gods who foretell the future - for which he purified himself in their days when *Ikh* (decan) rose heliacally beside Benu (Venus) from earth and he contented the lands with his utterances;
>
> who observes the culmination of every star in the sky, who knows the heliacal risings... all their manifestations throughout the year,
>
> who foretells the heliacal rising of Sothis at the beginning of the year, so that he observes her (Sothis) at the day of her first festival, knowledgeable in her course at the times of designating therein, observing what she does daily, all she has foretold is in his charge;
>
> knowing the northing and southing of the sun, announcing all his wonders (omina) and appointing for them a time, so that he declares what they cause when they have occurred, coming at their times;
>
> who divides the hours for the two times (day and night) without going into error at night ...for all that is brought at the beginning of every month;
>
> knowledgeable in everything which is seen in the sky, for which he has waited, skilled in their winds and their foretellings.

The foretellings mentioned are those defined by the Greeks as '*Salmeschiniaka*', predictions based on the observation of the Sun and the movement of the planets. Nothing was known of these books until research conducted on the papyri in the Egyptian Museum in Turin enabled me to identify manuscripts of the Ramesside Period (c. 1300-1100 B.C.: CGT 54065; cf. entry I.2.2), the content of which dates at least in part to the beginning of the second millennium B.C., which, as we have seen, is when the first books were written[6] (fig. 6).

Despite huge gaps, the documentation retrieved enables us to declare the Egyptians' astronomical science one of the great fields in which they excelled. Our limited knowledge seems, as a result, open to major advances. The aim is not to make a global evaluation of the actual knowledge and its limitations but to reconstruct and understand how this science took shape and developed into a structured vision of the universe based on society's needs and changes.

–

Bibliography

Bommas 1999; Brugsch 1856; Brunner 1973, pp. 25-30; Derchain 1989, pp. 74-89; Hornung 1982; Jasnow-Zauzich 2005; Leitz 1991a; Leitz 1991b; Leitz 1995; von Lieven 1999, pp. 77-126; von Lieven 2000; von Lieven 2007; Panaino 1987, pp. 139-155; Kriech Ritner 1993; Roccati 1994, pp. 493-497; Shaltout-Fekri-Belmonte 2006, pp. 93-112.

[1] Shaltout-Fekri-Belmonte 2006.

[2] The 'sharp' meaning in the Egyptian term *Sepdet* is linked to the sense of 'arrow', common to a vast number of pre-classical cultures: cf. Panaino 1987.

[3] Von Lieven 2007.

[4] Von Lieven 2000.

[5] Statue found at Tell el-Faraun, in the Delta. Comment by Derchain 1989; cf. K.H. Janssen-Winkeln, ZÄS 125 (1998), pp. 9-10 and Ritner 1993, p. 36, note 167. Cf. also Brunner 1973.

[6] Roccati 1994.

SVSCI PITE O LI C TE RAS
ET LE GES EGIP TII
DEUS OMNIUM CREATOR
SECUM DEUM FECIT
VISIBILEM ET HUNC
FECIT PRIMUM ET SOLUM
QUO OBLECTATUS EST ET
VALDE AMAVIT PROPRIUM
FILIUM QUI APPELLATUR
SANCTUM VERBUM.
HERMIS MERCURIUS TRIMEGISTUS
CONTEMPORANEUS

THE ANCIENT WORLD

1 | THE DAWN OF ASTRONOMY: MESOPOTAMIA, EGYPT AND THE BIBLICAL COSMOS

THE LEGACY OF EGYPTIAN ASTRONOMY

Edoardo Detoma

Egyptian astronomers left modern astronomy a crucial legacy – two measurements that have defined the evolution of astronomy and the everyday life of Western civilization. These were the definition of the yearly calendar as we know and use it today, and the division of day and night into 12 hours each.

> Now with regard to mere human matters, the accounts which they gave, and in which all agreed, were the following. The Egyptians, they said, were the first to discover the solar year, and to portion out its course into twelve parts. They obtained this knowledge from the stars.
>
> (Herodotus, *History*, Book II, 4)

The definition of the calendar that measures time on the basis of the annual solar cycle is controversial and serious doubts exist as to whether the Egyptian calendar was of astronomical or of agricultural origin. The yearly cycle may be based on the observed period between the floods in the Nile valley, floods that were crucial to the survival of the Egyptian civilisation. Recognising the imminent occurrence of the flood, predicted by observing the heliacal rising of the star *Sepdet* (the Greek Sothis, known to us as Sirius), was the link between the astronomical definition of the calendar and its purely agricultural origin, and connects the annual cycle to the religious cycles of death and resurrection that include the diurnal cycle of the sun, people's lives, the annual flood cycle and the 'open' cycle of the cosmogony. Everything had its origin in water, whether it be the primordial ocean Nun from whose depths the Earth was created, or the water carried by the annual inundation that regenerated the Egyptian land. So, we are led to believe that the annual cycle that was the foundation of the calendar was determined simply by counting the days that elapsed between two successive floods, and then in some way averaging the figure obtained every year. One cannot but marvel at the fortuitous circumstance by which the heliacal rising of Sirius falls so close to the inundation, and the fortuitous circumstance that this event is so very regular, astronomically speaking. Nor can we ignore the happy coincidence by which the magnitude of Sirius makes its heliacal rising so much easier to observe.

Thanks to these three remarkable circumstances, from a certain time on the observation of the heliacal rising of Sirius on the eastern horizon, seen as the union of Hathor/Isis, the fertility goddess, with the rising sun, Ra, the giver of life and creator of the world, replaced the counting of days and astronomical observation predicted the imminent rise of the waters of the Nile.

This produced the first calendar in the history of mankind, based on a period of 365 days and remarkably similar to the mean solar year, or tropical year, of 365.2422 days. As Egypt adopted a decimal numerical system, the duration of the Egyptians' 'vague' year was divided into 'weeks' of 10 days, with 36 'weeks' in all. The length of the months, in some way linked to an archaic lunar calendar, was 30 days and they had three 'weeks' each. Three seasons known as 'Inundation', 'Emerging from the waters' and 'Great Heat' or 'Dryness' comprised four months each, totalling 360 days, to which the Egyptians added five final ('epagomenal' in Greek, which means 'added', like the equivalent Egyptian expression 'that are upon the year') days to complete the cycle of 365 days. The division of the day into 24 hours stemmed directly from this calendar structure.

The first written documents describing this calendar were found on coffins of the 12th dynasty. The inner lids of these coffins (of which 17 are known to exist) portray the so-called 'diagonal clocks' or 'star calendars', which in this context have a purely ritual function. Nevertheless, these 'calendars' provide a wealth of information on the Egyptian calendar and astronomy.

Although, as we have said, these calendars were first discovered in coffins of the Middle Kingdom, careful study of their structure (including one of the two kept in the Egyptian Museum in Turin) suggests that the original prototype on which they were based is much older[1], dating possibly from 2830-2780 B.C. This date is close to the current estimate of the 'invention' of said calendar which, for reasons of form, ought to be when the flood coincides with the first day of the first month of the first season.

These calendars have a matrix of 14 rows and a variable number of columns; the more complete calendars, such as that on the I'qer coffin in the Turin museum, have between 39 and 41 columns. Others, such as that of Mereru, also in the Turin museum, have a smaller number of columns, usually fewer than 24.

Some of these rows and columns have no astronomical significance. The central row contains invocations by the deceased to the gods of the sky and the centre column lists the four main deities of the sky: Osiris, Isis, Nut and a representation of the celestial Pole. The top row, or date line, contains the caption for each column in terms of weeks of the Egyptian year, read from right to left, starting with the first week of the first month of the first season (column 1) and going on to the third week of the fourth month of the third season in column 36.

The body of the matrix contains, in columns 1 to 36, the name of a star (or group of stars), 36 in all, called decans in analogy with the division of each Zodiac sign into three parts in the later Greek-Babylonian culture. The final three (four) columns relate to the extension of the principal decan series to cover the epagomenal days. There are 12 rows, corresponding to the hours of the night. The rising on the eastern horizon of the star shown in the 12th row marks the end of the corresponding hour of the night. These calendars, among the oldest known, show the first indication of a vague year of 365 days and the division of the night into 12 hours.

Very little is known that would allow identification of the stars painted on the diagonal calendars. We can identify Sirius /Sothis with the name *Sepdet*, and Orion, but it is difficult to link the other Egyptian names to known stars.

One thing that we do know is that, when this calendar was developed, the Egyptians associated the decanal stars with a period of invisibility lasting 70 days between the heliacal setting and rising of the star:

> It rises and it comes into existence in the horizon like Sothis – that is to say, every one of them. It means, Sothis – it happens that she customarily spends 70 days in the Duat and she rises again.
>
> (Pap. Carlsberg I, V, 43-44, cf. Pap. Carlsberg I, VI, 3-4 and Pap. Carlsberg I, VI, 38-40)

The fact that the last hour of the night was determined by the heliacal rising of a decanal star meant that the Egyptian day started at dawn, and the Egyptian year started with the heliacal rising of Sothis, coinciding in this with the start of the agricultural year and of the cosmic cycle of Creation that began in the waters of the primordial ocean Nun, from which was separated the Earth made fertile by those same waters and hence the bearer of new life.

The creation of these calendars/clocks was hindered by the anomaly of the epagomenal days (which, in effect, introduced a 'half decade' into the order of 36 decades that formed the Egyptian year) and by the fact that the difference between the solar year and the Egyptians' vague year meant that the diagonal clock only returned to its initial configuration after 1461 Egyptian years, equal to 1460 solar years.

The difficulty of managing these calendars, already clear in the specimens of the First Intermediate Period, resulted in the modification of the decanal star series used in these archaic calendars during the 18th Dynasty. The new star sequence no longer marked the hours when the stars rose on the eastern horizon but at their culmination, that is the meridian transit.

In the following years, the observation of the stars at their culmination became increasingly elaborate, as seen in the star calendars on the walls of the tombs of the 19th dynasty. The tables reproduce the observations over the course of the 360 days of an Egyptian year, with two tables per month and a 15-day interval between one observation and the next. A human figure serves as a reference marker for the observation, which is recorded in relation to parts of the human body. A star is said to rise 'in the centre', 'above the left eye' or 'above the right elbow'. The accuracy of the observations reproduced in the tombs is questionable since they were painted for funerary purposes. The axis of the human figure represented as a reference for the observations is thought to coincide with the meridian and the observations are believed to have been taken with the aid of an instrument, called a '*merkhet*', a specimen of which is preserved in the Berlin museum.

The Egyptians soon developed clocks that measured time independently of the path of the stars. The appearance of clepsydrae[2] and sundials in a papyrus of the 19th dynasty[3] is proof of the introduction of the concept of hours of equal duration (wnwt), the length of the days and nights being determined in equinoctial hours throughout the year.

In the year 46 B.C. Julius Caesar launched an ambitious plan to restore order to the Roman calendar. At that time, the Romans were already in contact with Eastern civilisations and certainly with Egypt, because the reform was entrusted to an Egyptian astronomer of the School of Alexandria, which in Hellenistic times had become the hub of Mediterranean culture. Although the Julian reform has been described in all texts as a 'reform' of the calendar, in actual fact, the lunar-based Roman calendar was abandoned in favour of a calendar founded on the duration of the tropical year. As the lunar calendar was based on a cycle of 354 days, the length of the months had to be modified by adding the missing days at the end of each month in such a way that the festivals would not be affected. Only the designation of the festival changed, e.g. a festival celebrated on 21 December was not moved but the date was changed from X Kal. Jan. to XII Kal. Jan, because the new month no longer had 29 days but 31[4].

1. Page 34, representation of Hermes Trismegistus on the floor of the Cathedral of Siena, 1488.

2. Water clock (clepsydra) of Amenhotep III from Karnak; Cairo Museum.

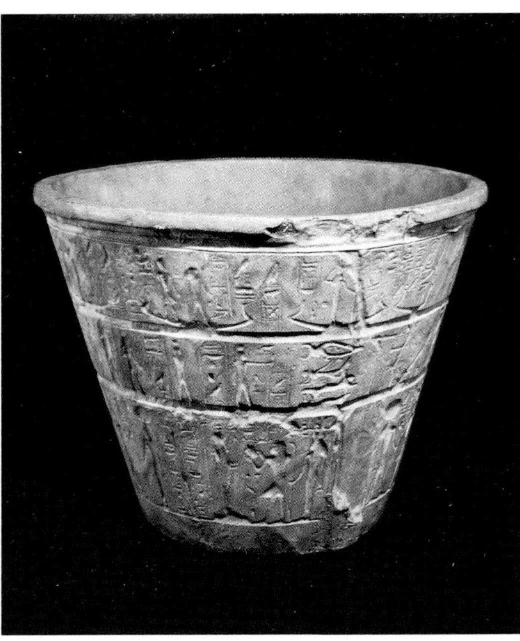

3. Pinturicchio, *Isis with Hermes Trismegistus and Moses*, 1492-1494; Stanza dei Santi, Borgia Apartments, Vatican City.

Months of 31 and 30 days alternated starting in March, the first month in the Roman calendar. February had 29 days to complete the cycle of 365. Every fourth year, they added an intercalary or leap day after VI Kal. Mart. (i.e., 24 February) and this day was called 'bis sextum Kal. Mart'. In that year, February had 30 days.

Ninety days were added to the year 46 B.C. to align the months with the proper seasons and the reform became effective in the year 45 B.C. A further correction was required in the year 9 B.C. during the reign of the Emperor Caesar Augustus, as the Julian reform was incorrectly applied, adding a leap day every three years instead of four. The leap year was omitted for 16 years to 'offset' the error. Not until the year 8 A.D. was the Julian calendar applied again as originally intended by the author of the reform. In the same period, probably taking advantage of this state of confusion, the length of the month of August was changed after it had been dedicated to the Emperor Caesar Augustus, so that he was not given a month that was a day shorter than the preceding one (July) dedicated to Julius Caesar. As a result, February lost a day and its length became 28 days in normal years and 29 in the years that started to be known as '*annus bissextus*' during the Empire.

The Julian reform was not applied simultaneously all over the Empire and many provinces continued to use the old local calendars, especially the western provinces. Egypt, which had resisted Ptolemy III's attempt to reform the calendar as recorded in the Decree of Canopus, did not introduce the Julian reform until the year 26 B.C., adding a sixth epagomenal day every four years (3, 7, 11 and so on) to the Egyptians' vague year and thus initiating the so-called 'Alexandrian year' as it was later called, which begins on 29 August. The Alexandrian year differed from the Roman calendar because every month was the same length (30 days), effectively reforming the Egyptian's 'vague' calendar and correcting its then known difference from the tropical year.

Strange as it may seem, the Egyptians' 'vague' year of 365 days survived in astronomical practice, serving the same science that with the precise measurement of the tropical year had prompted its correction and replaced it in common usage with the Julian year. In this sense, over the centuries, the Egyptians' 'vague' year of exactly 365 days provided the link, via the Arabic astronomy, between the Greek and Ptolemaic astronomy and the development of the Copernican system at the height of the Renaissance.

In the *Almagest* (150 A.D.) Ptolemy used the Egyptians' 'vague' calendar, dating the origin of its time scale to the epoch of Nabonassar (Nabû-Nāṣir), with a starting date[5] (Nabonassar 1, Thoth 1) of 26 February – 746 (747 B.C.) in the Julian calendar[6]. Ptolemy[7] himself explained why he chose the epoch of Nabonassar as the starting point for the time scale adopted; in the computations of the mean motion of the Sun, he made use of the observations available to him 'from the beginning of the reign of Nabonassar [...] because this is the epoch starting from which the ancient observations are, generally, preserved to our times'.

Why use the Egyptians' vague year, which had so little in common with the motion of the celestial bodies? The answer to this question remains a fundamental point in the science of measuring time, namely, in general, should preference go to a time scale that is accurate but not uniform and continuous or to one that is the reverse? Copernicus provided it in a book that radically changed the structure of the then-known Universe during the European Renaissance. In *De Revolutionibus Orbium Coelestium* (1543), almost 1400 years after Ptolemy, Copernicus wrote[8]:

> Moreover, in our computations of the celestial movements we shall employ the Egyptian years, which alone among the legal years are found equal. For it is necessary for the measure to agree with the measured; but that is not the case with the years of the Romans, Greeks, and Persians, for intercalations are made not in any single way, but according to the will of the people. But the Egyptian year contains no ambiguity as regards the fixed number of 365 days, in which throughout twelve equal months—which they name in order by these names: Thoth, Phaophi, Athyr, Chiach, Tybi, Mechyr, Phamenoth, Pharmutbi, Pachon, Pauni, Epiphi, and Meson—in which, I say, six periods of 60 days are comprehended evenly together with the five remaining days, which they call the intercalary days. For that reason Egyptian years are most convenient for calculating regular movements. Any other years are easily reducible to them by resolving the days.

But, while Copernicus, Kepler and Galileo were reforming the understanding of the Universe and redefining the Earth's position in it, the humanists of the Florentine Renaissance were re-discovering the Egyptian culture in a most bizarre way.

For the first time after the dark centuries of the European Middle Ages, the humanists were rediscovering the ancient civilisations and the Greek and Roman texts offered a new vision of the world that went beyond the limits set by Aristotle and the Scholastic philosophy of the Middle Ages. In these texts, the humanists saw the legend of a lost civilization, a mythical golden age rich in wonderful knowledge and lost secrets. Egypt was certainly the first of these civilisations to lure those trying to shed light on this past by researching and translating the ancient texts. It is no coincidence that Plato reports a curious conversation[9] between an elderly Egyptian priest and the Greek Solon in the dialogue in *Timaeus* in which Plato introduces the myth of Atlantis:

> And a very old priest said to him, 'Oh Solon, Solon, you Greeks are all children, and there's no such thing as an old Greek.' 'What do you mean by that?' inquired Solon. 'You are all young in mind,' came the reply: 'you have no belief rooted in old tradition and no knowledge hoary with age... 'This is the reason why our traditions here are the oldest preserved;'....'But in our temples we have preserved from earliest times a written record of any great or splendid achievement or notable event which has come to our ears whether it occurred in your part of the world or here or anywhere else...

Apart from the wonder at the monuments that defied time and so amazed Herodotus (and us still today), the Egyptian language prevented direct access to the texts, piling mystery upon mystery, despite the first rudimentary attempts to decipher it. However, Greek texts came out of Egypt and these could be read. In a colossal error, the humanists, and Marsilio Ficino and Pico della Mirandola in particular, dated these Hellenistic texts, the *Corpus Hermeticum*, earlier than they should have[10] (fig. 1).

The figure of Hermes Trismegistus, the Hellenistic association of the Greek god Mercury (Hermes) with the Egyptian god Thoth, the god of knowledge and inventor of writing, became the cornerstone of an ancient philosophy that, in some ways, seemed a forerunner of the advent of Christ and Christianity.

In this form, elements of the Egyptian religion that appear in the *Corpus Hermeticum* were, in a certain sense, accepted by the Christian religion and the Church itself.

Hermes Trismegistus justifiably entered the churches and his portrait appears in a famous relief in the floor of the cathedral of Siena. Pinturicchio painted him with the Zodiac in the Sala delle Sibille in the Borgia apartments in the Vatican, along with Egyptian symbols and the god Hapi in adoration of the Cross (Sala dei Santi). The decans, three per Zodiac sign, were painted by Francesco del Cossa in Palazzo Schifanoia in Ferrara.

The Church's acceptance of Hermetism was certainly influenced by the writings of one of the Fathers of the Church, Lactantius, although somewhat undermined by the criticisms of St Augustine in *De Civitate Dei*. Although critical, Augustine accepted Hermes as a pagan prophet who told 'many truths about God'. This acceptance became an 'imprimatur' for the works of Ficino and Pico, and endorsed the humanists' desire to uncover the secrets hidden by the Egyptian civilisation and only partially known through Greek texts.

The search for the lost knowledge of a legendary 'golden age' gradually developed magical and esoteric connotations in the quest for the secrets of a knowledge hidden in obscure texts (fig. 2).

It was the age when Reuchlin wrote *On The Art of the Kabbalah*, Pythagoras' numerology was rediscovered and Agrippa von Nettesheim wrote the *Three Books on the Occult Philosophy*. There was a very fine line between science and magic, as too between orthodoxy and heresy. While Ficino and Pico remained within the boundaries imposed by the Church, Giordano Bruno and Campanella saw the *prisca theologia* as the true religion of the golden age corrupted by Christianity, and were persecuted for it.

Galileo was left virtually untouched by these influences, but he lived in a world and a society that were imbued with them, and science was no exception. It is puzzling, to say the least, to see that immediately after the presentation of the new universe that placed the Sun in the centre of the cosmos, Copernicus explicitly defined the Sun using the words of Hermes Trismegistus, who called it 'Visible God'[11].

In the introductory pages to the *Harmonices Mundi*, Kepler writes[12]:

> I am free to give myself up to the sacred madness, I am free to taunt mortals with the frank confession that I am stealing the golden vessels of the Egyptians, in order to build of them a temple for my God, far from the territory of Egypt.

Kepler's 'folly' provided Copernicus and Galileo with the missing proof to restore the Sun to the centre of the Universe: the elliptical orbits, the only ones that could explain the retrograde motion of the planets (fig. 3).

In so doing, Copernicus, Kepler and Galileo ended a journey that had commenced thousands of years before Christ on the banks of the Nile with the first observations of the heliacal rising of a bright star that joined with the Sun god at dawn to bring new life to the land of Egypt. At last, Renaissance astronomy placed the Sun back at the centre of the cosmos where, for the Egyptians, it had always been.

> But a vision of the sun is not a matter of guesswork. Since it is the visual ray itself, the sun shines all around the cosmos with the utmost brilliance, on the part above and on the part below. For the sun is situated in the centre of the cosmos, wearing it like a crown.

> (*Corpus Hermeticum* XVI, Definitions of Asclepius
> to the king Ammon on God, matter, fate, the Sun,...,
> from Copenhaver 1991, page 59)

Bibliography

Neugebauer-Parker 1960-1969; Bickerman 1980; Toomer 1998; Naval Observatory 1987; Clagett 1995; Allen 1963; Budge 1989; Copernico 1995; Platone 1977; Kepler 1995; Yates 2006; Copenhaver 1991; Borchardt 1899, pp. 10-17.

1 Neugebauer-Parker 1960-1969, p. 111.

2 Water clocks; an important description was found in an inscription in the tomb of Amenemhat, a dignitary of the 18th dynasty, in Thebes and copied by Schiaparelli. In the inscription, later studied by Sethe and Borchardt, Amenemhat proudly describes a water clock created in honour of his king Amenhotep I and boasts of the discovery of the changing duration of the night during the year.

3 Neugebauer-Parker 1960-1969, p. 119.

4 Bickerman 1980, p. 47

5 The 'historical' dates reported often differ by a few years in different authors. Compare, as an example, the dates reported in Toomer 1998 table p. 11, and the similar dates reported in Bickerman 1980, tav. V, p. 127.

6 For the time reference systems adopted by Ptolemy, see Ptolemy 1998b, pp. 9-14.

7 Ptolemy 1998b, chap. III 7, p. 166.

8 Copernicus 1995, p.131.

9 Plato 1977, p.35.

10 Note, indeed, the caption at Hermes Trismegistus' feet that defines him as a contemporary of Moses.

11 Copernicus 1995, p. 25.

12 Remembering the construction of the golden calf, and perhaps hinting at the referred text in Platos' *Timaeus*.

326

Obv.

ERASURE

ERASURE (?)

THE ANCIENT WORLD

–

1 | THE DAWN OF ASTRONOMY: MESOPOTAMIA, EGYPT AND THE BIBLICAL COSMOS

—

BABYLONIAN ASTRONOMY

–

Hermann Hunger

–

Astronomy can be defined as an endeavor to understand the movements of the celestial bodies and to predict them. The Babylonians did have such an astronomy; its main development took place during the second half of the first millennium B.C., a period when Babylonia was no longer politically independent, and it was carried out by people who seem to have had no politically important position.

The beginnings of observation of the sky in Mesopotamia are of course not documented. According to the definition just used, giving names to groups of stars and telling a story about them is not yet astronomy. Names of stars and constellations are attested in texts from the 3rd millennium B.C., but we do not know what people knew about their movements and what they thought about the physical side of stars. The stars were considered representations of gods. The Mesopotamians looked to the sky for omens indicating the future, as they did in the liver of sheep or in the behavior of animals. Such celestial omens, derived, for example, from the appearance of the moon, are attested since the beginning of the 2nd millennium B.C.

What could the Babylonians see in the sky and what did they look for? It is essentially the same as what we see, apart from the difference in geographical latitude.

The motion of the Sun (which corresponds to the motion of the Earth, both in its daily rotation and in its orbit through the year) accounts for the visibility of fixed stars. As long as the sun is below the horizon, stars can be seen. This would make only about half of the stars visible each night. Since the earth moves around the sun, and therefore for an observer on earth the sun moves among the stars, all of them are seen in the course of the year, except those which are too close to the other pole of the sky; for an observer on the northern half of the earth this means that some stars of the southern sky remain permanently invisible.

The moon is sometimes invisible for two or three days, and then appears as a thin crescent in the west, just after the sun has set. This crescent moon sets soon after the sun. Every night the moon is seen for a longer and longer time. After about 14 days it is full. Thereafter, the moon rises later and later, becoming thinner as well. Finally, it is seen as a thin crescent in the morning, just before sunrise. There follow the few days of invisibility, during which the conjunction of sun and moon occurs. With the reappearance after conjunction the moon's cycle begins again. The whole cycle lasts for 29 or 30 days; the average length of such a month is just a little more than 29½ days.

There are five planets visible to the naked eye. Like the moon, the planets become invisible when they are close to the sun; but they also seem to stop in their movement and move backwards. The Babylonians knew about their phenomena, and they saw the differences in motion between inner and outer planets.

The phenomena of moon and planets are important for Babylonian astronomy (and for astrology as well).

The calendar in Mesopotamia is based on two clearly defined units: the day and the month. The Babylonian day begins at sunset. The month begins with the evening on which the crescent moon is seen for the first time after the conjunction of sun and moon. Such a month is called a synodic month, and it has either 29 or 30 days. To find out whether a month will have 29 or 30 days is one of the goals of the mathematical astronomical texts. A Babylonian year contains an integer number of months, usually 12. But 12 synodic months add up to only about 354 days. Such a year very quickly is out of step with the course of the sun, and therefore with the seasons – which is what people will notice without any knowledge of astronomy. In order to keep the seasonal events like the harvest at the same time in the year, a month was added to the year whenever it was thought to be necessary. So some years have 13 months. The decision when a month had to be intercalated lay with the king. Until about 500 B.C., intercalation was irregular. At this time, an intercalation cycle of 19 years was introduced which contained 7 additional months in a fixed pattern so that one could know in advance which years would be intercalary. The cuneiform texts relating to astronomical observation.

Towards the end of the second millennium B.C. we find pieces of astronomical knowledge embedded in omens derived from events in the sky. There are tables for the visibility of the moon during the course of the month, and very approximate schemes for the time intervals between the phases of planets.

From this time we also have lists arranging the constellations more or less according to their place in the sky, and also according to the time of the year when they appear and disappear. Since the lists want to assign three constellations to each month, it is clear that they have to be rather schematic and cannot correspond exactly to reality. Such a scheme is projected onto the celestial sphere in the exhibition.

A more sophisticated approach is found in a compilation text called 'Plough star'.

It is preserved in copies from the 7th century and later, but some of its contents was probably compiled a few hundred years earlier. This text too begins with lists of constellations or stars, but they are arranged in three sections called 'paths' or 'roads', the first comprising northern stars, the second stars on both sides of the equator, and the third southern stars. This does not imply anything about the concept of equator: it is only convenient for us to describe the 'roads' in this way. The Babylonians observed the stars mostly on the horizon.

There are more interesting features in this 'Plough star' compendium. After listing the constellations in general, there follows a list arranging constellations in the order of their first visibility in the course of the year. Another list tells which stars rise when certain others set. One more list combines stars which culminate with those that rise at the same time. It is clear that all these lists can help us to identify the stars, and on the whole the identifications are well established. There are nevertheless some doubtful points, because the text still is somewhat schematic in its attempt to find for every month stars related to each other in the ways just mentioned. Next we find in the text an enumeration of the constellations in the 'path of the moon', as it is called, which more or less corresponds to what we call the zodiac; but at this time, the subdivision of the zodiac into twelve signs does not exist yet; 17 constellations are listed. Further sections describe the movement of the sun during the year in relation to the stars; rules for intercalation depending on the first visibility of certain stars; the times for the visibility and invisibility of the planets - these time intervals are very rough approximations; then the length of day and night in the course of the year, measured by the amounts of water in a water clock; and a table of the length of the shadow of a stick at certain times of the day, for the solstices and equinoxes only. Finally, there are a number of omens appended at the end. This shows that no separation existed between omens, what we would call astrology, and astronomy.

From the 7th century B.C. we have remnants of the archives of the Assyrian kings. Among the hundreds of letters which were sent to the kings and kept in these archives there are also messages from experts in celestial omens. Omens from signs observed in the sky were an important device to come to terms with the uncertainties of the future, and the contribution of Giovanna Biga in this volume will explore the importance of omens.

On the other hand the letters contain not only omens, but are also indications of a certain level of astronomy on the part of their senders.

It is evident that these experts knew about the phenomena of the planets and their sequence. About the time intervals between the planetary phenomena they had only rough knowledge, quite similar to what one can read in the 'Plough star' compendium mentioned before. One can see this from the following quote from one of these letters:

> Mars has reached Cancer and entered it. I kept watch: it did not become stationary, it did not stop. It touched the lower part of Cancer and goes on.
>
> Its going out of Cancer remains to be seen. When it will have gone out I shall send its interpretation to the king my lord.
>
> Maybe someone will write to the king as follows: "If Mars comes close to Cancer: the ruler will die." If it had become stationary and stopped, that would have been a bad sign. This (what was observed) is bad for Babylonia.

They do pay attention to the following planetary phenomena: a planet being in a particular constellation; first or last visibility; retrograde motion; conjunctions with other planets or the moon; planets in the halo of the moon; planets visible during an eclipse. They frequently predict the length of a month (29 or 30 days) or the date of the full moon, sometimes one or two months in advance. We do not know how these predictions were made; probably the distance between sun and moon at last visibility was used, but this is not enough for a secure prediction. The writers were also able to tell the king several days in advance if a lunar eclipse would be likely. They could, with more confidence, also say when a lunar or solar eclipse would not be possible. Contrary to what is sometimes said, they (and all Babylonian astronomers down to the very end of Babylonian civilisation) were not able to predict solar eclipses, because for this one has to have some idea about the spherical shape of the earth, and to know where on it one is located. This however was not known in Babylonia.

It is evident from these letters that the phenomena of celestial bodies were observed carefully, and this probably had been done for centuries. However, there were no records sufficiently precise concerning time and place in the sky of these phenomena; so predictions could not be based on calculation. The senders of the letters were clearly interested in predicting the ominous phenomena which they observed. But they did not have very much to go by.

It is therefore quite likely that exactly these experts initiated the sys-

1. Page 40, *Astronomical diary* for 191/190 B.C.

2. Astronomical calculations for 104/102 B.C.

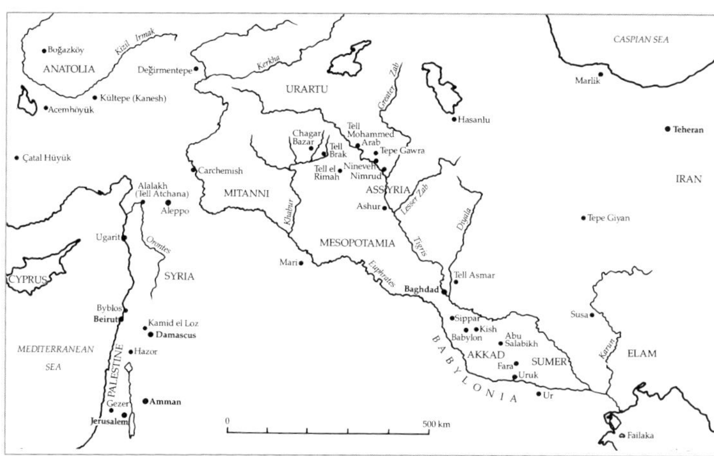

3. Geographic chart of the ancient Near East.

tematic observations which were carried out during the later part of the first millennium B.C. The oldest observations that we have are reports on lunar eclipses, beginning in the middle of the 8th century. Babylonian observations of lunar eclipses were still available to the famous Greek astronomer Claudius Ptolemy, who lived in the 2nd century A.D.; of course this does not mean he could read clay tablets, but only that these reports about eclipses reached him in some form. Apart from the eclipse reports, there are also tablets with planetary observations from Babylonia, beginning in the 7th century. The source of all these collected observations seems to be the so-called Astronomical Diaries.

More than a thousand diary tablets have been found, but most of them are fragments and quite small. A typical *Diary* covers 6 or 7 months making up the first or second half of a Babylonian year, with a section for each month. The following astronomical phenomena are recorded:

1. For the moon: At the beginning of each monthly section, there is a statement about the length of the preceding month, whether it had 29 or 30 days. Then the time interval between sunset and moonset on the first evening of the month is recorded.

Around full moon, the time intervals between rising and setting of moon and sun before and after opposition. Toward the end of the month, the date of the morning of the last visible crescent is recorded, together with the time interval from moonrise to sunrise.

Duration and magnitude of lunar eclipses are noted, the planets that were visible during the eclipse, weather conditions etc.

2. For the outer planets Mars, Jupiter, and Saturn, the *Diaries* give the dates of first and last visibility, of the stationary points and of opposition; for first and last visibility, the zodiacal sign is also recorded. For the inner planets Venus and Mercury, we find the dates and zodiacal signs of first and last visibility as a morning star and as an evening star.

3. The dates of the equinoxes and solstices and the appearances of the star Sirius are all given according to a schematical computation; so these are not observations.

4. In addition to these phenomena, the passings of the moon and the planets by certain stars near the ecliptic are recorded. The distance of the moon and the planets from these stars is measured.

5. Apart from astronomical observations, the *Diaries* frequently mention weather conditions, the prices of some basic commodities, like barley and dates, and the water level of the river Euphrates.

6. Lastly, for each months so-called historical events or rumours of such events are reported. These events can be of great importance, like the death of Alexander the Great. We find notes about battles, military expeditions, changes of reigns, and much more. Unfortunately, the bad state of preservation of the tablets leaves many details in these historical reports uncertain. Since the diaries can be dated on astronomical grounds, the historical events mentioned can also be dated securely.

From the *Diaries*, other types of non-mathematical astronomical texts are derived.

One group consists of the so-called Goal-year texts.

This is again not a Babylonian name but a modern one. They contain materials for the prediction of planetary and lunar phenomena for a certain year, the goal year. Planetary phenomena, like a first visibility or a stationary point, occur after a certain number of years at almost the same calendar date within a Babylonian year. Every planet and the moon have a separate section in the Goal-year texts. In it, the phenomena of the planet are collected from a year which is by one period earlier than the goal year. So the first section contains the phenomena of Jupiter from a year which preceded the goal year by 71 years. In a similar way data for the other planets and for the moon are presented, in each case by one period earlier than the goal year. The periods are 71 or 83 years for Jupiter, 8 years for Venus, 46 for Mercury, 59 for Saturn, and 79 or 47 for Mars. The procedure is as if a modern astronomer, instead of making computations for the year 2009, would use the data of 1938 for Jupiter, those of 2001 for Venus, of 1963 for Mercury, of 1950 for Saturn, and of 1930 for Mars.

The goal year texts are obviously excerpted from the *Diaries*. They use exactly the same expressions, and they even contain remarks about bad weather which prevented an observation, as do the *Diaries*.

A third group are called *Almanacs* (by modern scholars); they do look somewhat like calendars. They contain predictions for a whole Babylonian year in 12 or 13 sections, one for each month. At the beginning of each monthly section, the length of the preceding month, 29 or 30 days, is given. Then follows a summary of where the five planets were at the beginning of the month. The remaining data are then arranged chronologically. For most of the planetary phenomena, the zodiacal sign in which they occurred is mentioned. It is also indicated when a planet moved from one zodiacal sign into another. The *Almanacs* also contain data for eclipses. Lunar eclipses which are visible in Babylon are predicted, sometimes with an indication of their magnitude. If a solar eclipse is considered possible, the almanacs add the remark 'to be watched for' because the Babylonians were never sure whether a solar eclipse would actually be visible.

In the *Almanacs*, remarks about bad weather are completely absent. From this and the remark about solar eclipses it can be seen that the *Almanacs* are predictions, not observations. How the predictions were made, is uncertain, but it is very likely that the goal year texts were used in their construction. One of the possible purposes of these *Almanacs* could be the construction of so-called horoscopes, because these Babylonian texts contain exactly the data that are provided by the *Almanacs* and apply them to the date of a birth of a child. About two dozen such texts are known; they list the positions of the planets, sun and moon for a particular day, on which a child was born, and also mention other astronomical phenomena, like eclipses, some time before and after that day. They only rarely make predictions about the child's future.

The most successful predictions of astronomical phenomena are found in the mathematical astronomical texts, which are one of the great intellectual achievements of the Babylonians. So far about 400 tablets and fragments of such computations have been found. They make use of very simple mathematical tools, but by combining these computation methods they succeed in describing rather complicated astronomical relations.

Most phenomena of the celestial bodies are periodic, i.e. they are repeated after a certain time interval. These time intervals however are usually not constant but of varying length. In addition, the phenomena do not occur every time at the same place in the sky, as represented by the fixed stars, but they can be seen in different places.

Nowadays, if astronomers want to compute time and place of a certain phenomenon, they start from the Laws of Physics, and compute the forces that act on the celestial bodies. The Babylonians did not know of such forces. They just measured the position of a planet along its path in degrees, and they measured time in units of their calendar, months and days, and fractions of them. The mathematical astronomy of the Babylonians is directed towards the computation of positions and times of phenomena of the moon and planets, and not to the explanation of the geometric properties of their motion.

To calculate the periodic variation in time and position of celestial phenomena, Babylonian astronomers used sequences of numbers separated by constant differences.

As an example, let us consider the length of daylight in the course of the year. Somewhat simplified, at summer solstice there is a maximum of 16 hours, at winter solstice a minimum of 8. In between, the daylight lasts for 12 hours at the equinoxes.

Months	Hours	Months	Hours	Months	Hours
I	12	V	14 2/3	IX	9 1/3
II	13 1/3	VI	13 1/3	X	8
III	14 2/3	VII	12	XI	9 1/3
IV	16	VIII	10 2/3	XII	10 2/3

The Babylonians assumed a constant difference from month to month. Starting from a given value, one reaches the next by adding the difference. Whenever the maximum is reached, the difference is subtracted until the minimum occurs. Then the direction is again reversed, and the difference added. A graphic representation looks as follows.

Of course, no such drawing ever occurs in Babylonian texts; this is a typically modern device. The Babylonian texts only contain sequences of numbers. Such sequences were combined by the Babylonian astronomers cleverly to compute complicated movements like that of the moon and the planets.

For their complicated computations, the Babylonians needed less observational data than one might believe. Since the phenomena are periodic, it is important to establish the periods as accurately as possi-

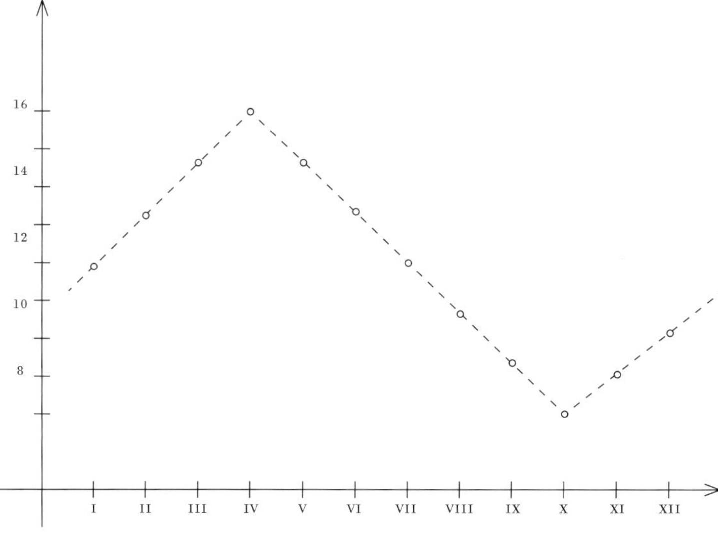

ble. Once this is done, the details of calculation can be adapted to the arithmetical possibilities. It is obvious that the values in the Babylonian tables are not directly taken from observations: no observations would have yielded values of a seeming precision of seconds of time. The fractions are the result of computational requirements in order to keep the period relations intact.

The Babylonian tables for the Moon are by far the most complicated. In them, different components were taken into account for the movements of the moon. It is in itself an important idea to think of a movement which cannot easily be understood as being composite, and to try to analyse it and isolate its components. The Babylonians did not do this in the same way as later astronomers, but they were the first to use this idea.

The tablet (fig. 2) computes the date of the new moon, i.e. the evening on which the thin crescent of the moon can be seen for the first time after it had been invisible for two or three days.

While the computation of these tables is an impressive achievement, it does raise a number of questions about the historical aspects of Babylonian astronomy. Who wanted to have such tables computed? Who would be interested to know when the synodic phenomena of the planets happen? It is true that omens were derived from some of them. But again, as celestial omens mostly concerned the country as a whole or the king as its representative, for whom was it necessary to know about such omens? Or did the astronomers do the computing for their own satisfaction? We have tantalizingly few documents relating to these questions. There are a few contracts dating from the 2nd century B.C. about the employment of men who are, according to these contracts, paid for producing astronomical tables and observations. Their employer is the Marduk temple in Babylon. So it seems that the temple was interested in the service of the astronomers. How they were of use to the temple is not known to us. But it is clear that only through the association with the temple the astronomical activities in Babylonia remained alive until the end of the first century A.D., when all other native institutions had long ceased to function.

Can any relations be shown between Greek and Babylonian astronomy? There are basic differences. In Greece geometrical models of the movements of moon and planets were used early on, whereas the Babylonians relied on arithmetical procedures to find the desired results. We cannot tell from the Babylonian astronomical texts what their authors thought about the spatial relationship among the planets; it did not influence their calculations.

Given these differences it is even more surprising that important numerical parameters were taken over by Greek astronomers from Babylonia. The first to have done so seems to have been Hipparchus in the second half of the 2nd century B.C.. Some of the periods he used for computing the moon's movements are known from Babylonian calculations. He is the first of whom we know that he used sexagesimal fractions, which certainly come from Babylonia, and also the measure 'cubit' known from the Babylonian *Diaries*.

How may Hipparchus have learnt about all this? There certainly existed connections between the Greek world and the East, especially after Alexander's conquests. A few years ago an Egyptian papyrus from about the 2nd century A.D. was found which contained a column of a Babylonian lunar table in Greek writing. In the meantime, a number of similar papyri in the collection of the papyri from Oxyrhynchus have been published. Of course this does not prove that Babylonian methods were widespread already at the time of Hipparchus; neither he nor Ptolemy refer to such methods. To understand a Babylonian table one needs a person to explain it, and it must remain speculation whether Hipparchus himself met with Babylonians sufficiently versed in Greek to provide him with such explanations. It is more likely that he acquired his information in ways about which we do not know. It remains certain that he took over important details from Babylonia.

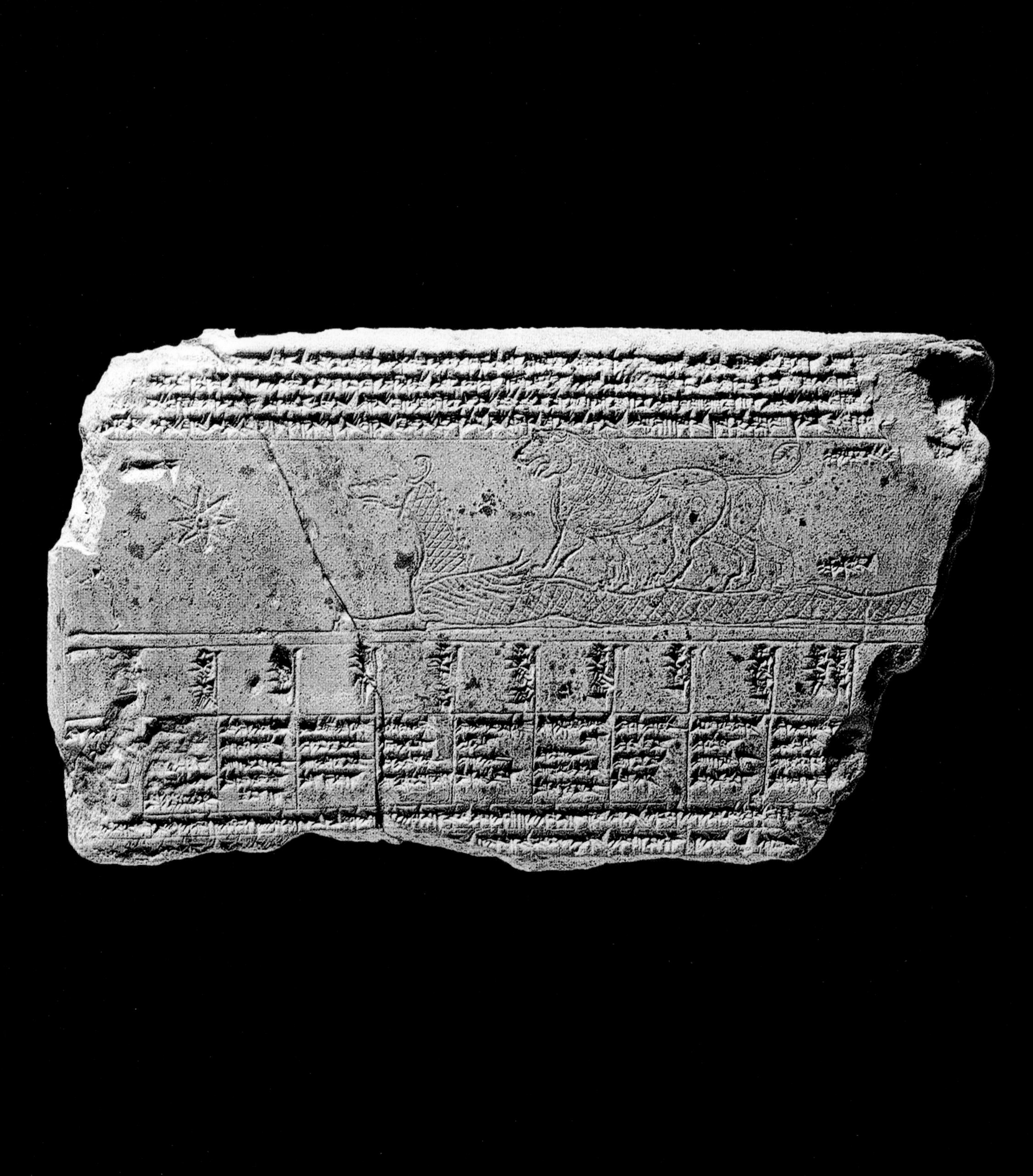

THE ANCIENT WORLD

1 | THE DAWN OF ASTRONOMY: MESOPOTAMIA, EGYPT AND THE BIBLICAL COSMOS

ASTROLOGY AND DIVINATORY PRACTICES IN THE ROYAL COURTS AND AMONG THE PEOPLES OF THE ANCIENT NEAR EAST

Maria Giovanna Biga

The peoples of the ancient Near East believed the sky to be the original home of the gods, as shown by the cuneiform sign for 'god', the representation of a star in the sky. This sign was used in the language of the Sumerians, the people that inhabited southern Mesopotamia in the late fourth millennium B.C., both to indicate the god of the sky (the Sumerian An) and as a determinative qualifying all the names of deities from the very origins of cuneiform writing until its demise in the first centuries of the Christian era.

The world of Near Eastern polytheism was dominated by a multitude of gods who conveyed their wishes to men by sending signs. Accordingly, various divinatory practices were carried out to comprehend these signs and understand episodes from the past, to interpret the present and predict the future. Any sign sent from heaven, it was thought, must surely be followed by an event. Some omens were requested of the gods, others not; earthquakes or eclipses of the Moon or the Sun, for instance, foretold dreaded terrestrial and celestial *omina*. Every celestial sign, examined on the heavenly vault by studying the motion of the stars and planets, foreshadowed some event. The astronomical texts were based on the concept that, if a certain thing happens in the sky, then another specific thing is bound to happen on Earth. The celestial *omina* were thought to exert their influence on the whole country and its representatives: the king, the royal court and their policies.

Already in the earliest recorded texts of Mesopotamian and Syrian history, omens from the gods were being sought in the entrails of animals and in the sky. In the most ancient lists of Sumerian words and gods, the names of astral deities had appeared since the early third millennium B.C.

In the second millennium hepatoscopy predominated, that is, examination of the liver of an animal sacrificed for this purpose. Remaining the favourite practice for interpreting the will of the gods up to the first millennium, it was then superseded by astrology, especially for omens concerning the king and the state, although astrological signs were frequently subjected to confirmation by hepatoscopy. Every Near Eastern sovereign had at his service experts who interpreted for him the signs found in the entrails and livers of animals. Some rulers, such as the Mesopotamian King Shulgi from the Third Dynasty of Ur (21st century B.C.), boasted of being able to verify the diviners' interpretation of entrails, ensuring that a positive sign could not be mistaken for a negative one.[1]

For all of the ancient Near Eastern peoples, the supreme astral deity was the Moon, whose appearance, disappearance and changing phases were observed and studied, and which regulated the cycles of the months, the agricultural calendar crucial to the Sumerians, whose lives depended on cultivation. The Sumerian moon god Nanna, whose chief temple stood in the sanctuary of Ur, was greatly revered. The temple was built in the form of a *ziqqurat*, a tower topped by a *sancta sanctorum*. By the Semitic populations, and in particular the Akkadians (recorded as present in Mesopotamia from the middle of the third millennium B.C.), the moon god was called Sin, and was deeply revered. The name of a great sovereign from the Akkadian period (23rd century B.C), Naram-Sin, means 'Beloved by the god Sin', showing how greatly the god was venerated by the ruling dynasty as well. The name of the god Sin appears repeatedly in proper names, including those of many kings, such as Amar-Sin, Shu-Sin, Ibbi-Sin from the Ur Third Dynasty (21st century B.C.), whose capital was the city of Ur, of which Sin was the poliadic god. Up to the first centuries of the Christian era another important sanctuary of the moon god existed at Kharran, in today's Turkey but in the Syrian cultural area. And it is no coincidence that the Bible states that the patriarch Abraham departed from Ur and travelled with his people to Kharran before Joshua led them to the Promised Land.

The god's name was also written as the number 30, the conventional number of days in a month in the Near Eastern calendar, which was a lunar calendar. We know of many hymns and prayers to this god who lit up the night, and who soon became the protector of divinatory practices as well.[2]

Nanna was considered the father of the sun god, called Utu in Sumerian and Shamash in Akkadian, the deity who saw everything in his daily journey and thus presided over justice and diurnal divining. For this divinity too, beautiful hymns are known; the most ancient of them, recorded in texts from the middle of the third millennium found at the site of Abu Salabikh in central Mesopotamia, was translated by the scribes of the Syrian kingdom of Ebla (24th century B.C.). Curiously enough, the sun god was male in Mesopotamia but female in the Syrian world. A long hymn to the sun god found in second-millennium Mesopotamian texts describes his journey through the day and the night, his activity as vigilant guardian and protector of merchants and wayfarers travelling the roads, and as the implacable judge who punishes the usurer, the cheating merchant, the unjust judge, and rewards the honest.[3]

The other greatly revered astral deity was the Sumerian goddess Inanna. Early identified with the planet Venus, called Ishtar by the Semites, she was the most idolized goddess in the history of the ancient Near East. To her too were dedicated numerous hymns describing her diverse functions and often, in the Akkadian language versions, depicting her as queen of the skies and the stars and daughter of the sun god Sin. Many prayers, lamentations and supplications to her are also known.[4] The gods of the night, the constellations, were worshipped too. To them above all the diviners addressed their prayers, asking their assistance in nocturnal divinatory practices.[5]

Astrology, among the various divinatory practices, concerned almost exclusively the destiny of the king and the state. It was believed, in fact, that the stars moving through the heavenly vault announced divine decisions concerning the whole community: the victory or defeat of armies, tumult and insubordination in the cities, stability or insecurity of the throne, wars or reconciliation between kings, numerous births and prosperity or famine. While people of every rank consulted the diviners who interpreted signs found in the entrails and livers of sacrificed animals, the flight of birds, the direction of smoke from burning incense, the pattern of oil poured on water, etc., to know how to act before the gods and to ward off impending evil, the lives of the king and the royal court were heavily influenced by the astrologists.

The names of many stars, planets and astral deities are Sumerian, showing that observation of the motions of celestial bodies for divinatory purposes had begun already in the third millennium B.C.; but it was the Old Babylonian period, starting in the early years of the second millennium, that – based on today's findings – handed down to us the first astrological texts containing predictions based on observation of the Moon, the Sun and atmospheric phenomena.

In the lexical texts of the time, studied by scribes in the schools, appear many names of celestial bodies, among them the Moon, the Sun, the five planets visible to the naked eye, the stars and numerous constellations. Mesopotamian science always proceeded by accumulation, piling up new information generated in every field of knowledge, and thus enabling the scribes – mainly from schools annexed to the great temples such as that of Enlil, in the Mesopotamian city of Nippur – to compile large collections of astrological omens already at this time.

Texts from Old Babylonian times have been found in the royal archives in the palace of Mari, the capital of a kingdom in the Middle Euphrates. A great political and cultural centre during the first centuries of the second millennium B.C., Mari was later destroyed by King Hammurabi of Babylon. These texts provide abundant information on the various divinatory techniques, foremost among them hepatoscopy, but also observation of the flight of birds and interpretation of dreams. They also contain numerous predictions requested by the king of prophets from the chief temples of the time, especially that of the storm god Adad at Aleppo, and at Terqa and Tuttul, where the prophets and prophetesses of the god Dagan conveyed his omens. Some of the Mari texts deal with predictions on eclipses of the Moon, considered ominous signs.[6]

The best-known text in Mesopotamian literature, the Epic of Gilgamesh (first millennium), the legendary hero of the city of Uruk in Lower Mesopotamia, also shows the importance of omens sent by the gods to the hero, often under the form of dreams involving the heavens. For instance, Gilgamesh tells his divine mother Ninsun one of the dreams sent him to inform him of the presence of a coming antagonist, Enkidu: 'Mother, I dreamed last night that I was wandering joyfully here and there in the midst of heroes. Then there appeared stars in the sky and the firmament of An fell onto me. I tried to lift it, but it was too heavy for me; I tried to move it but could not'.[7] Frequently, during his adventures, Gilgamesh prays the sun god Shamash to send him an omen.

In the cuneiform texts, all of the omen series were referred to by their first lines. Poems and hymns to the gods were also known by their first lines. But what distinguishes Mesopotamian and Syrian divination as a whole was the belief that signs, even ominous ones, sent to men by the gods, were not inevitable and could in some way be averted by making sacrifices or performing special rituals addressed to the gods, or to the particular god thought to have sent the message. For this purpose the specialists in every divinatory technique had to know the procedures to be carried out to avert these evils, the exorcisms to be recited and the rituals to be performed. A special group of exorcists, for example, dealt with omens concerning diseases.

Although it was always possible to examine the entrails of an animal simply by choosing one suitable for sacrifice, the sky could be observed only in good weather.

1. Page 46, astrological plaque from Uruk,
Seleucid age, with representations of constellations;
in particular, at left, the planet Jupiter and the symbols
of the constellations of Hydra (the winged serpent with
lion's paws) and of Leo.

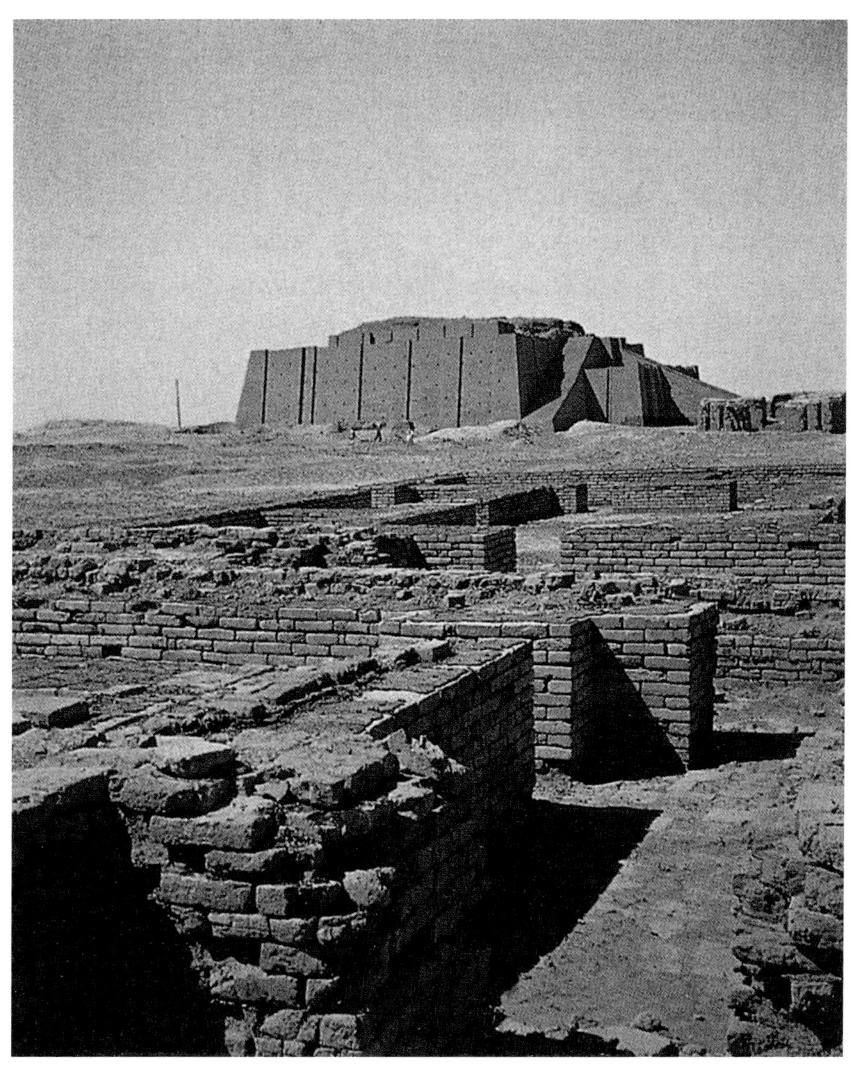

2. The ziqqurat of Ur as it appears today, partially reconstructed.

The earliest collections of astronomical omens date from the Old Babylonian period. It was probably at this time that a first core group of prayers and hymns in honour of Marduk, the poliadic god of Babylon, was formed. Much later, in the 12th century B.C., under the reign of King Nebuchadnezzar I, this original group of prayers assumed more organic form in a long hymn to Marduk, known to the ancient Mesopotamians by the first line, 'When above the heaven had not yet been named'. Today this hymn is known to scholars as *The Epic of Creation*, because it starts by narrating how fresh water and salt water emerged from the original chaos, for successive generations, up to the birth of the god Marduk. The latter, after defeating his enemy Tiamat, creates the heavens and earth from her body, establishes the places of the astral deities and the various stars and constellations, and creates the calendar. The text provides a clear picture of the knowledge of astral geography of the times.[8]

But it was starting from the Neo-Assyrian age (10th–7th century B.C.) that astrology made rapid progress in observation methods, leading to the gradual transformation of this discipline into astronomical activity based on mathematics.[9] Since celestial signs were thought to be addressed directly to the king and the whole state, the science of divining was restricted to groups of individuals connected to the palace and the great temples of the kingdom.

Starting in the late 8th century and throughout the 7th the sovereigns Sennacherib, Esarhaddon and then his son Ashurbanipal became custodians of the knowledge of the Sumerian and Akkadian tradition from the preceding millenniums, ordering their scribes to collect texts on divination and propitiatory rites of all kinds for the libraries of the capital city Nineveh.

In excavating a well in the Assyrian capital of Kalkhu (today's Nimrud), British archaeologists unearthed a magnificent ivory polyptych inscribed, in dense, perfect writing with some 1000 lines from the astrological series Enuma Anu Enlil. The inscription 'Palace of Sargon' shows that the splendid work was destined to the new capital Dur-Sharrukin then being built by the sovereign. King Sennacherib too was kept constantly informed by his astrologers and haruspexes of every good and bad omen they observed.

But the most plentiful information on the experts who worked at the Assyrian courts, especially that of Nineveh, is provided by the two last great sovereigns of the Neo-Assyrian Empire, Esarhaddon and Ashurbanipal (7th century B.C.). Both kings ordered experts in the various divinatory disciplines to copy for the library of Nineveh, or to bring there, ancient texts from the libraries of Babylon and other cities in southern Mesopotamia such as Uruk, Borsippa, and Sippar, as well as from other parts of the kingdom. And it is for this reason

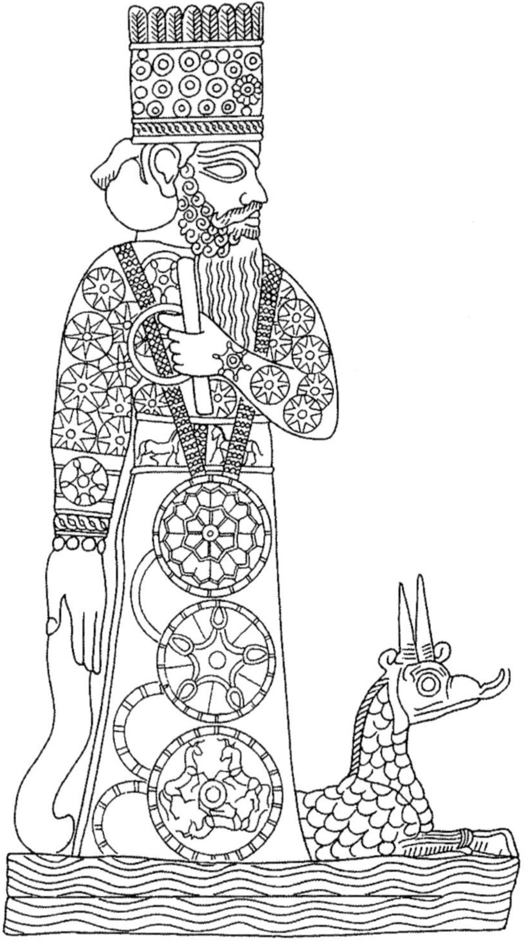

3. Graphic representation of detail of a seal portraying the god Marduk, 9th century B.C; Babylon, Iraq.

that in the Nineveh library have been found, brought to light by the British excavations of Sir Henry Austin Layard, the most important collections of divinatory texts, including works on astrology and astronomy now at the British Museum in London. Collections of divinatory texts were found in other cities of the empire as well, such as Assur (which had a great library annexed to the temple of Assur, the empire's chief god), Kalkhu (also a capital of the Assyrian Empire), and in the homes of the diviners. At the Assyrian court were experts (*ummânu*) specifically trained in the various divination techniques, both prayers for warding off evil and rituals performed to avert the consequences of inauspicious omens. The experts instructed a group of scribes in these occult arts. A clear example is provided by the letter written by one of these experts, a diviner, to his lord King Esarhaddon. The diviner, who had fallen into disgrace, wrote a supplication to the king describing his skills: 'May the king my lord summon me and if I must die, let me die. If I am to live, let me continue to observe the stars in the sky and should I see there a sign, let me inform the lord of kings, my lord! The profession of my father, the discipline of religious lamentation, I have perfectly mastered. [There follows a list of rituals, including purification of the king's palace, and of divinatory treatises with which he is thoroughly familiar] ... I have read the Enuma Anu Enlil series... and I have conducted astronomical observations. [This is followed by another list of rituals for various forms of divination].[10]

We know the names of many wise men who played a crucial role in the policies of the two great sovereigns Esarhaddon and Ashurbanipal, who had set up a network of stations for observing the sky in the various parts of the empire. The astronomers of the Assyrian cities of Nineveh, Assur, Arbela, Khalkhu and those of Babylon, Borsippa, Dilbat, Nippur, Uruk and Ur in Babylonia sent, in fact, regular reports to the sovereigns. We also know the names of many astronomers who powerfully influenced the policies and decisions of their sovereigns: for example, Nabu-zeru-leshir and his son Ishtar-shumu-eresh, the learned experts of Esarhaddon and Ashurbanipal. Akkullanu, high priest of the god Assur, also wielded great influence. Although the power of these experts was controlled and limited, some of them took part in political decisions, with decisive consequences.[11] It was a group of astronomers, for instance, who decided when to carry out a ritual that came to be enacted much more frequently under the reign of King Esarhaddon: that of the 'substitute king'. This sovereign appears to have been strongly conditioned by some of his diviners, most notably the all-powerful Adad-shumu-usur.[12] Esarhaddon had become king after the assassination of his father Sennacherib by his elder brothers, who had refused to accept their father's decision to name his younger son Esarhaddon his successor. The brothers had gone so far as to slay their father in the temple of the god Ninurta, a sacrilegious act for which Esarhaddon exacted atonement from the guilty. In 674 B.C., in the seventh year of his reign, there was a total eclipse of the Moon, generally thought to portend the death of the king. Esarhaddon, deeply shaken by this event, immediately called in his diviners. To ward off the effects of this dreadful omen, they advised him to perform the ancient ritual of the 'substitute king'. It consisted of sending the king away from the capital city for a while to a safe place and installing on the throne a substitute, chosen from among the notables (and later the servants) who would draw onto himself the inauspicious omen. When the situation had returned to normal, the substitute king was removed and almost certainly killed (along with the substitute queen), while the true king resumed his place. Under the reign of Esarhaddon there were twelve eclipses, total or partial, of the Moon and two of the Sun. Esarhaddon performed this ritual no less than four times, as we know from the letters sent him by his advisers. In one of these letters[13] we read, 'To our lord, your servants Issar-shumu-eresh, Urad-Ea and Marduk-shakin-shumi. All health to our lord! May Nabu and Marduk bestow blessings on our lord! In accordance with what our lord has written us: 'On the 29th day an eclipse of the sun has taken place', we will carry out the necessary apothropaic ritual. Some one must occupy the throne to avert the portended evil.'

Other letters inform the king – who is now far from the throne and is referred to as 'the farmer' – that the situation has returned to normal, the substitute king can 'go to meet his fate' (that is, most probably, be put to death), and the true king can resume his rule. There are cases in which the substitute king remained on the throne for as long as a hundred days. This ritual was also carried out by King Ashurbanipal.

Many of the classical authors, among them Herodotus, hint at the existence of a similar practice among the Persians. And some authors who wrote of the life of Alexander the Great – in particular Plutarch, Arrianus and Diodorus Siculus – reported that a comparable procedure was carried out in Babylon when the young king Alexander lay gravely ill, in danger of death. The wise men of the kingdom suggested performing the ancient Mesopotamian ritual of the substitute king, but the stratagem was doomed to failure and Alexander died in Babylon in 323 B.C.

Under the two sovereigns Esarhaddon and Ashurbanipal, the Sun god, who saw all from above, was called upon to confirm some of the predictions made by observing the entrails and livers of sacrificed animals.[14] These omens and requests for confirmation by the god are

4. Plaque with hymn to the sun god from Ebla.

reported on tablets. The queries concern the political problems of the empire, especially difficulties with bordering populations, such as the Phrygians and other peoples of Asia Minor and Cappadocia, with Urartu, Scythia and Mannea to the north, Media and Elam to the East and with Egypt and the Levant. The petitions all begin with the phrase, 'O god Shamash, great lord, give me a firm positive answer to what I ask of you', followed by indication of the time within which an answer from the god is expected (usually less than a month) and questions on the movement of troops, the outcome of sieges and other military operations. Lastly, the god is requested to verify and confirm the oracular response furnished by the haruspexes who have examined the entrails and liver of a sacrificial animal.

This *corpus* of texts dating from the time of kings Esarhaddon and Ashurbanipal, along with the hundreds of letters written them by the diviners to report and interpret ominous signs, clearly shows the extreme attention to the oracles paid by these sovereigns, who frequently consulted astrologists, without neglecting any of the other forms of divination. At the courts of these sovereigns the astronomers who interpreted the meaning of eclipses, meteors and other natural phenomena such as earthquakes in relation to the life of the king, the court and the whole country, worked in close contact with other specialists from every branch of divination.

In the following epoch as well, that of the Chaldeans, who put an end to the Assyrian Empire by establishing the great Neo-Babylonian Empire (6th century B.C.), great importance was assigned to astral omens, on which depended the choice of a king and the welfare of the kingdom. A significant example is found in an inscription of King Nabonidus, the last ruler of Chaldean Babylonia, who witnessed the downfall of the vast Neo-Babylonian Empire and the entry of the Persian King Cyrus into Babylon in 539 B.C. Nabonidus, who had seized the throne some years after the death of Nebuchadnezzar, was not a member of the royal family. To convince the notables and people of the realm that his ascent to the throne was legitimate, he had carved on a stele, found badly damaged in Babylon, a long inscription stating that his predecessor Nebuchadnezzar and the god Marduk had told him in a dream that he was destined to assume power. The dream describes an astronomical configuration with an astral conjunction, a phenomenon deemed a sign sent by the gods. In the dream, an expert is immediately consulted, who interprets the conjunction as a good omen. 'I saw in a dream the conjunction of the Great Star and the Moon and decided. Then a man came to stand beside me, and turning to me he said, 'This conjunction bears no bad omen linked to it!' In the same dream there appeared before me King Nebuchadnezzar my predecessor with one of his followers, both standing in the royal chariot. His faithful follower turned to Nebuchadnezzar saying: 'Speak to Nabonidus who will tell you the dream he has seen'. Nabuchadnezzar listened to him; and spoke to me in these words: 'Tell me what good omens you have seen'. Then I answered him saying, 'In my dream the Great Star, the Moon and the planet Jupiter were rising to the firmament. I watched them with joy, and they called me by name ... I have raised altars to the planet Venus, the planet Saturn, the Star SHU-PA, the Star ..., the Great Star, inhabitants of the sky, the chief witnesses of my dream and I have prayed to them that my life may be long, my throne be stable, my reign be long-lasting and my words be favourably accepted by my lord Marduk' '.[15]

Although the documentation on astronomers and astrologers in the Neo-Babylonian period is much scarcer than in the Neo-Assyrian age, we know that astronomers continued to work in the temples in Seleucid times. A text dating from 110 B.C., during the era of the Arsacid Parthians, records the appointment of a new astrologer in the Esagila temple of Marduk in Babylon, and establishes forms of payment in silver and arable land.[16]

The last cuneiform tablet that has come down to us is one of astronomical content, dating from 75 A.D. It proves that the Mesopotamian science to survive the longest was astronomy, a group of doctrines that was transmitted to the later peoples of Greek and Latin tongue.

The Bible too records the Babylonian astronomers, although in harshly negative terms. In Isaiah 47, 13, where the fall of Babylon is described, we read: 'Let now the astrologers stand and save thee / they that gazed at the stars and counted the months / that from them they might tell the things / that will come to thee. / Behold, they are as stubble / fire hath burnt them / they shall not deliver themselves.'

–

Bibliography

Biga-Capomacchia 2008; Biga 2001, pp. 409-415; Bottéro-Kramer 1992; Castellino 1972; Castellino 1977; Durand 1988; Fales 1974, pp. 453-496; Fales 2001; Foster 1993; Joannès 2000; Hunger 1992; Hunger 2001, vol. I, chapter XIII, *Astronomia e astrologia*, pp. 419-426; Koch Westenholz 1995; Meyer 1988; Panaino 2001, vol. I, chapter XII, pp. 416-418; Parpola 1993; Pettinato 1992; Pettinato 1998; Pinnock 1995; Reiner 2005; Rochberg 2001, vol. I, chapter XIII, *Astronomia e astrologia*, pp. 426-433; Star 1990.

[1] V. Shulgi, Hymn B ll. 144-147, in Castellino 1972, pp. 44-45.

[2] Foster 1993, pp. 154-155, 680-684.

[3] The translation of this hymn is found in Castellino 1977, pp. 383-391.

[4] For the various types of texts dedicated to Inanna and Ishtar see Castellino 1977 and Foster 1993; for the astral divinities see Biga-Capomacchia 2008, pp. 107-109, 118-119, 187-189; for the lunar god see Pinnock 1995.

[5] See for example Foster 1993, pp. 146-147.

[6] For divination at Mari see the complete collections of texts translated and commentated by Durand 1988.

[7] For this translation see Pettinato 1992, p. 241.

[8] For the translation and commentary on the text see Bottéro-Kramer 1992, pp. 640-722.

[9] For a thorough discussion of all of the divinatory texts of the Neo-Assyrian period, and thus of astronomical texts, see chapter VII, 'I testi della divinazione', by Fales 2001, pp. 244-283.

[10] Fales 2001, p. 257.

[11] For a study of Neo-Assyrian astronomers see Pettinato 1998, pp. 140-157.

[12] For this figure see Fales 1974, pp. 453-496.

[13] V. Parpola 1993, p. 20, letter n. 25.

[14] For a study of the models of livers for hepatoscopy see Meyer 1988, Starr 1990, pp. XIII-LXXV; the volume contains all of the oracular petitions to Shamash.

[15] Joannès 2000, pp. 97-101.

[16] Joannès 2000, p. 169.

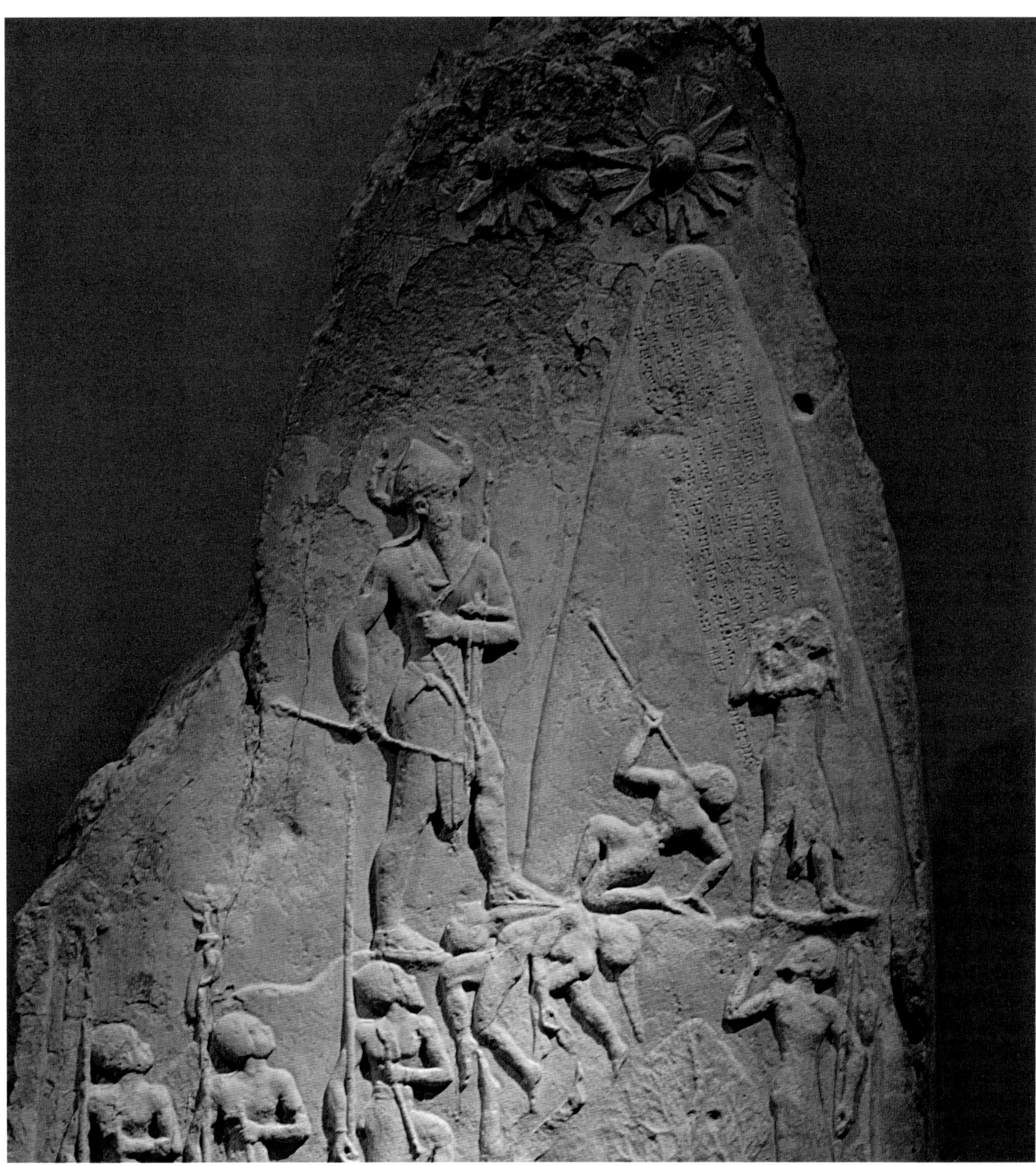

THE ANCIENT WORLD

–

1 | THE DAWN OF ASTRONOMY: MESOPOTAMIA, EGYPT AND THE BIBLICAL COSMOS

–

A PRESAGE OF HERESY METAPHYSICAL NOTES AND ICONOGRAPHIC THEMES FOR AN ARCHAEOLOGY OF THE MESOPOTAMIAN SKIES

–

Marco Ramazzotti

–

Empirical observation of the skies has been a relatively recent conquest of modern science, but one of crucial importance, since – as we know – it replaced the theoretical and iconographic centrality of the Earth with the multi-dimensional expanse of the universe. As regards perceptions, and to introduce our exploration of the skies over the land between two rivers, we may recall that *cosmos* is a Greek term, although when and where it assumed the connotation of order, and then of Celestial Order, is unknown. In this brief article, then, we intend to trace, *ex oriente*, the most ancient part of the tradition that linked Babylon to Jerusalem, two epicentres of Near Eastern astronomy and premonitory ideology that were undoubtedly known to the Alexandrine sphere.

Although the sky *nostrum*, ancient and Near Eastern, evokes the nocturnal atmosphere of *The Arabian Nights*, by convention, tradition and fatal absence of other information, one of the first poetic separations between earth and sky can be dated – with good approximation – to the 'Creation Poem', the *Enuma Elish*, compiled at the time of Nebuchadnezzar I of Babylonia (1124-1103 B.C.). It envisages the creation of a humanity at the service of the gods, and – according to even more ancient myths – the building of the *Esaghila*, home of the *Anunnaki*, the six hundred deities of heaven and earth. It is this division, this separation of the two unities, that gives rise to the celestial order and its twin, the human one, resting on a flat disc, floating in the primordial ocean, rendered finite only by the boundary marked by the stars.

The Sumerian logogram for the universe is *An-ki*, a compound term meaning both sky and earth. For us, accustomed to expressing the unity of the beginning, the origin, by the word *genesis*, it is immediately surprising to see that ideography (the writing of ideas) has absorbed the heavens and the earth in such hybrid form, without specifying either one or the other. Surrounding *An-ki* is *Apsû*, the ocean (the sea), suggesting that while it may be the primordial place of origin, *Lil* (translated as wind, air and spirit and today as ghost) is its energy, physical force deified; in the act of separating the sky from the earth, it infuses life. In such a context, it appears that this configuration of the universe is only one of the possible physical (and geometric) forms governing the complex relationships between the pre-eminent deities: *An* the sky god, *Enlil* the ghost god, *Enki* the water god and *Ninkhursag* the earth god.

In the religious literature and iconography this cosmic order often seems to burst out in a myriad of lyrics, hymns, lamentations and vulgate compositions that animate ever new traditions, as well as popular 'translations'. An example may be seen in a clay plaque carved in relief (fig. 2) from the city of Khafajah on the Diyala a tributary of the Tygris (18th century B.C.), which not only represents the allegory of a still unknown mythological battle, but demonstrates – at the same time – how in this narration the god is slain, if he can be correctly interpreted as the one-eyed monster with head shaped like the Sun who is pierced by the blade of another god. In any case, the land that covers part of *Apsû* also becomes the round site, flat and finite, of that 'Just Order' which is fixed in the primordial ocean below it, but which, for humans, must necessarily depend on observation of the heavens above it.

This vision was not only to play a decisive role in formulating a figurative aesthetic canon of harmony (and *cosmeo* was to be the Greek root of cosmos) – as demonstrated by many of the famous masterpieces of Old Babylonian and Old Syrian goldwork from the second millennium B.C., such as the necklaces of Dilbat and Ebla, unmistakeably inspired by astral forms (the Sun, the Moon, the planets and Venus) – but was also to forge the ideology of kingship, always in dialogue with the astral dimension of the divine. At the same time, observation of the motions of the celestial bodies could not fail to enrich predictive practices and thus also to replenish the images of kingship, their appearance and representation. Observation in fact always converged on and diverged from a single centre, from the political exigency of 'being' at the only centre of the universe, of being able to interpret everything in the belief that Babylonia coincides with the Earth, and that the Earth ends where the Ocean begins; which in fact flows all around it in the more ancient, in some respects still enigmatic, but famous *Mappa Mundi*, probably from Sippar (fig. 3). It is a Neo-Babylonian copy from the 5th century B.C. of a schematic map of the world, certainly inspired by remote systems of topograph-

1. Page 54, Stele of the Victory of Naram-Sin from Susa, detail, c. 2230 B.C.; Paris, Musée du Louvre, Sb. 4.

2. Clay plaque with mythological scene from Khafajah, 18th century B.C.; Baghdad, Iraqi Museum, I.M. 27783.

ical classification and by more archaic psychological maps of kingship. As concerns the celestial vault instead, the so-called 'Assyrian Planisphere' (K8538) found in the Library of Ashurbanipal at Nineveh is severely fragmented, but what emerges distinctly by integrating several sources is precisely the fact that the *focus* of observation of the sky irradiates from a centre, as in the *Mappa Mundi*. A hypothetical astrolabe would thus be divided into three concentric regions under the dominion of Anu, Enlil, and Ea, separated in turn into 12 sectors having areas equivalent to the 12 months of the year and, in the 36 regions resulting from the intersection of the 12 months with the 3 concentric circles, would appear the constellations for each month, inscribed in the area proper to the triad.

At every epoch, in Babylonia, the temple is the residence of the gods, where human destinies (*me*) are decided. This is well documented by myths narrating the spectacular events of their founding (such as the Eengurra temple of Enki in Eridu, immersed in Apsû, or the Ekur temple of Enlil at Nippur, emerging from Apsû at his command) and the just order of their positions, indicated both by the epic feats of the sage Enki – alleged to have built a temple in the midst of the sea orientated on the constellations of Pegasus and Ursa Major – and by the experimental attempts of man to design their layouts based on astral distances, as mentioned in the *Hymn to the Temple of Keši* and the so-called *Manual of Divination*. The sky was, we repeat, the twin sister of the earth, but man, other than admiring it, could do no more than measure its distances, replicating their proportions to calculate space and time. In this specific sense it is not by chance that, already in the late 4th millennium B.C., in the maze of concentric corridors (*Steingebäude*) buried under the high terrace of the White Temple in the Kullab region of Uruk, the four corners were oriented with striking precision in the directions of the cardinal points. It is equally interesting to recognise in the Pillar Hall (*Pfeiler-Halle*) at Eanna (the House of Heaven), the other sacred quarter of the First City dedicated to Inanna, a solar calendar.

The place for observing the space and time of this vault, which was then mythologized as the mangled half of the body of Tiamat, defeated in combat by Marduk, the greatest of the Babylonian gods, is not known with certainty; but even today there is no particular reason not to consider the tops of the ziqqurats as the best places for contemplating the sky. Nor does this exclude the performance of rituals linked to the festival held for the beginning of the new year (ziqqurat of Anu at Uruk); nor celebrations in honour of the moon god Nanna-Sin (Ziggurat of Nanna in Ur), nor those in honour of the sun god Utu-Shamash (Ebabbar at Larsa). These were imposing religious edifices, visible from every corner of the city and from inland, destined to serve

3. Babylonian map of the world, probably from Sippar, 700-500 B.C.; London, British Museum, W.A. 92687.

as models for more ambitious building projects such as the later ones of the Double Temple of Sin and Shamash and the Temple of Anu and Adad at Assur, the venerable capital of the Assyrians. Thus when *Genesis* would later call the Tower of Babel a 'symbol of the arrogance of a people that with a building wanted to touch the sky' (11: 1-9), it can be seen as a devastating moral judgement on the arrogance of a people, but also as a precise reference to a profound transformation in the relationship between astronomy and religion. Identification of the stars as gods, the motions of planets as omens for predicting events, the infinite reading of space and time based on celestial omens, was supplanted by an only God, creator of heaven and earth.

In Babylonia – to conclude – we find, always and everywhere, a very close correlation between propaganda and prediction. These two factors constitute the links of an inextricable chain, at the end of which rational action can be implemented only after predictive thought. But this is only the last reverberation, the most conspicuous one, in the relationship between ideology and astronomy in ancient Mesopotamia. The other, and not the least important, is the one that sees the stars as beneficial aids and protectors of human endeavours. One of the first historical personages to introduce us to this world is Enheduanna, the daughter of Sargon of Akkad who, invited as priestess to the sanctuary of the god Nanna at Ur, was so strongly opposed by the local priests of Nanna that she had to return to her own country; an episode that, as has been noted, exemplifies the conflict between the Sumerian priesthood and the Akkadian dynasty. The homage paid to Sin (the Moon), Ishtar (Venus) and Shamash (the Sun) is however only the political, and in a certain sense exterior, expression of a more intimate attention focused on the relationship of dependency between the celestial deities and victory.

The most ancient exaltations in this sense, such as the Stele of Naram Sin originally erected in the sanctuary of Sippar (fig. 1), already transform the disposition of the guardian stars into an iconology that was to become the compositional model for representing victories and justice, down to the first millennium B.C. The sovereign on a mountaintop, having crushed the enemy, is represented triumphant under three suns. Later this same syntax, polarized on the visual centrality of the major celestial bodies (the Sun and Moon) was also to dominate scenes of libation to the god, as shown by the Stele of Justice found at Susa and the probable reconstruction of the upper registers of the more ancient Stele of Ur-Namma from Ur, erected in honour of Nanna and Ningal, protectors of the capital, as well as Ninghirsu and Shamash. It may also have been an astral symbol, perhaps the morning star, the one placed on the top of the Votive Stele of Ishtar at Ebla – a palimpsest of Early Syrian cosmogony devastated by the Hittites

4. Detail of offerer wearing star-strewn gown, gold and copper figurine from Susa, 12th century B.C.; Paris, Musée du Louvre, Sb. 2758.

5. Front of plaque dedicated to the Sun god from Sippar, 9th century B.C.; London, British Museum, W.A. 91000.

around 1600 B.C. – where the goddess appears within a winged aedicule supported by two androcephalous bulls. In the Code of Hammurabi in the Louvre, instead, the upper logo is missing, but the consignment of the tools of power to Hammurabi by Shamash follows the same narrative as the Stele of Justice.

It may be from this sphere, from its best known representations, from those that have been integrated and those that can be reconstructed, that these astral symbols become, in regal deeds, the Babylonian *kudurru* of the Cassite period, signs of a divine guarantee that sets a seal to the donation of lands. These inscribed pillars, classified in various ways, were legal deeds kept in the temples; but what is most interesting today is the maze of symbols they bear, metamorphous, hybrid or individual: the man-lion, the centaur-snake, the lion-dragon, the fish-goat image of Ea, and again the serpent, the ear of grain, the sheaf of thunderbolts, and so on. That this association between kingship and legality fell under predictive astronomy and knowledge of the constellations, especially in Neo-Babylonian times, is also confirmed by the *omina*, texts relating how a certain apparition, form and/or position of the stars, eclipse or other event, will inevitably be followed by a certain occurrence. But archaeology is more sparing of information, although the rare cases of which we dispose are sufficient to demonstrate at least the 'preciousness' of the rituals performed. The bronze model of Sît-Shamshi from Susa dating from the 12th century B.C. may reproduce the sacred precinct of a ceremony held in honour of the rising Sun, as states the inscription, in which two kneeling personages raise their hands in prayer before an altar near a sacred woods and a Ziqqurat. This is the outdoor space where a special cult, probably a regal one, is practiced in honour of the Sun. The contemporary silver, gold and copper figurines of offerers from Susa, depicted wearing spectacular star-strewn gowns (fig. 4), could be interpreted in the same sense. The model and the two masterpieces tell us, the one of a ritual procedure, the other of a regal dimension in the office that now seems to have integrated the classic iconography of the king as offerer (the Good Shepherd) with a particular priesthood, perhaps mystical, of which we can unfortunately guess only the form, that is, the splendour of its garments, unique of their kind.

In any case (and apart from the details) this is the context that leads us toward the admirable mythological-symbolic elaboration of the 9th century B.C. of which the limestone plaque of Nabû-apla-iddina from *Ebabbar* (middle of the 9th century B.C.) is an exceptional document (fig. 5). The cuneiform inscription below evokes the decadence of the temple, the search for the precious simulacrum of the god Shamash at Nippur probably sacked by the Sutei nomads, and boasts that a new one has been made of gold and lapis; while in the upper registers, over a classic representation of the wavy sea (one of the possible forms of Apsû), the sovereign – followed by a goddess and preceded by a priest – is 'presented' to Shamash. The latter, who appears in the usual position on both the Stele of Justice and the Code of Hammurabi, is now flanked by three astral symbols (the waxing moon, the solar disc and the eight-pointed star) and sits, with the sceptre and ring of command, on a throne decorated by two androcephalous bulls similar to those of the Stele of Ishtar that bear his emblems. Leaning out from the top of the baldachin are two genies holding a solar disc on which appears a four-pointed star and four streams of water. The disc, perfected subdivided, is placed on an altar and separates the introductory scene from the iconic representation of the god.

Here we find a synthesis that closes our orbit. In this masterpiece carved in relief on gray schist, placed by Nabû-apla-iddina in the Ebabbar temple of Shamash at Sippar, salvaged by Nabupolassar (625-605 B.C.) or Nabonidus (555-539 B.C.) during one of the frequent restorations of the temple and deemed so important as to be assigned a new place and protected with a clay covering that has left its mark, between the sovereign and the god looms the icon of the solar disc, whose system is believed to have unveiled the mystery of life, of death – and of kingship.

–

Bibliography

Brecht 1955; Frankfort 1948; Horowitz 1998; Kohbach *et al.* 2007; Kramer 1956, pp. 45-62; Kramer 1964, pp. 149-152; Lambert 1975a, pp. 191-200; Lambert 1975b, pp. 42-65; Matthiae 1985; Matthiae 1992; Matthiae 1994; Matthiae 1995; Rochberg 2004; Wiggerman 1992, pp. 279-304; Winter 2002, pp. 3-28; Woods 2004.

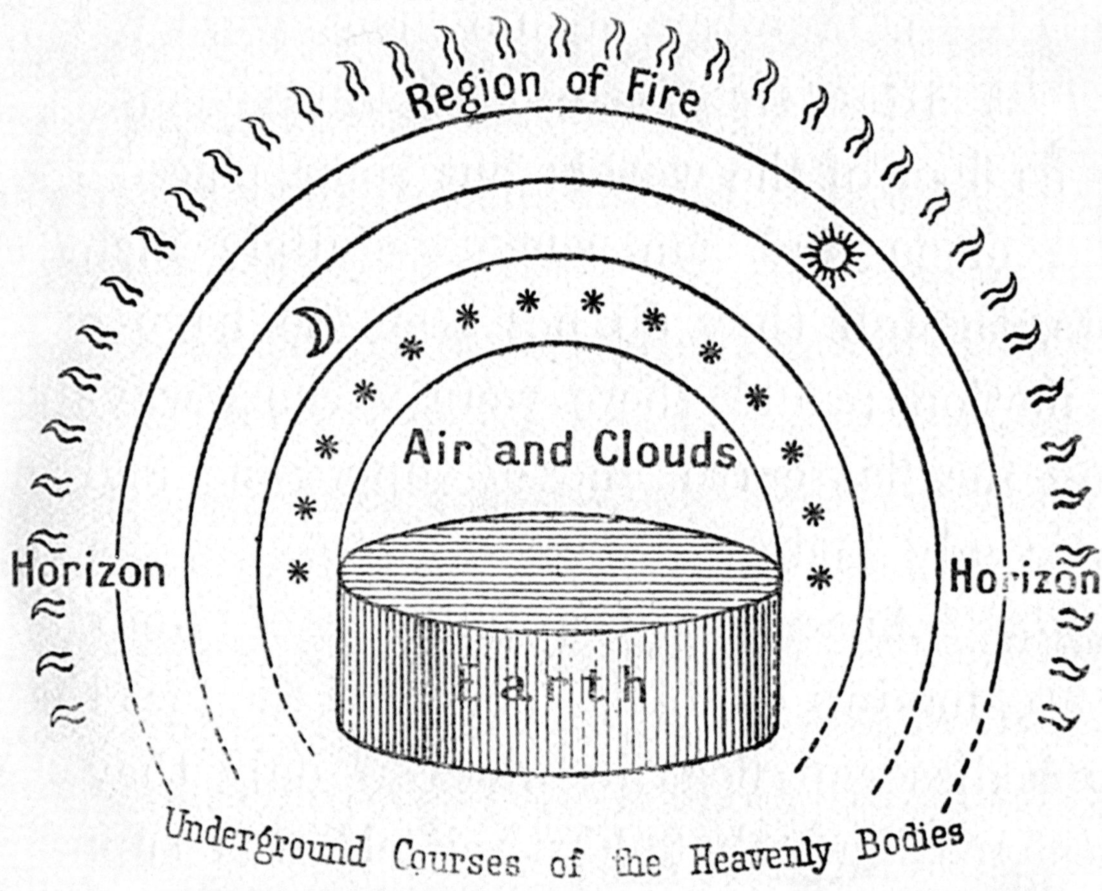
Region of Fire
Air and Clouds
Horizon
Horizon
Earth
Underground Courses of the Heavenly Bodies

THE ANCIENT WORLD

–

2| THE COSMOS BECOMES A SPHERE

–

IMAGES OF THE COSMOS AMONG THE GREEK PHILOSOPHERS

–

Giovanni di Pasquale

–

The generating principle will always be debated, and doubtful will
remain what is concealed and is so far above a man and a god.
(Manilius, *Astronomicon*, 1, vv. 145-146)

The image of the world handed down from classical civilisation to medieval Christian Europe, strongly influenced by the works of Plato, Aristotle and Ptolemy, is that of a spherical universe with the Earth standing immobile at the centre and the fixed stars and planets revolving around it. Outside of this sphere nothing existed worthy of investigation. It was only in the 17th and 18th centuries that this image began to change, consequent to a period of extraordinary innovative research masterfully summarised by A. Koyré in his famous work *From the Closed World to the Infinite Universe*[1]. The image of the cosmos that persisted for so many centuries is thus a product of Hellenic civilisation, developed on the basis of reflections covering a great span of time, from the Homeric poems to the days of Claudius Ptolemy.

The Homeric cosmos consisted of the Earth and the dome-shaped sky, on whose inner sur-
1 face could be seen to move the Sun, the Moon and the stars. The *Iliad* and the *Odyssey* mention the celestial vault only in relation to its height, showing the great distance between it and the Earth[2], a distance illustrated by Hesiod through the well-known example of the anvil that, falling from the top of the sky, would take nine days and nine nights to reach the Earth[3]. The sky of Homer and Hesiod is thus a half-sphere and the Earth, presumably a sort of thin circular layer, constitutes its plane. This is also the representation on the shield made by Hephaestus for Achilles, on which were depicted 'the Earth, and the sky and the sea, the Sun that never sets, the Moon in full splendour, and all of the constellations with which the heavens are crowned'[4].

As regards the meeting point between heaven and Earth, both Homer and Hesiod speak expressly of Atlas, who at the boundary of the ecumene supports the sky with his head and the celestial vault with his arms.

Like Hesiod in the *Theogony*, the philosophers of Ionia were concerned with the origin and formation of the universe. The images produced by these thinkers are profoundly innovative. Striving to understand the world and its laws, having put aside the mythological stories, the pre-Socratic philosophers subjected nature to a new kind of investigation, which was to yield revolutionary answers. The great innovation lay in the concept of *archè*, the eternal principle from which all was generated, which became the subject of profound study. Attentive to what was happening in the city, the centre par excellence of the new knowledge developed by technicians, the naturalists of Ionia sought in the mechanical arts the key to understanding the operation of the cosmos and the evolution of the phases that had generated it[5]. Free from religious concerns, they enquired into the course of the Sun, the reasons for the light of the Moon, the appearance and disappearance of the celestial bodies, and the matter of which the cosmos was made. According to tradition, the first attempts to reply to these questions were made by Thales who, viewing the liquid element as the unifying principle of the universe, albeit in a world still filled with gods, placed water at the origin of all things. Already present in the cosmogonic myths as generating forces, as in Homer's Ocean, water was for Thales the force that generates the multiplicity of substances and their ceaseless transmutation.

So expert in astronomy as to predict the eclipse of the Sun that occurred in 585 B.C., according to a tradition not universally accepted but already known in antiquity, Thales wrote a text on *Nautical Astrology* and the books *On the Solstice* and *On the Equinox*[6]. Although strikingly innovative, Thales' image of an Earth floating on water in the midst of the cosmos remained problematical; above all, it was unclear what the water supporting the Earth would itself have floated on.

The objective of abandoning the language of mythology to construct a rational discourse on the origin of the world and its causes continued with the work of Anaximander, active in the first half of the VI century B.C. at Miletus. His cosmological concept is devoid of any divine purpose. The Earth, suspended and immobile at the centre of the cosmos, is imagined as a cylindrical column of thickness equal to one-third the diameter of its base, inhabited on the upper surface and located at an equal distance from all points of the celestial vault[7]. Accordingly, there was no reason whatsoever why the Earth should move to the right or the left, upward or downward. In this universe viewed as geometric space, the Earth was declared immobile by reason of the properties between the centre and the outer points of a sphere. The process of geometrizing the cosmos was thus launched. Suspended and devoid of any support, the Earth stands immobile at the centre of the universe, stationary amid the eternal rotation of the heavens (fig. 1). With this image, moreover, Anaximander eliminated the ancient need to explain what lay under the Earth.

Anaximander's interest in these subjects is further confirmed by the literary sources. The Byzantine lexicon *Suidas* (10th century) attributes him with knowledge of the equinox and the solstices as well as a first attempt to give a topographic representation of the Earth. With the introduction of a gnomon set up in Sparta as a sundial, according to Diogenes Laertius (2, 1), Anaximander completed the first steps leading to the dawn of scientific astronomy.

At the origin of the universe, Anaximander posits an indeterminate primary substance, *àpeiron*, the eternal and indistinct infinite from which the elements had developed. Thales' water still existed, but only as a substance deriving from an original process in which it had not been present. According to Anaximander, in fact, the principle that generates the differences between things cannot be a defined entity, but something in which all of the elements exist in a formless state. Lastly, Anaximander compares the stars to hollow wheels filled with inner fire. The Sun, Moon and stars are visible thanks to holes on their surfaces. This gives rise to an image of the cosmos with the immobile Earth inside a system of wheels surrounding it like rings[8]. The last of the great Milesian physiologists, Anaximenes (middle of the VI century B.C.) imagines a cosmos supported by the necessary action of the air, considered divine, dynamic and dispenser of life. The Earth, an enormous living being that breathes, still cylindrical in shape, stands at the centre of the cosmos held up by the air, like the Sun, the Moon and all the planets, being flat in shape, while the stars are fixed like nails in the crystalline heavenly vault[9]. Anaximenes' air serves the same function as Anaximander's *àpeiron*, as the primary and indeterminate substance of the cosmos. In this case, however, all of the elements derive from the air through mutual processes of transformation based on condensation and rarefaction. With Anaximenes the season of the Milesian philosophers concludes; the political and economic heart of the Mediterranean moves to Athens, which after its victories over the Persians in the early V century B.C. becomes pre-eminent culturally as well.

From Ionia the philosopher Anaxagoras di Clazomenae (500-428 B.C.) moves to Athens. While working within the earlier tradition, he elaborates a cosmology distinguished by remarkably innovative elements.

In the original state of formless chaos of the cosmos, Anaxagoras posits the presence of seeds of life from which all things in the world will grow, qualitatively different but not yet aggregated in the proportions and relations proper to each object. The universe assumes form thanks to the aggregation of the seeds according to established modes and proportions. Imposing order on the whole is *Nous*, the intellect that forms the world without generating it, implementing a process of mechanical type that excludes any reference to the gods.

Clashing with official religion, Anaxagoras was condemned for impiety for having sustained that 'the Sun is a blazing incandescent mass' measurable in terms of area and 'greater in size than the Peloponnesus' and, on the occasion of the fall of a meteorite, for having declared that the sky too is made of stones[10].

Rescued by Pericles from condemnation, Anaxagoras is the first testimonial to the conflict that these studies could arouse with official religion, which frowned upon the concepts through which the philosophers tried to explain all of the celestial phenomena.

On the opposite shore of the Mediterranean, in Campania, Parmenides (540-450 B.C.), the greatest figure in the Eleatic school, may have arrived at conceiving of the cosmos as a sphere. Still today, the question depends on the definition of Parmenides' Being, declared 'complete on every side, similar to the mass of a perfectly round sphere, having the same force at the centre and in all directions'[11]. Aristotle and other authors (*Physica*, 3, 6, 207 a, 15-17) identified it with the universe, but already in antiquity some doubted that Parmenides attributed to it any physical nature (for instance Simplicius, in *Aristotelis Physicorum libros quatuor priores commentaria*, edited by H. Diels, Berlin 1882, p. 143).

In the fifth century B.C. the cities of Magna Graecia as well produced their philosophical systems, thanks to the westward migration of such figures as Xenophon and Pythagoras. With the Pythagoreans we find a concept of the Universe viewed as an ordered whole, in keeping with the meaning of the term *kosmos*. Although accepting the principle of the divinity of the celestial bodies[12], the Pythagoreans sought in the diverse manifestations of nature the mathematical relations that determined its essence. Introducing mathematics into cosmology, they formulated a theoretical concept in which numbers played a key role in the structure of the world, superseding the primary elements of Ionian philosophy. The number, having a physical dimension, constitutes the structure of any object. The union of mathematics, geometry and astronomy found confirmation in language as well: μάθημα, 'object of learning' generates the broader term with which the ancient Greeks and Romans defined the astronomer, namely μαθηματικόσ and *mathematicus*.

Pythagorean thought was permeated with the idea of order and measure. If in the cosmos the limited and the unlimited are opposed, number becomes the cornerstone of order in the universe. The number one, starting from which all the other numbers are generated, is the principle

1. Page 60, replica of the cosmos according to Anaximander.

2. The world system of Philolaus.

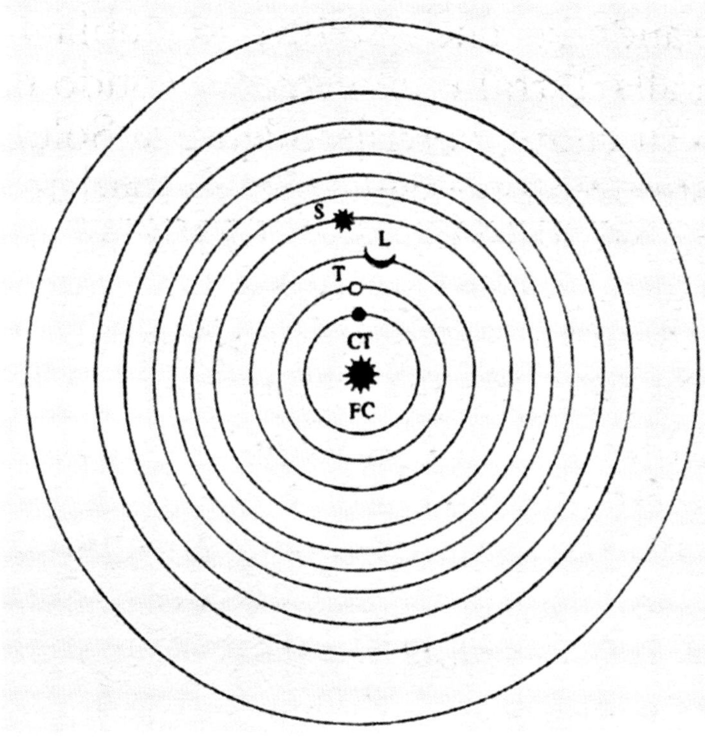

of everything and of the opposition between odd and even, which also reflects the duality between male and female, finite and infinite, straight and curved, light and darkness.

The spectacle of ordered, regular and immutable motion of the celestial bodies was thus translated into numerical ratios. Moreover, the discovery of the existence of a constant ratio between the length of the strings of a lyre and the basic chords (1:2 for the octave; 3:2 for the fifth; 4:3 for the fourth) could only confirm the marvellous properties of numbers, which also governed the connection between music and astronomy. Since musical relationships expressly involved the first four numbers, the entire cosmos had to be the expression of a harmony based on them. From this came the belief that the spheres in their motion constantly emitted music, a celestial harmony imperceptible to the human ear. The numerical harmony that governs all, from the phenomena of music to the entire universe, led Pythagoras to construct the 'cosmic figures', five regular solids which Plato was to associate with the four basic elements and the sphere of the world. The harmony of the celestial spheres is manifest also in the body and soul, and for this reason, according to Heraclites, for Pythagoras 'beatitude is knowledge of the numbers of the soul'.

The first Pythagorean to publish his ideas in a treatise was, as far as we know, Philolaus (IV century), who imagines a world system in which the Earth is dislodged from its central position in the cosmos to become a planet like the others, orbiting in twenty-four hours around a fiery sphere that is not the Sun. Also rotating around this sphere, the 'Central Fire' and centre of the universe, are the Moon, the Sun, the five planets and the compact sky of the fixed stars. In addition, interposed between the Earth and the Central Fire, Philolaus collocated a new entity that he called Counter-Earth (*Antichton*, αντίχθων in order to make ten celestial bodies, the magic number that is the sum of the first four numbers. Remaining always on the Earth-Central Fire alignment, Counter-Earth was invisible to any terrestrial observer.

Although Philolaus' system may seem fantastic, it contains elements of decisive importance for the subsequent heliocentric hypotheses (fig. 2).

In the IV century B.C. the concepts of sphere and circular motion introduced by the pythagoreans became central to the development of astronomical studies. Moreover, as noted by Claudius Ptolemy, the image of a spherical vault derived from the realisation by terrestrial observers of the systematic repetition of the astral revolutions. It was, moreover, the uniform circular motion of the visible stars around an apparently fixed pole to suggest, according to Ptolemy, the image of a sphere that turns, entraining the stars in its motion.[13] In the work of Plato, the idea of a single, material principle was replaced by a theoretical structure capable of fully explaining the origin of the cosmos. The extraordinary story of the creation of the world is found in *Timeaus*, where the cosmos is described as being generated and yet eternal. The first book is devoted to the story of the myth of Atlantis, with the cataclysmic changes that serve as prologue to the creation of the cosmos narrated by Timeaus.

The story of Atlantis is not intended as a fable, but as a description of real events known only to the Egyptians, in comparison to whom the Greeks, a young people, can have no memory of the ancient catastrophes that engulfed the Earth and that, explained as deviations of the bodies from their circular motion, spared only Egypt[14].

In the second part of the dialogue Timeaus sets forth his cosmogonic theory. The question of the nature of the cosmos, whether it had always existed or had instead been created, brings to light the key point: how could eternity be reconciled with creation? While for Parmenides the cosmos had not been created by an external force but had always existed, for Plato instead the universe came into being through the work of a creator capable of realising the beautiful and the good, drawing inspiration from models, the ideas, paradigms of what is eternal and perfect, unlike the creations of man, which as such are destined to perish. A divine craftsman who moulds matter, observing the eternal ideas, the Demiurge is capable of imposing order on all that lives. The sensible world has been created in a place called the *chora*, within which are found the imitations and copies of the paradigms that instead existed already before the intervention of the Demiurge. The elements pass from disorder to order through forms and numbers, that is, geometry and mathematics, the sciences that will allow man to know the universe. The building bricks of the cosmos have the form of the regular solids, and to each of them is associated an element: to the tetrahedron fire, to the hexahedron earth, to the octahedron air, to the isocosahedron water; the dodecahedron is linked instead to the universe and to the fifth element, aether.

For this construction, all of the fire, water, air and earth are required. The body of the world is forged out of the four elements according to firmly established proportions, and the whole cannot be dissolved except by the one who has constructed it. This universe, unique, perfect and animated, has the form of a sphere, as is proper to the divine nature of the celestial bodies whose only motion is a circular one. From the motion of the celestial bodies, not wandering but divine, eternal and living, come the day, the night, the seasons and the years. It is time that renders eternal the creation of the Demiurge.

In line with Pythagorean philosophy, Plato thus proposes a theory of motion to which a good part of ancient astronomy is limited: a circular, uniform motion that, as is proper to the celestial soul, has neither beginning nor end, in contrast to terrestrial rectilinear motions. Introducing a new element not contemplated by Pythagoras, Plato urges astronomers to devise rigorous mathematical methods capable of explaining the irregularities (standing still, retrograde motion and apparent variations in speed) that had been observed in planetary motion, in order to preserve the two Pythagorean axioms mentioned above.

A firm believer in the utility of theoretical astronomy, Plato was convinced that the true motions of the planets could not be understood by observation of the heavens alone. 'Each of them traverses in circular motion its path, not many but one alone and always the same, while it appears to traverse many paths'[15]. The basic assumption for explaining this statement, determinant for the development of astronomical research, was the belief in the divine nature of the celestial bodies, whose rational souls command them to perform just this kind of motion.

In the *Epinomis*, the dialogue now attributed to Plato's pupil Philip of Opus, who lived near the middle of the IV century B.C., the genesis of Plato's cosmos is systematically stated. The heart of this work is the knowledge of mathematics, a gift from the heavens bestowed on man to facilitate his earthly existence. Mathematics, in fact, furnishes the numbers on which depend the motion of the stars and the alternation of the seasons that offer what is needed to live on the Earth. The celestial bodies are living beings, which have received from God a body, soul and motion established since the very beginning. To the astronomer pertains knowledge of the supreme science, astronomy, the only one able to describe the orbits of the planets, formulating models and laws of mathematical type: '[...] the true astronomer is perforce a great sage as well. This regards not those who practice astronomy in the manner of Hesiod and his followers, who limit themselves to observing the rising and setting of the stars, but to those who, of the eight orbits, have identified at least seven, each with its own revolving motion. Under these conditions it is certainly not easy for any man to contemplate these phenomena, without possessing extraordinary natural qualities'[16].

The divine nature of the celestial bodies and the circularity of their motion are the presuppositions of the studies conducted by Eudoxus, the first astronomer in the ancient world to try to solve the crucial problem of the irregularity observed in planetary motion, sufficient to cast serious doubt on the credibility of Plato's system.

In the lost treatise on *Velocity*, Eudoxus presents a geometric model designed to salvage the circularity and uniformity of motion of the stars and planets. While Plato in the *Timeaus* had stated that the circular motion of the celestial bodies resulted from the composition of two uniform motions rotating in opposite directions around the axis of the Equator and the Zodiac, Eudoxus modifies this concept, which could explain only the apparent displacement of the Sun. The solution consisted of introducing a series of concentric circles, four for each planet. Integral with one another, having a common centre but different poles, they transmit to one another their motion around their respective axes. The planet is fixed to the equator of the innermost sphere, whose motion descends from the outermost one. It is this ensemble of motions that gives the appearance, illusory, of the irregularity that had been noted.

Albeit with a solution of exclusively mathematical nature, Eudoxus consolidates that 'geometrizing' of the universe to which Anaximander and Pythagoras had significantly contributed by imposing uniformity on the motion of the planets and restoring to the heavens the order and regularity required by the Academy.

Aristotle's cosmology starts from developments in Plato's philosophy. The arrangement of the universe on two levels still differing in hierarchy no longer concerns the empirical world and that of ideas, but the sphere of the skies and the sublunar world. The distinction between heavy bodies and light ones having been made (fire is always light, earth heavy, air and water both heavy and light), the sky and the Earth are separated by their different natures. Their elements and the motions that take place in them are different, celestial motions being eternal and circular, terrestrial ones rectilinear and of limited duration. In the sublunar world are found the four elements of pre-Socratic philosophy: air, water, earth and fire, with their natural motions, while the celestial world is composed of a fifth element called ether, incorruptible and unalterable as is required by the perfect nature of the heavens.

The problems dealt with in the *Physics* and the *Metaphysics* find their astronomical collocation in the *De caelo*, where the precise hierarchies of the cosmos are described. That which stands above is more perfect than that which lies below; motion is a consequence of the nature of bodies, which tend to reach their own natural place. The structure and operation of the universe could not be understood without this premise.

In the eternal rotation of the heavens the Earth, whose centre coincides with the centre of everything, remains immobile. Contrary to the Pythagoreans, Aristotle declares that the Earth does not rotate on itself nor does it orbit around a central fire. Contradicting the theory of the Earth's rotation are, for Aristotle, physical phenomena such as the fact that weights dropped through the air, fall vertically, something that would not happen, he believes, if the Earth were rotating. Aristotle accepts the theory of Eudoxus but, introducing a crucial innovation, attributes a physical nature to the mathematical theory of the astronomer from Cnidus. The spheres and circles that had previously held only theoretical value now became concrete. The insurmountable boundary of the universe was the sphere of the fixed stars. Between it and the Earth were the seven planets, embedded in their spheres which, crystalline and perfect in their ethereal substance, determined the motion of the celestial bodies fixed to them. Having established the structure of the universe, Aristotle then confronted the problem of its mechanical operation. Immortal and divine, the universe moves by itself. The Unmoved Mover (*Physics*, VII, 5, 256a 10), the origin of all celestial motions, is God himself, guarantee of the eternal motion of the sphere of the fixed stars. From the motion of the sphere of the fixed stars, at the outer limit of the celestial globe, descends that of the others, actuated in turn by planetary souls or intellects[17]. The Unmoved Mover does not move the sphere of the fixed stars by direct contact. Like the Intellect of Anaxagoras, the God of Aristotle is separated from the world. Motion results from the aspiration of celestial matter toward God. Closed, perfect, finite and eternal, the cosmos of Aristotle has always been and will always be, like the circular motion that has had no beginning and will have no end. This is the image of the universe to which, around the middle of the 2nd century A.D., Claudius Ptolemy was to apply a mathematical basis destined to meet with enormous success in the following centuries.

–

Bibliography

Koyré 1957; Mondolfo 1982; Lerner 2000, p. 16; *I dossografi greci* 1961; *I presocratici* 1969, vol. 1, p. 276.

[1] Koyré 1957.
[2] Homer, *Iliad*, 8, 13 and ff.
[3] Hesiod, *Theogony*, vv. 722 and ff.
[4] Homer, *Iliad*, 18, 671 and ff.
[5] Mondolfo 1982.
[6] Diogenes Laertius, 1, 23.
[7] Aristotle, *De caelo*, 295 b 10; Diogenes Laertius, 2, 1.
[8] Lerner 2000, p. 16.
[9] Hippolytus, 1, 7, 4; Aetius, 2, 14, 3-4 in *I dossografi greci* 1961.
[10] Diogenes Laertius, 2, 10-12.
[11] *I presocratici* 1969, vol. 1, p. 276.
[12] Diogenes Laertius, 8, 27.
[13] Ptolemy, *Almagest*, 3, 13.
[14] Plato, *Timeaus*, 21e, 22d.
[15] Plato, *Republic*, 7, 529 c.
[16] Plato, *Epinomides*, 8.
[17] Aristotle, *Metaphysics*, XII, 8, 1073a 30.

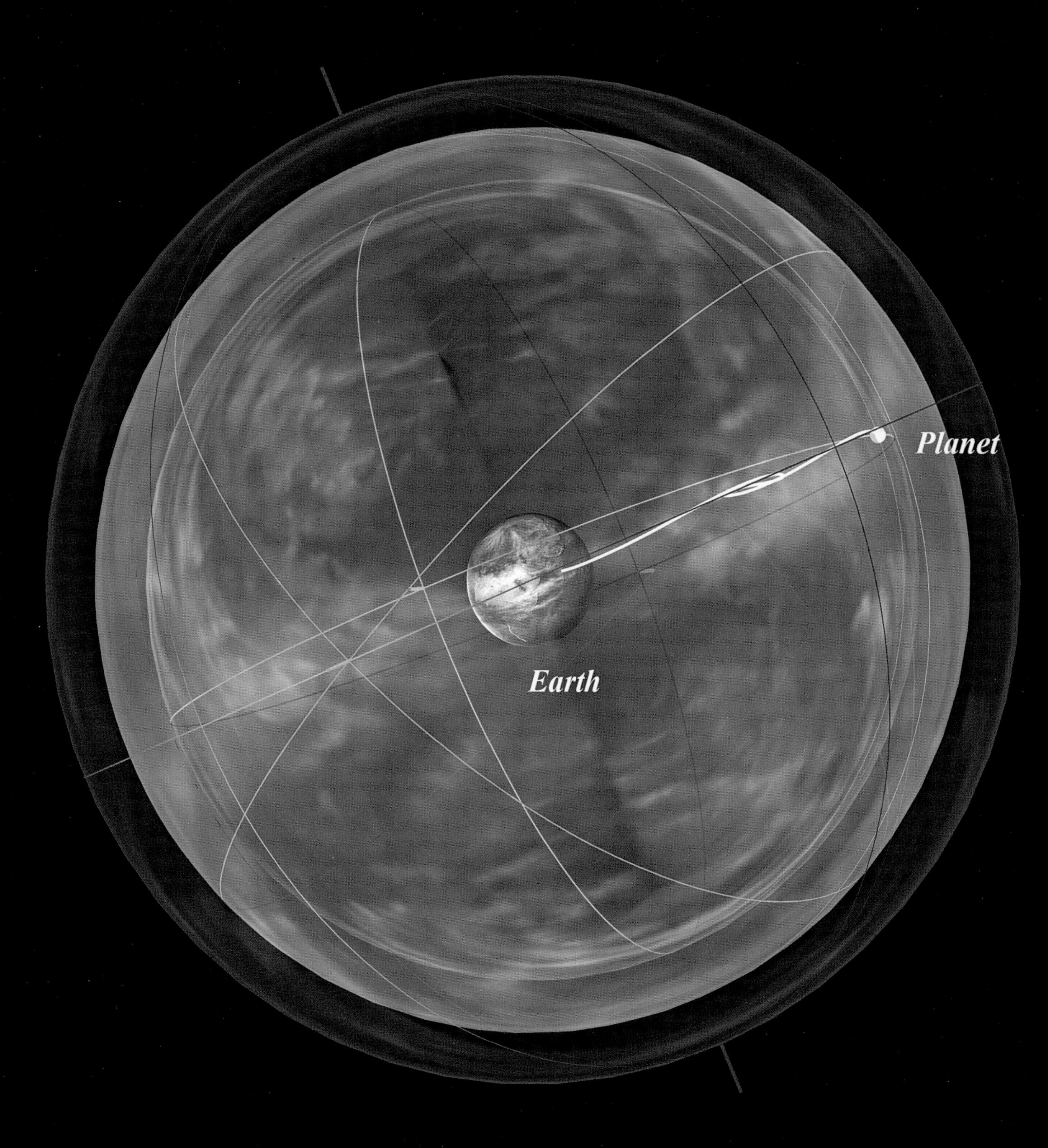
Planet
Earth

THE ANCIENT WORLD

–

2 | THE COSMOS BECOMES A SPHERE

–

GRAECO-ALEXANDRINE MATHEMATICAL ASTRONOMY

–

Giorgio Strano

–

The Geometry of the Cosmos

The idea that the Earth stood perfectly immobile at the centre of the cosmos occupied the minds of the philosophers and astronomers of antiquity almost undisturbed up to the 16th century. The extraordinary duration of this concept was partly due to the immediate responses suggested by the senses to the queries posited by man. The Earth appeared to stand still, while the Sun, Moon, planets and stars seemed to revolve around it. A further reason may be found, however, in the plausibility of the theories elaborated by mathematicians to explain and predict the course of the stars. The ancient Greeks were of course aware that the impressions of the senses could suggest false conclusions; but when they added functional mathematical models to these subjective impressions, the geocentric concept became very hard to eradicate.

The history of the first planetary models – that is, the first mathematical hypotheses formulated to precisely describe observed phenomena – starts with definition of the basic characteristics of celestial motion by Plato (427-347 B.C.). This philosopher dealt with cosmological problems in various works; but it was above all in the *Timaeus* that, albeit in metaphysical language, he described the perfectly spherical form of the cosmos and the two principal motions imposed on celestial bodies by the will of the 'Demiurge' creator[1]. The first motion consisted of the uniform rotation of 'Sameness' toward the right, that is, the motion of all the celestial bodies from east to west parallel to the circumference of the celestial equator. The second motion was instead the rotation of 'Difference' to the left diagonally, that is, the motion of some celestial bodies from west to east parallel to the circumference of the Zodiac, inclined in respect to the celestial equator (Fig. 2). While the first motion involved all of the celestial bodies in the same way, causing them to complete a revolution around the Earth in one day, the second motion differed for the various planets[2]; the Moon in fact appeared to transit through the Zodiac in about one month, the Sun in a year, Mars in about two years, Jupiter in twelve and Saturn in thirty. The combination of the two principal motions generated the paths that the stars and planets appear to follow around the Earth.

With this description, Plato established the principles that inspired Greek and Alexandrine mathematicians in delineating the structure and operation of the cosmos. Each planet had to move around the Earth through a combination of spheres or circumferences travelling in uniform circular motion. Some mathematicians also tried to determine the basic geometry of the cosmos using other geometric figures. For example, Euclid (4th century B.C.) dedicated a proposition in the *Elements* to the pentadecagon, the regular polygon with fifteen sides[3]. As Proclus (c. 410-485 A.D.) noted centuries later, this proposition was highly useful in astronomy; when this polygon was inscribed in the celestial sphere on a plane perpendicular to the celestial equator and to the Zodiac, the side of the pentadecagono established the mutual inclination of 24° of the latter two circumferences[4]. But the real problem posed by Plato to the mathematicians was not the basic geometry of the celestial sphere, but if and how it was possible to combine spheres or circumferences to faithfully replicate the motion of the planets.

In a first approximation, the Sun and the Moon appeared to transit across the Zodiac moving uniformly from west to east. This was not true of the planets, which move across the Zodiac at variable speeds. If, for instance, we trace the course of Mars, Jupiter or Saturn in relation to the stars, we note that when each of these planets appears in the west immediately after sunset, it moves rapidly eastward. Its speed decreases as the planet, becoming brighter, advances month by month along the Zodiac. At a certain point the planet seems to stop, remaining roughly in the same position in relation to the stars in the background for several days (first stationary point). Then for several more days it appears to move backward, from east to west, reaching its greatest brightness when it rises while the Sun is setting (opposition). The planet then seems to stop again (second stationary point) and lastly to resume its eastward course, diminishing in brightness and gradually accelerating in speed, until it rises in the east a little before the Sun. The behaviour of Venus and Mercury is similar, except that these two planets appear to move away from the Sun for no more than a certain angle (maximum elongation).

How was it possible to explain this varying motion, now 'forward' (to the east), now 'retrograde' (to the west), on the basis of uniform circular motion alone?

Homocentric spheres

The destiny of an illustrious mathematician – great fame, but a short lifetime – is marked in youth by having the hem of his gown licked by an ox. But the animal must be Apis, the sacred ox, and the mathematician must be called Eudoxus of Cnidus (c. 408-c. 355 B.C.), on a voyage of study through Egypt[5]. Famous in the history of mathematics for having elaborated the theory of proportions further developed by Euclid and the method of exhaustion for analysing curved figures which was then utilised by Archimedes of Syracuse (287-212 B.C.)[6], Eudoxus was a pupil of Plato. Not only did he take seriously his master's ideas on the cosmos, but also developed geometric models able to explain the alternating forward and backward motion of the planets on the basis of uniform circular motion alone. Unfortunately, Eudoxus' writings on this subject have been lost, and the little surviving information on his planetary models is found in the *Metaphysics* of Aristotle (384-322 B.C.) and the commentary by Simplicius (6th century A.D.) to Aristotle's *De caelo*.

'Eudoxus', states Aristotle, 'sustains that the motion of translation of both the Sun and the Moon takes place within three spheres, the outmost of which, he believes, is that of the fixed stars' while 'the motion of translation of each planet takes place by means of four spheres, and the first two are identical to the first two of the Sun and the Moon'[7]. Aristotle also mentions the arrangement of the planetary spheres, all concentric to the Earth, and thus called 'homocentric' (having the same centre). The first sphere of each planet is that of the 'fixed' stars, so called because they always appear at the same distance from one another. This sphere presides over the first motion of the skies. It completes one revolution a day, moving westward parallel to the celestial equator, resulting in the rising and setting of the planet. Below this first sphere, and entrained by it, moves the second, inclined as far as the Zodiac is inclined on the celestial equator (24°). This sphere completes one revolution in thirty years in the case of Saturn, twelve years in the case of Jupiter, and so on. In other words, this sphere presides over the second principal motion of the skies, proper to an individual planet. Thanks to it, the planet transits through the Zodiac with an assigned period; it does so without slowing down or speeding up, stopping or moving backward. The discontinuity of motion, called 'anomaly', depends on the two innermost spheres, which however Aristotle does not describe in detail: 'The third sphere of all the planets has its poles in the circle that bisects the Zodiac and, lastly, the fourth sphere moves along a circle that is inclined in relation to the equator of the third'[8]. How do these two inner spheres produce variations in the velocity, the stationary points and retrograde motion of a planet?

In reflecting on *De caelo*, and more generally on Aristotle's astronomical writings, Simplicius furnishes supplementary indications taken from now lost treatises. The third sphere, entrained by the second, revolves in a direction perpendicular to the Zodiac with the 'synodic period' proper to each planet, that is, in the interval of time between two successive retrogressions. The fourth sphere, which bears the planet embedded at its equator, is slightly inclined in respect to the third and completes one revolution during the same period, but in the opposite direction. This combination of equal and opposite motions constitutes Eudoxus' stroke of genius: due to the two inner spheres, the planet oscillates forward and backward, describing a closed curve termed 'hippoped' (horse-foot), from the name of the figure 8 traced by a horse trotting around two stakes fixed in the ground. When the two inner spheres are entrained by the second sphere of medium motion, the hippoped opens and the planet performs the complicated revolutions revealed by observation, periodically stopping and moving backward along the Zodiac[9] (fig. 1).

The planetary models of Eudoxus provided acceptable results for Jupiter and Saturn, but not for the other planets. The three-sphere models did not explain in fact why, without any retrograde motion, the Sun and the Moon appear to move at variable speed along the Zodiac. And the three-sphere models were unable to reproduce the retrograde motion of Mars and Venus[10]. Callippus of Cyzicus (4th century B.C.), who had studied mathematics with a colleague of Eudoxus and had worked in Athens with Aristotle[11], tried to eliminate the various discrepancies by adding two spheres to the Sun and the Moon, and one sphere to Mars, Venus and Mercury[12]. Unfortunately, neither Aristotle nor Simplicius explain the role of the additional spheres, particularly those of Mars and Venus. Reconstructing the final stage of the homocentric models thus remains still today conjectural, and is the work of the Italian astronomer Giovanni Virginio Schiaparelli (1835-1910), known to history for having discovered the 'canals' on Mars[13].

As a mathematician, Eudoxus probably thought of his planetary models in the abstract sense: as geometric constructions useful for performing calculations, as shown by the fact that the sphere of the fixed stars was the outermost one for all of the planets. Unlike Eudoxus, Aristotle was not concerned with predicting the future positions of the stars, but with delineating an organic, functioning cosmic machine. Nonetheless, the homocentric spheres offered him the possibility of constructing such a machine, set in motion by the first of all beings, the external mover, eternal and immobile[14]. Motion was transmitted from a higher sphere to the one below it, and was increasingly attenuated as

1. Page 66, reconstruction of the motion of a planet according to Eudoxus.

2. The two most principal celestial motions.

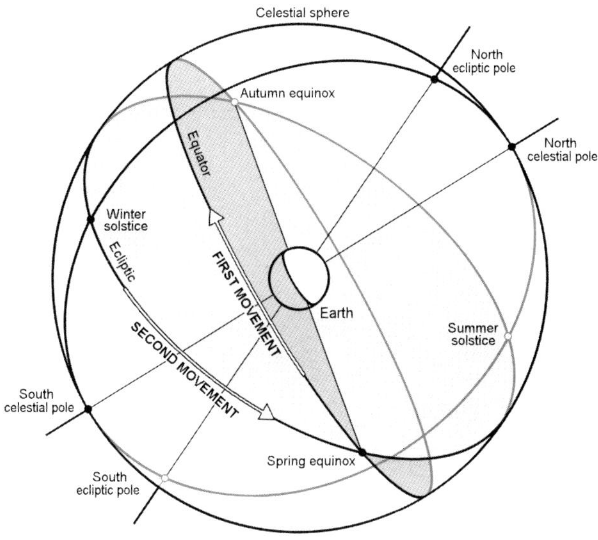

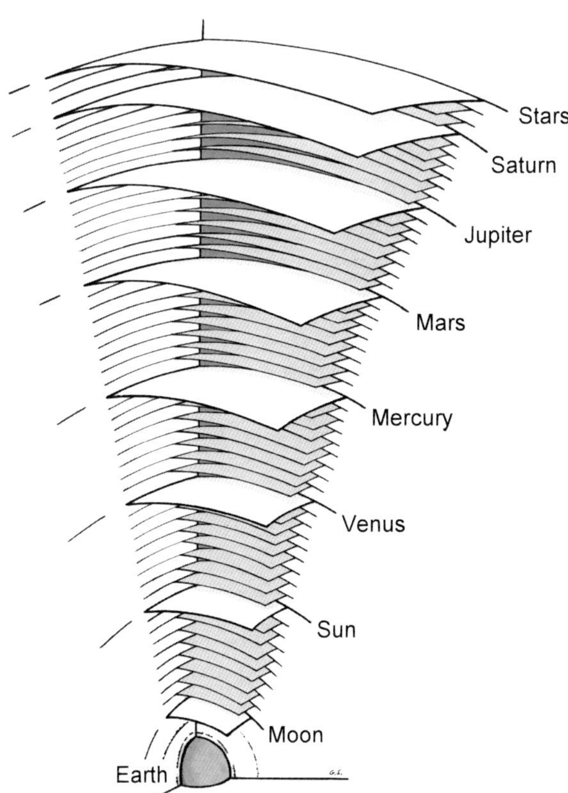

3. Section diagram of Aristotle's cosmos.

its distance from the prime mover increased, down to the total immobility of the Earth at the centre[15]. From pure geometrical conceits, the celestial spheres were transformed into material entities constituted of a fifth element, eternal and incorruptible, the crystalline aether or quintessence[16], differing from the four elements – earth, water, air and fire – of which inconstant earthly things were made[17].

In the *Metaphysics*, more specifically, Aristotle is concerned with organising the individual planetary models into a consistent system. As a rule, the models were inserted one inside another, starting from the sphere of the fixed stars down to the innermost sphere, that of the Moon. But it was impossible to make the system function correctly by introducing the four spheres governing the motion of Jupiter immediately below the four spheres governing the motion of Saturn; the five of Mars immediately below the four of Jupiter, and so on, for a total of 33 spheres. By doing this, the motion of a planet would have been added to the motions of the planets above it. It was thus necessary to interpose between the various groups of governing spheres other groups of reacting spheres: three under Saturn and Jupiter, four under Mars, Mercury, Venus and the Sun. The reacting spheres nullified the motion of the planet above them, so that the motion of the planet below again derived from the sphere of the fixed stars. On the whole, Aristotle introduced 22 reacting spheres and posited a cosmological system formed of no less than 55 crystalline spheres[18] (fig. 3).

The theory of epicycles

Polemarchus of Cyzicus (4th century B.C.), pupil of Eudoxus and master of Callippus, soon noted that the models based on homocentric spheres failed to explain all of the celestial phenomena. The most obvious problem, which then found its way into Aristotle's cosmos, was the impossibility of explaining variation in the brightness of the planets – Mars and Venus in particular – and in the apparent diameter of the Moon. These variations suggested that the planets periodically approached the Earth; but unfortunately, in a system of concentric spheres, the distance of the planets from the observer is unchanging[19].

A first alternative hypothesis able to explain all of the phenomena – both the retrograde motion and the changes in the brightness of planets – in a system of concentric, uniformly revolving spheres, called for a general rearrangement of the cosmos. It was necessary to move the centre of the planetary orbits from the Earth to the Sun, to place the Earth in motion and to enormously increase the radius of the sphere of the fixed stars. Very few traces of this first heliocentric concept have survived. Out of all of the works of its author, Aristarcus of Samos (3rd century B.C.), only the treatise *On the dimensions and distances of the Sun and the Moon*[20] has survived. The little that is known of Aristarcus' cosmological ideas comes from a text of Archimedes on a numerical notation useful for quantifying enormous amounts, such as the number of grains of sand that could fit in the cosmos. 'Aristarcus of Samos', states Archimedes at the beginning of the *Arenarius*, 'sets forth in writing some hypotheses, according to which it can be deduced that the cosmos is several times larger than has been said. He supposes in fact that the fixed stars and the Sun remain immobile and that the Earth turns, following the circumference of a circle, around the Sun, which stands at the centre of the orbit; and that the sphere of the fixed stars, around the same centre of the Sun, is so large that the circle along which the Earth is said to turn has in relation to the distance of the fixed stars the same proportion as the centre of the sphere in relation to its surface'[21].

Even these few remarks show how Aristarcus thought to solve the cosmological problems. If all of the planets, including Earth, revolve around the Sun, their positions and mutual distances will change cyclically over time, so that phenomena such as retrogressions and variations in brightness become necessary facts. For example, approximately every two years the Earth passes beside Mars and overtakes it. During the overtaking stage, Mars appears to remain behind against the background of the zodiacal constellations. Since as it passes Mars, the Earth reaches its closest distance from the planet, Mars appears brighter just in coincidence with its maximum retrograde speed. And again, while passing Mars, Earth finds itself exactly between Mars and the Sun, so that these two planets appear at opposite points of the Zodiac.

Since the heliocentric concept explained phenomena so well, why was it not immediately taken into more serious consideration? A first obstacle consisted of the need, pointed out by Archimedes, to vastly enlarge the sphere of the fixed stars. In the geocentric system, the stars may be found relatively close to the Earth. The greatest astronomer mathematician of antiquity, Claudius Ptolemy (2nd century A.D), notes in fact that it is enough for Earth to be like a point in relation to the sphere of the stars. If this were not true, two stars would subtend a smaller arc when they are on the horizon than when they are high in the sky, since in the latter case they would be closer to the observer[22]. In Aristarcus system instead, it is the Earth's orbit that must be like a point in respect to the sphere of the stars. Otherwise, two stars would subtend different arcs depending on the position occupied by the Earth in its orbit. In the final analysis, the sphere of the stars would have to have a radius at least a thousand times greater in the heliocentric cosmos than in the geocentric cosmos. Such vastly increased size disturbed the philosophers, embarrassed at having to explain the necessary existence of such an enormous 'empty' space.

A second obstacle was the impossibility of explaining why, although the Earth revolved around the Sun and around its own axis at dizzying speed, the things on its surface appeared to be at rest. For Aristotelian physics, a body not subject to any natural motion – on the vertical in earthly regions and along a circumference in celestial regions – had to be set in motion by a motive force applied to it[23]. If the Earth moved, all of the objects not kept in the direction of terrestrial motion by something exerting a motive force on them would have had to show the same behaviour. 'The result would be', noted Ptolemy, 'that objects not firmly anchored to the soil would appear to move in the same direction, opposite that of the Earth: nor could the clouds, nor other objects flying or thrown into the air, ever be seen to move eastward, because the Earth's eastward motion would always be greater and would overcome them, so that all of these objects would seem instead to move westward, that is, backwards'[24]. In order to be convincing, the concept of Aristarcus would have had to be accompanied by the definition of a new physics of motion; something that no one had yet contemplated.

An ultimate and fatal obstacle to the ideas of Aristarcus was however the introduction of planetary models alternative to the homocentric spheres and able to explain all of the phenomena observed, including the varying brightness of the planets, without denying the immobility of the Earth. Ptolemy reports that these models were developed by mathematicians. The most eminent of them, Apollonius of Perga (3rd century B.C.), had demonstrated that the anomaly of retrograde motion, curiously dependent on the mutual positions of a planet and the Sun, could be reproduced by superimposing two circumferences. A circumference concentric to the Earth, and thus called 'concentric', bore on it a second smaller circumference, called 'epicycle' (circle above), on which the planet was situated. It flowed in uniform motion along the epicycle from west to east, while the centre of the epicycle, in turn, flowed at uniform motion along the concentric, always from west to east. The positions of Saturn, Jupiter, Mars, Venus and Mercury along the Zodiac could be replicated by assigning suitable values to the speed of rotation and the ratio between the radiuses of the two circumferences[25]. Accordingly, each planet, in the course of its own geocentric revolution, passed from a point of maximum distance from Earth when it was in conjunction with the Sun, to a point of minimum distance from Earth when it was in opposition to the Sun. The notable decrease in distance explained the substantial increase in brightness shown by the planet in coincidence with its maximum retrograde speed (fig. 4).

The Sun and the Moon, which travel along the Zodiac at variable speed, but never in the retrograde direction, constituted special cases. According to Ptolemy, the first authoritative interpreter of the motion of these two celestial bodies was another illustrious mathematician, Hipparchus of Nicea (2nd century B.C.). He had in part conducted accurate observations on the Island of Rhodes, in part employed data already ac-

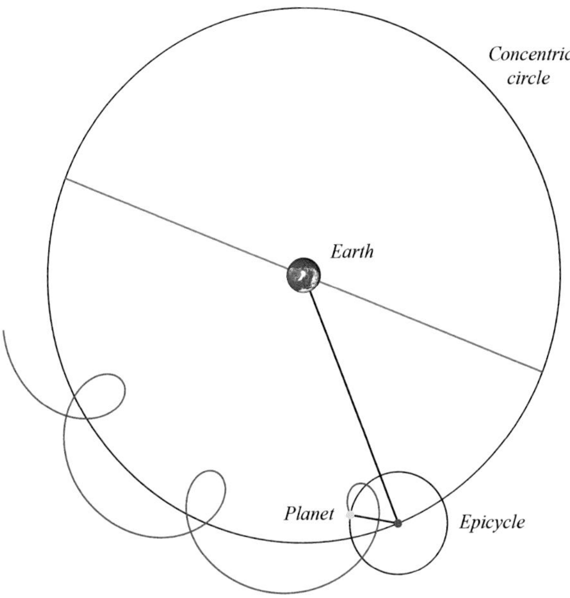

4. The motion of a planet in an epicyclical-concentric system.

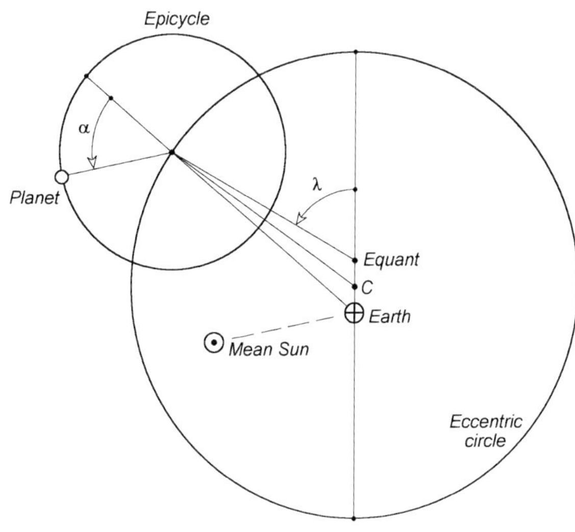

5. Diagram of a planetary model according to Ptolemy.

quired by Eratosthenes of Cyrene (4th century B.C.), librarian of the Museum at Alexandria in Egypt, famed for having estimated the length of the Earth's circumference. To describe the variations in speed and distance of the Sun and the Moon, Hipparchus had employed two equivalent models. The first consisted of an epicycle-concentric system of a particular type, in which the celestial body completed one revolution from west to east along the epicycle in the same time during which the centre of the epicycle completed one revolution from east to west along the concentric. The second model consisted of considering the celestial body as travelling in circular uniform motion along a circumference whose centre was displaced in relation to the centre of the Earth by an amount equal to the radius of the epicycle in the preceding model[26]. In both cases, the Sun and the Moon appeared to move along the Zodiac at different speeds depending on which constellation they were traversing (zodiacal anomaly). Moreover, depending on their greater or lesser distance from the Earth, they presented a smaller or larger diameter to the observer.

Ptolemaic astronomy

The epicyclic-concentric and eccentric models offered notable advantages over that of the homocentric spheres, especially in calculating the planetary positions. Studying the curves generated by two circumferences rotating on a plane was easier than studying curves generated by four or five spheres rotating through space. As regards the model of Aristarcus, those of Apollonius and Hipparchus call for no changes in the traditional concepts of the motion of bodies, at least in the case of terrestrial physics. More problematical was the relationship of the new models to the principles of the cosmological machine delineated by Aristotle. If the concentric spheres models could compose a plausible mechanical unit while also respecting the Platonic dictate of the uniform circular motion of celestial bodies, the same could not be said of the models composed of circumferences. Epicycles, concentrics and eccentrics also complied, in blander manner, with the Platonic dictate; but what did they correspond to in actual reality? Who or what obliged an epicycle to move along the concentric or a planet to move along the epicycle? How did the Sun and the Moon move at uniform speed along circumferences that were eccentric in respect to the Earth and to the sphere of the stars? How was motion propagated to the various circumferences starting from the prime mover outside the sphere of the stars?

All of these questions went unanswered by the mathematicians, concerned with formulating a geometric explanation complying as closely as possible with the results of accurate observations conducted with various types of graduated instruments, rather than with defining the physical structure of the cosmos. The same attitude prevailed in Ptolemy's

6. Diagram of a celestial sphere according to Ptolemy.

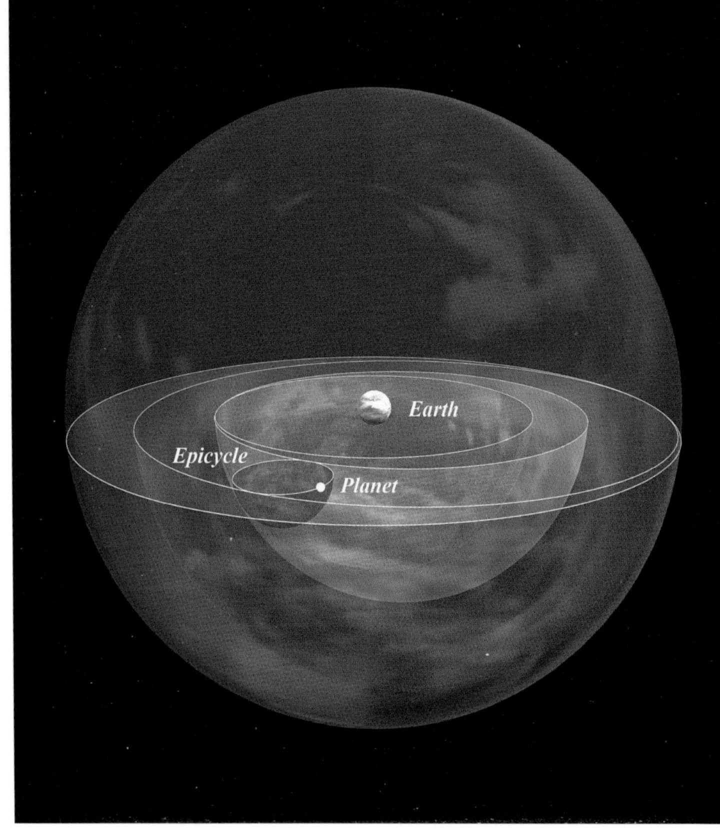

most important astronomical work. As happens with great works of synthesis, especially those that are useful and successful, the *Mathematical Composition* – better known as the *Almagest* (from the Arab *al-Megisti* = The Great), the name given it by the medieval Islamic astronomers – swept away almost all of the work of Ptolemy's predecessors. The astronomical texts of Apollonius and Hipparchus, for example, were no longer transcribed and were lost, having been absorbed and superseded by the new and more exhaustive treatise. In fact, Ptolemy drew just from these two authors the data and the concepts on which he based his own planetary models, in whose development he also attempted to explain new phenomena.

Attentive observations, probably conducted at the Museum of Alexandria, and comparison with the data recorded by the Alexandrine and Babylonian astronomers of the past, had shown Ptolemy that the planets were affected by not one, but two anomalies. The most obvious, that of retrograde motion, was found to be synchronized on the course of the Sun and could be explained by the motion of the planet along the epicycle. But in analysing the amplitude of the arcs of retrograde motion shown by a planet at various points in the Zodiac, it was found that their amplitude depended on the constellation at which the retrogression took place. The brightness of a planet too appeared greater in coincidence with the retrograde arcs of greatest amplitude. These observations suggested that it was not only the distance of a planet from the Earth that varied in synchrony with the motion of the Sun (solar anomaly), but also the distance of an epicycle from the Earth varied in synchrony with the position of its centre in relation to the Zodiac (zodiacal anomaly). To explain the latter phenomenon, Ptolemy modified the models of Apollonius by supposing that the centre of the epicycle moved not along a concentric, but along an eccentric. In addition, to better calibrate the motion of a planet in relation to data from observations, Ptolemy supposed that the centre of the epicycle moved uniformly not in respect to the eccentric, but in respect to an 'equant' circumference, whose centre coincided neither with the centre of the Earth, nor with the centre of the eccentric[27] (fig. 5).

This ulterior complication was a blatant violation of the Platonic precept on the uniformity of celestial motions, and as such it was perceived in the following centuries. Nonetheless, the notable capacity for prediction of the Ptolemaic planetary models meant that the equant constituted a problem more for philosophers, interested in explaining the physical causes of planetary motion, than for mathematical astronomers, interested in predicting the geometric course of such motion; and even more so because eccentrics and epicycles made it possible to overcome another shortcoming in the homocentric spheres of Eudoxus and Callippus. In moving in longitude across the Zodiac, the planets did not follow a circumference of the celestial sphere, as did instead the Sun. They described complex trajectories that departed in latitude from the circumference at the centre of the Zodiac. Such trajectories could be very well explained by the models developed by Ptolemy, in which it was hypothesized that the planes of the eccentric and the epicycle were slightly inclined from each other[28].

Although he was more interested in his models' capacity for prediction, Ptolemy also tried to redefine the structure of the cosmos. Although the graduated instruments at his disposal did not allow him to measure the distance of any celestial body from Earth except the Moon, in his *Mathematical Composition* Ptolemy first advanced an aesthetic hypothesis on the order of the planetary spheres. He placed above the Earth, in order, the Moon, Mercury, Venus, the Sun, Mars, Jupiter and Saturn. 'Because, if we place the Sun at the centre', explained Ptolemy, 'it is more accordant with nature to separate the planets that can reach all possible distances from the Sun [Mars, Jupiter e Saturn] from those that cannot do so, but remain always in its vicinity [Venus and Mercury]'[29]. To this collocation, destined to become canonical, Ptolemy added in another work, the *Hypothesis on the planets*, an updated theory of his own on the conformation of the world-machine. He imagined a cosmos made up of concentric spherical shells, each containing the eccentric and the epicycle of a planet, packed one within another so that no empty space remained between them. The thickness of an individual spherical shell was established by the difference between the maximum and minimum distance of the planet from Earth. The circumference of the epicycle was in reality to be understood as the equatorial section of a small sphere rotating within a cavity in the spherical shell formed of two eccentric spheres[30] (fig. 6). This was, in synthesis, an ingenious fusion of Ptolemy's planetary models and Aristotle's world-machine.

–

Bibliography

Boyer 1976; Dreyer 1970; Hoskin 1999; Linton 2004; Neugebauer 1975a; North 2008; Schiaparelli 1997; Yavetz 1998, pp. 221-278.

[1] Plato, *Timaeus*, 33B-34B.

[2] Plato, *Timaeus*, 36B-36D.

[3] Euclid, *Elements*, IV, 16.

[4] Proclus, *Commentary to the Euclid's first book of 'Elements'*, 8.

[5] Dreyer 1970, p. 79.

[6] Boyer 1976, pp. 105-110.

[7] Aristotle, *Metaphysics*, 12 (Λ), 8, 1073b.

[8] *Ibid.*

[9] Simplicius, *On Aristotle's 'De Caelo'*, II, 12 (495-497).

[10] Dreyer 1970, pp. 93-94.

[11] Simplicius, *On Aristotle's 'De caelo'*, II, 12, (pp. 493).

[12] Aristotle, *Metaphysics*, 12 (Λ), 8, 1073b.

[13] Schiaparelli 1997, v. 2, pp. 5-93. On homocentric spheres, see also: Dreyer 1970, pp. 78-97; Neugebauer 1975b, pp. 675-685; Hoskin 1999, pp. 29-33; Linton, 2004, pp. 25-32; North 2008, pp. 73-79. For an alternative view, see Yavetz 1998, pp. 225-275.

[14] Aristotle, *Metaphysics*, 12 (Λ), 8, 1073a; Aristotle, *De caelo*, II (B), 6, 288a-288b.

[15] *Ivi*, 10, 291a-291b.

[16] *Ivi*, I (A), 2-3, 269a-270b.

[17] Aristotle, *Meteorology*, I (A), 2, 339a.

[18] Aristotle, *Metaphysics*, 12 (Λ), 8, 1073b-1074a; see also: Simplicius, *On Aristotle's 'De caelo'*, II, 12 (497-504).

[19] *Ivi*, (504-505).

[20] V. Dreyer 1970, pp. 123-124.

[21] Archimedes, *Psammites*, I, o.

[22] C. Ptolemy, *Mathematikė Syntaxis*, I, 6.

[23] Aristotle, *Physics*, VIII (θ), 4, 254b-256a.

[24] C. Ptolemy, *Mathematikė Syntaxis*, I, 7.

[25] *Ivi*, XII, 1.

[26] *Ivi*, III, 3.

[27] *Ivi*, IX, 5.

[28] *Ivi*, XIII, 1. On the theory of epicycles, see also: Dreyer 1970, pp. 135-150, 175-188; Hoskin 1999, pp. 33-44; Linton 2004, pp. 45-81; North 2008, 92-118.

[29] C. Ptolemy, *Mathematikė Syntaxis*, IX, 1.

[30] V. Hoskin 1999, pp. 45-46; Linton 2004, pp. 81-83.

THE ANCIENT WORLD

2| THE COSMOS BECOMES A SPHERE

MYTHS AND STARS IN CLASSICAL GREECE

Eugenio Lo Sardo

Among the first to sing of the universe and its origins were Homer, Hesiod and Orpheus, the father of the mystery cults.

For Homer, as we read in the *Iliad*, Oceanus is the father of all the gods, generated in the primordial union with Tethys[1]. From this element, with its deep-flowing current *bathurroos* the Sun (*Helios*) rises every day to light up the world. Homer reveals his concept of the cosmos and its structure in another passage found in Book XVIII, where he describes the decoration on Achilles' shield, divided into five circles. Around the edge of the great bronze disc appear, in addition to Gaia, Uranus and Thalassa (the salt sea), the principal constellations, among them the Pleiades, the Hyades, Orion and the two bears, Ursa Major and Ursa Minor. The poet shows knowledge of some details of the celestial sphere's rotation and justly notes that the constellations mentioned above 'are never plunged into the wash of Ocean', that is, they never set.

While Homer sang of the feats of heroes and warriors beneath the walls of Troy, Hesiod drew inspiration from the rituals and traditions of an agricultural land, Boeotia. In the former we see the grandiose machine of the universe moving with the impersonal power of the great Ocean current, in the latter a throng of gods gradually emerging from the original *caos*.

'And so', we read in the *Theogony*, 'first of all was Chaos'[2], which in Greek means chasm, abyss, dark void; the name of the district of Pirandello's villa, in fact. Chaos was succeeded by 'broad-breasted' Gaia, a solid, safe home for both men and gods; then Tartarus, the dark place concealed deep within the caverns of Gaia, and lastly Eros 'the most beautiful (*callistos*) of the immortals'. Our world, which is not yet a cosmos, has a top and a bottom, a right and a left, and under the surface of the Earth and around its borders lies primordial chaos.

Gaia, the most prolific of the divinities, is mother earth. Alone she generates Uranus (*Ouranos)*, the starry sky, her mirror-image companion, the vault that will embrace her 'all around', making her fertile. From the Earth/Sky couple were born: Pontus, 'the barren sea, of swelling waves', that with its billows marks the boundaries of its mother; Oceanus, 'of the deep whirlpools', Mnemosine, the enchanting Tethys, and 'for last, ... Cronos of the twisted thoughts, the most terrible of the sons'.

Uranus and Gaia give birth to many other offspring, too many to be mentioned here. Their destiny, as primigenial divinities supplanted by their descendents in ruling the world, seems modelled on older myths from the Mesopotamian area, and on the Egyptian celestial couple, Nut, the Sky and Geb, the Earth. They had been separated without violence by the atmosphere, the god Shu, who prevented them from mating. In the Greek world Uranus instead lay heavily on Gaia, preventing their children from emerging from their mother's womb to see the light, which had not yet appeared due to the presence of the dominating entity. Cronus/Saturn, the elder son, urged on by his mother, broke the bonds that joined Heaven and Earth, castrating his father. But from Uranus' seed was born the goddess of love, the beautiful Aphrodite, the morning star. Graziano Arrighetti, who translated and commentated the *Theogony*, establishes a parallel between this passage and a Hittite cuneiform text, dating from the XIII century B.C., which tells the story of Alalus, the king of heaven, and the powerful Anu, first among the gods. Here too the events, after a series of divine battles, conclude with a castration.

In the *Theogony*, references to astronomical knowledge are recurrent. For the Greeks, Cronus, the planet Saturn, was the lord of the last ring in the sky, the closest to Uranus, who with his wandering had broken the cosmic equilibrium of the eternal present, giving rise to the flowing of time that engulfs its children. Cronus, by castrating Uranus, had shifted forever the axis of the celestial pole, which has ever since appeared inclined[3]. It was his fault that the stars far from Ursa Major, such as the Decans, died and were born, sharing the fate of living beings.

Hesiod's universe is divided into two parts, separated by the disc of Gaia, evoking the AN-Kid couple of the Babylonians. On one side is the starry vault, with its deities and its lights, on the other is Tartarus, always obscured in darkness. We even know the size of this cosmos. Hesiod writes that if a bronze anvil should fall from the sky for nine days and traverse the earth on the tenth, it would take just as many days to reach Tartarus. This hellish place is not really a part of Gaia, but something different; it is like a jar, those used in antiquity to bury the dead in a cellarium, or those where the fruits of the earth are stored. It is the vessel from which seeds sprout and plants are born; in it reside the deceased[4]. 'It is encircled by a bronze fence, and night runs round its neck in a triple strand; and above emerge the roots of the earth and the barren sea'[5]. It is a physical place in which are found the origins and boundaries, the dark, melancholy places that even the gods abhor. It is an enormous chasm and to reach its bottom not even a year would suffice, even to one who managed to enter its gates, avoiding the terrible storms that guard it. It harbours the terrible home of Night, wrapped in leaden clouds. Before it Atlas holds up the sky on his head and his tireless arms, near the bronze gate where Day and Night greet each other in passing, 'the one bringing for earth-dwellers the light that sees much, the other sleep'[6].

While the stories told by Homer and Hesiod follow traditions whose origins are recognisable in the civilisations near that of Greece, Orpheus ventures onto paths apparently unexplored.

Today we think of the origins of the universe in physical terms, and no one advances hypotheses of biological nature. In the Orphic myths instead we find an egg at the origin of everything. It is a very particular egg, resplendent, generated by Uranian forces, but nonetheless an egg. It is told that dark-winged Night was loved by the Wind and laid a silver egg in the womb of Darkness. From it emerged Eros, who set the Universe in motion. Primordial Love appeared in the form of a hermaphrodite with four heads that roared like a lion, bellowed like a bull, hissed like a snake and bleated like a ram. Night lived with him in a cave and assumed the triple guise of Night, Order and Justice[7].

Since silver was the lunar metal, the silver egg of Night recalls the lunar disc, Semele, the Cadmean virgin 'queen of the world'[8]. Eros, also called Protogonos, was defined 'heteroplancton', for his dual nature, 'generated from an egg, furnished with golden wings, bellowing like a bull', origin of the blessed and of men. He had dissipated the dark shadows by beating his wings around the world and emanating a shining light.

Orphism sings of Aether, the matter of the stars, the Sun and the flaming Moon, supreme element of the world. It recalls Uranus, father of the cosmos who moves with an infinite rumble, bearing in his breast the terrible necessity of nature. The celestial bodies of sacred splendour, the beloved children of black Night, move around her flaming throne, radiating immortal splendour, benevolent guardians of the shadows[9]: the Sun (*Helios*), indefatigable Titan, father of dawn and of Night, lord of the world; the Moon with its bull's horns, wandering pilgrim of the sky, glowing lamp, queen of the stars; Pan, the totality of the world, who generates and produces all, on whom rest the infinite stretches of the earth, who causes the waves of the sea to withdraw, and Oceanus with his deep whirlpools.

The naturalists

Greek naturalism was born, around the VI century B.C., from a rib of shamanism and poetry. It marks an epochal transition from *mythos* to *logos*, that is, from a mythological description of reality to a logical one[10]. The philosophers who brought about this prodigious transformation are known as the Pre-Socratics, because they lived and worked before the time of Socrates, the master of Plato. In the history of philosophy they are hailed as the first to open a path that was to lead not only to critical analysis of thought (*logos*) but also to careful observation of nature and its phenomena, in other words, to science. Much of their attention was focussed on understanding the world in which we live, on cosmology, and their works are frequently titled *peri fuseos*, concerning nature.

But we should nourish no illusions. Their thought is often obscure and incomprehensible, and not only due to the fragmentary state in which it has come down to us, so that hosts of interpreters, starting from remotest antiquity, have attempted to explain it. To use a fitting expression of Jean-Pierre Vernant, the Greek world has a unique characteristic: it is different enough to give us a 'change of air', the sense of a substantial distance and, at the same time, is not overly extraneous. We can penetrate it without too many obstacles, since our own mental categories to a large extent derive from concepts elaborated by them (such as democracy, poetry and economy).

In the VI century we thus witness the birth of philosophy, a young and fragile shoot that was to lead Greek civilisation along a course never before explored.

In the first decades of that fortunate age, the idea that the cosmos resembled a sphere and that our planet stood at the centre of a circular space began to spread. With Parmenides, for the first time (or according to other sources, with Pythagoras), the Earth assumed the form of a globe. Some basic concepts came from the nearby Middle Eastern and Egyptian civilisations, but the Greeks, 'eternal children', managed to transform that set of observations into a unitary theory that not only explained the motions of the celestial bodies but also examined the problem of the origin of the cosmos.

The first physicists reasoned on the essence of nature, attempting to find a unifying element, an *archè*. This was an important step, since from that time on the universe was presumed to be substantially homogeneous, formed of the same components to be seen on Earth. The sky, the dwelling place of the gods, ought not to have a structure different from that of the inhabited world. The proportions might vary, air or fire might predominate over water and earth, but the divine world and the human one were based on the same elements.

The modern world begins precisely here, with these Greek philosophers, who began to rough out an idea of the world similar to our own

1. Page 74, Plato's Academy, mosaic; Naples, Museo Archeologico Nazionale, inv. 124554.

2. Head of a philosopher, bronze, 4th century B.C.; Reggio Calabria, Museo Archeologico.

today, and tried to harmonise the image of a spherical Earth with the motions of the stars and planets.

Hesiod's model, presented in the *Theogony* and the *Works and Days*, left many unsolved problems, which translated into just as many questions for anyone observing the celestial phenomena, or even the cycle of the year with its changing seasons. In the keen minds of the naturalists, highly complex problems arose. If the Sun rises in the east and sets in the west, how can it make its return journey, since it does not pass under the Earth, through deep, dark Tartarus? Why do the stars revolve around an axis that is inclined from that of the observation point? In particular, why do they turn around the Pole Star, which remains immobile at the same height in the sky the whole year round? And, linked to the first phenomenon, why do some stars appear and others disappear, as the seasons change? The inclination of the axis of the firmament (the ideal line running from the observer to the Pole Star) varies, moreover, depending on the observer's latitude, a phenomenon that could be explained only by hypothesising that the Earth is spherical, not flat. The other planets, and most notably those we can see best, such as the Moon, are obviously round, perhaps spherical. Why should the Earth be different? The phases of the Moon raised further dilemmas hard to exorcise, with its waxing and waning as if the shadow of a great body had come between the Moon and the light of the Sun. And what other body, if not the Earth, is so close to both of them?

The first to ask these questions was, according to tradition, Thales of Miletus, who lived between 624 and 546. Plutarch, in *De Iside et Osiride*, pairs his name with Homer's, the two who believed the liquid element to be the unifying principle of the universe, an idea derived, he adds, from the Egyptians[11].

Gaia, for Thales, rests on water like a floating log, surrounded by a beneficial liquid element from which everything is born. In this way he answered many of the above questions and laid the conditions for explaining the motions of the celestial bodies which, through a liquid universe, revolved around the Earth.

Thales, an 'elusive' personage, was famous above all as astronomer and for the geometric instruments he perfected to measure distances and heights. Pliny, in his *Naturalis Historia*, states that Thales, applying the geometric theorem that now bears his name, was able to measure the height of a pyramid by comparing the shadow of the monument with that of a rod stuck in the ground nearby.

For his great wisdom, Thales was hailed by his native city Miletus as 'the wisest of all the astronomers'[12]. He could predict the solstices and eclipses of the Sun and tried to determine the size of our star, estimating it as equivalent to the 720th part 'of the circle it traverses'[13].

Thales had opened the way, had broken off the roots of Tartarus;

thanks to him the Earth had begun to fluctuate and the universe around it no longer needed the vigorous shoulders of Atlas to hold up the sky. Anaximander, his most singular and hieratic pupil, went much further, applying to cosmology the principles of Greek science *par excellence*: geometry. His studies in astronomy led him to construct gnomons and sundials, timekeepers based on the shadow cast by the light of the Sun or Moon. He even built a celestial sphere, if we are to believe the words of Diogenes Laertius.

Of Anaximander's sphere we know only too little, and of the man himself we have only indirect testimony, some of which seems sufficiently trustworthy, such as that of Aristotle, who in the *Physics*[14] refers to the theory of the *apeiron*, the unlimited or infinite, as the origin of things according to the Milesian; or of Strabo, who credits him with having drawn the first geographic chart.

According to Anaximander, the Earth remained immobile at the centre of the universe exclusively thanks to the position it occupied, like a point at the centre of a sphere, equidistant from all the other points along the edges. Its stability could be explained by the geometric properties of space. He also stated that the motion in which the skies have been formed is eternal and the Earth rests suspended in the unlimited, is supported by nothing and remains in its place with no external intervention. Just as urban space had been deconsecrated,

notes Vernant, by placing at its centre the *agorà*, the shared hearth, so in the same way the universe of Anaxagoras had become a uniform space. High and low, heaven and earth, the space of the gods and that of mortals, right and left, the one propitious and life-giving, the other inauspicious and pointing the way to Hades, with all their symbolic meanings, had lost their traditional connotations. From a geometric viewpoint, seen from the centre, high and low, right and left, are reversible, so that all the points on the celestial sphere were, for the Milesian philosopher, *homoioi*, exactly similar[15]. In this he departed radically from the theories of his fellows, Thales and Anaximenes, the former his master, the latter his disciple. For him, everything in the universe was in motion and transformation, except *apeiron*, which remained immutable and immobile.

The Italic philosophers

The early philosophers shared many aspects of the poet and the demiurge, and in presenting their ideas they resorted to oral teaching or to poetic language. This is the case of the two pre-eminent members of the Italic school, Pythagoras and Parmenides.

Pythagoras, who lived in the late VI – early V century, mainly in Croton, was viewed by his contemporaries as a semi-divine personage. His theories on the universe, or at least those reported by his pupils and by later sources, had a deep and lasting influence. It is said that one of his followers, Philolaus, who lived in Taranto and Croton at the time of Plato, decided to divulge the secret books of the school, dealing with naturalist topics. There emerges a totally new and revolutionary concept of the cosmos, with a Central Fire, hypostatized, called the 'guardian of Zeus' and generator of the universe, around which revolve nine divine bodies: Counter-Earth, Earth, Moon, Sun, Mercury, Venus, Mars, Jupiter and Saturn. The whole was enclosed within the sphere of the fixed stars. The Sun, in this hypothesis, appeared as a great mirror reflecting the light of the Central Fire, while the Moon was entirely similar to the Earth, inhabited by living beings and filled with plants much larger and more beautiful than the terrestrial ones[16]. The stars were great bodies rotating at distances and speeds proportional to one another.

In Philolaus' theories can be glimpsed the first images of a solar system, of the Earth's rotation and of other inhabited worlds. He also speaks of the harmony of the spheres, the musical sound emitted by the celestial bodies in their vertiginous motion.

The implications of this theory, the exaltation of the *tetraktys*[17], the famous Pythagorean triangle, the statement that 'the entire sky is harmony and number', although imbued with mystical and religious concepts, were unquestionably and authentically valuable to the history of scientific knowledge for over two millenniums.

Another outstanding figure in the Italic school was Parmenides, born around 520 B.C., who lived in the city of Velia, south of today's Salerno. Plato, who dedicates a dialogue to him, describes him as a handsome man and a remarkably profound thinker. A stele found in his native town refers to him as a physician and son of a physician. His masters, according to the sources, were Xenophanes of Colophon, who introduced him to the doctrines of Anaximander, and the Pythagorean philosopher Aminia, to whom he erected a funerary monument. Xenophanes was a personage of great importance, known for his famous statement on the nature of the gods, whom men and animals would portray (if they could) with their own features. Of Aminia we know very little, but certainly he must have been familiar with the cosmological theories of Pythagoras.

Fortunately, some fragments of Parmenides' famous poem *On Nature* have survived, in particular nine-tenths of the first part in which the philosopher discusses the way of truth, which must be based exclusively on logic. The second part, where he describes the way of opinion (what we can deduce on the form and nature of the universe through observation) is too fragmented to allow adequate reconstruction of the Eleatic philosopher's theories.

For him the universe is round and the Earth stands at its centre. This was a revolutionary concept, resulting from the collective efforts of a number of philosopher-naturalists who during those years were slowly dismantling mythological thought. The light of the Moon, moreover, which in the collective imagination was opposed to that of the Sun, was described in the poem as the 'reflected nocturnal light that wanders around the earth ... always turned toward the radiant gaze of the sun'[18]. Eclipses were considered normal astronomical phenomena, and not dire omens. The rainbow was merely an optical effect caused by humidity in the air. The stars, until then known as divine entities exerting their influence on the lives of human beings, became blocks of fire, all identical, embedded in the celestial spheres[19]. The evening star Hesperus and the morning star Phosphorus were, according to Parmenides, the same celestial body, which then took the name of Aphrodite, the Venus of the Romans.

Socrates and Plato

In one of the works of his maturity, the *Phaedo*, Plato narrates the last hours in Socrates' life. In this dialogue he describes the development of the master's thought and his early enthusiasm for the doctrines of Anaxagoras, who hypothesised a supreme mind (Nûs), composed of purer air, from which the cosmos had been generated. For Anaxagoras, a whirling circular motion had separated at the very beginning the opposing elements existing in nature: the rarefied from the dense, cold from hot, and light from shadows. Socrates, at first fascinated by these theories, had soon been disappointed, feeling he had grounded his hopes on falsehood. His studies were devoted to other themes and, in the very last hours of his life, he felt the need to communicate their deepest meaning to the friends around him.

Having drunk the bitter hemlock, Socrates has left the world behind him, and now in quiet communion with himself, speaks in the form of myth. The Earth, he says, 'is not so made nor so small as it is thought to be by those accustomed to reason on it'[20]. It is situated in the middle of the universe, is spherical, and 'has no need of either air' or any support to remain in its place, 'being sufficient to support it the fact that the universe is all the same in every part and the earth is in perfect equipoise'[21]. Furthermore, it must be very large, and we inhabit only a small part of it, around the Mediterranean Sea, 'like ants or frogs around a swamp'. Many other people live elsewhere, in 'many places similar to this one'. Socrates then explains that our senses do not allow us to grasp the secrets of the universe and the Earth that forms part of it. Only the soul, once freed from the body, will be able to comprehend the mysteries of the cosmos. Viewed from above, what form has the 'true earth'? He believes it resembles a ball, one of those made out of twelve pieces of leather, 'iridescent and as if inlaid with different colours', so luminous that those used by the painters are only a pale imitation. The allusion to the dodecahedron[22], the geometric solid, the form of the universe mentioned in the *Timaeus*, is obvious. Everything is more beautiful in this higher sphere: plants, trees, flowers, fruits, mountains, lakes and the sea. It is a spectacle for the blessed. The seasons there are so mild that no one falls ill and men live much longer. There are beings that inhabit the universe and share in many of the qualities of the divinities. From there 'the Sun, the Moon and the stars' can be seen 'without shields, as they are in reality'. The land to which Socrates alludes is without a shadow of a doubt the well-ordered cosmos, within in which move the souls, the demons and the gods. Within this 'earth' are 'many regions, some deeper and more open than this one that we live in', pierced here and there by underground channels, now narrower, now wider, which communicate with one another and through which flow masses of water, as from one basin into another. Under this 'earth' there are 'enormous masses of perennial rivers and waters hot and cold and great rivers of fire', like lava in Sicily. And all of these waters are moving up and down 'like a kind of seesaw inside the earth'[23]. These rivers, Socrates says, flow through Tartarus and emerge from it, and even flow all around the Earth, 'either one time or more, winding like snakes'[24].

The great historian of scientific thought Giorgio De Santillana, who commented on these pages from the *Phaedo* in *Hamlet's Mill*, believed that Socrates was alluding to the great thoroughfares in the firmament envisaged by many ancient cultures, such as ancient Egypt, as immense cosmic rivers, like the waters held up on her back by the goddess Nut or to the 'waters above' mentioned in the Bible.

The *Timaeus*

In the *Timaeus*, Plato directly confronts, with imposing theoretical force, the problems of the universe, its origin and its nature.

The first question he asks is the following: Was the universe created or has it always existed?' This is a problem of a logical, rather than a physical nature, on which the best minds of Greek naturalism had pondered, among them Parmenides. It was a question of reconciling two opposing elements: eternity and becoming. For Plato there were no doubts. The universe had been generated, 'because it can be seen and touched and has a body'[25]. If it has been created there must have been a cause, a father, a creator, who is hard to define. He is a hidden god with an innate tendency toward the beautiful and the good, who has indubitably looked, in creating, to the 'eternal model', that of perfect objects, the ideas, and not the perishable one of things that are born and that die. The demiurge, however, having carried out his initial act, has withdrawn and appears no more on the scene of the world, animated by ceaseless motion and dictated by precise laws, not by the sporadic, subjective intervention of a creator. Everything was established from the beginning because the demiurge himself is not free in his choices, has

3. House of the months, mosaic, calendar from the 3rd century; El Djem, Tunisia.

not created matter nor invented the model. The demiurge is a craftsman who moulds wax, fuses metals and carves wood, and at the same time a magistrate who dictates laws. He desires that all things be good and no one, as far as possible, be found imperfect. He thus transforms everything that lives in 'motion without order or rule', leading it from disorder to order. He does not create from nothing, but operates within the context of already existing elements on which he imposes order. He contemplates the world of ideas to reproduce its image in the empirical world and the ideas continue to constitute a sort of original paradigm. The elements on which he acts, with his ordering hand, are three: the eternal ideas, the empirical world generated from models, and a third element, 'difficult and obscure' in which generation takes place[26], the χώρα (*chora*), a space composed of an indefinable matter, evocative of the *heteroplancton* of Orphic tradition.

In the χώρα lie the imitations and copies of the paradigms, which existed already, before the intervention of the demiurge, mingled together, confused and constantly changing. The *chora* itself is in ceaseless agitation, transmitting its motion to the things present in it.

The demiurge acts by imposing order on the elements according to form and number, that is, according to a precise geometric-mathematical structure. Accordingly, the study of these sciences allows us to penetrate the mysteries of the universe, since our mind reasons in the same terms it recognises in the great book of nature, written in the same characters.

Having established these premises Timaeus, the philosopher from Locri to whom the dialogue is dedicated, goes on to describe the constitution of the body of the world, forged by god out of the four fundamental elements (water, earth, fire and air) in well-established proportions to render it harmonious and in self-accord, united by friendship and for this reason indissoluble, except by the entity that has composed it. The basic elements, the bricks of the universe, are four in number, associated in form to the regular geometric solids: the tetrahedron, hexahedron, octahedron, icosahedron; and a fifth element, the dodecahedron, formed of twelve regular pentagons and reserved as for a special function. It is the most similar in form to the universe, most similar to the sphere, and for this reason the demiurge uses it as ornament.

God utilised all of the fire, all of the water, all of the air and all of the earth, without excluding any portion, ensuring above all that the universe was alive and perfect, composed of perfect parts and that it was unique, 'because nothing was left out from which another similar world could arise'[27]. The figure of the cosmos could be no other than a well-turned sphere, with each part of the circle equidistant from the centre and the ends, and with an absolutely smooth boundary, so that nothing could separate from it and nothing could be added. The universe has been, from the moment of its creation, an entirely self-sufficient and independent sphere with a single motion: the circular one. It is complete, perfect, composed of perfect bodies and endowed with a soul that pervades and envelops it. It is capable of standing alone with no need of anything else, 'sufficiently knower and lover of itself'. And, thus operating, the god who created the universe was pleased.

The soul of the world (*anima mundi*), Timaeus adds, was not generated after the body, and only in narrating it has it been given a temporal sequence. In reality it is 'older' than the body, which it commands and dominates. The soul is formed by combining three elements– Sameness, Existence and Difference – forcefully adapting 'the nature of the different that resists mixing, to the identical'[28]. This is done according to precise mathematical proportions, which have been clearly described by Luc Brisson[29] .On the basis of these arithmetical elements the Demiurge constructs a figure resembling an armillary sphere, which Timaeus describes in detail, as if explaining to an expert craftsman how to make a planetarium. The demiurge, he says, 'ended by using all' of the mixed material resulting from the fusion of the three elements. He divided it in two, lengthwise, and joined the two parts together, just at the centre, forming a kind of 'X'. Then he curved into a circle the two parts that lay one upon the other 'joining the ends to each other at their intersection' and imparted a uniform circular motion to the two circles, the inner and the outer one. The latter was the circle of Sameness, that is, of the fixed stars, the other that of Difference, that is, of the planets. The two circles were set in motion in opposite directions. The motion of the circle was divided six times, giving rise to seven unequal circles and the demiurge ordered the circles to proceed in opposite directions from one another, the first three – the Moon, the Sun and Mercury – at the same speed, the other four – Venus, Mars Jupiter and Saturn – at different speeds[30].

Then the father, like God the creator in the Bible, 'saw this world, living and moving, become the image of the eternal gods and he was pleased, and filled with joy he thought to make it ever more like the model'. Since he is eternal, he tried to make it eternal too, within the limits granted him. But it is impossible to adapt what is eternal to what has instead been created. He then thought of producing a 'mobile image of eternity': time. With the sky and the motion of the stars were thus born the days, the nights, the months and the years, which had not existed before. All of these phenomena are portions of time and the past, present and future cannot refer to eternity, because it lives only in the present. Time is thus measured by the Sun, the Moon and the planets, called wanderers. After having formed the bodies of each of them the god placed them in their destined orbits. The Earth, positioned around the axis that traverses the universe, became the custodian and producer of day and night, the first and most ancient of all the divinities in the sky[31].

Plato's pupils continued to follow in their master's path, developing the precepts for a religion of the stars that was to distinguish the Academy for many centuries, until it was finally dissolved in the year 529 A.D.

The astronomers

The complex planetary models that were developed in parallel during the fifth and fourth centuries were to be utilised up to late Renaissance times.

One of the geniuses of this season was Eudoxus of Cnidus (c. 391-338), who elaborated the system of homocentric spheres. The main problem was to explain in a geocentric perspective the motions of the planets, their appearing sometimes larger, sometimes smaller, and their changing speeds (slowing down, accelerating, apparently moving backward). The observation data and the proposed model were then inserted into speculative systems that attributed to the celestial spheres the perfect and eternal motion of divinity: circular motion. To explain the more obvious irregularities in the motion of the Moon and the planets, Eudoxus hypothesised a complex mechanism resembling that of an armillary sphere, in which the celestial bodies were fixed, each in its own sphere, revolving evenly around two poles, but these poles were in turn entrained by a larger sphere, rotating at a different speed around two other poles[32].

Another extraordinary innovator was Heraclides Ponticus, the first to declare that the Earth rotated daily, as stated by Simplicius in *Aristotelis de coelo commentaria.* He was also the first to formulate the hypothesis that the innermost planets revolved around the Sun, and then the Sun, Mercury and Venus, along with the other planets, orbited around our globe. 'Attributing for the first time motion to the Earth', writes Lucio Russo, 'required a profound transformation in the concepts of space and motion', and not by chance Ptolemy, 'who shares the Aristotelian concept of space, not only rejects heliocentrism but also denies that the Earth rotates'[33].

Heraclides opened the way to the revolutionary theories of Aristarcus of Samos, who studied and worked at Alexandria, and supposed, as writes Archimedes, 'that the fixed stars and the sun remain immobile and the earth turns, following the circumference of a circle, which lies at the middle of the orbit'[34]. The ideas of Heraclides and Aristarcus, taken from a Babylonian astronomer, Seleucus, remained milestones in the long journey of astronomy that was to lead to the epochal discoveries of Nicolaus Copernicus, Johannes Kepler and Galileo Galilei.

The fifth element

Aristotle confronted the subject of the universe, its form and size, in the *Perì ouranou* (*On the Heavens*), a work that powerfully influenced the thinking of astronomers for many centuries, starting from Late Antiquity, in both the western and the eastern world. From a geometric-mathematical viewpoint, he refers to the theories of Eudoxus, but increasing the number of 'homocentric' spheres to better adapt the theoretical model to data acquired through observation.

His idea of the cosmos is based on assumptions apparently irrefutable from the logical point of view, but in reality entirely syllogistic, as pointed out by Galileo in his *Dialogo sopra i due massimi sistemi del mondo* [Dialogue on the two chief world systems].

Aristote begins by assuming that each element – earth, water, fire and air – has a motion of its own. Earth moves straight from above to below, fire on the contrary from below to above, and the mixed bodies move according to their composition. To justify the apparent circular motion of the skies and their presumed eternity, he then introduces, like other pupils of Plato, a fifth element: aether. The motion proper to this fifth element is said to be circular and perfect[35]. The universe is envisaged as a closed space, finite and eternal, exempt from creation and corruption. It has always existed and always will.

The sky, composed of aether, spins in a circular fashion and its inhabitants, the celestial bodies, are divine and immortal. Furthermore, the empyrean has no weight and thus no need of an Atlas to hold it up, nor of the forces generated by a vortex as posited by Empedocles[36].

The Earth remains immobile at the centre of the universe because the element of which it is made moves naturally toward the centre. For the same reason it is spherical, since all of its particles tend by nature to move downward and form a sphere. If any experimental proof of this were needed, it would be enough to observe the shadow of our planet projected on the Moon during the various phases of its monthly cycle.

For Aristotle, then, we find ourselves in a great globe made up of many concentric spheres, 'we' on Earth condemned to the pain of becoming, of birth and death, and 'they' in the sky above, imperishable and satisfied. But we can legitimately aspire to rise up to the heaven, while 'they' instead, firmly set in the great sphere of the firmament, are by an ironic paradox obliged to gaze down on the things of the world, for all eternity.

Bibliography

Vernant 2001, p. 205; Graves 1955, p. 24; Colli 1992; Pasquinelli 1958, p. 10; Riedweg 2007, p. 150; Brisson 1992; Russo 1996, p. 107; Iori 2002, 284*a*, p. 19 and ff.

[1] This is not the Nereid who was of Achilles' mother, cf. Book VII, 421-22.

[2] Verse 116. The quotation is taken from the edition of the *Theogony* edited by G. Arrighetti, Milan, 2004. For the *Opere e i Giorni* and *Lo scudo di Eracle*, Milan 2004, introd. by W. Jaeger, trans. by L. Magugliani.

[3] The apparent inclination depending on the latitude of the observation point.

[4] Vernant 2001, I ed. Paris 1965, p. 205.

[5] *Theogony* 723-24.

[6] *Ivi*, 735-50.

[7] Graves 1955, p. 24.

[8] *Inni orfici*, edited by G. Faggin, Rome 1991: *A Semele*, p. 121.

[9] *Ivi*, p. 37

[10] Cf. Colli 1992. Colli aims to establish that 'the sages were not physicists' (p. 24) and to confute 'the materialistic, physical label' applied by Aristotle 'to the age of the sages' (p. 23). The reconstructions of Aristotle and Theophrastus have however the advange of isolating some aspects of the thought of the 'sages' by showing the evolution in cosmological thought of the VI and V centuries. In this way they offer a consistent justification of the subsequent debate, in which complex geometric mathematical models, such as that of Eudoxus of Cnidus, were developed.

[11] Plutarch, *De Iside e Osiride*, edited by D. Del Corno, Milan 1985, 34, p. 92. The 'first very ancient theologians', Homer in particular, had expressed a similar opinion 'because they called Oceanus and Thetis the progenitors of generation'.

[12] Pasquinelli 1958, p. 10.

[13] Diogenes Laertius I, 22.

[14] 202 b 36, p. 29, cit. in Vernant 2001, p. 238.

[15] *Ivi*, p. 221.

[16] *I Presocratici*, cit., Philolaus, 16 and 17, pp. 477-79; cf. also ff.

[17] The tetrad is the series of the first four numbers added together from which emerges a perfect equilateral triangle. Cf. Riedweg 2007, p. 150.

[18] Parmenides, *Poem on nature*, edited by G. Cerri, Milan 1999, Fr. 14-15.

[19] *Ivi*, fram. 12.

[20] Plato, *Phaedo*, trans. by M. Valgimigli, Rome-Bari 2000, 108 *d*.

[21] *Ivi*, 109 *a*.

[22] The dodecahedron, one of the five regular geometric solids, also known as Platonic solids, is composed of twelve regular pentagons.

[23] Leonardo was probably fascinated by this passage when, in observing fossils, he elaborated a theory on the emerging of mountains and the ceaseless changes in the earth's crust.

[24] *Phaedo*, 112 *e*.

[25] Plato, *Timaeus*, edited by F. Fronterotta, Milan 2006, 28*a*. The one can be accounted for by rational thought, 'since it remains always identical to itself; the other is the object of opinion that derives from a sensation which cannot be rationally accounted for.'

[26] Fronterotta, Introduction to *Timeaus*, p. 51.

[27] *Timaeus*, 32*d*.

[28] *Ivi*, 35*b*.

[29] Plato 1992: in *annexe* 2, pp. 284 and ff. he furnishes a very clear scheme of the mathematical, harmonic and arithmetical proportions. In the subsequent *annexe* he reproduces with the aid of graphic reconstructions the fabrication by the demiurge of the armillary sphere that represents the soul of the world.

[30] *Ivi*, 36*d*.

[31] *Ivi*, 40*c*.

[32] Eudoxus manages to represent the motions of the Moon and Sun by assigning to each of them three spheres; for the other planets he had need of four spheres and for the fixed stars, one. In all, he needed 27 spheres. His pupil Callippus raised them to 33, and Aristotle to 55.

[33] Russo 1996, p. 107.

[34] *Opere di Archimede*, edited by A. Frajese, Turin 1988, p. 448.

[35] Galileo dismantles Aristotle's great cosmic clock piece by piece, first severing the links that he had established between the individual natural elements (water, air, earth, fire and aether) and the motion proper to each of them. According to Salviati, who lays bare the fabric from which are woven the arguments in the *Perì ouranou*, the great philosopher had begun his discourse well and methodically but 'had more the objective of terminating and striking for a purpose', that is, of arriving through forced demonstrations at a demonstration, than of effectively ascertaining the laws of nature. In *Dialogo sopra i due massimi sistemi del mondo, Tolemaico e Copernicano* [Dialogue on the great world systems, the Ptolemaic and the Copernican] edited by L. Sosio, Turin 1975, p. 42.

[36] Iori 2002, 284*a*, p. 19 and ff.

ASTROLOGY, POWER AND IMAGE OF THE COSMOS IN ROME

Giovanni di Pasquale

The age of Octavian Augustus

The calendar reform ordered by Julius Caesar in 46 B.C. constitutes one of the key moments for investigating the relationship between cosmos and power that strongly marked the history of Rome in the Imperial Age. For many years, the Senate had managed the lunar calendar, manipulating it to the point of producing severe discrepancy between the astronomical year and the civil year. Thanks to the collaboration of the astronomer Sosigenes of Alexandria, who had calculated the duration of the solar year as 365 and one-fourth days, Caesar was able to institute a calendar reform that finally brought the civil year to coincide with the solar year; the nearly six hours left over would make up one day to be inserted every four years, after february 24th.

Although this solved the problems involved in using the old calendar attributed to King Numa, based on the cycles of the Moon[1], it was insufficient to cover the duration of the year[2], making it necessary to introduce an intercalated month, called Mercedonius, destined to create many errors among the pontifeces responsible for the calendar. It is no coincidence that Macrobius called the year when Caesar's reform was introduced *annus confusionis ultimus*, while Plutarch had already stated that 'the Romans are the people that make fewer mistakes than the others in irregular measurement of the year'[3].

At the death of Julius Caesar astronomy, astrology and catasterisms had long been part of the culture of the time and it can properly be said that the entire life of his successor, Octavian Augustus, was marked by a particular relationship with the celestial bodies essential to the future ruler's political project.

Symptomatic, for example, is the young Octavian's exploitation of a comet that appeared in the skies over Rome in 44 B.C., a few months after the death of Caesar. Plutarch remarks on its brightness and size, Julius Obsequens, referring to the autobiographical passage of Octavian Augustus reported by Pliny the Elder[4], states that it appeared at the eleventh hour of the day, that is, between 5 and 6:30 pm, while Cassius Dion records its motion toward the western part of the sky. The comet appeared just during the days when games were held in honour of Venus, the mythological ancestress of the Gens Julia, promoted by Octavian to commemorate before the people his adoptive father. It is easy to imagine what a striking impression the comet, immediately christened *Sidus Iulium*, must have been made. Although such episodes were usually associated with disastrous events, its passage could only indicate that Julius Caesar was continuing in heaven the beneficial activity he had carried out on earth, as Virgil was to say in the IX *Eclogues* (vv. 46-50)[5].

The comet of 44 B.C. was thus exploited by the young Octavian, who had a star placed on the head of a statue erected in honour of Caesar (Suetonius, *Caesar*, 88,2; Servius, *Aen.*, 8, 681) and another on the tympanum of the temple inaugurated in the Forum in 42 B.C. and consecrated to the dictator, to confirm the astral apotheosis of his adoptive father and its full accord with the feelings of the people. The comet now heralded not only the reign of Octavian, but also a time of general well-being fittingly described by Virgil in the *Georgics*, where, among other things, the poet narrates (1, vv. 32-35) the future catasterism of Augustus with the consequent creation of a new constellation in the celestial space lying between the Scorpio, who will withdraw his claws to make room for it, and Libra.

A coin struck to celebrate the victory in 36 B.C. of M. Vipsanius Agrippa over Sextus Pompeius and the pirates in the Mediterranean shows thc statue of the future emperor with at his feet a celestial sphere, the sign of aspiration to absolute power whose consonance with the planetary motions is emphasised (fig. 2). To convey this message even more clearly, on one of coins minted by Octavian before 31 B.C. appears the portrait of the young military hero and the goddess Victory who, winged and standing on a sphere, is running to meet him. Other coins from the same period bear on one side the head of Victory and on the other the future emperor with one foot on a globe. These are clear, simple, basic messages for whose diffusion Octavian chose, not at random, coins, the most effective propaganda for political messages.

The very title of Augustus only confirmed the divine nature of Octavian. When the Senate proposed to change the name of the month called Sextilis to Augustus, this also entered the calendar permanently.

Among other things, at the death of Julius Caesar, the pontefices had erroneously applied the calendar reform instituted by the dictator, inserting the intercalated day every three years instead of every four. The error was corrected by Augustus who, having had himself elected pontifex in 12 B.C. expressly for the purpose of rectifying the calendar, was finally able to impose the new system in the year 8 A.D.[6].

As previously mentioned, a connection with the celestial bodies had accompanied Augustus since youth. Suetonius reports the emblematic episode of the young Octavian who, a stranger in the city of Apollonia, saw the astrologer Theogenes kneel at his feet after having observed the constellation under which he was born, indicating the future lord of the world. The same is said to have been confirmed by the astrologer Nigidius Figulus, who had cast Octavius' horoscope from the hour of his birth[7]. From that time on, Octavian meticulously worked to disseminate his horoscope, by having coins minted with the image of Capricorn (fig. 3), which was to become the sign of recognition of his followers, carved on ornaments and gemstones, and appearing as decorative element in paintings in private homes[8].

While the image of Capricorn was supposed to show that Octavian's destiny had been assigned him by the stars, he was actually born in September, and thus under a different constellation. In the abovementioned passage in the *Georgics*, Virgil indicates that he knows Augustus was born under the sign of Libra.

It is plausible that Capricorn was chosen as the time of Augustus' conception, a moment deemed crucially important in one of the most authoritative manuals of astrology, the text of Nechepso and Petosiris.

King Nechepso and his priest Petosiris had lived in the 7th century B.C. Their work, later edited in Greek around 150 B.C., touched on all the themes of Mesopotamian and ancient Egyptian astrology, constituting the most widely consulted manual up to the *Tetrabiblos* of Claudius Ptolemy. The fruit of a revelation destined exclusively to royal spirits for whom the ancient wisdom of Thoth was revived, the text narrates how Nechepso had learned of the eternal and immutable order of the motions in the cosmos from a divine voice coming from the dark night sky. It would thus be the importance of moment of conception, in January, to justify associating Augustus with the sign of Capricorn, a link that finds further confirmation in the *Astronomicon* of Manilius (2, 507).

The propaganda through which Augustus intended to spread the image of a reign inaugurated under the benevolent auspices of the stars involved the architectural sphere as well. Starting in 28 B.C. Octavian had begun to restore the ancient temples of Rome, completing projects begun by Julius Caesar. To these operations Augustus added the erection of new and more ambitious monuments, symptomatic of the now consolidated relationship between the cosmos and personal power. Consecrated in 10 B.C. in the vicinity of his Mausoleum rose the Solarium Augusti, the largest sundial ever seen. As gnomon, an obelisk thirty meters high, now in Piazza di Montecitorio, was used; imported from Heliopolis in Egypt, it projected its shadow onto a bronze network of lines, serving simultaneously as both clock and calendar. The obelisk was consecrated to the Sun; the inscription on its base commemorated the crucially important victory over Egypt at Actium. On Octavian's birthday, September 23rd, the shadow projected by the gnomon pointed to the centre of the Ara Pacis Augustae, showing that the Sun saw the emperor as the custodian and guarantor of a new time of peace on Earth. Along this enormous monument, the inscriptions were translated into Greek so that all could understand. Rome became filled with symbols that indicated the advent of a new age for mankind, proudly hailed by Horace in the *Carmen Saeculare*. Moreover, the monumental sundial was not the first sign of this kind. One of the architectural works of most powerful astral connotation was the Pantheon, the great temple ordered built by Marcus Vipsanius Agrippa just after the battle of Actium. Dion Cassius (53, 27) states that it was dedicated to the twelve planetary deities and that the dome covering it was meant to be an image of the sky, as seems confirmed by the five concentric circles of lacunars forming the ceiling, the twenty-eight ribs and the twelve large windows in the tambour. The building we see today is the one designed by Apollodorus of Damascus and built at the order of the Emperor Hadrian after the fire of 123-125 A.D. Within this monumental architectural image of the Universe, all could admire the spectacle that took place each year at noon on April 21st, when the rays of the Sun lit up the doors on the anniversary of the foundation of Rome.

The symbolism residing in the Pantheon and the Solarium Augusti was clear: as Jupiter guarantees peace in the sky, so the emperor will do on earth, in a play of equilibrium that related the two spaces by suggesting kinship between the ruler's family and the stars.

A relief carving found on the Via Cassia and now displayed at the Museo Nazionale Romano seems to constitute a perfect synthesis between the rule of Augustus and the evocative power of the images employed propaganda not only for the empire as a geographical and political entity, but also for that *consensus universorum* based on which Octavian claimed to exercise absolute power. At either side of the scene are two construction site machines shown building a section of wall. At the centre a Winged Victory flies to crown a triumphant general, presumably Augustus, while the goddess Rome lays at his feet the sphere of the Universe, and the trophy with the barbarian arms of the defeated appears on the right. The sphere alludes to the power of Rome and to that of the emperor who is its guarantor, the representative on earth of a universal empire that has no equal and that, thanks to the work of the sovereign, builder of the world, brings benefits everywhere through the submission of the barbarians and the civilising effects of Roman architecture.

This is a repetition of the message already conveyed by the beautiful gemstone in Vienna (fig. 4), which however, as a precious object, could not reach the public at large. In the guise of Jupiter, Octavian Augustus is depicted with Capricorn, the Sun and a star, the *Sidus Iulium*, above his head; at his right are Oceano and Ecumene, to indicate rule over the world after victory over the barbarians, now tamed, as shown by the scene in the lower register.

The sovereign and the sphere, a clear political message, reiterates in the official art of the court as well as that of the people the message that beneficial work on earth is accomplished in full harmony with the divine will. The accord between the state and the gods, between universal and earthly order, has arrived at completion through the work of Augustus, in the epoch of a new world order of which the *Gens Iulia* is the guarantor on Earth.

This new political order is also mentioned in the extraordinary poem of Manilius, which summarised the knowledge of a now millenary tradition that had come to Rome from Greece and the Orient. In the *Poem of the Stars* Manilius is the spokesman for the conclusive phase of a long-standing cultural debate in Rome that also involved Lucretius and Virgil. In *On the Nature of Things* Lucretius had proposed a design of the universe based on the teachings of Epicurus. Resolutely materialistic, Lucretius had described an infinite universe composed only of atoms and a void, scattered with perishable worlds that aggregate and dissolve according to immutable natural laws leaving no room for the presence of either divine minds providential to man, or religious feelings. Everything in the world must, sooner or later, return to the primordial elements of which all things are composed. Writing some fifty years after Lucretius, Manilius invites the reader to contemplate the stars, within which are enclosed the destinies of every man and of all creation. In him the need to understand everything, which had driven Lucretius, disappears. Any terrestrial occurrence is the result of a celestial gift. This crisis in reason had already appeared in Virgil and had taken shape in the *Georgics*, the manifesting a reality that, emerging with the rule of Octavian Augustus, had narrowed the space of the political and cultural debate that had animated republican Rome. Manilius, writing at a time when Augustus had long been ruler, expresses in his poem the connection between nature ruled by a god and the empire, an earthly cosmos governed by a sovereign for the good of humanity. The poet of the stars can thus do no more than describe the regular motions of the celestial vault and its earthly reflections, manifested in the *Pax Augusta*. Regular motions of the celestial vault that will find room, and not by chance, in a hall of Nero's supremely elegant Domus Aurea (Suetonius, *Nero*, 31) and in the palace of Domitian (Martial, *Epigrams*, VII, 56), to underline the syntony between cosmos and power.

After Augustus

The reigns of the emperors who succeeded Augustus unfolded under the sign of a complex relationship with the astrologers, whose popularity appeared unchallengeable. During the time he spent on Rhodes, Tiberius met the astrologer Trasillus, who was to enter his close circle of intimates and to become one of the most influential personages at court[9]. Through astrological predictions, Tiberius struck at his presumed or true enemies, ordering the death of those whose birth charts authorised them to nourish hopes of power[10]. On the contrary, he tolerated Gabba, the future emperor in the difficult year of 69 A.D., because the stars had predicted that he would become ruler only years after the death of Tiberius[11]. According to Tacitus, moreover, at the departure of Tiberius for Capri the astrologers announced that the emperor would not return to Rome (*Annales*, 4, 58, 2). Depicted negatively by the literary sources whose authors refused to pardon his long stay away from Rome, Tiberius was criticised by Juvenal as well, who describes him as idling away the time in his villa on Capri surrounded by astrologers (*Saturae*, 10, 93 and ff.).

Already in the reign of Claudius (41-54), fears were spreading over the potential danger of the predictions and prophecies made outside of the ruler's direct control. Reiterating a provision already taken by Augustus in 11 A.D. prohibiting divinatory practices at times of severe internal crisis, Claudius prohibited horoscopes concerning his own person, as suggests the episode of Furius Scribonianus, exiled from court for this very reason.

And yet this same Claudius had allowed Balbillus, the son of Trasillus, to follow him on his expedition to Britannia. Having predicted Nero's rise to the throne (Tacitus, *Annales*, 6, 22, 4; 14, 9, 2), Balbillus even received a highly prestigious appointment to the post of *praefectus Aegypti* from 55 to 59 A.D., remaining at court even when the astrologers were exiled from it in 52.

The reign of Nero, only seventeen when acclaimed emperor, represents the most organic attempt yet made to confer on princedom an autocratic connotation. While Octavian Augustus had never let the cult of his person be separated from that of Rome, Nero abruptly destroyed this delicate equilibrium. The year of this sudden change was 58, when he began to govern in personal and increasingly absolutist manner;

beyond the whims and eccentricity, there emerges the image of a divine monarch. The burning of Rome in 64 gave him a chance to enormously enlarge the new imperial palace, which now stretched from the Palatine Hill to the area occupied today by the Coliseum. Within this incredibly luxurious residence was an octagonal hall whose ceiling revolved in imitation of the sky, an extraordinary work fabricated by Nero's *machinatores*[12]. In a dominating position on one of the heights of the Palatine Hill, the Velia, Nero had an enormous statue built dedicated to the Sun, but bearing his own features. Although the long-term judgement of Nero's rule is a negative one, he had demonstrated for the first time that an emperor could govern as absolute monarch and that there existed forces willing to support him. Not by chance, the urban proletarians long mythologized the figure of Nero, whose horoscope had been cast at the moment of his birth by Trasillus, the astrologer who was one of the most influential personages of the time[13]. Nero was born on december 15th of the year 37[14], and the astrologers claimed that his horoscope showed both empire and the wickedness he was later to display. Wishing to appear as the 'new Sun', Nero believed he had come into the world in almost apollonian manner, being born under the aegis of the winter solstice, the moment of the Sun's rebirth (Suetonius, *Nero*, 6, 1; D. Cassius, 61, 2, 1). Faithful to this image, Lucan describes Nero driving the chariot of the Sun, keeping to the middle zone of the sky so as not to disturb the *equilibrium* of the cosmos[15].

.Moreover, the middle position suggested by Lucan can also be traced to the Milky Way, the region of the sky, according to Manilius, destined to welcome the souls of great men[16]. The reign of Nero too saw the appearance in the sky of two comets, which Tacitus records in the years 60 and 64, linking them to disasters that occurred[17]. Tacitus reports in fact 'the opinion of the people that comets foretell the change of a king' and Suetonius confirms how after these apparitions deemed messengers of his downfall, Nero ordered many noble citizens killed.

The century came to an end with the Flavi and the tragic story of the Emperor Domitian (81-96 A.D.), of whom the chaldean astrologers at court had predicted, while still a child, his assassination in the manner in which it actually took place at the hands of his own officials[18]. Already his father Vespasian, between 72 and 74, had ordered philosophers and astrologers driven out of Rome. Obsessed by these predictions throughout his reign, Domitian had put to death many members of noble families whose horoscopes he had obtained. Many innocents were condemned to death on the basis of horoscopes to which the court astrologers could link a vague presentiment of empire. According to Suetonius, a certain Metius Pompeianus was first exiled and then put to death because, in addition to having an important horoscope, he kept in his room a geographical chart of the ecumene, a clear sign of aspiring to power.

In the following centuries, even during the most tormented moments in Roman history, the celestial sphere continued to be one of the most striking symbols of power. A coin minted under the Emperor Trajan (98-117) shows the globe encircled by the zodiac at the feet of a woman personifying Providence, the divine *prónoia* of the Stoics, who orders and disposes all for the good of the human race. This was a cultured reference; the emperor provides for the good of the subjects of an empire that had now reached its greatest geographical extension exactly as the goddess renders the cosmos benevolent for humanity. Antoninus Pius (138-161), in turn, had coined a medallion on the back of which appears Atlas holding up the celestial globe, in evident comparison to the labours of the emperor who bears on his back the fate of humanity. Starting in the late 2nd century, the *Providentia Augusti* becomes *Providentia deorum* and the globe, a small one, alternates between the hands of the goddess and those of Eternity and of the personification of Rome.

It is symptomatic to recall that, near the end of the pagan era in Rome, the celestial sphere was, along with other symbols of power, an ornament atop the sceptre of Maxentius (fig. 6). Found in 2005 during excavations on the Palatine Hill, the sceptre was inside a box wrapped in silk-and-linen cloth, buried with other emblems of command to be retrieved if Maxentius had managed to defeat Constantine. Having proclaimed himself emperor in 306 A.D., Maxentius died in the Tiber, defeated by Constantine at the Milvian Bridge in 312. The pagan emblems of Maxentius, with their glass and chalcedony spheres, remained buried underground while the celestial globe turned in the hands of an emperor, Constantine the Great. With the spread of christianity, however, to the sphere was added a cross, to recall the dominion of the Christian god over the world.

Texts, spheres and stars in popular culture

Highly popular among the people were the *Phenomena* and the catasterisms in the versions of Aratus and of G. Julius Hyginus, a repertoire that nourished art as well. With the work of Aratus the astronomical tradition in literature had returned to the path laid out in the Homeric poems and in Hesiod. Between 275 and 270 B.C. Aratus had in fact composed the *Phenomena*, setting to verse the lost treatise of the same name in which Eudoxus had described the celestial vault. After the opening hymn to Zeus (vs. 1-18) viewed as spirit (*pneuma*) that pervades the cosmos and with his divine providence (*prónoia*) renders the Universe comprehensible and benevolent for mankind, Aratus describes the sky in sections containing the constel-

1. Page 84, Urania with the celestial sphere, detail, 1st century B.C.; Pompeii, Villa of Murecine.

2. Denarius of Octavian coined for his victory over Sextus Pompeus in 36 B.C. The statue of the future ruler rests on a celestial globe whose main circles can be recognised.

3. Coin of Augustus depicting Capricorn with a cornucopia, sign of the advent of a new age of happiness for humanity.

4. Gemstone from the Augustan Age, c. 10 B.C., Vienna, Kunsthistorisches Museum.

5. Floor mosaic with armillary sphere, 2nd century B.C.; Solunto, Italy, House of Leda.

6. Sceptre of Maxentius, detail of the dark glass sphere, 4th century.

lations, the circles of the sphere and the Milky Way, but without furnishing details on the positions of the individual stars. The work, whose scientific component is minimum, closes by describing the synchronisms between the times when the various constellations rise.

How successful was Aratus' *Phenomena* in Rome is also demonstrated by its numerous translations, from which derive Cicero's *Aratea*, Germanicus' *Phaenomena Arati*, Ovid's *Phaenomena*, of which only two fragments remain, and Avienus' *Aratea*.

The work of Hyginus also met with notable success. Hyginus, the librarian of Octavian Augustus, wrote a treatise called *De astronomia* that was widely successful, especially the part dealing with catasterisms ('placings among the stars'), where he describes the ascent to heaven of persons, animals and things and their transformation into stars. Adopting a widely successful literary genre that had been introduced at Alexandria by Eratosthenes, Hyginus declares his intention of facilitating the reading of Aratus' *Phenomena*. Divided into four books, his work offers the reader the necessary rudiments for observing the celestial vault and understanding of the mechanics of the Universe with the fundamental aid of a celestial sphere.

Drawing inspiration from Aratus, Ovid composed the *Fasti* and Virgil the *Georgics*. These themes attracted prose writers also, as demonstrated by Book XI of Columella's *De re rustica*, dedicated to the works to be carried out in relation to the apparition of the astronomical signs that govern their succession during the course of the year. Although the works of Virgil, Ovid and Columella cannot be considered real astronomical texts, they are the mirror of an age that viewed knowledge of the skies as an effective aid to such practical matters as navigation and agricolture.

The dissemination of these texts in popular culture also inspired the representation of celestial and armillary spheres in art. The celestial sphere passes from the hands of Urania (fig. 1), the goddess who in numerous frescoes and mosaics proudly displays the object of her protection, to those of astronomers and philosophers. While the famous mosaic from Stabia depicting Plato in the Academy, or, as others believe, the Seven Sages, shows a lesson in astronomy where the celestial globe is placed in a box, the centre of attention from the onlookers, the magnificent armillary sphere with the little immobile Earth at the centre represented in a floor mosaic in the house of Leda at Solunto brings us instead to Eudoxus and his ties with the Academy of Athens (fig. 5). A symbol of the new astronomy and of agreement between Plato and Eudoxus, the armillary sphere is the concrete sign of an astronomical science that is perfecting its instruments. Expressly for having introduced the armillary sphere into his astronomy lessons, Eudoxus was severely criticised by Epicurus in Book XI of the *Perì fuseos*; nonetheless, instruments were now being included in discussions of this subject. In explaining the structure of the Universe to his companions, Timaeus declares he cannot continue describing the celestial sphere and the orbits of the planets because he needs a model (Plato, *Timaeus*, 40 c). Study of the various world systems could thus be conducted either through a geometric approach, or by using models such as celestial and armillary spheres. The collection of texts known today as *Minor astronomy* (to it, containing works by Autolicus, Theodosius of Bithynia, Hypsicles and Euclid refers Pappus at the beginning of Book VI of the *Collectio Mathematica*), confirms the validity of an approach based on study of the laws that govern the motions of the celestial sphere, on observation of a sky of which we see only a part, and the construction of a model that simplifies the whole. The sky can also be studied by observing the celestial globe and the armillary sphere, instruments used to reproduce a number of astronomical events as support to direct observation.

Not by chance, in clarifying that his text is addressed to students, in the foreword to *De astronomia* Hyginus accuses Aratus of being overly obscure as regards the sphere, the learning instrument par excellence. We know that Hipparchus[19] fabricated a globe on which to place the stars, based on his meticulous observations of the celestial vault, and that Ptolemy also built spheres of this kind, giving detailed indications for their construction. Starting from a globe of dark colour to recall the night, he suggests positioning the stars on it using the colours yellow and red with a different intensity according to their brightness, and connecting them with lines but without drawing figures, which become a hindrance to observation[20]. Note that the celestial sphere is a representation in which the spectator seems to gaze from a point out in the Universe. He thus sees from the outside the globe that envelopes all, at the centre of which stands the Earth, the imaginary axis around which revolves the sphere of the heavens, and the tiny size of the Earth in relation to all the rest.

Some idea of this is provided by the little spheres displayed in the exhibition coming from Mainz and from the collection of the Parisian antiquarian Kugel; the latter, dating from the 2nd century B.C., is the work of an artisan who presumably limited himself to copying other similar spheres, without following any particular literary tradition. Despite some imprecision in depicting the constellations, its documentary value is notable[21]. These little bronze and silver spheres must have been costly gifts, as suggested by a passage in the *Palatine Anthology* mentioning the gift of an *ouranion mimèma*, 'an imitation of the skies' received by Poppaea for her birthday[22].

The sphere in the hands of the Farnese Atlas in the Museo Nazionale Archeologico of Naples, the copy of an original from the Hellenistic Age, dates from the middle of the 2nd century. On the globe, partially obscured by the titan's hands, are the representations of several constellations and of the zodiac with the line of the ecliptic, the circles of the equator and the tropics, as well as the solstitial colure. The arrangement of the constellations suggests that the work may have been designed following the text of Aratus, while their representation, seen in reverse, is in keeping with the suggestions of Hipparchus.

Spheres were now commonly found in Rome: technology, art and science were based on their realization, which became progressively freer and more imaginative. Not by chance, in defining the form of the constellations, the Latins often recurred to the term *deformatio*. Hyginus (*Pref.*, 2, 23, 2; 2, 43) is aware of the fact that the figures to be represented on the sphere are deformed in the drawing; and the same term is used three times by Vitruvius, expressly in the part of *De architectura* describing the astronomical figures of the anaphoric clock (9, 8, 8). It was to avoid complications of this kind that Ptolemy suggested, as has been seen, not to draw the constellations but merely trace their contours.

Lastly, the mechanical cosmos unanimously attributed by literary tradition to Archimedes must be mentioned. Information reported by Cicero, Ovid and other authors indicates that in Rome it must have been possible to observe the two spheres fabricated by Archimedes and confiscated from Syracuse as part of the booty of war by Consul Marcellus after having defeated the city in 212 B.C. The simplest of these, mentioned by Ovid in the *Fasti* (6, v. 277-278) and described also by Claudianus in a curious epigram called *In sphaeram Archimedis*, was presumably an armillary sphere. The poet describes the sphere in fact as an image of the cosmos with the Earth at the centre, equidistant from the top and the bottom. Kept in the temple of Vesta, it was made a 'museum piece', bearing witness to both the mythicizing, already in act, of the great scientist from Syracuse, and to the admirable artifices that could be expressed by technology.

Much more complex must have been the other planetary sphere, to which Archimedes presumably dedicated the lost treatise *On the construction of the sphere*. It is mentioned in a passage from the *Tusculanae*[23] and one from Cicero's *De republica*[24], where it is defined as a 'new type of globe' capable of showing simultaneously the Sun, the Moon, the planets and the eclipses, each with its own motion and its own velocity.

The finding of the Antikythera mechanism, whose dating (middle of the 2nd century B.C.) and provenance (Rhodes) suggest a connection with the astronomer Hipparchus, shows that precise measurement and complex calculations were not extraneous to the conceptual horizon of the ancients and to their technical capabilities. The complexity of this machine can be explained only by the attempts and achievements of many technicians whose names have been lost, but and who must have engaged in the very ancient attempt to endow technological objects with motion. The finding of this complex device thus renders plausible not only reports on the mechanical cosmos of Archimedes, but also those, furnished by Cicero (*De natura deorum*, II, 87-88), on the planetary mechanism 'recently constructed by Posidonius, which at each revolution reproduces the motions of the Sun, the Moon and the five planets as they occur in the skies every twenty-four hours'. Although a planetary mechanism could not solve all of the problems discussed by the astronomers of the time, it certainly contributed to nourishing debate on the operation of the great world machine. We have already seen how Epicurus criticised Eudoxus for having utilised armillary spheres in his school of astronomy at Cyzicus. The target of Epicurus' criticism was the doctrine of Eudoxus, who had taught to read the sky and place in it a geometrically treatable model, including the basic elements of an armillary sphere made of a few rings. The passages from Cicero quoted above show that in the 1st century B.C. the higher cultural milieu still utilised these world machines in connection with argumentation on the nature of the universe that called into question the philosophic thought of Epicurus and his school. With the construction of the planetary mechanism, the question *a quo moventur planetae?* would have found matter for more animated confrontation.

The idea of the machine world found further support in Vitruvius. After having dealt with the matter of building in the first eight chapters of *De architectura*, Vitruvius addresses, following an order probably not chosen at random, questions of astronomy and mechanics. In a passage from Book IX (9, 1, 2) the Universe is described as a machine that rotates around two axes hinged to the immense sphere of the fixed stars. Moreover, at the beginning of the part dedicated to machines, Vitruvius declares that the model of the machine exists in nature : by transferring to earth the cosmological premises of the mechanical heavens, the machine allows knowledge of that nature of which man was progressively becoming the master.

–

Bibliography

Sedley 1976, pp. 23-54; Cuvigny 2002, pp. 22-27; Cuvigny 2004, pp. 345-377.

[1] Cicero, *De legibus*, 2, 9; Ovid, *Fasti*, 3, 151; Plutarch, *Cesare*, 59, 4 ; *Numa*, 18.

[2] Dion Cassius, 43, 26, 1.

[3] Macrobius, *Saturnalia*, 1, 14, 3 and Plutarch, *Cesare*, 59,5.

[4] Julius Obsequens, *Liber Prodigiorum*, 68 and Pliny the Elder, *Naturalis Historia*, 2, 93.

[5] A similar reference is also found in the *Georgics*, 1, 488 and in *Aeneid*, 8, 68; see also Horace, *Carmina*, 1, 12, 46-48, Ovid, *Metamorphoses*, 15, 749 and 848-850 and Valerio Massimo, *Memorabilia*, 3, 2, 19.

[6] Pliny, *Naturalis Historia*, 18, 211 and Suetonius, *Augustus*, 31, 2.

[7] Suetonius, *Augustus*, 94.

[8] Dion Cassius, 56, 25, 5; Suetonius, *Augustus*, 14, 18.

[9] Tacitus, *Annales*, 6, 21.

[10] Tacitus, *Annales*, 6, 20; Dion Cassius, 57, 19, 3.

[11] Tacitus, *Annales*, 6, 20; Suetonius, *Galba*, 4.

[12] Suetonius, *Nero*, 31.

[13] Suetonius, *Nero*, 62; Tacitus, *Annales*, 6, 22, 6.

[14] Tacitus, *Annales*, 14, 96.

[15] Lucan, *Bellum Civile*, vv. 1-45

[16] Manilius, *Astronomicon*, 1, 758 and ff.

[17] Tacitus, *Annales*, 14, 22, 1; 15, 47, 1.

[18] Suetonius, *Domitian*, 14, 2.

[19] Sedley 1976, pp. 23-54,. in particular pp. 31-43.

[20] Ptolemy, *Almagest*, 7, 1.

[21] Ptolemy, *Almagest*, 8, 3.

[22] Cuvigny 2002, pp. 22-27; see also Cuvigny 2004, pp. 345-377.

[23] *Palatine Anthology*, 9, 355.

[24] Cicero, *Tusculanae disputationes*, I, 63: 'When Archimedes enclosed in a sphere the motions of the moon, the sun and the five wandering planets, he, like the God of Plato who constructed the world in the *Timaeus*, made it so that one revolution of the sphere controlled various motions differing in speed and slowness. Now, if these phenomena can take place only with the aid of the divinity, not even Archimedes could have recreated the same motions in a sphere without divine genius'.

[25] Cicero, *De re publica*, 1, 22.

[26] Vitruvius, *De architectura*, X, 1, 4-6.

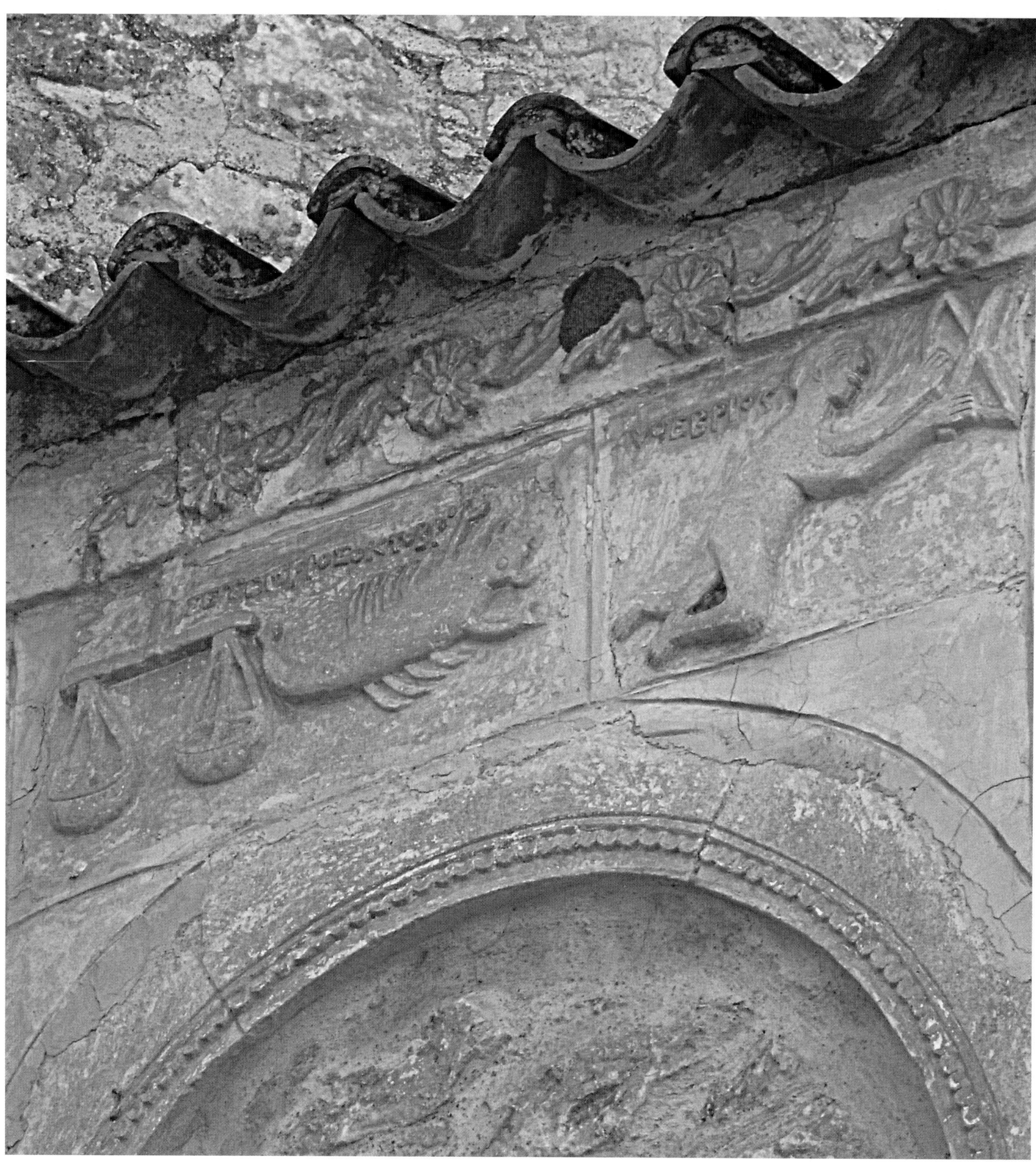

THE ANCIENT WORLD

3 | THE GEOMETRY OF THE COSMOS

AGRICULTURE AND THE STARS

Annamaria Ciarallo

We have also explained the system of the constellations and the seasons in simple manner, such as to leave no reason for doubt even in those not expert in the matter. For he who truly understands, the countryside contributes to a knowledge of the sky no less than the science of astronomy to cultivation of the land.
(Pliny, Naturalis Historia, XIX, 1)

And although the Ancients based their operations on the positions of the Stars, they are not to be followed nor imitated, both for the little knowledge of the stars common to many of them, and because the positions of the Stars are not now as they were then, because each century the Stars advance their positions by degrees and since the time of the Romans, not to speak of the Greeks from whom the Romans took this science, many centuries have passed, and the Stars observed by them have advanced some twenty-two or twenty-three degrees. And what Farmer of this region would wait to plant, as advised by Virgil, until the twenty-first of October, at which time, according to Columella, the Vergiliae set, or the eighth of November, when they also set in the morning according to the same Columella? And who does not know that it is not the time to plant Beans, Lentils and hemp at the end of February, when Arcturus appears, as was ordered by the Ancients?
(Tanara 1651, p. 448)[1]

For Tanara, writing some sixteen centuries after Columella, it was better to plant beans, lentils and hemp at least a month later, a need dictated by the different climatic conditions prevailing on those same dates, due to the precession of the equinoxes, of which the author was well aware[2].

Confirmation of this is also found in popular sayings. '*A San Benedetto la rondine sotto il tetto*' (On St. Benedict's Day, swallows under the roof) states a famous proverb, but for Pliny and Columella the swallows did not arrive on March 21st, but on February 22nd (*VIII Kalendae Martii*)[3]. Furthermore, although the night of August 10th is still considered that of the falling stars, it can easily be seen that this phenomenon has moved forward a couple of days. And while for us the seasons begin on the days of the solstices and equinoxes, for the ancients the 27th of January (*VI pridie Kalendae Febrarii*, in Columella) was a mid-winter day and spring started on the 9th of February (*V Idus Febrarii*, in Pliny)[4].

Observation of the sky was vitally important for the agricultural and pastoral activities of the ancients, and was common to all civilizations. In the stars and the planets[5] they sought reassuring signs for the outcome of harvests, often threatened by bad weather.

Testimony of the presence of the celestial bodies in the daily life of the ancients comes to us from Pompeii. In addition to the frescoes and some oil lamps decorated with astronomical and astrological themes, a graffito records, for example, the rising of Dane, a star in the constellation of Cygnus[6].

This tradition lived on through the centuries, producing a great number of agricultural calendars and literary descriptions evidencing the connection between work in the fields and the course of the stars. They show how the calendar for the various agricultural practices changed, also in relation to the precession of the equinoxes, a phenomenon imperceptible to us due to the brief span of human life[7].

But ancient Pompeii furnishes tangible proof of the precession of the equinoxes. An ensemblc of naturalist findings confirms a philological reading of the letters of Pliny the Younger, which place the date of Vesuvius' eruption at August 24th of the year 79 A.D., while also demonstrating that, on the same date, taking account of changes made in the calendar over the centuries, the season was already autumn, as was moreover indicated by Varro, Columella and Pliny, for whom this season began between the 11th (*III Idus Augusti*) and the 12th (*Pridie Idibus Augusti*) of August[8]. And in fact, this appears obvious; if 13,000 years from now, on the same date the season will be the opposite of today's, then the change amounts to about one month in a little over 2,000 years.

The first agricultural calendar in the broad sense may be attributed to Hesiod. In his *Works and Days* this author described in poetic form the agricultural and pastoral activities that were probably carried out in Boeotia, the Greek region from which he came.

For Hesiod, the right times for harvesting and ploughing coincided with the rising and setting of the Pleiades, which for the astronomer Fresa[9] corresponded to May 17th and November 3rd respectively, for the region of Boeotia in 800 B.C.

The rising of Arcturus in the evening marked the time to prune the grapevines, while the rising of Orion, around June 19th, signalled the beginning of threshing time. For Columella instead, this should be done, in temperate zones, during the second half of June, while the proper time for ploughing and sowing was the end of November.

The difference in the times specified by Hesiod and by Columella depended on various factors of local significance, on inevitable climatic differences over the short term (for instance, Columella records that the climate around Rome, in August, was particularly rainy; XI, 2, 64), and on the fact that after eight centuries the effects of the precession of the equinoxes were already being felt, although to a minor degree, calling for more precisely compiled agricultural calendars.

Columella and Pliny, almost contemporaries, both tried to take account of these variables in their agricultural calendars, a need that had become even more urgent in the first century A.D., when the expansion of the Empire was at its peak and its vast Provinces lay at widely differing latitudes.

But while Columella, in specifying the rising and setting of the stars, seems to refer to the latitude of the capital, and in suggesting a schedule for agricultural operations makes no reference to specific geographic places but rather to areas having similar climates and soils, Pliny accurately delimits the boundaries of the regions he refers to and describes the course of the stars in relation to them.

The peasants, however, could read at the most a few inscriptions. The accurate precepts of the classical authors could be useful to an educated ruling class, but certainly not to them. Illustrated agricultural calendars instead, probably addressed to them, satisfied their needs, providing a compendium of information useful for civil life and farming; the one found at the Museo Archeologico of Naples, coming from the Farnese Collection, is a significant example.

On the four sides of a marble cube are represented the three months of each season. The year began with January and for each month, placed under the protection of a god, was indicated its constellation of entry, its number of days, the duration of the diurnal and nocturnal hours (but not the minutes, so that the hours added up to 24 only at the equinoxes and solstices), the chief agricultural and pastoral activities and the major religious festivities. On the dating of this marble calendar, which seems based on the precepts of Pliny and Columella, various hypotheses have been advanced; the locality from which it came is unknown.

The classical agronomists indicate the same dates as the Neapolitan calendar for the arrival of the swallows, in February, and the washing of the sheep, in April. But on the Neapolitan calendar some other operations are postponed, such as the reaping of barley and harvesting of broad beans in July, the harvesting of grain to August, the tarring of terracotta vats to September, the harvest to October and the sowing of wheat and barley to November. This could mean that the Neapolitan calendar refers to places with a colder climate, but if so, there would have been no cultivation of olives to be harvested in December; or that it was compiled at a later time, although in this case the arrival of the swallows in February seems strange.

The tradition of illustrated agricultural calendars, at times transformed into a 'representation of the months' lasted for centuries, at least up to the Renaissance, although in the transition from the Roman to the Christian world the incitement to industrious labour, more in keeping with Divine precepts, assumed greater importance. Splendid examples of Christian agricultural calendars are found in the so-called *Books of Hours* and in the more famous medieval cathedrals.

In a mosaic from Carthage dating from the 5th century A.D. the representations of the months are not linked to the signs of the Zodiac, but to the activities typical of each month, for example, reaping in July, harvesting in September, hare hunting in October, while in November attention was focused on gathering pinecones, obviously an important element in the local economy[10].

In the great floor mosaic in the Cathedral of Otranto (1163)[11], perhaps the best known among those that have come down to us, the representation of the months – the year begins with March – is based on the scheme of the *arbor vitae*, in which each branch bears a tondo corresponding to a month, within which are represented the sign of the zodiac and human figures intent on the agricultural activities of the period.

If we compare the Otranto Calendar with the cycles of the months appearing in the sculptures of the Cathedrals of Parma (1120) and Ferrara (1220), to mention only two (although this is generally true for all those of Central Italy), we note that, while the former replicates the scheme of the marble calendar in Naples, in the others the constellation of entry is the subsequent one. It would thus seem that a scheme from centuries before is replicated at Otranto, perhaps for religious reasons linked to Early Christian or Romanesque rituals, while in the other places real observation of the heavens was conducted, resulting in that discrepancy, due to the precession of the equinoxes, between the entry of the Sun into a zodiacal sign, the domain of modern astrology as well, and its real entry into the relevant constellation.

An interesting and unedited zodiacal calendar, represented on the outer wall of the apse of the little Orthodox church of Areopolis, a tiny village on the peninsula of Mani deep in the Peloponnesus, indicated to the inhabitants the time to begin and to end work in the fields. The calendar is carved on rectangular marble panels distributed over three sides of the hexagonal apse. The signs of the Zodiac are oriented on the annual course of the sun. At the centre is a frowning sun, to the onlooker's left, and a blazing sun to the right, separated by the figure of an angel.

On the left side, proceeding toward the right, we find a panel on which are carved the signs of Libra and Scorpios, then one with Sagittarius alone (fig. 1); then come two more panels, one with Capricorn alone, the other with Aquarius and Pisces.

On the right side, again starting from the left, we find a panel with Aries, one with the signs of Taurus and Gemini, and another with Cancer and Leo; the series concludes with a panel bearing the sign of Virgo alone.

It is clear that on the left side, which records the passing of the autumn and winter months, the panels bearing the signs of the beginning (Capricorn) and end of the year (Sagittarius) meet at the centre, thus closing a cycle, while on the right side they open (Aries) and close (Virgo) the spring and summer months, dedicated to work in the fields.

In some later representations, the problem of the zodiacal sign of entry and the real one is solved by indicating for each month both of the zodiacal signs, as in the 'Great Calendar and shepherds' almanac' from the 15th century or the Duke of Berry's famous illuminated calendar, compiled in the late 13th – early 14th century. Instead, in the pictorial cycle of the great Hall of Months in Palazzo Schifanoia at Ferrara (1464), each month is placed in the sign of the constellation that is entering, but in homage to classical times it is placed under the tutelage of the corresponding deity, according to the ancient Roman calendar. For example, the month of March is placed in Aries, but entrusted to the protection of Minerva.

In these illustrated calendars, as has been noted, the main agricultural activities change according to the place, and consequently the climate, in which they were compiled. Accordingly, while in a large part of Italy the countrymen were occupied with swine and wild boars or gathering firewood, at Parma and Ferrara the turnip harvest was important, while the dates for grape harvesting ranged between August and September and those for reaping and threshing between July and August.

Obviously the illustrated agricultural calendars, as compared to literature, were more immediately effective, so that they were used for centuries. An example known to all is the so-called 'Barbanera', found up to a few decades ago in every farmhouse, and still published today. In its on-line version, under the heading 'cultivation with the biodynamic method', it states, testifying to a bond that has never been broken, 'This calendar offers advice on work and the best times for cultivating, applying a method that takes account of the course of the moon through the constellations.'

Bibliography

Alvino 1887; Barale 2000, pp. 147-155; Cernuti 2002, pp. 44-52; Ciarallo-De Carolis 1998, pp. 63-73; De Santillana-von Dechend 2006; Fresa 1959, pp. 249-255; Fresa 1970, pp. 253-265; Fresa 1973, pp. 7-15; Invernizzi 1994; Parrish 1984; Tanara 1651.

[1] In 1654 Vincenzo Tanara wrote a work on activities to be carried out in the country. He reviews the classical texts, those of Pliny and Columella in particular, adapting them to his own time; G.B. Della Porta carried out a similar operation. Both authors refer essentially to the places in which they lived: Della Porta to the area around Naples and Tanara to the Bologna countryside.

[2] The astronomer Alfonso Fresa, former Director of the Capodimonte Observatory, clearly described the effects of the precession of the equinoxes. In the dividing of the Zodiac, effected some 2000 years ago, the ecliptic, the line of symmetry of this celestial zone, intersected the equator at the points gamma and omega, the beginning of spring and of autumn, in the constellations of Aries and Libra respectively. Due to the effect of the precession of the equinoxes, since the time of Hipparcus (II century B.C.) the gamma point has moved into Pisces and omega into Virgo.

[3] Pliny the Elder (23-79 A.D.) dedicated to the agricultural calendar the XVI book off his *Naturalis Historia*, and Columella (4-70 A.D.) the XI book of his *De re agricola*.

[4] For correspondence on the calendar cf. Alvino 1887, Invernizzi 1994, Cernuti 2002.

[5] Aveni has written, for example, on the Mesoamerican archaeoastronomers, especially those of the Maya in ancient Mexico (Aveni 1994).

[6] Fresa 1959, pp. 249-255.

[7] Cf. *Hamlet's Mill*, the extraordinary book by G. de Santillana and H. von Dechend.

[8] Ciarallo-De Carolis 1998, pp. 63-73.

[9] Fresa 1973, pp. 7-15.

[10] In Parrish 1984, pp. 116-120, pl. 19.

[11] On the mosaic of Otranto cf. Willemsen 1980.

1. Page 92, outer wall of apse of the church of Areopolis (Greece); on the left side can be seen Libra and Scorpio, on the right panel, Sagittarius.

For 'twas the wish of many gods that not alone in heaven's light should the golden coronet from Ariadne's temples stay fixed, but that we also should gleam, the spoils devote from thy golden-yellow head; when humid with weeping I entered the temples of the gods, the Goddess placed me, a new star, amongst the ancient ones. For a-touching the Virgin's and the fierce Lion's gleams, hard by Callisto of Lycaon, I turn westwards fore-guiding the slow-moving Bootes who sinks unwillingly and late into the vast ocean.
(Catullus, *Carmina*, 66)

THE ANCIENT WORLD

3| THE GEOMETRY OF THE COSMOS

STAR MYTHS IN VESUVIAN PAINTING

Ernesto De Carolis

The astronomers of antiquity created the constellations, by joining groups of neighbouring stars with lines and identifying them with mythological personages. These figures, although pure inventions of the human imagination, had the great advantage of being easily identifiable by anyone observing the nocturnal sky to find references for orientation on land or sea.

Although the Romans' role in the history of astronomy was much more limited than that of the Greeks, they were not indifferent to these subjects, as shown by numerous references found in literary works, as well as some didactic poems[1].

An authoritative treatise was written by G. Julius Hyginus[2], a native of Spain and slave of Caesar, later freed by Augustus, who held the position in Rome of superintendent of the Palatine Library, succeeding Pompeus Macer. We do not know the original title of his work, which is generally called *De Astronomia*, since different versions appear in the manuscript traditions. It is not even certain that the work was divided into four books, a scheme that may have been imposed by the transcribers. Hyginus, presumably writing in the last decades of the first century B.C. and the early years of the first century A.D., draws on both the *Phaenomena* of Aratus and the *Catasterismi* of Eratosthenes. He divides the celestial vault into 41 constellations and mentions the five planets known in his day as well as the Milky Way.

The second book in particular, the longest, dedicated to star myths, narrates the ascent into heaven and transformation into stars of persons, animals and things. In addition to its astronomical interest, the literary aspect of this work is highly interesting, since in recounting the star myths he refers not only to the well-known stories, closely linked to the contemporary *Metamorphoses* of Ovid[3], but also to less familiar versions, furnishing a broad panorama of mythological themes in the ancient world.

The exact description of the constellations, with the individual stars linked to particular parts of the body, and the presence of illustrations in the manuscript transcriptions[4] suggest that Hyginus's original text must have been accompanied by images, derived from the Greek texts on which he drew, datable within a span of time ranging from the fourth to the second century B.C.[5]

Starting from this assumption and from the broad dissemination of his text in the early Imperial Age[6], as well as the recognisable link with Ovid and the erudite circles of the Augustan Age, we have examined Vesuvian pictorial iconography with the aim of revealing possible connections with the representations of the constellations found in the manuscripts we have been able to examine.

The cities of the Vesuvian area constitute some of the Roman world's most important archaeological sites, due to the exceptional state of conservation of the urban fabric in all its components, subsequent to the eruption of Vesuvius that began on August 24th of the year 79 A.D. Of special importance is the group of frescoes that make up the most ample and chronologically homogeneous *corpus* that has survived to our own day, datable between the second century B.C. and 79 A.D.

For this reason – and for the hypothesis we have advanced, that Hyginus' text was compiled between the last decades of the first century B.C. and the early years of the first century A.D., and thus contemporaneous with the Third Style in painting (25/20 B.C.-40/50 A.D.) – it seems useful to survey the paintings still conserved or precisely described in reports of archaeological excavations. We will first examine the constellations associated with the paintings, which represent several personages from the same episodes.

The most obvious connection is with the four neighbouring constellations named for the mythological personages Andromeda, Perseus, Cepheus, and Cassiopeia, to which may be added the constellation of Cetus, identified as the sea monster sent by Poseidon to devour Andromeda.

Hyginus, in describing these groups of stars[7], states that Andromeda is bound with open arms, while Perseus, her saviour and future husband, is flying to kill the sea monster, gripping in his right hand the *harpè* and in his left the Gorgon's head. Cepheus, Andromeda's father, is standing with arms outstretched, and Cassiopeia, her mother, is seated on a throne.

This famous mythological episode appears frequently in Vesuvian wall paintings, represented according to three different iconographic schemes[8].

In the most commonly found composition, Perseus and Andromeda are seated romantically embraced in a pyramidal scheme, with the hero's raised arm, holding up Medusa's head as a trophy[9], at the vertex. This iconography was used by the painting workshops of the Vesuvian area exclusively in wall decorations of the Fourth Style, datable between the middle of the first century A.D. and 79 A.D., since the clients of this period preferred a 'light', narrative reading of the episode, portraying the conclusion of the story.

The second scheme, found in both the Fourth Style and the last stage of the Third, represents an intermediate moment, immersed in a quiet atmosphere far removed from the preceding dramatic events, with Perseus helping Andromeda to descend from the rock to which she was bound, taking her politely by the hand[10].

Lastly, the third scheme vibrates with tension and action, representing not the stage subsequent to the freeing of Andromeda but the central episode of the myth, with Andromeda bound with open arms to the rock at the centre or on the right of the composition, and Perseus in flight, on the left, armed with the *harpè* and the Medusa's head, which he flings at the sea monster below, while in a secondary position Cepheus and Cassiopeia fearfully observe the terrible scene. This version is found in four paintings from the central stage of the Third Style[11], classifiable as Mythological Landscape compositions, and, in a much simpler version, two more from the Fourth Style[12].

Only the third scheme, then, shows a link with Hyginus' description of the relevant constellations, especially as regards the figures of Andromeda[13], bound with open arms, Perseus, armed in flight, and the seated Cassiopeia watching the dramatic unfolding of the events. The similarity is quite close in the four Third Style paintings, especially the compositions found in the House of the Priest Amandus at Pompeii and the so-called Villa of Agrippa Postumus at Boscotrecase (fig. 3). It is important to note, moreover, that this group of paintings dates from the Augustan Age, the late first century B.C. – early first century A.D., coinciding with the central stage of the Third Style.

Another two constellations to be considered are the neighbouring ones of the Kneeling Man and Draco, identified as Heracles and the serpent Ladon set to guard the apples in the Garden of the Hesperides[14]. The constellation, as described in the text, represents Heracles kneeling with the lion's skin in his left hand and the club in his right, while he tries to crush with his left foot the head of the serpent, positioned below the hero. This famous myth[15] is documented in the Vesuvian area by two Third Style paintings[16], which depict the epilogue to the event in a static composition, with Heracles standing and the three Hesperides grouped around the plough over which the serpent's body coils. According to this interpretation, the most common among the surviving representations, the golden apples are not won by violence, but thanks to the aid of the Hesperides who cause the serpent to fall asleep[17]. Accordingly, we find no iconographic connection between the picture illustrating the text and the known paintings from the Vesuvian area, but only a generic reference to the central episode of the myth.

It is interesting to note, however, that the iconography proposed by Hyginus is instead more closely linked to the portrayal of Heracles struggling with the Lernean Hydra, the monstrous serpent with many heads[18]. In Attic black and red figure vase paintings, Heracles is in fact frequently depicted in the act of striking the Hydra with his leg[19]. Even more pertinent are a gemstone from the mid-fourth century B.C. and a 'Campana' relief from the first century B.C., with the hero portrayed in the kneeling position[20]. Particularly significant examples of this scheme in Roman times are found in the decoration of a silver *scyphus* found in the House of Menander at Pompeii, dating from the first century B.C.[21], and in a painting on marble found at Herculaneum in the House of the Jewel dating from the time of Nero but derived from iconography of the sixth century B.C.[22]

For these two constellations then – in addition to the customary choice of the heroic moment, as has been seen for the myth of Perseus and Andromeda – we may note that the text, although clearly referring to the episode of Heracles in the Garden of the Hesperides, describes the two constellations according to an iconography pertinent instead to the hero's victory over the Lernean Hydra.

The last example concerns the constellations of Aquila and Acquarius, which represent Jupiter and Ganymede[23]. But in this case too the link is very faint, consisting only of the presence of the myth in Fourth Style wall paintings, since the rare compositions that have survived[24] differ notably from Hyginus' description of the two constellations. The eagle, in fact, is always portrayed with wings closed and not open, while Ganymede is shown reclining or seated and not in the act of pouring liquid from a vessel. The connection here is based only on the familiarity of the episode, one highly suitable for use in the

1. Page 96, Pompeii, House of the Gold Bracelet, VI, 17, Ins. Occ., 42, triclinium c, Fourth Style; moulding panel with representation of Capricorn.

2. Pompeii, House VI, 17, Ins. Occ., 41, tablinum 6, Second Style; large-figure painting on the middle register on the wall with representation of a ship's bow.

3. On the following page, Boscotrecase, Villa of Agrippa Postumus, cubicle 19, west wall, Third Style; panel in middle section of wall representing 'Perseus and Andromeda'.

painters' workshops, since the clients preferred themes of love, and the passions of gods and heroes in particular.

Continuing our *excursus* through the individual constellations, we have found another series of comparisons with repetitive decorative motifs and paintings of mythological subject.

Delphinus[25] and the Corona[26] are in fact commonly represented in secondary decorations of the Fourth Style, while Lyra[27], found more rarely, is present also in the Third[28]. Very frequent in the Fourth Style is the scheme of a centaur galloping or fighting a wild beast, in the act of shooting an arrow, which is the way Hyginus represents the constellation of Sagittarius[29].

The constellation of Capricornus[30], instead, with the body shaped like a he-goat in front and like a fish with a sinuous finned tail in back, seems to have been popular as a secondary decorative motif in the Fourth Style (fig. 1), if we can identify it in some of the representations inserted in the class of the so-called sea monsters[31].

The Horse, identified with Pegasus[32], and the lion, Leo[33], are not only very frequently found in Fourth Style architectural partitions, but are also the subjects of some rare paintings linked to the myths of Bellerophon[34] and Heracles[35] respectively.

Cygnus the swan and Taurus the bull evoke Jupiter, who placed them in the firmament because it was in the form of these animals that he had seduced Leda[36] and Europa[37]. In the pictorial iconography Leda[38] is standing and embracing the swan. Europa[39] is portrayed on the bull's back, being carried off to Crete through the waves of the sea. For these two constellations we can only note that the iconography of Cygnus, the swan, depicted with curved neck and open wings, is similar to the image found in the text, while for Taurus the resemblance is highly generic, since the constellation is formed only of the forepart of the animal's body. Cygnus, moreover, like the other constellations, is commonly found, with the same iconographic scheme, in Fourth Style secondary decorations.

The constellation of Aries is identified with the Ram of the Golden Fleece, who flew through the air carrying on his back Phryxus and Helle, the children of Athamas, to escape the sacrificial altar to which they had been condemned by a false oracle[40]. During the flight Helle fell from the ram's back into the sea at a place known ever since as the Hellespont. Her brother instead reached Colchis where the ram, according to the tradition of Eratosthenes reiterated by Hyginus, took off his fleece, left it to Phryxus in memory of their exploit and then flew off into the sky. In this case too the pictorial compositions[41] represent the central moment of the episode, with Phryxus flying on the ram's back and Helle, fallen into the sea, stretching her arms out to her brother, while in the constellation only the ram appears.

Centaurus, according to the most accredited version of Hyginus, is identified with the centaur Chiron[42], who raised Achilles and was placed in the sky at his death in honour of his wisdom and justice. As in the preceding myth, the constellation of Centaurus represents only this personage, while the paintings[43] include Achilles as well.

The two last constellations for which reference has been found in the pictorial decoration are those of Gemini[44], identifiable with the Dioscuri, and of the ship called Argo[45].

For Gemini we have only one reference to two Fourth Style paintings found in the House of the Dioscuri[46] (VI, 9, 6), where however they appear with their horses and not embraced, as in the constellation. For the ship Argo instead, the connection between the pictorial compositions[47] and the image of the constellation is much closer, since only the bow of the ship up to the mast is depicted in all cases (fig. 2).

As conclusion to this *excursus* the first consideration to be made concerns the constellation myths used as pictorial subjects in the Vesuvian area, 22 as compared to the 41 of Hyginus's text. As regards common themes, only rarely have we found close resemblance between the images of the constellations appearing in the manuscripts examined and the surviving paintings. The closest links are found in the myths of Perseus and Andromeda and of the ship Argo. Interestingly, the iconography of the personages in the former myth is found especially in Third Style Mythological Landscape compositions, dating from the Augustan Age, while it tends to disappear in the following stage. The rare portrayals of the ship Argo are instead typical of the Second Style.

Based on these findings, we may hypothesise a closer link to the representations of the first century B.C.-early first century A.D., nearer in time to the compiling of the text.

In other pictorial compositions we have found only a generic connection with the constellation myth, since the iconographic scheme is different or more complex, with the inclusion of several personages. In other cases instead, especially for Delphinus, Corona, Lyra, Capricornus and Cygnus, we find a close link not with paintings, but with secondary background motifs commonly used in pictorial decorations.

In conclusion, the research conducted has confirmed the initial hypothesis of a wide-ranging connection between the iconographic schemes of the paintings and the constellation myths illustrated in Hyginus' text and those of his contemporaries dealing with the same subject[48]. In any case, the *pictores* must have been familiar with these texts, considering the many similarities found, and it may be that some mythological episodes were chosen over others due to their great familiarity[49]. Continuing along this train of thought, it may be that the development of compositions based on mythological figures in painting, which took place with the Third Style starting from 25 B.C., was influenced by the dissemination of texts on the constellation myths. This is of course a working hypothesis, which would merit further investigation, as would the possible connection between the representations of the constellations found in Vesuvian paintings and the function assigned to the relevant rooms by the owner of the house.

–

Bibliography

Napoli 2006; Bragantini 1995, pp. 175-197; *Collezioni Mann* 1986; Coralini 2001; Dawson 1965; De Carolis-Esposito-Ferrara 2007, pp. 117-141; Ghedini 1997, in part. pp. 825-828; La Rocca 2008; Le Boeuffle 1977; Igino 1983; LIMC 1981-; Maiuri 1932; Maiuri 1958; Pagano-Prisciandaro 2006; Picta Fragmenta 1997; Pompei 1990-2003; Ward Perkins-Claridge 1978; Nava-Paris-Friggeri 2007; Sauron 2007; Bonifacio-Sodo 2001.

1 Cicero composed, around 80 B.C., the *Aratea*, a translation of Aratus' *Phaenomena* of which ample fragments remain. Another version of the same work, also in hexameters, was written by Julius Caesar Germanicus, the son of Drusus Major and Antonia Minor, who died at Antioch in 19 A.D.

2 The following translation has been used: Hyginus 1983.

3 Ovid (43 B.C.-17 A.D.) began to compose the *Metamorphoses* in 3 A.D.

4 Hyginus' text gave rise to various codices, often illustrated, compiled since the 9th century, outstanding among them the manuscript Voss. Lat. Q79, dating from the 13th century, now at the Leiden University Library.

5 On the mythological images and traditions present in ancient literature in relation to the heritage of classical iconography see Ghedini 1997 (with ample bibliography), pp. 825-828.

6 The spread of texts on star myths and their influence of the society of the times is also demonstrated by information on the pictorial representation of the constellations on the ceiling of the rotating dome in one of the rooms of Nero's Domus Aurea: 'The main banqueting hall was circular and rotated continuously to show the day and the night' (Suetonius, *Nero*, 31). A similar composition was found in the palace of Domitian, as recalls Martial (*Epigrammata*, VII, 56): 'You had in your pious heart the image of the stars and the sky, O Rabirius, as you built with your marvellous art the Arcadian palace'. In private homes as well there were compositions evoking the sky and the constellations, as shown by the fresco found at Stabia in a section of the ceiling of the portico at Villa San Marco depicting an armillary sphere (cf. entry III.4.2). Starry skies in the form of rosettes or stars with many rays were often painted on the ceilings of public buildings, as in the *frigidarium* of the Stabian Baths

in Pompeii (Pompeii 1995, p. 418, n. 245) and in the vestibule of the Palestra at Herculaneum (Maiuri 1958, p. 120, no. 67).

[7] Le Boeuffle 1977, pp. 200-201; Hyginus 1983, pp. 37-38, 73, 91-95, 107-108.

[8] Another two iconographic schemes in Fourth Style, imbued with an atmosphere of abandonment, consist of a panel (House I, 3, 25, cub. i) representing Perseus comforting Andromeda, with the sea monster lying at their feet (Pompeii 1990, I, p. 102, no. 18), and another composition (House of Menander, area 15), with Andromeda bound and the hero standing (Pompeii 1990, II, p. 322, no. 129). Not included in the compositions presented here is a panel coming from an unidentified house in Pompeii (Naples, Museo Archeologico, inv. 9477), since we have no other examples depicting Perseus, without the *harpè* and the Medusa's head, struggling against the sea monster. It has thus been deemed appropriate to identify the episode as the freeing of Hesione by Heracles (Dawson 1965, p. 107, no. 54, pl. XX; Bragantini 1995, p. 188, fig. 5; Pagano 2006, I, p. 45, 3 December 1763).

[9] House of the Ephebus, tabl. 4; House of Menander, *oecus* 11; House of the Dancers, tricl. 12; House of Meleager, perist. 16; House of the Prince of Naples, tricl. k; House of the Iron Furnace, room 9; House of the Coloured Capitals, *oecus* 17 (Pompeii 1990, I, p. 635, no. 26; 1990, II, p. 314, no. 114; 1993, IV, pp. 254, 720, nos. 47, 118; 1994, V, p. 663, n. 25; 1996, VI, pp. 994, 1020, nos. 2, 30).

[10] Third Style: House of Pompeius Axiochus, tricl. h; House IX, 9, d, tricl. l (Pompeii 1994, V, p. 221, no. 35; X, p. 86, no. 32). Fourth Style: Caupona *Sotericus*, tabl. 5; House of the Dioscuri, perist. 53; House of the Five Skeletons, cub. 12; Main Excavation of Montenegro, *oecus* 6; House of the Postumii, ala 9 (Pompeii 1990, II, p. 725, no. 32; 1993, IV, pp. 975, 1042, nos. 224, 21; 1997, VII, p. 841, no. 2; 1998, VIII, p. 475, n. 40). Herculaneum: Palestra, *Ins. Or.* II (Rosso Pompeiano 2008, p. 109).

[11] House of the Priest Amandus, tricl. b; House of the Sailor, exedra z; House IX, 7, 16, cub. a (Pompeii 1990, I, p. 602, no. 20; 1997, VII, p. 761, n. 108; 1999, IX, p. 786, n. 7). A fourth composition comes from the Villa of Agrippa Postumus at Boscotrecase (Dawson 1965, p. 100, no. 41; Pompeii AD 79 1978, pp. 164-165, no. 128).

[12] House of the Black Wall, *oecus* m; House of the Centenary, perist. 9, with Perseus in flight on the right (Pompeii 1997, VII, p. 113, no. 32b; 1999, IX, p. 971, no. 128).

[13] In the text Andromeda is described as tied by the arms to two trees, in keeping with the representations on Greek ceramography of the 5th century B.C. and the vase production of Southern Italy. In the latter she also appears chained to the rock, in a scheme similar to that of the pictorial compositions (LIMC 1981, I, 1-2, pp. 774 -781, 623-633).

[14] Le Boeuffle 1977, pp. 191, 193; Hyginus 1983, pp. 22, 31-33, 88-90.

[15] Coralini 2001, pp. 70-72, 150-151, 180-181, 239.

[16] House of the Priest Amandus, tricl. b; House V, 2, 10, cub. q (Pompeii 1990, I, p. 593, no. 7; 1991, III, p. 844, no. 24). The identification of a third panel in Fourth Style, found in the calidarium of Villa A at Oplontis, with this myth is uncertain instead due to the lack of details in the scene (Coralini 2001, p. 71).

[17] In Roman times there was also a heroic version of the myth with Heracles alone, depicted standing or in the act of striking the serpent coiled around the tree (*LIMC* V, 1, pp. 106-108).

[18] *LIMC* V, 1, pp. 34-43, 2, 52-60.

[19] *LIMC* V, 2, in part. nos. 2003, 2009, pp. 54-55.

[20] *LIMC* V, 2, nos. 2045, 2076, pp. 58, 60.

[21] Maiuri 1932, p. 314, no. 6; Argenti 2006, pp. 198-199, nos. 280-281.

[22] Coralini 2001, pp. 69, 239, E. 010.

[23] Le Boeuffle 1977, pp. 195-196, 218-219; Hyginus 1983, pp. 51-52, 72, 98, 106.

[24] House of Meleager, cub. 12; House of the Coloured Capitals, *oecus* 17; House of Ganymede, room g; House of the Fountain of Love, cub. i; House IX, 5, 11.13, room f (Pompeii 1993, IV, p. 688, no. 60; 1996, VI, p. 1016, no. 27; 1997, VII, p. 624, no. 15; 1998, VIII, p. 1077, no. 20; 1999, IX, p. 553, no. 49). Stabia, Villa Arianna, room 3 (Stabia 2001, pp. 133-134).

[25] Le Boeuffle 1977, pp. 196-197; Hyginus 1983, pp. 52-54, 98.

[26] Le Boeuffle 1977, pp. 191-192; Hyginus 1983, pp. 28-31, 89.

[27] Le Boeuffle 1977, pp. 193-194; Hyginus 1983, pp. 33-36, 90-91.

[28] Hyginus, in listing the various mythological traditions of these two constellations, identifies Delphinus as the person sent by Poseidon to search for Amphitrite, the Corona as the precious gift of Aphrodite or Dionysus to Adriadne and the Lyre as the instrument fabricated by Mercury and then given to Orpheus.

[29] Le Boeuffle 1977, p. 217; Hyginus 1983, pp. 70-71, 104-105. In the text Hyginus identifies it with the centaur Crotus, who lived on Mount Helicon with the Muses. To reward him for his skill at hunting and in the arts of the Muses, Jupiter had him ascend to the skies, transforming him into a constellation.

[30] Le Boeuffle 1977, pp. 217-218; Hyginus 1983, pp. 71-72, 105. Capricorn is identified with Pan and its particular form as a constellation is linked to an episode in the struggle between the Titans and the Gods: to flee at the sudden arrival of Typhon, during a meeting, the gods transform themselves into animals; Pan throws himself into a river, the lower part of his body assuming the aspect of a fish.

[31] A clear representation of Capricorn, with the head of a goat and lower part of the body in the form of a fish, is found in the central scene on the moulding of triclinium c in the House of the Golden Bracelet at Pompeii (Pompeii 1996, VI, p. 52, no. 17). It is thus clear that, to determine the frequency of these representations in wall painting, the whole decorative class of serpents and sea monsters should be re-examined.

[32] Le Boeuffle 1977, p. 197; Hyginus 1983, pp. 55-56, 99. The horse Pegasus is

linked to the myth of Bellerophon who, after having slain the monstrous Chimera, in the attempt to fly ever higher in the sky, turns his gaze toward Earth but, terrified at the height, falls and dies, while his horse flies on and is placed in the heavens by Jupiter.

[33] Le Boeuffle 1977, p. 212; Hyginus 1983, pp. 67-68, 103. Jupiter placed him among the stars because he was considered the king of the animals; according to another version of the myth, he is identified with the Nemaean lion slain by Heracles as his first labour.

[34] Third Style: House IX, 7, 16, triclinium b (Pompeii 1999, IX, p. 795, no. 21). Fourth Style: Thermopolion I, 8, 8, triclinium (Picta Fragmenta 1997, pp. 119-120, no. 69).

[35] Fourth Style: Heracles and the Nemaean Lion, Herculaneum, Basilica (Collezioni *MANN* 1986, p. 148, no. 184).

[36] Le Boeuffle 1977, p. 194; Hyginus 1983, pp. 36-37, 91. In addition to this well-known version of the myth, the text also reports the story of Jupiter seducing Nemesis, thus generating an egg that was then transferred to Leda' womb by Mercury.

[37] Le Boeuffle 1977, p. 207; Hyginus 1983, pp. 61-64, 100-101. The text also cites a second version of the myth, identifying the constellation as the heifer into which Io, beloved by Jupiter, is transformed to escape the jealousy of his wife Hera.

[38] Fourth Style: House of Venus in the Shell, cub. 14; House of Meleager, cub. 14; House of the Iron Furnace, cub. 4; House of the Gilded Cupids, cub. r; House of the Coloured Capitals, exedra 31; House of the Ancient Hunt, room 4; House of the Sailor, wing h; House of Joseph II; House of the Fountain of Love, tricl. k (Pompeii 1991, III, p. 166, no. 82; 1993, IV, p. 697, no. 73; 1994, V, pp. 165, 839, no. 10, 224; 1996, VI, p. 1085, no. 130; 1997, VII, pp. 14, 725, ns. 9, 42; 1998, VIII, pp. 353, 1086, ns. 87, 32). The representation of Leda with the swan also appears in the form of a vignette: House of Queen Margherita, room o; House of the Glass Vases, tricl. 12; House of the Vettii, room e (Pompeii 1994, III, p. 776, no. 5; 1993, IV, p. 335, no. 16; 1994, V, p. 491, no. 33); Stabia, Villa Arianna (Stabia 2001, p. 90).

[39] Third Style: House of Jason, cub. g (Pompeii 1999, IX, p. 707, no. 46). Fourth Style: Thermopolio I, 8, 8, tricl. 10; House of Menander, tabl. 8; House of Loreius Tiburtinus, cub. a; House V, 4, 3, tricl. d; House of the Gladiators, pluteo; House delle Dancers, tricl. 12; House of the Tragic Poet, cub. 6a; House of the Dioscuri, atrium 37; House of the Labyrinth, cub. 6; House VI, 16, 28, room i; House of the Clay Models, room 5; House of the Fisher Woman; House of the Postumii, room 32; House IX, 5, 14-16, cub. g (Pompeii 1990, I, p. 821, no. 31; 1990, II, p. 291, no. 78; 1991, III, pp. 44, 1051, 1071, ns. 45, 7, 3; 1993, IV, pp. 255, 596, 884, ns. 48, 129, 52; 1994, V, pp. 13, 942, ns. 19, 22; 1997, VII, pp. 151, 382, ns. 16, 4; 1998, VIII, p. 509, no. 104; 1999, IX, p. 641, no. 68). Herculaneum: Sannite House, cub. 1 (Maiuri 1958, p. 204, fig. 160). Stabia, Villa San Marco, nymphaeum, glass paste panel, diet. 50 (Stabia 2001, pp. 62, 73).

[40] Le Boeuffle 1977, pp. 205-207; Hyginus 1983, pp. 57-60, 100.

[41] Fourth Style: House of Sallustius, *viridarium* 32; House of Modestus, tabl. 7; House of the Tragic Poet, cub. 6a; House dei *Postumii*, tricl. 14; House of the Red Walls, room b; House of M. Lucretius, cub. 7; House IX, 5, 6.17, wing d (Pompeii 1993, IV, pp. 132, 344, 596, ns. 75, 3, 131; 1998, VIII, pp. 485, 636, ns. 55, 33; 1999, IX, pp. 222, 415, ns. 121, 23). Another panel comes from the *Ins. Occ.* (Rosso Pompeiano 2007, p. 137). The same composition appears in a wall panel from the nymphaeum of the Villa San Marco at Stabia (Stabia 2001, p. 62). The vignette with Frixus on the ram inserted in a Fourth Style decoration in the House of the Golden Wedding, room Q, seems instead to be a *unicum* (Pompeii 1991, III, p. 708, no. 66).

[42] Le Boeuffle 1977, pp. 204-205; Hyginus 1983, pp. 79-80, 111. Heracles, while visiting Chiron, accidentally drops an arrow that wounds him on the foot, causing his death, since it was dipped in the poisonous blood of the Lernean Hydra.

[43] Fourth Style: House of Adonis, *viridarium* 14; House of M. Lucretius, cub. 4; House IX, 5, 6, cub. g (Pompeii 1993, IV, p. 430, n. 42). Another composition comes from the Basilica of Herculaneum (Collezioni *MANN* 1986, p. 148, no. 177).

[44] Le Boeuffle 1977, pp. 208-209; Hyginus 1983, pp. 64-65, 101-102. The Dioscuri ascended to the sky for their bond of great affection, without rivalry. Castor dies, during the siege of Sparta; his brother Pollux, the only immortal one, saves him by giving him half of his own life. For this reason, they shine in the sky on alternate days.

[45] Le Boeuffle 1977, pp. 203-204; Hyginus 1983, pp. 78-79, 110. In the text it is identified with the first ship to sail the seas, named for Argo, its inventor. According to another version, it is instead the ship built by the Argonauts to sail to Colchis in search of the Golden Fleece.

[46] Pompeii 1993, IV, p. 14, nos. 14-15.

[47] Second Style: House VI, 17, *Ins. Occ.*, 41, tabl. 6. The bow of a ship, with the figure of Triton, is represented in the House of the Labyrinth, cub. 42 (Pompeii 1996, VI, p. 17, no. 21; 1994, V, p. 39, no. 64). Fourth Style: VI, *Ins. Occ.*, 10 (Collezioni *MANN* 1986, p. 128, no. 34).

[48] A connection between the paintings and the constellations has recently been proposed in the allegorical explanation of parts of some Second Style paintings in some of the rooms of Villa A at Oplontis (Sauron 2007, in particular pp. 61-65, 113-120).

[49] On the organisation of the painters' workshops in the Vesuvian area see lastly: De Carolis-Esposito-Ferrara 2007, pp. 117-141.

I.1.1
Tablet with literary text 'Enuma elish'
7th century B.C.
Clay; 9.8 x 7.3 cm
London, British Museum, inv. K3567

It is one of the seven tablets, each of about 150 verses, that composed the text of the hymn in honour of the god Marduk and celebrated his rise to head of the Babylonian pantheon. It is a great literary composition known to the ancients as *Enuma elish* ('When on high'), from the initial line. The long text, (about 1100 verses), begins with the narration of how, in the beginning, the skies did not exist, because they had no name, just as the Earth; in a great primordial silence, a male element of fresh water mixed with a female element of salt water. From these, and for many following generations, pairs of gods are born, up to Marduk, generated by the great god Ea and by his companion-wife Damkina. When the goddess Tiamat decides to destroy the young gods, their father Ea asks Marduk to defend them; in exchange, he will be recognized as head of the gods and will have enormous power. Thanks to the help given by the father, who also performs magic, Marduk faces and defeats Tiamat in an epic duel. After having killed her, he cuts her body in two: with the upper part he creates the sky and with the lower part, the Earth. He establishes the dwelling of the great gods in the sky, he creates the constellations and the stars, he defines the year of twelve months, he fixes the position of the Polar star, he makes the Moon and the Sun appear and he establishes their movements (that will be object of astronomic predictions), he creates the winds, the rains, the fogs and all the atmospheric elements. On Earth he creates the rivers, the mountains and establishes the place of the city of Babylon; finally, he gives life to Man. It is an exceptional text that contains a cosmogony, a theogony and an anthropogony and presents, in poetic form, the knowledge of the sky, of the stars, of the zodiac, of the calendar present throughout Mesopotamic culture of the second half of the second millennium B.C. The composition of the text probably dates back to the twelfth century B.C. when, with the second dynasty of Isin and its sovereign Nebuchadnezzar I, the city of Babylon and its god Marduk become prevalent throughout central Mesopotamia. Nevertheless, astronomical knowledge and ideas of the third millennium and, in particular, of the Babylon of King Hammurabi (18th century B.C.), the most important city of Mesopotamia, all converge in the text as well. (M.G.B.)

Bibliography: Bottéro-Kramer 1992, pp. 640–722.

I.1.2
The star of Aratus
Babylonia, c. 500 B.C.
Clay; 3.2 x 2.3 cm
London, British Museum, inv. BM 86378

First tablet of the astronomical compilation Mul.Apin. It contains six lists of stars and constellations. The first ist arranged approximately by the place in the sky where the stars are, beginning from the north. The second list contains the dates when certain constellations rise heliacally, in an idealized calendar. The third list gives constellations which rise and set simultaneously. A fourth list is based on the second, giving the time differences between the heliacal risings. The fifth list combines stars that culminate with those that rise at the same time. Finally, there is a list of 17 constellations in what is called the path of the moon, i.e. the ecliptic. Parts of the text were probably composed in the 13th century B.C.
(H.H.)

Bibliography: King L.W. 1912a, pl. 1-8; Hunger-Pingree 1989.

I.1.3
Celestial omens
Assyria, c. 7th century B.C.
Clay; 17.1 x 9.2 cm
London, British Museum, inv. K160

The text mainly consists of *omina* according to the following pattern: 'In month *MN*, the nth day, Venus disappeared in the west, stayed away n days in the sky, and in month *MN*, the nth day, Venus became visible in the east.' After this there follows a non-astronomical prediction of the type: 'there will be rains and much water in the springs, kings will send reconciliatory messages to each other.' The text continues: 'In month *MN*, the nth day, Venus disappeared in the east, stayed away n days in the sky, and in month *MN*, the nth day, Venus became visible in the west.' This is again followed by a prediction. In this way, last and first visibilities alternate with each other. The dates, months and days, are not random, but agree pretty well with dates expected from the natural sequence of the Venus phenomena. It is therefore very likely that the dates are based on observations, to which predictions were added. Apart from two easy-to-correct errors, the calendar dates are what one expects from celestial mechanics. The last date is not followed by an omen, but by a year-name referring to a 'golden throne'. The year was identified with the 8th year of Ammiṣaduqa. This set of dates, after correction, can be considered to reflect observations from the first 8 years of Ammiṣaduqa's reign. Scholars tried to use them to find the date of Ammiṣaduqa. Unfortunately, the dates do not suffice to uniquely identify these years in our calendar because the dates of the Venus phenomena in the Babylonian calendar are repeated after 64 or 56 years. As research went on, three possible datings of Ammiṣaduqa emerged, labelled as 'high','middle' and 'low' chronologies. Depending on what other evidence scholars adduced, they arrived at different choices among these three. Applying the three chronologies to the well-known king Hammu-rapi of Babylon, his reign is dated as follows: 'High chronology': 1848-1806 'Middle chronology': 1792-1750 'Low chronology': 1728-1686 Which chronology of the three (if any) is correct is not clear yet.
(H.H.)

Bibliography: Reiner-Pingree 1975.

I.1.4
Kudurru of Meli-Shipak
1186-1172 B.C.
Limestone; 51 x 24 cm
London, British Museum, inv. BM90829

Documents of this type, found in Mesopotamia from as early as the 4th millennium B.C., usually recorded the grant of lands. The Babylonian *kudurru* on display here – probably preserved, like many others, in a temple – also mentions the donation to a certain Khasardu of a large landed property in the district of the Mesopotamian city of Shaluluni by the Kassite king Meli-Shipak (1186-1172 B.C.). What we have, therefore, is a sacralized legal and administrative act which, as stated in the inscription at the bottom, lists the four functionaries who arranged the transfer of the property, the seven high officials summoned in to guarantee the transaction and all the thirteen deities called upon to protect it (Anu, Enlil, Ea, Šamaš, Marduk, Nabu, Anunitum, Ninib, Ninkarrag (Gula), Adad, Nergal, Shukamuna, Shumalia). Carved in the conical upper part are eighteen celestial signs and beings, particularly striking among which, along with the solar disk and crescent moon, are the eight-pointed star and lightning flash, a winged centaur with bow and arrows and a being half human and half animal. These stand for figures, signs, events and rites which are difficult to interpret, but their presence here, certainly inspired by the tradition of cosmogonical literature, and maybe also by the inductive observation of the celestial bodies, clearly reveals an intention to make of these documents some sort of living symbol, a summary of a cosmic order both wonderful and inviolable. (M.R.)

Bibliography: King L.W. 1912b; Seidl 1989; Gelb-Steinkeller-Whiting 1991; Slanski 2000.

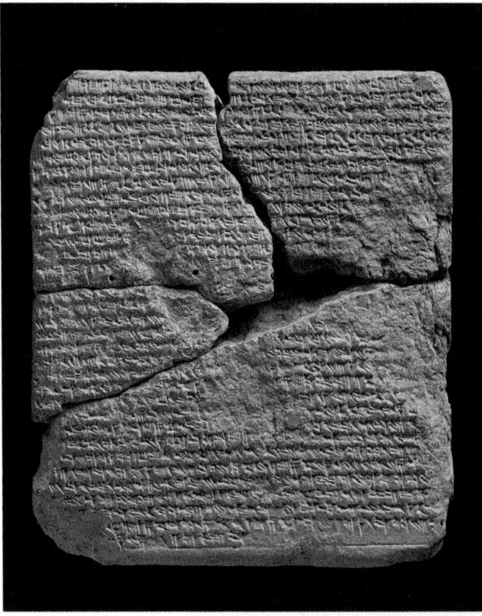

I.1.5
Astronomical diary
Babylon, middle of 4th century B.C.
Clay; 18.5 x 16.5 cm
London, British Museum, inv. BM 46229

Astronomical Diary for year 12 of king Artaxerxes III (= 347/6 B.C.). Such diaries contain:
1. At the beginning of each monthly section, there is a statement about the length of the preceding month, whether it had 29 or 30 days. Then the time interval between sunset and moonset on the first evening of the month, when the lunar crescent became visible for the first time. Around full moon, the time intervals between rising and setting of moon and sun before and after opposition. Toward the end of the month, the date of the morning of the last visible crescent is recorded, together with the time interval from moonrise to sunrise. Lunar and solar eclipses, not only those visible in Babylon but also invisible ones. Duration and magnitude of the eclipse are noted, the planets that were visible during the eclipse, weather conditions etc.
2. For Mars, Jupiter, and Saturn, the Diaries give the dates of first and last visibility, of the stationary points and of opposition; for first and last visibility, the zodiacal sign is also recorded. For Venus and Mercury, we find the dates and zodiacal signs of first and last visibility as a morning star and as an evening star.
3. The dates of the equinoxes and solstices and the appearances of the star Sirius are all given according to a schematical computation; so these are not observations.
4. In addition to these phenomena, the conjunctions of the moon and the planets with certain stars near the ecliptic are recorded. The distance of the moon and the planets from these stars is expressed in the measures 'cubit' and 'finger' which correspond to 2 degrees and 5 minutes of arc, respectively.
5. Apart from astronomical observations, the diaries frequently mention weather conditions, especially clouds which prevented seeing the stars or the moon. But we also find wind, rain, lightning

and thunder, rainbows etc.
6. At the end of each monthly section, the prices of some of the basic commodities, like barley and dates, are given. If the prices changed in the course of the month, this will be described in detail.
7. Most diaries also give the level of the river Euphrates during the course of the month.
8. Finally, for each month so-called historical events or rumours of such events are reported. We find notes about battles, military expeditions, changes of reigns, the overthrow of the Seleucid empire by the Parthians, and much more. Unfortunately, the bad state of preservation of the tablets leaves many details in these historical reports uncertain. Since the diaries can be dated on astronomical grounds, the historical events mentioned can also be dated securely.
(H.H.)

Bibliography: Sachs-Hunger 1988, pp. 142-153.

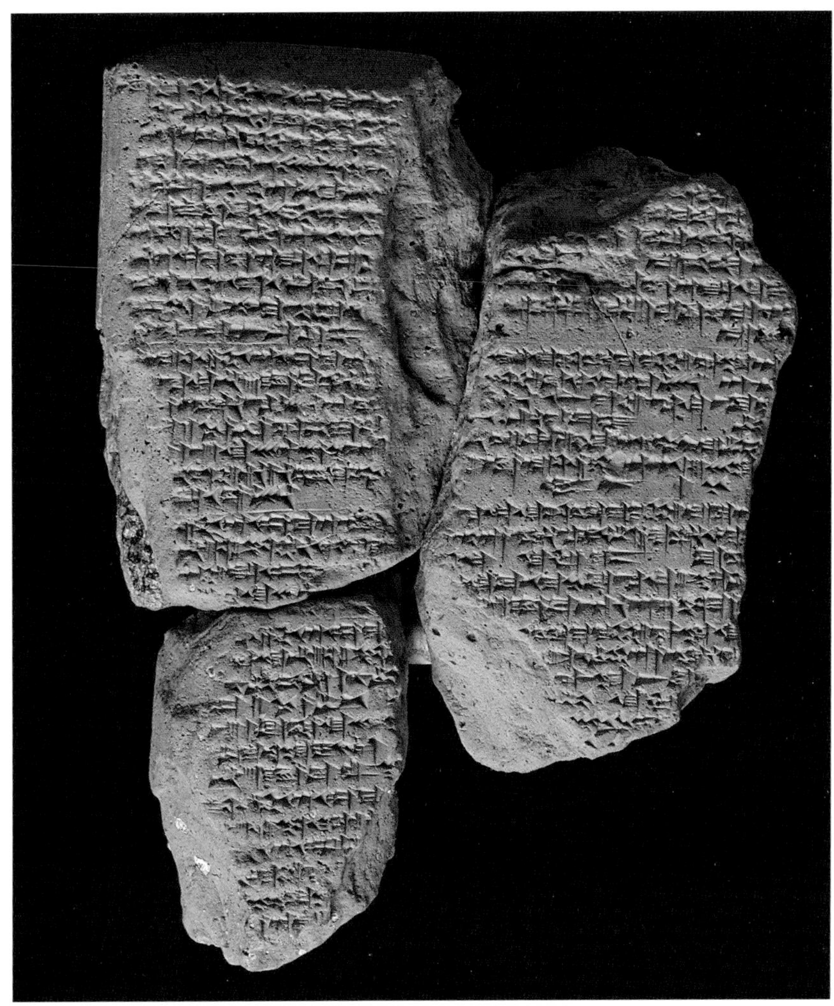

I.1.6
Forecasts of eclipses
Assyria, 7th century B.C.
Clay; 6.9 x 5 cm
London, British Museum, inv. K3561

Omina from lunar eclipses, 20th tablet of the series 'Enuma Anu Enlil'.
Eclipses can occur in all months; the omina are arranged by the months of the calendar. Since the Babylonian calendar has lunar months, lunar eclipses are possible only around the middle of the month, on days 12 to 15. Nevertheless, the text considers eclipses on days 14 to 21. This cannot be based on observation but may be an attempt to cover additional possibilities. Apart from the day number, the omina frequently take notice of the watch in which an eclipse occurs; nighttime is divided into three watches. The duration of an eclipse is expressed by referring to the watches. Setting or rising of the moon during the eclipse is also ominous. The magnitude of an eclipse is described in the text, but not measured.
The movement of the shadow across the lunar disk was the most important element for the decision concerning which country would be affected by the evil announced by the eclipse. The disk was divided into four quadrants; each was associated with a country. The country whose quadrant was obscured first was the one that would suffer the misfortune. Similarly, the direction from which the wind was blowing during an eclipse was used to determine the country which would be affected.
The tablet is from the 7th century B.C., but its contents may be several centuries older.
(H.H.)

Bibliography: Rochberg 1988, pp. 181-216.

I.1.7
Model of sheep's liver
Babylon, c. middle of 1st millennium B.C.
Clay; 8.5 x 7.3 cm
London, British Museum, inv. BM 50494

In a clay model of a sheep's liver, the names of its parts and their significance for the interpretation of omina are written. This is sometimes simply expressed by 'right' and 'left': while in general 'right' was favorable and 'left' was unfavorable, they could signify the opposite in some parts of the liver. With the help of this model, the diviner could find what was predicted by an actual liver of a sacrificed sheep.
(H.H.)

Bibliography: Nougayrol 1968; Koch U.S. 2005, pp. 480-518.

I.1.8 a-c
Tablet of the Sun God with covers
860-850 B.C.
BM91000: grey schist; 29.5 x 17.8 cm
BM91001: clay; 17.5 x 11.8 cm
BM91002: terracotta; 13 x 17 cm
London, British Museum, inv. BM91000, BM91001, BM91002

As stated in the cuneiform text at the top left, this tablet comes from ancient Sippar (today's Tell Abū Habba), seat of the temple of Ebabbar consecrated to the sun god Šamaš. We see King Nabû-apla-iddina (887-855 B.C.) being led into the presence of Šamaš accompanied by a goddess with raised hands according to a very ancient iconological model. The god is shown wearing a tiara adorned with bull's horns, bearing the insignia of power, and seated on a throne the supports of which are in the form of two human-headed bulls. Beneath the canopy are the three celestial bodies also mentioned in the text: the disk of the Moon (symbol of Sîn, the moon god), that of the Sun (symbol of Šamaš) and the morning star (symbol of the goddess Ištar). The Primordial Ocean is suggested by the lower border decorated with an undulating motif interrupted at the base by four stars, perhaps denoting the universe as divided into four parts. From the upper tips of the canopy emerge two genies supporting an idol, a typical representation of the solar disk having at its centre

a four-pointed star and four triple wavy lines radiating from it. The long inscription for the most part relates the exploits of Nabû-apla-iddina, who after finding beside the Euphrates a clay model of the precious statue of Shamash, which had originally been at Ebabbar but was subsequently lost, replaced it with an equally precious copy made of gold and lapis lazuli.

The tablet was discovered in a clay container together with two impressions of the relief. The first of these (BM91001) is the one used by Nabû-apla-iddina to stamp the tablet and bears a faithful negative impression of the bas-relief. The second, BM91002, is far better preserved and much later. It is thought that another sovereign – Nabopolassar (626-605 B.C.) or, as recently suggested, Nabonidus (626-605 B.C.) – having unearthed the precious object during one of the frequent restorations of the Ebabbar had broken the clay casing and subsequently taken another impression before enclosing the whole lot in a casket.
(M.R.)

Bibliography: Barnett-Wiseman 1960; Horowitz 2000; Seidl 2001; Woods 2004.

a

b

c

I.1.9
Disc with stars and constellations
Nineveh, c. 7th century B.C.
Clay; diameter 14.1 cm

Drawing of stars and constellations, approximately in natural sequence. Most of them can be identified, the purpose of the disc is however unclear. It may even have been used for magic. Only part of the inscription is understandable.
(H.H.)

Bibliography: King L.W. 1912b, pl. 10; Koch J. 1989.

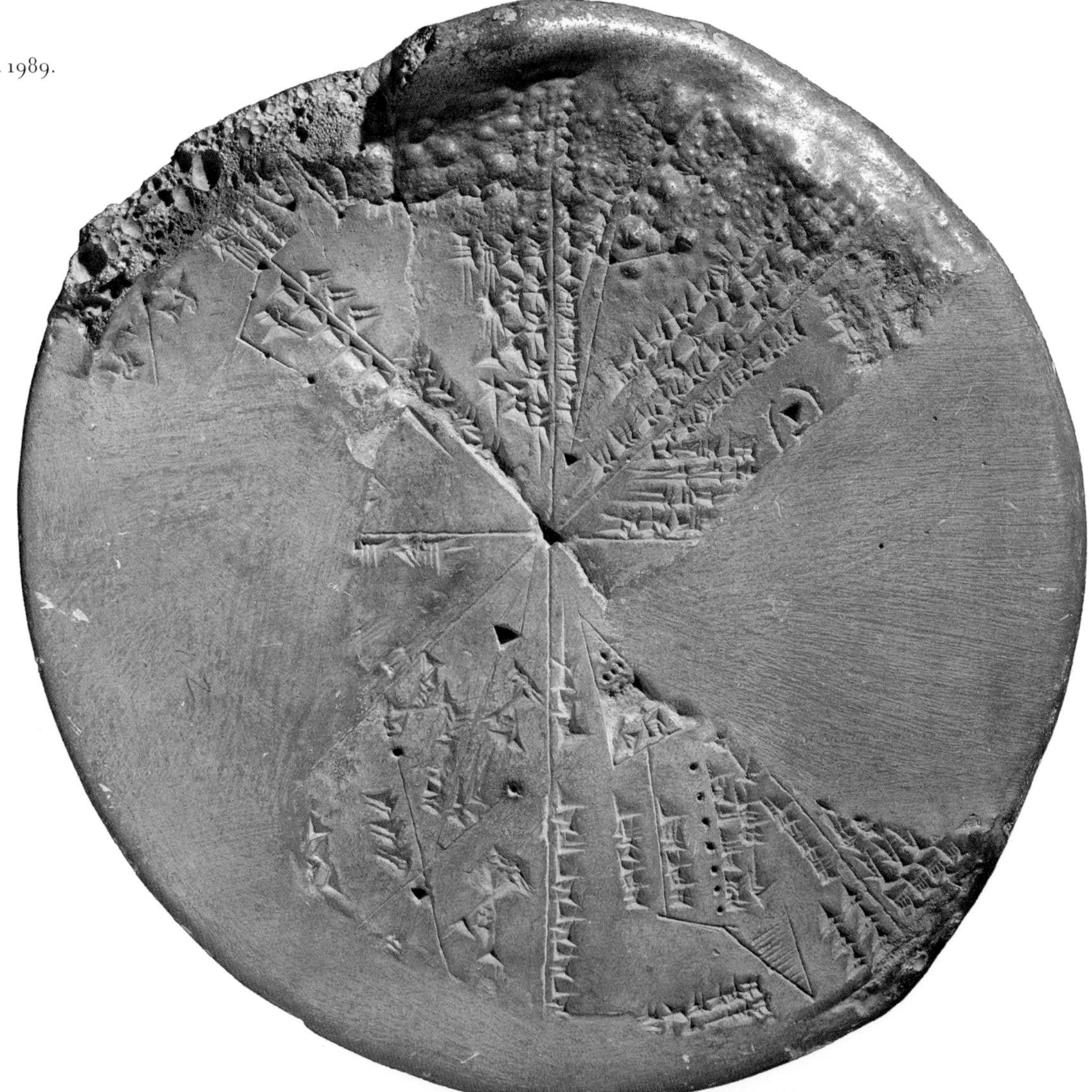

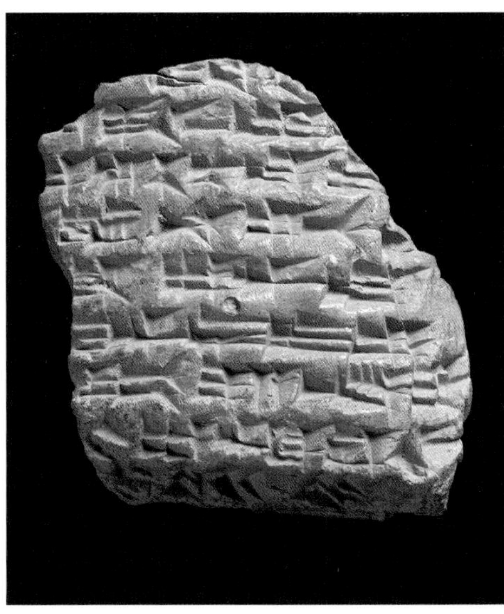

I.1.10
Tablet with a letter to the Assyrian king Esarhaddon
680-669 B.C.
Clay; 2.8 x 2.5 cm
London, British Museum, inv. K13174

This cuneiform text belongs, with the one following , to a group of more than 170 letters sent to the king of Assyria, in the capital city Niniveh, by the astrologers that resided at the court or in other cities of the kingdom. They observed the skies constantly, informing the king of any sign they discerned there, considered an omen sent by the gods, and important for the life of the kingdom. The letter is written by Balasi, master of the scribes, tutor of the crown prince and head of the royal astrologers, and by Nabu-akhkhe-eriba, another court astrologer. They are answering the king, who had asked for an explanation regarding the predictions connected to the apparition of a star. The two scribes quote the astronomical compendium *Mul.Apin*, literally 'Plough Star', taken from the first line of the text, which is a catalogue of the stars distributed according to three paths recognized in the sky. That proves that the compendium was the collection of Babylonian astral cognitions of the first centuries of the first millennium, studied by all astrologers and known even by the king. According to this compendium, the sign of Aries will appear on the first day of the month of Nisan (first month of the year), while on the twentieth day the constellation of the Auriga will appear.
(M.G.B.)

Bibliography: Parpola 1993, p. 45.

I.1.11
Tablet with letter to the Assyrian king, Esarhaddon
680-669 B.C.
Clay; 6.3 x 3.1 cm
London, British Museum, inv. K496

Letter written in cuneiform characters to the king, Esarhaddon, by two court astrologers, Balasi and Bamaya, who observed the full Moon on the fourteenth day of the month. Now the two astrologers will observe the apparition of the new Moon in the following month and will immediately inform the king. If the Pleiades will light up and appear before Venus in the morning, the prediction will regard the city (it is not clear which city but probably is the capital city Niniveh); in any case, it is a conjunction of Mars and Venus that will probably bring no good. The two astrologers will write another letter to the king after further observations of the skies.
(M.G.B.)

Bibliography: Parpola 1993, pp. 45-46.

I.1.12
The Mesopotamian universe
Demonstration model
Steel, acrylic; 265 x 200 cm
Opera Laboratori Fiorentini

This model of the Mesopotamian cosmos is set up around three viewpoints which taken together give a pretty fair summary of some aspects of Babylonian cosmological traditions. Projected on the lower level is the map of the Babylonian world, floating like a raft on the Primordial Ocean and enlivened by images of the places and things shown in it (Babylonia, Assyria, marshes, canals, cities etc.). All around, corresponding to the regions beyond the Primordial Ocean, are depicted heroes, gods, cosmic scenes and symbols reproduced on *stelae* rising from the triangular points of the map, extending beyond the Ocean. These images are intended to convey the physical and mythical atmosphere interposed between the earth and the sky. Above, attached to the tops of the *stelae*, a circular, rotating celestial vault shows a kind of astrolabe which marks a few of the major constellations (Leo, Virgo, Gemini, Taurus), as well as the ecliptic, the equator and the two parallels within each of the three regions ascribed to the most important deities of the Mesopotamian world (Ea, Enlil and Anu).
(M.R.)

Bibliography: Lambert 1975; Horowitz 1988; Hunger 1989; Wiggermann 1992; Matthiae 1994; Horowitz 1998; Horowitz 2006.

I.2.1

Sarcophagus lid with representation of the sky goddess Nut

Egypt, Necropolis of Thebes; c. 740-700 B.C.

Stuccoed and painted wood; length 178 cm, width 44 cm

Turin, Museo delle Antichità Egizie, inv. C. 2220 (Collezione Drovetti, 1824)

This lid belongs to the sarcophagus which contained the mummy of the 'mistress of the house' Tararo, daughter of Shepenimendiesher (the mother). The typology and characteristic features of the work suggest a dating to the end of the 3rd Intermediary Period (c. 740-700 B.C.), corresponding to the end of the 22nd Dynasty and the contemporary 23rd-25th Dynasties. Considering the high quality of the work, it is possible that the coffin was in its turn preserved inside a larger sarcophagus, according to a custom of the period evidenced also by similar depositions from the Theban necropolis which the Turin museum acquired as a part of the Drovetti Collection. The beautiful image of the sky goddess Nut with which the inside of the lid is decorated had the function of protecting the dead person, giving him or her assurance of eternity in the astral sphere. The name of the goddess is written in hieroglys above her head, with the last sign representing the vault f heaven. Above the inscription is the solar disk, which Nut supports by raising her arms in a clear evocation of the Sun rising above the horizon, as an augury of the cyclic continuity of life. The correlation between the head of the dead person and the solar disk ensured the supply of warmth and vital energy to enable the person to go on living for 'millions of years', a term the Egyptians used to mean eternity. The goddess is often to be found as decoration either on the bottom or the lid of sarcophagi of this period, usually with arms spread as enfolding the dead in a welcoming embrace. Unlike the examples cited, which depict the goddess with peculiar features of Egyptian art, with body and head shown in profile, Nut is seen in front view, perfectly composed according to a pattern in which volumes and parts are rigorously portrayed. Also auguries for eternal life are the colours of the long linen tunic worn by the goddess, painted red with a white ribbon, evoking the luminosity of sunlight. As the 'mistress of the sky' Nut was the goddess chiefly associated with the Sun and its daily cycle from dawn to sunset. Her body, decorated with stars, figures in other funerary contexts, and together with Geb, god of the Earth, and Shu, god of the Air, she is part of complete cosmogonic depictions which embrace the divine mystery of life.

(E.D.A.)

Bibliography: Fabretti-Rossi-Lanzone 1882, p. 301, no. 2220; Gasse 1996, pp. 158-162, no. 25; Tiradritti 1999, p. 93, no. 76; Graefe 2001, pp. 23-26, plates 5-13, figs. 9-10; D'Amicone-Fontanella 2005, pp. 64-69.

I.2.2
Fragmentary magical-religious papyrus scroll
Ramesside period
Papyrus, black and red ink; 35 x 70 cm
Turin, Museo delle Antichità Egizie, CGT 54065

Dozens of fragments of papyrus have been joined together to make this extraordinary collection of magical-religious texts in hieroglyphic writing. On the recto (horizontal fibres) they are concerned with the origin of the world and protection against the forces of evil. Here we find the famous *Monologue of Atum*, formerly known only from a document a thousand years more recent. In it the creator god issues from the inertia of primordial Chaos and generates by himself the cosmos in the form of couples of deities and all existent things by pronouncing their names ('The things that exist are as many as are the words of my mouth'). Men (*rmt*) on the other hand are born from his tears (*rmwt*). The similarity between the words is thought to be evidence of a substantial relationship. There follows the *Ritual to defeat Apophis*, the snake personifying the forces of evil. The texts on the verso (vertical fibres) are written by another hand. They include a manual of divination by the interpretation of the forms oil takes on when poured onto water.
(G.R.)

Bibliography: Roccati 1980, pp. 224-231; Roccati 1989; Demichelis 2002, pp. 153-158.

I.2.3
Illustrated funeral papyrus
21st dynasty, probably second half
Papyrus, black ink; 25 x 97 cm
Turin, Museo delle Antichità Egizie, Cat. 1770

This papyrus belongs to the category also called 'mythological papyri', that after the New Kingdom appeared among objects placed in tombs together with the more famous *Book of the Dead*. Four illustrated parts predominate: the deceased who adores the god Osiris; the four funeral demons called 'Sons of Horus'; a classic scene regarding cosmogony, with the god Shu (probably the light), first-born of the Sun, who separates his children, the Sky-goddess Nut (characteristically arranged to form an arc), from the Earth-god Geb; lower there is the Sun-god Horus seated in his boat. The forth 'picture' includes scattered figures that belong to the vignettes of chapters 148 and 149 of the *Book of the Dead*. The owner of the papyrus is a priest of Amon whose name has been read *Pa-mer*.
(G.R.)

Bibliography: unpublished; cf. Fabretti-Rossi Lanzone 1882, p. 208; Niwinski 1989, pp. 366, 197-203.

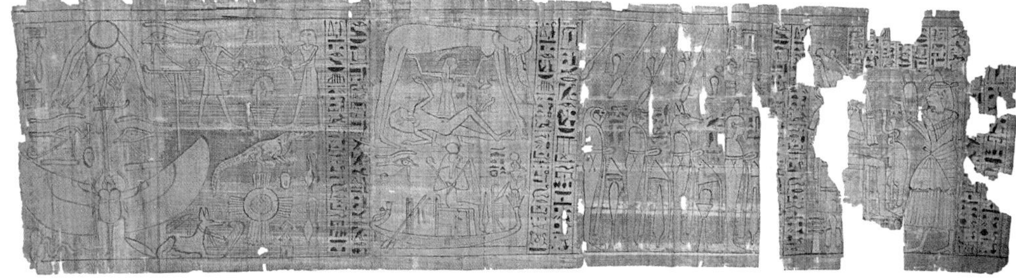

I.2.4
Funerary stela
Late Period
Carved and painted limestone; 44.5 x 32 cm
Florence, Museo Egizio, inv. 2502

A stela with curved top and a winged solar disk in the lunette. One observes two scenes arranged as mirror images showing on the right the god Atum and on the left Harakhty as objects of worship by the owner of the stela, the 'dean of the timekeeping priests of Osiris at Abydos' Penbu, son of Hemsa, who bears the same title. In the great temple of Abydos, therefore, both father and son were overseers of the priests responsible for determining the hours, especially during the night, for the correct performance of the temple rites. Penbu displays the emblem of his office, the star-sighter (called the *bâi*, translated into Greek as *phoinix*), which is shown behind his back on the right, and behind his left arm on the left.
(G.R.)

Bibliography: Bosticco 1972, pp. 21-22, n. 11, tav. 11.

I.2.5
Copy of merkhet
c. 600 B.C.
Ivory, palm leaf stem; length 11.5 cm, height 34 cm
London, Science Museum, inv. 1913-573

The term *merkhet* was used in ancient Egypt to generally indicate instruments for orientation and for measuring time: in fact, it means an instrument 'with which ones knows' (just like the Greek *gnomon*).
The copy, made in 1913, reproduces the original instrument preserved in the Berlin museums (inv. 14084/5), still the only complete example of *merkhet*, made in two parts: a level (similar in shape to sundials with a horizontal plane) furnished with a plumb-line (integrated), and a sight made from the woody rib of a palm leaf (*bâi*). By aiming on the plumb-line through the slit cut into the widest part of the *bâi* and orientating oneself towards the Pole Star, the observers were able to establish the north-south line and to measure the nocturnal hours by means of the 'passage' of certain stars on the vertical. In fact, on the wood there is inscribed: 'To reveal the start of a celebration, to put everyone in their hour (of service)', and on the level: 'I know the motion of the Sun, Moon and stars, each in their place'.
(G.R.)

Bibliography: Borchardt 1899; Borchardt 1920, pp. 53-54, table 16; Sloley 1931, p. 169, pl. 16.

I.2.6
Model of a cubit
Late 18th Dynasty
Calcite; height 44.5 cm x 4 cm
Florence, Museo Egizio, inv. 3078

Made for the funeral equipment of the Royal Scribe and Chief Steward Amenhotpe, called Huy, this reproduces the unit of measure used by the Egyptians also for astronomical calculations. One face linear and one side are occupied by three vertical hieroglyphic inscriptions expressing classic funeral formulas, while the opposite face bears the subdivision of the royal cubit (52.3-5 cm) as far as one digit (about 1.88 cm); below right, from the digit to the *djeser* (4 hands), the fractions of the digit as far 1/16th are inscribed, evidenced by vertical segments in the lower side. Now reduced to seven pieces, most of them worn by probable re-use, it lacks one segment more to make up the proper measure.
(G.R.)

Bibliography: Lepsius 1865, pp. 14-15, tav. II; Bagnani 1934, pp. 40-46, fig. 5; Hayes 1938, pp. 10-11.

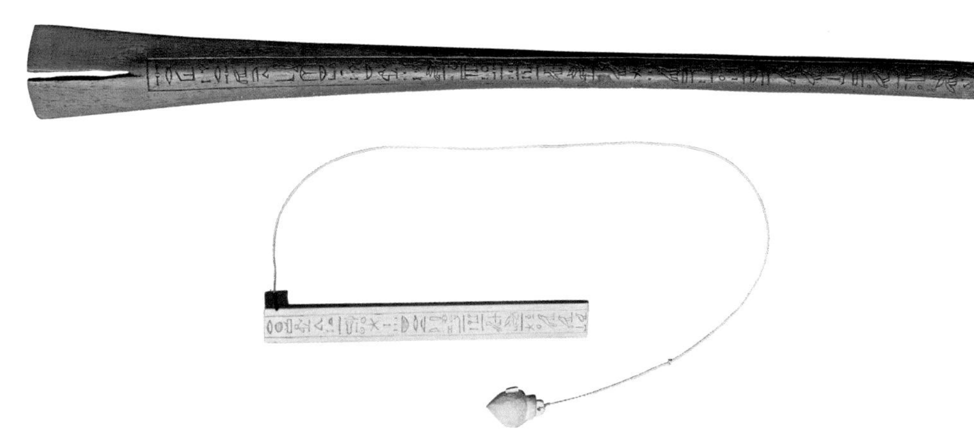

I.2.7
Sundial
Ptolemaic period
Grey granite; 6.6 x 10 x 3.5 cm
Vatican City, Musei Vaticani, inv. MV 55462

The object, of unknown provenance, represents a fragmentary example of sundial (in Egyptian, *merkhet*) with the projection of the shadow line on an inclined plane, for measuring the time during hours of day-light. An instrument of this kind, that functioned only in a perfectly horizontal position, was used for cultural purposes, to mark the different sacerdotal activities and their relative recitations.
The back is filled by the standing figure of the falcon-headed god Ra-Horakhty, with the solar disc and uraeus, the *uas* sceptre in his right hand and the *ankh* symbol in his left. This deity, that appears on other examples, must have been associated to this kind of instrument precisely for his solar character. Holding particular interest is the hieroglyphic inscription that runs along the base, with a dedication to the god 'Horus of Semen-hor, who stands at the head of lower Naret', which connects the object with the area of the 21st nome of Upper Egypt. Some graphic characteristics of the inscription and some stylistic characteristics of the god Horakhty make the sundial datable from the Ptolemaic period.
(A.A.)

Bibliography: Bosticco 1957, pp. 33-49; Graefe 1984, coll. 1105-1106.

I.2.8
Mobile shadow-clock
Probably early Ptolemaic period
Basalt; 6.3 x 3.4 cm
Turin, Museo delle Antichità Egizie, Cat. 7353

The plinth is cracked and the rectangular prism is missing, as well as the oblique surface on which it cast its shadow (cf. entry I.2.7). A feature of this little object, intended for real use, is an oblique hole drilled from the upper face to a vertical grooved surface on the right hand side. A lead plummet must have been attached to this to ensure that the base was perfectly horizontal. The Sun god Horus is depicted on the outer face, and the hieroglyphic inscription tells us it belongs to a 'scribe of the altar' and 'scribe of the countryside', who certainly made use of it in his daily life, and who is called 'privileged with Thot', the presiding deity of scribes and responsible for the measurement of time.
(G.R.)

Bibliography: Borchardt 1920, p. 43, Abb. 17.4; Bosticco 1957, pp. 44-47.

I.2.9
Fragment of clepsydra
Early Ptolemaic dynasty
Granite; maximum height 12.5 cm
Florence, Museo Egizio, inv. 12290

A fragment of the side of a clepsydra similar to the one in the Museo Barracco (see entry I.2.11) and probably of the same period. On the main face, arranged in columns to be read from right to left, is a list of the decans, which are the stars the rising (or, later, the transit) of which indicated the hour of the night. They are correlated with the 36 periods of ten days into which the 12 months of the ancient Egyptian civic year was divided. The names of decans from the 6th to the 16th are still preserved, appearing in pairs in the first three columns. The list tallies with the one the famous Senenmut, 'spokesman' for the female pharaoh Hatshepsut, had made at Thebes for his second tomb (Theban Tomb 353) in about 1470-60 B.C. The god Horus, falcon-headed, must refer to the 12th decan, Lower Khentet.
(G.R.)

Bibliography: Neugebauer-Parker 1960-1969, III/Text, pp. 60-61, no. 45; III/Plates, pl. 22 D.

I.2.10
Portable sundial
Basalt; 8.8 x 13.5 cm
Florence, Museo Egizio, inv. 14501

The object, still completely unknown to the public-at-large, has recently been donated to the Egyptian Museum of Florence and was brought to notice thanks to an indication by M.C. Guidotti, director of the Museum. It is a portable sundial with an inclined plane, of which the front part of the base, with a projecting prism, is missing. The decoration consists of six frames holding figures of divinities: the goddess Neith and the crocodile-god Sbek, also mentioned in the inscription in hieroglyphics that must have occupied the entire base. On the inclined plane, neither marks nor dots for reading the time can be found, therefore it is probable that a mobile cursor was applied in the central groove (cf. the exemplar in the Vatican Museums, entry I.2.7).
(G.R.)

Bibliography: unpublished.

I.2.11
Clepsydra
Reign of Ptolemy II Philadelphus, 285/82-246 B.C.
Basalt; height 36.4 cm
Rome, Museo Barracco, inv. 27

'Water clocks' of this type were used to measure the hours of the night, probably in a temple setting. The water issued from the hole at the bottom (which must have been lined with a metal tube) and the hour was read on the monthly horal scales marked by notches on the inside. On the outside and on the opposite side to the scale is depicted the patron deity of the month, to whom the sovereign Ptolemy II is paying homage, or who is accompanying him in the rite. In the surviving painted areas the first two deities of the year (the goddess Tekhyt and Ptah) and the last four (Khonsu, Horus-Khentykhety, Ipet-hemetes and Ra-Harakhty) may be recognized. This fine specimen, found in the Iseo Campense area in Rome, may have been made in Alexandria and probably functioned accurately for over 120 years.
(G.R.)

Bibliography: Mengoli 1986; Sist 1996, pp. 71-74.

I.2.12
Coptic ostracon
10 March 601
Limestone, black ink; 11 x 9 cm
Turin, Museo delle Antichità Egizie, Cat. 7134

This splinter of limestone was written on in Coptic on both sides by Petros son of Paulos, who held the office of *lashane* (temple administrator) at Djeme, on the edge of the ancient necropolis of Thebes. He records the fact that during his service there was an eclipse of the Sun at midday on the 14th day of the month of Phamenoth in the 4th cycle of indiction, corresponding to 10 March 601.
(G.R.)

Bibliography: Stern 1878, pp. 11-12, n. 1; Rossi 1894-95, p. 801; Till 1962, p. 172; KSB II, 2004, p. 200, n. 1238.

I.2.13
Model of the Zodiac of Dendera
Wood; 255 x 255 cm (reproduction in scale 1:1)
S. Battaglia, G. Miglietta and Opera Laboratori Fiorentini

The Zodiac of the temple of Hathor in Dendera is perhaps the first representation of the sky in which it is possible to find use of stereographic projection. The temple dates from 54 B.C. and the Zodiac, as deduced from astronomical data, was made in the summer of the year 50 B.C. The large stone slab, today found in the Louvre, occupied a part of the attic of the East chapel of Osiris located on the temple's roof. The figures and the hieroglyphics are arranged on circular registers. The first, the out-most circle, contains the representation of the 'decans' that scan 36 intervals of 10 days each; the first 'decan' is in correspondence with Sirius, the star that announced the beginning of the year and the arrival of the Nile-flood. The second register contains the constellations of the southern hemisphere included between the Tropic of Capricorn and the Equator, while the third includes the constellations of the northern hemisphere with the Ursa Minor (North Pole) at the centre. The figures of the Zodiac are aligned along the eccentric circle of the ecliptic. The axis that unites Cancer and Capricorn (solstices) indicates the North-South direction that forms an angle of circa 18° in respect to the longitudinal axis of the temple. The transversal axis of the temple is, in fact, perfectly orientated towards the heliacal rising of Sirius, that rose at circa 18° East-South-East. Sirius, represented as a crouching cow, is correctly represented in the point of maximum culmination on the celestial meridian of the southern hemisphere.
(F.C.)

Bibliography: Neugebauer 1955, 1975a; Auborg 1995; Cauville 1997; Trevisan 1997.

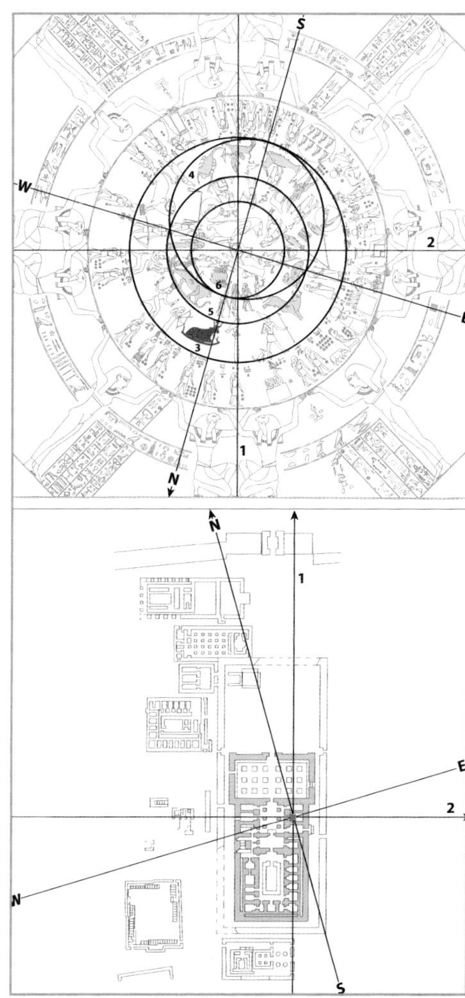

I.3.1
Model of the cosmos according to the Judaic tradition
Reconstruction
Steel, acrylic, resins; 100 x 200 cm
Opera Laboratori Fiorentini

Interested in understanding the universe in order to grasp the signs it shows of the greatness of God, the Judaic civilization has elaborated a geocentric image of the cosmos whose essential traits can be reconstructed through, above all, passages from the *Bible* and, in particular, from the book of *Genesis*.
The reconstruction shows, in the centre of it all, the Earth thought of as a flat disc supported by columns (*Job*, 9,6). Above this there is the sky, the firmament of solid matter (*Genesis* 1: 6-8), also resting on pilasters (*Job*, 26, 11). The Sun and the Moon are found, with the stars, under the firmament (*Genesis*, 1, 14-17), that also acts as an element of separation between the waters above from those below it (*Genesis* 1, 6-7). Above, among the higher waters, there are containers of snow of hail and of wind: special gates regulate its flow towards Earth. Some of the waters under the firmament were united in the beginning to create the seas (*Genesis*, 1, 9-10) the circle the earth; a part of these waters also flows under the earth (*Exodus*, 20, 4; *Deuteronomy*, 4, 18), connected with the depths (*Genesis*, 1, 2). Streams of water of various flow again arise from these underground waters. Finally, in the depths of the earth there are the infernal regions (*Numbers*, 16, 28-34; *Isaiah*, 14, 9-11).
(G.D.P.)

I.3.2
The creation of the world according to Genesis
Images by Hartmann Schedel, *Das Buch der Croniken*, Nuremberg 1493

The images visualize the creation of the world in six days, as narrated in the Book of *Genesis* of the Old Testament, attributed to Moses.
First Day:
In the beginning God created the Heavens and the Earth. And separated the light from the darkness.
Second Day:
God separated the waters under the firmament from those above it. And thus he created the heavens.
Third Day:
The hand of God gathered the waters under the firmament in one place and divided the land from the waters. And he ordered the earth to yield herbs and fruits.
Fourth Day:
The hand of God created lights in the heavens, the greater to rule the day and the lesser to rule the night.
Fifth Day:
God said: 'let the waters bring forth every kind of fish and let birds fly in the heavens.'
Sixth Day:
God created the land animals and then said: 'let us make mankind in our image'. And so He created man.
Seventh Day:
The creation is complete and God rests in contemplation of his own perfect work.
(P.G.)

II.1.1
Sarcofagus of Phaethon
Early 4th century
White marble; 102 x 247 cm (casket)
Rome, Villa Borghese, in deposit to the Museo Pietro Canonica, inv. VB340
Reproduction 1:1 (Opera Laboratori Fiorentini)

The Sarcophagus of Phaethon belongs to the historical nucleus of the collection created by Scipione Borghese (1574-1633). It is decorated on three sides and closed by a kline lid (not on display) on which a deceased couple reclines.
The front represents a mythological scene with the figures of numerous characters. In the centre, the fall of Phaethon, received on earth by the personification of the Eridanus, to which the personification of Thalassa, with an oar in her hand, is counterposed. Behind Phaethon's extended leg, the interior of the over-turned chariot is seen. To the left of Phaethon, *Helios* is depicted with a chlamys on his shoulders, his right arm raised and a tortoise at his feet. In the lower left-hand corner, Phaethon's two sisters, the Eliades, are depicted in tears at the moment of being transformed into poplars. To the right of the sun chariot is a bearded male figure identified as *Zeus*, with a sceptre in his left hand; immediately to the right, a female figure, interpreted as the personification of the West (*Dysis*). In the upper left-hand corner, the fact preceding the fall is portrayed: Phaethon asks his father *Helios* permission to drive the chariot.
The left side of the sarcophagus represents *Helios* while he drives the biga and holds the horses' reins

in his left hand; beneath him there is a female river deity. On the right side, the Moon drives a biga drawn by a pair of oxen; and below this scene there is *Thalassa*.
In the classical age the fall of Phaethon represents Helios' daily dive into the great Ocean that turns red with fire, or – according to Euripides' version – the morning and the evening star. After the spread of the myth of Mithra, a negative connotation emerges. Phaethon is, in fact, the foolish charioteer that, incapable of driving the chariot of the Sun, threatens to burn the fruits that Mithra gave to the Earth.
(A.N.)

Bibliography: Manilli 1650, p. 170; Montelatici 1700, p. 116; Musso 1993; Campitelli 2003, p. 265.

II.1.2
Red-figured crater with Helios on a chariot
5th century B.C.
Clay; height 33 cm
London, British Museum, inv. GR 1867,0508.1133

On its principal face, the vase presents one of Apollo's most important daily tasks, that of preparing his chariot and of leading the Sun across the sky. 'Swift and untiring', 'good courier', according to the definitions in antique Hellenistic poetry, Apollo crosses the sky with a golden chariot drawn by four speeding horses. (Homeric Hymns, *Apollo*, 15; Euripides, *The Phoenician Women*, 3) their nostrils smoking (Pindar, *Olimpian Odes*, 7, 71), nourished with a magical plant that grows only in the Islands of the Blessed (Athenaeus, 7). Every morning Helios comes out of the Ocean in the East and every evening, in the West, he dives again into the great circular sea disappearing under the Earth, where the rest, necessary for facing the efforts of the next day, is found during the night. The vase shows Helios, whose solar disc is reduced to the radiate crown on his head, at the moment of departure, between, Eos, Phosphoros and Selene. (G.D.P.)

Bibliography: Cumont 1919a, p. 1379, fig. 6489.

II.1.3
Anonymous
Relief with Phanes
c. 2nd century A.D.
Marble; 74 x 48.7 cm
Modena, Museo Civico Archeologico, inv. 2676

The relief shows the iconograph of Phanes, first giver of life in the universe according to Orphism, which spread throughout the Roman world after the first century A.D. Phanes emerges from the cosmic egg at the beginning of time created by Chronos (Time), and Ananke (Necessity). Generator of new life, Phanes owes the appellation of Protogonos, frequent in literary sources, to the fact of being the first-born. Often identified with Eros and with Mithra, he is portrayed as a youth with golden wings and a serpent coiled around his body. Bearer of light in the universe, Phanes holds a torch in his hand. His marriage with Nyx, the dark Night, is a new motif in Greek theogony: the primordial couple is no longer formed of sky and earth, but of light and darkness, according to the scheme of Orphic mythology.
(G.D.P.)

Bibliography: Cumont 1909; Cumont 1997.

II.1.4
Anonymous
Relief with Mithra
End of 3rd century A.D.
Stone; 90 x 148 cm
Rome, Museo Nazionale Romano, inv. 205837

The importance of Mithra in the Roman world is testified to by the abundance of statues, inscriptions, altars and architectural elements recovered in great quantity in places of worship. The encounters of the god's followers took place in the mithraeum, an underground cavity or cave, a veritable universe in miniature that served as a background to the tauroctony represented in the relief: having seized the bull, Mithra strikes its neck with a sword. From the contact of the bull's body and the Earth, all beneficial plants will grow, from its marrow, wheat and from its blood, grapevines. To contrast this profusion of vitality, the god of evil sends to Earth a scorpion with the task of trying to contrast the beneficial action of the bull's sacrifice by poisoning its semen, so as to impede every form of life on Earth. A dog, the god's hunting companion, attacks the wounded bull, like the snake that, according to Cumont, is a later addition to the original scheme in which there were just bull, dog and scorpion. On Mithra's cape there is the crow, messenger of the Sun, that communicates to the god – whose head is in fact turned towards the bird – the order to sacrifice the bull. The two figures to the left and to the right of Mithra are the torch-bearers, Cautes and Cautopates: the first has a torch upraised, the other lowered, to represent the solar cycle from sunrise to sunset. Finally, in the upper vertices of the relief there are the personifications of the Sun, on the left, and of the Moon, on the right, to complete the portrayal of the universal space to which Mithra's tauroctony alludes: above the *Sol* and *Luna* there is the region of infinite light that extends to the sphere of fixed stars, where the immortal souls to which Mithra has revealed the path of salvation reside.
Offering the prospective of life after death, the cult of Mithra had a great following at all social levels. Popular especially among the Roman soldiers, Mithraism was banned by Theodosius in the year 391 together with all pagan rites.
(G.D.P.)

Bibliography: Cumont 1909; Cumont 1919b; Boll-Bezold-Gundel 1979, pp. 23-41; Le Boeuffle 1989; Cumont 1997; Bastianelli Moscati 2008.

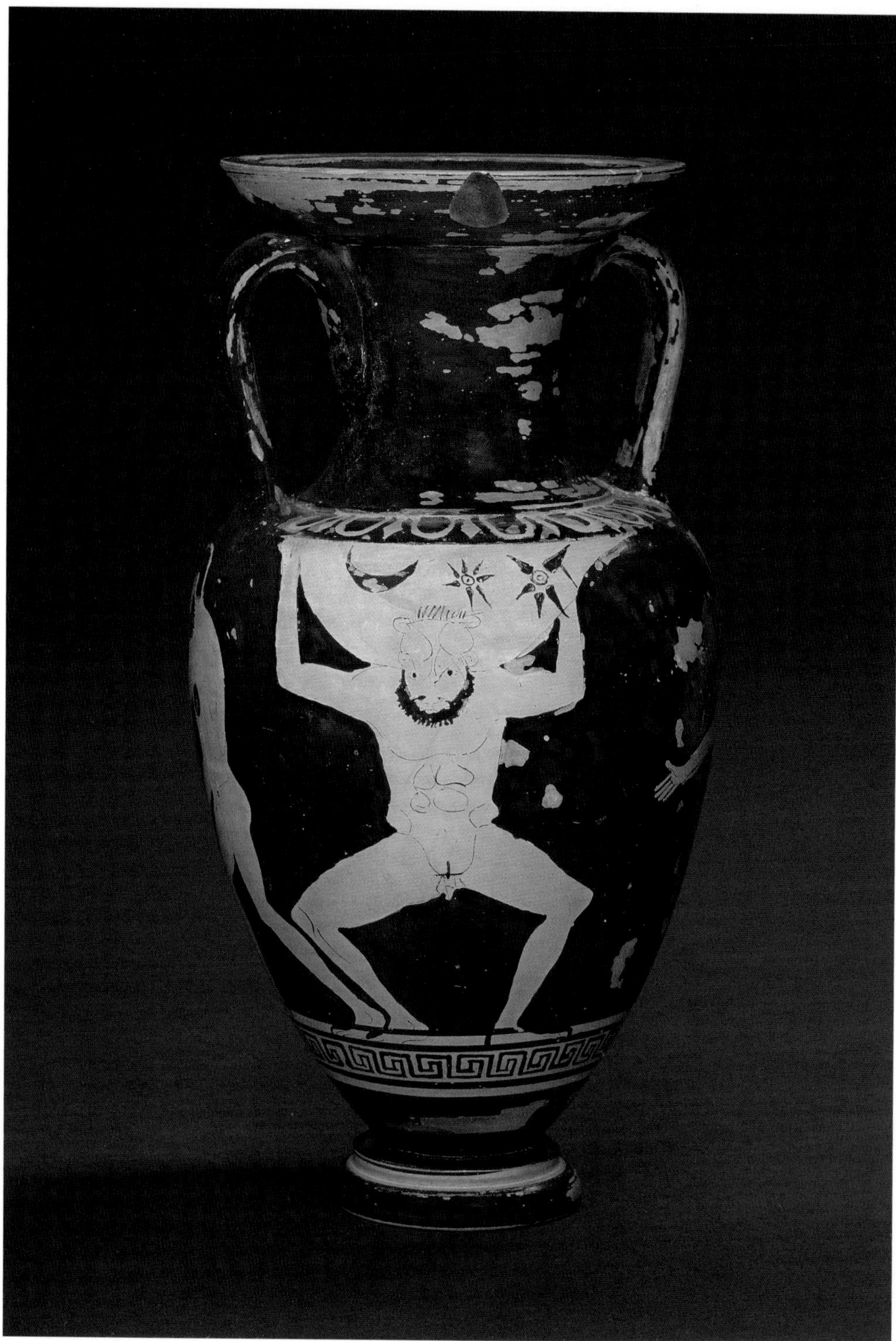

II.1.5
Campanian amphora with Atlas, Heracles and the celestial sphere
5th century B.C.
Clay; height 33 cm
London, British Museum, inv. GR 1722,0320.432

Atlas is portrayed while he runs to take the wonderful golden apples from a tree in the garden of the Hesperides: he will give them to Heracles, who is momentarily taking his place in the tiring task of supporting the celestial sphere. Referring to the last of Heracles' labours, this episode was quite well-known in antiquity; mention of it is made by the Byzantine author John Tzetzes (*Chiliades*, V, v. 268), who records how Heracles learned the science of astronomy from Atlas and refers that, in the Classic Age, even Servius and Philostratus knew this version of the myth.
The vase from the British Museum shows Heracles with his knees bent under the enormous effort, while he supports the star-covered celestial sphere with both hands. On his right Hera observes the scene, while Atlas and one of the Hesperides approach the tree of the golden apples watched over by a monstrous many-headed snake.
(G.D.P.)

Bibliography: D'Hancarville 1766.

II.2.1
Anonymous
Relief with Anaximander
Ist century A.D.
Pentelic marble; 17 x 18 cm
Rome, Museo Nazionale Romano, inv. 506

The name impressed on the upper part of the fragment reveals that the relief portrays the philosopher Anaximander, practising in Miletus in the first half of the sixth century B.C., here represented in the typical thoughtful attitude, according to the canons of iconography in the Hellenistic period. With Anaximander's works, the abandon of the language of myths was definitely affirmed, with the success of rational discourse on the causes that originated the world. Without any divine design, Anaximander's cosmological concept places the Earth, for the first time, in the middle of the cosmos: imagined like a cylinder without support and immobile, it is equidistant from all the points of the celestial vault.
(G.D.P.)

Bibliography: Lucchetta 2001, p. 619, fig. 1.

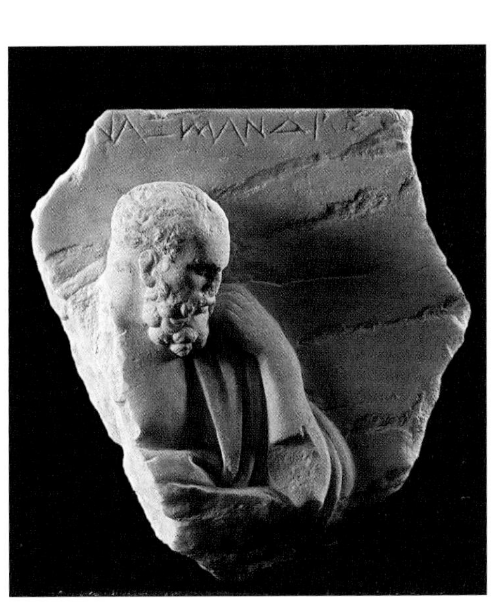

II.2.2
Anonymous
Herma of Pythagoras
1st century A.D.
Greek marble; height 49 cm
Rome, Musei Capitolini, inv. M.C. 594

In the fourth century B.C., a portrait already existed of Pythagoras, who had lived in the sixth century B.C. This portrait was then replicated in series. The head in the Capitoline Museums portrays the philosopher with his head covered by a turban, presumably a homage to Eastern culture, that had borne such great influence on him. Although none of Pythagoras' writings have reached us, the vision of the cosmos shared by the philosopher and his circle has had enormous influence on naturalists and astronomers of the following ages. Conceived as an ordered whole, the *kosmos* of the Pythagoreans is perfectly spherical and governed by precise numerical relationships, fundamental to the order of the universe. The numerical harmony that governs everything, from musical phenomena to the entire universe, guides Pythagoras in the construction of the 'cosmic figures', the five regular solids to which Pythagoras will associate the four fundamental elements and the sphere of the world.
(G.D.P.)

Bibliography: Stuart Jones 1912, p. 151, n. 80, tav. 59; Buccino in Roma 2001, pp. 302-303; Firenze 2007b, p. 217.

II.2.3
Anonymous
Astrological globe
2nd century B.C.-2nd century A.D.
Crystalline white marble; diameter 30 cm
Matelica (MC), Civico Museo Archeologico, inv. 77238

Recovered in 1985 during works for the consolidation of the foundations of the Palazzo del Governo in the historical centre of Matelica, this sphere presents etched lines, concentric circles, letters and words in Greek. It is a very ancient sundial, a brilliant instrument for astronomical, astrological and chronological observations and calculations. This 'computer of stone' is capable of indicating, with a good level of accuracy, the time of day starting at the Sun's rising, and its entrance into the constellations of the zodiac, the calendar, the dates of the solstices and of the equinoxes, the length of day and night in the various periods of the year. Belonging to the category of sundials, the globe must be exposed to the sun-light, using the 'border', generated by the illuminated part and the shaded part of the sphere, when it intersects the circles and the lines etched on the surface. The particular feature that distinguishes this object is its spherical and convex shape. Only one other example of spherical sundial is known, which is the globe found at Prosymna, in Greece, a locality between Argos and Mycenae. These two globes, even though they present clear similarities, differ both in their dimensions (the Greek one is almost twice the size of the one from Matelica), as well as for the geometrical configurations present on their surfaces.
It is plausible that the particular shape of the globe displayed constitutes a precise reference to the acquisition of the notion of the spherical shape of the Earth. Designed to function only at the latitude of Matelica (43°15'), the globe is not, therefore, a part of war booty but documents the remarkable astronomical knowledge of the ancient populations that, in succession, inhabited this region.
(D.B.)

Bibliography: Azzarita 1987; Baldini-Carusi 1989; Fantoni 1990; Baldini-Carusi 1991; Marengo 1998.

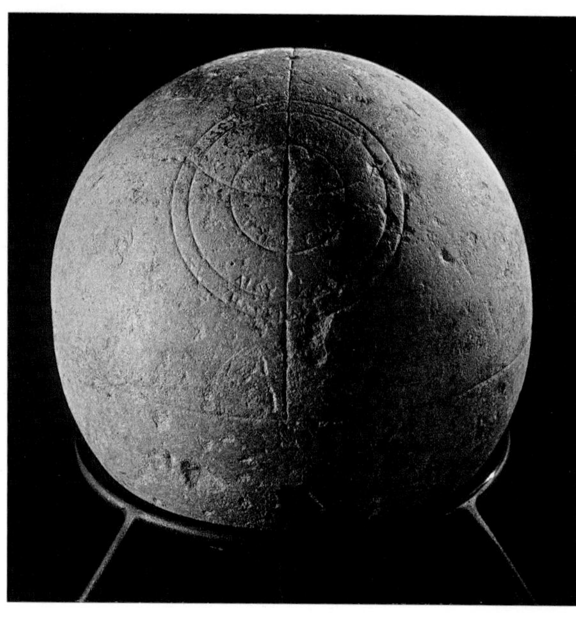

II.2.4
Celestial medicine
S. Battaglia, G. Miglietta, F. Wenig-Lynds
Fiberglass, wood, iron; diameter 150 cm

This exhibit illustrates the concept of the existence of correspondences between man (microcosm) and the universe (macrocosm), that goes back to the farthest ages (it was already wide- spread in the civilizations of Mesopotamia and of the Nile delta). Starting from Classical Greece, this doctrine, known as 'melotesia' (disposition of the limbs), obtained a more precise statute with the definition of the influences exercised by the zodiacal signs, by the planets and by the Moon on the various organs of the human body. The celestial 'influences' predisposed those born under a certain sign to specific pathologies. Physicians had to consider the configurations of the stars to administer effective remedies. Melotesia enjoyed wide success in the Middle Ages and in the Renaissance. Although with often significant variations, celestial medicine was based on the following system of correspondences: Aries influences the head and the brain; Taurus the neck; Gemini the arms and the lungs; Cancer the chest; Leo the heart (also influenced by the Sun); Virgin the intestines and the spleen; Libra the kidneys and the lumbar region; Scorpion the genital organs; Sagittarius the liver, the sciatic nerves and the thigh; Capricorn the knee and the joints; Aquarius the ankles and the circulatory system; Pisces the feet.
(P.G.)

Bibliography: Murdoch 1984, pp. 315-316.

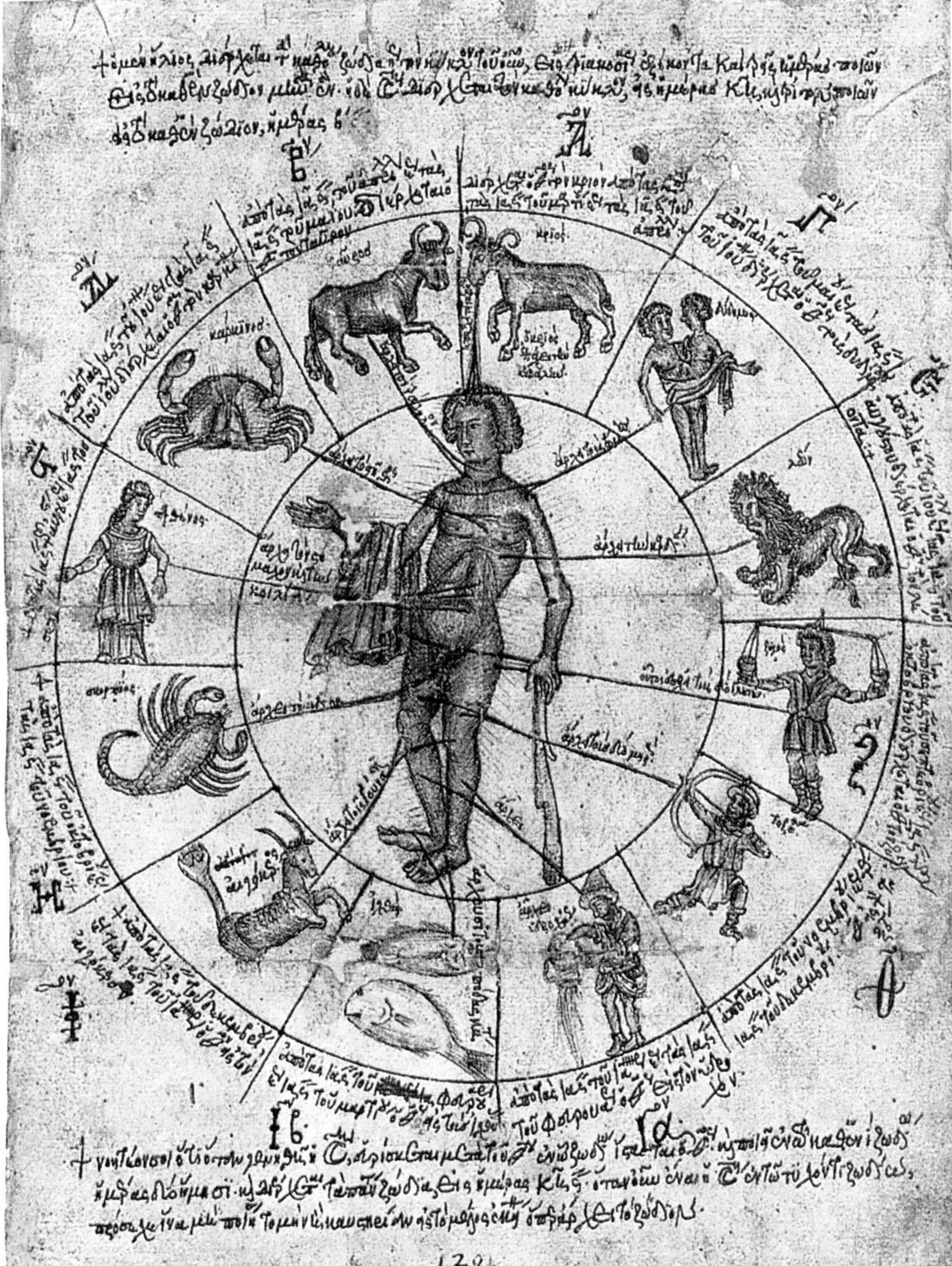

II.2.5
The five regular bodies
Wood and plexiglas; diameter 60 cm
R. Folicaldi, Fermo

The five regular polyhedrons of Platonic and Euclidean thought – tetrahedron, cube, octahedron, dodecahedron and icosahedron – symbolically represent the image of the cosmos. In the *Timaeus*, Plato associates four of these to the elements that constitute the terrestrial world according to Empedocles and precisely, the tetrahedron to fire, the cube to earth, the octahedron to air, the icosahedron to water, while the dodecahedron is given the function of representing the *quintessence*, or rather, the 'ether' that for Aristotle was the essence of the celestial world. For Euclid, regular bodies became object of geometric reflection in Book XIII of the *Elements*, where it is proposed to inscribe each polyhedron in a sphere of a given diameter. During the Renaissance it will be Piero della Francesca to bring renewed attention to these geometric bodies, making them the subject of geometric investigation (*Libellus de quinque corporibus regolaribus*) and an object of perspective representation (*De prospectiva pingendi*).
(F.C.)

Bibliography: Folicaldi 2001, Firenze 2005.

II.2.6
Dominicus Sanctes Sanctini
Heraclides' system
c. 1675
Brass; horizon ring diameter 43.3 cm, height 53 cm
Oxford, Museum of the History of Science, inv. 57517

This armillary sphere is constructed according to the planetary system of Heracleides of Pontus, who lived in the 4th century B.C. According to this arrangement, Venus and Mercury revolve around the Sun, while the Moon, the Sun, Mars, Jupiter and Saturn revolve around the Earth. In the seventeenth century this system was supported by the Italian astronomer Andreas Argolus (1570-1650). Despite dealing with such an ancient proposal, the armillary sphere is up-to-date in other respects. Jupiter is represented as having four satellites and Saturn as having three. While Galileo had discovered the satellites of Jupiter, the third satellite of Saturn was discovered in 1672 by Cassini, who discovered the fourth in 1684. This suggests a date for the instrument between 1672 and 1684.
(J.B.)

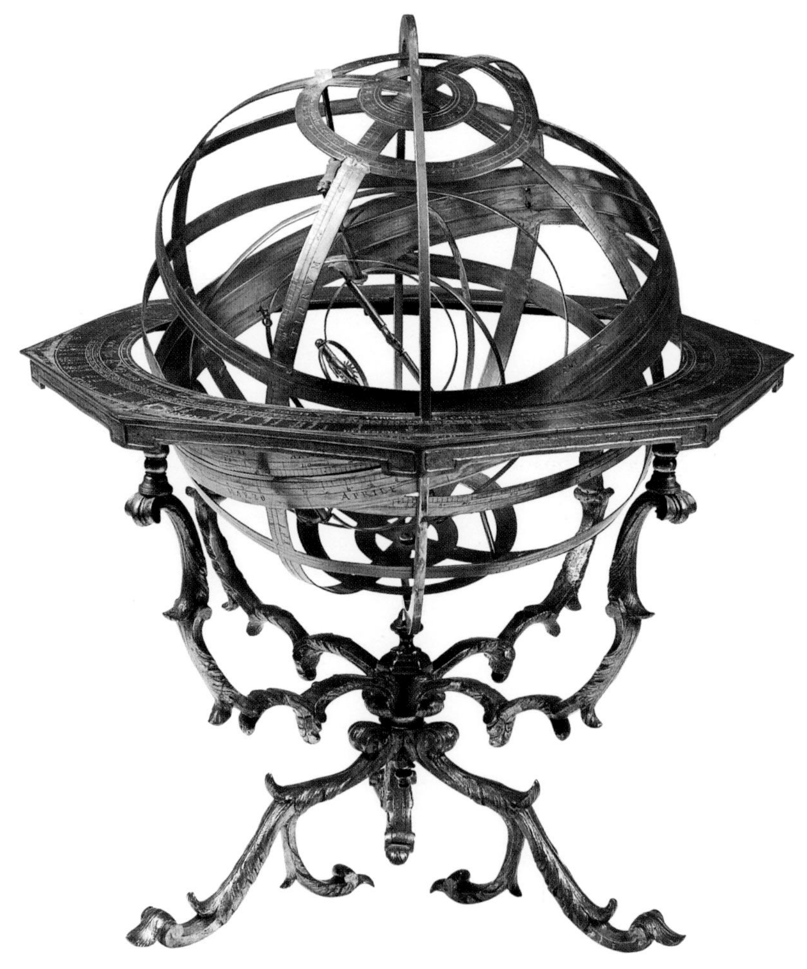

II.2.7
Anonymous
Bust of Aristotle
c. 2nd century A.D.
Onyx, marble; height 73 cm
Florence, Galleria degli Uffizi, inv. 9

The head, inserted in an onyx bust with marble drapery, is of unknown origins and depends, like many others of the Imperial Age, on an original portrait of the philosopher made in bronze by Lysippos around 330 B.C. The identification with Aristotle derives from the finding of a sixteenth-century drawing depicting a bust, found on the Quirinal Hill, a part of this series and with the name of the philosopher on its base.
Presented in the *De caelo*, Aristotle's cosmology contemplates the Earth, immobile at the centre of the universe, stationary in the eternal rotation of the skies: Aristotle, basing his work on objections of a physical nature, such as the trajectory of vertical fall of bodies thrown in air, declares – against the Pythagoreans – that the Earth is without any movement of rotation on its own axis. The sphere of fixed stars marks the invalicable confines of the universe. Convinced of the validity of Eudoxus' system of the world, Aristotle introduces the fundamental new idea of conferring concreteness to spheres and circles that previously had only theoretic value. Contained, perfect, finite and eternal, Aristotle's cosmos has always existed and will always exist, like the circular motion that had no beginning and will have no end.
(G.D.P.)

Bibliography: Gullini 1949, p. 137; Mansuelli 1961, p. 21, fig. 2; Richter 1965, p. 173, n. 9; Firenze 2004b, p. 221, n. 1.62; Firenze 2007b, p. 215.

II.2.8-9
Jan Brueghel the Younger (attr.)
Allegory of Earth and of Water
Allegory of Air and of Fire
Panel painting; 57 x 94 cm
Florence, Galleria degli Uffizi, inv. 1890
nos. 1223 and 1204

The theme of the four elements characterizes the production of Jan Brueghel the Elder in works conserved in the Louvre and in the Biblioteca Ambrosiana. The two paintings displayed here, attributed to his son, Brueghel the Younger (1601-1678), visualize the qualities of the four elements (water,earth,air,fire) according to classic iconography that draws inspiration from Aristotle's concept. The great Greek philosopher considered the four elements to be the fundamental components that, moving continuously and mixing together in infinitely different ways, shape the sublunar world (i.e. our planet) whereas the skies above the Moon was filled with another substance, the quintessence, or fifth element.
(P.G.)

Bibliography: Firenze 1977, p. 319.

II.2.10
Eudoxus' homocentric spheres
Demonstration model
Alloy steels, light alloys, brass, bronze, polycarbonates; diameter 100 cm, height 130 cm
Centro Studi per il Restauro e la Valorizzazione degli Orologi Antichi e Strumentaria, Istituto Statale di Istruzione Superiore 'L. da Vinci', Florence

The geometry of planetary models with homocentric spheres conceived by Eudoxus of Cnidus (c. 408-c. 355 B.C.) was reconstructed at the end of the nineteenth century by the Italian astronomer Giovanni Virginio Schiaparelli (1835-1910) on the basis of the few indications given by Aristotle (384-322 B.C.) and by Simplicius (6th century). This exhibit constitutes the first complete and functioning mechanical reproduction of an Eudoxean planetary model. It shows the motion of Jupiter against the background of the sphere of fixed stars. The motion is controlled by a sphere for the mean motion of revolution, that completes a full revolution in about twelve years, and by two more internal spheres for anomalous motion, that complete their revolutions, moving in opposite directions, in about a year. Periodically, the combination of movements makes the planet, in comparison to the Zodiac, seem to stop, reverse its motion, stop again, and finally, resume its initial direct motion. In the model, each sphere is stylized by a pair of rings, one perpendicular to the other.
(G.S.)

Bibliography: Schiaparelli 1997, v. 2, pp. 5-93; Dreyer 1970, pp. 78-97; Neugebauer 1975a, pp. 675-685; Hoskin 1999, pp. 29-33; Linton 2004, pp. 25-32; North 2008, pp. 73-79.

II.3.1
The precession of the equinoxes
Demonstration model
Steel, wood; 270 x 120 cm
Opera Laboratori Fiorentini

The phenomenon of the precession of the equinoxes was determined by Hipparchus of Nicaea (2nd century B.C.) by comparing his own measurements of the stellar coordinates with those of some of his predecessors. Within the overall framework of geocentric astronomy the precession was interpreted as a very slow rotation from west to east of the entire crystalline sphere of the fixed stars around the poles of the maximum circumference at the centre of the Zodiac, that is, the ecliptic. This phenomenon caused the points of intersection between the ecliptic and the celestial equator (the equinoxes) to shift very gradually forward with respect to the signs of the zodiac. In the same way the celestial North Pole, the point round which the whole celestial sphere seems to turn in 24 hours, appeared over the course of centuries to shift with respect to the stars. From the heliocentric point of view the same phenomenon is explained by the change of direction of the earth's axis, which over a period of 26,000 years describes a right circular cone.
(G.S.)

Bibliography: Dreyer 1970, pp. 185; Hoskin 1999, p. 39; North 2008, pp. 99-100.

II.4.1
Aratus of Soli
Phaenomena
9th century
Latin codex membranaceous; 32 x 28 cm
London, The British Library, Harley MS 647, fols. 3v-4r

A spectacular Carolingian manuscript, already in the possession of the Abbey of St Augustine at Canterbury in the 10th century. It contains the oldest surviving exemplar of Cicero's Latin translation of the *Phaenomena* of Aratus (c. 315-240 B.C.). The translation of Aratus' poem, depending on a lost late antique source, occupies the lower half of each page, while the upper part is filled with an enchanting depiction of a constellation (there are twenty-two in all). In the border of the depiction are extracts from the *Astronomica* of Hyginus, a treatise on the myths of the constellations. Folios 3v-4r show the constellations of Perseus and Pisces.
(P.G.)

Bibliography: Murdoch 1984, p. 251; Pattie 1980, p. 22; Whitfield 1995, p. 35.

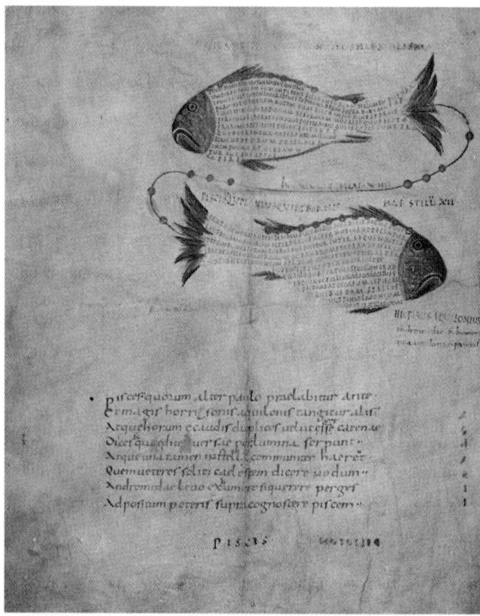

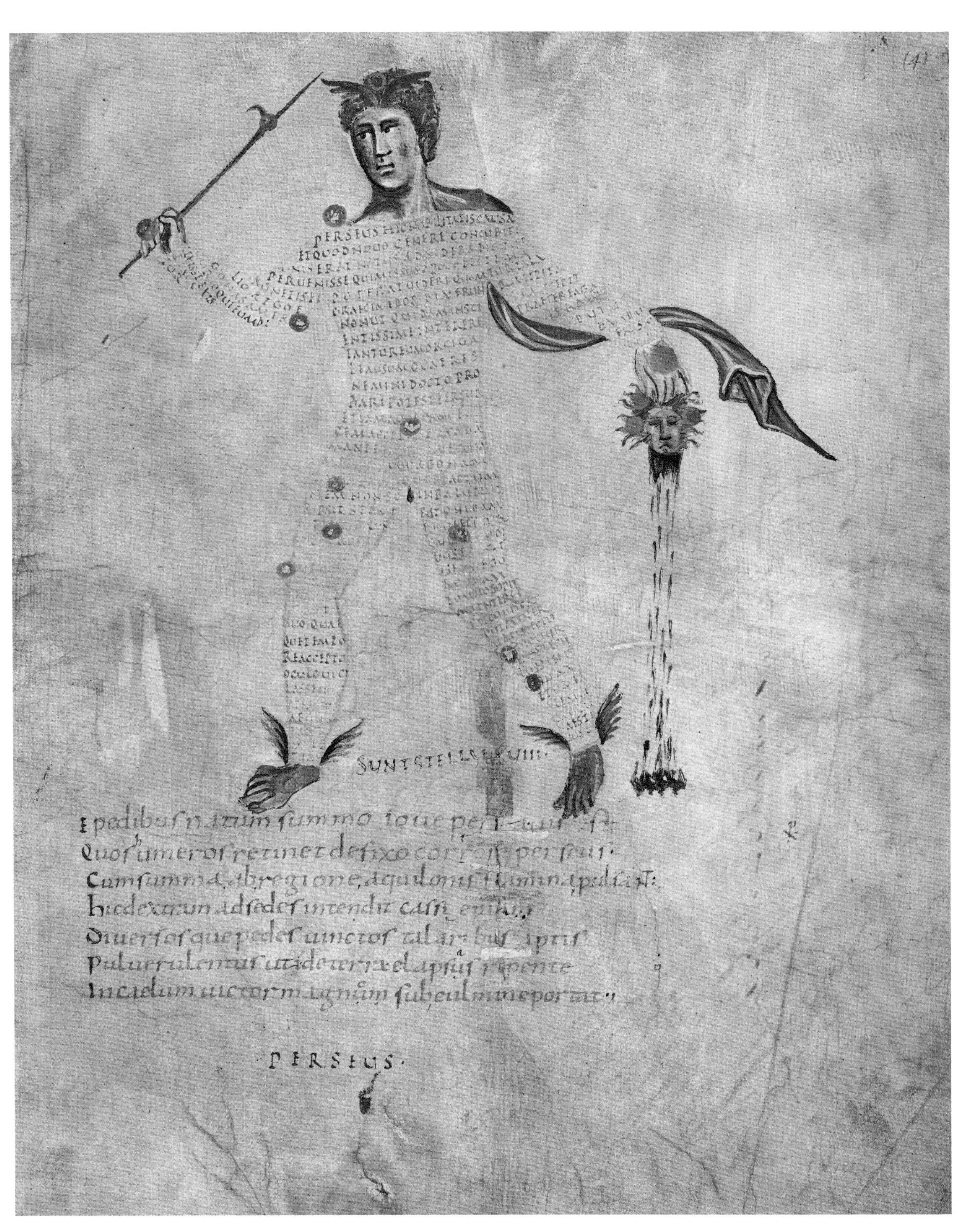

pedibus natum summo ioue per
Quos umeros retinet defixo
Cum summa ab regione aquilonis
hic dextram ad sedes intendit
Diuersosque pedes uinctos talar
Puluerulentus uti de terris lapsus
In caelum uictor magnum sub culmine portat
PERSIUS

II.4.2
Anonymous
Celestial globe
2nd century B.C.- 1st century A.D.
Silver; diameter 6.3 cm
Paris, Kugel Collection

On the surface of the globe, of unknown origins, the personifications of constellations are represented, distributed with some imprecision in regards to the knowledge of the times. Nevertheless, the positions of the constellations suggest the knowledge, on the artist's part, of Eratosthenes' *Catasterismi* and of their iconographic tradition in Hyginus, as well as the works of Hipparcus. Besides, it can be seen that the constellations are not depicted according to the prospective of an observer outside the celestial sphere, as was usual, but as seen from inside the sphere.

Small spheres in bronze and silver were considered precious gifts, as indicated in a passage from the *Palatine Anthology* (9, 355) in which the gift is mentioned of a *ouranion mimèma*, 'an imitation of the skies', received by Poppaea for her birthday.
(G.D.P.)

Bibliography: Cuvigny 2002; Cuvigny 2004.

II.4.3
The Antikythera Mechanism
Bronze, maple-wood; 33.3 x 22.5 x 12.4 cm
Model by M.T. Wright, London

The original fragmentary Hellenistic artefact, recovered from a shipwreck dateable to about 70 B.C. and probably made some decades earlier, is the oldest elaborate astronomical instrument, intended for computation or demonstration. This reconstruction is based on Wright's examination of the original (Wright 2007), but incorporates the results of further research by others (Freeth et al. 2006, 2008).
The inner ring of the front dial represents the Zodiac, divided into 360 degrees and with the Zodiacal constellations named. Small letters correspond to a list of annual astronomical events which survives only in part on a detached plate and cannot be restored. The outer ring represents a year of 365 days: twelve named months of 30 days and five extra days. In this, the Egyptian calendar, the dates of the solstices and equinox were reckoned to change by one day every four years, corresponding to a year-length of $365\frac{1}{4}$ days; so the calendar ring is moveable.
Hands show the date and the places of the Moon and the Sun; and a small rotating ball within the Moon hand, half black and half white, displays the phase of the Moon. This much is certain. The date hand shows the place of the mean Sun, but since the motion of the Moon hand was modified by a single anomaly, as in the lunar theory of Hipparchus, probably there was a separate Sun hand with a similarly modified motion, as seen here. Epicyclic mechanism, mostly lost, realized a single-anomaly theory of the place of at least one planet. The model illustrates a conjectural restoration, with hands for the five planets then known, all worked in the same way (Wright 2003).
On the back two spiral displays, both divided into long sequences of synodic months, offer supplementary information. Sliding indicators on the hands, guided by tongues running in spiral slots, show which turn of each scale must be read. The upper display represents the Metonic calendrical period; 235 named months, taken to equal 19 years, are laid out in five turns so as to show which months should have 29 days instead of 30, and which years should have 13 months instead of 12. A subsidiary dial to the right shows a four-year cycle of several Panhellenic games. A second subsidiary dial to the left, restored conjecturally, displays the 76-year Callippic period which is cited on a detached fragment.
The lower spiral represents the Saros period of 223 synodic months, after which the pattern of eclipse-possibilities is repeated. Possible lunar and solar eclipses are identified, together with the expected times of day. (The sequence cannot be fully restored.) The whole pattern falls about one-third of a day later in each successive cycle, and the subsidiary dial indicates corrections in hours to be added to the eclipse-times in each cycle.
Separate bronze plates (not shown) covered both dials. Surviving fragments suggest that they were inscribed with information about the displays and perhaps notes on working the instrument.
(M.T.W.)

Bibliography: Wright 2003; Freeth et al. 2006; Freeth *et al*. 2008; Wright 2007.

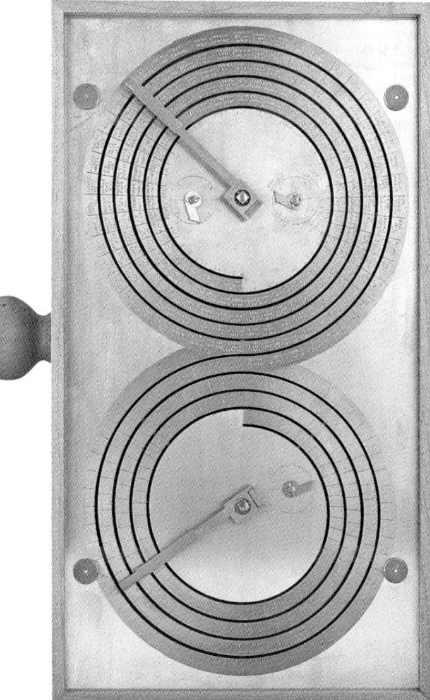

III.1.1
Cygnus
1st century A.D.
Fresco; 39 x 27.5 cm
Soprintendenza Speciale per i Beni Archeologici di Napoli e Pompei, inv. 8560

The constellation of Cygnus (the Swan) represents the only animal into which Jove transformed himself to seduce Leda, wife of King Tindareus of Sparta. Later, Leda lays an egg from which Helen of Troy and the twins Castor e Pollux were born. Hyginus, though he knows this famous episode, prefers instead to match the constellation of Cygnus to the story, similar, of Zeus' love for Nemesis (2, 8). The swan is portrayed on a dark red background, with outspread wings and neck bowed, on a flowering bough. The fragment of fresco, of unknown origins (Vesuvian area), was part of a larger, decorative Fourth Style mural painting.
(E.D.C.)

Bibliography: Inedited.

III.1.2
Europe on the bull
1st century A.D.
Fresco; 69 x 76 cm
Soprintendenza Speciale per i Beni Archeologici di Napoli e Pompei, inv. 9900

'The Bull (Taurus) was put in the sky, it is said, because it carried Europe safely to Crete', thus Hyginus begins the story of the event originating this constellation (2, 21). This panel is composed of many fresco fragments, belonging to a single black background wall decoration of the Fourth Style found in 1749, probably in Pompeii in the so-called Villa of Cicero. The middle fragment portrays the episode of the abduction of Europe by Jove, disguised as a bull, while he carries her to Crete over the sea's waves. In this case, the representation of the bull differs from that of traditional iconography for the fish-tail shape that the rear part of his body assumes. The constellation is constituted of only the front part of the animal; Hyginus, in fact, referring that the event giving origin to everything could also be that, almost parallel, of the abduction of Io by Zeus, states (2, 21): 'Jove tried to repay Io, when he transformed her into a heifer, placing her body among the stars so that the front part rests visible, like that of a bull, and the rest remains in the shadows'.
(E.D.C.)

Bibliography: Inedited.

III.1.3
Centaur
1st century A.D.
Fresco; 23 x 26 cm
Soprintendenza Speciale per i Beni Archeologici di Napoli e Pompei, inv. 9132

According to Hyginus, the constellation of Sagittarius (2, 27) is represented by a centaur, that he identifies with the satyr Crotos, nurse of the Muses on Mount Helicon, transformed by Jove and placed among the stars in such a way as to unite all his activities in a single image: besides the tail of the Satyr, the legs of a horse for his skill in riding and the arrow for his precision in hunting.
In this fresco found in Herculaneum, the young Centaur is portrayed in the act of drinking from a goblet in a large basin placed on a column-shaped altar. With his right arm he grasps a goblet while with the left he supports a cornucopia. The representation, typical of the Fourth Style, constitutes a very frequent motif in Roman painting, in particular as a vignette in the decorative architectural panels in the middle and higher areas of the wall.
(E.D.C.)

Bibliography: Inedited.

III.1.4
Capricorn
1st century A.D.
Fresco; 53 x 104.5 cm
Soprintendenza Speciale per i Beni Archeologici di Napoli e Pompei, inv. 8868

The Capricorn (*Capricornus*), characterized by the horns, by the beard and by the fish-tail, is portrayed between two Sea-centaurs on a black background and was probably part of the base of a Fourth Style wall decoration (Herculaneum, unknown provenance). Even in this case, as for the Dolphin (*Delphinus*), the Swan (*Cygnus*), the Crown (*Corona*) and Pegasus, the representation of the constellations in wall painting of the 1st century A.D. is not found as a composition illustrating the most important moment of the myth, but as a simple, secondary decorative motif. The Capricorn is identified with Pan and the particular aspect of the constellation, with its upper body in the form of a goat and the lower body of a fish with a sinuous tail and is connected with an episode of the battle between the Titans and the Gods: to escapes the sudden arrival of Typhon during a gathering, the gods transformed themselves into animals and Pan threw himself in a river, the lower part of his body taking on the form of a fish.
(E.D.C.)

Bibliography: Inedited.

III.1.5
Pegasus
1st century A.D.
Fresco; 41 x 19 cm
Soprintendenza Speciale per i Beni Archeologici di Napoli e Pompei, inv. 8781

Hyginus relates the version according to which the constellation of the Horse 'for Aratus and for many others is Pegasus, son of Neptune and of the Gorgon Medusa' (2, 18). Pegasus is linked to the myth of Bellerophon who, after having killed the monstrous Chimera, in the attempt to fly even higher in the sky, looked down at the earth, became frightened for the height, fell and died. The horse, instead, continued his flight and was changed by Jove into a constellation. His whole body does not appear among the stars, but only the front half without the wings. This painted panel (Herculaneum, unknown provenance) is formed by two fragments of fresco, each portraying Pegasus, the winged horse, in flight. The figures have been detached from Fourth Style white background wall decorations and probably constitute the centre vignette of two panels from the middle zone of the wall.
(E.D.C.)

Bibliography: Inedited.

III.1.6
Ceres as Dapifer
First quarter of the 4th century A.D.
Fresco; 53 x 73 cm
Soprintendenza Speciale per i Beni Archeologici di Napoli e Pompei, inv. 84286

In the 1st century A.D., the passion for astrology breaks out in Rome as well as in its surrounding areas. It also finds expression in art, that echoes the extraordinary success of the Latin version of the genre of the *Catasterismi*, the literature of Alexandrian origin that, spread through Rome mainly thanks to the works of Hyginus, told the stories of the celestial myths.

This fresco portrays Ceres, who Hyginus, even admitting a variety of interpretations, proposes to identify with the constellation of the Virgin (*Virgo*), describing her in movement, covered by a long robe and bearing a sheaf of wheat (2, 25). The figure, of which only the upper part remains, carries a tray with a container surrounded by sheaves of wheat. Originally, the pictorial cycle was made up of a procession of servants bearing food and drink to the *dominus* for a banquet. The offering of the sheaves of wheat can be interpreted as an auspicious reference to the abundance that, associated to the evidently feminine traits of the face, identify the painting as a distant remembrance of a symbolic representation of Ceres personified in the figure of the servant. The fresco was found in 1783, together with six others, in an aristocratic *domus* of late-antiquity near the Lateran in Rome.
(E.D.C.)

Bibliography: Roma 2000, pp. 454-455.

III.1.7
Roman celestial globe
Replica of the original
Plaster; diameter 11 cm
Mainz, Römisch-Germanisches Zentralmuseum, inv. 42695D

The celestial globe shows the forty-eight constellations known to the ancients: the oldest, the representation of the Milky Way, is of great importance. Despite the reduced dimensions, the sphere presents the circles of the solstices and of the equinoxes, and the position of the constellations is very meticulous. Although the context of its finding is not known, on the basis of confrontations with the other known spheres this globe is attributed to the Imperial era, in a period between 150 and 220 A.D. Presumably manufactured in Egypt or in the eastern part of the Empire, it has a hole; therefore it must have crowned a sundial or, considering its small size, an imperial sceptre. Among the constellations, Libra, that closed the zodiac, is not depicted.
(G.D.P.)

Bibliography: Künzl 1998.

III.1.8a
Anonymous
Farnese Atlas
c. 2nd century A.D.
White marble; height 164 cm
Naples, Museo Archeologico Nazionale, inv. 6374

III.1.8b
Cast of the sphere of the Farnese Atlas
c. 1930
Alabastrine plaster ; height 75 cm, diameter 65 cm
Rome, Museo della Civiltà Romana, inv. M.C.R. 2896

The statue, presumably brought to Rome in the times of Antoninus Pius (2nd century A.D.), is a document of exceptional importance for approaching the astronomical knowledge of ancient times. It is, in fact, the oldest and most comprehensive representation of the sky, a perfect synthesis of the relations between art and science. Having become part of the Farnese collection in1562, the sculpture portrays Atlas almost kneeling under the weight he must sustain, the great celestial globe on which the principal circles and the personifications of the constellations are represented. In fact, the celestial equator, the elliptic with the belt of the zodiac, the Arctic and Antarctic circles, the colures and the constellations (19 northern, 14 southern) and the twelve signs of the zodiac are represented in light relief. Compared to the star catalogue by Claudius Ptolemy, this sphere lacks the constellations of the Equuleus and of the Triangulum. The upper part of the globe, damaged, impairs the view of Ursa Minor and part of Ursa Major. The position of the constellations on the sphere reveals the knowledge, on the part of the author of the sculpture, of the phenomenon of the precession of the equinoxes discovered by Hipparchus of Nicaea around mid-first century B.C. and later described and measured by Claudius Ptolemy in the second century A.D. It is therefore justifiable to see in Hipparchus the source that has guided the work of this unknown sculptor, who presumably followed the stellar catalogue by the Nicean astronomer. Finally, the position of the constellations shows the work's place of production, located between 33° and 34° latitude north, corresponding to central Phoenicia.
At the centre of considerable interest on the part of naturalists, astronomers and mathematicians, the sphere of the Farnese Atlas was described by Ulisse Aldrovandi in 1550, by Francesco Bianchini and by Cassini near the end of the 1600's, and by Martin Folkes, member of the Royal Society, in the first half of the 1700's. It was Folkes who, in 1733, had a plaster copy of the sphere made. From this copy, today lost, the Sloane Sphere of the British Library was taken.
(G.D.P.)

Bibliography: Passeri 1750; Bianchini 1752; *Museo della civiltà romana* 1982, p. 570, n. 7; De Caro 1994, p. 330; Schaffer 2005; Valerio 2005, pp. 233-239.

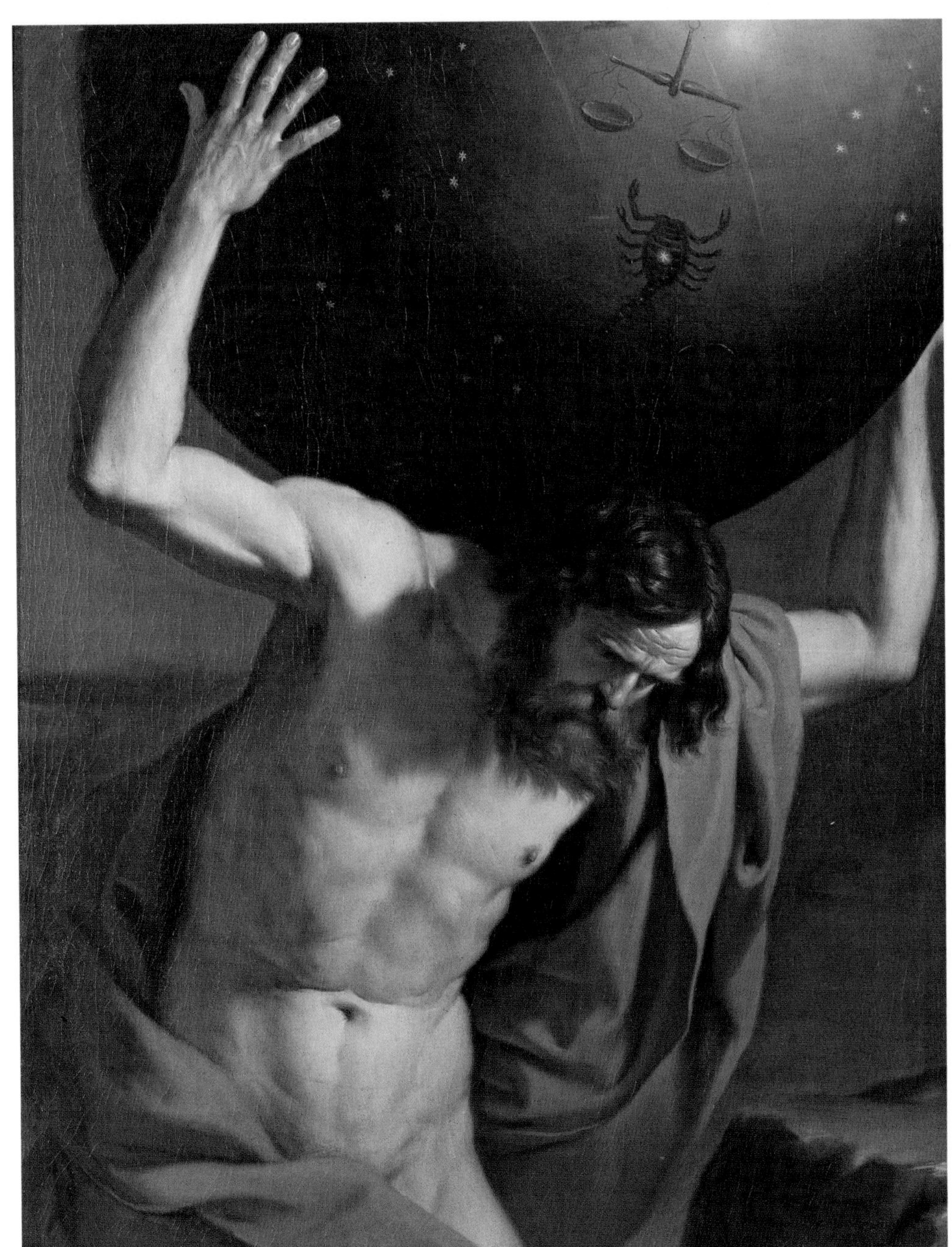

III.1.8c
Giovanni Francesco Barbieri
known as il Guercino
Atlas
1646
Oil on canvas; 127 x 101 cm
Florence, Museo Mozzi Bardini

The myth of Atlas condemned by Zeus to support the celestial vault for all eternity was a fairly popular subject for painting in the 17th century. One of the most famous of such works is this version painted by Guercino (1591-1666) for Don Lorenzo de' Medici in 1646. A commission, therefore, which shows the Medici's interest in astronomy. The canvas, in the past mistakenly considered a *pendant* of the *Hercules*, which also came from the Capponi Collection and was transferred to that of the antiquarian Stefano Bardini, shows Atlas supporting the sphere of the stars, marked by the ecliptic with the zodiacal constellations of Libra and Scorpio. With the exception of Antares, the heart of Scorpio, all the stars on the sphere appear to be distributed at random.

Bibliography: Salerno 1988, pp. 304-305, n. 230; Bologna 1991, pp. 280-282, n. 103; Carofano in Forte di Bard 2007, pp. 197-199 (with bibliography).

III.1.9
Gaius Julius Hyginus
Astronomical poetics
Second half of the 15th century
Membrane manuscript, fols. III, 169, I'; 25.5 x 17.5 cm
Florence, Biblioteca Medicea Laurenziana, Plut. 89 sup. 43, fols. 85v-86r

Gaius Julius Hyginus (1st century A.D.) was librarian to the emperor Augustus. A friend of scholars and poets, he composed a work of astronomy with the scope, declared, of making more comprehensible the *Phaenomena* by Aratus. The treatise, dedicated to non-expert readers, deals with the basis elements of ancient astronomy. In the chapters of the work that met with greater success, the second and the third, returning to the literary genre of the catasterismi, the Alexandrian literature of astral myths that was having so much success even in Rome, Hyginus narrates the celestial legends that describe their protagonists' ascension to the skies. Following the traditional order, starting from the Arctic circle to the Antarctic circle, the author, in the third book, describes the number of stars in every single constellation, justifying the form and facilitating their recognition even on a sphere that reproduces the celestial vault, that he considers a fundamental instrument for specifying the structure of the asterisms and for drawing their appearance.
The signs of Sagittarius and Capricorn are represented in the displayed images.
The Laurentian manuscript, that also contains the *Poetic Astronomy* by Hyginus (not complete), explains the success of this text through history. An abundant tradition of codices, from the ninth century on, confirms this fact; importance is also given to the presence of the treatise in the incunabulum and printed editions, starting with that of Carnerius realized in Ferrara in 1475.
(G.D.P.)

Bibliography: *Catalogus codicum manuscriptorum BML* 1774-1778, vol. III, coll. 310-311; Firenze 2007a, pp. 18-19, n. 5.

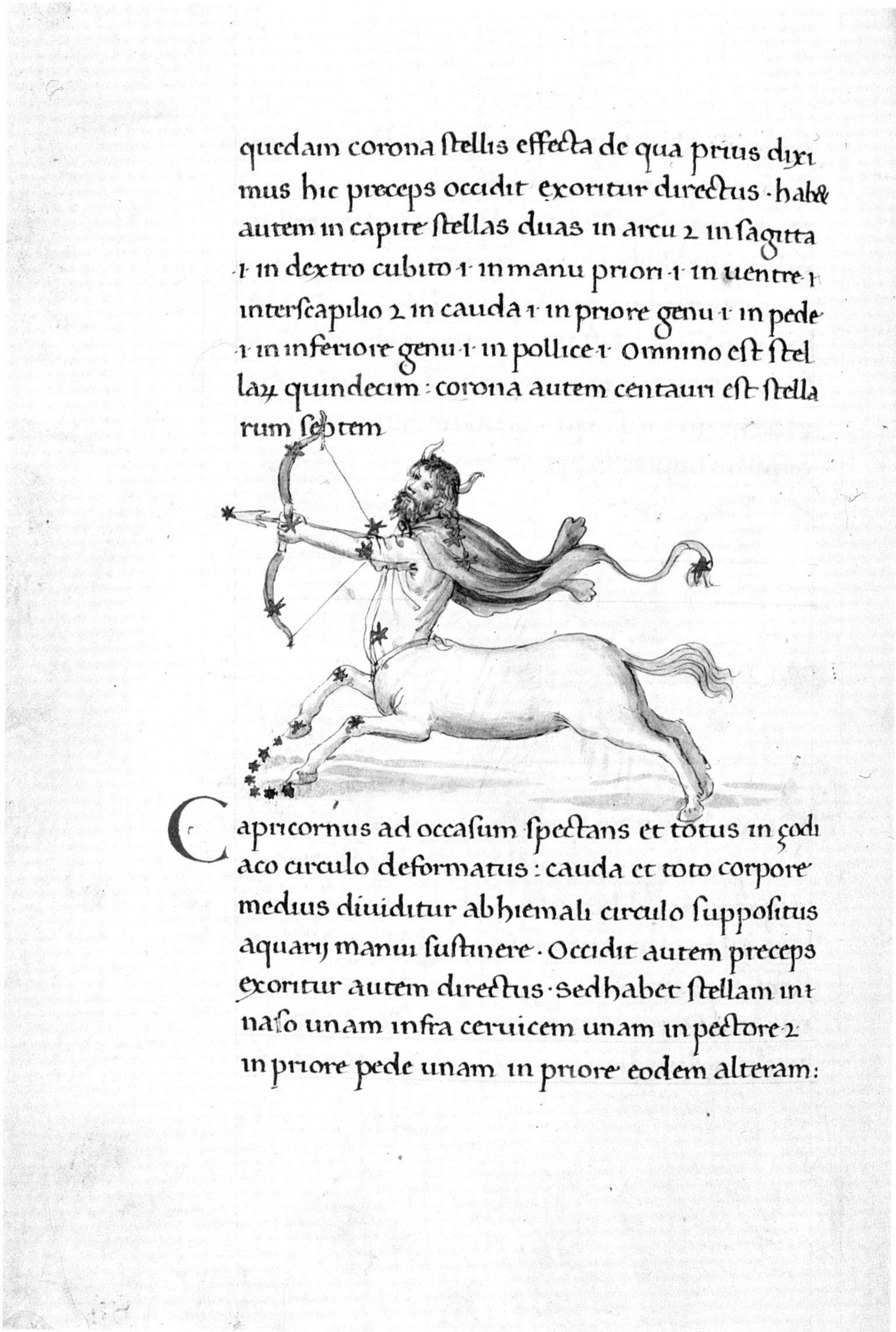
quedam corona stellis effecta de qua prius dixi
mus hic preceps occidit exoritur directus · habet
autem in capite stellas duas in arcu 2 in sagitta
1 in dextro cubito 1 in manu priori 1 in uentre 1
interscapilio 2 in cauda 1 in priore genu 1 in pede
1 in inferiore genu 1 in pollice 1 omnino est stel
larum quindecim : corona autem centauri est stella
rum septem

Capricornus ad occasum spectans et totus in zodi
aco circulo deformatus : cauda et toto corpore
medius diuiditur ab hiemali circulo suppositus
aquarij manui sustinere · Occidit autem preceps
exoritur autem directus · sed habet stellam in t
naso unam infra ceruicem unam in pectore 2
in priore pede unam in priore eodem alteram:

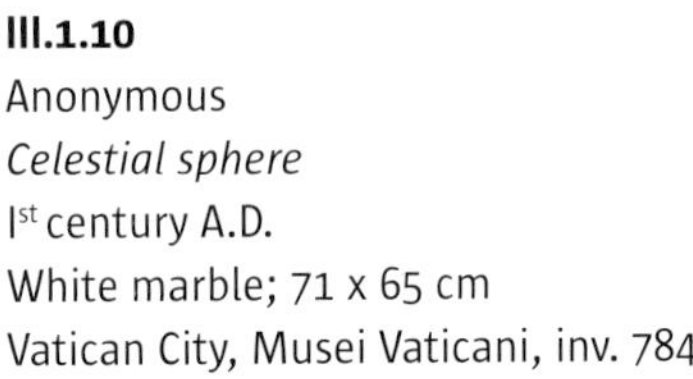

III.1.10
Anonymous
Celestial sphere
I[st] century A.D.
White marble; 71 x 65 cm
Vatican City, Musei Vaticani, inv. 784

Of unknown origins, the large sphere is crossed by the belt of the zodiac, sculpted in light relief, containing the signs relative to the twelve constellations. On its surface, scattered without any apparent order, a series of stars. Probably this globe was designed to be observed only from the front.
(G.D.P.)

Bibliography: Visconti 1835; Denza 1894; Tabarroni 1955.

III.1.11
Apollo-Helios with sphere
1st century A.D.
Fresco; 81 x 58 cm
Soprintendenza Speciale per i Beni Archeologici di Napoli e Pompei, inv. 8819

The fresco, found in 1830 in Pompeii (*Casa dell'Argenteria*, VI,7,20.22, atrium, south wall), portrays Apollo-*Helios* with his mantle fastened around his neck, his head radiate and surrounded by a halo. With his left arm he supports a sphere, while with his right arm he grasps a whip, referring to his activity as guardian of the herds of Admetus, recalled in literary accounts. Since the 5th century B.C., Apollo has been identified with the god of the Sun, thus replacing *Helios* as bearer of light and charioteer of the quadriga that pulled the Sun through the sky every day. In the first Imperial Age this assimilation became stronger with the institution of the cult of Apollo Palatine, and then, from the second half of the 2nd century A.D., blended with the solar divinities of Eastern origin, such as Mithra and Elagabal of Emesa. The presence of the sphere refers to the aspect of Apollo-*Helios* as responsible for the movement of the stars and heart of the cosmos, arbiter of human destinies and model of regality (LIMC IV, 1, pp. 592-595, 599-601; IV, 2, pp. 366-385, nn. 47-460, in particular p. 369, n. 90). In Pompeii there are some significant images of Apollo-*Helios*, not of a full figure but just of the bust, in the bedroom of the House of the Wild Boar (*Casa della Caccia Antica*) and in the Felter's Shop (*Officina coactilaria*) IX,7,1-2 of *Via dell'Abbondanza*, where it is depicted on the facade together with the busts of Jupiter, Mercury and Artemis (*Pompei* 1997, VII, p. 16, n. 14; *Pompei* 1999, IX, p. 770, n. 2). With the vignette of Apollo-*Helios*, another depicting the personification of Autumn was found (but no longer preserved), permitting us to hypothesize that in the same room there were also portrayals of Spring, Summer and Winter, creating a single pictorial cycle that drew inspiration from the passage by Ovid with the description of the heavenly palace where the god sat in his throne among the Seasons (*Met.* II, 1-30).
(E.D.C.)

Bibliography: *Collezioni MANN* 1986, p. 158, n. 257; *Pompei* 1993, IV, p. 450, n. 2.

III.2. BIANCHINI'S PLANISPHERE

III.2.1
Anonymous
Bianchini Planisphere
2nd century A.D.
Marble; 78.5 x 78 cm
Paris, Musée du Louvre, inv. Ma 540

Found on the Aventine Hill in 1705, already in a fragmentary state, this slab was given to the French Academy at Rome by the astronomer Francesco Bianchini. It is an astrological table composed of a few fragments of the original planisphere dating back to the 2nd or 3rd century A.D. that incorporates the so-called 'Barbarian Sphere', the representation, that is, of the Greek, Egyptian and Mesopotamic constellations. The centre of the system is on the pole of the elliptic, a consequence of the knowledge of the phenomenon of the precession of the equinoxes. Four concentric bands and an external ring with figures are seen there, in the centre of it all there are the constellations of Ursa Major and Ursa Minor and Draco. In the first circle, images of the Caldean zodiac are found; in the second and third bands there are two identical Greek zodiacs representing, presumably, the fixed ecliptic and the mobile one according to Ptolemy's distinction. A part follows with numbers that indicate the influences of the planets on the single signs of the zodiac, while the figures in the fourth belt represent Egyptian decans, each with his own name. On the outer circle there are the faces of the Greek decans or, as some hold, of the personifications of the seven planetary divinities. The lines that go from the centre to the outer margin of the circle divide the surface into twelve sectors, while at the four corners there are the heads of the principal winds.
The definition of 'Barbarian Sphere' indicated a map of the sky, foreign in respect to the Hellenic cultural environment. This is in contrast with the Graecanic sphere, that is, the celestial globes with the constellations known in the Greek, Hellenistic and Roman cultural environment, consequent to the diffusion of the texts of Eudoxus and Aratus. It is possible that the Latin scholar Nigidius Figulus (1st century B.C.) dedicated a work to both these spheres, even Teucros the Babilonian wrote a text dedicated to the Barbarian Sphere (1st century B.C.): his work was crucial, in particular, for the diffusion of the knowledge of the system of the decans (the division of the zodiac and of the celestial vault into thirty-six decans, three for each sign of the zodiac).
(G.D.P.)

Bibliography: *Histoire de l'Académie Royale* 1708, pp. 110-111; Dupuis 1795; Boll 1903.

III.3. PTOLEMY: THE GEOMETRY OF THE SPHERES

III.3.1
Ptolemy's parallactic instrument
Scale model
Wood, steel; 150 x 150 x 150 cm
Opera Laboratori Fiorentini

For making precise measurements, Claudius Ptolemaeus (2nd century A.D.) devised an instrument large in size but simple and solid in structure. In his *Mathematical Composition* or *Almagest*, he describes it as three wooden rulers four cubits in length (about 150 cm) attached together. The vertical ruler was graduated in 60 parts and their fractions. In the upper swivelling ruler were two pinholes through which to view the Moon. Finally, the lower swivelling ruler served to determine the angle of the upper ruler with respect to the upright one. Ptolemy used the instrument to find the lunar parallax by taking two measurements of the angular distance from the zenith on particular occasions, and thus to determine the distance of the Moon from the Earth. Ptolemy's earliest commentators, Pappus and Theon (both of Alexandria and 4th-century A.D.) found it more practical to move the graduated scale from the vertical ruler to the lower swivelling ruler.
(G.S.)

Bibliography: Ptolemy, *Almagest*, V, 14; Del Santo-Strano 2004, p. 95; Strano 2007b, pp. 87-88

III.3.2
Claudius Ptolemy
Almagest
Early 14th century
MS on parchment, sheets IV, 337, III';
41 x 29 cm
Florence, Biblioteca Medicea Laurenziana,
Plut. 28.1, fols. 74v-75r

Ptolemy's *Mathematical* or *Great Composition* (2nd century A.D.) – better known as the *Almegest*, from the title *Al-Megisti* (= The Great) conferred on it by the Islamic astronomers – sums up all the geocentric astronomical notions arrived at in the Hellenistic world. In its thirteen Books the work in fact refines the geometrical models as conceived by Apollonius of Perga (3rd century B.C.) and Hipparchus of Nicaea (2nd century B.C.), which were based essentially on an eccentric circumference and an epicycle, and proved capable of providing an exact picture of the positions of the planets along the Zodiac. In addition to the *Almagest* this Greek manuscript contains an introduction to the first Book attributed to Eustochius of Ashkelon (5th century A.D.) and the commentary of Theon of Alexandria (4th century A.D.) on the first two Books. It also contains some minor works of Ptolemy's and extracts from the *Elements* of Euclid (4th century B.C.). The manuscript, which belonged to the Byzantine statesman Demetrius Cydones – who probably annotated it – belonged to the Medici library.
On fols. 74v-75r, epicycles and eccentrics.
(S.B.&G.S)

Bibliography: *Catalogus codicum manuscriptorum BML* 1764-1770, Vol. II, col. 9-12; Ptolemy 1984b, pp. 1-6; Fryde 1996, Vol. II, pp. 436-439 and pp. 773-774; Jackson 1998, pp. 199-204.

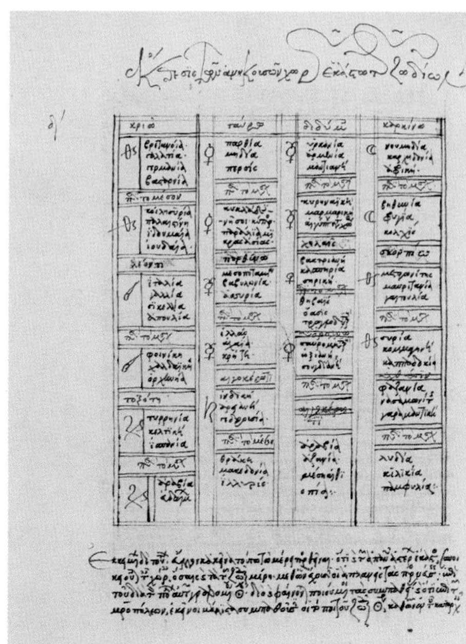

III.3.3
Claudius Ptolemy
Tetrabyblos
15th century
Parchment codex, fols. II, 72, I'; 28.5 x 21 cm
Florence, Biblioteca Medicea Laurenziana,
Plut. 28.43, fol. 16v

One of the main uses of astronomy in ancient times was for the prediction of the configurations of the stars and the planets with a view to formulating prognoses. Ptolemy, however, made a clear distinction between the mathematical aspects of predicting the positions of the celestial bodies, which he entrusted to the *Mathematical Composition* (cf. item III.3.2), and the rules of judicial astronomy, which he treats in the *Tetrabyblos* (= Four Books). The latter work contained tables for elementary calculations, information regarding the types of influence originating from each planet in its relation to its position in the Zodiac, and the different ways such influences act in the various regions of the Earth. This Greek manuscript combines the *Tetrabyblos* with the text of the *Hypotyposis astronomicarum positionum* of Proclus Diadochus (c. 410-485), in addition to astronomic tables. It may have been part of Lorenzo de' Medici's own library.
On fol. 16v, the table of the rising of the planets.
(S.B.&G.S)

Bibliography: *Catalogus codicum manuscriptorum BML* 1764-1770, Vol. II, col. 66; Müller 1884, p. 376; Feraboli 1985, pp. X-XVIII; Ptolemy 1998, p. XII.

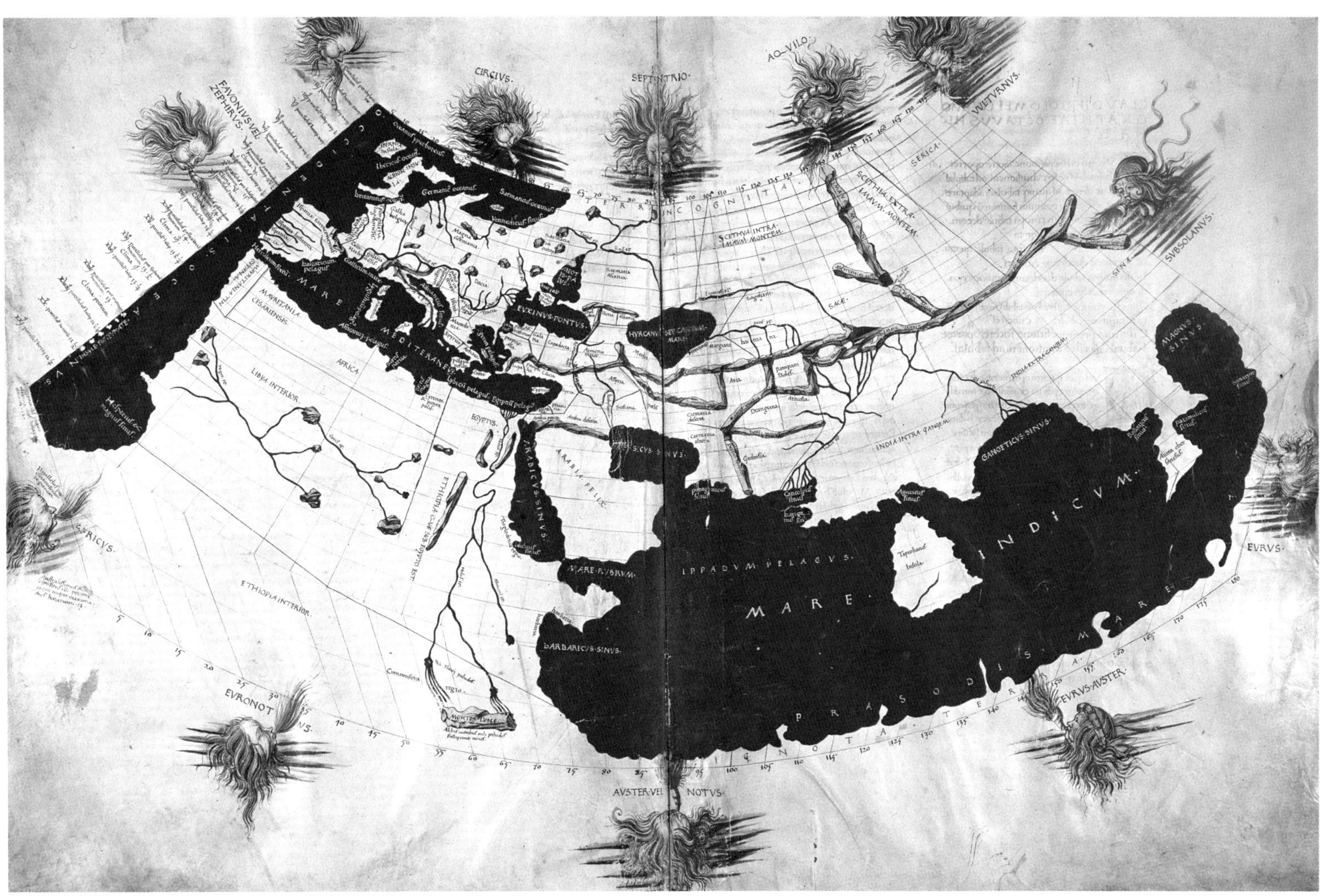

III.3.4
Piero del Massaio (attr.)
Ptolemei Cosmographie
c. 1455-1462
Codex membranaceus, fols. 117; leather binding, with Medici coat-of-arms and bronze cantonals (c. 1570); 66 x 42 cm
Florence, Biblioteca Medicea Laurenziana, Plut. 30.2, fols. 68v-69r

The codex contains the eight books of Ptolemy's *Geography* in the Latin translation by Jacopo Angeli da Scarperia. It belonged to Lorenzo di Pier Francesco de' Medici (fol. 117r) and later, to Cosimo I (fol. 1r). The text is accompanied by 27 tables attributed to Piero del Massaio (b. 1425), including a planisphere, 12 tables of Europe, 4 tables of Africa and 10 tables of Asia. The planisphere is drawn according to Ptolemy's first projection (book I, chapter 23), that considers a case of geometry similar to that of the sky maps, that is, the plane representation of a spherical surface. The terrestrial globe developed on a plane, within a grid formed by concentric circular arcs representing the parallels, and straight radial lines, representing the meridians. This grid, that maintains the distances between places unaltered, delimits the classic Ptolemaic oecumene, or rather, the known and inhabited part of the world: from 63° latitude north, in proximity to the island of Thule, to 16° south, in correspondence to the city of Meroe; and from meridian 0, passing through the Fortunate Isles (the present Canary Islands), to the meridian that marks 180° in correspondence with the Asian city of Kattigara. The systems of projection illustrated by Ptolemy will also have great importance in celestial cartography.
(F.C.)

Bibliography: *Catalogus codicum manuscriptorum BML* 1774-1778, II, col. 68; Ptolemy 1932, I, pp. 219, 409-414; II, tables IV.51-52; Gentile 1992, pp. 202-207, n. 101; Aujac 1994, pp. 187-204; Valerio 1995, 63-82; Ptolemy 2000; Gautier Dalché 2007, pp. 321-322; Cattaneo 2008.

III.3.5
Niccolò Germano
Geographia
Second half of the 15th century
Codex membranaceus, fols. 134, Medicean binding with chain; 43.5 x 39 cm
Florence, Biblioteca Medicea Laurenziana.
Plut. 30.3, fols. 75v-76r

Dedicated to Borso d'Este, the codex contains the second version of 'Nicholaus Germanus' edition of the eight books of Ptolemy's *Geography*. In respect to the previous version, that had 27 tables, here modern maps of Spain, of Italy and of Northern Europe have been added. The planisphere was drawn on the base of Ptolemy's second projection, also known as *homeoteric* projection (book I, chapter 24), that considers a geometric case similar to that in sky maps, that is, the plane representation of a spherical surface. The terrestrial globe developed on a plane inside a grid formed by concentric circular arcs representing the paralells, and curved 'radial' lines representing the meridians. The latter become progressively more curved as they move away from the centre, the only straight meridian, towards the extremities. According to Ptolemy, this projection was preferable to the first, because more suitable for expressing the spherical nature of the Earth.
The systems of projection illustrated by Ptolemy will also have great importance in celestial cartography.
(F.C.)

Bibliography: *Catalogus codicum manuscriptorum BML* 1774-1778, II, col.69-70; Ptolemy 1932, I, pp. 215-216, 315-356; II, table IV.24; Gentile 1992, pp. 207-212.

III.3.6
The epicyclic theory
Demonstration model
Alloy steel, light alloy, brass, bronze, polycarbonate; diamer 100 cm, height 105 cm
Centro Studi per il Restauro e la Valorizzazione degli Orologi Antichi e Strumentaria,
Istituto Statale di Istruzione Superiore
'L. da Vinci', Firenze

Claudius Ptolemy (2nd century A.D.) states in his *Great Composition* or *Almagest* that it was Apollonius of Perga (3rd century B.C.) who first designed a geometric model with two circles capable of explaining the motion of a planet along the Zodiac. This mechanical planetarium shows the motion of the two circles for Jupiter. The planet revolves uniformly along a small circle, the epicycle, which in turn revolves uniformly along a larger circle concentric to the Earth. In addition, the segment joining the planet to the centre of the epicycle always remains parallel to the segment joining the Sun to the Earth. The combination of these movements causes the planet periodically to halt with respect to the Zodiac, to turn back (at a maximum retrograde speed at the moment when it is closest to the Earth), halt again, and finally return to its initial forward motion.
(G.S.)

Bibliography: Ptolemy, *Almagest*, IX, 5 and XII, 1; Hoskin 1999, pp. 35-37; Del Santo-Strano 2004, p. 95; North 2008, pp. 92-94.

III.4.1
Cherub with sphere
1st century A.D.
Fresco; 37 x 24 cm
Soprintendenza Speciale per i Beni Archeologici di Napoli e Pompei, inv. 9237

The fresco, found in 1762 in Pompeii in the House VII, 6, 28, shows a Cupid with quiver, bow and, in his left hand, a sphere. On the basis of Vesuvian pictorial evidence it is unique. Considering that usually, in Roman painting, Cupids are secondary divinities depicted in the act of bearing the deities' characteristic objects, this fresco perhaps can be explained, given the important significance of the sphere compared to the secondary importance of the Cupid, by hypothesizing the presence, in the same room, of a central representation of Apollo-*Helios* with, to each side, the figures of the *Eroti* as bearers of the god's attributes.
(E.D.C.)

Bibliography: *Collezioni MANN* 1986, p. 154, n. 223.

III.4.2
Armillary sphere
1st century A.D.
Fresco; 197 x 210 cm
Soprintendenza Speciale per i Beni Archeologici di Napoli e Pompei, invv. 62525, 62464, 63718

The panel was part of the decoration of the ceiling of the arcade of the Villa San Marco in Castellammare di Stabia. In the centre of the panel, an armillary sphere is depicted, clearly showing the structure composed of intersecting circles, within a square frame. On the left there is a female figure next to a Cupid carrying a large sheaf of wheat, while in the centre there are the head crowned with vine-leaves and part of the body of another female figure. On the right there is another Cupid with a hare in his arms and a hand on his shoulder of another female figure, of whom only the arm and part of the cloak remain. The preserved figures, thanks to the presence of the attributes, are identified respectively with the personifications of Summer, Autumn and Winter, while Spring, which should have been on the lower part of the sphere, is missing. The central element of the fresco, a unique case in Vesuvian painting, is the armillary sphere, introduced by Eudoxus both as a teaching tool and for observation of the sky. The name derives from the Latin *armilla* (circle, bracelet), because the instrument presents a series of circles that connect the poles and represent the equator, the ecliptic, the meridians and the parallels. In this fresco, the two large intersecting circles represent the equinoctial colure and the equator.
(E.D.C.)

Bibliography: Elia 1957, pp. 26-29, graph B; Castellammare 2000, p. 116, n. 213.

III.4.3
Sundial
1st century A.D.
Marble; 34.5 x 19.5 cm
Soprintendenza Speciale per i Beni Archeologici di Napoli e Pompei, inv. 71257

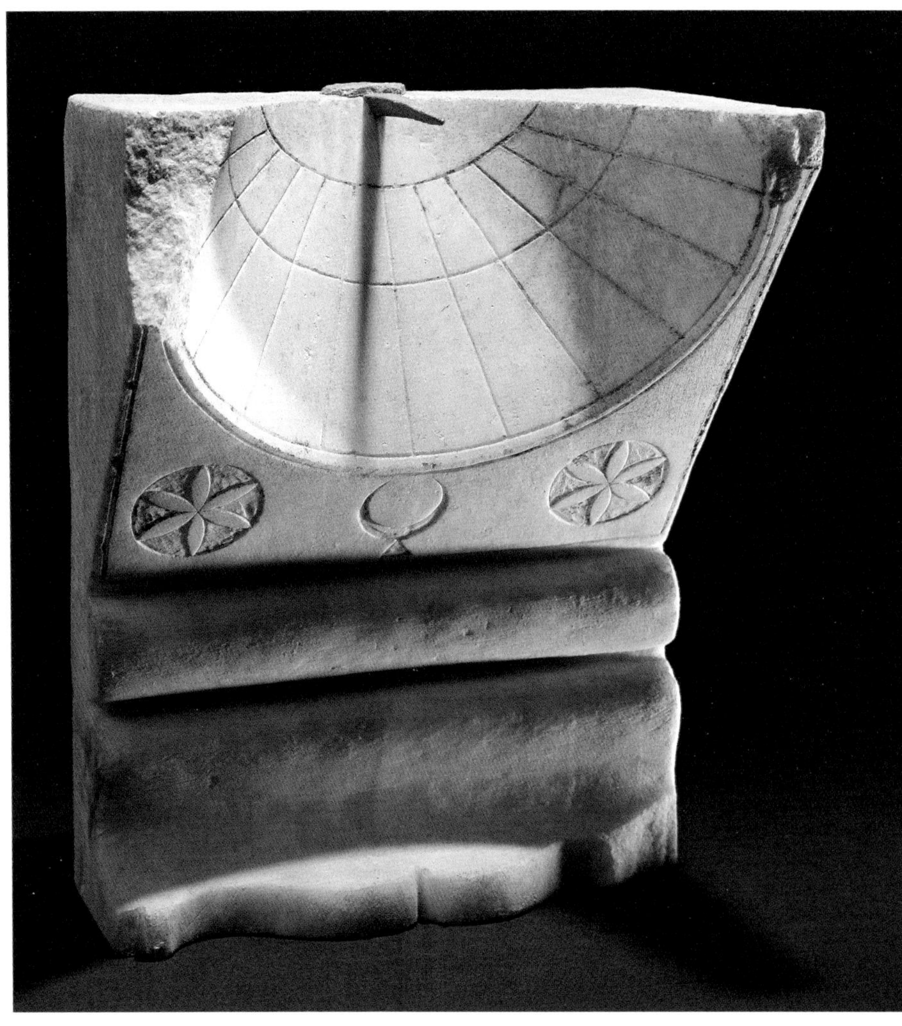

The sundial, found in the garden of the Villa A in Oplontis, is made of a style in bronze that projects its shadow on a hemispheric quadrant with engraved hour lines. The base presents a moulding decorated with a crescent moon between two rosettes. Of this common instrument, used in the ancient world to indicate the time of day, about thirty examples in marble or stucco-covered tuff have been found in the Vesuvian area, in the gardens of homes or of public buildings. Particular interest is due to a bone sundial in the shape of a small box, discovered in the so-called *Bottega di Verus* (I, 6, 3), together with an iron *groma*, which testifies to the existence of a portable version of this instrument (Napoli 1999, p. 243, n. 299). The meridians were used to measure time during the hours of day-light, variable according to the location or the period of the year. In fact, the length and the direction of the sun's shadow projected by the gnomon depend on three factors; the latitude of the locality, the day of the year and the time of the observation.
(E.D.C.)

Bibliography: Ferrara 1996, p. 269, n. 604.

III.4.4
Slab with signs of the zodiac and planets
c. 1930
Alabaster plaster cast; 26 x 28.5 cm
Rome, Museo della Civiltà Romana, inv. M.C.R. no. 2898

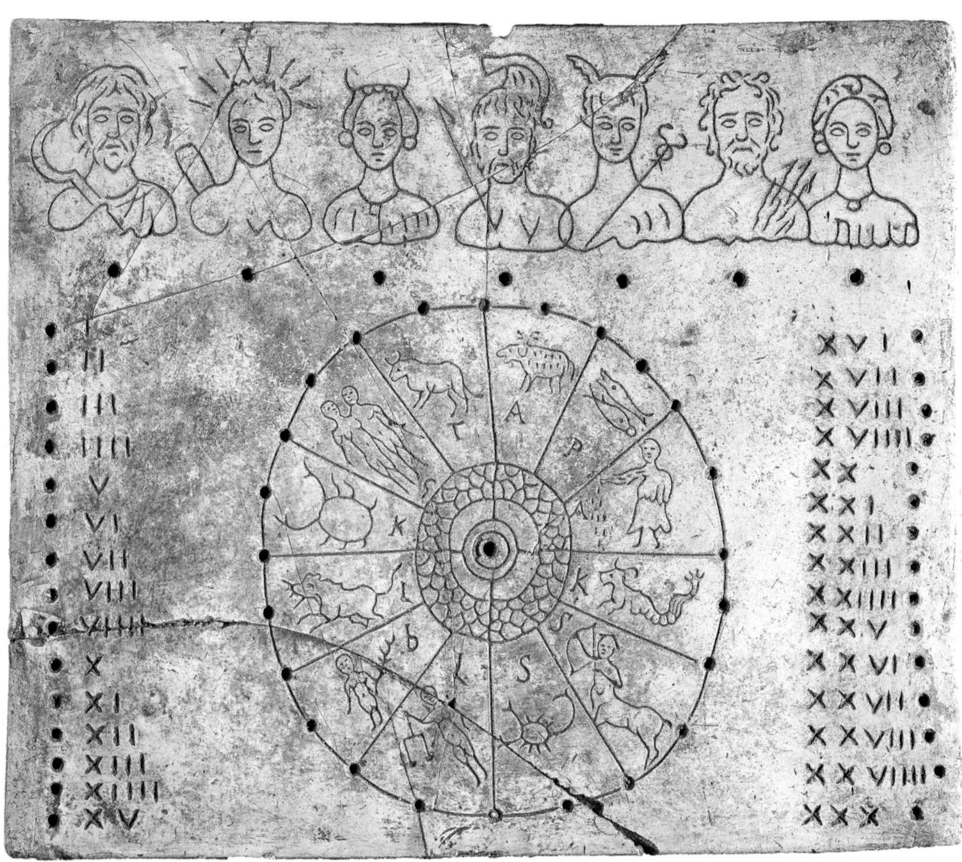

This slab is an interesting example of an astrological lunar calendar.
In the upper part are seven busts representing the heavenly bodies connected to the days of the week: Saturn, the Sun, the Moon, Mars, Mercury, Jupiter and Venus. Beneath each bust is a small hole. The central section of the slab is occupied by a circumference divided into 12 segments converging in a number of inscribed circles surrounding the pierced centre of the circumference. Within each segment there are a sign of the zodiac and the first letter of its Latin name. Round the large circumference are 24 small holes, two at the edges and one in the centre of each segment. At the sides of the slab are two series of numbers, respectively from 1 to 15 and from 16 to 30, corresponding to the same number of small holes along the outside edge. These make up an almanac, as seems to be confirmed by the numbering along the sides of the slab, marking the passing of days according to the synodic movement from one new moon to the next (about 29 1/2 days). The method of measuring time was derived from the one used by the Greeks, who alternated a month of 30 days with one of 29. The large central circle therefore marks the passage of the moon through the signs of the zodiac, while the 24 holes indicate the sidereal movement occurring in 27 days.
The use of two different pegs produced this computation by means of the 24 holes. The first peg marked the entry of the moon into the constellation of the moment, while the second, inserted into the sixth hole along, marked a quarter of the rotation of the moon. The first peg was then moved daily until it caught up with the second, at which point it could be inserted into the hole at the centre of the circumference. Here it remained for one day, after which it took the place of the second peg, which was then moved forward another six holes until another quarter was completed, and so on.
There is some controversy about the use of the holes beside the numbers I to XXX referring to the days of the month, whereas those situated under the busts representing the heavenly bodies were used to show the day of the week. The procedure described above was probably used also to assess the influence of the stars on various events in human life. There is evidence of the use of this type of calendar from the 1st century A.D. on.
The slab is taken from a terracotta copy preserved in the von Wagner Museum of Würzburg University, which in turn is based on a graffito of the Imperial era found on the wall of a *domus* on the Esquiline Hill in Rome.
(A.M.L.)

Bibliography: *MCR Catalogue* 1982, p. 570, no. 9; Mancioli 1984, pp. 18-22.

III.4.5
Unsigned, Roman
Portable sundial: vertical disc dial
c. 250
Bronze; diameter 6 cm
Oxford, Museum of the History of Science,
inv. 51358

A rare example of the tiny number of surviving portable sundials from the Roman era. There are two discs, the smaller turning in a central recess in the larger. This adjustment allows the instrument to be set for a range of latitudes, according to a scale on the larger disc marked 'XXX' – 'LX'. The curved piece which rotates above the smaller disc is a combined hour scale and gnomon (the part of a sundial that casts the shadow). This is set for date (solar declination) against a scale on the smaller disc, ranging from 'VIII K IAN' (=25th December) for the winter solstice to 'VIII K IVL' (=24th June) for the summer solstice in the Julian calendar. Once these adjustments have been made, the dial can be suspended vertically and turned until the shadow of the gnomon falls on the curved hour-scale, indicating the time. On the back of the large disc are engraved the latitudes, given in degrees, of 30 provinces of the Roman Empire. For nearly every province, the latitude cited is the mean of the range of latitudes given for that province by Ptolemy.
(J.B.)

Bibliography: Turner A. 1994.

III.4.6
Sundial
c. 1929
Alabaster plaster cast; height 44 cm,
diameter 27 cm
Rome, Museo della Civiltà Romana,
inv. M.C.R. no. 2897

Disk-shaped sundial bordered with the signs of the zodiac.
The centre of the sundial consists of a semicircular face divided into 12 equal parts. By the use of an upright spike (gnomon) set on a small base to register the length of the equinoctial shadow it was possible to determine the 12 hours of the day, according to latitude and the different times of year.
The use of sundials goes back to very ancient times, but it was Vitruvius (*De architectura*, IX, 7) who codified the form of the analemmas, the circle of the months and the proper placing of the lines marking the hours, dependent on latitude. The largest and most important sundial in antiquity was that of Augustus in the Campus Martius in Rome.
The copy on display here, taken from an original probably dating from the 1st century A.D. and preserved in the Museo Nazionale Romano, was made on the occasion of the first National Exhibition of the History of Science, which took place in Florence in 1929.
(A.M.L.)

Bibliography: *MCR Catalogue* 1982, p. 570, no. 8; Dosi-Schnell 1992, pp. 70 ff.

III.4.7
Rustic calendar
c. 1930
Alabaster plaster cast; 65.5 x 41 cm
Rome, Museo della Civiltà Romana,
inv. M.C.R. no. 3485

This *menologium rusticum* consists of a parallelepiped cippus listing three months of the year on each of its four sides. On the top is a relief representing the 12 signs of the zodiac appertaining to the constellations ruling the various months. Each month is marked, starting from the top, with its name and number of days. There follow indications of the day of the nones, corresponding to the first quarter of the moon, the length in hours of the day and night, the sign of the Zodiac, the patron deity, the work to be done in the fields and the principle festivities. The month of January, for example, is described as follows: 31 days; nones on the 5th; length of day 9 ¾ hours; length of night 14 ¼ hours; sun in Capricorn; under the patronage of Juno; sharpening stakes; cutting willows and canes; sacrifice to the Penates.
Calendars of this type, already in use in the Greek world, were widespread also among the Romans under the name of *menologia*. They gave precise information about the farm work to be done on the basis of the phases of the moon and, according to Varro (*De lingua Latina*, I, 36) one had to be available to the manager of every big farm.
The specimen on display is a cast from the original, datable in the 1st century A.D. It was found in the Colocci garden in the Campus Martius in Rome, hence the label *Colotianum*.
(A.M.L.)

Bibliography: *MCR Catalogue* 1982, p. 633, no. 38; *C.I.L.* 2007, VI, 2305; Invernizzi 1994.

III.5.1
Martianus Capella
De nuptiis Philologiae et Mercurii
11th century
Codex membranaceous, I, 116, I' fols.;
27 x 18.5 cm
Florence, Biblioteca Medicea Laurenziana,
San Marco 190, fol. 102r

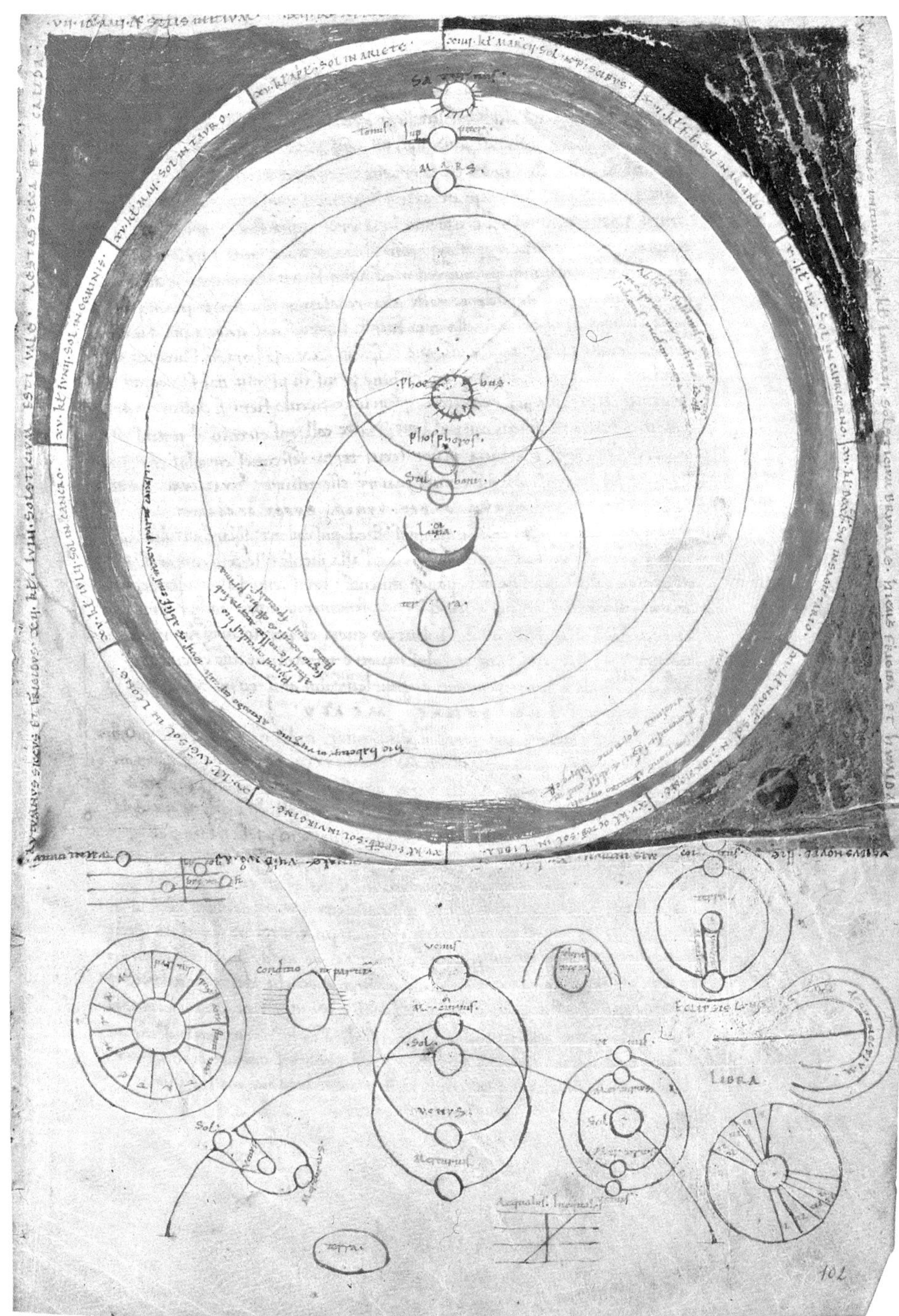

Once belonging to Niccolò Niccoli, glossed by Pietro Crinito and used by Poliziano for his *Miscellanea*, the codex, which came from the Convento di San Marco, passed to the Biblioteca Laurenziana in 1808.
Martianus Capella, a Carthaginian jurist living in the fifth century and a Neo-Platonic pagan not without Stoic leanings, created his treatise like an encyclopaedia in nine books that reviewed Classical knowledge according to the plan of the trivium and the quadrivium, in the farcical situation created around the wedding of the swiftest of the gods and the most erudite of brides-to-be.
In book VIII, Astronomy in person described the structure of the universe, explaining to the gods 'their own motions', because the sky, and not Olympus, was their place. The system of planets took inspiration from that of Heracleides Ponticus. The Earth, immobile, held the lowest position, central in respect to the lunar motion, but eccentric in respect to the rotations of the Sun and of the other planets. The only exceptions, Venus and Mars, orbit around the Sun instead.
(S.B.)

Bibliography: Firenze 1955, pp. 48-49, n. 38; Leonardi 1960; Björnbo 1976, pp. 50, 120-121; Boccuto 1985; *Biblioteca medicea* 1986, p. 104, pl. LVI; Firenze 1992, pp. 31-32, n. 4; Capella 2001.

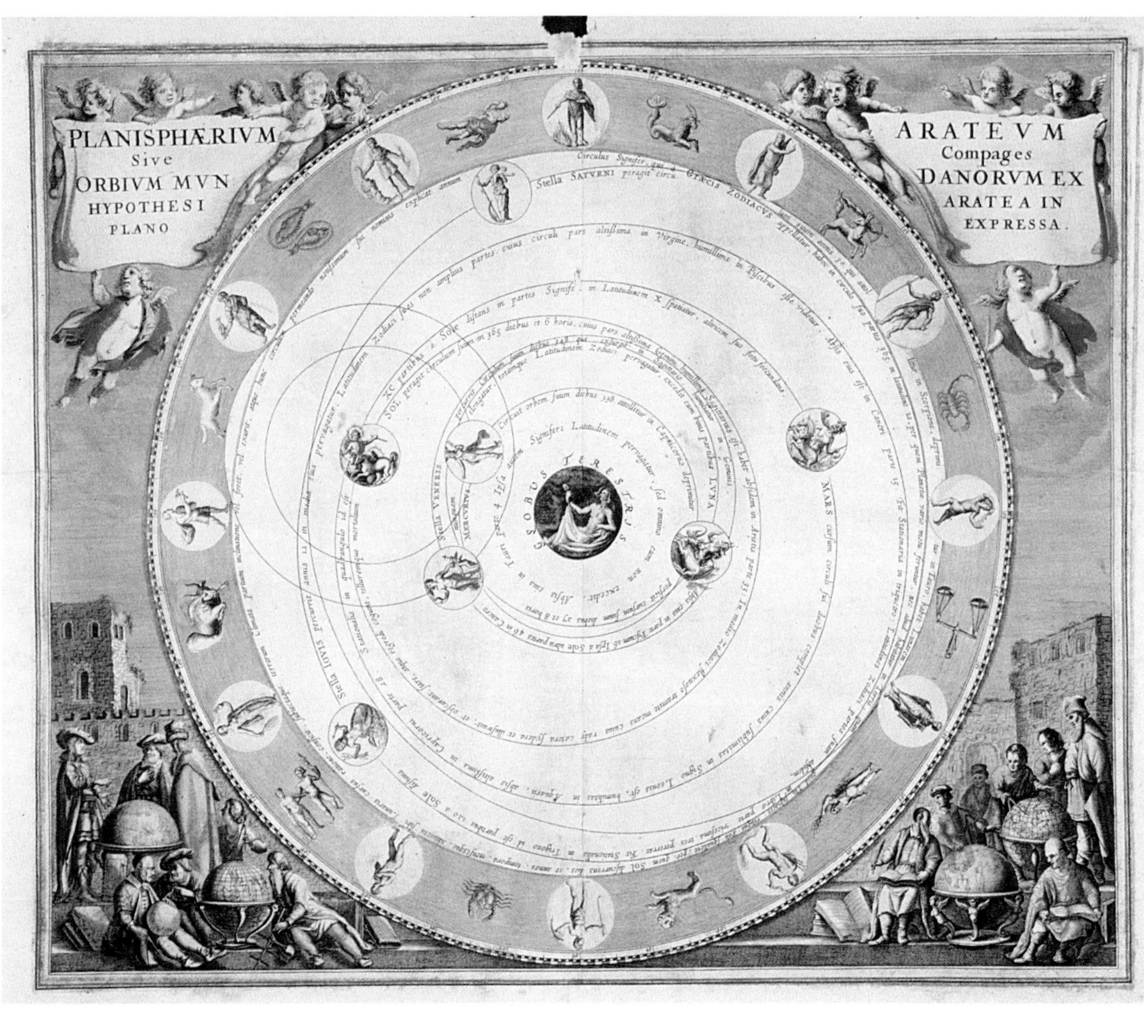

III.5.2
Andreas Cellarius
Atlas coelestis seu Harmonia Macrocosmica
Amsterdam, Johannes Janssonius, 1660
Florence, Biblioteca Nazionale Centrale,
Magl. 5._.81, pl. 9 (*Planisphaerium Arateum*)

A cosmographic work, monumental in size and with a wealth of tables of superior artistic quality. It was conceived by the Dutch publisher Janssonius as the seventh volume of an ambitious encyclopaedia (most of which was realized), the *Novus Atlas Absolutissimus*, that would have visually described the geography of the Earth and the skies. Little is known of Cellarius (1596-1665). Rector of the Latin School in Hoorn, in the Rhine Palatinate, he devoted himself to military architecture and map-making The preparation of the *Atlas* began as far back as 1647. The project provided for a second volume in which Copernican astronomy would have been described in detail (the first only reserved it marginal mention, concentrating on Ptolemy's and Tycho's systems), that, however, was never realized. The *Harmonia* consists in 29 double-page tables, made by various engravers and coloured by hand. Those showing the Earth from outside a transparent sphere, on which the constellations are visible, are particularly spectacular. The tables are accompanied by the author's vast commentary in Latin that provides not always up-to-date astronomical information. There is an obvious, almost total absence of references to the telescope, and a lack of visual documentation of the most important discoveries obtained thanks to the new instrument (with the exception of Jupiter's satellites). The *Atlas coelestis* was probably produced as an aesthetically attractive publication, designed to satisfy the curiosity of the nobles and of wealthy merchants, rather than to provide an up-to-date picture of astronomical knowledge after the Galilean and Keplerian revolution. The inscription in the ornamental cartouche attributes the Greek poet Aratus of Soli with the paternity of the geo-heliocentric planisphere represented, in which all the planets carry out their revolutions around the immobile Earth at the centre of the world (Sun included), while Venus and Mercury rotate around the Sun. In actual fact, the system represented is that of the Roman philosopher Marziano Capella (cf. entry III.5.1).
(P.G.)

Bibliography: Cellarius 2006, pp. 71-76.

III.5.3
Andreas Cellarius
Atlas coelestis seu Harmonia Macrocosmica
Amsterdam, Johannes Janssonius, 1660
Florence, Biblioteca Nazionale Centrale,
Magl. 5._.81, pl. 2 (*Planisphaerium Ptolemaicum*)

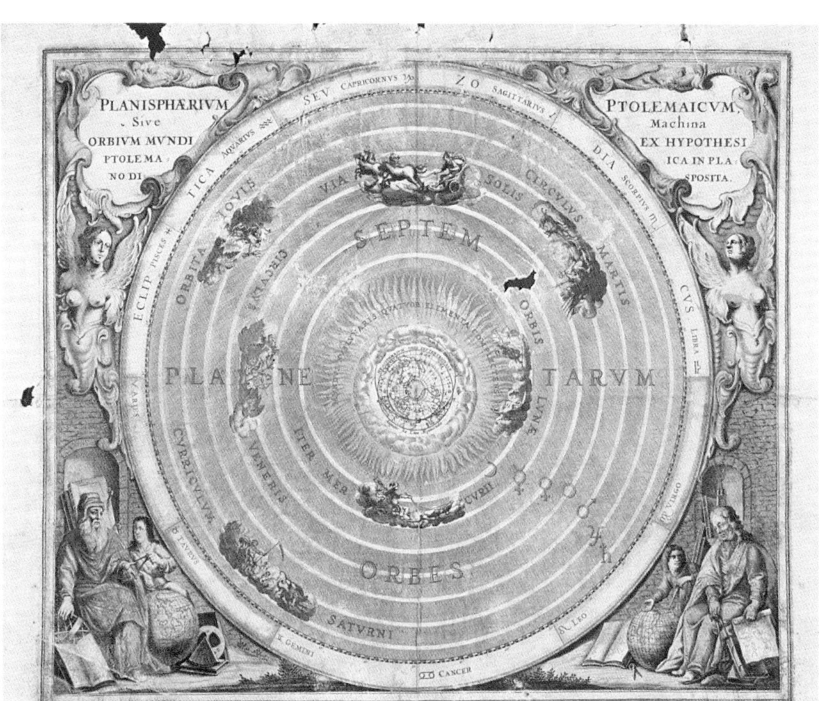

Cf. entry III.5.2.
A plane view of the Ptolemaic system, simplified (without deferents, epicycles, etc., that are illustrated in the following tables), and surrounded by the fixed stars, with the indication, in the centre, of the region of the elements (in sequence: earth, water, air, fire). In the lower right-hand corner, there is a picture probably of Ptolemy, while the person with a long white beard in the opposite margin may be identified as Aristotle.
(P.G.)

Bibliography: Cellarius 2006, pp. 29-34.

III.5.4
Atlas coelestis seu Harmonia Macrocosmica
Amsterdam, Johannes Janssonius, 1660
Florence, Biblioteca Nazionale Centrale,
Magl. 5._.81, pl. 15 (*Hypotesis ptolemaica ... sive communis planetarum motus per eccentricos et epicyclos demonstrans*)

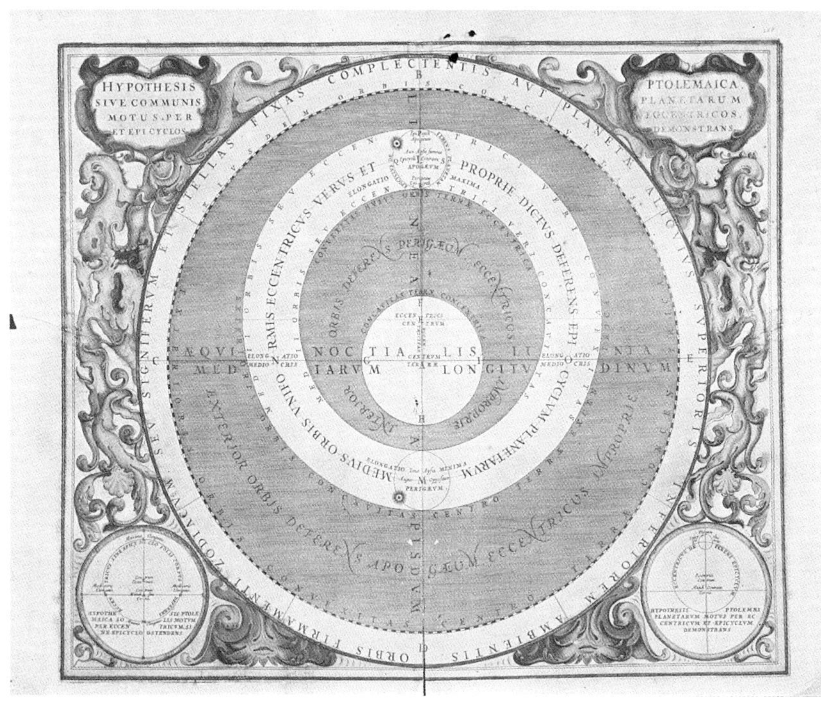

Cf. entry III.5.2.
Cellarius illustrates the geometrical solutions found by Ptolemy for explaining the retrograde motion of the planets. The image shows the Earth surrounded by the orbit of a single planet that, dragged by the deferent, advances along the epicycle. The scheme in the lower right-hand corner shows the different solution, based on the eccentric position of the Earth and on the motion of the planet along the epicycle, used by Ptolemy to explain the apparent motion of the planets. The scheme in the lower left-hand corner proposes the same solution for the motion of the Sun.
(P.G.)

Bibliography: Cellarius 2006, pp. 107-112.

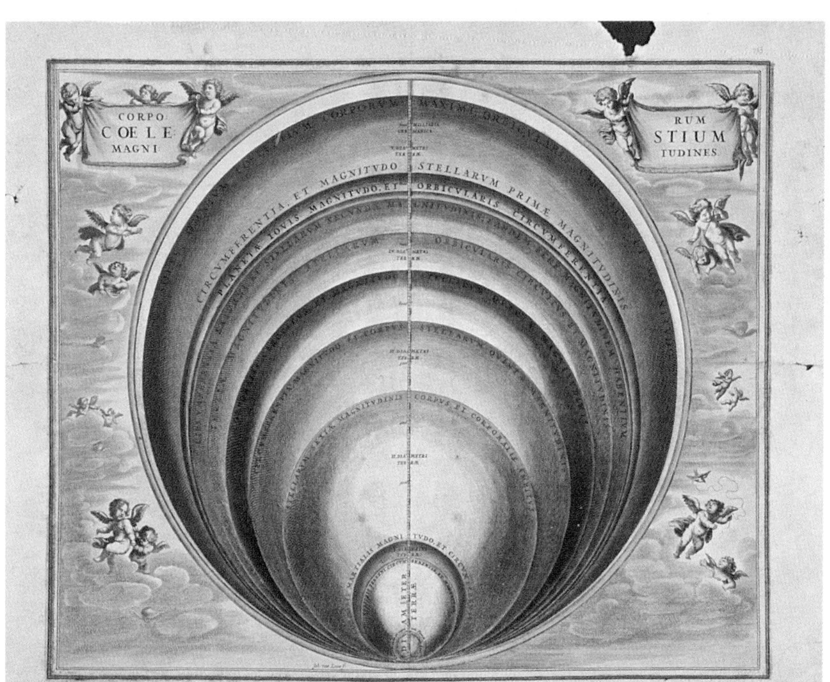

III.5.5
Andreas Cellarius
Atlas coelestis seu Harmonia Macrocosmica
Amsterdam, Johannes Janssonius, 1660
Florence, Biblioteca Nazionale Centrale,
Magl. 5._.81, pl. 11 (*Corporum coelestium magnitudines*)

Cf. entry III.5.2.
With this beautiful multicolour illustration Cellarius indicates the relative sizes of the planets in respect to the Earth, according to Ptolemy's calculations in the *Ipotesi planetarie*.
(P.G.)

Bibliography: Cellarius 2006, pp. 83-87.

III.5.6
Andreas Cellarius
Atlas coelestis seu Harmonia Macrocosmica
Amsterdam, Johannes Janssonius, 1660
Florence, Biblioteca Nazionale Centrale,
Magl. 5._.81, pl. 20 (*Typus selenographicus Lunae phases*)

Cf. entry III.5.2.
A beautiful illustration of the phases of the moon. Besides the large central diagram, Cellarius repeats the demonstration of the lunar phases in the two opposite lower margins. The one on the right illustrates the waxing and the waning phases with 12 discs, while the one on the left presents as many as 36 successive positions of the Moon in the course of its cycle.
(P.G.)

Bibliography: Cellarius 2006, pp. 137-141.

III.5.7
Plane projections of the celestial sphere
Forex and Plexiglass; 150 x 150 x 102 cm
S. Battaglia, G. Miglietta

The model shows three cases of plane projection of the celestial sphere through the projection of the shadow of an armillary sphere. In the first case (a. *stereographic polar projection*), The source of light is placed in correspondence to the South Pole, and the shadow produced by the armillary sphere corresponds to the design of the rete of an astrolabe, the openwork disk that in that ancient instrument reproduces the circumpolar movement of the fixed stars. In the second case (b. *stereographic equatorial projection*), the source of light is placed on the Equator in correspondence with the equinoctial colure; the shadow reproduces the design used in the Middle Ages in the so-called *saphaea azarchielis* (plate of Azarquiel), the universal astrolabe that could be used in every latitude. In the third case, (c. *gnonomic projection*) the source of light is placed at the centre of the armillary sphere and the shadow reproduces the plan of the quadrant of a sundial.
(F.C.)

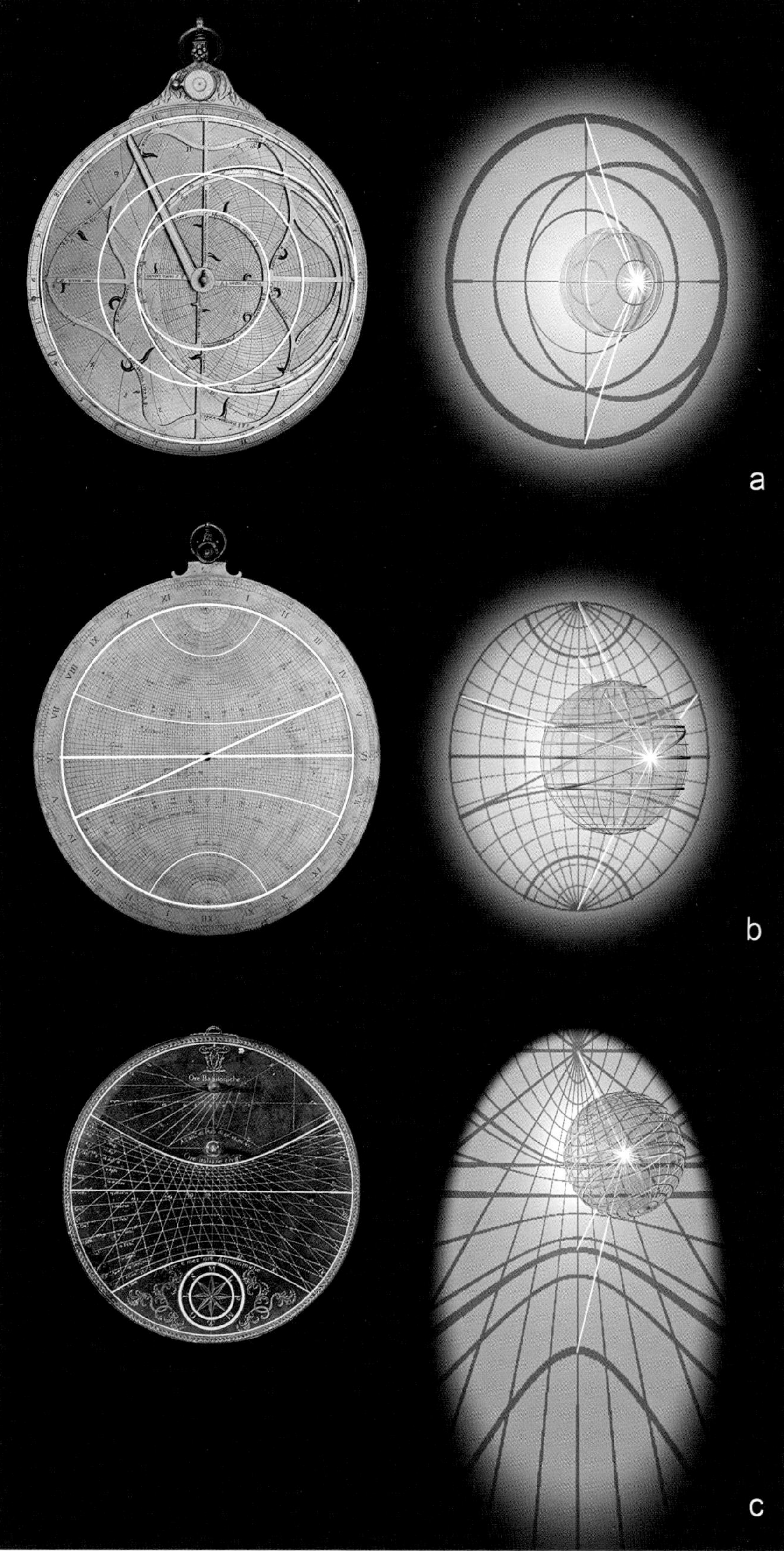

ARIE
SATU

AQVARI
VS

AQVARIVS
IVBITER

PISIS

AQVS
MARS ARIES

TERARM
LENUS TAVRVS

ARIE
MARCURIO

THE MIDDLE AGES

–

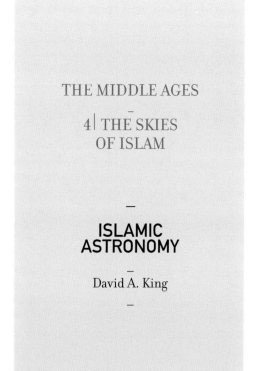

THE MIDDLE AGES

–

4| THE SKIES OF ISLAM

–

ISLAMIC ASTRONOMY

–

David A. King

–

Within a few decades of the death of the Prophet Muhammad in the year 632 the Muslims had established a commonwealth stretching from Spain to Central Asia and India. They brought with them their own folk astronomy, which was then mingled with local traditions, and they discovered the mathematical traditions of the Indians, Persians and Greeks, which they mastered with remarkable facility and adapted to their needs. Early Islamic astronomy was thus a potpourri of pre-Islamic Arabian starlore and Indian, Persian and Hellenistic astronomy, but even by the 9th century Islamic astronomy had acquired very distinctive characteristics of its own. There is no need to apologize for the expression 'Islamic astronomy'. From the 8th century to the 15th, Muslim scholars excelled in this discipline, as in mathematics. They achieved this in a multi-racial, highly-literate, tolerant society with a predominant cultural and scientific language, Arabic.

Astronomy flourished in Islamic society on two different levels: *folk astronomy*, devoid of theory and based solely on what one can see in the sky, and *mathematical astronomy*, involving systematic observations and mathematical calculations and predictions. We shall concentrate on the latter aspect, in other words, on the background to fig. 1.

Arab starlore

The Arabs of the Arabian peninsular before Islam possessed a simple yet developed astronomical folklore of a practical nature. For the Bedouin of the desert this included an intimate knowledge of the stars, particularly the 28 lunar mansions, the apparent motion of the sun throughout the year, and the lunar phases. Later Islamic folk astronomy also involved a knowledge of the associated meteorological and agricultural phenomena, and simple time-reckoning using shadows by day and the lunar mansions by night. The *Quran* mentions the sun and moon and ordains that men should use the stars for guidance; hence an extensive literature dealing with Islamic folk cosmology arose, and the scholars of the sacred law (*fuqahâ'*) occupied themselves with folk astronomy. As we shall see, they had their own proposals for astronomy in the service of Islam. The astronomers also played their part in applying their discipline to certain aspects of religious practice.

Persian and Indian sources

The earliest astronomical texts in Arabic seem to have been written in Sind and Afghanistan, areas conquered by the Muslims already in the 7th century. Our knowledge of these early works is based entirely on citations from them in later works. They consisted of text and tables and were labelled *zîj* after a Persian word meaning 'cord' or 'thread' and by extension 'the warp of a fabric', which the tables vaguely resemble. A Sasanian *zîj* was translated from Pahlavi into Arabic as the *Shâh Zîj*, and the astronomers of the Caliph al-Mansûr used this to chose an auspicious moment to found his new capital Baghdad. The various horoscopes computed by Mâshâ'allâh (Baghdad, c. 800) in his astrological world history are also based on it.

Significant for the subsequent influence of Indian astronomy in the Islamic tradition was the arrival of an embassy from Sind at the court of al-Mansûr c. 772. This included an Indian well versed in astronomy and bearing a Sanskrit astronomical text. The Caliph ordered al-Fazârî to translate the text into Arabic with the help of the Indian. The resulting *Zîj al-Sindhind al-kabîr* was the basis of a series of *zîj*es prepared in Iraq before the end of the 10th century. The *Sindhind* tradition flourished in Muslim Spain, mainly through the influence there of the *Zîj* of al-Khwârizmî (see below).

Greek sources

The *Almagest* was translated at least five times in the late 8th and 9th centuries. The first was a translation into Syriac and the others were into Arabic, the first two under al-Ma'mûn in the middle of the first half of the 9th century, and the other two (the second an improvement of the first) towards the end of that century. The translations gave rise to a series of commentaries on the whole text or parts of it, many of them critical and one, by Ibn al-Haytham (c. 1025), actually entitled *Doubts about Ptolemy*. The most commonly-used version in the later period was the recension of the late-9th-century version by the polymath Nasîr al-Dîn al-Tûsî in the mid-13th century. Various other works by Ptolemy, notably the *Planetary Hypotheses* and the *Planisphaerium*, and other Greek works, including the short treatises by Autolycos,

Aristarchos, Hypsicles, and Theodosios, and works on the construction for reducing problems in three dimensions to a plane known as the 'analemma', were also translated into Arabic; most of these too were later edited by al-Tûsî. In this way Greek planetary models, uranometry, and mathematical methods came to the attention of the Muslims. Their redactions of the *Almagest* not only reformulated and paraphrased its contents but also 'corrected, completed, criticized, and brought (the contents) up to date both theoretically and practically' (George Saliba).

DEVELOPMENTS IN ASTRONOMY

Theoretical astronomy

The geometrical structure of the universe conceived by Muslim astronomers of the early Islamic period (c. 800-1050) is more or less that expounded in Ptolemy's *Almagest*, with the system of eight spheres being regarded essentially as mathematical models. However, already in Ptolemy's *Planetary Hypotheses* these models are taken as representing physical reality; this text also became available in Arabic. Several early Muslim scholars wrote on the sizes and relative distances of the planets, and one who proposed a physical model for the universe was Ibn al-Haytham (*fl.* c. 1025). Other significant modifications to Ptolemaic planetary models, devised to overcome philosophical objections (to the notion of an equant and the excessive variation in lunar distance inherent in Ptolemy's lunar model), belong to the later period of Islamic astronomy. There were two main schools, one of which reached its fullest expression in Maragha in N.W. Iran in the 13th century (notably with al-Tûsî and his colleagues) and Damascus in the 14th (with Ibn al-Shâtir) and the other developed in Muslim Spain in the late 12th century (notably with al-Bitrûjî). The latter tradition was doomed from the outset by a slavish adherence to (false) Aristotelian tenets and mathematical incompetence. The former was based on sophisticated modifications to Ptolemy's models, partly inspired by new observations. In the 1950s E.S. Kennedy discovered that the solar, lunar and planetary models proposed by Ibn al-Shâtir were mathematically identical to those of Copernicus some 150 years later. The Polish astronomer gave himself away: his description of his complicated Mercury model shows that he misunderstood the model of Ibn al-Shâtir. We still do not know how Copernicus came to know of the models of the Damascene astronomer.

Mathematical astronomy – the tradition of the *zîjes*

Zîjes – sets of astronomical tables with accompanying text – well illustrate the richness of Islamic astronomy. In 1956 E.S. Kennedy published a survey of about 125 Islamic *zîjes*. We now know of over 225, and Benno van Dalen is currently completing a revised version of the *zîj* survey. Many of them are lost and are known solely by their titles, and many of the extant ones are derived from other *zîjes* by modification or borrowing. Nevertheless, there are enough independent *zîjes* available in manuscript form to reconstruct a reasonably accurate picture of Muslim activity in this field.

The major *zîjes* consist of several hundred pages of text and tables, and most *zîjes* deal with: (1) chronology; (2) trigonometry; (3) spherical astronomy; (4) solar, lunar and planetary mean motions; (5) solar, lunar and planetary equations; (6) lunar and planetary latitudes; (7) planetary stations; (8) parallax; (9) solar and lunar eclipses; (10) lunar and planetary visibility; (11) mathematical geography (lists of cities with geographical coordinates), determination of the direction of Mecca; (12) uranometry (tables of fixed stars with coordinates); (13) mathematical astrology.

The earliest *zîjes* from the 8th century, based on Indian and Sasanian works, are lost, but with the *zîjes* compiled in Baghdad and Damascus in the early 9th century under the patronage of the Caliph al-Ma'mûn and based on either the tradition of the *Almagest* and *Handy Tables* or the Indian tradition, we are on firmer ground. Manuscripts exist of the *Mumtahan Zîj* of Yahyâ ibn Abî Mansûr and the *Damascus Zîj* of Habash, each of which was based on essentially Ptolemaic theory rather than Indian. The *Zîj* of al-Khwârizmî, based mainly on the Persian and Indian traditions, has survived only in a Latin translation of an Andalusian recension. The *Zîj* of al-Battânî of Raqqa c. 910 is also in the *Almagest* tradition. The most important later works of this genre, and also the most influential are: the *Hâkimî Zîj* of Ibn Yûnus, compiled in Cairo at the end of the 10th century; the *zîj* called *al-Qânûn al-Mas'ûdî* by al-Bîrûnî, compiled in Ghazna about 1025; the *Zîj* of Ibn Ishâq, compiled in Tunis c. 1195; the *Îlkhânî Zîj* of Nasîr al-Dîn al-Tûsî, prepared in Maragha in N.W. Persia in the mid-13th century; and the *Sultânî Zîj* of Ulugh Beg from early-15th-century Samarqand.

Although the *zîjes* are amongst the most important sources for our knowledge of Islamic mathematical astronomy, it is important to observe that they generally contain extensive tables and explanatory text relating to mathematical astrology as well. Islamic astrological texts form an independent corpus of literature, in which often highly sophisticated mathematical procedures are involved. In spite of the fact that astrology was anathema to Muslim orthodoxy, it has always been (and still is) widely practiced in Islamic society. We shall now consider various aspects of the *zîjes* and the related literature.

1. Page 162, miniature depicting the observatory of Istanbul around the year 1577; Ms Istanbul U.L. Yıldız 1404.

2. Cartographic grid structured to show the direction and distance of Mecca, appearing here at the centre for every place in the Islamic world; Kuwait, Museum of Islamic Art.

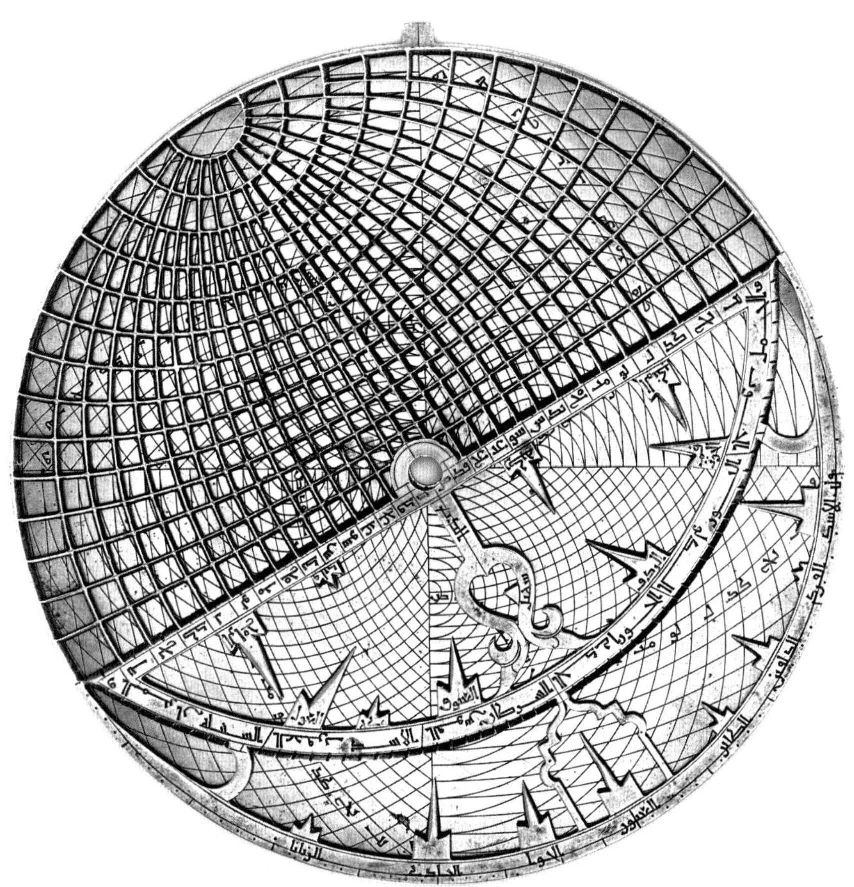

Trigonometric tables

All early Islamic astronomical tables have entries written in Arabic alphanumerical notation and expressed sexagesimally, that is, to base 60. Already in the early-9th-century Muslim astronomers had restyled the cumbersome Indian sine function using base 60 (which the Greeks had used for their chord function). Likewise the Indian shadow functions, unknown in Greek astronomy, were adopted with different bascs (usually 12 or 7). Most *zîjes* contain tables of the sine and (co)tangent function for each whole, or half, or quarter degree of arc. Entries are generally given to three sexagesimal digits, corresponding roughly to five decimal digits. The magnificent trigonometric tables in the *Zîj* of Ulugh Beg display the values of the sine and tangent to five sexagesimal digits (equivalent to about nine decimal digits) for each minute of argument and are generally accurate in the last digit.

Planetary tables and ephemerides

Given the Ptolemaic models and tables of the mean motion and equations of the sun, moon, and planets such as were available to Muslim astronomers in the *Almagest* and *Handy Tables*, or the corresponding tables based on Indian models that exemplify the *Sindhind* tradition, Muslim astronomers from the 9th to the 16th century sought to improve the numerical parameters on which these tables were based.

All Islamic *zîjes* contained tables of mean motions and equations for computing solar, lunar, and planetary positions for a given time. Auxiliary tables were sometimes available for generating ephemerides without the tedious computation of daily positions from mean-motion and equation tables. From the 9th to the 19th century Muslim astronomers compiled ephemerides displaying solar, lunar, and planetary positions of each day of the year, as well as information on the new moons and astrological predictions resulting from the position of the moon relative to the planets.

Stellar coordinates and uranography

Most *zîjes* contain lists of stellar coordinates in either the ecliptic or the equatorial systems, or occasionally in both. In his *Book of Constellation Figures* the 10th-century Shiraz astronomer al-Sûfî presented lists of stellar coordinates as well as illustrations of the constellation figures from the Hellenitic tradition and also information on the lunar mansions following the Arab tradition.

Spherical astronomy and spherical trigonometry

Most *zîjes* contain the solutions of the standard problems of spherical astronomy, such as the determination of time from solar and stellar altitude. There were two main traditions. In the first, the problems relating to the celestial sphere are reduced to geometric or trigonometric problems on a plane using an analemma construction. In the second, the problems are solved by applications of rules of spherical trigonometry.

Already Habash in the 9th century was at ease with both analemma constructions and spherical trigonometrical methods for solving problems of spherical astronomy. In the *zîjes* of scholars of the calibre of Ibn Yûnus and al-Bîrûnî we find various methods for solving each of the standard problems of medieval spherical astronomy. The auxiliary tables compiled by Habash and al-Khalîlî (c. 1360) for solving all of the problems of spherical astronomy for any latitude are a remarkable testimony to their mastery of the subject.

ASTRONOMY IN THE SERVICE OF ISLAM

The lunar calendar

The Muslim calendar is lunar and the civil months begin with the first sighting of the lunar crescent. The precise determination of the beginnings and ends of the months is particularly important for Ramadân, the month of fasting, and various other religious festivals. The legal scholars were content to rely on direct sighting of the crescent or on alternating 29- and 30-day months to regulate the calendar. But the subject of lunar crescent visibility was generally treated in *zîjes*, and a wide variety of methods and tables were devised to facilitate the solution of this problem. Al-Khwârizmî, for example, compiled a table of the minimum ecliptic elongation of the sun and moon for each zodiacal sign, computed for the latitude of Baghdad. A few early Islamic astronomers, notably Thâbit ibn Qurra and Ibn Yûnus, postulated far more complicated conditions. Unfortunately no Muslim astronomer has left us any observational data on crescent visibility.

Nowadays there is sometimes confusion about the beginning of Ramadân, which stems from the fact that the crescent may be seen in some locations and not others, and no less from the reluctance of the religious scholars, who have the final say in announcing the new month, to listen to the astronomers.

The times of prayer

In Islam the times of prayer are astronomically determined. The standard definitions of the five prayer-times, still in use today, are as follows: The Muslim day begins at sunset, and the interval for the first prayer (*maghrib*) lasts from sunset to nightfall. The interval for the second prayer (*'ishâ'*) begins at nightfall and lasts until daybreak. The third prayer (*fajr*) is performed in the interval between daybreak and sunrise. The permitted time for the fourth prayer (*zuhr*) begins when the sun has crossed the meridian and ends when the interval for the fifth prayer (*'asr*) begins, namely, when the shadow of an object equals its midday shadow increased by the length of the object. The interval for the fifth prayer may last until the shadow increases again by the length of the object or until sunset.

Clearly the times of the prayers can be regulated without difficulty by observation, assuming a clear sky. A genre of literature dealing with time-keeping from a non-mathematical point of view was compiled by specialists in folk astronomy, some of whom were also noted legal scholars.

The astronomers prepared tables displaying the length of the prayer-times for each day of the year or each degree of solar longitude. Already al-Khwârizmî computed the shadow at the *zuhr* and the *'asr* in Baghdad for each 6° of solar longitude. In the 10th century 'Alî ibn Amâjûr compiled two tables displaying the time of day as a function of solar meridian altitude and instantaneous altitude. The first, based on an accurate formula, was computed specifically for Baghdad, and the second, based on an approximate formula, is universal and works well for all reasonable latitudes.

These early Islamic tables for time-keeping, of which so few examples survive, began a tradition that reached its zenith in 13th-century Cairo and 14th-century Damascus. Most of the corpuses of tables for time-keeping compiled for these two centres and others such as Jerusalem, Alexandria, Maragha, Tunis, and Taiz, belong to the later period of Islamic astronomy. Some remarkable tables were produced: one, compiled by Najm al-Dîn in Egypt in the 13th century, has three arguments (solar or stellar altitude and meridian altitude and arc of visibility) and displays the time of day or night for any terrestrial latitude; it contains over 250,000 entries.

It was apparently in Egypt in the 13th century that the office of the *muwaqqit* or mosque astronomer responsible for the times of prayer was developed. Most of the Egyptian and Syrian astronomers of consequence from the 14th and 15th centuries were *muwaqqit*s.

The tables that modern Muslims use to regulate their prayers, published in newspapers, pocket-diaries, wall-calendars and now on the Internet, have a history of over a millennium. The call to prayer at five specific times is one of the most distinctive features of modern Islamic urban life.

The sacred direction

The Quranic injunction that prayer and other ritual acts should be performed facing the sacred Kaaba in Mecca led the legal scholars to devise schemes of sacred geography, in which the world was divided in sector around the Kaaba. Each sector had a sacred direction or qibla defined by astronomical risings and settings of the sun and various bright stars. These qibla directions were inevitably at variance to those that could be derived by mathematical geography.

By the early 9th century Ptolemy's list of geographical coordinates was available to Muslim scholars and the coordinates of Mecca and Baghdad had been investigated by a team commissioned by the Caliph al-Ma'mûn. Furthermore, exact geometrical and trigonometric procedures had been devised for determining the qibla from geographical coordinates. Al-Bîrûnî's treatise on mathematical geography, the ultimate goal of which was the determination of the qibla at Ghazna, is the most important work of its kind from the medieval period. Since these exact procedures for determining the qibla were rather complicated, approximate methods were also derived. Already in the 9th century a table was compiled based on one such method and it displays the direction of Mecca as a function of terrestrial latitude and longitude. The splendid qibla-table of al-Khalîlî for the entire Islamic commonwealth is based on the exact formula.

Of particular interest are three circular qibla-indicators in brass made in Isfahan c. 1675 which bear a cartographic grid with 275 localities marked according to their longitudes and latitudes and with Mecca at the centre, so devised that the qibla can be read from the outer scale and the distance from Mecca can be read from the non-uniform scale on the diametrical rule (see fig. 2). The mathematics underlying the grids is found in two treatises on conics from 10th-century Baghdad and 11th-century Isfahan.

The different methods for finding the qibla proposed by the legal scholars and the astronomers are reflected in the orientations of medieval mosques, only a minority of which are aligned in directions that could have been proposed by the astronomers. Only in the 18th century did it become possible for the first time to measure longitude differences correctly, and only then could it become obvious that most medieval longitude coordinates were incorrect and that even the qiblas based on these coordinates were also off by a few degrees. Nowadays some Muslims use pocket-compasses provided with lists of qiblas for the major cities of the world.

OBSERVATION PROGRAMMES

In the early 9th century the Caliph al-Ma'mûn patronized observations first in Baghdad and then in Damascus, gathering the best available astronomers to conduct observations of the sun and moon. Some of the results were incorporated into the *zîj* called *al-Mumtahan*, 'tested', and the *Damascus Zîj* of Habash.

These observations, like later ones, were mainly directed towards determining the local latitude and current value of the obliquity, and towards deriving improved parameters for the Ptolemaic planetary models and more accurate star-positions. The armillary sphere, the meridian quadrant and the parallactic ruler were known to the Muslims from the *Almagest*, and they added new scales and other modifications, often building larger instruments even when smaller ones would have sufficed.

Other series of observations were conducted in different parts of the Muslim world and we can cite only a few.

Al-Battânî carried out observations during the period 887 to 918 in Raqqa in N. Syria. He appears to have financed his observational activity himself, and although we have no description of the site where he made his observations, the instruments mentioned in the *zîj* based on his observations include an armillary sphere and mural quadrant, as well as a parallactic ruler, an astrolabe, a gnomon, and a horizontal sundial.

The Egyptian astronomer Ibn Yûnus made a series of observations of eclipses, conjunctions and occultations, as well as equinoctial and solstitial observations. We are extremely fortunate to have not only his reports of these observations but also his citations of earlier observations of the same kind made by individuals such as Habash. Ibn Yûnus' purpose is somewhat obscured by the fact that he does not present the calculations with which he derived his new solar, lunar, and planetary parameters. Neither does he mention any locations for his observations other than his grandfather's house in Fustat and a nearby mosque in al-Qarâfa. Ibn Yûnus mentions at least one instrument, probably a meridian ring, that was provided by the Fatimid Caliphs al-'Azîz and al-Hâkim. The latter made an abortive attempt to found an observatory in Cairo, but this was after the death of Ibn Yûnus in 1009. At some time during his reign there was an armillary sphere in Cairo with nine rings, each large enough that a man could ride through them on horseback.

The observations of al-Bîrûnî were conducted between 990 and c. 1025 in several localities between Khwarizm and Kabul. His recorded observations served determinations of the obliquity and local latitude, and determinations of equinoxes, solstices and eclipses.

The corpus of tables known as the *Toledan Tables* was compiled in the 11th century, based on observations directed by Sâ'id al-Andalusî and continued by Ibn al-Zarqâlluh. Only the mean motion tables in this corpus of tables are original; most of the remainder were lifted from the *zîj*es of al-Khwârizmî and al-Battânî.

In the 13th century there was a substantial observational programme at Maragha. The results are impressive only in so far as theoretical astronomy is concerned (see above). Otherwise the trigonometric and planetary tables in the major production of the Maragha astronomers were modified or lifted *in toto* from earlier sources. This is not a happy outcome for a generously endowed observatory fitted with the latest observational instruments, known to us from texts.

In the early 15th century the scene had moved to Samarqand where a group of astronomers directed by the astronomer-prince Ulugh Beg did impressive work. Only the 40-metre meridian sextant survives from the observatory. These men produced a *zîj* which remains to be properly studied. The short-lived observatory in Istanbul under the direction of Taqi al-Dîn (1577) produced another *zîj* that also awaits study.

ASTRONOMICAL INSTRUMENTS

We now turn to instruments smaller than those used for observational purposes. An important work on such instruments was compiled in Cairo c. 1280 by al-Marrâkushî, who incorporated numerous treatises on instruments into his book. The 14th-century Cairo astronomer Najm al-Dîn described every kind of instrument known to him as well as those invented by himself, altogether over 100 different types.

Armillary spheres and globes

In the 8th century al-Fazârî wrote a treatise on the armillary sphere. No early Islamic armillary spheres survive, but several other treatises on it were compiled over the centuries. The earliest treatise in Arabic dealing with the celestial globe was written by Qustâ ibn Lûqâ in the 9th century. Of the various surviving celestial globes, which number over 100, none predates the 11th century.

Astrolabes

The Muslims learned of the astrolabe in Harrân (now in S. Turkey), and it was again al-Fazârî who first made one and who also wrote on the use of the instrument. Several early astronomers, including Habash, al-Khwârizmî and al-Farghânî, wrote on the astrolabe, and introduced the features not found on earlier Greek instruments, such as the shadow squares and trigonometric grids on the backs and the azimuth curves on the plates for different latitudes, as well as the universal plate of horizons. Also al-Farghânî in the 9th century compiled extensive tables to facilitate the construction of astrolabes.

Another important development to the astrolabe occurred in Andalusia in the 11th century, when Ibn al-Zarqâlluh devised the single universal plate (*safîha*) with markings for both equatorial and ecliptic coordinate systems. His contemporary, 'Alî ibn Khalaf, devised a universal astrolabe that did not need plates for different latitudes. The instrument was further developed in Syria in the early 14th century: Ibn al-Sarrâj devised in Aleppo a remarkable astrolabe that can be used universally in five different ways.

The astrolabes made by Muslim craftsmen show a remarkable variety within each of several clearly-defined regional schools. We may mention the simple, functional astrolabes of the early Baghdad school; the splendid astrolabe of al-Khujandî of the late 10th century, which started a tradition of zoomorphic ornamentation that continued in the Islamic East for several centuries; the very different astrolabes of the Andalusian school in the 11th century and the progressive schools of Iran in the 13th and 14th centuries; and the remarkable instruments from Mamluk Egypt and Syria in the 13th and 14th centuries. After about 1500 the construction of astrolabes continued in the Maghrib, in Iran and in India until the end of the 19th century. Many of these, especially those from the Isfahan, were beautiful objects of the finest workmanship.

3. Sundial built by Ibn al-Shâtir for the minaret of the mosque of the Omayyads at Damascus in 1371-1372.

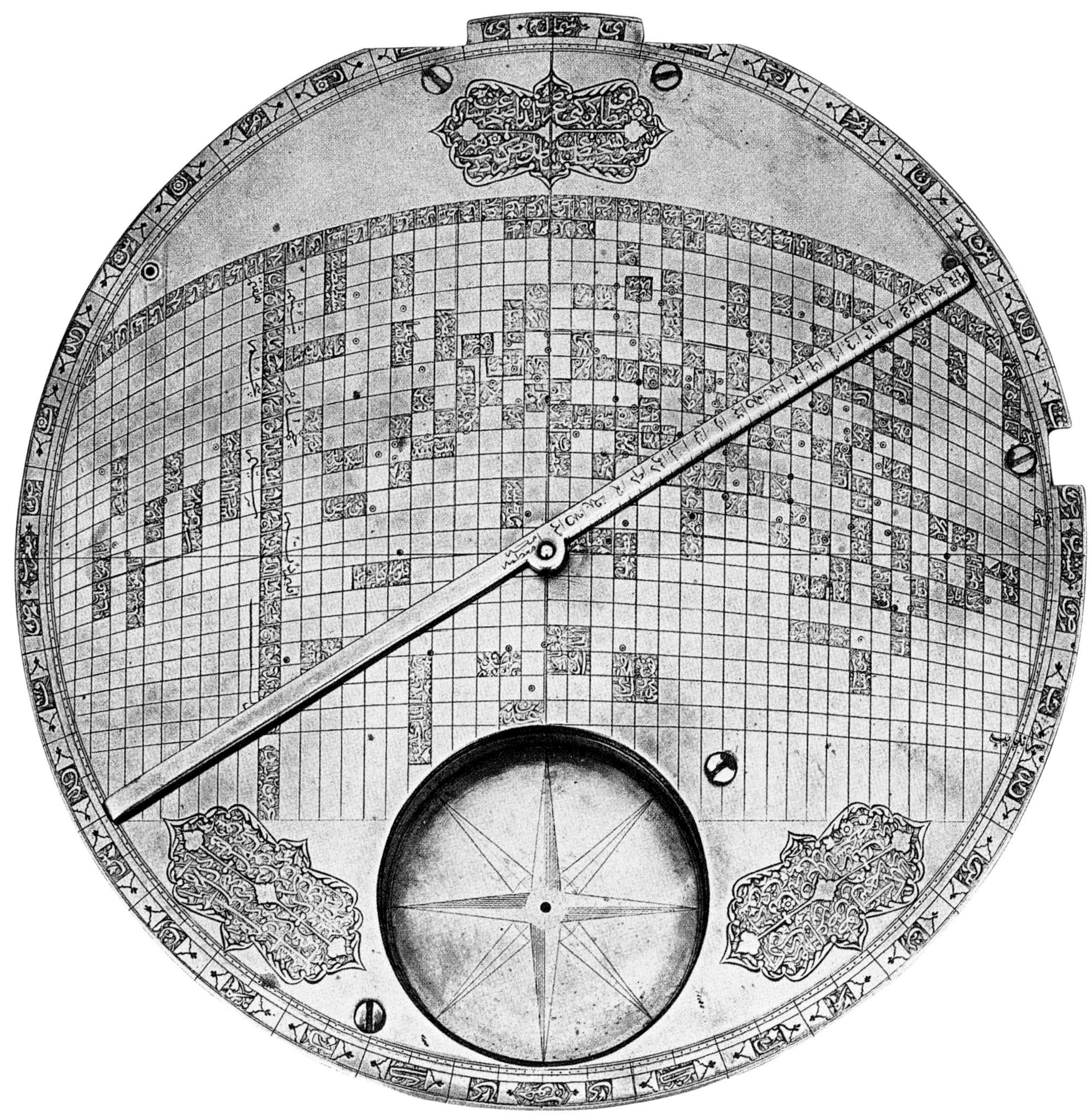

Quadrants

Another category of observational and computational devices to which Muslim astronomers made notable contributions was the quadrant, of which we can distinguish three main varieties. Firstly, the trigonometric quadrant with an orthogonal grid. Secondly, the horary quadrant with fixed or movable cursor. Both of these instruments were invented in 9th-centur Iraq, and both are found on the backs of astrolabes. Thirdly, the astrolabic quadrant displaying one half of the altitude and azimuth circles on an astrolabe plate for a specific latitude, and a fixed ecliptic. The quadrant with astrolabic markings on one side and a trigonometric grid on the other generally replaced the astrolabe in the Ottoman Turkey.

Sundials

The earliest sundials described in the Arabic astronomical sources are planar, usually horizontal, but also vertical and polar. Already a treatise on sundial construction by al-Khwârizmî or Habash contains extensive tables displaying the polar coordinates of the intersections of the hour lines with the solstitial shadow traces on horizontal sundials for 12 different latitudes. The treatise on sundial theory by Thâbit ibn Qurra contains all the necessary mathematical theory for constructing sundials in any plane; likewise impressive from a theoretical point of view is the treatise on gnomonics by his grandson Ibrâhîm.

The earliest surviving Islamic sundial, apparently made in Cordova about the year 1000 by the Andalusian astronomer Ibn al-Saffâr, displays the shadow traces of the equinoxes and solstices, and the lines for the seasonal hours as well as for the times of the two daytime prayers. The magnificent sundial made in the late 14th century by Ibn al-Shâtir was so devised that it could be used to measure time with respect to any of the five daily prayers (see fig. 3). In the late period of Islamic astronomy a sundial was to be found in most of the major mosques.

Miscellaneous

Several multi-purpose instruments were devised by Muslim astronomers. Notable examples are the linear rule of al-Fazârî, fitted with a variety of non-uniform scales for various astronomical functions, and the compendium of Ibn al-Shâtir, comprising a magnetic compass and qibla-indicator, a universal polar sundial, and an equatorial sundial.

There are several Islamic treatises on eclipse computers and planetary equatoria for determining the positions of the planets for a given date. With these the standard problems of planetary astronomy dealt with in *zîj*es are resolved mechanically, without calculation Treatises on eclipse computers are known from the early 10th century, and al-Bîrûnî in the early 11th describes such an instrument in detail. Early Islamic treatises on planetary equatoria are from 10th-century Baghdad and 11th-century Andalusia. Al-Kâshî, the leading astronomer of early-15th-century Samarqand, has left us a description of a planetary equatorium with which not only ecliptic longitudes but also latitudes could be determined and eclipses calculated.

Regional schools of astronomy

After the 10th century there developed regional schools of astronomy in the Islamic world, with different interests and concentrations. They also had different authorities (for example, in the furthest East al-Bîrûnî and al-Tûsî, and in Egypt Ibn Yûnus). The main regions were Iraq; Iran and Central Asia; Muslim Spain; Egypt and Syria; the Yemen; the Maghrib; and later also the Ottoman lands. In the past 25 years the complex tradition of Muslim Spain (10th-14th centuries), the colourful tradition of Mamluk Egypt and Syria (13th-early 16th centuries), the distinctive tradition of Rasulid Yemen (13th-16th centuries), and the staid tradition of the Maghrib (12th-19th centuries) have been studied. The traditions of Ottoman Turkey and Mogul India are currently being researched.

In the period after c. 1500 Islamic astronomy declined. All of the problems had been solved, within the medieval context, some many times over. Not that interest in astronomy died down. From Morocco to India the same old texts were copied and studied, recopied and restudied, usually different texts in each of the main regions. But there was no new input of any consequence. Astronomy continued to be used as the handmaiden of astrology, and for the regulation of the calendar and the prayer-times.

Transmission to Europe

The Muslims 'transmitted' nothing astronomical to Europe. It was the Europeans who took what they could find and what they thought would be useful to them. The Europeans learned of Islamic astronomy mainly through Spain, where the most up-to-date writings from the Islamic East were not generally available. This explains, for example, how it came to pass that the Europeans came across two major works of Muslim astronomers from the East, al-Khwârizmî and al-Battânî, at a time when these works were no longer used in the Islamic East. It also explains why so few Eastern Islamic works became known in Europe. None of the Eastern Islamic developments to Ptolemy's planetary theory were known in Muslim Spain or in medieval Europe. Also serious astronomical time-keeping does not seem to have been of much concern to the Muslims in Spain; hence nothing of consequence was transmitted.

In the European Renaissance there was no access to the latest Islamic works. So the Europeans contented themselves with new Latin translations of the ancient Greek works, with occasional references to Albategnius (al-Battânî), Azarquiel (Ibn al-Zarqâlluh), Alpetragius (al-Bitrûjî) and the like. A few technical terms derived from the Arabic survived, such as alidade, azimuth, almucantar, nadir, saphea, and zenith, and a few star-names such as Aldebaran, Algol, Altair and Vega. When the Europeans did come to learn of some of the major Islamic works and to try to come to terms with them it was as orientalists and historians of astronomy, for by this time the Islamic materials other than observation accounts were of historical rather than scientific interest. Thanks to orientalists, works that had been completely unknown to Europeans and mainly forgotten by Muslims were published, translated and analyzed. This work was continued by various scholars of different nationalities during the 20th century – notably the American E.S. Kennedy – but there is still much to be done.

In 1845 L.A. Sédillot, whose privilege it was to have access to the rich collection of Arabic and Persian scientific manuscripts in the Bibliothèque Nationale in Paris, wrote: 'Each day brings some new discovery and illustrates the extreme importance of a thorough study of the manuscripts of the East.' Given the vast amount of manuscripts – and instruments – available in libraries and museums elsewhere in the world, and the small number of people currently working in this field, Sédillot's statement is no less true nowadays than it was a century and a half ago.

Bibliography

BEA; Berggren 1986; *DSB*; *Enc. Islam*; Goldstein 1985; Gunther 1932; Kennedy 1956; Kennedy 1983; Kennedy 1998; *Kennedy Festschrift*; King D.A. 1986; King D.A. 1996, pp. 143-174; King D.A. 2004-2005; Kunitzsch 1989; Kunitzsch and Smart 1986; Mayer 1956; Pingree 1973, pp. 32-43; Ragep 1993; Saliba 1995; Saliba 2007; Samsó 1992; Samsó 1994; Samsó 2007; Savage-Smith 1985; Sayılı 1960; Sezgin 1974, 1978 and 1979; Storey 1958; Suter 1900, pp. 157-185; Dalen 1993; Varisco 1993; Vernet 1978; Wright R.R. 1934. For the latest research see www.islamsci.mcgill.ca.

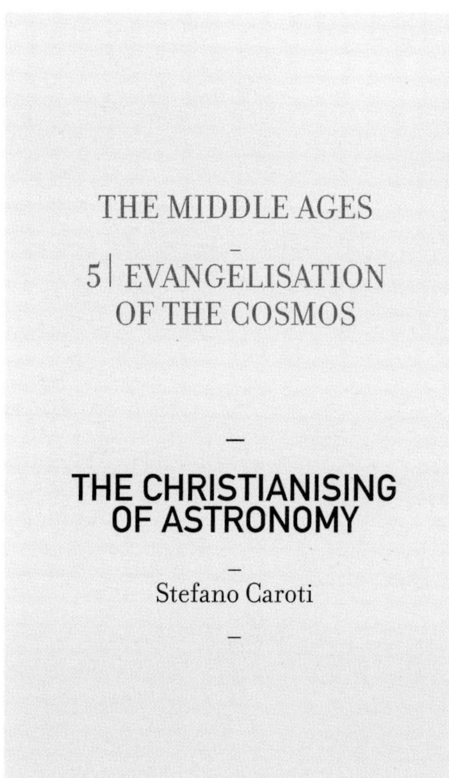

THE MIDDLE AGES

–

5 | EVANGELISATION OF THE COSMOS

–

THE CHRISTIANISING OF ASTRONOMY

–

Stefano Caroti

–

> While in the ancient, Oriental and Greek worlds, the supremacy of the heavens is defined against the background of a complex solar and astral theology, transcribed in philosophical terms in Book XII of Aristotle's *Metaphysics*, on the Christian horizon the heavens and the celestial movers assume a more precise collocation and value, becoming tools of the Creator who entrusts to them *dispensatio temporalis divinae providentiae*... In the thirteenth century, the Platonism of twelfth-century cosmologies soon gave way to the more precise cosmology of the Aristotelian-Arab tradition with all of its metaphysical implications[1].

This quotation aptly summarises the salient features of cosmological thought in the Middle Ages, and more specifically the transition from a vision of reality focussed, even in naturalist studies, on the message of redemption, to one in which physicist concepts are evaluated apart from their possible utilisation for an allegorical interpretation of the Holy Scriptures. Such an epochal transition could even evoke the Scientific Revolution, had the latter not had as its own target of criticism the Ptolemaic-Aristotelian cosmos. Nonetheless, the transition from the 12th to the 13th century, when the scientific – as well as astronomical – paradigm changed from Plato's *Timaeus* to Aristotle's physics and metaphysics remains historically determinant for the evolution of scientific thought in the western world. The methodological 'revolution' – that is, the abandonment of any pretence of subordinating knowledge to theology and interpretation of the Bible – was crucially important. The new model, moreover, presented a complete, organic, picture of scientific knowledge, offering much greater potential than that of the *Timaeus*, also for teaching purposes; and this was a need keenly felt in the 13th century, when the system of higher education was becoming consolidated with specific *curricula* and authors of reference in the individual disciplines, a system that has come down to our own day. The primacy of the Aristotelian model in the Faculties of Arts, whose courses were preparatory to the more specialised ones of law, medicine and theology, determined a very particular situation in the field of astronomy. In fact, the institutional organisation (with the rudiments based on the manual of Johannes de Sacrobosco, 1195-1256, and the main subject matter on the commentary to *De caelo*, with precise references to religious issues) came to weigh so heavily on the scientific aspects as to form a real obstacle to new discoveries and new research in the 17th century.

The 'standardising' of cosmological thought with the adoption of the Aristotelian model in the universities starting from the mid-thirteenth century was the outcome, in certain respects inevitable, of over a century of fervent research, after the twelfth-century revival of interest in Plato's physicist concepts, as found in the *Timaeus* translated and commentated by Calcidius (4th century). The *De mundo et elementis*, that is, Book II of the *Naturalis historia* by Pliny (23-79), the commentary of Macrobius (5th century) to the *Somnium Scipionis* and the *De nuptiis Mercurii et Philologiae* by Martianus Capella (4th-5th centuries) are the sources of the early medieval encyclopaedias, from the *Etymologiae sive Origenes* to the *De natura rerum* by Isidore of Seville(550-636) and the *De universo* by Rabanus Maurus (780-856).

William of Conches, a leading representative of the School of Chartres, argued against the theologians' reduction of nature to a dense network of symbols to be interpreted allegorically ('Being ignorant of the forces of nature, they want all to be companions in their ignorance; they want no research to be done, but rather that the faith of the peasants prevail and no recourse to reason be taken... we instead say that in everything reason should be sought, as far as possible'[2]). His declaration bears witness to a renewed interest in nature, reinforced by the *Timaeus* of Plato, an author still thought by Abelard (1079-1142) to be chiefly interested in natural philosophy. In place of a traditional reading of *Genesis* – based exclusively on allegorical interpretation – William of Conches preferred, in his *Philosophia*, one more respectful of physical causality. In his view, Divine action was limited to creating the four elements, whose motions imposed form and order on the cosmos ('Since water was raised to the upper part of air, the air was dense, as was also fire, and in that density was some of the substance of the earth and of water which, coagulated and hardened by the heat and dryness of fire, formed the astral bodies that are visible and luminous'[3]). The introduction of the *lectio physica* into Biblical exegesis had obvious historical importance, marking the inversion of a trend that was to result in extending the list of texts to be considered in the commentary to the *Book of Sentences* by Peter Lombard (c. 1110-1160), a basic reference for the Faculty of Theology. In addition to the Fathers of the Church, philosophers and even authors of scientific texts were now taken into account. In his commentary on the *distinctiones* of Book II of the *Sentences* dealing with the creation of the world, Thomas Aquinas (1224-1274) quoted amply from the works of Aristotle, Avicenna (980-1037), Maimonides (1138-1204) and Averroes (1126-1198) (commentaries on Aristotle's writings, but also the *De substantia orbis*).

This renewed interest in physicist doctrines gave rise not only to a trend toward reconciling faith and religion – historically much more important and far-reaching than the one instigated by some Fathers of the Church, which reached its peak in the 13th century – but also to the central place of astronomy among the scientific disciplines deemed indispensable to the study of nature. This centrality was assured by the very broad meaning assigned to the term, which included study of the influence of the heavens on the sublunar world. In the *Didascalicon* by Hugo of Saint Victor (1141), an encyclopaedia widely used even after the triumph of the Aristotelian model in the universities, the dependency of the sublunar world on the celestial one is vividly portrayed in the relationship between *natura* and *opus naturae* ('The astrologers divided the world into two parts, namely, one above the sphere of the Moon and one below. The sopralunar world they called 'nature', because all of the things found in it are regulated by primordial law; the sublunar one they called 'work of nature', that is, of the higher realm, because all of the things that in it are animated by the vital spirit draw their nourishment from the admirable action of the heavens, not only as concerns their development after birth, but even their very survival'[4]). This was a widespread belief, found in the writings of such authors as Gundissalinus (12th century), Herman of Carinthia (c. 1100-1160) and Daniel of Morley (c. 1140-1210), who utilised Arab sources imbued with Neoplatonic concepts, sources that found definitive confirmation in a passage from Aristotle's first book of *Meteorology* (2, 339a21-23), sanctioning substantial continuity between the 12th and the 13th centuries, at least in this specific area.

The shared conviction that the world below the moon depended on the motions of the celestial bodies led to a substantial change in the meaning of the term astronomy, which came to encompass a number of disciplines entirely unknown to the ancient and modern traditions. In the wake of the *Enumeration of the Sciences* by Al-Farabi (c. 870-950), Domenicus Gundissalinus listed eight sciences that make up natural science, including not only medicine, optics, agriculture, navigation and alchemy, but no less than three different astrological disciplines: the science of astrological responses, physical magic and the science of images[5]. In his *Philosophy*, Daniel of Morley ascribes directly to astrology the division into eight parts that Gundissalinus had attributed more generally to natural science, almost as if the scope of the latter were fully comprised in the former (ed. Sudhoff, p. 34).

The 'unquenchable thirst for research'[6] nourished by this new attitude toward astronomical and scientific knowledge urged some authors to leave their own countries on a quest for Greek and Arabic scientific writings that did not yet circulate in the Latin world. Gerard of Cremona (1114-1187), one of the most prolific translators from the Arab of astronomical, mathematical and medical works, journeyed to Spain to seek for the *Almagest* of Ptolemy (100-178), the *summa* of astronomical knowledge prior to Copernicus (1473-1543). And even before him, Gerbert of Aurillac (940-1003), before rising to the Papal throne as Sylvester II, had introduced the use of instruments such as the armillary sphere and the astrolabe as aids in teaching astronomy, probably inspired by models of Arab origin with which he may have come into contact during his stay in Catalonia.

This fervent interest in works of profane knowledge, encompassing sciences – astronomy and physics – as well as such divinatory practices as the various forms of astrology, was bound to arouse the suspicions of theologians, who saw their supremacy as exclusive interpreters of the Holy Scriptures imperilled. William of St-Thierry (1080-1148), one of the outstanding figures in medieval mysticism, was not only responsible for the second condemnation of Abelard but was also the author of a text *On the Errors of William of Conches*, accused of having given an explanation of *Genesis* that was exclusively physical, and thus ignoring its redeeming message, certainly more important than any concepts of natural philosophy that might be drawn from it.

The library of astronomical-astrological texts described in the *Speculum astronomiae* is vast in scope. Strictly as regards astronomy, it includes Ptolemy's *Almagest* as well as commentaries on and compilations of Arab authors such as Geber (d. 1150), Messehalla (d. 815), al Battani (868-929), al Bitrugi (d. 1204), al Fargani (c. 800-880) and Thebit ben Qurra (836-901). Among the rediscovered texts were some of practical nature, tables recording observations on planetary motion, which, along with works on calculation, constitute fundamental elements of the medieval *corpus astronomicum*.

The universities arising during these same years could not of course dominate a material so abundant and at the same time so composite. The complete and multi-faceted encyclopaedia made up of

1. Page 172, the winds, the four elements and, at the centre, the Sun and the Moon; Florence, Biblioteca Medicea Laurenziana, Ms. Pl. 17,3, c. 1r.

2. Engraving representing Astronomy, at right Ptolemy and at left Urania, the Muse patroness of astronomical science; Milan, Civica Raccolta delle Stampe Bertarelli.

Aristotle's writings – from logic to the pseudoepigraphical books on plants, to the medieval compendiums of minerals, passing through cosmology, physics, psychology and metaphysics – constituted a rival that was too powerful, insofar as being comprehensive and systematic, and thus particularly well suited to scholastic use.

But even Aristotle's works met with some attempts at suppression, at first in summary manner (1210, 1215, 1230), then by endeavouring to correct those of his positions deemed contradictory to the teachings of the Church – such as the eternity of the world, or the dependence of natural motions on celestial ones. The great syllabus of the Bishop of Paris Étienne Tempier (1279), which condemned no less than 277 propositions deemed dangerous or even heretical, was in reality a kind of surrender to the new philosophy, which could now be opposed only by attempting to mitigate some of its boldest concepts.

Aristotle, however, was not the only authority recognised in astronomy taught as a university discipline. Another text was in fact employed to instruct students on the structure of the cosmos and the motion of the planets. This was the *Tractatus de sphaera* by Johannes de Sacrobosco, a manual widely disseminated in manuscript form and then reprinted several times from 1472 to 1669. The first three books of *De sphaera* deal with astronomical geography (the sphere of the fixed stars and its motion, the Earth and its central position in the universe in the first; the celestial equator, the ecliptic, the zodiac, and the division of the Earth into zones according to their distance from the poles and the equator, in the second; the rising and setting of the planets and the duration of day and night in the Earth's different zones in the third). The fourth contains a brief description of the motion of the Sun and the planets and an explanation of the phenomenon of eclipse. It was immediately noted that these subjects were discussed too briefly, and Sacrobosco's text was accompanied by the anonymous *Theorica planetarum*, which describes more clearly the motion of the Sun (according to the model of Hipparcus, 190-120, for whom the Sun moves at regular speed around a deferent eccentric to the Earth, and thus to the centre of the universe) and of the planets, whose irregular motions are explained by a system of epicycles (the circumference along which a planet moves) whose centres move along a circumference, called deferent, eccentric to the Earth. In the case of Mars, Jupiter and Saturn, the centre of the epicycle moves along the diameter of the deferent. In addition to the *Tractatus de sphaera*, other manuals by Johannes de Sacrobosco formed part of the *corpus* of texts utilised in teaching astronomy: a treatise on arithmetic, the *Algorismus vulgaris*, and a manual for determining the calendar, the *Compotus*. With this particular organisation of the discipline, uniting the mathematical

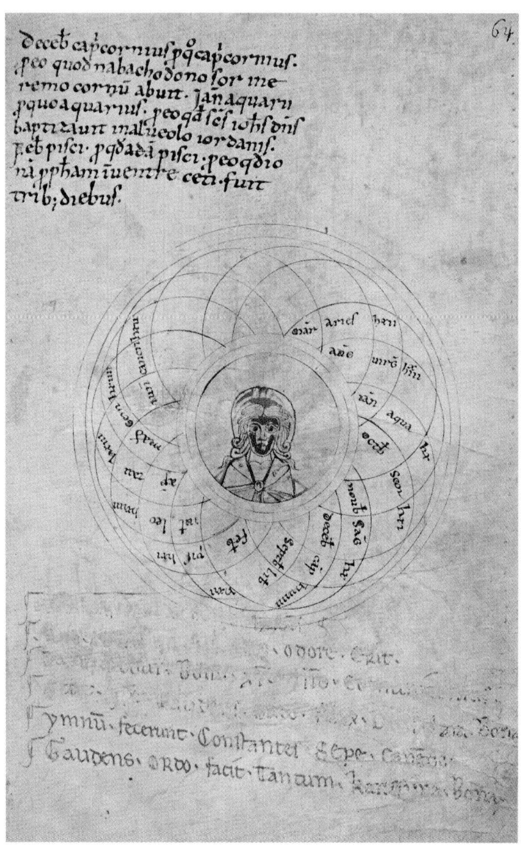

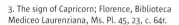

3. The sign of Capricorn; Florence, Biblioteca Mediceo Laurenziana, Ms. Pl. 45, 23, c. 64r.

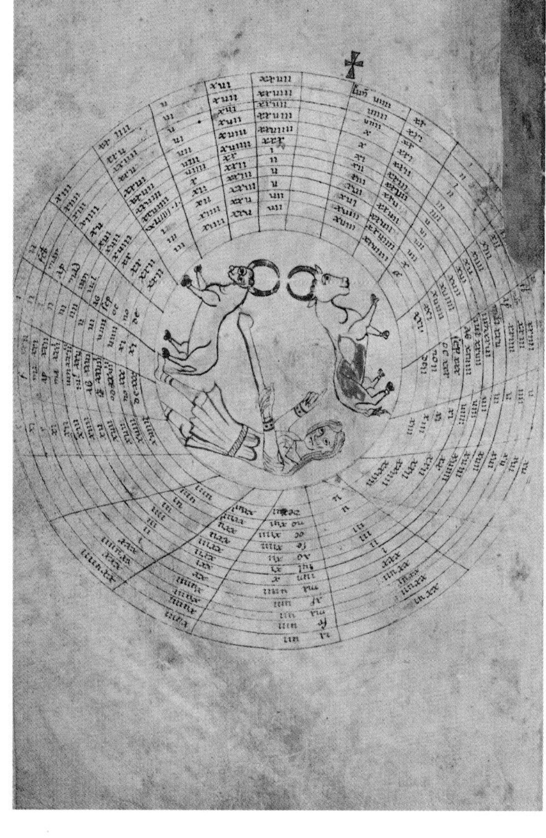

4. Calculating wheel: this is a method used for calculating the date of Easter and the other movable feasts; Florence, Biblioteca Medicea Laurenziana, Ms. Pl. 45,23, c. 62v.

and the physical sciences, astronomy could be considered a *scientia media*, and thus especially interesting for the possibility of interrelating mathematical and physicist research, strictly impossible in the Aristotelian scientific model, where the two sciences occupy distinctly separate spheres.

In the *De caelo* Aristotle applies to the description of the cosmos the basic concepts of his physics. Its salient features can be summarised as: *a*) distinction between the elementary world and the celestial world, the latter being distinguished by a fifth essence (quintessence) of immutable nature; *b*) the different nature of motion in the two different parts of the cosmos and, as regards the sublunar world, in all types of change. In the elementary world change depends on the two principles of being, form and matter, with the relevant concepts of power – typical of matter – and act – typical of form. In the celestial world, where there is no matter and thus no potentiality, the only kind of change is local motion, which, because of lack of contrariety due to the immateriality of the quintessence, can only be circular – the perfect motion – and regular, again due to the absence of any kind of resistance. Within this system there was no place for the eccentrics and epicycles of the Ptolemaic system, introduced expressly to explain the anomalies in observations deriving from having assumed a homocentric model.

The pre-eminence of Aristotle's writings in the universities, along with other texts on logic, physics, psychology and metaphysics, determined a certain preponderance of cosmological and physicist interests in astronomical research. This predominance was then sanctioned by adopting the problems discussed in the commentaries to *De caelo* in those addressed to the cosmological and astronomical sections of Peter Lombard's second book of *Sentences*, chosen as a teaching manual for the higher faculty, that of Theology[7]. And it is just this particular historical and institutional conjuncture (wide dissemination of Aristotle's writings and adoption of their premises in higher education) to establish, as has been said, the boundaries of astronomical science that were to prevail from the Middle Ages down to modern times, when a new vision of the world found itself opposing an ensemble of convictions on which generations of philosophers and scientists had been trained.

The Aristotelian model on which the Christianising of the cosmos was based posed various problems, foremost among them the eternity of the world, sustained by Aristotle, which negated one of the basic tenets of Christian doctrine: the creation of the universe in time. In his demonstration of the temporal nature of the created world Bonaventura of Bagnorea (1221-1274) called philosophers' attention to the absurdities deriving from the Aristotelian solution, for which it would have been necessary to admit the possibility of infinites constituted by a greater or lesser, and thus larger or smaller, number of elements, (for example, if the past is considered infinite, the revolutions of the Moon are more numerous than those of the Sun). For St. Thomas, the beginning of the world in time is not demonstrable but only an object of faith, insofar as God would have been able to create without a temporal beginning, since the status of creature is not contradictory to that of existence without a beginning in time.

Even the absolute power of God seems to be called into question by an eternalist concept of the cosmos, since one of the arguments against its temporal nature is the immutability of the will of the First Cause. If this immutability can be deemed perfection, when it does not constitute a limitation to Divine power, then just for this reason the Aristotelian belief in the finiteness of the cosmos is more problematical. In spite of acknowledging the *potentia Dei absoluta* also as concerns the size of the cosmos, many authors, among them Johannes Buridan (c. 1300-1361) in his commentaries to the *Physics* and the *De caelo*, defended Aristotle's finitist position, pointing out the indefensible nature of some consequences of a different hypothesis, such as the inadmissibility of a centre, or the fact that an infinite space is traversed in a finite time. Even the *Coimbra Commentaries*, a text widely used in universities and Jesuit colleges in the 17th century, recommended a negative response to the question of whether God could have created an actual infinite[8].

Based on the same risk of limiting the infinite power of God was condemnation of the proposition: 'that the prime cause cannot make several worlds'[9]. Admitting this possibility would have gravely undermined the Aristotelian model in many respects, but above all as regards the theory of natural places (with fire above and earth below), which would lose their absolute character. Moreover, empty spaces in which to place the worlds other than the one inhabited by man would have to be postulated. A possible solution to these problems was advanced by Nicole Oresme (1320-1382), who believed it would not be contradictory to introduce two concentric worlds, since the centre of the innermost one would coincide with that of the outermost[10]. This hypothesis, according to Albert of Saxony (1315-1390) can not be defended, since each of the different worlds would have to have its own prime mover, a concept that in this case would lose all sense, with dangerous repercussions also on the theological level. Albert also denies the possibility of a successive plurality of worlds, since they would have to be corruptible.

The incorruptibility of the celestial sphere, unlike that of the elementary one, is a basic tenet of Aristotelian cosmology, and was to form one of the greatest obstacles to the new astronomical theories of the modern age, based also on observations that seemed to confute the theory of the fifth essence. For the purposes of Christianising the cosmos, instead, this opposition could be efficacious. In the inquest promoted by the General of the Dominican Friars Giovanni da Vercelli (c. 1200-1283) in 1271, after the first condemnation of Aristotelian thought, Thomas Aquinas explicitly endorsed identifying the celestial movers with the angels of Christian tradition. Although he had always shown a certain hesitation over the nature of the relationship between celestial movers and celestial bodies, Thomas fully accepted the philosophical thesis of the 'intelligent' nature of the movers of the stars, which allows such an identification to be made. It was a difficult decision however, by no means incontrovertible, and neither Albertus Magnus (1193-1280) nor Robert Kilwardby (c. 1215-1279), the others interrogated by the General of the Order, showed enthusiasm for Thomas's position. Albertus Magnus in particular saw in the regularity of the celestial motions something very like a law of nature, wholly incompatible with the freedom of the angels. Even leaving aside this question, it remained very hard to establish criteria for determining the various levels of perfection among the celestial movers, incommensurably inferior to the Prime Mover, but certainly differing among themselves. The criterion of order established according to distance from the Earth did not seem to take into due account the central role of the Sun.

5. Planetary melothesia; Florence, Biblioteca Medicea Laurenziana, Ms. Strozzi 153, c. 33v.

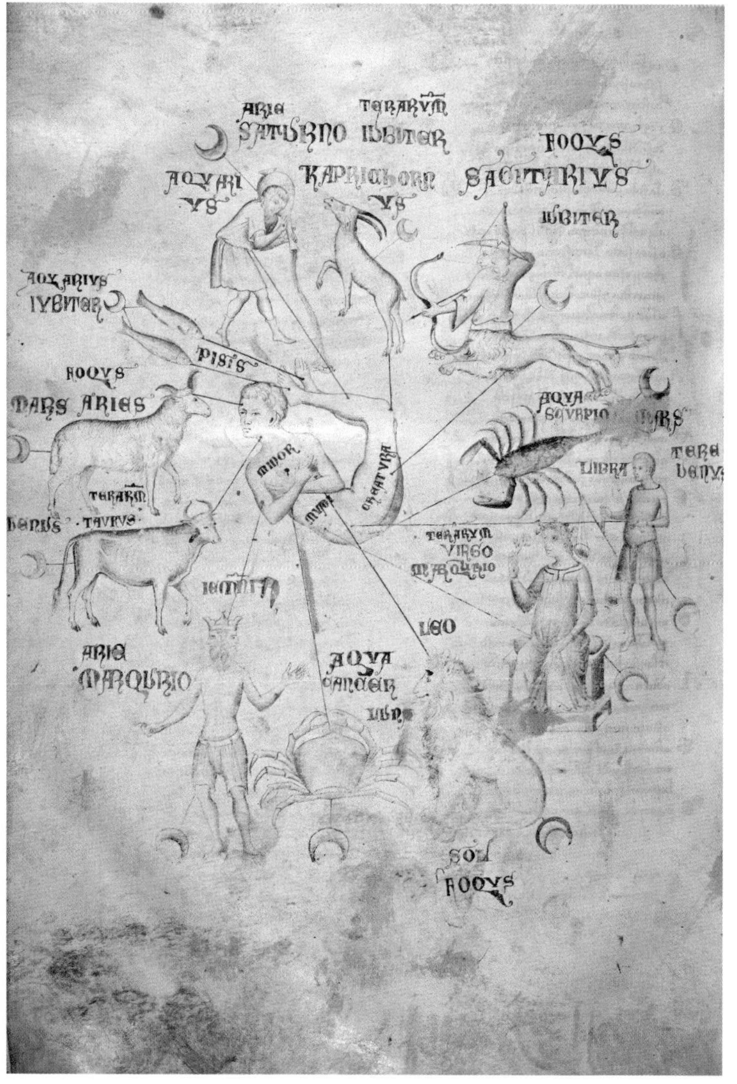

The incorruptibility of the sopralunar world seemed to cast doubt on the Aristotelian ontological principle of the matter-form synolon. Averroes, who served as guide to interpreting the texts of Aristotle throughout the Middle Ages, posited the exclusively formal nature of the heavens, while Thomas, although admitting a principle of potentiality, limits it to place alone (giving rise to the circular motion of the celestial bodies). In this way he underlined the difference between the matter of the sublunar world – characterised by potentiality as regards both qualitative aspects (alteration) and substance (generation and corruption) – and the celestial world. In spite of dissenting opinions, such as that of Aegidius Romanus (c. 1245-1316), for whom there exists no difference between terrestrial and celestial matter (an opinion shared, although on different grounds, by William of Ockham, c. 1285-1349), the belief in a sharp division between the two spheres was to be a notable obstacle to the new science and the astronomical discoveries largely enabled by the perfecting of instruments for observation.

The impossibility of accounting for the motions of the celestial bodies on the basis of the homocentric system, defended by Aristotle, could not be resolved by adopting the Ptolemaic system of eccentrics and epicycles. Already Vincent of Beauvais (d. 1264) in his *Speculum naturale*[11] had rejected this model for its implications on the nature of the fifth element: it would have assumed, in fact, characteristics too similar to those of elementary matter to be able to explain the irregular motions of the celestial bodies, without having to admit the existence of a void (the presence of alteration due to condensation and rarefaction). Albertus Magnus admits the existence of a certain type of matter, differing from quintessence, among the celestial spheres, expressly to obviate the consequences of the clearly irregular motions of the celestial bodies. The centrality of the Earth was then retained through a complex system in which, considering the totality of the sphere (*orbis totalis* in the language of the commentary by Pierre d'Ailly, 1350-1420, to the *Tractatus de Sphaera* of Johannes Sacrobosco, a text known and annotated by Christopher Columbus, 1451-1506), the centre was the Earth, but inside the sphere the planet revolved in an epicycle that, at the Earth's points of greatest distance and nearness, rotated along two eccentric circles. This was a widely accepted solution, which made it possible to save appearances without having to reject a postulate of Aristotelian cosmology.

Jean Buridan, while accepting the eccentrics, refuted the existence of epicycles, based on observation of the unchanging appearance of lunar spots (the 'man in the Moon') at the apogee and the perigee, while at the apogee they should instead have appeared upside down[12]. Buridan's rejection is justified also by his conviction that the stars do not rotate on their axes in a direction opposite that of the epicycle. Albert of Saxony, on the contrary, admits this motion, also based on the different effects of the Moon on the sublunar world depending on its distance from or nearness to the Earth[13].

Even the total number of spheres, not considering the various subsystems of eccentrics and epicycles, was the subject of debate. The different solutions were closely dependent on the number of motions attributed to the last of them, that of the fixed stars. Admitting only daily motion in the counter-clockwise direction, the number is fixed at eight. If the motion of the precession of the equinoxes and that of trepidation, introduced by Thebit ben Qurra (Roger Bacon, c. 1215-1294, Albert of Saxony and Pierre d'Ailly) are included, it rises to ten. Since they were entirely invisible, these spheres above the firmament were identified with the crystalline heaven of the Holy Scriptures (the division of the waters in *Genesis* I,7), although for Peter of Abano (c. 1250-1315) such an identification derived from the improper irruption of theology into science. Above these moving spheres was soon added an immobile sky, the empyrean, home of the blessed, shining resplendent with its own light, it too transparent and invisible but indescribably more perfect than all of the spheres below it, inferior not in place alone. Its mention in the *Sentences* of Peter Lombard accredited this concept, which was to serve as inspiration to greater philosophers (Alexander of Hales, c. 1185-1245, Albertus Magnus, Bonaventura, Thomas, Duns Scotus, 1265-1308).

This was the culminating moment in the Christianising of the cosmos. Even Thomas Aquinas, who in his commentary on the *Sentences* (II, dist. 2, q. 2 art. 3) had doubted that the empyrean could act on the lower spheres, since it is immobile (while every action implicates change and thus motion), was to radically reconsider this position in the *Quaestiones Quodlibetales* (VI, q. 11, art. 19), thus facilitating a synergy between the laws of nature and Divine Providence.

–

Bibliography

Gregory 2007; Gregory 1992; Grant 1996; Grant 1994; North 1989a; North 1989b; Lindberg 1992; Pedersen 1993; Wagner 1983; Lindberg 1978; Haskins 1927; Haskins 1960, p. 75; Teodorico di Chartres-Guglielmo di Conches-Bernardo Silvestre 1980, p. 234; Hissette 1977, p. 64; Oresme 1968, I, 24, pp. 167-171; Thorndike 1923-1958; Verdet 1992, pp. 38-109; Duhem 1913-1959; Dreyer 1953; Lerner 1996.

[1] Gregory 2007, pp. 52, 54.
[2] William of Conches, *Philosophia*, I, 44-45, in Gregory 2007, p. 17.
[3] William of Conches, *Philosophia*, I, 40, in Teodorico di Chartres-Guglielmo di Conches-Bernardo Silvestre 1980, p. 234.
[4] Hugo of Saint Victor, *Didascalicon*, in *Patrologia Latina*, CLXXVI, p. 748.
[5] 'Of the sciences, some are universal, others particular. The universal ones include many sciences, and thus natural science is universal, since it comprises eight sciences: medicine, astrology, physical sorcery, the science of images, agriculture, navigation, optics and alchemy, which is the science of the transmutation of things', transl. by Baur, p. 20.
[6] 'Insaciata philosophandi aviditas', from the prologue by Hugo of Santalla (1119-1151) to the *Liber Aristotelis de 255 Indorum voluminibus*, cited by Haskins 1960, p. 75.
[7] See the catalogue of *quaestiones* of cosmological and astronomical nature discussed from the 13th through the 17th century in commentaries on works of phsyics and theology, compiled by Grant 1994, pp. 681-741.
[8] Grant 1994, p. 110.
[9] Hissette 1977, p. 64.
[10] Oresme 1968, pp. 167-171.
[11] Vincent of Beauvais, *Speculum naturale*, III, fol. 104.
[12] Johannes Buridan, *In Metaphysicam quaestiones*, XII, q. 104.
[13] Albert of Saxony, *In De coelo quaestiones*, II, q. 7.

Marcius

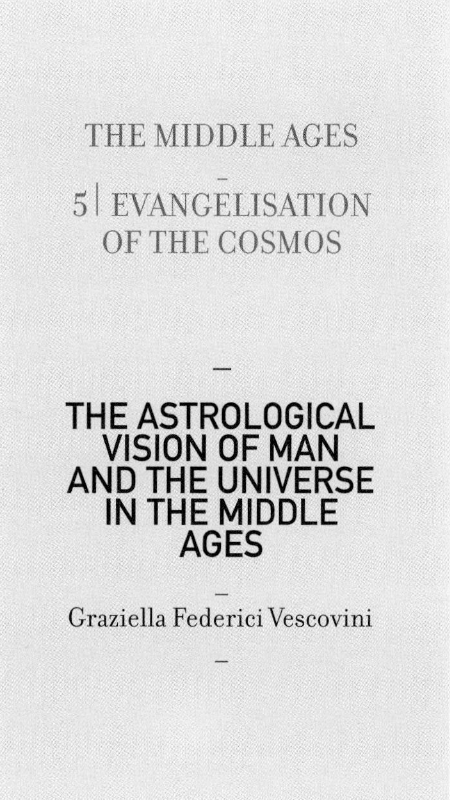

THE MIDDLE AGES
–
5 | EVANGELISATION OF THE COSMOS
–
THE ASTROLOGICAL VISION OF MAN AND THE UNIVERSE IN THE MIDDLE AGES
–
Graziella Federici Vescovini
–

The medieval vision of the universe had a complex dynamics that cannot be explained merely as the transition and transmission of the cosmology of antiquity to that of the Renaissance. Based on recent studies it appears instead as a profoundly innovative revision of the earlier Aristotelian-Ptolemaic cosmology. This new cosmological vision depended on its astrological component, based not on the Greek or 'Greek-style' sphere of the epigones of Aristotle and Ptolemy, but rather on the 'barbaric' sphere, according to the excellent reconstruction of Franz Boll. In the centuries before the Copernican revolution, the universe was a closed sphere, perfect, finite, without a vacuum, and made up of contiguous spheres. The medieval astronomy onto which astrology was grafted introduced, along with names of signs and stars from the classical sphere, those of the oriental world: Egyptian, Babylonia, Persian and Indian. In the 1st century B.C. the Graeco-Roman sphere was called 'Greek-style', and not Greek, by Nigidius, probably in contrast to the barbaric sphere of Oriental Egyptian and Babylonian astronomy.

This new vision of the medieval universe was constructed according to complex and well defined astrological techniques, on the basis of philosophical doctrines of rather syncretistic nature, in the voluminous *Treatises of introduction to astrology*. The basic concept was derived from some principles of Jewish and Arab astrologists of the 8th and 9th centuries (Messahalla, Alkindi, Albumasar) and their later Arab and Latin-Christian interpreters. The new vision of the astrological world depended on the idea that the motion of the skies, eight in number according to Aristotle and Ptolemy, or nine according to the ninth-century reform enacted by the Arabs (probably by Ibn al-Haytham el-Alasan, called Alhazen or Alacen by the Latins, c. 965-1040) exerted an influence on the sublunar or terrestrial world, on the universal level, over the millenniums, and on the general level, during the century or half-century (in this case for the rise and fall of kingdoms or empires), as well as on the individual level. In the latter case, the influence was thought to give a meaning or an explanation to the future life of a man, starting from the signs in the sky at his birth (*De nativitatibus*).

The astrological vision of the world that developed in highly refined form with the analytical, well-structured techniques of the Jewish and Arab scientists and astrologers of the 8th through the 11th century who lived in Baghdad was based on Ptolemaic cosmology. Such an astrological vision was in fact closely linked to the mathematical-geometric models of Ptolemaic astronomy. Ptolemy, in the *Almagest* (the *Mathematical Syntax*), had proposed a world system whose more strictly scientific-mathematical nature was explained through the geometry of eccentrics and epicycles. This model served to explain the anomalies in the 'apparent' motions of the planets not considered in the astronomy of Eudoxus and Calippus adopted by Aristotle: that is, the retrograde motion, acceleration and stationary points of the planets, and the precession of the equinoxes discovered by Hipparchus and then recalculated by Ptolemy.

This explanation of the celestial world was extended to the terrestrial one, whose events were thought to depend on the motions of the celestial bodies. From this came an explanation of human history, of physical-geographical meteorological events and a calendar or measurement of time on an astrological basis that laid the foundations for medieval medicine, meteorology and geography. Based on it were the numerous medieval astrological calendars. The bas-relief of the months and activities presided over by the planets on Giotto's Bell Tower in Florence can also be considered a calendar. The astral bodies whose revolutions governed the course of the years, the days and the diurnal and nocturnal hours, manifested in all their beauty in the celestial spectacle, reassured men of their material existence, and raising their eyes to the great fresco of the skies, their imagination saw in it familiar objects and shapes. From this came the fantastic figures of the constellations, planets and stars.

The *Quadripartitum*

This astrological doctrine was developed in another work of Ptolemy, expressly dedicated to explaining the influence of the sky. It was called *Quadripartitum* by the Latins, who translated the title from the Greek *Tetrabiblos*, or book divided into four parts; but the appropriate title was (as Ptolemy explained in the preface) *Treatise on omens*, which were based on the mutual effects of the apparent motion of planets as they appear in the firmament. But while Ptolemy's *Quadripartitum* can be considered the fundamental text of the medieval astrological vision, many innovations were introduced by Jewish and Arab astrologers from the 8th to the 12th century. Ptolemy's *Quadripartitum* was read, in fact in the Commentary of Alì (perhaps Alì ibn Ridwan or Ali Ametus Yusuf, 12th century).

Many aspects of Ptolemy's doctrine are underlined by Alì. Ptolemy does not mention the 'divine' influence of the decans, does not assign great importance to the influence of the 48 images of hermetic-oriental origin, and mentions only very briefly elections and interrogations, as was to be noted later by Pietro d'Abano in his *Lucidator dubitabilium astronomiae* (1303-1310).

In the 12th century and the early 13th, the Latin terminology of the *Almagest* and its Latin versions (the *De sphaera* of Sacrobosco and the *Theorica planetarum* attributed to Gherardo da Cremona) was not yet entirely consolidated. Astronomy was not separated from astrology as *scientia de iudiciis* because astrology formed an integral part of mathematical astronomy, even though, like physics and science of nature, the two terms were synonymous.

In Roman culture the astrological vision of the world had derived expressly from the philosophy of the Middle Stoa, most notably from the teaching of Posidonius (135-51 B.C.), the master of Cicero, whose doctrines were reaffirmed in the *Astronomicon* of Manilius (early 1st century A.D.) and the *Anthologiarum libri* of Vettius Valens (2nd century A.D.), but above all, prior to Manilius, by the most ancient of the Roman astrological thinkers, Publius Nigidius Figulus, who lived in the 1st century A.D. and died in 47 A.D.

But the fatalistic astrological view of the Roman Stoic philosophers of the 2nd century B.C. and 2nd century A.D. had no followers in the Middle Ages, either Latin or Arab, since this astrological determinism was confuted and rejected, also due to the opposing arguments of Cicero and later of St. Augustine.

Christian astrology

The Christian encyclopaedists of the 8th to the 12th century, such as Isidorus of Seville, Hugo of Saint Victor and Domenicus Gundissalvi, classified the Graeco-Latin astrology known at their time, which did not include these works, among the superstitious disciplines. Both Iamblicus in the *Mysteries of the Egyptians* (3rd century A.D.) and Hermes in the *Discourse to Thoth*, reported in a fragment of Stobeus, had introduced the idea of a magic ceremonial to invoke the planetary entities through appropriate prayers. In the works attributed to Hermes Thebit (12th century) that circulated in the Middle Ages, inspired by the hermetic Arab Egyptian star worship of the followers of the Queen of Sheba from Harran (8th-9th century), predictions were also based on the deities of the decans, who resided in the twelve signs of the Zodiac, multiplied by three, numbering in all 36 (*De trigintasex decanis*). But all of the magic astrological practices had been banned as superstition by Christian thought. In the mid-thirteenth century, on behalf of King Alfonso X of Castile, a magical, necromantic, astrological, divinatory treatise, *Picatrix*, which contained a magic-necromantic star worship of this type, was translated into Latin. We now know that the *Picatrix* was one of the main sources of inspiration for Alfonso's *Lapidarius*. However the work did not circulate directly in the Middle Ages, until Marsilio Ficino, Cornelio Agrippa and the wizards of the Renaissance rediscovered it, and the magic-divinatory astrology of hermetic Greek-Arab inspiration invaded Europe.

In the second half of the 13th century and then in the 14th, some Latin philosophers and scientists, first among them Pseudo-Albertus, thought to be Albertus Magnus, Pietro d'Abano, Thomas Aquinas and others carried out a doctrinal operation consisting of expelling divinatory magic from prediction of the effects of planetary motion (astronomy) on the Earth, so that astrology was rehabilitated as compared to superstition as a rational science, legitimate and permissible, possessing the same scientific dignity as the other mathematical and metaphysical sciences. The astrology of the Arabs was thus adapted to the religious horizon of Medieval Christianity as an acceptable discipline.

In iconography as well the image of this astrological cosmos is adapted to the Bible of the Old and the New Testament, its greatest fresco being that of the Empyrean in Dante's *Divine Comedy*. It shows God the Father seated in majesty on the throne, dominating the Earth and the celestial spheres, surrounded by the Empyrean of the Blessed. Here we find expressed a synthesis between the Christian concept of salvation and the astrological system of Ptolemaic-Arab-Latin astronomy. A poetic representation of this astrological universe, but with a strong tone of astrological determinism, dating from the time of Dante, appears in the poem *L'Acerba* by Cecco d'Ascoli, a fine illuminated manuscript of which is found in the Biblioteca Laurenziana of Florence (Ms. Pluteo 40, 52).

Albumasar

The most grandiose representation of the medieval 'barbaric sphere' is given by Albumasar (Muhammad al Balkhi or Jafar, 786-886) in his *Great introduction to astrology* (*Introductorium maius in astrologiam*) and his *De magnis coniunctionibus*. These works exerted an influence on the western world up to the 16th century.

1. Overleaf,
Giotto, Astrological cycle, 1312-1313,
detail of the upper register
with the sign of Aries (March-April);
Padua, Palazzo della Ragione.

2. Fascia of the Decans of Cancer, fresco,
15th century; Ferrara, Palazzo Schifanoia.

Albumasar reintroduces the mathematical astronomy of Ptolemy and the physical-natural one of the *Quadripartitum* within a cosmology where the relationships between the quintessence of the eternal, perfect heavens and the qualities of the four terrestrial elements combining to make up the sublunar forms are not clearly defined, constituting one of the major interpretive problems for the erudite Christian Latins, due to the contamination between Aristotelian and Neoplatonic-Stoic physics in regard to the concept of 'subject' material.

Between the necessary divine world and the contingent natural world, what nature should be attributed to the fixed stars and the planets? Are they substances or qualities; are they divine, or only physical, realities? To these questions Albumasar gave no clear answer, with all of the ensuing consequences for the science of astronomy. If science is the science of the necessary, then astrology is not a science, being a form of contingent knowledge. Nonetheless Albumasar offers a series of interpretations on the necessary or merely possible nature of events, of Neoplatonic-Stoic inspiration, when he speaks in favour of the contingency of events. Before events occur, they are potentially '*in ducatu siderum*'. Only when they have occurred, are they necessary. Accordingly, astrology is said to the science of 'possible' occurrences in one direction or its opposite (*ad utrumlibet*), on the basis of a probable 'sufficient' reason.

On the technical level Albumasar elaborated an astrological explanation for the history of the millenary events of the world, alleged to depend on planetary revolutions or conjunctions, millenary and centennial, and on aspects of 'triplicity'. Translated from Arab to Latin twice, in 1133 by John of Seville and in 1140 by Herman of Carinthia, one of its greatest commentaries contaminated with other doctrines is the *Liber introductorius in astrologiam* by Michael Scotus. In a fine fourteenth-century codex in the State Library of Munich, of Paduan provenance, this 'barbaric sphere' described by Albumasar is represented in beautiful coloured images. Albumasar transposes the *Almagest*'s original astronomical system of the eight skies (whose actions and influences on agriculture, illnesses and navigation are described in the *Quadripartitum*) onto a level that is merely physical, natural, geographic, medical and anthropological. He contaminates it with Islamic religious issues, with Aristotle's philosophical doctrines but also with Neoplatonic ones. And on the level of the history of technical procedures he introduces elements of Oriental Babylonian, Persian, Indian and Egyptian astrology, such as the hermetic-Egyptian Decans, the *paranatellonta* of the Greek and Latin astrology of Manilius and Firmicus Maternus. He develops the complicated technique of 'triplicity' grafted onto that of the great conjunctions. Albumasar's astrological innovation in the Ptolemaic concepts, which was accepted by many medieval astrologers such as Michael Scotus, consists of a remarkable syncretism. He differs from Ptolemy in accentuating, through the doctrine of the great conjunctions of the slow planets, the universal aspect of the astrological explanation of the world, giving rise to doctrines of catastrophic transformations in the universe, or cosmic revolutions. Ptolemy instead had been interested mainly in explaining particular events or genethliacal aspects, as he himself stated. Albumasar and the other great philosopher, mathematician and astrologist, Alkindi, introduced into the complex doctrine of oriental inspiration the complicated rules of the Arab Parthians, including techniques for finding the point of fortune or of misfortune, the point of death, the determination of a lifetime, and the position of the parents, themes already discussed, but only generically, in the *Quadripartitum*.

Albumasar thus introduced a complex survey of the planetary aspects of Fortune or Misfortune depending on the degrees of the stars, while imposing order on the differing opinions of Persian and Egyptian astrology through the doctrine of the *putei* or *precipitia* degrees, that is, the degrees that have no constellations or planets, and thus no influence, and for this reason diminish that of the degrees occupied by neighbouring stars. He also established rules for elections and interrogations, which were being elaborated contemporaneously by Jewish astrologers such as Messahalla (726-815) and Zahel (Sahl ben Bisr, c. 822-850). These treatises, under the title *De electionibus*, were widely disseminated up to the 16th century.

A singular iconographic documentation of the doctrine of the planets and their positions in the signs, according to the *facies* or terms, that is, their domicile in the thirty degrees divided by three (that is, for ten degrees, or decimal *facies*) according to their respective 'dignities' is found in Ms. Lat. 7330 of the National Library of Paris, which contains part of the preface to Albumasar's *Introductorium* compiled by an erudite Greek, Giorgii Zothori Zapari Fenduli, who boasted of having translated it from the Persian. The planets are represented for each sign, in domicile, exaltation and fall.

This sophisticated system of degrees, signs and constellations and their 'domification', or division into houses, taken from Arab astrology by the Latins, was scathingly denounced by Marsilio Ficino in his Neoplatonic-Plotinian reform of astrology, considering them to be signs and not causes, although instrumental and secondary, as was believed by the most famous Latin Aristotelian astrologers (Pietro d'Abano, Guido Bonatti), theologians such as Thomas Aquinas and all those who had adapted Aristotle's cosmology to Christianity by interpreting it.

Messahalla, Albumasar and Alkindi, almost contemporaneously, inaugurated the tradition of astrological teaching of the books of the 'Three Judges', become 'Nine Judges' in the widely disseminated medieval anonymous compilations that were then published in rare incunabula and sixteenth-century editions. 'Judge' in this tradition means an astrologer who pronounces the *iudicium*, the verdict, which is a prediction based on interpreting or explaining a celestial figure or image (horoscope) with the sun on the horizon (ascendant). For this reason medieval astrology was called 'judiciary' astrology or science of judgements, to distinguish it from the physicist-mathematical astronomy of the *Almagest*, of which it was the practical or operational section.

Astrological medicine, melothesia

The magical-hermetical-astrological doctrine of praying to the planetary deities to obtain certain results, found also in the *Libri Hermetis de orationibus planetarum*, *Liber Lunae, Veneris, Mercurii*, etc., had medical aspects as well. An astro-mathematics began to develop, based on the hermetic principle of correspondence between microcosm and macrocosm, which can be traced in the Middle Ages in the covert transmission of the Latin *Asclepius* and the *Picatrix*, which contained the magic formulas of these hermetic books.

Assigning parts of the body to the zodiacal signs produced a zodiacal melothesia, where reference to the planetary qualities is inserted into the relationship between the zodiacal signs and the body parts of the healthy man. For example, Aries is assigned the head, divided into seven parts corresponding to the seven planets: the right eye to the Sun, the left to the Moon, etc. In the texts of medieval hermetic medicine, this zodiacal melothesia was accompanied by decanic melothesia, that is, the influence of the planetary images deemed divine distributed among the three decimal parts of each sign (fig. 2), a theory discussed by Arab interpreters such as Alkindi and Alhazen.

Hermetic medicine also established the critical days, linked mainly to the phases of the Moon, and the climacteric periods, and prescribed rules for taking pharmaceuticals at the most propitious times. It is thus associated with the technique of 'elections' (*electiones*). These indications, in which some medical doctrines from the *Quadripartitum* were contaminated with the hermetic-magical doctrine of manipulating stones, plants and animal substances, were reiterated and presented in didactic form in the Arab compilation that was the *Centiloquium*, or *One hundred sentences*, of Pseudo-Ptolemy with the commentary of Ali (perhaps Ali ibn Ridwan, 12th century). It served as basis for teaching medicine in the Italian universities up to the early 16th century. It was in the 16th century, in fact, that the great physician Girolamo Cardano imposed reform on the Renaissance astrological magical medicine that had developed from commentaries to the *Centiloquium* by writing a monumental new commentary to the *Quadripartitum*, eliminating the magical-hermetic interpretations of the *Centiloquium* from the correct astrological teaching of medicine.

The 'children of the planets' and the astrological images (*facies*)

The term *facies* was used by Aby Warburg and Fritz Saxl, based on the works of physiognomy and astrological medicine of Pietro d'Abano and then of Michele Savonarola in particular. They describe the characteristics, both universal and particular, of earthly events as concerns the human species, the masculine qualities and, later, the feminine ones, and their aptitude for the professions and trades, depending on their birth.

The *Astrolabium planum* by Johannes Engel is a significant example of the physiognomic doctrine inspired by Pietro d'Abano. It presents a calendar of figures, one for each decimal *facies* of the Zodiac, that signify a characteristic, a quality or a particular aptitude of the individual, the dominant traits of a personality depending on its sign and the ascension of each star or constellation that accompanies each degree of the sign (*paranatellonta*).

In the *Astrolabium planum* we find the Ptolemaic planetary order, so that, beginning from Mars Lord of Aries, the three first decimal *facies* are Mars, the Sun, and Venus, according to the succession of the planets established by the anonymous medieval text *Trigintasex decanis* and by Alkindi. Thus the order of the planetary skies is followed from Saturn to the Moon; then it goes on to the slower planets, ascending to Saturn, then descending to the faster ones, that is, from Saturn to Jupiter, Mars, the Sun and Venus, down to the Moon. Note that the *Astrolabium planum* still has the traditional representation of the planets (which was that of Pietro d'Abano), described according to their prerogatives, which coloured each face (*facies*) and were common to almost all the traditions.

In other words, the representation of the *facies* in the *Astrolabium* comes from the traditional iconography of the planets according to their prerogatives, that is, the attributes assigned them, from which derived their influence on the 'natives' or 'children of the planets'. The astrological iconography of the *facies* in the *Astrolabium planum* is a 'planetary' iconography, since in each sign the images of the planets are represented according to their traditional attributes. Accordingly, there is no trace of those mysterious images that are the decans of medieval Arab-Latin magical hermeticism, which do not coincide with the planetary skies but are the powers that reside in the ten degrees of each sign. Testimony of the decans is found instead in the *Picatrix* and in the images of the sky in the Palazzo Schifanoia frescoes.

According to the medieval planetary theory of the *facies*, the succession of the planets within each decimal *facies* of each sign follows

3. The 'children of the planets': the sons of Mars.
De sphaera; Modena, Biblioteca Estense,
Ms. Lat. 209, c. 7v.

the order of the Lords (*Domini*) of each sign, and thus Mars for Aries, Venus for Taurus, and Mercury for Gemini. In the writings of Alkindi we find explanation for this succession, which was instead criticised by Albumasar, Alkabizio and Alì ben Ragel. With the commentaries of these authors, well known to the Latins in their various compilations of Ptolemy's astrology, this doctrine was complicated and enriched by the theory of the triplicities, the dignities, the domiciles, the exaltation, fall, and exile of the planets, of which we have an extraordinary representation in the illumination of Ms. Lat. 7333 in the National Library of France, which contains some parts of Albumasar's *Introductorium maius* edited by Giorgio Fendulo.

Highly important documentation of this vision is found in the astrological frescoes of Palazzo della Ragione in Padua attributed to Giotto, whose upper register was filled (between 1306 and 1308, when the building was remodelled by Fra Giovanni) with that grandiose astrological scene we can still admire today. It is a kind of invitation to the heavens, after life in the depths of the earth (below this scene, justice was administered in the Palace). It is a very particular sky, however, not the translucent one filtered through stained-glass windows of a Gothic cathedral, but a sky thronged with figures illustrating the effects of astronomical influences (of the constellations and the planets in domicile, fall or exaltation) on the life of man, described also in his behaviour and his aptitude for the trades and professions (fig. 1).

We find here a first description of the 'children' of the planets and their characteristics in relation to the signs and the lords of the signs governing their birth. It differs from the images of the figures expressing the symbolic characteristics of individuals according to their ascendants, which are thirty for each sign, in all 360 for the cycle of the twelve signs according to the hermetic theories of their Three-hundred-sixty degree ascendants, as illustrated by the figures in the codex of hermetic astro-magic in the Biblioteca Vaticana Palat. Lat. 1283a.

At Padua instead we find only the figures representing the natural influences of the Forty-eight images on the children of the planets, according to the theory of the decimal 'faces' (*facies*), since the planets are not decanic deities, according to Pietro d'Abano's hypothesis, but natural forces. In comparing the images of the planets and the characters of their children in Palazzo della Ragione with the middle register of Palazzo Schifanoia, which represents the decans, the difference is apparent.

Pellegrino Prisciani, astrologer to the Court of Ferrara, was probably the inspirer of the grandiose astrological fresco in Palazzo Schifanoia. The second middle register admirably represents these decanic figures of the twelve signs, as described in Albumasar's *Introductorium maius*. In the upper register appear the planetary deities of the classical Olympus and in the lower, the earthly events influenced by them. However, this Renaissance astrological iconography differs from the medieval one of the 'children of the planets'. It is suffused with a magical-hermetic atmosphere very different from that of Palazzo della Ragione in Padua. The Schifanoia fresco was in perfect harmony with the general climate that was pervading all of the cultural centres of Italy near the end of the 15th century. It was at Ferrara, in fact that Ficino's version of the work of Hermes Trismegistus was translated into Italian in 1472.

Moreover, the doctrine of the proliferation in the skies of deities that generate other kinds of demons, which in turn generate human beings, was a *topos* of the *Asclepius*, which can be considered a paradigm of the magical-astrological climate prevailing in the late 15th century.

The term 'decan', which derives from the Greek, is according to scholars extraneous to Ptolemy (as Nallino also pointed out) and to medieval astrology, which always employs the term *facies* in relation to the division of a thirty-degree sign into three *facies* (images) of ten degrees each. The expression *facies duodecim signorum* was in fact commonly used to indicate the representation (or image) of a planet within the ten degrees of each of the twelve signs. Before the Schifanoia frescoes we find no trace of these figures in medieval astrological iconography, except for what is known of the descriptions in Manilio's *Astronomicon* (dealing with the Egyptian decans) and in the above-mentioned *Picatrix*, the Arab-Spanish manual of ceremonial necromantic-astrological magic.

A splendid, grandiose illustration of the 'children of the planets' and planetary influence on terrestrial life in general is found in the so-called *Sfera estense* manuscript in the Biblioteca Estense at Modena, marked Alpha X.2.14 = Lat. 209 (fig. 3).

This codex, which dates from the 15th century, was most likely inspired by the descriptions of astrological physiognomy in the widely-known *Compilatio physiognomiae* by Pietro d'Abano, dedicated to Bardelone de Bonacossi (Captain General of Mantua from 1292 to 1299), which the author probably finished in Paris in 1295, as indicated in the *explicit* to one of his manuscript copies.

The physiognomic tradition was not unknown to the classical world prior to Ptolemy, since Aristotle had dealt with it in his biological works (*Historia animalium*, I, 488b-12) and in a passage from the *First analytics*, establishing a parallel between the traits of animals and the customs of men. But Ptolemy and the medieval physiognomists such as Pietro d'Abano introduced a new element, which distinguishes medieval physiognomy from those of antiquity and the Renaissance: namely, the astrological basis of physiognomy. This gave rise to the astrological physiognomies of the signs represented graphically as well, a singular instance of which is found in the *Sfera estense*. This exceptional example of the 'children of the planets' typology, composed by Cristoforo De Predis in the 15th century, most probably derives from the tradition of astrological physiognomies of previous centuries, and from Pietro d'Abano's *Compilatio physionomiae*.

Other notable figurative examples of the children of the planets are found in the monochrome frescoes on the moulding of the Church of the Eremitani in Padua attributed to Guariento. Although iconographic interpretation of the figures has posed some problems, I believe that the scheme is that of the general astrological physiognomies as described by Pietro d'Abano in his physiognomy.

A curious example with similar but more archaic iconography is found in the illustration to the astronomical work of Prosdocimo de' Beldomandis, contained in Ms. Canon. Misc. 554 of the Bodleian Library at Oxford, of Paduan provenance, fols. 171v-172r. He was a famous professor of astronomy in Padua in the early 15th century, who read the commentary to the *Sfera* in 1418, a work reprinted in Venice in 1531.

One of the most interesting innovations in these astrological physiognomies is the exclusion of the traits of animals from those of men (unlike the biological physiognomies of the Renaissance centuries, which return to the original Aristotelian scheme) and the application of Hippocratic-Galenic medical theories to human constitutions and to the breakdown (*crasis*) or harmony of the humours, on which depended beauty. In these treatises physiognomy appears as a medical science that identifies the characteristics of the constitution according to balance or unbalance in the humours, depending on the influence of the dominant planets. Saturn, Jupiter, Mars, Mercury and the Moon are in fact considered to be made of the same combinations of elements as terrestrial bodies, and so to possess the constitutional qualities of cold, hot, humid or dry, like those of human constitutions on earth.

The significance assigned to physical characteristics, balanced and symmetrical or isomorphic of human forms, the insistence on the concept of harmony between body and soul, between interior motions and exterior signs, the idea of a harmonious relationship with the surrounding world and, in particular, with the motion of the planets in the sky, introduced a concept of man highly attentive to his physical aspect, to the outer signs of an individual's vices and virtues, affected by the influence of the stars through the Divine will. Attention began to be focussed on the physical signs that betray the emotions. This was to be a significant factor for artists at the end of this century and the beginning of the 14th: among them the great Giotto, who was working on the Chapel of the Scrovegni in Padua just at the time when Pietro was active in the same city.

Investigation *de nativitate* is the central point of this physiognomy. It establishes that the constitutions and temperaments of individuals have a clearly determined physiological typology that depends on their dominant sign: martial traits come from Mars, jovial ones from Jupiter, melancholic or saturnine from Saturn, lunatic from the Moon, venusian from Venus, etc.

This concept was entirely reinterpreted and re-elaborated by Pietro d'Abano, in the light of Galenus' *De complexionibus*. In the Greek text of the ancient physician, Pietro found the term 'symmetry' in relation to the proportions and harmony of the qualitative, quantitative and humoural components of the temperate or balanced constitution depending on the influence of the planets. This aesthetic concept of symmetry is applied to the physical conformation of the man of temperate or 'justicial' nature, from which derives the external physiognomy that he calls 'median' and that represents the ideal norm of bodily perfection. It constitutes the rule for the man who is perfect, and therefore wise, healthy and beautiful.

This constitution of the beautiful man is, however, exceedingly rare (*rarissime inventa*). It is never found in two persons at the same time, nor do there exist many men endowed with it. It requires the cooperation of appropriate transits of the major planets such as Saturn and Jupiter at the beginning of Aries, and the assistance of the Divine will. It was the character of Jesus Christ, and can be admired in the portrait of St. Francis (Assisi), the image of Christ, in the Chapel in Assisi painted by Zoto, as Pietro calls him, that is, Giotto.

The astrological physiognomy of Codex Estense 693 in Modena

A distinction between the traits of man and of woman can instead be found in a document that bears figurative witness to this theory of astrological physiognomy. This is the beautiful codex in the Biblioteca Estense of Modena, exquisitely illustrated, whose watercolours have been compared in style to Pisanello, dating from the first half of the 15th century. It is a miscellany of astrological works, including the physiognomies of the 'subjects' of the 48 astronomical images and a brief text attributed to Pietro d'Abano on the diet and regime to be followed during the twelve months of the year.

This text takes for granted the general philosophical theories of astrological influences on the daily life of men and women, on the salient events of life, on health, and on physical appearance, or physiognomy. The work, along with the one that follows it and deals with the 'subjects' of the constellations *paranatellonta*, grouped by 48 astronomical *ymagines*, constitutes a little manual of interpretation, of hermeneutics of the 'significance' of the astrological characteristics of men. In other words, it belongs to the astrological literature of explanatory nature dedicated to interpreting the general characteristics of the individual according to signs with medical aspects. It does not include the rules and the 'technical' mathematical, geometric and astronomical systems for casting a horoscope or 'nativity' theme. The text is finely illustrated, and we will leave to the scholars of art history the task of evaluating its graphic aspects.

It is, in fact, a text of astrological *physiognomica*, certainly in line with the medical tradition of Pietro d'Abano. In the Estense codex the physiognomies of individuals born under each of the twelve signs are described. But the text differs in some ways from the passages on astrological physiognomy in Pietro d'Abano's *Compilatio*. The physiognomic description of the Estense codex dwells only briefly on the somatic features of the natives of the twelve signs, focussing instead on their moral and intellectual qualities, vices, virtues, and probable illnesses, and indicating the major events of their lives divided into different periods of years according to the cycles of the planets dominating the signs. Unlike Pietro d'Abano's text, where the physiognomic descriptions of the natives of the twelve signs make no distinction between men and women, the masculine portrait is clearly distinct from the feminine one in this work.

If there is no discrepancy, and we believe there is none – between text and illustration, the three figures at the bottom in each of the twelve signs follow the same scheme: the figure on the onlooker's left represents the physiognomy of the native man, the one in the centre the planet lord (*Dominus*) of the sign, and the figure on the right the physiognomy of the native woman.

In comparing the illustration with the text, we have the physiognomic representation of the natives, man and woman, portrayed according to some characteristic elements, at times taken freely from the written text, as well as the image of the planet.

The two small animal figures appearing on the corona around the planet, a scorpion and a ram, symbolise (like the other illustrations to the codex) the signs dominated by Mars: Scorpio and Aries.

This astrological vision of the world and of man in the Middle Ages was to endure throughout the following centuries, in the Renaissance of letters, philosophy and the arts of the 15th and 16th centuries, despite the heated attacks on it by Giovanni Pico della Mirandola. With the introduction of hermetic-magical texts translated by Marsilio Ficino, with direct knowledge of the works of the great Greek Neoplatonic philosophers such as Plotinus, Iamblicus, and Proclus, this astrological vision was to change only in sign and direction, no longer aimed at studying physical and medical effects on the Earth and on men, but rather at spiritual ascension toward the celestial souls, toward all of the entities that reside in the stars, according to a mystic and magical elevation to the upper spheres, home of the Divine intellects.

–

Bibliography

Albumasar 1995; Alfonso X di Castiglia 1982; Alfonso X di Castiglia 1981; Barzon 1924; Boll 1903; Burnett 1994; Caiazzo 2003; D'Ancona 1954; Dominguez-Rodriguez 1982; Engel 1488; Federici Vescovini 2002; Federici Vescovini 1996; Federici Vescovini 2008a, with ample bibliography; Federici Vescovini 1986; Federici Vescovini 1991; Kennedy-Pingree 1971; Frosini 2005; North 1986; al-Magriti 1986; Pietro D'Abano 2008; Poulle 1984; Ptolemy 1927; Ptolemy 1985; Rotondò 1960; Sadan 2000, Samek Ludovici 1962; Tardieu 1986; Venturi-D'Arcais 1965; Venturi-D'Arcais 1917; Weill-Parot 2002.

1. THE SKY OF THE ASTROLABE

IV.1.1
Model of a stereographic projection
Forex and Plexiglass;
diameter of the sphere 30 cm
S. Battaglia, G. Miglietta

The model visualizes the geometric procedure known as 'stereographic projection'. Explained by Ptolemy in the *Planisphaerium* (second century), but perhaps already known to Eudoxus of Cnidus (fourth century B.C.), the method permitted a plane representation of the celestial sphere. Astronomers in the Middle Ages and in the Renaissance used it especially for constructing some essential components of the astrolabe, such as the *rete* and the *planispheric plates*. The model visualizes the projective relationship between the stars located on the eighth sphere and the same ones projected on the equatorial plane, where the design of the *rete* takes form. The stars and their projections are connected by straight lines converging at the South Pole, an ideal observation point from which the plane design of the rete apparently coincides with the tri-dimensional geometry of the celestial sphere.
(F.C.)

2. STARS AND HUMAN TEMPERAMENTS

IV.2.1
Abd al-Rahām al-Sūfī
Book of the constellations and of the fixed stars
10th century
Paper manuscript; 23.5 x 16.5 cm
Paris, Bibliothèque Nationale de France,
Arab Ms. 5036, fols. 40v-41r (facsimile)

The text by al-Sūfī (903-986), of whose life very little is known (but he was active in Baghdad and in Iran), enjoyed enormous success for the splendid colourful apparatus of the most ancient manuscripts and for the precision of the stellar observations (he furnished longitude, latitude and magnitude of the single stars) that allowed him to make significant additions to Ptolemy's star catalogue. To al-Sūfī we also owe the identification of the Arabic names of the stars with the Greek names used by Ptolemy. His treatise presents a catalogue of the fixed stars, a series of representations of the 48 Ptolemaic constellations and of the zodiac. Al-Sūfī's text and illustrations enjoyed intense and prolonged success in the astronomic tradition of Islam.
On fols. 40v and 41r representations of the constellation of Hydra, on whose back the Crater and the Aquila rest. The stars of the three constellations are indicated by different-sized discs, that have different colours according to the constellations to which they belong.
(P.G.)

Bibliography: Kunitzsch 1961; Wellesz 1965; Washington 1991, pp. 217-219.

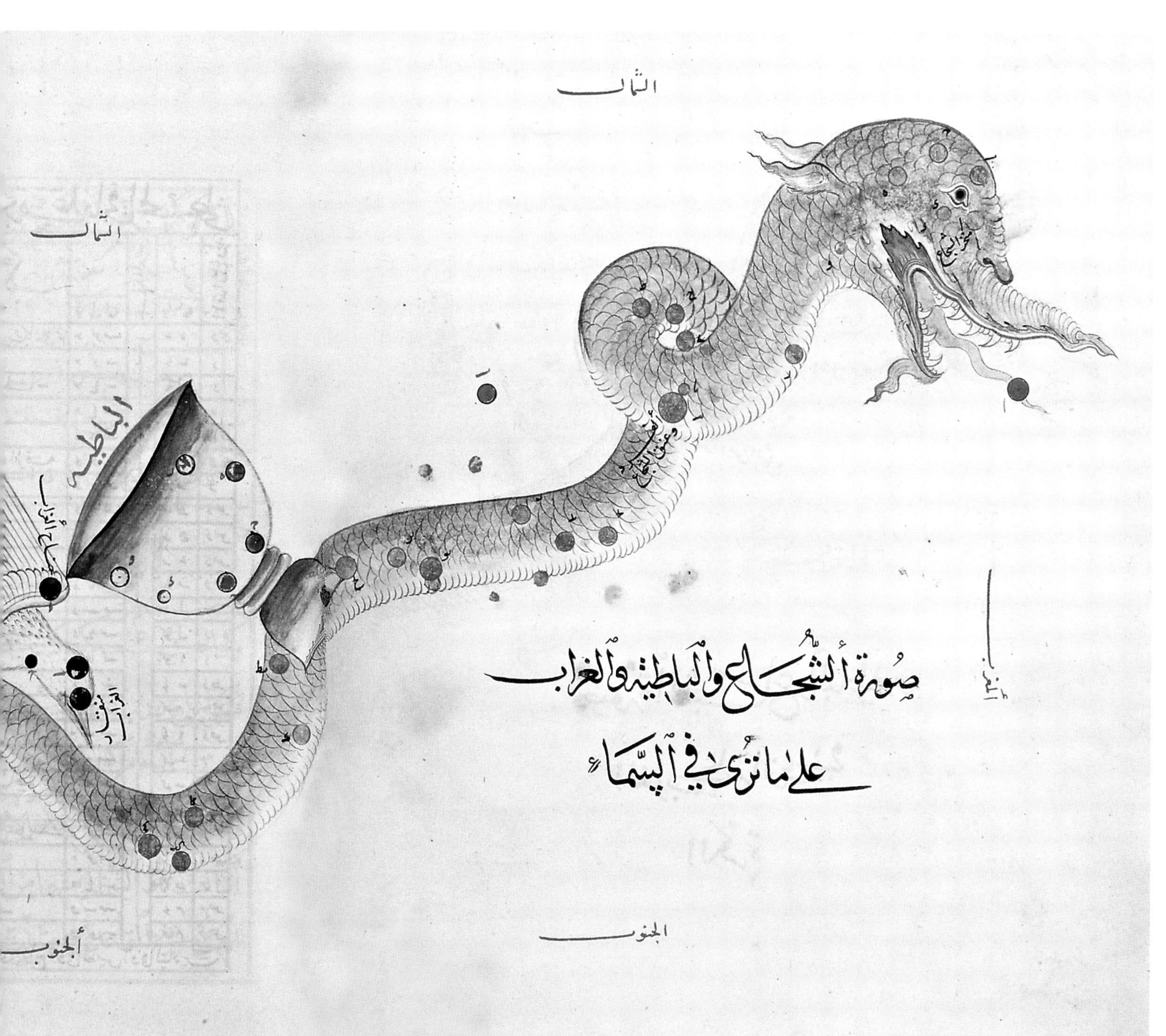
الشمال
الشمال
الباطية
صورة الشجاع والباطية والغراب
على ما ترى في السماء
الجنوب
الجنوب

IV.2.2
Al-Quazwīnī
The wonders of creation
16th century
Arabic codex chartaceus; 32.5 x 23.5 cm
Florence, Biblioteca Medicea Laurenziana,
Orientali 45, fol. 17v

A treatise on cosmography which enjoyed wide circulation. The Persian author (c. 1203-1283) reports the opinions of Greek and Arab writers. The first part of the treatise is entirely devoted to the illustration of questions of astronomy (the celestial world), while the second deals with the sphere of the elements (sublunary world). The frame of reference is the geocentric concept outlined by Aristotle and Ptolemy, whose works were well known to al-Quazwīnī.
On fol. 17v, diagrams illustrating the configurations of Sun, Earth and Moon which result in the eclipses of the moon.
(P.G.)

Bibliography: Murdoch 1984, pp. 57, 292-293; Maqbul Ahmad 1975, pp. 230-233.

IV.2.3a
Andreas Cellarius
Atlas coelestis seu Harmonia Macrocosmica
Amsterdam, Johannes Janssonius, 1660
Florence, Biblioteca Nazionale Centrale,
Magl. 5._.81, pl. 16 (*Typus aspectuum, oppositionum et coniunctionum in planetis*)

Cf. entry III.5.2.
A table that presents explicit astrological finalities. It illustrates the 'aspects' or reciprocal angular configurations of the planets, according to the Ptolemaic theory. Cellarius highlights, with different colours, thc 'trigons' (thc groups of three signs of the zodiac, each corresponding to one of the four Aristotelian elements), associating them to the four 'humours' of the human body (on whose equilibrium health depends) and to the four 'temperaments' determined by astral influences: choleric (Aries, Leo, Sagittarius), melancholic (Taurus, Virgin, Capricorn), sanguine (Gemini, Libra, Aquarius), phlegmatic (Cancer, Scorpio and Pisces).
(P.G.)

Bibliography: Cellarius 2006, pp. 113-118.

IV.2.3b
Planets and human temperaments
Demonstration model
Fiberglass; diameter 150 cm
S. Battaglia, G. Miglietta

The exhibit visualizes the theory that establishes a precise correlation between planets and human temperaments. Elaborated in the Hellenistic period, it was extensively developed in the Islamic world and enjoyed great success in the Medieval and Renaissance world. According to this theory, each planet, just as each human temperament, is characterized by a pair of qualities (hot/cold/dry/humid) and dominated by one of the four elements (fire/earth/air/water). These correlations are at the base of the planets' influence on psychosomatic temperaments in man. According to the most wide-spread conception, Jupiter, hot and humid and dominated by the element of air, presides over the sanguine temperament, also hot and humid, dominated by air and characterized by equilibrium, extroversion, liberality. Saturn influences the melancholic temperament, inclined to introversion (planet and temperament are dry and cold, while in both the earth is the dominant element); Mars dominates over the choleric temperament (quality: hot/dry; dominant element: fire). The Moon, over the phlegmatic temperament (quality: cold/humid; dominant element: water). Final result of this conception is the planet's influence on professional activities, expression of the temperamental inclinations of man.
(P.G.)

IV.3.1
Alam al-Din Qaysa
Celestial globe
1225-1226
Brass; diameter 22.1 cm
Naples, Museo Nazionale di Capodimonte,
inv. A.M. 112091

This splendid globe was made for the Ayyubid Sultan of Egypt al-Kamil in 1225. Its maker, 'Alam al-Din Qaysar known as Ta'asif, was a famous as an architect and mathematician. Inlaid silver points inside small circles indicate the positions of about 1025 stars with five different sizes used to indicate their magnitude. A full set of Ptolemaic constellation figures is engraved and damascened in copper. Their names, as well as the names of the brightest stars are damascened in silver. The inscriptions indicate that the longitudes of the stars are those of Ptolemy (c. 125) adjusted by 16°46' for the effect of precession. The globe bears the names of the constellations in a European hand; also, part of the meridian ring and stand are not original. The instrument served didactic purposes: to use it, the axis of the globe must be set to the latitude of one's locality on the meridian ring. One rotation of the globe around its axis will then represent the apparent daily rotation of the celestial sphere about the observer. In particular, risings and settings of the Sun and stars over the local horizon can be seen, as well as their culmination across the meridian.
(D.K.)

Bibliography: Mayer 1984, pp. 80-81; Savage Smith 1984, pp. 218-219.

IV.3.2
Mūsa
Spherical astrolabe
1480-1481
Brass, silver; diameter 9 cm
Oxford, Museum of the History of Science,
inv. 49687

Astrolabes generally present the stars and the path of the Sun on a flat surface by means of planispheric projection, in the manner of a map of the world. This is the only complete example of a spherical astrolabe. It is signed 'Work of Mūsa. Year 885 [= A.D. 1480/1]' and from the style of lettering and the system of numerals used, it is understood to have been made in Eastern Islam. The spherical astrolabe is used for the same set of astronomical calculations as the more common planispheric model but is less convenient to use and less robust. It is thought to be an Islamic invention and there are treatises on the instrument by an-Nairīzī (d. c. 922) and al-Bīrūnī (973-1048). The sphere is of brass with inscriptions and engraved lines damascened in silver, while the surrounding 'rete' or star map is of brass, laminated with silver on the ecliptic and equatorial circles and on the vertical quadrant; the suspension piece is of silver. The rete has pointers for 19 fixed stars, all named and all above the ecliptic, and the astrolabe can be adjusted for use in any latitude.
(J.B.)

Bibliography: Maddison 1962.

IV.3.3
Ibrahim ibn Saîd
Arab astrolabe
Valencia, 463 A.H.
Gilt brass; 33 x 24 cm
Rome, Museo Astronomico e Copernicano,
inv. 157/688

The mater contains seven tympanums and the rete; the limb is graduated and at the top there is the 'throne'. On the rete, the names of the stars are engraved near their indexes. On the verso, there is the alidade, that bears a graduation (with engravings in Arabic) on a rim and, near the ends, two sights, each with two holes for sighting. All the components of the astrolabe are hold together by a pin that passes through the centre. A tympanum engraved on the bottom of the matrix's hollow indicates various cities and the projections of the equator, of the two tropics, of the meridian of the place, besides the azimuths and almucantars for a given latitude. The tympanums also indicate the hour lines. Five of the seven tympanums – made for ten different latitudes – are similar to each other; a sixth tympanum, on one face, bears engravings entirely similar to the other five, whereas on the other face it is divided into four quadrants. The seventh tympanum serves to determine the time of the rising and setting of the Sun, of the rising and setting of a star, and to establish the length of a day. In the fourth quadrant there is the shadow square surrounded by the names of 28 constellations and the relative points (stars). An engraving on the verso states that the astrolabe was constructed 'in Rajab in the year 463 of the Hegira ... in Valencia by Ibrahim ibn Saîd'. Regarding Ibrahim ibn Saîd al-Mouazinî, it is known only that he was author of important astrolabes and of several globes. This astrolabe was transferred to the Museo Astronomico e Copernicano in 1886 from the Museo Kircheriano. (M.C.)

Bibliography: Roma 1981, p. 32, n. 8, p. 26 fig. 2; Barbanera-Venafro 1993, p. 197, fig. 9; Calisi 1991, p. 128, n. 285; Calisi 2000, p. 147, n. 302.

IV.3.4
Ahmad ibn Khalaf
Astrolabe
Baghdad, 9th-10th century
Brass; 19 x 12.5 cm
Paris, Bibliothèque Nationale de France,
inv. GE A 324

This beautiful astrolabe from the 9th-10th century was fabricated for Jafar (905-987), the son of Califf Muktafi Bi-llah, who reigned from 900 to 907 A.D. It has seventeen stars on the rete (a characteristic common to the astrolabes of this period) and a tympanum set for the various latitudes, including those of Mecca (21°) and Medina (24°).
There is no grid on the back except for an altitude scale, as in Greek astrolabes and in the most ancient Islamic astrolabes.
(D.K.)

Bibliography: Sédillot 1844; Gunther 1932, vol. I, p. 230, n. 99; Mayer 1956, p. 37; Destombes 1962, pp. 11-12; Makariou 1998, p. 82.

IV.3.5
Anonymous
Planispheric astrolabe
14th century
Gilded brass; diameter 17 cm
Florence, Istituto e Museo di Storia della Scienza, inv. 1109

The planispheric astrolabe was particularly widely used in the Islamic world, where even into the 20th century it was employed by the *muwaqqit*, the mosque astronomer, to establish the hours for prayer. From the 11th century on, European mathematicians who turned to the study of mathematical astronomy began to acquire functional instruments. Aware of the superiority of Islamic astronomy, many of them imported instruments to be converted to serve their own requirements. This astrolabe, equipped with five tympanums, four of which are for latitudes 0° and 18°, 21° and 24°, 30° and 32°, and 34° (corresponding to regions between Ethiopia and Syria), bears witness to this kind of appropriation. The Arabic inscriptions originally to be found on the rete of the instrument have been erased and replaced by their Latin translations. Nevertheless, the task of adaptation seems to have been interrupted after the engraving-etching of the Latin names of the signs of the Zodiac. This instrument belonged to the Medici collections.
(G.S.)

Bibliography: Righini Bonelli 1976, p. 163, no. 97; Miniati 1991, p. 8, no. 5; Acidini Luchinat-Morolli 2006, p. 149

IV.3.6
Muhammad Abī Bakr al Ibarī
Astrolabe with geared calendar
1221-1222
Brass, damascened with silver, gold; height 27.5 cm, width 18.5 cm
Oxford, Museum of the History of Science, inv. 48213

This Persian astrolabe with a geared calendar movement is the oldest geared machine in existence in a complete state. One side is an astrolabe and is connected to the calendar by a train of gears. It illustrates an important stage in the development of the various complex astronomical machines from which the mechanical clock derives. The design is based on a text by al-Bīrūnī (973-1048 A.D.), who explained how a special train of gearing might be used to show the revolutions of the Sun and Moon at their relative rates and to demonstrate the changing phase of the Moon, phenomena of fundamental importance in the lunar calendar used in Islam. The wheels have teeth shaped like equilateral triangles, recalling the teeth on the wheels in the Hellenistic astronomical computing machine found in a wreck of c. 80 A.D. at Antikythera and now in the National Museum, Athens (cf. entry II.4.3). When assembled, the geared calendar is operated by turning the 'rete' of the astrolabe. One circular opening on the back reveals a lunar phase diagram, while a rectangular opening gives the age of the Moon (and therefore the date in a lunar calendar). Below, within a zodiacal calendar scale, are two concentric rings, the outer ring inset with a small gold disc representing the Sun, the inner ring formerly having a similar inset representing the Moon. The rotations of these rings show the relative positions of the Sun and Moon, and the position of the Sun in the zodiac. The highly decorated rim has pictorial representations of the signs of the zodiac, between figures of warriors, while the astrolabe itself has two plates, for use in latitudes 30°, 32°; 36° and 40°.
(J.B.)

Bibliography: King H.C. 1978, pp. 15-17.

IV.3.7
Muhammad ibn Abi'l Qasim Ibn Bakran
Planispheric astrolabe
1102-1103 (496 of the Hegira)
Gilded brass; diameter 12.2 cm
Florence, Istituto e Museo di Storia della Scienza, inv. 1105

Perhaps already known to Ptolemy, who seems to refer to it in his *Planisphaerium*, but attested to with certainty only in the years 640-650 by two treatises devoted to it by John Philopon and Severus Sêbôkht respectively, the planispheric astrolabe was for centuries the most advanced and widespread instrument for astronomic calculations. The pierced 'rete' of the instrument shows a stereographic projection of the chief circles of the celestial sphere (tropics, equator and ecliptic) and a few stars as reference points. The rete can be rotated round a circular tympanum bearing the grid of the azimuth coordinates for the particular latitude of the observer. This small astrolabe, perhaps of Persian origin, has four typanums engraved on either face, for latitudes 24° and 30°, 31° and 35°, 32° and 36°, and 0°. On the back the instrument includes a rotating arm equipped with a sight for measuring the height of a celestial body (the Sun or a star) in order to determine the hour of the day or night. This instrument was donated to the Istituto e Museo di Storia della Scienza by Prince Tommaso Corsini.
(G.S.)

Bibliography: Gunther 1932, Vol. I, pp. 59-103 and p. 122, no. 122; Righini Bonelli 1976, p. 163, no. 93; Miniati 1991, p. 8, no. 3.

IV.3.8
Unsigned, Persian
Sundial and Qibla indicator
18th century
Brass; 13.1 x 9.9 cm
Oxford, Museum of the History of Science, inv. 48472

Times of prayer and the sacred direction for praying – towards Mecca – are important elements of Islamic observance and the astronomical and geometrical challenges they present have given rise to a variety of ingenious instruments. This one combines a sundial and a 'Qibla indicator' (for direction). The horizontal pin-gnomon dial is on the upper section of the plate and would have indicated the time in 'Babylonian hours', i.e. counted from sunrise, but the hinged gnomon for casting the shadow is missing, as is the magnetic compass that was set in the circular hole. The lower section of the plate, though now incomplete, was used to find the Qibla, in combination with a table of geographical data on various places in a table engraved on the reverse.
(J.B.)

IV.3.9a
Ibrâhîm 'Ibn Saîd al Sahlî
Celestial globe
Valencia, 1085 (478 of the hegira)
Gilded brass, wood; diameter 13.5 cm, height 29.5 cm
Florence, Istituto e Museo di Storia della Scienza, inv. 2712

Ever since ancient times celestial globes were instruments essential to astronomical calculations. In their most complete form – which we can date back at least to Hipparchus of Nicaea (2nd century B.C.), as described by Ptolemy in the *Almagest* – the globe shows the principal circumferences of the celestial sphere and, suitably distinguished into constellations, the stars of which the coordinates were precisely known.
This globe, the work of Ibrâhîm 'Ibn Saîd al Sahlî and his son Muhammad, is the most ancient of all the very abundant Islamic production of astronomic instruments. It shows 47 of the 48 classic constellations and contains 1015 of the 1025 stars included in the stars catalogue of the *Almagest*, each marked by a small circle. On the surface may also be seen the great circles of the celestial equator and the ecliptic, accurately graduated, as well as the Arctic and Antarctic Circles.
(G.S.)

Bibliography: Meucci 1878; Savage Smith 1985, p. 217, no. 1; Righini-Bonelli 1976, p. 156, no. 43; Miniati 1991, p. 8, no. 1; *Istituto e Museo di storia della scienza (Firenze)* 2004, pp. 112-118, no. 24.

IV.3.9b
Ferdinando Meucci
Gores of Ibrâhîm ibn Sa'îd al-Sahlî's celestial globe
Exploded model
Opera Laboratori Fiorentini

Ibrâhîm 'Ibn Saîd al Sahlî's celestial globe (cf. entry IV.3.9a) was bought in 1876 by Ferdinando Meucci (1823-1893), director since 1844 of the Imperiale e Regio Museo di Fisica e Storia Naturale in Florence. Meucci, who was the first to study the globe, added to it a ring of the meridian and the horizon, as well as a turned wooden base. He also made an exact reproduction of its surface, divided into 12 gores, which he published in 1878.
(G.S.)

Bibliography: Meucci 1878, p. 7

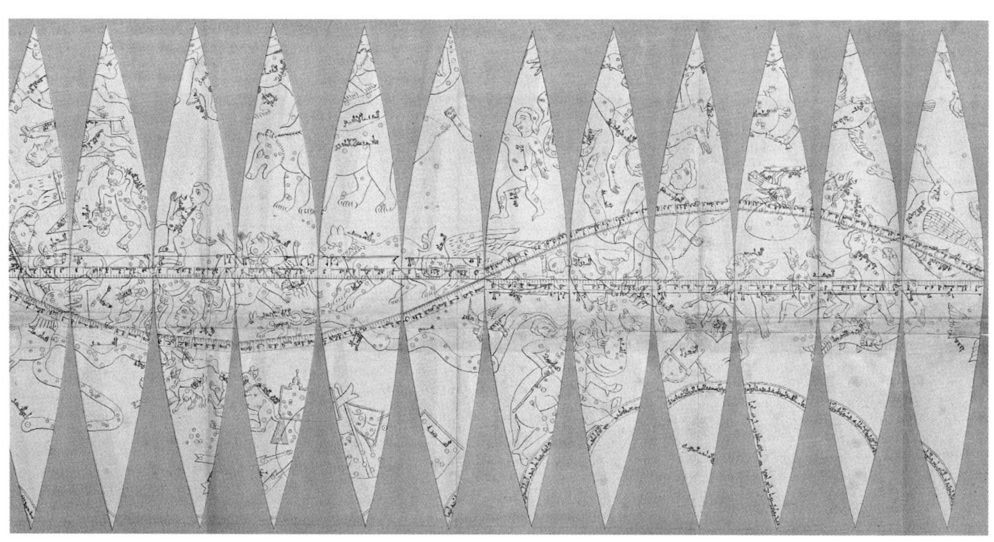

V.1.1a
Giovanni Dondi
Astrarium
14th century
Membrane manuscript, 34 fols.; 35 x 24.2 cm
Padova, Biblioteca Capitolare, Ms. D. 39,
fols. 12v-13r

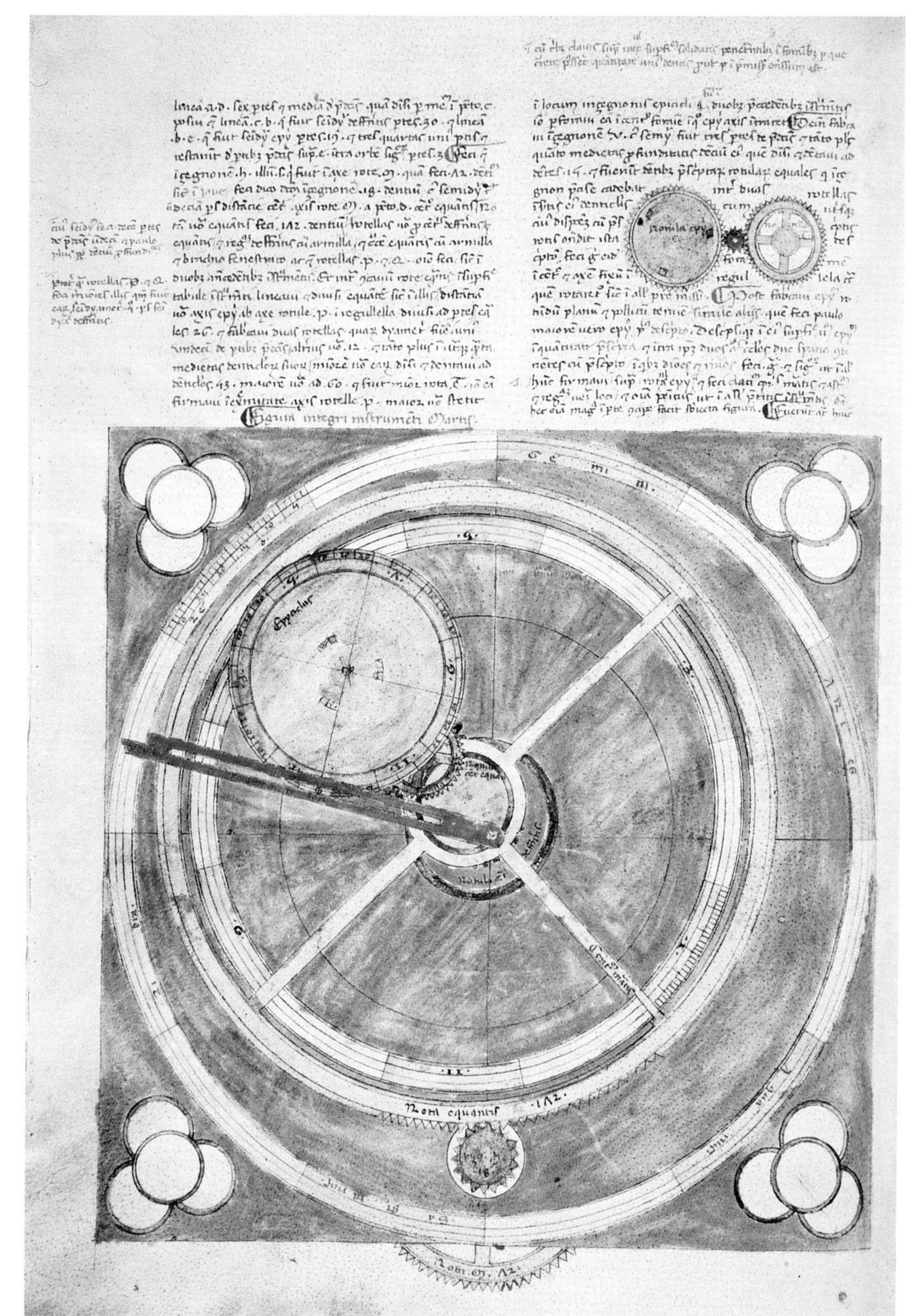

The astrarium is the first planetary clock (it shows the positions of the five planets, of the Sun and of the Moon), moved by a mechanical clock, to have ever been conceived. Designed and realized in 16 years (1365-1381) by Giovanni Dondi (c. 1330-1388), whose father Iacopo had constructed an astronomical clock (that only presented the positions of the Sun and the Moon), the planetary clock seems to have already been lost in the sixteenth century. Fortunately Dondi had prepared an extremely detailed report, accompanied by precise technical drawings, of the complex construction, committing it to a manuscript jealously guarded by his descendents and presently kept in the Biblioteca Capitolare of Padova.
In the folios 12v and 13r, driving wheel of the epicycle and instrument of the planet Venus.
(E.P.)

Bibliography: Poulle 2003; Dondi dall'Orologio 2003.

V.1.1b
Giovanni Dondi
Astrarium
Steel, brass; 100 x 90 cm
Working model; reconstruction by A. Segonds, E. Poulle, J.P. Verdet
Paris, Observatoire de Paris, inv. 404, anc.20-36

This spectacular reconstruction of the *astrarium* was realized, under the direction of E. Poulle, not only on the base of drawings from the Paduan manuscript, but also by scrupulously following the indications furnished by Dondi's text. In the clock, the planetary movements are distributed to the same number of dials around the 'common' machine that moves all the mechanisms of the astrarium, in exactly the same way as, according to the ancients' belief, the 'prime mover' conferred movement to all heavenly bodies. The mechanism of each single planet faithfully reproduces the complex movements attributed by Ptolemy, through the use of deferrents, equants and epicycles.
(E.P.)

V.1.2
Cosmas Indicopleustes
Christian Topography
9th century
Latin codex membranaceus; 25.5 x 19 cm
Florence, Biblioteca Medicea Laurenziana, Pl, 82.10, fols. 95v-96r (facsimile)

A 6th-century Alexandrian traveller and merchant who visited India on business (hence the title Indicopleustes), Cosmas represents one of the spearheads of the cultural movement which turned its back on the pagan culture of the classical world and set about constructing a physics and cosmology compatible with Holy Writ. He rejected the concept of the universe as a sphere rotating about its axis with the Earth motionless in the middle. In adherence to the biblical texts which describe the sky as a vault, Cosmas constructed a novel image of the Earth and the universe. In it our planet is a rectangular body to the sides of which the heavenly vault arises. His universe thus takes on the appearance of a tabernacle, as is vividly illustrated on fol. 96r of the Laurentian Codex, the earliest and most authoritative source of *Christian Topography*.
(P.G.)

Bibliography: Cosmas Indicopleustes 1968; Cosmas Indicopleustes 1992

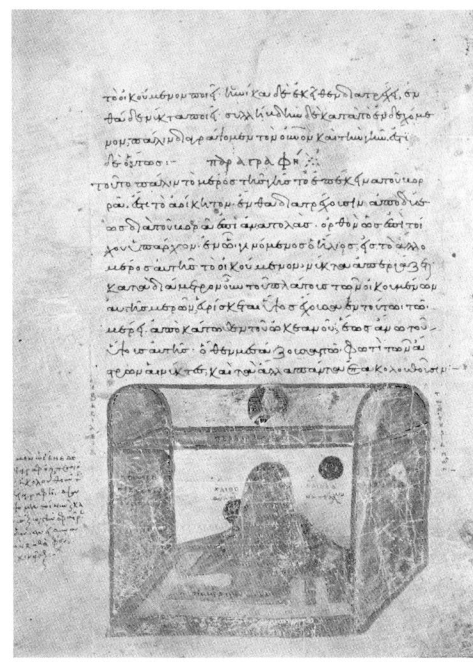

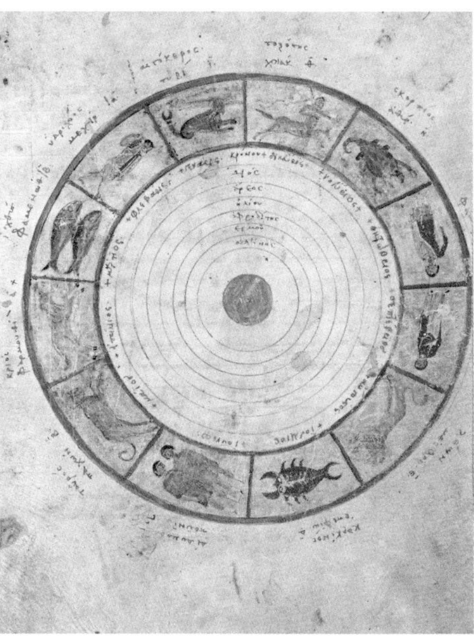

V.1.3
Matfre Ermengau de Bézier
Les bréviares d'amor
codex membranaceus; 35 x 25.5 cm
London, The British Library, Royal MS 19.C.I., fol. 34v

This beautiful codex contains a Provençal poem of 34,000 lines begun in 1288. In addition to expounding the doctrine of the Troubadours, Ermengau (d. 1322) gives us a *Traité de Dieu et de la Création*, followed by a *Traité de la nature* which includes numerous illustrations of astronomical subjects all based on the Aristotelian-Ptolemaic concept of the cosmos seen in the light of the Christian notion of the creation of the universe. Folio 34verso shows the universe with the Earth at the centre. In accordance with the Christian belief in angels, the Earth's sphere is rotated in the hands of four angels.
(P.G.)

Bibliography: Murdoch 1984, p. 336; Parigi 1998, p. 28.

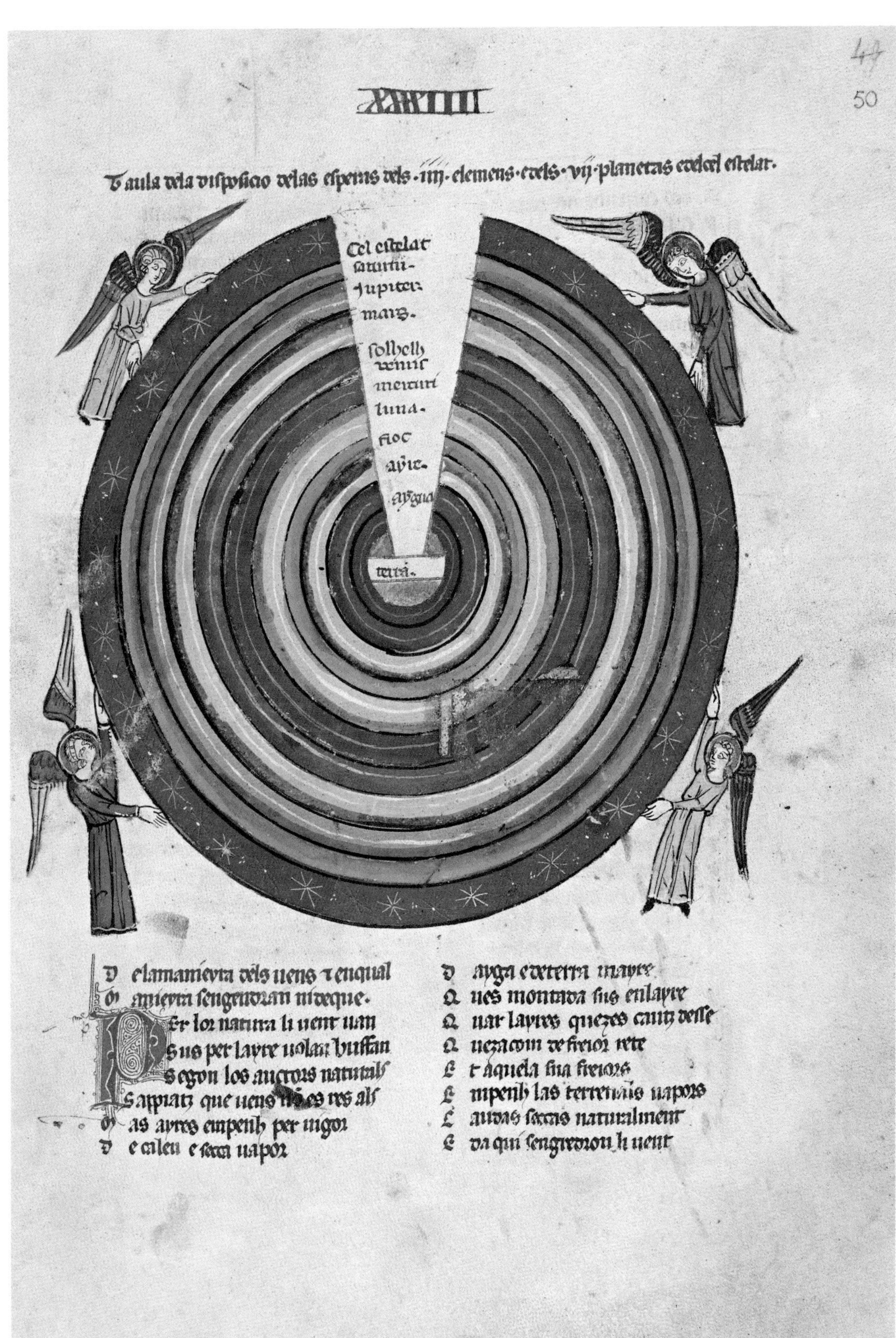

V.1.4
Hildegard of Bingen
Liber divinorum operum
13th century
Codex membranaceous; IV, 164, V; 40 x 26 cm
Lucca, Biblioteca Statale, Ms. 1942, fol. 9r

Hildegard of Bingen (Bermersheim 1098 - Bingen 1179), born into a family of Rhenish free nobles, demonstrated from a tender age an extraordinary visionary capacity. For this reason, her parents dedicated her to monastic life. She was first a Benedictine recluse in the convent of Disibodenberg, then abbess of the monastery she herself founded near Bingen. Hildegard maintained contacts (and was often in contrast) with the highest-ranking religious and civil figures. Her visions found expression through works where philosophy and theology interacted with music, medicine, astronomy, botany, etc., giving life to an encyclopaedic system of exceptional organicity, extraordinary for a female figure. The *Liber divinorum operum*, which should probably be associated with the beginning of her process of canonisation in 1227, is the third and last prophetic work by Hildegard. Divided into three parts, it presents ten visions that explain the position of man as a 'microcosm' at the centre of the celestial spheres and of the other forces of the macrocosm. The manuscript belongs to the library of the Regular Clerks of the Mother of God of Santa Maria Corteorlandini Monastery in Lucca. It is probable that it was previously in the possession of the erudite Archbishop of Lucca, Giovan Domenico Mansi (1692-1769). The study of the graphic and artistic aspects indicates the origin as the Rhine area, in the second or third decade of the 13th century. The manuscript is enriched by ten full-page illustrations (one for each vision). At folio 9r, the Spirit of the world opens its arms to embrace the cosmo; at the centre, man is measure of the Whole, while each of the four elements (five with the ether) is explained in its physical and allegorical meaning. In the lower left-hand corner, Hildegard is sitting at her desk with a tablet and a stylus in her hands recording her visions.
(G.P.)

Bibliography: Calderoni Masetti-Dalli Regoli 1973; Ildegarda di Bingen 1996; Ildegarda di Bingen 2003.

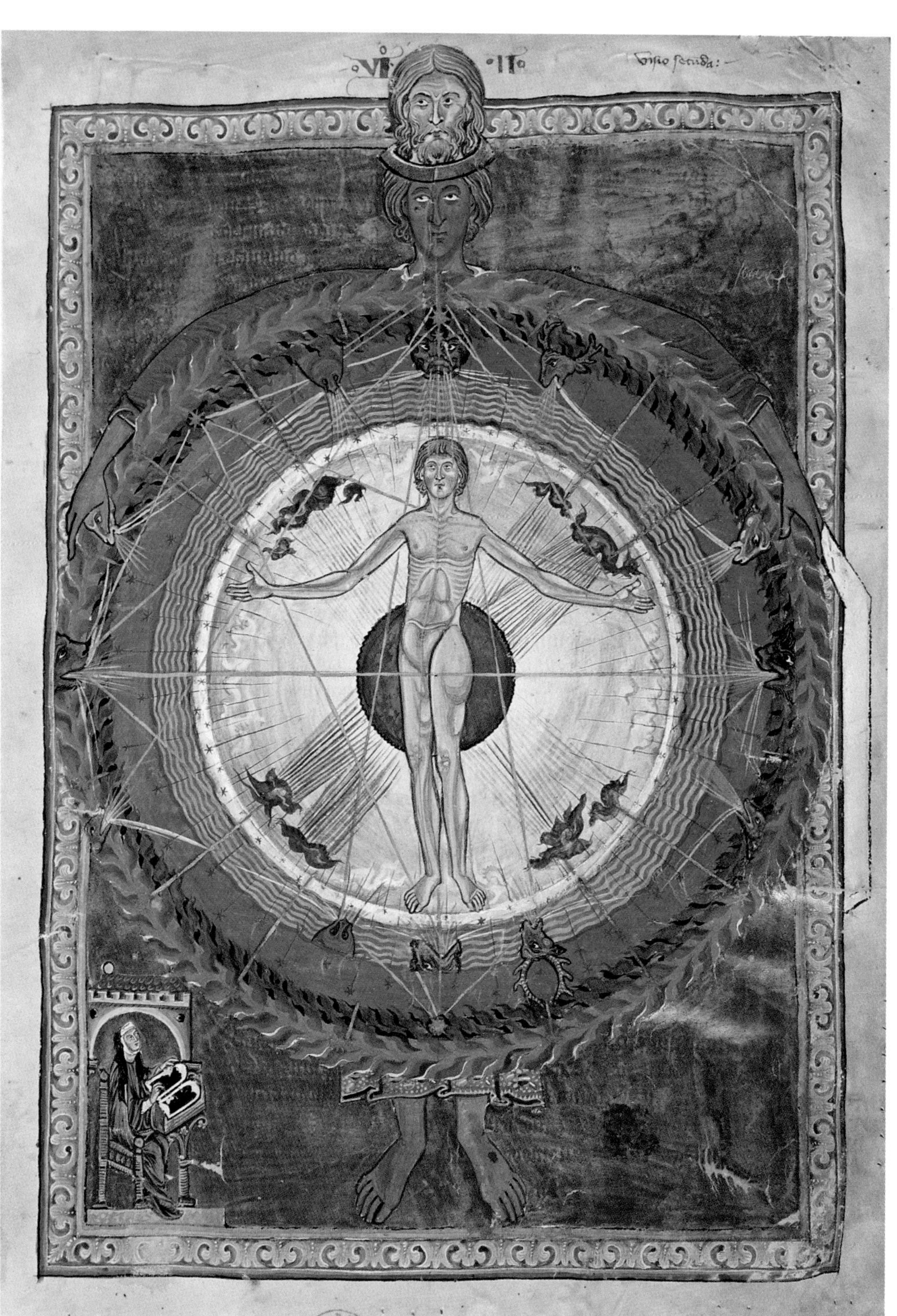

V.1.5
Giovanni Sacrobosco (John of Holywood)
Tractato de la sfera
14th century
Codex membranaceous; III, 39, III'; 39 x 27 cm
Florence, Biblioteca Riccardiana,
Ms. Ricc. 2425, fols. 35v-36r

The *Sfera* is a treatise of elementary cosmology written by Giovanni Sacrobosco (Holywood), born at the end of the 12th century (precise date is unknown) and who died in 1256. It is a simple and clear compilation of Ptolemy's *Almagest*, with his theory of eccentrics and epicycles. The treatise presents the transformations brought about by the Islamic commentators in the 9th and the 11th centuries, who introduced the *primum mobile* or ninth sphere attributed to Alhazen (10th-11th century), the division of the climatic zones (*climata* or latitudes) determined by Al-Farghani, or Alfraganus (9th century), well known also for having established the distances between the planets in terms of semi-diameters of the planetary spheres. The new calculations of the precession of the equinoxes established by Al-Battani, or Albategnius, are reported here. The *Sfera* represented the elementary manual of astronomy for nearly four centuries, up to the Galilean revolution.
The 35v folios of the manuscript, that contains the 'vernacularization' of the *De Sphaera* completed in the first half of the fourteenth century by the Florentine notary, Zucchero Bencivenni, illustrates the sphere of the world with the *primum mobile* with the motions of the Sun and of the Moon, the total and partial eclipses of the Moon and the eclipse of the Sun.
(G.F.V.)

Bibliography: Thorndike 1949; Poulle 1984; Ronchi 1999.

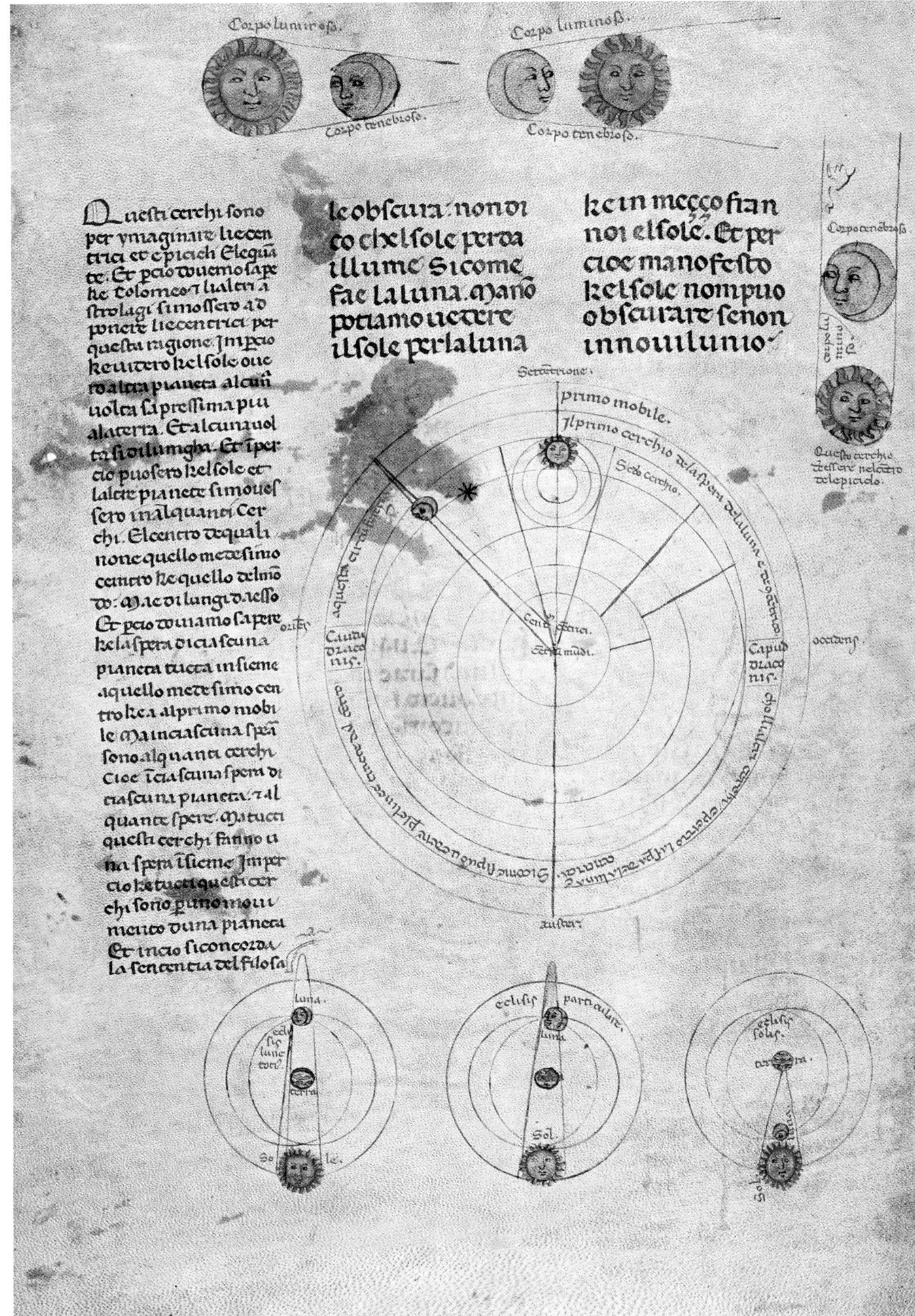

V.1.6
Michael Scot
Introductorium maius in astronomiam
15th century
Codex membranaceous; 29 x 20.3 cm
Florence, Biblioteca Nazionale Centrale,
Magl. XXII,24, fols. 30vab-31rab

Michael Scot (c. 1175-1235/37) was a philosopher, astronomer, magician in the retinue of Frederick II, and translator of Aristotle. His *Introductorium maius in astronomiam* is the greatest encyclopaedic work of the early thirteenth century. It spreads all the new facts regarding science and philosophy introduced by the translations done in Toledo, around the middle of the twelfth century, of Aristotle's philosophic works, as well as of scientific, mathematical and astronomical texts in Arabic and in Hebrew written from the eighth century through the twelfth century, and of Arab texts on magic, Hermetism and astrology.
The work is divided into three parts: the first deals with the sky and the earth and pictures the universe with all the skies, planets, constellations, and the Zodiac with its signs. Paradise is described there with angels, and Hell with the cohort of all the demons. All the sciences and forms of knowledge are classified and defined. The second, with the title *Liber particularium (rerum)*, treats the secrets of nature even with subjects such as alchemy, while the third, entitled *Physiognomia*, deals with the secrets of plants, animals and human nature.
In folios 30v-31r, images of the constellations.
(G.F.V.)

Bibliography: Edwards 1985; Federici Vescovini 2008b.

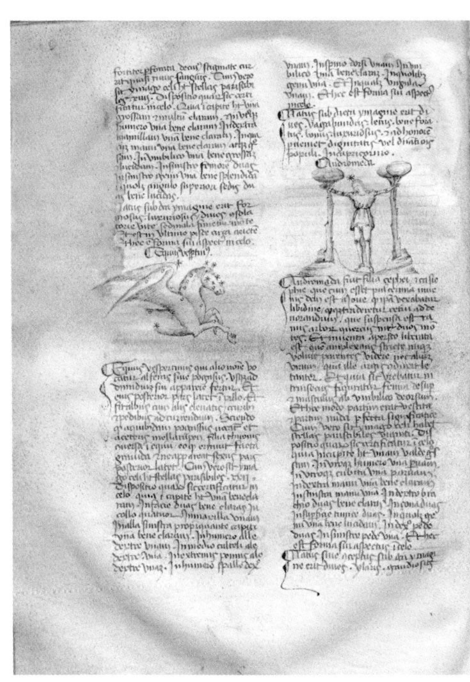

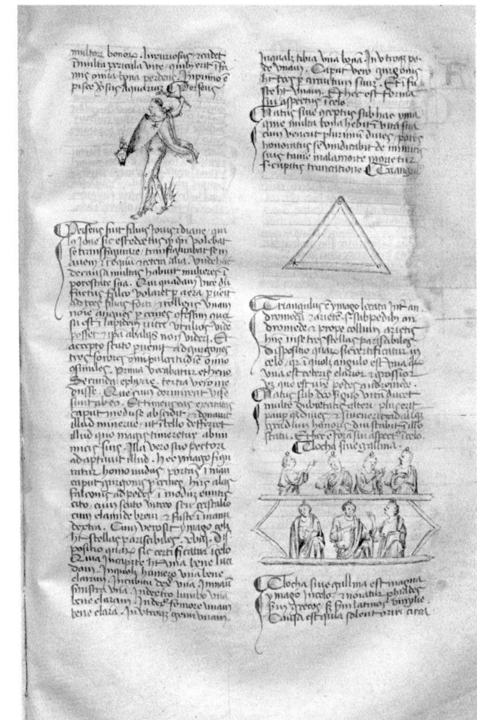

V.1.7
Andreas Cellarius
Atlas coelestis seu Harmonia Macrocosmica
Amsterdam, Johannes Janssonius, 1660
Florence, Biblioteca Nazionale Centrale,
Magl. 5._.81, pls. 23-24 (*Coeli stellati Christiani Haemisphaerium Prius - Posterius*)

Cf. entry III.5.2.
In these two tables Cellarius proposes the Christian interpretation of the constellations elaborated by the lawyer Julius Schiller of Augsburg in his *Coelum Stellatum Christianum* (that he had published in his own city in 1627). Following Schiller's model, Cellarius re-names the classic constellations with the names of characters from the New Testament (north of the Zodiac) and of the Old Testament (to the south), while the signs of the zodiac are substituted by the names of the 12 apostles. The planets (Sun and Moon included) are christened with Biblical images. Christ coincides with the Sun, whereas the Virgin is identified with the Moon.
(P.G.)

Bibliography: Cellarius 2006, pp. 155-165.

COELI STELLATI
CHRISTIANI HAEMISPHAERIUM PRIUS

V.2.1
Sandro Botticelli
Saint Augustine in his Study
c. 1480
Detached fresco; 152 x 112 cm
Florence, Chiesa di Ognissanti

The splendid fresco by Botticelli (1445-1510), commissioned by the Florentine family of the Vespucci, portrays Augustine in an ecstatic attitude with his eyes turned towards the sky. The portrayal well expresses the tension perceived in the writings of the Saint (354-430), between the tendency to consider curiosity for the natural world as a dangerous distraction from the search for beatitude and the awareness that to defend the faith from pagans it is necessary to know natural philosophy. The need to reach this goal must be connected with the importance that the Saint assigns to the mathematical disciplines, particularly to music. Though he never dedicated a specific work to astronomy, he underlines its importance, on the condition that the study of stars not give rise to superstitious beliefs (*De civitate Dei*, V, 1, 6-7).
The study in which Botticelli portrays Augustine is full of objects relating to the mathematical sciences and astronomy. Behind the saint, and beside an open text of geometry (probably Euclid's *Elements*) is a mechanical clock. In front of Augustine is an armillary sphere representing the geocentric universe.
(P.G.)

Bibliography: Firenze 2004, pp. 130-133; *Storia della Scienza* 2001, IV, pp. 130-134.

V.2.2
Anonymous
The motions of the universe
1450-1500
Flemish tapestry (perhaps Tournai);
415 x 815 cm
Toledo, Museo de Santa Cruz
(in deposit from Toledo Cathedral)

A complex geometrical and allegorical depiction of the structure and motion of the universe, this truly spectacular work, of enormous dimensions, is one of the oldest examples of Flemish tapestry. Its presence in the Cathedral of Toledo is recorded right back to 1501.The whole is dominated by the celestial sphere at the centre of the tapestry, which is projected onto a plane so that it assumes the form of an astrolabe kept in motion by two angels, one of whom is winding a handle while the other pushes round the circle of the Primum Mobile. At the centre of the sphere, and the tapestry itself, shines the Polar Star surrounded by three circles representing the Arctic Circle (the inner one), the Tropic of Capricorn (the middle one), and the course of the Sun along the ecliptic.
Identified by their Latin names are the extra-zodiacal constellations of the southern hemisphere according to Hyginus (Andromeda, Pegasus, Orion, Draco etc.). The Latin text above the astrolabe explains that the sphere of the earth revolves around the polar axis surrounded by the Zodiac, exercising its influence upon mankind. God is shown as the 'First Mover', giving motion to the sphere of the world supported by the kneeling figure of Atlas.
The Latin text in the upper margin tells us the meaning of the illustrations below. When, on God's orders, the angel winds the handle, the universe begins to move. On the right is depicted Philosophy, with Geometry and Arithmetic at her feet. To the left of Philosophy is shown the astronomer Abrachis (Hipparchus), above whom is Virgil, while on the right and towards the sphere Astrology points her finger skywards. The meaning of this part of the picture is explained by the text above: thanks to Philosophy and Wisdom, Hipparchus understood the nature of the celestial phenomena of which Virgil wrote; and thanks to Mathematics many people now possess this knowledge.
(P.G.)

Bibliography: Firenze 1980, p. 327; Washington 1991, pp. 214-215.

V.3.1
Byzantine Sundial-Calendar
5th-6th century
Brass, partly tinned; diameter of disc 13.5 cm
London, The Science Museum, inv. 1983-1393

The four fragments are all that remains of a portable sundial combined with a geared calendrical mechanism. The style of the Greek lettering, the style of the ring of incised heads, and the set of place-names, suggest an origin within the Byzantine empire in the late 5th or early 6th century A.D. The instrument bears witness that the use of geared mechanism in an astronomical context, first found in the Antikythera Mechanism (cf. entry II.4.3), continued into the Byzantine era and was then adopted by the Arabs (Field-Wright 1985).
The large circular disc formed the basis of the sundial. A lost part, combining shadow-caster and hour scale, was fitted to the central hole, and the scales around the hole, marked with abbreviations for the Julian months, enabled the user to set it to the Sun's declination for the time of year. At the edge of the disc is a scale of degrees for setting the instrument to the user's latitude, and there is a table of the names of cities and provinces with their latitudes. A second hole, for the stem of the mobile by which the calendar is worked (described below), is encircled by seven incised heads representing the days of the Judaeo-Christian week. A lost rim, fixed to the back of the disc, formed a shallow box.
The suspension arm lay behind the box, held in place by the stem of the shadow-caster. Its hooked end embraced the rim of the box, so that its pointer registered on the scale of latitude. When used as a dial, the instrument was held up by the ring.
The other two pieces were parts of the internal calendrical mechanism. One has two small gears, of seven and ten teeth, and a seven-lobed ratchet. Its stem, which projected through the offset hole in the disc and carried a pointer indicating the day of the week, was turned to set the calendar. A pawl, engaging the seven-lobed ratchet, ensured that the user always moved the calendar forward, one step each day. Thus the smaller gear, with seven teeth, moved forward by one tooth each day.
This gear engaged the larger one on the other surviving piece which, having 59 teeth, therefore made one turn in 59 days: an approximation to two synodic months. Its face, brightened by tinning, formed part of the display. The numbers 1 to 29 and 1 to 30, the days of two consecutive months, are engraved near the edge, and it has two large circular holes which were probably filled with some dark material. This wheel rotated behind two openings in the lost back of the box, showing the day of the month through a small hole and a crude representation of the phase of the Moon through a larger circular one.
Behind the large wheel is a smaller one of 19 teeth. This and the second gear on the other mobile worked additional display elements. Following a description by al-Bīrūnī (c. 1000 A.D.) of a similar geared calendar, these were probably indications of the places of the Sun and Moon in the Zodiac (Hill 1985). A reconstruction of the complete instrument is displayed nearby (cf. entry V.3.2). (M.T.W.)

Bibliography: Field-Wright 1985b; Hill 1985; Field 1990; Wright 1990.

V.3.2
Byzantine Sundial-Calendar
Brass, partly tinned, hard wax; 18.2 x 16.8 cm, diameter of body 13,5 cm
Model by M.T. Wright, London

The model is a reconstruction of the original fragmentary instrument, believed to date from the early sixth century A.D., which is displayed nearby (Field-Wright 1985).
The instrument comprises two practically independent parts: a sundial for use at any latitude, and a geared calendrical device showing the phase of the Moon, the day of the month and the places of the Sun and the Moon in the Zodiac.
This type of sundial is attested by a several examples, some inscribed in Latin and some in Greek (Field 1990). None is securely dated, but the archaeological record suggests that these instruments were widely distributed within the Roman and the early Byzantine empires. The design probably corresponds to that described by the Roman author Vitruvius (late 1st century B.C.) as 'pros pan clima' (for every latitude), suggesting a yet earlier Greek origin.
The dial occupies most of one face of the instrument. It comprises a piece that is both shadow-caster and hour-scale, the central pin of which passes first through the circular body and then through the swinging arm at the back to which is jointed a ring by which the instrument is hung upright. Two scales on the body enable the user to adjust the first part to the elevation of the Sun at noon, according to the place and the time of year: the shadow-caster is moved over a double scale of solar declination, marked out with abbreviations of the Julian month-names; and the arm is adjusted according to a quadrant scale of latitude near the rim of the body. The dial is then held up, and rotated until the shadow of the projecting part falls along the curved scale, whereupon the user may read off the morning or afternoon hours. Much of the rest of the face of the dial is taken up with a reference table of place-names and their latitudes. The known comparable dials are smaller and are based on flat circular discs. In this case, uniquely, a hollow box, which takes the place of the disc, contains a geared calendrical mechanism which is worked by turning a pointer on the face of the dial. The pointer moves over a circle of seven incised heads representing the seven days of the Judaeo-Christian week. A ratchet inside prevents the user from turning it backwards. Simple gearing in the ratio 7:59 rotates a disc making one turn in 59 days which displays the day of the month (alternately 29 and 30 days in length) and an approximate representation of the phase of the Moon, through openings in the back of the box. Following the description of a similar instrument by al-Bīrūnī (Hill 1985), the remainder of the mechanism is restored to drive indications of the places of the Moon and of the Sun in the Zodiac. A more elaborate reconstruction might include a display of the Moon's nodes (enabling the user to predict the possibility of eclipse) or mechanism whereby the position of the shadow-caster and hour-scale is set automatically by the calendar (Wright 1990); but these possibilities have no historical basis.
(M.T.W.)

Bibliography: Field-Wright 1985b; Field 1990; Hill 1985; Wright 1990.

V.3.3
Anonymous
Astrolabe
1062
Brass; diameter 37.5 cm
Brescia, Civici Musei d'Arte e Storia, inv. IC n. 2

This is the sole surviving astrolabe with inscriptions in Greek. It serves as a reminder that although most surviving astrolabes have inscriptions in Arabic or Latin, the instrument is of Greek origin. The design of the rete or star-map is simple, indeed identical to that of the earliest known Islamic astrolabe, which suggests that this was a standard Greek and Byzantine design. An inscription on the back indicates that it was made by order of a government official (*protospatarius*) named Sergios in 1062. The inscription on the front, compiled by Sergios, is in verse, and elegantly describes the astrolabe as an icon of the universe. The astrolabe was apparently brought from Constantinople to Italy by Cardinal Bessarion, who in 1460-61 took it to Vienna. There he showed it to the young German astronomer Regiomontanus, who decided to make a new astrolabe for the Cardinal (cf. entry V.3.4). The instrument was donated to the City of Brescia in 1844 by Francesco Sailer (1786-1915), a cavalryman in the Piemonte Army and a collector. (D.K.)

Bibliography: King D.A. 2007a; Miniati 2003, pp. 24-27.

V.3.4
Regiomontanus
(Johannes Müller de Königsberg)
Astrolabe presented to Cardinal Bessarion
1462
Brass; diameter 11.6 cm
Private collection

In 1460-61 the Greek Cardinal Bessarion served as Papal Legate to the court in Vienna and there met the astronomer and mathematician Regiomontanus (1436-1476). He showed the young German Regiomontanus an old Byzantine astrolabe that he had brought from Constantinople (c.f. entry V.3.3). Regiomontanus decided to present his new patron with a new astrolabe to replace the old one in every sense. The new piece is a typical production of the Vienna school (it is the most elegant of ten other known astrolabes), but it is the image of the angel and the Latin dedication on the back that are of monumental historical significance. First, the epigram is a brilliant acrostic with eight vertical axes containing hidden messages, some referring to the Byzantine astrolabe. But second, the letters of the epigram reveal the names of a series of eight personalities who were later used, in the same order, by Piero della Francesca in his *Flagellation of Christ*. The angel on the astrolabe is the Cardinal's patron saint, the 5th-century Egyptian St Bessarion, and the blonde angelic figure in the painting is Regiomontanus.
(D.K.)

Bibliography: King D.A. 2007a, pp. 31-73, 234-274.

V.3.5
Anonymous
French geared astrolabe
14th century
Brass; 21.5 x 3 x 15 cm
London, Science Museum, inv. 1880-32

The calendrical gearing on the front of this astrolabe is the earliest surviving example of mathematical gearing from the West.
The gearing, which is incomplete and shows traces of modifications or repairs, is worked by a train of wheels running around the inside of a ring of 180 teeth attached to the edge of the rete (see Field-Wright 1985a for a reconstruction). The gear train is moved by an arm which pivots around the astrolabe's central pin. The tip of this arm, now missing, gives the position of the Sun in the Zodiac where it crosses the rete's offset circular scale. A second arm, also missing, would have indicated the Moon's zodiacal position on the offset scale and the age of the Moon in days on a circular scale on the arm. This scale is divided into 30 intervals and uses Arabic numerals (read right to left).
This is a 'Northern astrolabe': the projection is from the North Pole, with the South celestial pole at the centre of the disc. The rete indicates the positions of 22 stars with flame pointers. The single tablet is marked *Engletiere* on one side and *hollande* on the other, and does not appear to be original to the instrument.
(A.B.)

Bibliography: Field-Wright 1985b; Field-Wright 1985a; Günther 1976, p. 347.

V.3.6
Anonymous
Astrolabe bearing monastic numeral ciphers
Picardy, 14th century
Brass; diameter 11.7 cm
Private collection

The style of this astrolabe rete or star-map indicates that it is from Northern France. Typical of this tradition are the vertical axis and the half quatrefoils. The month-names on the back are in the Picard dialect of medieval French, which helps pinpoint the provenance still further. What is remarkable about this piece is that all numerals on it are engraved in a cipher notation that was circulating in certain European monasteries from the 13th century onwards. In this notation the concepts 1-9 are represented by nine attachments composed of short line segments attached to a vertical stem that itself has no numerical value. The attachments to the upper right of the stem serve the units. The same attachments on the upper left represent the tens, on the lower right the hundreds, and on the lower left the thousands. The genius of the system is that a given integer from 1 to 9,999 can be represented with the appropriate appendages attached in the four different ways to a single stem. This notation was used in limited circles from Spain to Sweden and from England to Italy, and it features as a curiosity in several early printed works. The astrolabe bears an inscription indicating that it was presented in 1522 by the Humanist monk of Liège, Berselius, to his teacher of Greek in Louvain, Amerotius.
(D.K.)

Bibliography: King D.A. 2001, *passim*.

V.3.7
Georg Peurbach (attr.)
Astrolabe
Vienna, 1457
Brass; diameter 12.9 cm
Nürnberg, Germanisches Nationalmuseum,
inv. WI 129

This instrument is the earliest surviving astrolabe from the Vienna school of the 15th century, of which another eleven have survived. Alas, all of them are unsigned except for the astrolabe presented by Regiomontanus to Cardinal Bessarion in 1462 (cf. entry V.3.4). This piece is exquisitely made, which is proof enough that many earlier astrolabes were made in this school. Since it is dated 1457, it is generally associated with the master of that school Georg von Peurbach (d. 1461), rather than his pupil and successor Regiomontanus, who was at the time perhaps too young (21) to be making astrolabes. The arms of Vienna are featured on the throne, and one of the plates serves latitudes 48°, that is, Vienna.
(D.K.)

Bibliography: King D.A. 2007b; King D.A. 2007a, pp. 237-241.

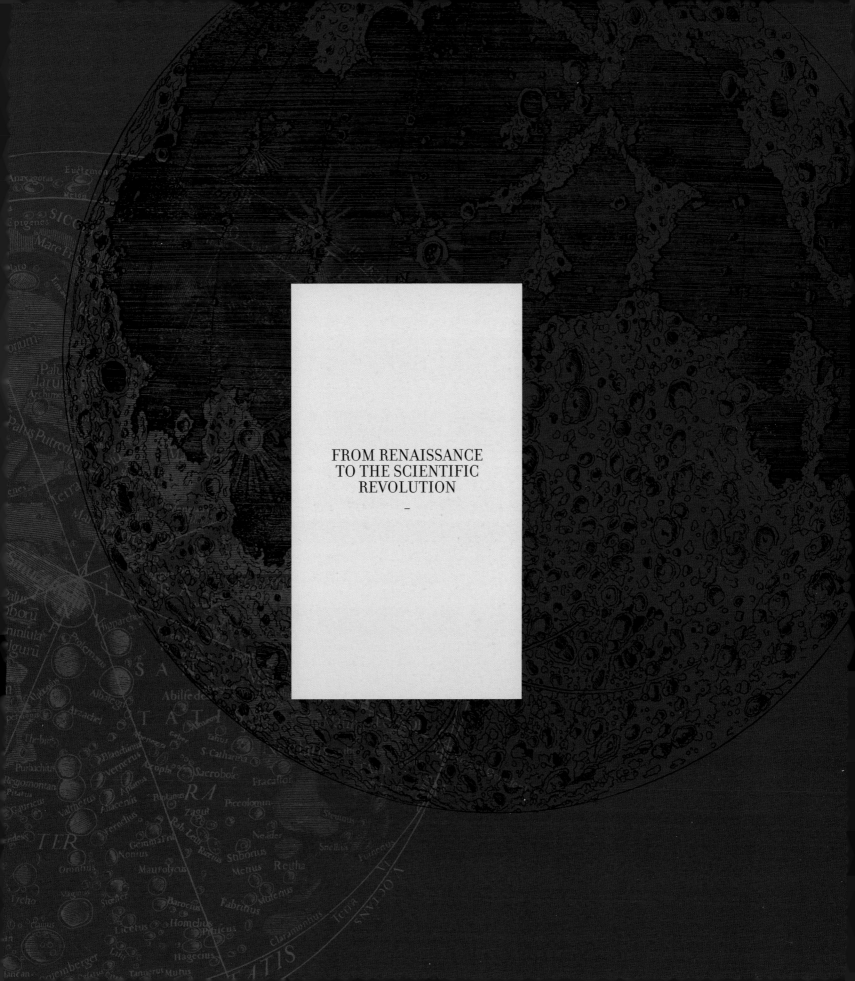

FROM RENAISSANCE TO THE SCIENTIFIC REVOLUTION

–

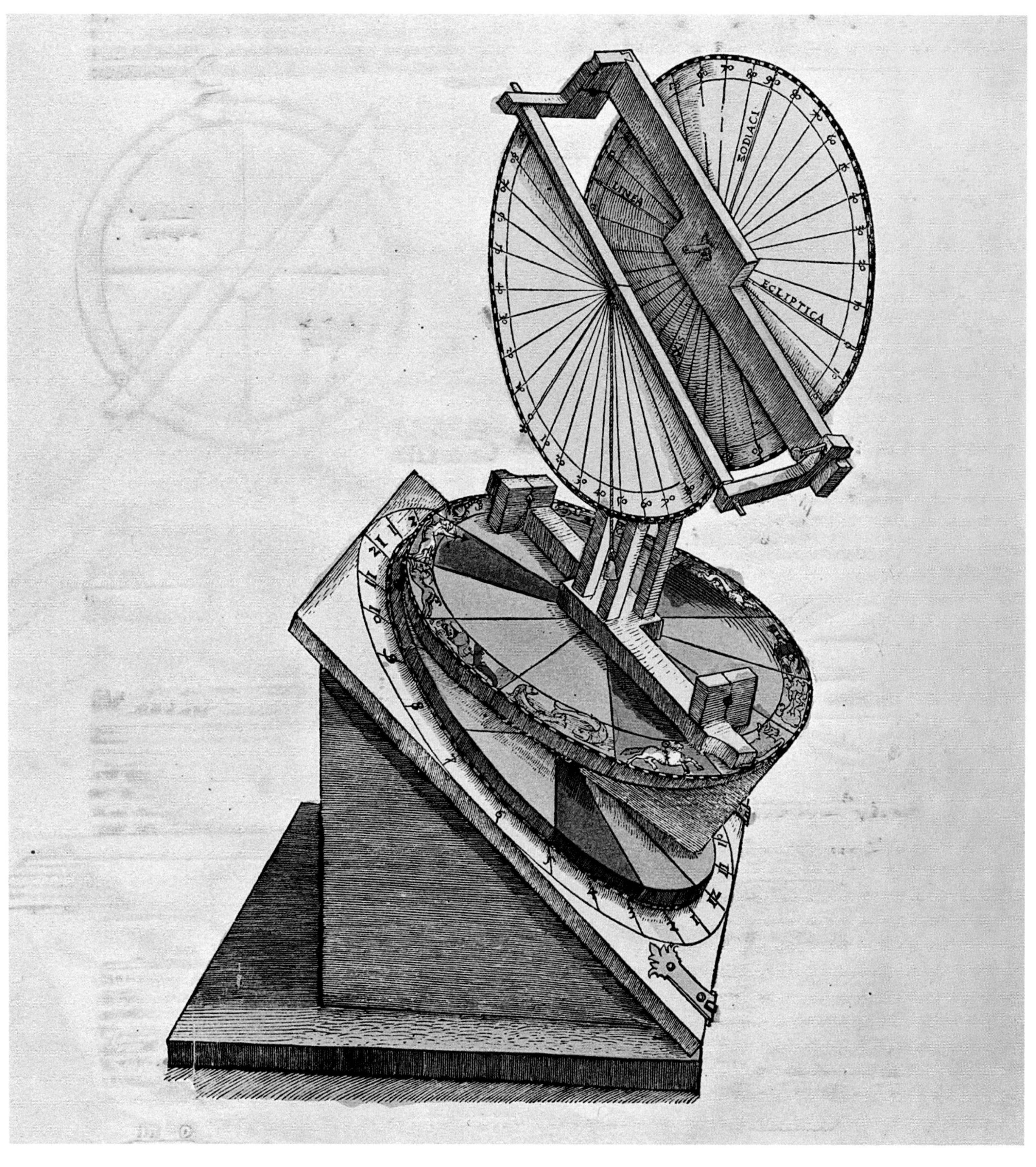
ZODIACI
LINEA
ECLIPTICA

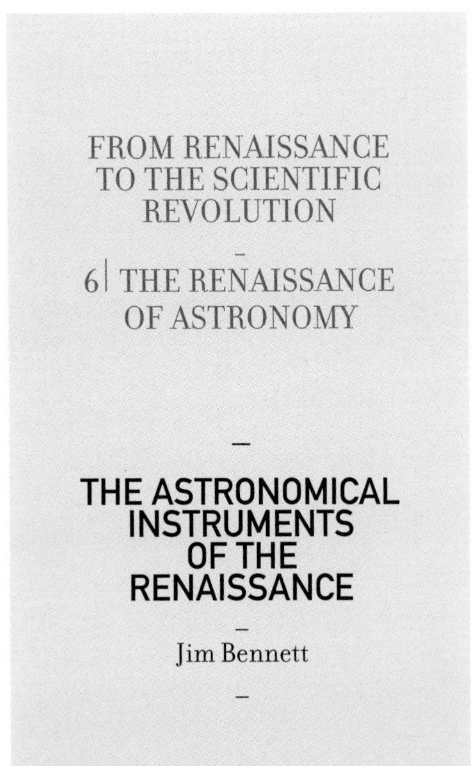

FROM RENAISSANCE
TO THE SCIENTIFIC
REVOLUTION
6| THE RENAISSANCE
OF ASTRONOMY
THE ASTRONOMICAL
INSTRUMENTS
OF THE
RENAISSANCE
Jim Bennett

The Renaissance impulse in astronomy was not confined to the recovery and mastery of Ptolemy's geometrical account of the planets and stars. Entailed in the same enterprise was the revival of what was understood to be the ancient practice of astronomical work in observation and measurement. Mathematical theory and instrumental practice shared the same fundamental documentary resource in Ptolemy's *Almagest*, written in the second century A.D., translated into Latin in the twelfth century and published in a printed edition in 1515. Even before *Almagest* was available in print, astronomers were at work building the instruments it describes and launching programmes of systematic observation. But the instrumentation of astronomy was not confined to tools for gathering measurements in observatories; the mastery of astronomical geometry and its range of applications involved techniques that were encapsulated and packaged for users in portable instruments, such as spheres, astrolabes, equatoria, quadrants and sundials.

The *Almagest* describes a range of instruments for making measurements of the heavens. The project for a systematic account of the motions of heavenly bodies must begin with measurement, so as to set out what is to be captured by this geometry and so as to test its results. Since the Earth is at the centre of the cosmos in the Ptolemaic view of the world, the only mode of measurement is angular – the only parameter available to the observational astronomer is the angle subtended at his instrument by distant objects. That may be measured and expressed in different ways – by the regular division of a circle (commonly into 360 degrees), by the passage of time indicated by a clock, by a ratio of lengths – but they are all varieties of angular measure.

Why is the scrutiny of the heavens in the vanguard of the use of geometry, and of angular measurement in particular? An intellectual or apriorist account might begin with a transcendent assumption about the geometrical nature of the heavens and declare that that philosophical assumption informs the work of astronomers. Alternatively, it might be noted more empirically that any observer of the sky can see that the passing of the day and the advance of the seasonal year is linked to progressive change in the celestial appearances and that an attempt to use that change in the regulation of time or the calendar will quickly lead to instruments for recording angles. More searching scrutiny of the heavens, particularly involving the motions of planets, and more ambitious accounts of the links between heavenly appearances and earthly experience will lead to ever more complex geometry and instrumentation.

If we begin with measuring instruments, Ptolemy describes several for taking specific types of measurement within his geometrical account of the heavens, and a further instrument of more general applicability. A form of quadrant, an instrument with a measuring arc of 90 degrees (a quarter of a circle), comprised a vertical plane of wood or stone set in the meridian (the north-south direction), an inscribed scale of 90 degrees, and a horizontal rod at its apex casting a shadow across the scale. The single measurement this could provide was the meridian altitude of the Sun – its 'height' at noon, which was the maximum for the day. An alternative was the meridian ring, where a close-fitting inner ring with diametrically-opposed sights, moved within a fixed ring carrying the degree scale. Again, this was confined to the measurement of meridian altitude.

The instrument of more general applicability relied on a complex combination of inter-connected rings and was known as an armillary sphere, that is, a sphere made of rings. Ptolemy describes an instrument whose outer rings are again located in the meridian but now support the pivot of an inner set of rings which can rotate in parallel with what we would call the apparent daily motion of the heavens (in Ptolemy's time the Earth was considered to be fixed and the daily motion of the stars not apparent, but real). The stars appear all to move in circles about a point in the sky called the pole, close to the Pole Star (Polaris), so for the rings of Ptolemy's sphere to rotate in parallel with the apparent paths of the stars, they must rotate on an axis which points to the celestial pole. Using such an instrument must have given the astronomer a very immediate sense of connection with the heavens. The position of the pole in the sky as seen from a particular location on Earth will vary with latitude – at the North Pole it will be directly overhead, at the equator is will be on the horizon (or would be were it not for the refractive effect of the Earth's atmosphere). The outer rings of Ptolemy's armillary sphere can be adjusted and the inclination of the axis set for a particular latitude, so that the rotation is parallel with the apparent paths of the stars. This means that the rotation is parallel to the equator and an instrument with such a motion is generally described as 'equatorial'.

While Ptolemy's *Almagest* is an ancient text, it had a powerful influence on the astronomy of the Renaissance, and already it has introduced to us concepts that will be fundamental to understanding Renaissance astronomical instruments. We shall encounter again instruments with adjustment for latitude, for example, as well as instruments with equatorial features. It is clear already that Ptolemy's armillary sphere was a sophisticated and complex construction but it had a further level of complexity – greater, in fact, than became common for such instruments in the Renaissance. The reference system Ptolemy used for positions in the heavens was based, not on the equator, but on the circle of the annual path of the Sun, known to astronomers as the ecliptic. This is inclined to the equator at an angle of about 23½ degrees. The stars and the imaginary circles astronomers used to describe their motions were considered to be on a sphere – the celestial sphere – with the Earth at its centre. The celestial equator was the circle on this sphere in the plane of the terrestrial equator, and the Sun was situated on that circle only at the equinoxes, in spring and autumn. At other times it was at different positions on the ecliptic, being furthest from the equator at the summer and winter solstices, while every day making its daily path, as did all the heavenly bodies, on circles parallel to the equator. The ecliptic circle itself, also on the celestial sphere, and the ecliptic pole, the point on the sphere 90 degrees from the ecliptic, made their daily rotations as well, so that any instrument for taking measurements of positions with respect to the ecliptic needed a second axis, displaced from the celestial pole by 23½ degrees, so that its graduated circles could readily be aligned with the ecliptic and the ecliptic pole. This complex facility was a feature of Ptolemy's instrument, which could rotate on two axes.

Ptolemy's armillary sphere is introduced in *Almagest* as a measuring instrument and it was occasionally built with that aim in the Renaissance but, while it became the most emblematic instrument of astronomy in the period, it was generally used for teaching or calculation, rather than for measuring. Its value for demonstration will perhaps be appreciated after reading the attempt in the previous paragraph at a written explanation of the celestial circles used by astronomers to manage the geometry of the heavens; an instrument where these circles could be shown and moved would be an enormous advantage to such an explanation. Even so, Renaissance armillary spheres generally, though not always, stop with the equatorial motion and do not embrace the further complexity of angular positions based on the ecliptic. Thus the most evident features of most surviving spheres are the celestial circles of the equator, the tropics and the ecliptic, while the sphere rotates on the celestial poles carried by a vertical meridian ring, set (and adjustable for latitude) in a stand with a prominent, flat, level band for the horizon in the latitude in question. One of the important features of such a sphere is that it is 'universal', that is, it can be set for any latitude and facilitate calculations for any position on the Earth.

What kind of an instrument was this? In the terminology of the Renaissance, it was 'mathematical' and 'artificial', belonging in the mathematical arts rather than to natural philosophy. This meant that it did not provide causal explanations of the workings of nature, but rather a convenient access to the geometrical techniques used by astronomers in coping with the complex motions of the heavens. Mathematical arts were underpinned and secured by the mathematical 'science' of geometry, but that did not mean that they offered insight into causes and the material nature of bodies, celestial or terrestrial. They regulated (through measurement) or taught (through demonstration) the geometrical system of the astronomers, not the character of the natural world, and all the Renaissance instruments we shall encounter have this 'artificial' character. It is only with the telescope that we have an instrument making different claims on knowledge: in the mathematical arts instruments could ignore a great deal of contemporary natural philosophy for the benefit of convenience of use. The rotation of the armillary sphere in its stand seems appropriate to the rotation of the heavens, but it is striking that terrestrial globes before Copernicus had exactly the same physical arrangement and rotated on the polar axis, even though everyone knew that that could not be true in nature. It did, however, make it much more convenient to perform calculations.

The story of the armillary sphere has taken us already from measurement to calculation and demonstration. But before moving on to astrolabes and sundials, we should consider the Renaissance use of Ptolemaic models for measuring instruments and the development of novel designs. The project of a Ptolemaic astronomical revival in Europe is generally associated with the mathematicians Georg Peurbach and Johannes Müller, called Regiomontanus, in Vienna in the

1. Page 218, torquet, illustration from the *Astronomicum Caesareum* by Peter Bienewitz, or Apianus (Ingolstadt, 1540).

2. Ptolemaic armillary sphere, illustration from Johann Schöner's edition of the treatises of Regiomontanus, *Scripta clarissimi M. Ioannis Regiomontani* (Nuremberg, 1544).

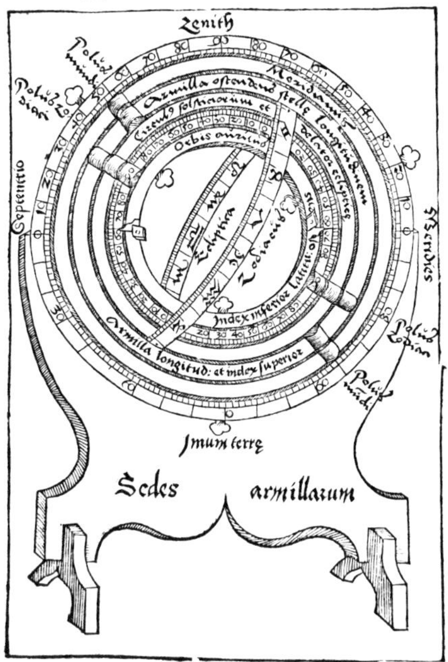

3. Armillary sphere of the type used for the calculation and demonstration made by Carolus Platus, 1588; Oxford, Museum of the History of Science, inv. no. 45453.

later fifteenth century. After spending time in Italy, Regiomontanus settled in Nuremberg in 1471, in part because of the availability of instruments and the skills of the local craftsmen. He wrote an accounts of the armillary sphere and of two other astronomical measuring instruments, the 'torquetum' and 'Ptolemy's rulers', and with his pupil Bernhard Walther he built an observatory in Nuremberg, which Walther took over after the death of Regiomontanus in his death in 1475. This observatory was equipped with a Ptolemaic armillary sphere for observation, which included an ecliptic axis, and an astronomer's cross-staff or 'astronomical radius'.

So already we have mentioned three further instruments for astronomical measurement, only one of which, the rulers, appears in *Almagest*. Also known as the parallactic instrument or the 'triquetrum', this was a set of three straight rods, one set vertical, so pointing to the local zenith, the point directly overhead on the celestial sphere. A second rod, pivoted close to the top for the first, acted as a sighting rule or 'alidade', while the third, pivoted near the bottom, could measure the angle between the other two – the 'zenith distance' of the target – as a chord, the value in degrees then being found from a table. Later sixteenth-century astronomers, such as Copernicus and Tycho Brahe, also used variants of this instrument. The torquetum, like the armillary sphere, could be set for latitude, so as to have an equatorial motion, but could then also be transposed into the ecliptic system of Ptolemy by providing an axis at 23 or so degrees to the polar axis. This was done, not by nested rings, but by a succession of hinged discs and, again like the armillary sphere, the torquetum was probably more useful for teaching than for observing. Surviving examples are exceedingly rare. The cross-staff, on the other hand, was definitely a practical instrument – first for astronomers and then in a smaller and simpler version for navigators, for whom it was made in considerable numbers. The simplest version combined a graduated rod – the 'radius' - with a cross-piece or 'transom', which moved along its length, across the scale, and by viewing from one end of the radius was made to cover the apparent distance between two targets in the sky and so subtend the angle between, registered by the scale, or available from a table if the scale was a linear one. Mounted on a universal joint, such an instrument could measure angles in any orientation, not just those in the meridian or parallel to the equator, and versions of the instrument were used by later astronomers such as Tycho Brahe and Thomas Harriot.

A number of sixteenth-century astronomers continued this tradition of Ptolemaic measurement but it was Tycho who exhausted its possibilities and then moved further with his own designs. Tycho had travelled extensively in Europe, visiting observatories and becoming familiar with their instrumentation, before setting up his own extraordinary institution on the island of Hven in the Danish Sound, under the patronage of King Frederick II. Here he built two observatories, a chemical laboratory, an instrument workshop, a paper mill and a printing press. Some two dozen instruments included armillary spheres, with and without ecliptic motions, Ptolemy's rulers and the cross-staff, but also new designs of quadrant and sextant (i.e. an instrument measuring up to 60 degrees). Both the traditional instruments and the new designs benefited from such innovations as new forms of sights and methods of dividing the scales. Sights that were simple vanes with viewing holes were inaccurate, because the target star could be viewed over a small range of alignments. Tycho replaced them with cylindrical foresights and near sights with two parallel slits separated by the diameter of the cylinder; the observer had to look through both slits and equalise the light visible on either side of the cylinder. Degree scales were subdivided by lines set obliquely between the scale divisions and these 'diagonals', being longer than the direct intervals, could themselves be divided into a greater number of equal intervals, say 10, that would serve to register the position of an alidade between two primary divisions.

One outcome of Tycho's extensive trials was the end of the armillary sphere with its complexity of motions as an observing instrument, alongside the realisation that for maximum stability and accuracy, instruments and their parts should move as little as possible as the instrument was used. Tycho's greatest success was his large mural quadrant, radius about 2 metres, comprising a wide brass arc engraved with a diagonal scale and mounted on a substantial wall built in the meridian. A second wall, at right angles to the first, had an aperture in which was set the cylindrical foresight at the centre of the quadrant arc, while moving on the arc itself were two double-slit near sights (each used for a different range of altitudes).

Tycho had a fresco of himself sitting in his study painted on the quadrant wall, and the illustration of this instrument, published first by Tycho himself in 1598 and reproduced in colour in editions of the *Atlas* of Willem Janszoon Bleau, who had worked in Tycho's observatory, has become one of best known images of Renaissance astronomy. It shows a further profound development – the use of clocks for astronomical measurement. Astronomers now based their co-ordinate system, not on the ecliptic as the fundamental reference circle, but on the celestial equator. The basic measurement from Tycho's mural quadrant was the altitude of a star as its daily apparent path took it across the meridian but, since this angle was in the same plane as the local latitude and the angular distance of the star from the celestial equator (the co-ordinate required by the astronomer, known as 'declination'), this last figure was easily found by simple subtraction. So a knowledge of the latitude readily converted a local measurement of meridian altitude into declination – an angle on the celestial sphere whose value would be useful to astronomers anywhere in the world. But since the quadrant had no equatorial motion, how was the complementary co-ordinate, parallel to the equator (known as 'right ascension'), to be found? This is were the clocks came into play. Time comes from the daily progression of the stars or the Sun in their motions, so an interval of time is equivalent to an angle parallel to the equator, and differences in right ascension can be measured by a clock. As one of Tycho's assistants noted the altitude from the scale of the quadrant, another would call out the time by a clock, and both measurements would be recorded by a third. The idea was fundamental to the development of astronomical measurement, and in turn the search for astronomical accuracy would be crucial to the advance of accurate clockwork, but in truth the clocks available to Tycho could not deliver the accuracy he needed for this measurement.

Having reached a clear breakthrough in instrumentation with the work of Tycho, one that was documented in his *Astronomiae instauratae mechanica* of 1598 and would stand for almost a century, we turn now to the portable instruments for calculation, demonstration and timekeeping.

Although not mentioned in *Almagest*, the astrolabe was known to Ptolemy and he wrote on the geometric projection on which it is based. The technique of projection involves the systematic transposition of a set of points or shapes on to a given surface. We are probably most familiar with its use in mapmaking, where the features of a spherical surface are transferred to a flat one, but it is used in a variety of mathematical instruments and conspicuously in the astrolabe. Here the chosen features of the heavens – a selection of prominent stars between the pole and the tropic of Capricorn and the full circle of the ecliptic – are projected on to the plane of the equator, to the intersections with the equatorial plane of lines joining these features to the south celestial pole. The result is a part of the astrolabe known as the 'rete' (Latin for 'net') – a fretted plate cut in brass, with pointers for the star positions and a band for the ecliptic. It is essentially a map of the heavens and is free to rotate about a pin situated at its centre (marking the north celestial pole). It moves above a second, 'latitude' plate, on which, using the same geometric technique, are the horizon for a particular latitude, the corresponding zenith point, and between them circles or arcs of equal altitude up to the zenith and of

4. Diptych sundial by Paul Reinmann, 1601;
Oxford, Museum of the History of Science, inv. no. 51148.

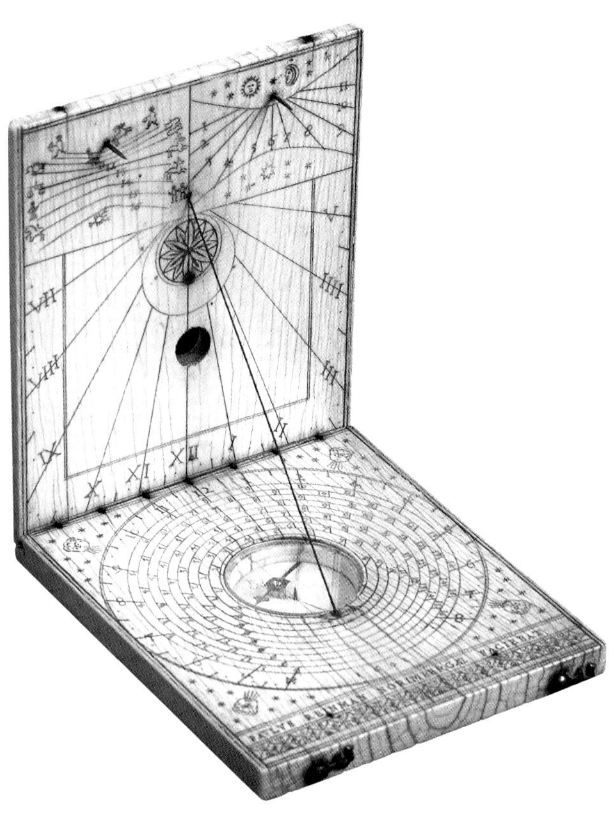

5. Astrolabe of Giovanni Domenico Feciolo, 1558;
Oxford, Museum of the History of Science, inv. no. 50257.

equal azimuth around the horizon ('azimuth' being the angle along the horizon). Thus the latitude plate has a characteristic co-ordinate grid of intersecting lines, marking out positions in the visible sky. It is stationary, since the Earth is stationary, but the rete can be moved to any position corresponding to the changing orientation of the heavens, giving the instrument many uses in astronomical calculations involving the stars and the Sun. Its range of application can be increased by alternative latitude plates, projected for different parts of the globe.

Like the armillary sphere, the astrolabe was an ancient instrument, but it had an influential role on the astronomical geometry of the Renaissance, and alternative designs and projections were introduced into the thriving European tradition of instrument making in the sixteenth century. 'Universal' projections offered celestial planispheres, covering the whole sky, so not confined to a single latitude, with different protocols for using them in calculation. This development took place alongside the introduction of new cartographic projections of the terrestrial globe, propagated in the many editions of Ptolemy's other, and much more popular, work, the *Geographia*, or *Cosmographia* as it was more generally known, the latter name being a reminder that the book deals with the cosmos as a whole and geometrical relationships between the Earth and the heavens. It is worth noting again the 'artificial' character of this mathematical practice. The use of a variety of coexisting projections in maps and in astronomical instruments was consistent with the contemporary role and status of mathematics – useful in many ways but not revealing about the material nature of things, true to its rigorous methods but not insightful on the causes of natural phenomena. Thus a single volume of *Cosmographia* could contain several world maps with very different shapes, adapted to different functions, and the two faces of a single astrolabe could present very different projections of the heavens.

But if mathematics and its instrumentation do not yield causal theories in the manner of Renaissance natural philosophy, they certainly aspired to rigorously systematic and reliable results. Geometry was, after all, a 'science' in the Renaissance meaning of the term, namely knowledge with a characteristic certainty and generality, that was not simply empirical, but systematised, generalised, and assured through some more transcendent account of things. Geometry employed a range of techniques for epitomising or encapsulating measurements in a systematic way; in astronomy these might take for form of circles whose movements generated planetary positions, a projection on an astrolabe, or a pattern of hour-lines on a sundial. These would not be 'theories' in our sense, as they make no pretence to explanation, only to convenient generalisation, but in the terminology of the time they would be called 'theorics', or in Latin, 'theoricae'. The projections of astrolabe planispheres and cartographic maps shared the characteristic feature of the theoric: the user could extract from them measurements that were not supplied or entailed in their construction, in the way that a mathematical curve might be based on a set of observations but will yield many more, interpolated results, when interrogated according to the proper protocols. Here was the power of the theoric as seen in the period – not in explanation but in its reliable output of valuable, practical results.

Moving on from the astrolabe, the Renaissance sundial also was a mathematical instrument in this sense, and it was also more than a device for simply finding the time. It deserves to be treated in any consideration of astronomical instruments, or perhaps even more to be seen as an instrument of cosmography, as it exemplifies important aspects of the relationship between the heavens and the Earth. Many important astronomers, from Regiomontanus on, concerned themselves with sundials, as did the leading cosmographers of the sixteenth century. Dialling was a discipline of remarkable diversity, creativity and technical challenge, as new ways were found for relating the solar (or lunar) motion to the time kept on Earth in a range of different systems and registers, according to a variety of ways of dividing up the day and night.

Like maps and astrolabes (and, for that matter, perspective drawing and painting) dialling relied on forms of projection, the fundamental task being to project the path of the Sun through a point (such as the end of a rod or pin) or through a set of points on a line (the straight gnomon or style, which casts the shadow) on to a surface. Different aspects of the Sun's daily motion were used for the parameter to be registered as the passage of time, such as the 'hour-angle' (as right ascension is termed in dialling), the altitude (angle above the horizon), or the azimuth (angle along the horizon). A dial might be designed to work in a single latitude or over a restricted range of latitudes, or to be 'universal', that is adjustable to any latitude. The scale or projection of lines for registering the passing of the hours might be drawn on a horizontal, vertical, equatorial, or some other plane, or be a curved surface, such as the outer face of a cylinder or a sphere, or the inner surface of a cone or a hemisphere. Polyhedral dials flaunt the maker's skill by having different dials on the plane and curved surfaces of some solid or other. There are a number of systems for counting the hours, beginning alternatively with sunrise, noon or sunset, and for dividing the day into different intervals. In other words, a great deal of geometrical astronomy is involved in the making and informed use of sundials in the period, and the discipline falls solidly within the mathematical arts, as practiced by such scholars as Regiomontanus, Peter Apian, Sebastian Münster, Gemma Frisius, Egnatio Danti, Oronce Finé or Christopher Clavius. The range of technical possibilities is more than matched by the variety of designs and the array of instruments stretches from small pocket dials to cathedrals where meridian lines mark the daily passage of the Sun throughout the year, and can be used for aspects of astronomical measurement, thus linking sundials directly with the work of observatories. Examples were installed in the churches of Santa Maria Novella and Santa Maria del Fiore in Florence and San Petronio in Bologna.

A further link between observatory measurement and instruments for time-telling is found in the range of quadrants, from large, fixed instruments to portable examples for the pocket. We have noted the quadrant as an instrument for measuring meridian altitude, but the variation of the Sun's altitude as the day progresses, rising to a maximum on the meridian and declining towards sunset, can he harnessed as a measure of time. For this purpose a portable quadrant will generally have sights fixed to one straight edge and a plumb-line hanging across the quadrant face and its pattern of hour lines. Because the Sun's altitude depends on the latitude and on the time of year, as well as the time of day, quadrants deal in different ways with these variables and the pattern or projection of hour lines varies with these different solutions, as well as with the system of hours to be registered. Other lines with additional astronomical functions may be added and often a fair degree of astronomical knowledge is expected of the user of a portable horary quadrant.

The nocturnal, for finding the time at night, is simpler than many designs of quadrant but its use assumes a familiarity with the night sky that would challenge the great majority of educated people today. It works on a completely different principle from any sundial, registering the rotation of the heavens about the pole, as though the sky were an enormous clock. As the stars circle the pole, they mark the passage of the night but, since we register time from the Sun, whose position in the rotating pattern of the stars moves throughout the year, the appearance of the starry heavens from a particular location is different at the same solar time at different times of the year. The nocturnal has a central hole through which the user, holding the instrument vertical, views the Pole Star, and a rotating index arm, which can be aligned with a star as it moves throughout the night. But the scale on the nocturnal against which the index arm will register the time, needs itself to rotate, so as to be adjusted for date before the observation can be made. Thus the nocturnal in its simplest form, is a kind of 'volvelle' – a disk with a handle and a date scale, a moving disk with the time scale, and an extended index arm. Needless-to-say other scales and functions are generally added. Enthusiasm for combining functionality has led to many astronomical 'compendia', where different instruments are brought together into an ingenious pocket gadgets with a range of different functions.

There were other designs of portable instruments that remained relatively unknown and little used, but one final example deserves to be mentioned, despite the fact that examples are exceedingly rare, because it brings our narrative back to where it began, namely with Ptolemy's *Almagest*. The astrolabe dealt with the Sun and stars, but to predict the positions of the other planets (the Sun was a planet in the Ptolemaic scheme) by an instrument, known as an 'equatorium,' would be a much greater challenge, involving the complexity of motions of interdependent circles and even the use of non-uniform motions set out in the technical heart of the *Almagest*. Such instruments were made but were feats of individual ingenuity, rather than designs for general production. The most famous of them were self-moving, through the use of clockwork, and the best known of these was the 'astrarium' of Giovanni de' Dondi, astronomer of Pavia in the fourteenth century. Roughly a century after its completion, Regiomontanus visited the astrarium in 1463, recording that it was still considered a marvel of the age. The large public clocks of the fifteenth and sixteenth centuries may not have been equatoria, since they did not generally display planetary positions, but they did present astronomical information, often for the Sun, Moon and stars.

But these clocks, whether equatoria or not, like all the Renaissance instruments we have encountered, were mathematical in character and competence: they were not tools of natural philosophy. The notion that a clockwork mechanism might actually exemplify the possibility of a mechanical natural world was a radical thought belonging to a later age. Understanding this profound limitation to the character of Renaissance instruments is vital for appreciating the fundamental challenge of the telescope. In insisting that the telescope offered discoveries in the natural world and uncovered new truths about the material nature of the heavens, Galileo was both attacking the Aristotelian cosmology and challenging the Ptolemaic tradition of astronomical instrumentation.

–

Bibliography

Bennett 1987; Hoskin 1997; Pedersen 1993; Thoren 1990; Turner A. 1987.

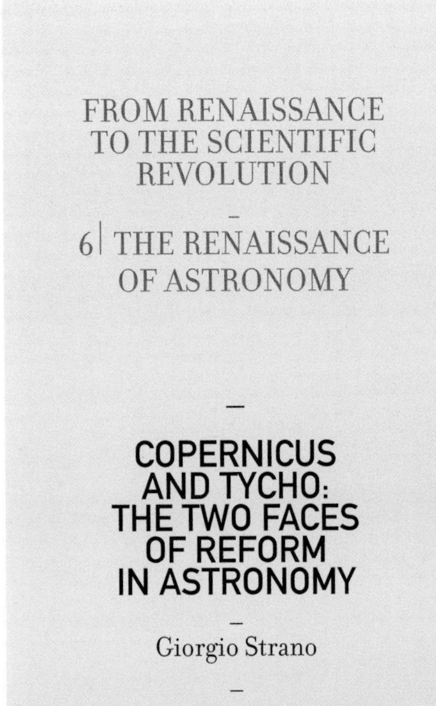

FROM RENAISSANCE
TO THE SCIENTIFIC
REVOLUTION
–
6| THE RENAISSANCE
OF ASTRONOMY
–
COPERNICUS
AND TYCHO:
THE TWO FACES
OF REFORM
IN ASTRONOMY
–
Giorgio Strano
–

The cosmological problem at the close of the 15th century

The Aristotelian-Ptolemaic system was the accepted cosmological theory for most philosophers and astronomers up to the early 16th century. But after having mastered the technical aspects essential to astronomy, the European mathematicians, like the Islamic ones before them, began to note the inconsistencies in this world system and to search for alternatives.

Georg von Peurbach (1423-1461), professor of astronomy at the University of Vienna, was inspired by Ptolemy's *Hypothesis on the Planets* to compose a short work, the *Theoricae novae planetarum* (*New theories of the planets*), published posthumously in 1472. Peurbach proposed updated versions of the spherical shells that transported the epicycles of the planets and, implicitly, showed how the equant introduced by Ptolemy contradicted the principle of the uniform circular motion of celestial bodies. His planetary models were composed of at least five spherical surfaces in motion which, when cut by the plane of the Zodiac's circumference, furnished a model that was basically epicycloid-eccentric. Each planet's sphere was bounded by two spherical surfaces concentric to the Earth, between which were collocated two eccentric spherical surfaces. The larger one touched the outer concentric surface at one point (the planet's apogee); the smaller one touched the inner concentric circle at a point opposite the former (the planet's perigee). The sphere of the epicycle was encapsulated between the two eccentric surfaces[1].

It could be imagined that the uniform motion of the outer concentric surface was in part transmitted to the first eccentric surface; from it, the motion passed on to the sphere of the epicycle which, in revolving, transmitted it to the second eccentric surface. The latter then transmitted the motion to the inner concentric surface. If the ratios of transmission of motion from one surface to the next were suitably selected it was possible, at least hypothetically, to explain the motion of all parts of the cosmological machine. In every case it was a question of uniform circular motion, since even though Peurbach's spherical shell models showed the presence of an equant circumference (or sphere), it was impossible to explain its mechanical action on the motion of the epicycle's centre.

Peurbach's *Theoricae* was only the premise for a widespread reaction to traditional cosmology that emerged in the late 15th - early 16th century, based on concepts already acquired in the Islamic world and new ones being formulated. This reaction was reinforced by a return to the original Greek sources, promoted by Peurbach himself and his pupil and collaborator Hans Müller from Königsberg, better known as Regiomontanus (1436-1476). The idea that many problems in astronomy had arisen from errors in transcription or translation of the ancient sources led the two scholars to embrace the project of Cardinal Giovanni Bessarione, an exile from Constantinople visiting Vienna in 1460, for a journey through Italy to be undertaken in search of ancient manuscripts. Due to the untimely death of Peurbach, Regiomontanus alone followed Bessarione, remaining in Italy for six years, where he established close relations with high-ranking prelates, studied Greek and collected documents. Regiomontanus thus discovered that some errors in Ptolemaic astronomy recorded by him in the *Epytoma in Almagestum Ptolomei* (*Compendium of Ptolemy's Almagest*), written around 1462 but published posthumously in 1496, had already been present in the original Greek sources. These errors undermined the geometric foundations of the traditional planetary models. In examining Ptolemy's lunar model, for example, it could be seen that the distance of the Moon from the Earth was halved in passing from apogee to perigee. Consequently, the apparent diameter of the Moon should have doubled[2]; a phenomenon that no one, Ptolemy included, had ever observed.

Regiomontanus confronted the problems of astronomy from three different angles. In the first place, he not only salvaged manuscript astronomical sources, but also had them translated and published. For this purpose he set up a printing workshop in Nuremberg, launching an ambitious publishing program around 1475[3]. In the second place, he decided to conduct new astronomical observations using updated versions of the instruments described by Ptolemy in the *Almagest*[4]. The contradictions inherent to astronomy, he believed, could be resolved only by systematic recording of the positions of the celestial bodies. Lastly, Regiomontanus intended to develop new planetary models able to respect Plato's dictum on the uniform circular motion of celestial bodies. In 1476 his sudden death in Rome, where he had been summoned by Pope Sixtus IV in connection with the project for reforming the calendar, prevented Regiomontanus from completing his various projects. The publishing programme was uninterrupted; the astronomical observations were continued by Bernhard Walther (1430-1504), his pupil and patron[5]; and only a few surviving letters suggest how Regiomontanus intended to adopt systems of concentric spheres to explain the motions of the Sun and Moon[6].

This attempt to return to a strictly concentric cosmology was not isolated, but involved some Italian scholars as well. In 1498 the Bolognese Alessandro Achillini (1463-1512), professor of philosophy at the University of Padua, published *De orbibus* (*On spheres*) where, without proposing new concepts, he recalled to the attention of astronomers the Aristotelian structure of the cosmos[7]. In 1536, *De motibus corporum coelestium* (*On the motion of celestial bodies*) was published in Venice by the scholar from Cosenza, Giovanni Battista Amico (c. 1512-1538), who had studied at the University of Padua. In this work, eccentrics and epicycles were discarded in favour of new planetary models based on homocentric spheres[8]. Then in 1538 the Veronese Girolamo Fracastoro (1483-1553) – philosopher, physician and astronomer, as well as professor of logic at the University of Padua from 1501 to 1508 – published the *Homocentrica* in Venice. This work contained a final elaboration, albeit an enigmatic one, of the planetary models originally conceived by Giovanni Battista Della Torre (died 1534). To conclude the ideas of his late friend, Fracastoro explained that all the phenomena described by Ptolemy could be replicated by means of planetary models employing as many as eleven concentric spheres[9]. To justify variations in brightness and size of the planets, all of these authors used the expedient of collocating below the sphere of the Moon a sphere of non-homogeneous material, more or less transparent[10].

The canon of Warmia: Nicolaus Copernicus

Since the 14th century, the University of Padua had been a centre of excellence for the study of astronomical questions. For example, one of its professors of medicine, Giovanni Dondi dall'Orologio (1318-1389), worked for sixteen years, from 1348 to 1364, to fabricate an 'astrarium', an intricate astronomical clock. The instrument served to demonstrate to sceptics that Ptolemy 's planetary models, no matter how complicated, could be transformed into mechanical equivalents[11]. In the late 15th and early 16th centuries the University of Padua also became a centre for advocates of cosmological theories alterative to the Ptolemaic system.

Nicolaus Copernicus (1473-1543) from Poland, canon of the capital of Warmia, studied medicine at the University of Padua for nearly four years, from 1501 to 1503 (fig. 1). He had already attended the University of Krakow, where he had studied with Albert of Brudzewo (1445-1497), the first commentator of Peurbach's *Theoricae*, and the University of Bologna, where he had followed the astronomy courses taught by Domenico Maria da Novara (1454-1504). After receiving a degree in canon law from the University of Ferrara in 1503, Copernicus returned to his native country in 1504, remaining there for the rest of his life[12]. Although Copernicus' interests in Padua are not precisely known, it seems plausible that his talent for mathematics and astronomy brought him into contact with the advocates of a cosmos made up of concentric spheres.

Throughout his life Copernicus actively engaged in politics, civil and ecclesiastical administration, economy, the practice of medicine, cartography, and plans for military defence against the Knights of the Teutonic Order, assuming a heavy burden of political and civic responsibilities[13]. But astronomy was always in his thoughts, and between 1512 and 1514 he wrote a brief treatise called *De hypothesibus motuum coelestium a se constitutis commentariolus* (*Brief account on the hypothesis of the celestial motions*) presenting new ideas on the structure of the world system. This was a first attempt, destined to remain in manuscript form, at unifying the concepts of the natural philosophers, engaged in furnishing a physical explanation of how the world-machine operates, and the theories of the mathematical astronomers, interested instead in developing geometric models able to predict the positions of the planets[14].

Copernicus believed that the concept of the cosmos structured in concentric spheres could be functionally revived by admitting a few postulates. The basic thesis consisted of placing the Sun at the centre of the cosmos and transforming the Earth, around which orbits the Moon, into one of the six planets known at the time. Many astronomical phenomena – the rotation of the celestial sphere from east to west in twenty-four hours, the transit of the Sun from west to east along the Zodiac and the retrograde motion of planets – were thus found to be only apparent, illusions produced by the rotation of the Earth on its own axis and its orbiting around the Sun[15]. To reinforce his concept, Copernicus added to the general postulates some geometric models for calculating the positions of the planets. It is still debated today whether those planetary models were entirely original or, on the contrary, derived from adapting in a heliocentric key some models developed by Islamic astronomers in the 13th and 14th centuries[16].

In the *Commentariolus*, Copernicus hypothesised that, within its own planetary sphere, or deferent (from the Latin *deferens* = that which carries), a planet was led around the Sun by three circumferences: 'Each deferent has in fact two epicycles, one of which entrains the other [...]. In fact the first epicycle, turning in the direction opposite that of the deferent, completes with it the same number of revolutions. The second epicycle instead, moving in the opposite direction to the first, entrains the planet in its motion, causing it to complete a dual revolution'[17]. With this solution the Platonic principle of the uniform circular motion of all celestial bod-

1. Page 226, Portrait of Nicolaus Copernicus, detail; Torun, Poland, Muzeum Okrgowe.

2. Structure of the Copernican cosmos, illustration from *De revolutionibus*; Krakow, Poland, Jiagiellonica Library, ms., fol. 9v.

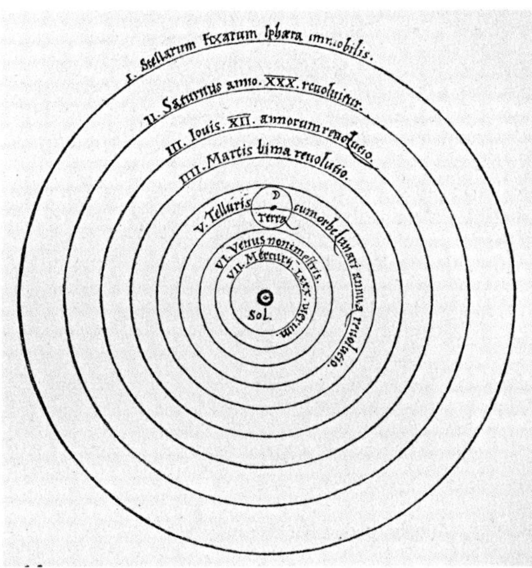

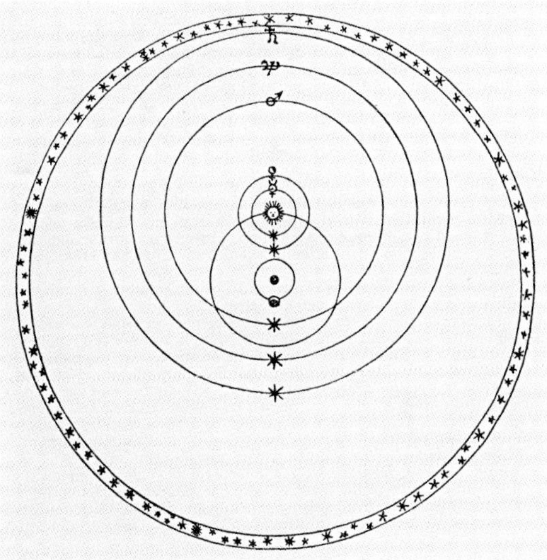

3. The world system of Tycho, *De Mundi aetherei recentioribus phaenomenis*, 1588, p. 189.

ies was salvaged because, having eliminated the great epicycle that in Ptolemy's planetary models served to regulate synodic anomaly – now explained by the orbital motion of the Earth – the new pair of epicycles took account of zodiacal anomaly without having to recur to eccentric and equant circumferences.

Copernicus continued to work on his heliocentric system. In 1514, he set up an observatory equipped with instruments of the Ptolemaic type[18] in a tower in the walls around Frombork cathedral, while between 1530 and 1532 he wrote an astronomical treatise in six books that, in content and mathematical complexity, emulated the *Almagest*[19]. Although he continued to perfect his work without deciding to publish the results, Copernicus' fame as mathematician spread so far that a professor from the University of Wittenberg decided to travel to Frombork expressly to meet him. Georg Joachim Lauscher (1514-1574) – better known as Rheticus from the Latinized name of his native region, Raetia – presented himself to Copernicus in the spring of 1539. Within a few weeks he came to realize the extraordinary scientific import of the new world system and decided to publish it, prudently in anonymous form, in a brief *Narratio prima de libris revolutionum* (*First report on the books on the revolutions*), published at Danzig in 1540[20]. This volume was so favourably received that Rheticus was able to convince Copernicus to print his astronomical treatise in unabridged form.

Rheticus departed from Frombork with Copernicus' manuscript in September 1541. The following year he managed to publish in Wittenberg the *De lateribus et angulis triangulorum* (*On sides and angles of triangles*), the part of Copernicus' work dealing with plane and spherical trigonometry. He entrusted the complete treatise instead to the printer Johann Petreius of Nuremberg, and was obliged by urgent university engagements to delegate editorial supervision to the Lutheran theologian Andreas Osiander. The work, called *De revolutionibus orbium coelestium* (*On the revolutions of the heavenly spheres*), came out in 1543 and, according to legend, Copernicus received a copy on his deathbed[21].

Osiander had however taken the liberty of prefacing Copernicus' text with a warning, 'To the reader on the hypotheses of this work'. The theologian had not failed to notice the contradiction between the heliocentric system and the Holy Scriptures, which contain several passages indicating that the Earth stands still and the Sun revolves around it. The warning served to mitigate the potentially subversive content of *De revolutionibus* and alluded to the traditional difference in perspective between the concepts elaborated by natural philosophers on the real structure of the cosmos, and the hypotheses of the mathematical astronomers. 'It is not in fact necessary', wrote Osiander referring to the functions of the latter, 'for those hypotheses to be true, nor even to be probable; it is enough that they show the calculation to be consonant with the observed phenomena'[22].

4. The observatory of Uraniborg, after T. Brahe, *Astronomiae instauratae mechanica*, 1598, p. H2v.

This was a betrayal of Copernicus' thought, since he had not intended to offer a mere hypothesis, but rather a cosmological solution acceptable to both philosophers and mathematicians.

In the body of *De revolutionibus* (books II through VI) Copernicus furnished, in fact, planetary models useful for predicting the positions of the celestial bodies, accompanied by calculation tables that were in some cases superior to those based on Ptolemy's planetary models[23]. The models of *De revolutionibus*, based on an epicycle-eccentric structure equivalent to the bi-epicycle-concentric structure of the *Commentariolus*, made it possible to eliminate the equant circumference and to restore intact the uniform circular motion of celestial bodies[24]. On the whole, the new models offered a simplification of the world-machine, which, moreover, acquired remarkable consistency; by placing the Earth in orbit around the Sun, the order of succession of the planets appeared irrefutably established. Mercury and Venus, which always stay within a limited angular distance (elongation) from the Sun and whose collocation had always been uncertain, were now seen to be planets with orbits 'inside' that of the Earth. Mercury is closer to the Sun since its orbit lies inside that of Venus too. But the order of the other three planets as well, 'outside' of Earth's orbit, was arbitrary, being established according to the amplitude of their arc of retrograde motion. Mars, which has the largest arc, is the one closest to the Earth (and to the Sun); Saturn, whose arc is the smallest, is the furthest; Jupiter occupies an intermediate position (fig. 2). This order reveals another harmonic property of the cosmos: the orbital periods of the planets increase as their distance from the Sun increases[25].

But the attempt to unify the two points of view, philosophical and mathematical, in *De revolutionibus* was only partially successful. The new cosmological system introduced a number of problems that Copernicus tried to make as unobjectionable as possible. Among them, the extraordinary size acquired by the sphere of the fixed stars – necessary to ensure the absence of phenomena dependant on the annual rotation of the Earth around the Sun – was perhaps the lesser difficulty[26]. Much worse problems arose from reflecting on what kept the celestial spheres in motion and why the Earth's motion was not felt by its inhabitants.

The general acceptance of Aristotelian physics and its explanation of the motion of celestial and terrestrial bodies was a severe obstacle to explaining the daily and annual motion of the Earth. How could the Unmoved Mover outside of the cosmos – objected the Aristotelians – transmit motion to the various celestial spheres if the first and outermost of them, that of the fixed stars, was perfectly immobile? Copernicus tried to answer this question by maintaining that it was no longer necessary to postulate an external Unmoved Mover, since rotating was an intrinsic and natural property of solids of spherical form[27]. And still further, if the Earth rotates on its own axis, and then around the Sun, why is it that bodies dropped from a height, clouds and everything suspended in the air, are not swept westward? And why does the Earth itself not shatter into fragments and its pieces be thrown as far as the sphere of the fixed stars[28]? Without abandoning the principles of Aristotelian physics, Copernicus countered these objections by arguing that the Earth's rotation and revolution are natural, and not violent motions. 'And things that take place according to nature have an effect unlike those that occur instead through violence. Those things, in fact, subjected to force or impetus are necessarily destroyed and cannot long exist. Those that occur according to nature instead take place appropriately and their composition remains at its best'[29].

Lastly, it is an aesthetic argument that should, according to Copernicus, convince philosophers and mathematicians to accept as true the new architecture of the cosmos. Once the Sun has been placed at the centre of the planetary orbits, Copernicus asks, 'Who, in this magnificent temple, could set this lamp in a different place or one better than that from which it can illuminate everything at once?'[30]. It is only in this arrangement that we find 'an admirable symmetry in the world and a precise harmonic relationship between the motion and the size of the spheres, which cannot be found in any other way'[31].

The noble Dane: Tycho Brahe

In *Hamlet*, Shakespeare introduces two friends of the protagonist whose names, Rosencrantz and Guildenstern[32], he seems to have taken from two of the heraldic emblems surrounding the portrait of a famous Danish nobleman. This nobleman was a striking figure, wearing on his breast the medal of the Order of the Elephant, conferred on him by Frederick II of Denmark, and displaying a metal prosthesis, very well dissimulated, that replaced part of his nose, damaged in a duel. The nobleman was Tycho Brahe (1546-1601), lord of Knudstrup, who had since youth devoted himself to eliminating the 'rottenness' that prevented the science of the stars from becoming a discipline of excellence for predicting the future. On this fundamental practical aspect of astronomy, that of astrological predictions, Tycho was ready to challenge anyone; and it seems in fact that he had lost part of his nose in defending the credibility of astrology after one of his predictions, the imminent death of Suleiman the Magnificent, had proven all too true, the subject of the prediction having already died six weeks before[33]. As for astronomy viewed as study of the positions of celestial bodies in order to determine their past, present and future positions, Tycho stated that he had been planning a reform of this discipline since, in August 1563, he had realised that the astronomical tables available at the time, modelled on the *Almagest* and the *De revolutionibus*, had predicted a conjunction of Jupiter and Saturn with errors of days and even weeks[34].

While the astronomical career of Copernicus had had to come to terms with his deep sense of civic commitment, Tycho's interest in science was so strong that the political and economic studies deemed proper for a Danish nobleman were unbearable to him. He began to study astronomy in secret, procuring books and portable instruments that he used while his preceptors were sleeping. After the death of his father in 1571 he moved to the Abbey of Herrevad, the residence of his uncle Steen Bille, who was devoted to alchemy. Tycho was just leaving his uncle's laboratory on the evening of November 11, 1572 when he saw a new star in the sky, appearing in the constellation of Cassiopeia. Neglecting his alchemistic studies, he then devoted himself to measuring the distance of the supernova from the Earth with a great instrument he had designed and installed in a window of the abbey[35].

Aristotle had stated in the *Meteorology* that, given the incorruptible and immutable nature of celestial things, the apparitions of novae and comets were to be seen as the result of meteorological phenomena produced by the ignition of dry exhalations that rose from the Earth's surface to the sphere of fire, located below the sphere of the Moon[36]. Tycho realized that, if Aristotle were right, the extreme vicinity of the nova to the Earth would have revealed a slight change in its position against the background of the fixed stars when it was observed at the beginning and then at the end of the night. The maximum angle of displacement – the so-called 'diurnal parallax' – should have been found greater than the one Ptolemy had managed to measure for the Moon[37]. In 1573, Tycho published a brief treatise on the results of his observations, *De nova stella* (*On the new star*), explaining that the rare phenomenon appearing in Cassiopeia did not present a measurable parallax, so that it must be located above the Moon's sphere, in the highest celestial regions, and perhaps even in the sphere of the fixed stars[38]. This conclusion had a revolutionary impact. Dealing a mortal blow to one of the fundamental concepts – that of the absolute immutability of all celestial bodies – it undermined the edifice of the Aristotelian cosmos at its roots. The sopralunar collocation of the new star demonstrated that the realm of the celestial spheres, like all things earthly, was subject to change.

Encouraged by his success, Tycho devoted himself to building increasingly precise astronomical instruments and conducting ever more accurate observations. In the meantime, his in-depth study of astronomy led him to appreciate the greatness of Copernicus' work *De revolutionibus*, although without accepting its heliocentric premise. Already in 1574, in inaugurating a course of lessons at the University of Copenhagen, Tycho had suggested the possibility of a synthesis between Copernicus' system and the physical requisite of retaining the centrality and immobility of the Earth.

Tycho was given the chance to bring about the long desired general reform of astronomy when Frederick II of Denmark, convinced of the practical utility of astrology in the work of governing, granted him the feud of the Island of Hven, in the Øresund, along with a substantial income from other feudal lands and the State treasury. Starting from 1576 the inhabitants of Hven were thus obliged to provide their new feudal lord with the labour and means required to build a perfectly equipped astronomical observatory, which was then called Uraniborg (fig. 4). It was a small castle with open terraces on which were placed instruments of great size furnished with remarkably precise graduated scales. The observatory was accompanied by a library and an alchemist's laboratory, to which was later added a print workshop[39], installed above one of the gates in the castle walls.

The observatory was still being equipped on the evening of November 13, 1577 when Tycho, who was fishing in an artificial lake on the island, suddenly saw before his eyes a great comet in the sky. He tracked the comet with some of his new instruments to verify whether comets too were really atmospheric phenomena, as Aristotle had believed. But determining the diurnal parallax of the comet, which moved day by day in relation to the fixed stars, was not easy. Before formulating a definitive conclusion, Tycho thought it advisable to make a new catalogue of the positions of the stars. For this reason, the results of his observations of the comet in 1577 appeared only in 1588, in the *De mundi aetherei recentioribus phaenomenis (On the most recent phoenomena of the aethereal world)*, printed at Hven. This work dealt a second dual blow to the Aristotelian cosmos. Not only had the comet shown itself to be a body of celestial nature, and thus a further indicator that change did occur in the skies, but its distance from Earth had varied considerably during the months it had remained visible. More precisely, the comet had described a circular orbit around the Sun. This meant it had traversed celestial regions that should have been occupied by some of the celestial spheres conceived as solid by Aristotle; in particular, those of Mars, the Sun and Venus. Obviously, the cosmos was not made up of solid spheres but of a fluid aether that could be traversed by comets[40].

The heliocentric trajectory of the comet was in keeping with the new cosmological system that Tycho had begun to formulate around 1584[41]. Its strong point was a new and very delicate series of observations of the planet Mars, conducted by Tycho and his assistants with the most precise instruments installed not far from Uraniborg in the newly built, more advanced underground observatory of Stjerneborg[42]. In the Ptolemaic system, Mars was always further away from the Earth than the Sun, while in Copernicus' system Mars was at times more distant, at times closer to the Earth than the Sun. Starting in November 1582, Tycho began to conduct observations to measure the diurnal parallax of Mars when the planet was in opposition to the Sun. If the parallax were found to be less than that attributed to the Sun, then Ptolemy was right. If, on the contrary, the parallax were greater than that of the Sun, then Copernicus was right. None of the instruments installed on the island of Hven were sensitive enough to measure the parallax of Mars and settle the question. Nonetheless, Tycho's great faith in the genius of Copernicus led him to believe he had verified that at opposition, when it reaches its greatest splendour at the centre of its retrograde arc, Mars was effectively closer to the Earth than to the Sun[43].

This dealt the final blow to the Aristotelian-Ptolemaic system, although it did not mean acknowledging total victory to Copernicus. Tycho's admiration for the mathematical genius of the author of *De revolutionibus* did not prevent him from rejecting the three principal motions assigned by the Polish astronomer to the Earth: rotation, revolution and a third motion that was indispensable, in a system of solid spheres, to keep the terrestrial axis always parallel to itself[44]. The basic reason for Tycho's rejection was his firm belief in the Aristotelian concept of motion. If the Earth moved, a lead ball dropped from the top of a tower would not have touched the ground at its base, but considerably further west, the Earth having moved while it was falling. To demonstrate the absurdity of terrestrial motion, Tycho suggested other experimental proofs as well. If the Earth moved, two cannonballs shot at the same elevation and with the same amount of gunpowder, one toward the east, the other toward the west, would have had different ranges: shorter for the one shot eastward, longer for the one shot westward. In the former case the motion of the Earth would have been subtracted from, in the latter added to, the motion of the cannonball. Since the ranges were instead the same, it followed that the Earth must be immobile[45]. Lastly, Tycho did not fail to point out that the heliocentric thesis contradicted Holy Scriptures, which must be considered incontrovertible[46].

In 1588, based on these considerations and his reflections on the comet of 1577, Tycho outlined a provisional scheme for a new world system, proposing a revision of the Copernican system to make it compatible with the thesis of the Earth's centrality and immobility. In the new system the Earth stood immobile at the centre of the cosmos, the Moon and Sun revolved around it, while all of the other five planets (as well as comets) orbited around the Sun[47] (fig. 3). But Tycho did not manage to complete this geoheliocentric system in detail. The death of Frederick II and the succession to the Danish throne of Christian IV, less interested in astrological predictions, along with severe financial problems of the State, sharply curtailed the funds allocated to the expensive research institute built on the Island of Hven.

In 1597 Tycho decided to leave Denmark, bringing with him his instruments and assistants. After two years of drifting he was finally welcomed in Prague by Emperor Rudolph II. Here Tycho decided to entrust to his best assistant, Christian Sørensen Langberg (Longomontanus, 1562-1647), who had helped him refine his theory on the motion of the Moon[48], the highly demanding study of the motion of Mars. To facilitate this work, in early 1600 Tycho added to the circle of his assistants a young and brilliant mathematician, Johannes Kepler (1571-1630). But mistrustful of his new assistant's Copernican sympathies, Tycho gave him only the few observation data necessary to study individual aspects of the theory on the planet's motion[49].

When Tycho died in Prague on October 24, 1601, Kepler was appointed his successor as Imperial Mathematician, and inherited the vast amount of precious observation data collected by the Danish nobleman in over twenty years spent on the Island of Hven. Probably Tycho would never have suspected that his brilliant assistant, although casting glory on the name of his master, for whom he expressed life-long admiration, was to become the protagonist of a radical revision not only of Tycho's system, but also that of Copernicus[50].

–

Bibliography

Copernicus 1975; Brahe 1598; Trento 2005; Christianson 2000; Di Bono 1990; Dreyer 1970; Brahe 1913-1929; Hoskin 1999; Gingerich-Voelkel 1998, pp. 1-34; Koyré 1966; Linton 2004; North 2008; Pepe 1996; Peurbach 1472; Regiomontano 1496; Regiomontano 1544; Shank 1998, pp. 157-166; Regiomontano 1949; Shea 2001; Swerdlow 1999, pp. 1-23; Strano 2005, pp. 7-47; Thoren 1990; Walker C. 1997.

1 Peuerbach 1472, 'De tribus superioribus'.

2 Regiomontanus 1496, V, 22.

3 Regiomontanus, *Haec opera fient in oppido Nuremberga Germaniae ductu Iohannis de Monteregio*, in Schmeidler 1949, p. 533.

4 Regiomontanus 1544, fols. 20v-21v, 27r-27v and 36r-43v.

5 *Ivi*, fols. 27v-34r and 44r-60v.

6 Swerdlow 1999, pp. 6-13. In general, on Peuerbach and Regiomontanus, see Dreyer 1970, p. 263; Walker C. 1997, pp. 264-275; Shank 1998, pp. 158-161; Hoskin 1999, pp. 85-86.

7 Di Bono 1990, pp. 63-65.

8 Dreyer 1970, pp. 275-277; Di Bono 1990, pp. 77 ff.

9 Dreyer 1970, pp. 270-274; Di Bono 1990, pp. 65-71.

10 On the salvaging of the homocentric spheres see also North 2008, pp. 298-301.

11 Trento 2005, pp. 137-138 and 141-143.

12 Dreyer 1970, pp. 278-281; Koyré 1966, pp. 17-19.

13 Copernicus 1975, pp. 76-78.

14 Koyré 1966, p. 22; Copernicus 1975, pp. 99-100.

15 Copernicus, *Commentariolus*, in Copernicus 1975, pp. 109-110.

16 Pepe 1996, pp. 69-70.

17 Copernicus, *Commentariolus*, in Copernicus 1975, pp. 118-119.

18 Copernicus 1975, p. 76.

19 Koyré 1966, p. 22.

20 *Ivi*, 1966, pp. 25-26.

21 *Ivi*, 1966, pp. 29-30; Copernicus 1975, p. 155.

22 Copernicus, *De revolutionibus*, 'To the reader ...', in Copernicus 1975, p. 165.

23 Shea 2001, pp. 63-64.

24 Copernicus, *De revolutionibus*, V, 4, in Copernicus 1975, pp. 562-566.

25 Copernicus, *De revolutionibus*, I, 10, in Copernicus 1975, pp. 208-214.

26 Copernicus, *De revolutionibus*, I, 6, in Copernicus 1975, pp. 192-195.

27 Copernicus, *De revolutionibus*, I, 4, in Copernicus 1975, p. 187.

28 Copernicus, *De revolutionibus*, I, 7, in Copernicus 1975, p. 197.

29 Copernicus, *De revolutionibus*, I, 8, in Copernicus 1975, pp. 197-198.

30 Copernicus, *De revolutionibus*, I, 10, in Copernicus 1975, p. 212.

31 Copernicus, *De revolutionibus*, I, 10, in Copernicus 1975, p. 213. In general, on Copernicus see also Dreyer 1970, pp. 278-315; Walker C. 1997, pp. 275-289; Hoskin 1999, pp. 86-93; Linton 2004, pp. 119-151; North 2008, pp. 302-320.

32 Shakespeare, *Hamlet*, II, 2.

33 Thoren 1990, pp. 22-23.

34 Brahe 1598, p. F2r.

35 *Ibidem*.

36 Aristotle, *Meteorology*, I, 6.

37 Ptolemy, *Almagest*, V, 13.

38 Brahe, *De nova stella*; in Brahe 1913-1929, v. 1, pp. 24-28.

39 Brahe 1598, pp. H2v-H3r. See also Christianson 2000, pp. 28-43.

40 Brahe, *De mundi aetherei*, VIII; in Brahe 1913-1929, v. 4, pp. 159-162.

41 V. Thoren 1990, pp. 236-264.

42 Brahe 1598, pp. H3v-H4r.

43 Gingerich-Voelkel 1998, pp. 1-25.

44 Brahe, *Apologetica responsio ad Craigum Scotum*; in Brahe 1913-1929, v. 4, p. 473. Cf. Copernicus, *De revolutionibus*, I, 11; in Copernicus 1975, pp. 214-222.

45 Brahe, *Epistolarum astronomicarum*; in Brahe 1913-1929, v. 6, p. 197 and pp. 219-220.

46 *Ivi*, p. 177.

47 Brahe, *De mundi aetherei*, VIII; in Brahe 1913-1929, v. 4, pp. 155-159.

48 Thoren 1990, pp. 312-333.

49 Koyré 1966, pp. 131-134.

50 In general, on Tycho, see also Dreyer 1970, pp. 329-340; Walker C. 1997, 289-301; Hoskin 1999, pp. 95-103; Linton 2004, pp. 153-168; Strano 2005, pp. 7-42; North 2008, pp. 321-338.

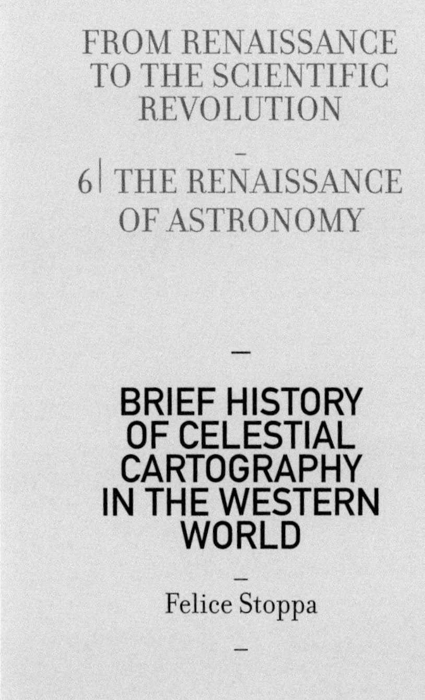

FROM RENAISSANCE
TO THE SCIENTIFIC
REVOLUTION
–
6 | THE RENAISSANCE
OF ASTRONOMY
–
BRIEF HISTORY
OF CELESTIAL
CARTOGRAPHY
IN THE WESTERN
WORLD
–
Felice Stoppa
–

Modern star atlases have accustomed us to classifying the stars and referring to the constellations we observe by clearly assigned proper names. This has not always been the case, but only since 1922/1930, when the International Astronomical Union established criteria for producing celestial charts that were homogeneous and comparable. In the preceding years and centuries, the science of astronomy had focussed on identifying with incontrovertible precision the positions of the stars in the sky in terms of coordinates, but had left the artistic spirit of the astronomer free to collocate groups of stars within imaginary boundaries and assign names to them. This evolved into a complex system of customs and traditions which, over the span of a few hundred years, saw the birth, death, rebirth and transformation of a changing assortment of names of constellations whose boundaries were not always the same in the different atlases. In 1922 the Astronomical Union, meeting in Rome, drew up a definitive list of 88 constellations which included almost all those described by Ptolemy in the *Almagest* plus a significant selection of those mentioned by astronomers starting from 1603, the date of publication of J. Bayer's *Uranometria*, the first atlas that proposed new groupings of stars to describe in particular the sky over the southern hemisphere.

The task of establishing the boundaries was entrusted by the Cambridge Assembly of 1925 to E. Delporte who, at Leyde in 1928, presented his work, which was approved by the international astronomical community. Delporte's work was published in 1930 at Cambridge under the title *Delimitation scientifique des constellations (tables et cartes)* [Scientific delimitation of the constellations (tables and charts)].

The Belgian astronomer delimited the constellations with geometric boundaries formed of hour circle arcs and parallel lines of declination calculated for the equinox of 1875. In his work he was careful to fully respect the data contained in the various catalogues in use at the time, and was obliged to extend or restrict the boundaries of some constellations in order to leave recognisable the names of many stars, those of the variables in particular (identified by a letter and by the genitive form of the name of the constellation to which they belonged), utilised in the vast scientific literature of the 19th century.

The precise, methodical work of Delporte left as legacy to the future research of astronomers a rigid, non-deformable sky ready to receive millions of stellar positions, whose history would depend only on greater precision in the observation instruments utilised, thanks to the evolution of technology. At the same time, his work marked the dramatic end of a long epoch in which art, history, myth, poetry and science, within a single frame of reference, had concurred to produce the most beautiful scientific works of the Western tradition.

We may begin this long history with the words of the Greek poet Aratus, c. 310-240 B.C., who in his didactic poem in hexameters *Phaenomena*, the most ancient of the surviving occidental works presenting the already millenarian astronomical knowledge of the Greeks, shows the need to understand the starry sky by assigning it a name and dividing it into constellations:

Many are the stars in every place, and of many identical
Is their size and brightness in their courses.
For this it was thought to render the stars
Grouped, so that, arranged one beside the others,
They represented figures, and in this way the stars
Became nameable.
(vv. 377-382)

The stars become nameable not by virtue of a name assigned to each, but by becoming points in a figure, always inspired by Greek mythology, which forms a constellation.

The ancient history of representation of the stars in the sky is thus a history of names and positions of constellations, and not of stars. And even when they are rarely named individually, the translations of their Greek names or those of the subsequent Latin and Arab traditions almost always identify the anatomical position occupied by the star in the figure, or one of its qualities: *Aldebaran* = the Bull's red eye, *Rigel* = Orion's left foot, *Betelgeuse* = the giant's hand, etc.

The complex history of celestial atlases prior to the work of Delporte can be divided into three great stages.

The first stage, before the publication of Bayer's *Uranometria* in 1603, is distinguished by two creative currents, represented on the one hand by the scientific production of Greek astronomers and philosophers such as Eratosthenes, Hipparcus and Ptolemy, responsible for the first great charting of the sky that culminated in Ptolemy's *Almagest*, a catalogue in which the Greek astronomer progressively enumerates 1022 stars, beginning again for each constellation. By the term *Informata* he indicates instead those stars, close to a constellation, whose positions have been calculated but which, due to graphic requisites, have not been inserted in the drawing of the constellation itself.

This catalogue, which was to serve as scientific heritage throughout the Middle Ages and the Renaissance, was updated by the original research of Arab astronomers such as Abd-al-Rahman al-Sufi, who in his *Liber locis stellarum fixarum* dating from 964 re-established the positions of the stars and their magnitudes, and even specified their colour. In Al-Sufi we find the first historical mention of a deep sky celestial object, the galaxy of Andromeda, M 31, which is described in the section on the *Great Fish*, in the zone of the constellation of *Andromeda*. Of this scientific current there remains very little iconographic documentation, basically a unique example of Roman celestial globe, the so-called *Farnese Atlas* at the Museo Archeologico Nazionale di Napoli, a statue of Atlas bearing on his shoulders a celestial globe on which appear the Ptolemaic constellations, and a very limited number of Arab metal globes, the most ancient of which is one dating from the year 1080 belonging to the Istituto e Museo di Storia della Scienza di Firenze, discovered and described by Ferdinando Meucci in 1878 in his famous *Il Globo Celeste Arabico del secolo XI* (The Arab celestial globe of the 11th century).

The other current during this period consists of Latin translations of the work of Aratus and numerous editions of the collection of fables by G. Julius Hyginus, the *Poeticon Astronomicon*, which was first published in print by Ratdolt in 1482.

In these poetic works, preserved in splendid manuscripts, aesthetic and astrological concerns predominate, and the positions of the stars are not indicated with precision. On the contrary, philological and literary interpretation is preferred to the point that the stars' positions are subordinated to the need to make them coincide with a certain anatomical detail in the mythological figure of which they form part. This tradition was to last throughout the Middle Ages and the Renaissance.

In the sixteenth century we find three works that break with this tradition, partially anticipating the innovations found in Bayer's atlas; these are the works of the German artist Albrecht Dürer and the Italians Alessandro Piccolomini and Giovanni Paolo Gallucci.

The two woodcuts made by Dürer in 1515, one for the Southern Hemisphere and one for the Northern, still reflect the Ptolemaic tradition as regards content and precision. In the corners of the northern panel appear Aratus, Manilius, Al-Sufi and Ptolemy, from whom the artist has drawn inspiration. But these woodcuts have the merit of presenting for the first time the entire known sky in only two flat panels, of remarkably high artistic quality.

The panel of the northern sky is the richer of the two, and is the one that shows the zodiacal constellations. The artist follows the school of Aratus and Vitruvius in naming some of the constellations, such as Cygnus, which is called Avis. Dürer respects the tradition, typical in the production of three-dimensional globes, of tracing the constellations as if seen from outside of the sky, while the stars are identified by a progressive number, in accordance with Ptolemy's *Almagest*. The coordinates and positioning of the celestial bodies in the panels were provided by two astronomers of the time, Stabius and Heinfogel, whose names appear, along with that of Dürer, in the scroll at the lower left-hand corner in one of the versions of the southern sky. The panel representing the northern sky was almost certainly inspired by an anonymous manuscript dating from around 1440. This unique and precious map, in some technical aspects even richer than that of Dürer, is now owned by the National Austrian Library of Vienna, and may be considered the most ancient representation on paper of the starry sky.

In 1540, *Delle stelle fisse* [On the fixed stars] by Alessandro Piccolomini was printed in Venice. The volume appears as a real guide to recognising the stars in the nocturnal sky. Its forty-seven plates represent the constellations without artistic concerns, traditional design is abandoned in favour of precision in positioning the stars, divided into four magnitudes and indicated by progressive letters of the Latin alphabet, starting from the brightest star. The plates are completed by a graduated scale, not always the same, and by indication of the position of the North Pole, so that, looking toward the south and aligning the book with the celestial vault, the constellation in the real sky and the one shown in the plate coincide. The plates are preceded by a section in which each constellation is briefly described by listing its stars, their positions and the more important mythological references.

The volume concludes with altazimuth tables in which, for the brightest stars, the celestial coordinates are given, month by month and for the whole span of the night. The last section indicates *'at what degree of the zodiac rise and set the principal stars in the sky'*.

Always in Venice, but in 1588, the *Theatrum mundi, et temporis* by Giovanni Paolo Gallucci was published. While Piccolomini's *Delle stelle fisse* has the merit of being a guide to reading the starry sky, Gallucci's text is a real encyclopaedia of astronomical knowledge. A description of the firmament appears only in Book V, the other books describing the Ptolemaic theories on the motion of the planets, the Sun and the Moon, with their eclipses. There are also two plates of the terrestrial globe and one of Dante's Inferno. The plates serving for calculating the Sun's transit over the meridian are followed by others on astrological influxes, but also by plates for calculating the golden number and trigonometric ones for sine. Book VI is curious, including a beautiful table for predicting the preces-

1. Page 234, Anonymous, *Manuscript of Vienna*; Vienna, National Library of Austria.
Based on the intersection of the line of the Ecliptic with that of the Equator, which varies in relation to the starry background due to the phenomenon of the precession of the equinoxes, this panel can be dated to around 1430. This is the oldest existing representation of the sky on paper.

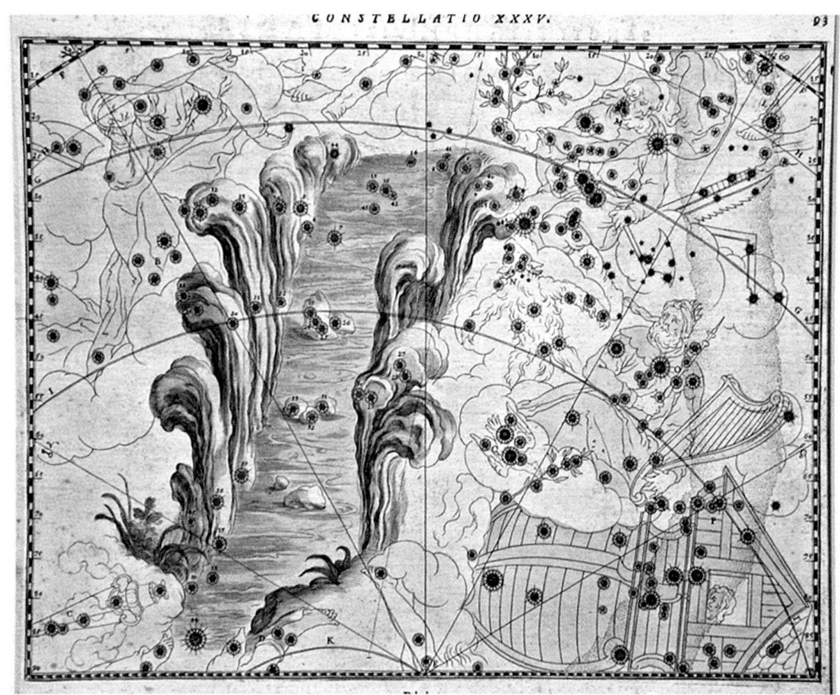

2. Julius Schiller, *Coelum stellatum Christianum*, Augusta Vindelicorum, 1627. The *Constellation XXXV* called *Transitus Israel nempe per mare rubrum* contains the stars normally belonging to the constellation of Eridanus

sion of the equinoxes from 1588 to 1800. It is a real compendium of the astronomical and astrological knowledge of the time.

Represented in Book V are the forty-eight constellations, each with a plate of its own. The innovation lies is the latitudinal and longitudinal coordinates, the data for which are taken from Copernicus' *De Revolutionibus*, appearing at the edges and the centre of the plates, to which are referred the very precise positions of the stars divided into four magnitudes. Some figures are drawn by Gallucci from behind, reversing the traditional Greek and Ptolemaic representation, and thus making it impossible to describe the positions of the stars based on anatomical details of the figures. This decision was to be confirmed by some later authors of celestial charts, but forcefully rejected by others. Flamsteed in the introduction to his *Atlas Coelestis* of 1729 was to boast that, by rejecting it, he had restored the Greek tradition, and Kepler, in *De stella nova* dating from 1606, having to indicate the position of the Nova that appeared in 1604 in the constellation of Ophicius, was to employ the principles introduced in Bayer's brand-new atlas, the latest and most updated of the cartographic productions, but was to draw the constellation turning it upside-down again and thus re-establishing the traditional canon.

The plates are interspersed with quantitative tables that indicate, in addition to the coordinates, the progressive number of each star, its magnitude, and its astrological 'nature'. Curious is the plate on page 209, that of *Aquila*, which shows *Antinous*, for whose stars the catalogue starts numbering again from the beginning, thus anticipating the tradition, which was to prevail for nearly two centuries, of representing this constellation independently.

The *Uranometria* of Bayer opens the second period in the history of celestial cartography. This cycle, both for the more exact positioning of the stars, taken from catalogues compiled by the best observers such as Tycho Brahe, and for the spectacular aesthetic quality achieved in representing the figures of the constellations, has been called the golden age of uranometry. Represented by the work of such astronomers and artists as Andreas Cellarius, Julius Schiller, Joannes Hevelius, and John Flamsteed, it concludes in 1801 with Bode's *Uranographia*.

Bayer's work is collocated in a historical period particularly crucial for astronomical research. As the telescope had not yet been invented, the number of stars to be positioned in the sky was not much greater than those of the preceding catalogues, such as that of Ptolemy, the reference for all of astronomers prior to Tycho Brahe, which lists 1022, and that of Bayer which contains 1706.

But a growing need was felt for precision and for assigning to the stars non-ambiguous names and symbols. Note that the first significant contribution of researchers for extending the description of the starry vault by inserting new stars and constellations observed in the southern skies dates from the late 16th century. Of the 1706 stars classified by Bayer, 135, located in the southern hemisphere, appear for the first time in an atlas. Moreover, phenomena such as the apparitions of *Nova* in the firmament observed by Brahe and then by Kepler, almost foreshadowing what would take place in 1610 in the skies over Padua through the work of Galileo, demanded that the fixed stars be catalogued with incontrovertible precision.

Bayer's atlas made a significant contribution in this direction.

The *Uranometria* of Johann Bayer published in 1603 marks the golden age of the great celestial charts. From this time on, the catalogue of stars was to be published in a separate volume, while the atlas proper, of great size and increasingly refined artistic quality, was to live a life of its own.

The work of our author, illustrated by Alexander Mair and published in Augsburg, comprises fifty-one rectangular plates of 38.2 x 28.2 cm. They are numbered alphanumerically in Latin capital letters which, upon coming to the end of the alphabet, are first duplicated and then tripled with lower-case letters, so that the first plate is numbered A, the twenty-fifth Aa and the fiftieth Aaa.

The plates are framed by graduated scales with marks of one degree, numbered every five degrees, and with a line traced every thirty degrees. The band around the ecliptic is shown for eight degrees to the north and eight degrees to the south, adding a continuous grey background that thus identifies the limit within which the planets can be distinguished. The coordinates and lines are the polar ones, but is appears a grid centred on the zodiacal poles that puts in evidence the ecliptic.

The stars are positioned utilising data that had been calculated by Tycho Brahe in his Danish observatory, attaining precision close to a minute of arc. They are denominated for the first time, inaugurating a tradition that continues still today, by letters of the Greek alphabet, and when all of these have been used, by Latin letters in increasing order of magnitude.

The fame of this atlas is also linked to the apparition of the two most important *Novae* of the time; the one observed in 1604 by Kepler and the use he made of Bayer's atlas has already been mentioned. The other Nova is the one observed in 1572 by T. Brahe at Uraniborg, for which the Danish astronomer had estimated a distance equal to that of the fixed stars, having been able to observe no parallactic displacement.

The *Nova* of 1572 sent shock waves through the Aristotelian theoretical framework and must have left a striking impression if, over thirty years after its disappearance, Bayer still included it in Plate K of his atlas, which represents *Cassiopeia*, brightly shining and with a graphic symbol larger than that of *Sirius*.

The *Novas* were not the only sign of the changing times recorded by Bayer. Plate Aaa is in fact dedicated to the new constellations observed in the skies of the southern hemisphere. They are twelve in number: *Phoenix*,

3. Johann Bayer, *Uranometry*, Augsburg 1603. Detail of the constellation of Cassiopeia showing the *Nova* observed by Tycho Brahe at Uraniborg.

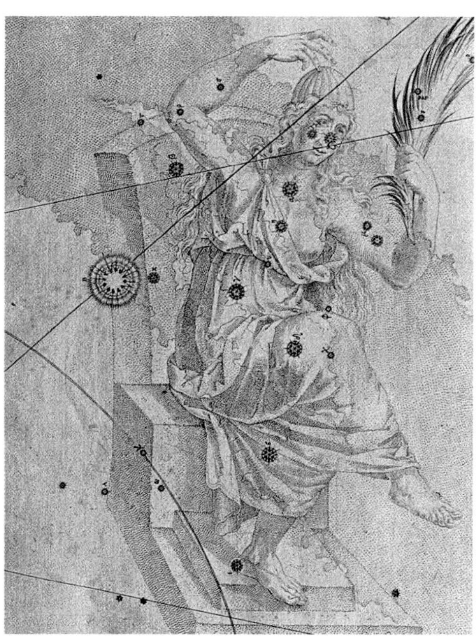

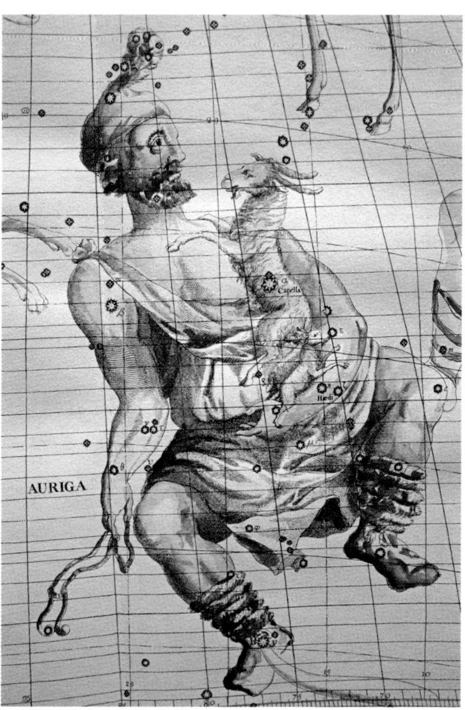

4. John Flamsteed, *Atlas Coelestis*, London, hand-coloured ed. of 1753. The constellation of Auriga with the star Capella.

Grus, Indus, Pavo, Toucan, Dorado, Hydrus, Piscis Volans, Chamaleon, Apis Indica, Triangulum Australe and *Apis*, which contain the 135 stars observed and catalogued with a certain precision, of around two degrees, by the navigators P.D. Keyser and F. de Houtman during a voyage to the Indian Ocean. The plate also includes the *Small* and the *Large Magellanic Clouds*, appearing as two little clouds and thus very different from the representation of the *Milky Way*. In this plate, unlike those of the constellations, the stars are not named, giving the idea that the information utilised by the author is still provisional.

The last two plates, dedicated to the northern and to southern sky, summarise all of the stars shown in the preceding plates, but without the drawings of the constellations.

The *Coelum Stellatum Christianum* by the Jesuit astronomer Julius Schiller was published in Augsburg in 1627. The work represents a real break with tradition, since progress in the scientific content (the plates are even larger than those of Bayer, 27 x 33 cm, and the positions of the stars are calculated in accordance with the observations of Brahe and Kepler) is accompanied by a true revolution in the names assigned the constellations. Already the title of the atlas informed the reader of its author's objective, that of doing away with the Greek mythological world and replacing it with the Biblical and Christian vision. The zodiacal constellations are called by the names of the twelve Apostles, those of the northern and southern hemispheres by the names of personages from the *New* and the *Old Testament*. The river *Eridanus* became the *Red Sea*, the *Milky Way* the *Way of St. James of Compostela*, the *Ship of the Argonauts* became *Noah's Arc*, and *Ursa Minor* became *St. Michael*.

The revolution won few converts, fading away after its peak success in 1661, when Andrea Cellario proposed his *Atlas Coelestis seu Harmonia Macrocosmica*, published in Amsterdam.

In this work the author dedicated two of the twenty-nine plates to the Christian sky, one for each hemisphere, and in the pages commenting on them he describes Schiller's project at length, presenting plates of comparison between the old and the new names, which show that the Jesuit also wanted to change the names of the bodies in the solar system as follows: *Sun-Christ, Mercury-Elijah, Venus-John the Baptist, Mars-Joshua, Jupiter-Moses, Saturn-Adam* and the *Moon-Blessed Mary*.

The presence of these two plates in Cellario's work does not imply that he had accepted Schiller's new vision, but are merely a recognition of it. In fact, the *Atlas Coelestis seu Harmonia Macrocosmica* is intended as a compendium of all of the systems proposed, the Ptolemaic, the Copernican and that of Tycho Brahe. It describes them, presents their advantages but without ever declaring the supremacy of one over the others. Moreover, unlike Schiller, in these two plates Cellario restores their traditional names to the constellations, flanked by the Christian names.

The twenty-nine plates of this atlas, of large format (double pages of approximately 52 x 42 cm), represent twenty-nine sections of the *Pars Prior* from the *Harmonia Macrocosmica*, where the author summarises, in Latin, every aspect of the theories proposed up to and throughout 1661. The content of these sections is highly technical but clearly still too closely linked to the theories of the previous century. There is no chapter on the new instruments of observation, nor any reference to the telescope.

The success of this atlas was due to the fine artistic content of some of the plates which, although printed on paper in one colour, black, were to be copied and coloured by hand by a number of artists, so that the European and American libraries possessing a Cellario in colour, own copies that are truly one of a kind.

The *Firmamentum Sobiescianum, sive uranographia*, in *Prodromus astronomiae*, was printed at Danzig in 1690. Hevelius, who owned a printing works, planned its publication himself, personally engraving the copper plates. But he did not live to see the finished work, which was published by his wife three years after his death.

Of the atlases described here, the *Firmamentum* is undoubtedly the most rare and beautiful. It is made up of fifty-six plates, in which appear 1564 stars. To the Ptolemaic constellations are added eleven new ones, notably augmenting the emerging tendency of thronging the firmament with new personages, often created to curry the favour of the political personage to whom the constellation was dedicated. Today, of these eleven new constellations, seven remain, among them *Scutum*, which Hevelius had however named *Scutum Sobiescianum* in honour of Jan III Sobieski, King of Poland.

The author positions the stars based on information from his own observations supplemented by data taken from the *Tabulae Rudolphinae*, published by Kepler in 1627 utilising observations conducted by Tycho Brahe. But the number of stars is not much greater than that of the earlier atlases, and the precision of their positions would have been better if Hevelius had used the telescope to determine it. For the stars in the southern hemisphere, the author used data from observations furnished by Halley in 1679 subsequent to his scientific expedition to the Island of St. Helena.

Another of the author's decisions, which was to be vehemently opposed by Flamsteed, was that of representing the constellations as viewed from outside of the ideal sphere they occupied, with the result that they appeared as mirror images of their real positions in the sky.

The *Atlas Coelestis* by John Flamsteed reproduced in twenty-five plates, format 62 x 48 cm, the entire northern hemisphere. The last two plates, on a different scale and drawn by another hand, summarise the skies of the northern and the southern hemisphere, representing them up to the equator. Published in London in 1729 by the executors of Flamsteed's will,

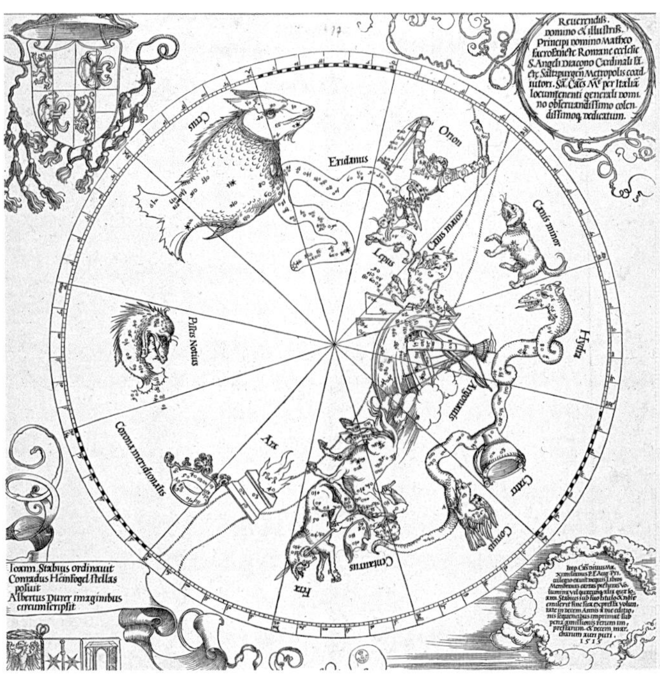

5. Albrecht Dürer, *Hemisphaerium australe*, Nuremberg 1515, Woodcut; the stars are in their real positions and are numbered according to the principles of Ptolemy's catalogue.

it completed the *Historia Coelestis Britannica* compiled in the preceding years, which contained the work carried out by the first director of the Greenwich Royal Observatory in his forty-three years of observations.

Flamsteed's atlas may be considered the first modern one. It shows some 3300 celestial bodies, double those of Hevelius, and for the first time the stars are positioned through their equatorial coordinates: right ascension and declination, whose grid is superimposed on the polar one in the plates. This innovation was made possible by the introduction in observations of the pendulum clock, making it possible to determine the difference in right ascension starting from the difference between the stars' times of transit over the meridian.

The precision of the astral positions is correct by a margin of 10', and this result was achieved by the author utilising a telescope connected to an enormous circular wall with radius of two metres, whose degrees were subdivided into five minutes each. With their graduated scales whose marks measured fourths of a degree, allowing the position of a star to be immediately determined by eye, these plates were easy to use.

The atlas was introduced by a preface written by Margaret Flamsteed and James Hodgson, which traced a brief history of celestial cartography starting from Hipparcus and Aristarcus, presenting the advantages of Flamsteed's work and its innovations, especially the use of the technique of sinusoidal projection perfected only a few years before by Sanson d'Abbeville, geographer to King Louis XIV. It resumes criticism of Hevelius for his representation of the stars as seen from outside of their sphere, emphatically stating that, in the *Atlas Coelestis*, the principles based on the Greek classic tradition have been restored.

A century before, Bayer had included in his atlas the two *Magellanic Clouds*, now Flamsteed, in the plate dedicated to *Andromeda*, drew as a small star, to the right of *nu Andromedae*, the galaxy M31, the only object outside of our *Milky Way*, apart from the two *Magellanic Clouds*, visible to the naked eye.

In the plate dedicated to the constellation *Taurus*, midway between the *Pleiades* and the *Hyades*, appearing below the line of the ecliptic, at the shoulder of the bull Taurus, the Astronomer Royal added a little star of the seventh magnitude, which in the relevant catalogue bears the name *34 Tauri*. The research of late eighteenth-century astronomers revealed that this was the planet *Uranus*, which Flamsteed had unknowingly detected almost ninety years before its official discovery. This unfortunate occurrence was recalled in a great many atlases dating from the early 19th century, for example in Plate XIV of the *Celestial Alas* by Alexander Jamieson, where the planet can be observed in the same position indicated by Flamsteed with a dual denomination: with the date of the unwitting discovery, 1690, and with a symbol, the one commonly used to indicate the planet.

The third period, which begins with Bode's atlas and concludes with that of Delporte (1930), is distinguished by the professional development of atlases. Bode's *Uranographie* represents the highest peak in the earlier tradition but, at the same time, marks the beginning of the dividing paths taken by atlases designed for professional astronomers and those addressed to the larger public of amateurs. It is for this second category that were designed the works in which the constellations are still marked by their iconographic images; in addition to Bode's atlas, we may recall the works of J. Fortin, Alexander Jamieson, K.F.V. Hoffmann and Eduard Hess.

With Bode's *Uranographie*, published in Berlin in 1801, there thus concludes the age of the great atlases that reconcile scientific requisites with artistic quality. Classified under eight magnitudes appear over 17,200 stars; binary stars, star clusters and some 2000 nebulae are indicated. Summarised in the twenty large-format plates is the work carried out by some thirty astronomers of the day, among them Lacaille, Lalande, Messier and in particular William Herschel for his contribution on the nebulae.

Shown in Bode's atlas are over one hundred constellations, the forty-eight Ptolemaic ones, the first twelve austral ones identified by Keyser in the late 16th century, the eleven of Hevelius, another fourteen collocated in the Southern Hemisphere by Lacaille subsequent to research conducted at Cape Town where, between 1751 and 1752, he classified nearly ten thousand new stars. The *Uranographie* contains all of those constellations that had been proposed by various astronomers during the last two centuries, even those whose lives were short-lived, such as the *Globus Aerostaticus* and the *Felis* proposed by J.J. de Lalande or the *Machina Electrica* and the *Lochium Funis* or the *Honores Friderici* and the *Officina Typographica*, as well as the *Musca Borealis* and the *Robur Carolinum* with the *Sceptrum Brandeburgicum*.

The creation of new constellations, dictated by the discoveries deriving from the research conducted by eighteenth-century astronomers, continued in later atlases as well, especially in the two editions of Fortin's *Atlas Céleste*. A first group appearing already in the 1776 edition is composed of the *Scutum of Sobiensky*, the *Bough* and the *Cerberus*, taken from the work of Hevelius, the *Renne*, proposed by Lemonnier in 1746 to commemorate the scientific expedition of French astronomers in 1736 to the arctic circle for the purpose of determining the measurement of the Earth. A second plentiful group was added to the second edition of 1795, the *Solitaire* of Lemonnier in 1776, *Le Messier*, taken from Lalande's Globe of 1779, and *Le Taureau de Poniatowsky* of the Polish astronomer Poczobut. Suggested by the *Ephémérides de Vienne* of 1790 edited by Hell, we find *Les telescopes de Herschel* and the *Harpe de George*, while the *Trophée de Frèdèric* was taken from a work published by Bode in 1787. Lastly, *Le Mural*, to commemorate the instrument used by Lalande to determine the positions of at least thirty thousand stars in the northern sky, a real monument of eighteenth-century astronomy.

The atlases of Fortin, manageable, precise, updated, were the principal reference used for many works of the following decades, from the Portuguese *Atlas celeste arranjado por Flamsteed...* (Lisbon 1804) to the British *A celestial atlas comprising a systematic display of the Heavens* by Alexander Jamieson (London 1822), to the Russian one, written in Cyrillic, drawn by Kornelius Reissig in St. Petersburg in 1829, to the curious *Atlas Celeste* by Franz Niklaus König, published in Berne in 1826, whose plates, printed on diaphanous paper with a black background, when suitably illuminated, projected the enlarged images of the constellations onto a wall. In 1782 Bode himself, before producing his *Uranographie*, completed in Berlin a work called *Worstellung der Gestirne* with thirty-four plates practically identical to those found in the first edition of Fortin.

This ceaseless proliferation of new signs along with the need to catalogue increasingly dimmer stars, discovered by ever more powerful telescopes, was to serve as obstacle to the representation in drawing of the figures of the constellations. Accordingly, within the first fifty years of the 19th century, rules were formulated for the production of atlases for scientific use, from which the drawings were soon to disappear, and those for amateur use, where they remained for ornamental purposes for several decades to come.

Bode was the first to insert dotted lines to indicate the constellations. These too were to change over the course of time, until 1922 when, in the first General Assembly of the International Astronomical Union, it was decided to freeze the evolution of the names in the sky by fixing the boundaries of the definitive eighty-eight constellations.

–

Bibliography

Ideler 1809; Meucci 1878; Hinckley Allen 1899; Brown B.J.W. 1932; Warner 1979; Sergeant Snyder 1984; Strohmaier 1984; Kunitzsch-Smart 1986; Sesti 1987; Werner-Schmeidler 1986; Flamsteed 1987; Bevis 1987; Ridpath 1988; Schaaf 1988; Lovi-Tirion 1989; Grasshoff 1990; Stott 1991; Galluzzi 1991; Galluzzi 1992; *Il Cielo* 1994; Whitfield 1995; Domenicucci 1996; Le Boeuffle 1996; Condos 1997; Lachièze-Rey-Luminet 1998; Charvet 1998; Domini-Milanesi 1998; Stoppa 2000a; Cellario 2000; Lafitte 2001; Wagman 2003; Appenzeller et al. 2003; Jamieson 2004; Olcott 2004; Mendillo et al. 2005; Stoppa 2006; Cellario 2006; Kanas 2007; Hoffmann 2007; Zucker 2008.

Gorgonea Alys
LA LICORNE: Fran
MONOCEROS
UNICORNIS Lat
CANE MAGGIO
LE GRAND CHI
Stringe la Sinistra
d'Orion un seudo o
Panno o Spoglia di Bue
ò di Leone
Geuze
LE PETIT CHIEN ou
LA CANICULE. Fran
Canis Minor, seu Altey Sep
tentrionalis, Sinister, Primus
Parvus Procyon, scilicet Antica
nis, ita vocitatus a Cicerone
Minusculus Canis à Vitruvio
sive Prœcanis, Canicula
Plin: Canis Orionis. Lat
ΠΡΟΚΥΩΝ. Gr
Cometa
osservata
a Danzica
da Hevelio
dalli 20 Dece
del 1652 sino li
7 Gen. dal 1653
Ras
Rasolga
Ixion,
56
3 n

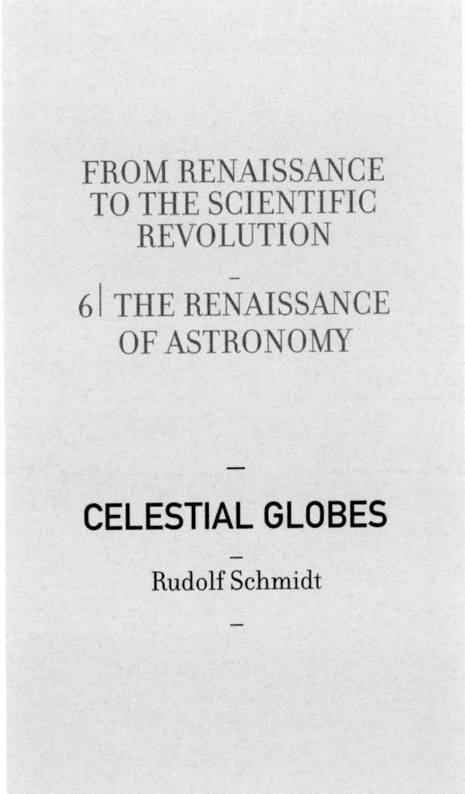

FROM RENAISSANCE TO THE SCIENTIFIC REVOLUTION

–

6 | THE RENAISSANCE OF ASTRONOMY

–

CELESTIAL GLOBES

–

Rudolf Schmidt

–

When were the first globes built? From what age do they date, the first three-dimensional models and the first representations of those celestial phenomena, already observed since remotest antiquity? Man began to reflect on the cosmos at a very early stage. Knowledge of the seasons was, in fact, essential for survival, for hunting to procure food, for planting and harvesting. All of the more advanced civilisations tried to determine the succession of the seasons and the length of the year based on the positions of the celestial bodies. Equally common was the belief that the stars exerted an influence on human destiny. Today there exists a new discipline specialised in this sector: archeoastronomy. In the Mesopotamian region, the Chaldeans were conducting systematic observations of the sky already around 3000 B.C., as was done in more recent times by the advanced civilisations of East Asia and Central America. The constellations still in use today are of Mesopotamian origin, and are also found represented on ancient Egyptian frescoes and bas-reliefs.

The Greeks instead did not stop at mere observation of the skies, but went on to formulate hypotheses on the operation of the universe. According to Greek and Roman philosophers, the Earth was the centre of the universe; it was spherical in form, freely suspended in space, immobile, and surrounded by crystalline celestial spheres. The most distant crystalline sphere was that of the fixed stars (1060, according to Pliny the Elder[1]), celestial bodies thought to be equidistant from the Earth, which were grouped into 48 constellations to make them easier to distinguish in the sky. The wandering stars (the planets, among which were included the Moon and the Sun) were instead thought to be embedded in crystalline spheres that revolved around the Earth at different speeds. The Greeks also associated persons, animals and things to the constellations. The deities that reigned over Earth, such as Zeus, Hera, and Athena, had raised to the skies Heracles, Orion and Andromeda as eternal custodians assigned the task of casting light on mortals.

Starting with Eudoxos of Cnidus (c. 408-356 B.C.), who seems to have fabricated the first celestial globe, and going on through Aristotle (c. 389-322 B. C.), Aristarcus of Samos (310-250 B.C.), Heraclides Ponticus, and Hipparchus of Nicea (190-125 B.C.), mathematicians, philosophers of natural science and thinkers added their own observations and discoveries to this world system, altering it, correcting it, extending it, reducing it and sometimes even confuting it. Already Heraclides had spoken of the Earth's rotation around its axis, while Aristarcus of Samos maintained that the centre of the universe was the Sun, that the Earth rotated around it and that the distance of the fixed stars was infinite. The idea of a heliocentric system was developed in fragmentary manner and then abandoned due to the hostility it encountered, precisely as was to happen with the Copernican theory many centuries later. Hipparchus compiled a stellar catalogue and worked out a system of coordinates to determine the positions of the stars and another identical one to establish the positions of various points on the terrestrial sphere. Lastly, he discovered the precession of the equinoxes. He had in fact realised that the spring and autumn equinoxes moved slowly along the orbit of the ecliptic. The amplitude of motion of the precession, long debated, has now been established as about one degree every seventy years[2].

The celestial globe is a model of the sky. This instrument is constructed from the viewpoint of an onlooker who is gazing from the fixed stars, considered equidistant from the Earth, toward a centre occupied by the Earth. Accordingly, the constellations on celestial globes are represented in a perspective reversed in respect to that of the Earth.

A particular model of celestial sphere is the armillary sphere, also called spherical astrolabe, consisting of imaginary auxiliary circles, the so-called great circles, such as the equator, the ecliptic, the tropics and the polar circles. If we pass these rings through the circles of the colures (the equinoctial colure that passes through the spring and autumn equinoxes is the solstitial one, which conjoins the summer and winter solstices), that is, the meridians perpendicular to the celestial equator that conjoin the celestial poles, we obtain an armillary sphere. Fixed to an immobile axis at the centre of the armillary sphere is the Earth. One of the very great achievements of the ancient philosophers was that of conceiving of and measuring celestial lines and trajectories, and then replicating them in a three-dimensional model. Armillary spheres are depicted in two ancient mosaics. One, representing the nine muses, was brought to light at Vichten, Luxemburg, only in 1995, and is now displayed at the Musée National d'Histoire et d'Art of Luxemburg[3]. The other is found at the archaeological site of Solunto, in the vicinity of Palermo[4]. These first armillary spheres are geocentric ones.

Other testimony to the astronomical observations conducted by the ancients consists of representations on coins, cameos, bas-reliefs and wall paintings. At present, three celestial globes from classical times are known: a small brass sphere, now at the Roman-Germanic museum of Magonza[5] (cf. entry III.1.7), represents some stars, celestial orbits and 48 constellations; a gilded silver sphere belonging to a private collection in Paris[6] (cf. entry II.4.2) shows constellations, the great circles, and some stars; and lastly, the marble statue of the Farnese Atlas[7] (cf. entry III.1.8a), portrays Atlas in the act of holding up the skies. The celestial vault, represented in the form of a sphere, is carved with the constellations and the great circles, but not the stars. These three archaeological treasures are displayed together for the first time in this exhibition.

It is highly probable that terrestrial globes as well existed in the classical world. For example, the Greek philosopher Crates of Mallus, c. 150 B.C., is attributed with having fabricated a stone globe depicting the world as it was known at the time.

Probably already in classical times, celestial globes were being used to calculate time. This is suggested by some representations of armillary spheres and celestial globes mounted on structures similar to those that, from the late Middle Ages to the second half of the 19th century, were used for this purpose. Calculating time could have been the purpose of the celestial globe in abbeys and religious centres, as well as in the Islamic cultural circles of the early Middle Ages. With the aid of a celestial globe, in particular with the circles of the ecliptic and the celestial equator, it is possible to calculate the time in any locality based on its geographic latitude. For local time, reference was usually made to the highest altitude of the Sun. With the celestial globe it was possible to calculate the time of dawn and sunset and even the duration of twilight. The method is simple: the axis of the globe, which can rotate within its meridian circle, is oriented toward the North Pole. On the ecliptic the position of the Sun, that is, the date, is marked, and the globe is turned until the point marked on it appears on the horizontal ring that divides it in two halves. The time is indicated by the digits found on the brass meridian circle of the globe. It is also possible to see where the Sun will rise on a certain day.

Ptolemy (c. 150 A.D.) synthesised all of the knowledge of the ancients in the *Almagest* and the *Geographia*, which were known to medieval scholars through Arab sources and the texts of Greek authors. Astronomy played a fundamental role in the Islamic world as well, and for this reason celestial globes were widely used to measure time. Islamic celestial globes are found in several museums; the most ancient of them, now in Florence, dates from 1080 A.D. (cf. entry IV.3.9a). Both in antiquity and in the early Middle Ages, each globe was one of a kind; they were expensive works of costly fabrication made of stone or metal. Celestial globes arrived in Europe only much later. In 1444 the cardinal and philosopher Nikolaus von Kues (Nicola Cusano, 1401-1464) purchased a celestial globe made of birch wood and another made of bronze. Both are now found at Bernkastel-Kues (Germany), in the Cusano Foundation. Numerous documents show that celestial globes, along with their terrestrial twins, were present in the princely courts, both religious and secular, of the 15th century. To Philip the Good, Count of Burgundy, Master Guillaume Hobit issued a receipt for 'a representation of the world in round form', for which he received 150 thalers[8]. The Vice Prefect of the Vatican Library, Monseigneur Josè Ruysschaert, discovered documentary material indicating that Niccolò Germano made a celestial globe and its terrestrial twin in 1477[9].

Dürer's representation of the skies marked the beginning of a new stage. The realisation of gores[10] (printed spherical triangles, in the form of wedges, to be applied to a sphere), allowed globes to be fabricated in larger numbers. The first printed gores were those of Martin Waldseemüller (c. 1470-1518/21), used in 1507 for a terrestrial globe 10 cm in diameter, four examples of which are known today. Of priceless value are the globes of Gemma Frisius (1508-1555) from Louvain. One of his celestial globes is now found at Greenwich. The terrestrial globes of the famous cartographer Gerhard Mercator (1512-1594), pupil and collaborator of Gemma Frisius, were more widely disseminated. Several examples of his globes have come down to us, including the terrestrial one of 1541 and the celestial one of 1551, both with diameters of forty-one centimetres. From this time on, globes were usually offered in pairs. They were not mere decorative objects, but were also used on the ships, which embarked on transoceanic voyages. The terrestrial globe was utilised to determine the direction of the prevailing winds and currents in the open sea or near the coastline, while the celestial ones served to calculate the ship's position on the open sea at night. With the invention of the telescope, the number of visible stars vastly increased and star atlases were enriched with new constellations, such as the Dove (1603, Johann Bayer), the Giraffe and the Tiger (1624, Bartsch). The astronomers who had named the new constellations were also indicated on the globes.

The great Dutch production of globes began in the late 16th - early 17th century, with the famous printers Jodocus Hondius (1563-1612) and Willem Jansz Blaeu (1571-1638) and their rivals Janssonius, Plancius, and Van Langren. Blaeu, pupil of the famous astronomer Tycho Brahe, and Hondius were the first to indicate on their celestial globes the circumpolar stars seen in 1595-97 by Frederick Houtman and Pieter Dircksz Keyser while circumnavigating the southern tip Africa, which Petrus Plancius then grouped in twelve constellations. To attract more customers, painters such as Jan Pietresz Sanredam (1565-1607) were commissioned to produce striking drawings of the constellations for the clothing and arms of some figures. The competitors quickly imitated this example. The Dutch globe producers, soon followed by Roman and Venetian cartographers and cosmographers, thus inaugurated a real competitive spirit, enlivened by discussions on the Ptolemaic and the Copernican representations of the universe. Matthäus Greuter (1557-1638), who worked in Rome and Venice, fabricated in the last years of his life marvellous celestial and terrestrial globes with diameter of 49 centimetres. In the scrolls he mentions Blaeu and indicates Tycho Brahe as the source for the positions of the stars, which were however calculated for 1636. Around 1700 the major centres of globe production moved from Holland to German, Italy, France, and Great Britain.

During this period, terrestrial and celestial globes had already made their entrance into the religious and secular princely courts. Gigantic celestial globes were built, like those of Erhard Weigel (1625-1699) which measured 18 and 33 feet in diameter (but only his celestial globes with diameters of 27.5 and 35.5 centimetres in have survived). Around 1650 a globe with diameter of 3.11 metres, which could be entered, was built for Count Frederick III of Schleswig-Holstein. It was decorated on the outside with a reproduction of the Earth's surface, while the inside, entered through a little door, could hold ten people, who admired the revolving firmament by candlelight (today this globe is found in St. Petersburg). In Paris, between 1680 and 1683, Vincenzo Coronelli (1650-1718), Father and later General of the Order of the Friars Minor, built a pair of globes with diameter of 3.85 m for Louis XIV. Although they could not be entered, they were the object of great admiration and still today constitute a great attraction for the public at the Paris National Library. Coronelli, cosmographer, maestro, inventor and eminent prelate, continued the work of the Italian globe makers, bringing it to the highest levels. His terrestrial and celestial globes with diameter of 110 centimetres are today the pride of various museums.

In the second half of the 18th century the celestial globe began to lose its place of importance. In navigation, clocks and increasingly precise tables provided better instruments for determining positions and for astronomical calculations.

Today, antique celestial and terrestrial globes have become collectors' pieces, testifying to the efforts and endeavours of the philosophers of antiquity and the astronomers of the modern age to realise scale representations of the Earth and the sky.

–

Bibliography

Allmayer-Beck 1997; Coronelli 1693; *Il p. Vincenzo Coronelli* 1951; Dekker 1995, p. 79; Dekker 1999; *Istituto e Museo di storia della scienza (Firenze)* 2004; Domini-Milanesi 1998; *Der Globusfreund* 1952; Fiorini 1899; Hamel 2002; Kier-Reinert 1995, pp.71-73; King-Millburn 1978; Krogt 1993; Parigi 2002b; Künzl 2003; Stevenson 1921; Savage-Smith 1985; Warner 1979; Krier *et al* 2002, pp. 44-47; Schmidt 2003, pp. 21-22; Boeselager 1983; Künzl 1998, pp. 7-80 (english edition pp. 81-155); Valerio 1987, pp. 97-114; Paviot 1995, pp. 19-29; Ruysschaert 1985, pp. 93-104; Babicz 1987, pp. 155-168; Glareanus 1527; Dürer 1525.

[1] Coronelli 1693, p. 39.

[2] Dekker 1995, p.79.

[3] Kier-Reinert 1995, pp. 71-73. Krier et al. 2002, pp. 44-47.

[4] Schmidt 2003 pp. 21-22; Boeselager 1983.

[5] Künzl 1998, pp. 7-80.

[6] Parigi 2002b, pp. 22-27.

[7] Valerio 1987, pp. 97-114.

[8] Paviot 1995, pp. 19-29.

[9] Ruysschaert 1987, pp. 93-104; and also Babicz 1987, pp. 155-168 (with abridged German version).

[10] Heinrich Loritius (Glareanus) invented an approximative solution in 1527 and Albrecht Dürer also describes the realisation with a compass of 'comb-shaped' elements. On this subject see: Glareanus 1527, chap. XIX, *De inducemda papyro in globus* and Dürer 1525.

1. Page 242, Vincenzo Coronelli, *Constellations*, detail of the gores in the Celestial Globe of 1693, Paris.

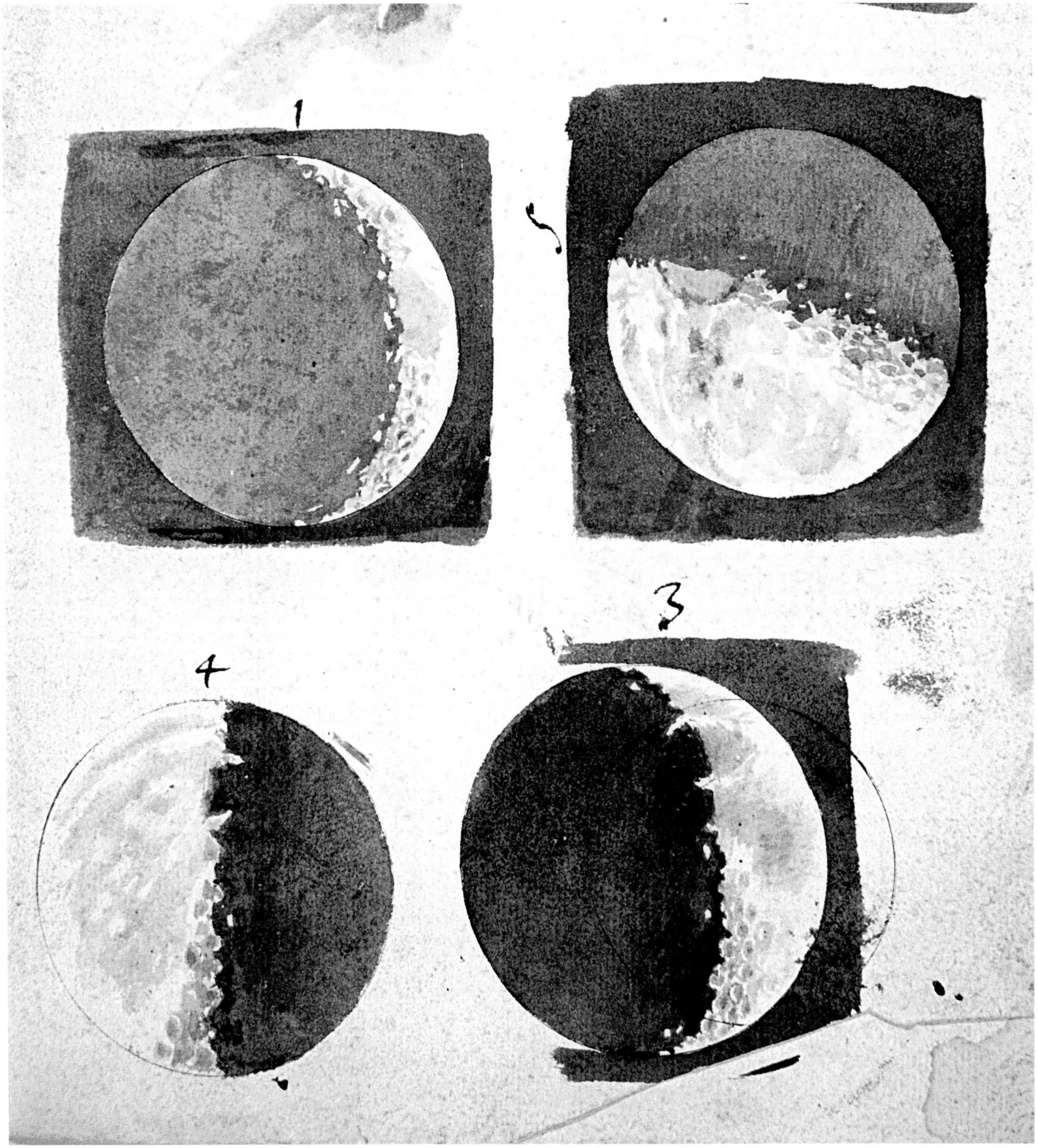

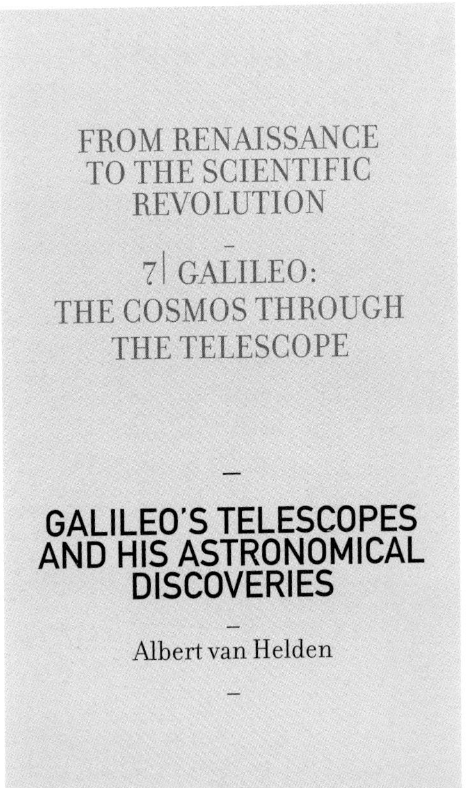

FROM RENAISSANCE
TO THE SCIENTIFIC
REVOLUTION
–
7| GALILEO:
THE COSMOS THROUGH
THE TELESCOPE
–
GALILEO'S TELESCOPES
AND HIS ASTRONOMICAL
DISCOVERIES
–
Albert van Helden
–

In October 1608, Hans Lipperhey applied for a patent on a spyglass he claimed he invented. The Hague was the scene of peace negotiations between Spain and the Netherlands, and the news of this new device spread rapidly through diplomatic channels: a printed newsletter describing the events in The Hague reached Fra Paolo Sarpi in Venice in November or December, and Sarpi told Galileo about it. Because there was no description of the spyglass, Sarpi and Galileo waited for confirmation from France, and this arrived late in the spring of 1609. Galileo quickly made a spyglass that magnified three times with lenses bought in a spectacle-maker's shop.

But lenses for a telescope required much higher optical quality than spectacle lenses. When we focus on an object through a spectacle lens, we use only an area about as large as our pupil. Over such a small area, optical defects are small, so that the imperfections do not affect our vision. With a telescope, all the light entering the convex objective takes part in image formation, and this means that imperfections in curvature must now be very small over the entire lens rather than a small area in a spectacle lens. Typically, the grinding of spectacle lenses produced more curvature near the edge of the lens than in the center, and making these better lenses meant retooling: better forms in which to grind the lenses with longer focal lengths, grinding more accurately and evenly, and taking care that the curvature was not changed during the polishing process. Spectacle makers were unable to meet these demands in 1609, and only a few learned men managed this feat.

The objective of Lipperhey's spyglass was covered for the most part, leaving only a small aperture in the center of perhaps a centimeter. This made the magnified image sharper, but it enlarged the light gathering power of the eye only slightly larger, perhaps by a factor of two or three. Galileo set out to make instruments with greater light-gathering power and higher magnifications, but this meant he had to learn to grind and polish his own lenses. He made bought the appropriate equipment and slowly train himself in the difficult and tedious task of grinding and polishing.

By the end of August, he had succeeded in making a spyglass that magnifies about eight times, and he presented this to the Senate of Venice. From thc tops of high towers, the senators satisfied themselves that one could identify a ship several hours earlier than without the instrument, clearly a device of strategic value. The saw to it that Galileo was finally given a permanent appointment (rather than a yearly renewable contract) as professor of the mathematical subjects at the University of Padua, with a doubling of his salary.

Up to this point, there was no significant mention of astronomical applications of the instrument. The newsletter from The Hague mentioned that a spyglass showed many more stars than were visible with the naked eye, and no doubt Galileo had from time to time directed a spyglass to the heavens, but he could surely not have seen much of interest in the fixed stars and planets, which are very bright for their size. Galileo's eight-powered spyglass was useful for seeing things on earth, but in the heavens the only body that could be observed during this early period was the Moon. An eight-powered instrument could show quite a bit of detail: the fact that the terminator, the line separating the dark from the light part was not smooth but jagged, and that some areas were smooth and others rough. But it is to be doubted that Galileo could see finer detail. It was not until he had made better and more powerful telescopes –up to 20-powered by November 1609– that he could begin a detailed research project. Now his telescope showed many small, round, spots (we know them as craters) and light points in the dark part near the terminator. He observed that the round spots were darkly outlined in the part toward the Sun, and that as the Moon waxed, the light part swallowed up the light spots ahead of the terminator. This was the play of light and shadow: the round spots were depressions and the light spots mountains.

Galileo now decided to observe the Moon through one waxing cycle and to draw what he saw. The drawings were to be the illustrations in a publication he was planning. From the end of November to the middle of December, Galileo observed and drew the Moon through a cycle of waxing (adding a few observations later). By the end of the year, he was writing up his results and sharpening his arguments for the similarity between the Moon's rough surface and the Earth's.

He did not stop his attempts to make better telescope lenses, however. The planets were not in good positions for observing, except for Jupiter, which was at opposition early in December and was the brightest body in the evening sky. The telescope that worked fine for lunar observations was not good enough for Jupiter, however, and it was not until after Christmas that Galileo managed to improve it sufficiently –perhaps with various sizes and shapes of aperture rings on the objective– to allow him to see Jupiter as a round disc, like a little full moon, and at that point he made an amazing discovery.

On 7 January 1610, Galileo wrote a long letter, probably to Antonio dei Medici, in which he related his observations of the Moon in great detail. He went on to speak briefly of the many fixed stars invisible to the naked eye, and gave as an example three bright little stars in a straight line with Jupiter, two on the eastern and one on the western side of the planet. He did not say that he had noticed these 'stars' before, and since they are always on a straight line with Jupiter, we can conclude that Galileo's telescope was now good enough to show stars near bright bodies such as Jupiter, where before these had been hidden in the colors and light spikes caused by optical problems. The formation interested Galileo enough to return to the observation the next evening. The stars were still there, on a straight line with Jupiter, but now they were all on the western side of the planet. Galileo thought that because these were fixed stars Jupiter had passed them. But that would mean that Jupiter was moving in the wrong direction. Over the next few nights of observing, Galileo found that, in fact, there were four, not three of these 'stars', and he determined that, in fact these they were moving along with Jupiter, while at the same time changing their positions with respect to each other and the planet. By 12 January, Galileo had concluded that these four bodies were moons going around Jupiter.

This was a very important discovery, not only for its bearing on the gathering debate between the Aristotelian/Ptolemaic and Copernican world systems, but also for Galileo's own career. For some years, he had wanted to return to his native Tuscany, where, during the summer vacations, he had instructed Cosimo, the son of Grand Duke Ferdinand de' Medici, in mathematical subjects. His previous attempts to obtain patronage from the Medici family had been unsuccessful. But things had changed. For one thing, his pupil, Cosimo, was the new Grand Duke, and for another, Galileo now had a very precious gift to offer. But he had to go into print quickly to make sure that others would not 'scoop' him.

Because he had discovered these moons, Galileo claimed the right to name them. While continuing his observations of Jupiter's moons, mapping configurations of stars to illustrate their multitude, and writing up his results, he approached the Tuscan Court again, telling the Grand Duke of his discovery, and asking him whether he would prefer the name 'Cosmic Stars', after the Grand Duke himself, or 'Medicean Stars,' after the Medici family. The first part of the book was already being printed, and Galileo, anticipating that the Grand Duke would choose the first alternative, named them 'Cosmic Stars' on the half-title. He had to make the correction by gluing over it a strip of paper with 'Medicean Stars' in each copy.

Sidereus Nuncius, or Sidereal/Starry Message/Messenger (the words can be translated either way), came off the press on 12 March 1610. It was dedicated to the Grand Duke, and the 550 printed copies sold out almost at once. Galileo began with a brief description of his telescope and an explanation of how one determined a telescope's magnification. He then launched in a narrative of his observations of the lunar surface, illustrated with four engravings of different phases. His argument was that the Moon's surface was rough and mountainous like the Earth's. For instance, the bright points of light in the dark region just beyond the terminator were mountain peaks: wasn't that how the Sun, when it was just rising, illuminated the mountain tops first, filling the valleys with light gradually as it rose higher in the sky? And he complemented this argument with an explanation of the so-called secondary light of the Moon seen just before and after the new moon: for an observer on the Moon, the Earth was, at this point fully illuminated, and it was the reflection of this light that was seen on the dark part of the lunar disc. Not only was the Moon like the Earth, but the Earth was like the Moon: Galileo had, so to speak, brought the Moon down to Earth and elevated the Earth into the heaven. This evidence did not fit into the traditional worldview with its rigid separation between the perfect and unchanging heavens and the corrupt and changing terrestrial region.

Galileo ended the section about the Moon with the question about the height of these lunar mountains. On numerous occasions, he had seen a bright mountain top in the dark part of the Moon, quite a distance ahead of the terminator, sometimes by as much as a twentieth part of the Moon's diameter. Since the Moon's diameter was roughly $2/7^{th}$ of the Earth's diameter, he knew two sides of a right triangle and could calculate the actual height, which he made 4 miles. But if there were such high mountains on the Moon, then why did they not appear outlined along the circumference of the lunar disc? Galileo presented two reasons: successive mountain ranges blended together near the rim, just as in a rough sea the horizon looks flat, and perhaps there was an atmosphere around the Moon so thin as to present an obstacle to our vision only when it was almost tangent to the lunar globe. This last argument, although reasonable at the time, proved to be incor-

1. Page 246, *Drawings of the Moon*, detail of the Moon; Biblioteca Nazionale Centrale di Firenze, Ms. Gal. 48, c. 28r.

2. The phases of Venus.

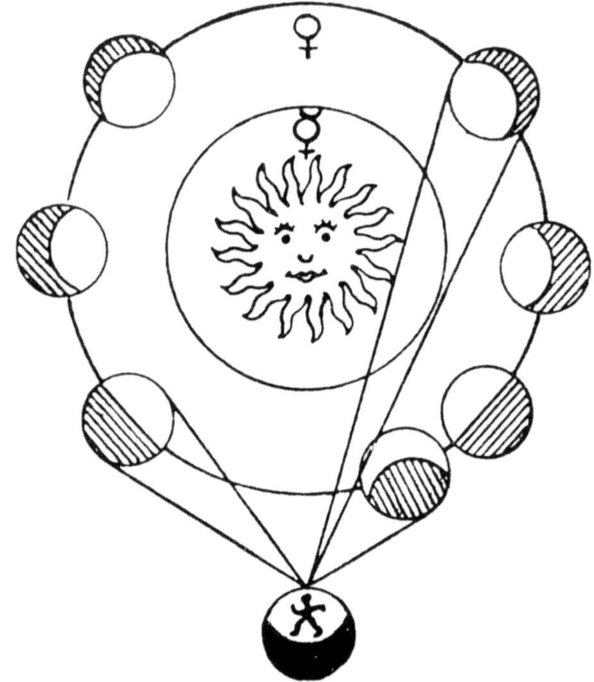

rect, and unfortunately it presented Galileo's opponents who adhered to the perfection of the heavens with an argument against any unevenness of the Moon's surface: Galileo's almost invisible atmosphere was turned by them into an entirely invisible crystalline layer that was perfectly spherical.

The next section of *Sidereus Nuncius* dealt with the stars. There were indeed innumerable fixed stars. Galileo wrote that he had planned to map the entire Orion constellation. His manuscripts show that on 23 January he had drawn an 8° by 10° grid and had begun to enter stars on it, and around it he wrote measurements of distances of smaller stars from a brighter one. This approach was far too ambitious: there were simply too many telescopic stars in the constellation to map, as it were, on the fly, while he was writing, overseeing the printing, and keeping track of Jupiter's moons (not to mention his teaching duties at the university and the private lessons at his house). On 7 February he made a sketch of the Orion's belt and sword region, showing 80 telescopic stars. In the Pleiades, drawn on 1 February, he showed no fewer than 36 stars, where naked-eye observes normally see six. Galileo also argued that nebulae, and the entire Milky Way, are agglomerations of stars too small to be discerned separately with the naked eye. Ptolemy's star catalogue, still unsurpassed after almost fifteen centuries, listed five nebular 'stars;' Galileo drew two of these, the nebula in the head of Orion (21 stars), and Praesepe (38 stars)[1]. (These are not in the manuscripts.)

In this section, too, Galileo had pointed out that the telescope revealed a distinction between planets and fixed stars: 'For the planets present entirely smooth and exactly circular globes, that appear as little moons, entirely covered with light, while the fixed stars are not seen bounded by circular outlines, but rather as pulsating all around with certain bright rays.'[2] In the old cosmology, all heavenly bodies, including the Moon, were made up of the same stellar material, and the fixed stars were just beyond Saturn. Now, the difference in appearance indicated that the planets were much closer than the stars, a notion that fit better with the heliocentric worldview.

It was one group of planetary bodies that was the subject of the last section of *Sidereus Nuncius*: Jupiter and its satellites. Galileo presented here 65 annotated observations from 7 January to 2 March 1610, specifying the time of night and estimates of the distances between them and the planet. Knowing full well that the existence of Jupiter's four moons would be the most spectacular and controversial among his claims, Galileo tried to convince the reader by the sheer weight of evidence. He then ended the book with some comments about the meaning of Jupiter's moons. They showed that there was more than one center of motion in the universe, no matter what cosmological system

Die 5. cœlum fuit nubilosum

Die 6. talis fuit constitutio H. 2. [* O *] 2. tm stellę aderāt. orienta=
lis una a ♃ distans 1', occidētalis altera a ♃ remota 3' erāt in ea=
dē recta cū ♃

Die 7. duę stellę aderāt orientales atq. ita constitutę [* * O]
interstitia inter ipsas et ♃ erāt ambo 1'. erātq. i eadē recta

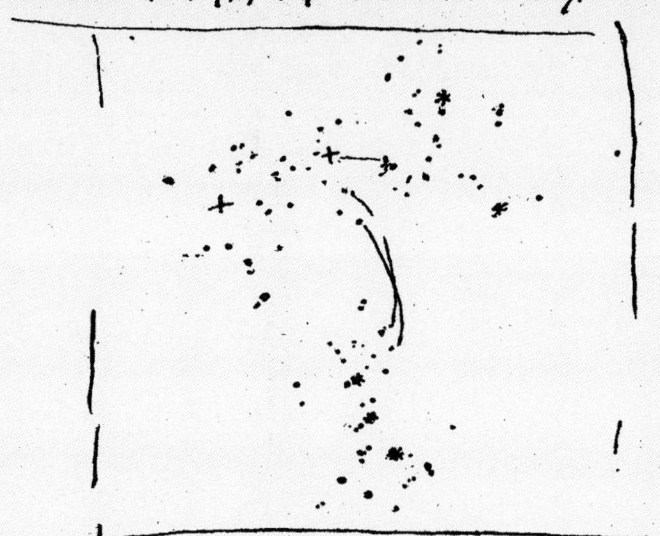

250

Die 8. H. 1. erāt 3. stellę orietales oēs,
ut in figura opposita ♃i prop.a
erat exigua distās ab eo 1'.0.
media ab hac distabat 4'. et erat satis magna, orientalior admodū exigua
distabat ab hac 20''. conspectę fuerāt h. o. 40. ab occasu; anceps erā nūqd ♃i
prop.a una tm. an 2. essent stellulę videbat. n. interdū huic aliā adesse
versus ortū mirā immodū exiguā et ab illa distās 10''. oēs in eadē rectā
tm ad expositionē eclipticę constitutę erāt.
Hora v.o 3. stella ♃i prop.a illū ferè tāgebat, distabat. n. 10'' tantū:
reliquę v.o paulo magis a ♃ aberāt, erat. n. media a ♃ distās 6'. tandē
Hora 4. omnino ♃i erat iūcta adeo ut amplius nō cernebat

Die 9. H. 0. 30 aderāt 2 stellę orientales, et una occidētalis ita [* * O *]
orientalior exigua a sequēti distabat 4'. media maior
erat et a ♃ remota 7'. ♃. ab occidētali quę parua
erat 4'.

Die 10. stellulę duę admodū exiguę cernebāt orietales atq. [* *O]
remotior distabat a ♃ 10'. vicinior v.o 0. 20''. erantq. in eadē recta
Hora autē 4. stella ♃i prop.a amplius nō apparebat, vero ut opinor sub ♃ latitabat
altera v.o adhuc 2 minuta erat ut vix cerni posset si aer preclarus esset, et a ♃ erat magis
elongata videbat. n. distare [illegible]

3. Drawings of part of the constellation of Orion; Biblioteca Nazionale Centrale di Firenze, Ms. Gal. 49, c. 33r.

4. Phases of the Moon, engraving; *Sidereus Nuncius*, Venice 1610.

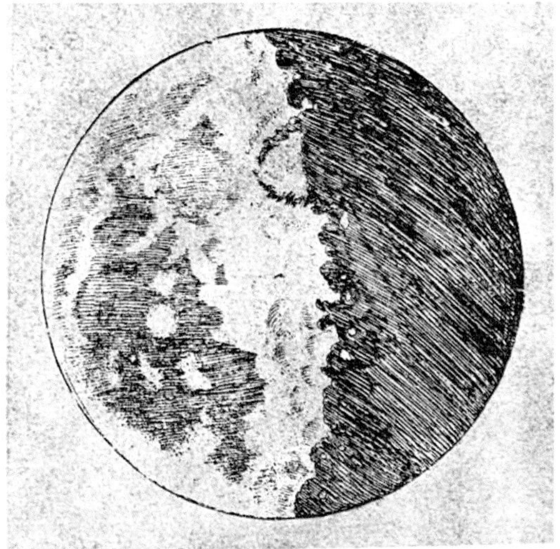

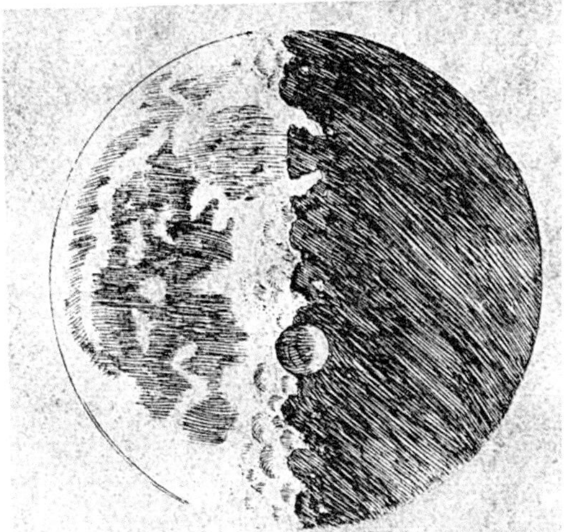

one subscribed to. Further, the objection that in the Copernican system Earth was the only planet with a moon now disappeared. Galileo tried to explain the fact that sometimes Jupiter's moons appeared larger and at other times smaller by postulating an atmosphere around the planet, just as he had argued that perhaps there was one around the Moon, and he extended this notion to all the planets. At the end of this brief section, Galileo ended the book with the sentence, 'The fair reader may expect more about these matters soon.'[3]

Sidereus Nuncius caused a sensation in learned circles. Some accepted the discoveries as evidence for the Copernican system, while others rejected them because they were impossible in the Ptolemaic/Aristotelian cosmology, in which the Earth occupied the center of the universe, was the sole center of rotation, and was a dark, corrupt body, very different from the perfect and unchanging heavens. Galileo had to answer objections, some of which were quite hostile. But he received important support from Johannes Kepler, the Imperial Mathematician in Prague, and he gained a powerful patron: Cosimo II de' Medici appointed him 'Philosopher and Mathematician to the Grand Duke.' In the meantime, he continued his observations, and in July of 1611 he discovered that Saturn has appendages that flank it and do not move with respect to it. The puzzle of these appendages, as they slowly changed their size and shape – and in 1612 disappeared entirely for some time– was not solved until half a century later.

In the autumn of 1610, after he had moved from Padua to Florence, Galileo turned his attention to the appearances of Venus. In the traditional cosmology, Venus occupied the spherical shell 'below' the Sun. It could therefore never appear like a little full moon. But in the Copernican system, the planet circled the Sun and should therefore appear like a small full moon when it was beyond the Sun (near superior conjunction) and like a much larger thin crescent when it was near its closest approach to Earth (inferior conjunction). The changes in appearance are very slow, and it took Galileo the entire autumn of 1610 to determine that the planet's appearances agreed with the Copernican system. Here was proof that the pure Ptolemaic system was wrong in this aspect.

By the end of that year, a few others had finally been able to verify Galileo's discoveries. Most important were Johannes Kepler in Prague and the mathematicians at the Collegio Romano. Indeed, when Galileo visited Rome, in the spring of 1611, these mathematicians, Christoph Clavius, Christoph Grienberger, Giovanni Paolo Lembo, and Odo van Maelcote, certified to Roberto Cardinal Bellarmine, director of the College, that the phenomena discovered by Galileo were real. (They did however indicate that the senior member, Clavius, did not necessarily agree with the interpretation of some these phenomena). Galileo

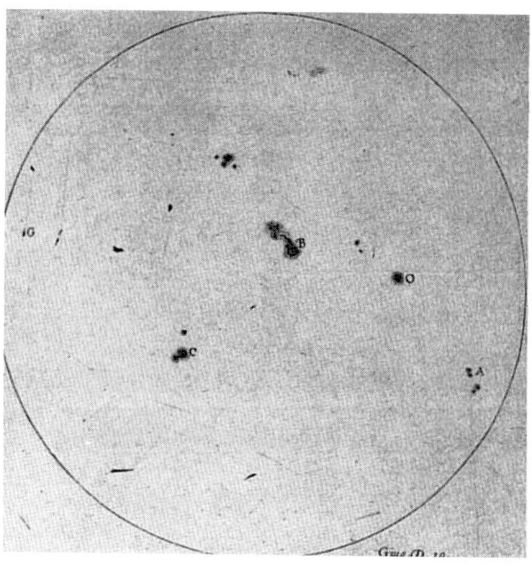

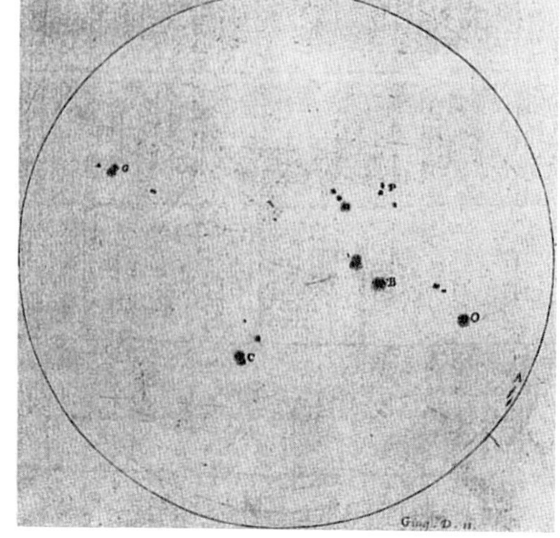

5-6. Sunspots, engraving, *Istoria e dimostrazioni intorno alle macchie solari e loro accidenti*, Rome 1613; Biblioteca Nazionale Centrale di Firenze, Post.155, pp. 64-65.

was therefore feted at the College, and the junior member, Maelcote, delivered a speech, *Nuntius Sidereus*, in which Galileo was, so to speak, praised to the heavens. At another feast in Rome, Galileo was inducted into the Accademia dei Lincei, Academy of the Lynxes, a group of scholars under the patronage of Prince Federico Cesi. At this feast, the name *telescope* was introduced.

While in Rome, Galileo showed sunspots to some of his friends. Large dark spots had been seen with the naked eye from time to time, but the few mentioned in the astronomical literature were interpreted to be transits of Mercury or Venus; after all, the Sun was a perfect body without blemishes. Since 1610 these had been observed through telescopes in London, Osteel (East Frisia), and Ingolstadt. It is not known when Galileo first observed them. Looking through a telescope directly at the Sun was very hard on the eyes, even if the aperture was very small and a piece of colored glass was used as a filter. Thomas Harriot in London, who made the first recorded telescopic observation of sunspots, could observe for only about fifteen minutes after sunrise over the low, flat Thames estuary. If the Sun was higher in the sky, one could only observe it when it happened to be covered by a thin veil of clouds.

In Florence, Galileo did not have low eastern and western horizons. By the time the Sun appeared from behind the mountains, it was higher in the sky. Thus, although he knew the phenomenon, he did not make a detailed study of them after his return from Rome in 1611. Moreover, he became involved in the controversy about floating bodies, on which he was to publish a book in the spring of 1612. He was rudely awakened, however, when a letter from the banker and Humanist, Marc Welser in Augsburg arrived early in the new year asking Galileo for comments on an enclosed tract, *Tres Epistolae de maculis solaris*, 'Three letters about solar spots,' signed by a certain 'Apelles latens post tabulam,' or Apelles hiding behind the painting, who argued that sunspots were swarms of satellites of the Sun going around it with a period of about a month. If the spots were not on the Sun, then the perfection of that body and the entire heavens (with the exception perhaps of the Moon) could be maintained.

As the Philosopher and Mathematician of the Grand Duke, Galileo was obliged to respond and defend his pre-eminent position in telescopic matters. In February 1612 he began making observations of the Sun. The earlier ones were little more than hasty sketches, but by April they were becoming more elaborate, with certain large spots carefully drawn and followed for several days. On 4 May, he sent his first letter to Welser, in which he argued that the spots were on or near the surface of the Sun and somewhat reminiscent of our earthly clouds. The letter had one sketch, showing the changes in shape of one large spot over several days. It was at this time that his student and associate, Benedetto Castelli, discovered that the Sun's image can be projected through a telescope. This meant that one could observe sunspots at all hours of the day, and Galileo now made a sustained series of observations on consecutive days. And whereas Apelles's sunspot illustrations were squeezed together on one big engraved plate, so that the sizes of the spots were not to scale, Galileo and Castelli traced the spots directly on the (roughly 12-cm wide) image of the Sun projected on the paper. The information content of these tracings was much greater than that of Apelles's (roughly 3-cm) depictions, in which the shapes of individual spots could hardly be made out.

Galileo sent the first series of tracings, made in May, to Maffeo Cardinal Barberini, who had showed himself to be an admirer of his. He then wrote a second letter to Marc Welser, in which he combined his verbal argument with mathematical demonstrations and an almost uninterrupted series of tracings (cf. entry VII.2.5), from 2 June to 8 July 1612. Galileo had made these observations at roughly the same time each day, so that the ecliptic was oriented the same way in successive drawings, and this meant that the daily motion of the spots was clearly visible. These illustrations also showed the spots' intricate shapes and how these shapes changed over time, and they also showed that all over the solar disc, spots sometimes suddenly appeared or disappeared. This meant that there was change on the supposedly unchanging Sun, and that there, too, things were, in the words of Aristotle, 'coming into being and passing away.'

Galileo's second letter to Welser crossed in the mail with a letter from Welser sending Galileo a new publication by Apelles (now known to be a Jesuit mathematician), *De Maculis Solaribus et stellis Iovem errantibus Accuratior Disquisitio*, or 'A more accurate inquiry into solar spots and planets wandering about Jupiter.' In this tract Apelles repeated his satellite theory of sunspots, although he seemed less convinced of its correctness, and defended it with further mathematical arguments and illustrations made by himself as well as others (on the same scale as those in *Tres Epistolae*). He also announced the discovery of a fifth moon of Jupiter, a claim Galileo easily refuted. By the time *Accuratior Disquisitio* reached Galileo, he already knew that Apelles was, in fact, Christoph Scheiner, SJ, a mathematician at the university of Ingolstadt. Galileo now wrote a much longer third letter on sunspots in which he argued cosmological issues as a 'philosophical astronomer' (*astronomo filosofico*) and gave devastating geometrical demonstrations as a 'mathematical astronomer' (*astronomo puro*).

By the time Galileo sent off his third letter, the decision to publish had already been made. Prince Cesi threw the weight and resources behind this project, and it would be an official publication of the Accademia dei Lincei. He and Galileo saw the importance of the illustrations at the end of the second letter, and Cesi called in the help of Galileo's friend, the artist Ludovico Cardi da Cigoli, to help supervise the engraving. They interviewed a number of engravers and decided on Matthäus Greuter, a well know engraver from Alsace, and they closely watched Greuter's work, insisting on corrections whenever Galileo or Cigoli thought a plate was not up to the quality they demanded. The book, *Istoria e dimostrazioni intorno alle macchie solari e loro accidenti*, or 'History and demonstrations about sunspots and their properties,' came off the press in the spring of 1613. Half the copies included Scheiner's two tracts. It appears that by this time Scheiner was already convinced that sunspots were really on or near the surface of the Sun. For the next thirteen years, Scheiner continued his research, eventually publishing his magnum opus, *Rosa Ursina* (1630), in which he reported that the Sun's axis of rotation was inclined 7°15' to the pole of the ecliptic, an astonishingly precise figure even by modern standards.

After 1613, no further important discoveries were made with the 'Galilean' or 'Dutch' telescope. It was a difficult instrument to use, and its restricted field of view, about 15 arc-minutes, made magnifications of more than 20 practically useless. Not until a new form, the astronomical telescope with its convex eyepiece, came into wide use after 1640, were new telescopic discoveries made.

–

Bibliography

Galilei 1993, pp. 123, p. 175.

[1] The nebula in the head of Orion is the area near α, φ e φ² Orionis. See *Ptolemy's Almagest*, tr. G.J. Toomer (London: Duckworth, 1984), p. 382. Praesepe is the area between γ and σ Cancri (*Aselli* or ass colts). See *Ptolemy's Almagest*, p. 366.

[2] Galileo 1993, p. 123.

[3] *Ivi*, p. 175.

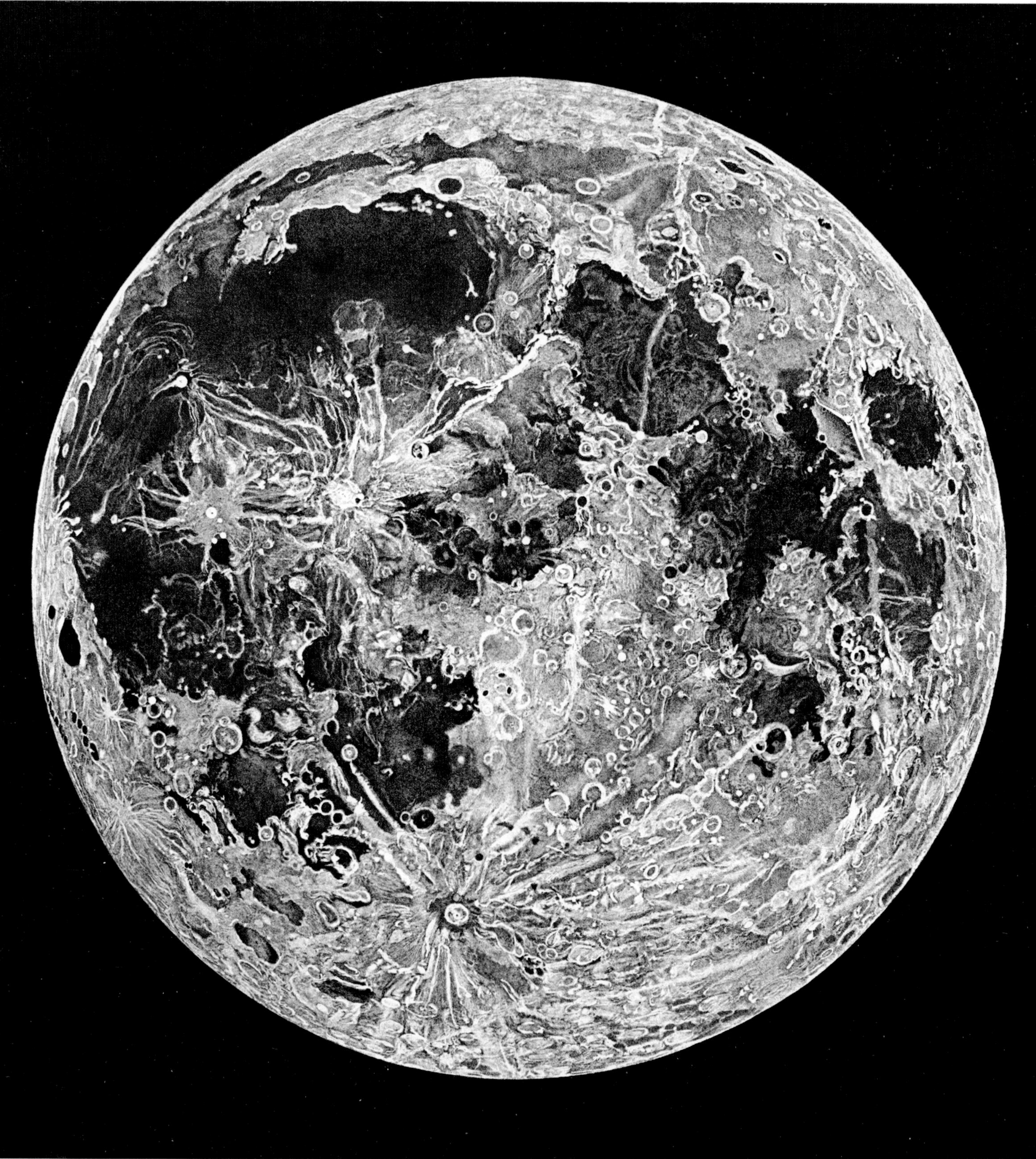

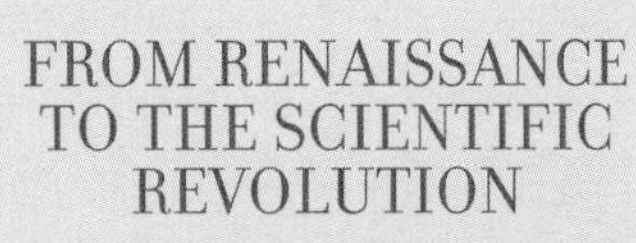

7| GALILEO:
THE COSMOS THROUGH
THE TELESCOPE

REPRESENTATIONS AND MAPS OF THE MOON. THE FIRST TWO CENTURIES

Ewen A. Whitaker

Of all the heavenly bodies, the Moon is the only one which exhibits surface detail that is plainly visible to the unaided eye. Its pattern of light and dark spots undoubtedly captured mankind's imagination since prehistoric times, as is evidenced by the ancient legends and folklore of many different cultures, where one often finds allusions to perceived images of familiar animals, human faces, or inanimate objects in this pattern. It is rather surprising, therefore, that the only known naked eye images of the Moon dating from the pre-telescopic era that display any real attempt at accuracy are a half-disk drawing by Leonardo da Vinci (1452-1519), and a rough map of the chief spots by William Gilbert (1544-1603, Fig. 4). Gilbert is best known as author of *De Magnete* (Concerning the Lodestone) and as physician to Queen Elizabeth I of England. I distinguish drawings from maps thus: images (or drawings) are artistic renderings of the Moon's appearance, whereas maps are conventional representations of lunar surface features, with names and/or a superposed grid of lines added for identification purposes.

The First Telescopic Observations

It is not known who was the first to look at the Moon through one of the newly invented (1608) Dutch telescopes. Galileo Galilei (1564-1642) was the first to observe the Moon methodically (in 1609) and to interpret what he saw, but Thomas Harriot (c. 1560-1621), an astute mathematician and scientist who is perhaps better known for his description of an expedition with Sir Walter Raleigh to Virginia in 1585, and for introducing the 'greater than' (>) and 'less than' (<) signs in mathematics, actually made the first known telescopic drawing of the Moon, dated 5 August 1609 (New Style).

That was four months before Galileo first pointed his own instrument towards that body. However, judging by the crudity of that sketch, and the impossible shape of the terminator, it is clear that Harriot failed to interpret what he was seeing. He did not return to lunar observation until July 1610, undoubtedly spurred to action after he had obtained, in late Spring of 1610, a copy of Galileo's new book (*Sidereus Nuncius*) and was no doubt amazed at everything that he had missed!

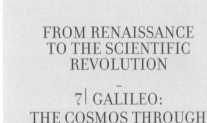

Thus Galileo remains the undisputed pioneer in the science of selenography. According to my research, he first directed a telescope of his own making (the 20-power) towards a non-terrestrial object during the evening of 30 November 1609, the object being the four-day-old crescent Moon. The fact that he observed that body until almost moonset, describing the progress of sunrise on what I have identified, with a fair degree of certainty, as a group of mountain crests in the Janssen area of the lower cusp, shows that he immediately grasped the importance of what was being revealed.

This was a time when confused notions about the true nature of the Moon were still held by most people – notions passed down from Antiquity. These included its being (a) a mirrror, reflecting the terrestrial oceans and continents; (b) a polished, translucent crystalline sphere; c) a body of condensed fire, etc., and (d) a terrestrial type of spherical body with seas, mountains, valleys, plains, etc.

Some of the more extreme ideas stemmed from the necessity of explaining such phenomena as the ashen light (by means of translucensy or self-luminosity), and why the Moon does not fall to Earth (because fire rises and is luminous). Another factor that influenced thinking was that, unlike the Earth with its many imperfections, all objects in Heaven were divine in nature, and therefore of necessity perfect and spotless. This led to the idea that the dark markings were due to permanent clouds floating between Earth and Moon. Galileo's telescope was showing him just how far from the truth most of these ideas were. The Moon's surface was by no means smooth, shiny or transparent – it was mostly very rough.

Galileo did not date any of his observations but left enough clues in his manuscripts and published a book on the subject (*Sidereus Nuncius*, or *Starry Messenger*; cf. entry VII.2.1) that I was able to assign dates to his drawings with a reasonable degree of confidence. This investigation is dealt with more fully in the catalogue of his drawings.

Galileo's descriptions of his lunar observations, and the conclusions he reached regarding the Moon make fascinating reading. He knew that he had to write very convincingly if he was about to bury two millennia of misconceptions. His conclusions may be summarised thus:

– The Moon is a solid, opaque, spherical body with a rough surface; the ashen light is due to reflected earthlight

– The roughness is mostly caused by hundreds of mountain-girt cavities and by large circular mountain ranges enclosing fairly level tracts

– The darker tracts are mostly smooth, avid are lower than the brighter areas; some are bordered by lofty mountain ranges; none extends as far as the limb

– The darker areas have lighter markings here and there; these cast no shadows and thus must be due to dissimilar materials

– The cavities merge into the background at Full Moon

– The highest mountains attain altitudes on the order of 6000 m

– The Moon has an atmosphere (the only incorrect statement in the list)

– Finally, in 1632, he announced that in observing the dark markings now named Grimaldi and Mare Crisium, he had noted that their apparent distances from the east and west limbs varied noticeably. Five years later he announced that he had also observed a 'nodding' motion of the Moon, with a period of one month.

The Next Forty Years

Galileo's revelations concerning the Moon, the discovery of Jupiter's four major satellites, and the starry nature of the Milky Way certainly sent shock waves around Europe and beyond, but little was done to extend telescopic lunar studies, possibly due to the scarcity of well-figured optical components for such instruments, and the general difficulty in mounting and using the telescope, to say nothing of trying to draw what is observed, with a wind-blown candle or oil lamp to illuminate the paper!

However, as I noted above, Harriot returned to observing the Moon after obtaining a copy of Galileo's book, making over a dozen rudimentary sketches of various phases from July 1610 to April 1611, mostly accompanied by short explanatory notes. At some time during or soon after this period he drew a map of the Full Moon (cf. entry VII.4.2), diameter 15 cm which he checked from observations made on 9 September and 14 December 1611, and 27 May 1612 (Old Style dates). It is annotated with both letters and numbers, which designate light and dark spots, plus various points on the edges of the dark markings (*maria*). These were used by Harriot as an aid in checking the placement of the points, and his MS records many observations such as 'e, h, 4, – a right lyne' (sic), and '3, a, 1, – a right angle'.

It is also very interesting that he writes here that 'the dark parts of 28 and 26 were nerer (sic) the edge then (sic) is described'. Calculation shows that maximum lunar libration to the north occurred only two days after that observation, meaning that he was the first to notice and remark on this phenomenon! As noted above, Galileo observed this motion 26 years later. Harriot's MSS on his lunar observations remain unpublished, except for the map and one or two drawings that have appeared since 1971.

It should be noted here that Galilean type telescopes, i.e. with concave lenses as eyepieces, have very small angular fields of view; both Galileo's and Harriot's could cover only about half to 2/3 of the lunar disk at any time, which made the drawing of the whole disk difficult.

It was not until about 15 years later that two quite independent programmes involving exhaustive telescopic lunar studies were conceived. The original aim in each case was to draw up an accurate map of the Moon, not so much for use as a starting point for lunar studies but rather as an aid in determining terrestrial longitudes!

One of these programmes was initiated by Pierre Gassendi (1592-1655), a leading astronomical thinker and observer of his day. The basic aim was to obtain the longitude difference between Aix-en-Provence and Paris by comparing the local times, at those locations, of the occultations and reappearances of small lunar spots during lunar eclipses, for which a reasonably accurate lunar map was needed.

Because of various setbacks, such a map was never realized, but three copperplate engravings of full, and near first and last quarter phases of the Moon, were made by Claude Mellan in the mid-1630s (cf. entry VII.4.7). One does not need to be a lunar expert to see that these images are remarkably realistic in appearance, and that they represent a great improvement in both accuracy and content over the imagery of Harriot, Galileo, and indeed of all their predecessors. It seems that very few prints were made from the plates, which ensured their obscurity until recent times. Incidentally, Mellan used a telescope constructed from optical parts supplied by Galileo, which suggests either that Galileo's lens-making techniques had improved since the 1610 era, or that they were better than average.

The First Real Lunar Map

The other programme for determining terrestrial longitudes was conceived by Michael van Langren (1600-1675), member of a prominent Flemish globe and map-making family. He proposed using the Moon's rotation as a celestial clock; by timing, in local time, the moments of sunrise or sunset on various identified lunar peaks and crater crests, and comparing them with the standard time (at some home base) of same the events (from an extrapolated ephemeris), then longitudes at sea or in overseas lands might be determined.

1. Page 254, John Russell, image of the full Moon.

2 Robert Hooke, first drawing (1662) of a lunar feature, the Hipparchus crater, compared with a modern photo (at right).

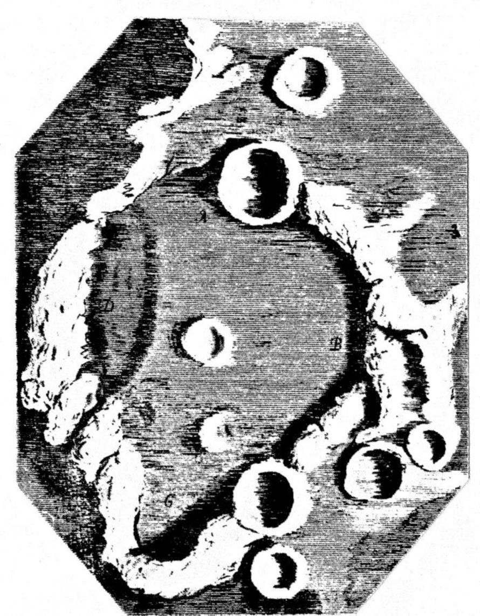

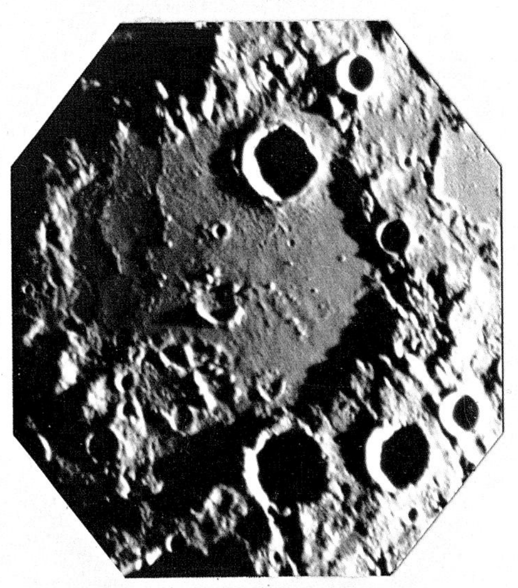

The scheme was quite impractical, but he made thirty drawings at various phases, which he later combined into a map, some 34 cm in diameter. This was quite a remarkable achievement, combining, as it does, the chief darker areas and bright spots with the main topographical features, and naming all 325 of them! Placing the features in reasonably accurate positions on the map was no easy task, especially as the Moon does not present exactly the same face to Earth all the time. Using the N-S terminator line as a cursor over the Moon's disk no doubt helped with longitudes, but fixing latitudes would have been more of a problem. Here are Langrenus' words on this:

'The face of the Moon is inconstant and ever variable. Its body has a libratory motion which causes the spots to appear first towards the east, then the west; first to the south, then the north.' (He had apparently read Galileo's earlier notes on these 'titubaziones'.)

Figure 3 illustrates the differences between Langrenus' placement and size of features (solid outlines) and true positions and sizes from a modern map (dotted outlines). His errors of placement can be seen to be predominantly in latitude, for the reason noted above. The map (cf. entry VII.4.8) was published in March of 1645, but very few copies were produced, due to lack of funds caused by the earlier death of his sponsor and monetary benefactor Princess Isabella of Spain.

This lack of publicity, together with the appearance in 1647 of a major volume devoted to telescopic observations of the Moon by a Danzig astronomer, totally eclipsed Langrenus' pioneering effort. Nevertheless, Langrenus was the true founder of lunar cartography having produced the first viable Moon map. His scheme of generally naming the various topographic features for scientists, mathematicians, patrons etc., and the dark patches as Maria, Lacus, Sinus or other watery names, has remained in effect to this day, as has his simple but effective mapping convention of representing craters as rings illuminated by a morning (i.e. rising) Sun.

Hevel's Magnum Opus

The large book noted above was by Hevelius (Johannes Höwelcke, 1611-1687), and represents a landmark in its content of lunar observations, descriptions of the surface, and other data. There are large images of successive lunar phases, plus two maps and one full-Moon image of the lunar disk. The latter is a remarkably accurate depiction, and is a tribute to his artistic and engraving skills. His *Selenographia* (cf. entry VII.4.10), as the book was titled, remained the authority on the subject for many decades, but his nomenclature scheme, in which he used the ancient classical names of geographical countries, regions, and seas, did not stand the test of time. Only ten of these names, such as Moris Apenninus, Promontorium Agarum, remain on our modern maps.

Riccioli Standardises the Nomenclature

Another landmark event that occurred just four years after the publication of Hevelius' monumental work was a new map of the Moon that appeared in an encyclopedic two-volume set titled *Almagestum Novum* (1651; cf. entry VII.4.12), produced by Giovanni Battista Riccioli (1598-1671), a Jesuit working in Bologna. There are actually two versions of a map which had been prepared by his younger fellow Jesuit Francesco Grimaldi (1618-1663), who is better known today for his discovery of the diffraction of light. They show a wealth of detail; one states that 'the best telescope' was used to view many phases of the Moon as a basis 'partly to confirm, correct and augment the selenographies of Langrenus, Hevelius, Eustachius Divini (cf. entry VII.4.11), Sirsilis and others, so that the evidence of the smallest details at any phase may be followed up.'. The other map notes that it is 'for the lunar nomenclature and libration'.

Riccioli did not adopt any of Hevelius' nomenclature, but opted to employ the same general scheme that Langrenus had pioneered. He used many of Langrenus' names, but moved most of them to different features in order to comply with his own more logical placement scheme, which grouped them by epoch, studies, philosophy etc. The Riccioli nomenclature was seen to be preferable to that of Hevelius with its mostly obsolete and lengthy names, and virtually all lunar maps dated after about 1800 use Riccioli's names exclusively.

Hooke and the Founding of Selenology

The design and optics of telescopes improved as time passed, and m 1664 Robert Hooke (1635-1703), the talented British scientist and inventor, used a telescope about 10 m in length to draw a detailed image of a single lunar crater – Hipparchus (fig. 2; cf. entry VII.4.14)). More importantly, he made quite graphic descriptions of this and other formations, with speculations on the nature of the surface and the origin of those formations, backed up by his own experiments with bullets being dropped into a slurry of pipeclay (impact theory), and bubbles of water vapour bursting from heated alabaster powder (volcanic theory). Thus he pioneered a new science – that of selenology.

Cassini's Large Map and LaHire's Huge Image

An early task undertaken by Gian Domenico Cassini (1625-1712), the leading astronomer at the Paris Observatory during the last three decades of the 17th century, was the preparation of a detailed map of the Moon. Using telescopes provided with objective lenses with diameters of about 9 and 18 cm made by Giuseppe Campani, he and two artist assistants – Jean Patigny and Sebastian Leclerc – produced some 60 drawings (cf. entry VII.4.16) of different areas of the lunar surface.

These were combined into a complete map by Patigny, engraved in copper, with a diameter of 54 cm. The map (cf. entry VII.4.17) is far more detailed than any of its predecessors, although comparison with modern maps or photos shows that some of this detail is illusory. Some points of interest are the volcano-like mountain in the crater Patavius, the lady's head at Prom. Heraclides, and the characteristic 'phi' marking in Mare Serenitatis. The map has no nomenclature. Once again, as with the three Mellan images and the Langrenus map, a very limited production of prints ensured this map's almost total obscurity.

Philippe de la Hire (1640-1718), professor of mathematics and architecture in Paris, made a drawing in 1686 of the appearance of the Moon at the full phase. It was 4 m in diameter, but apparently no longer exists; luckily, a greatly reduced (15 cm diameter) copperplate image was made and is printed in La Hire's *Astronomical Tables* (1686). Note that a number of features are numbered, while the *maria* are lettered. Identifications of these features are given in an accompanying table, using Riccioli's names.

A very similar but less detailed image, always referred to as 'Cassini's Map' in 18th century literature (fig. 5), first appeared in 1692 in an article by Cassini concerning a forthcoming lunar eclipse. The numbering and lettering of the various features is the same as in the LaHire image, suggesting that Cassini had no hand in this one. In any case, this image was copied and re-copied for over a century in textbooks, dictionaries, encyclopedias, and the 'Connaissance des Temps' until the quality was so degraded that it was unrecognisable as representing the Moon – except for the ubiquitous 'phi'.

Mayer, Pioneer of Scientific Selenography

By the middle of the 18th century, telescopic lunar observation and mapping had almost completely disappeared from scientific study. Hevelius' book and Riccioli' map were one century old, and the undersized, degraded maps noted above did absolutely nothing to promote interest in the subject. However, one person was motivated to produce an accurate map of the Moon.

This was Tobias Mayer (1723-1762), a gifted German cartographer/mathematician who made about 40 drawings of lunar areas as observed at different phases. He also calculated the absolute positions of 23 features, using an eyepiece reticle to measure their positions on the lunar disk. Because of the lunar librations and varying angles presented by the disk, many complicated calculations were required. His map was drawn in about 1749, but remained unpublished until 1775,

3. Verification of precision of van Langren's map.

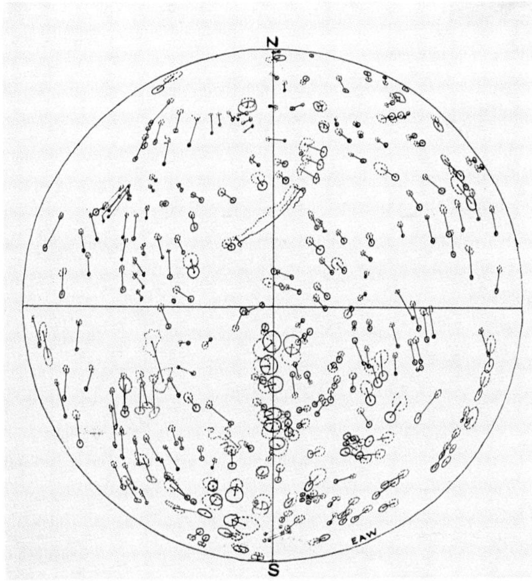

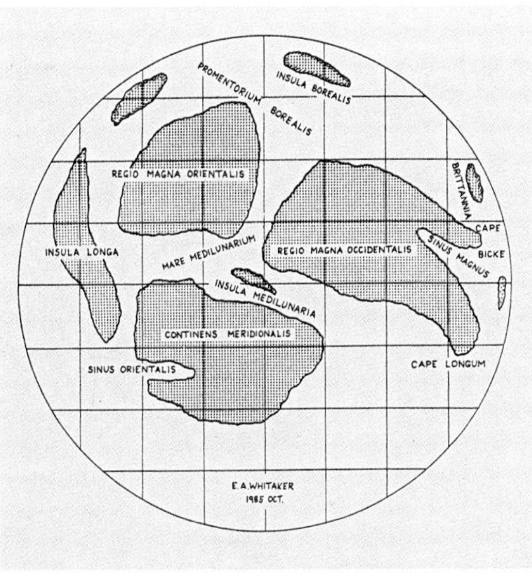

4. William Gilbert, map of the full Moon observed with the naked eye, c. 1600.

when Georg Lichtenberg had an engraved copperplate made, on which he added a latitude/longitude grid based on interpolations from Mayer's plotted positions of the 23 points (fig. 6). This map far exceeds all its predecessors in accuracy and content. It was published as an engraving, diameter 19,5 cm, in Lichtenberg's rather rare *T. Mayeri Opera Inedita* (1775), yet another case of limited availability, hindering the deserved widespread fame of a landmark lunar map.

An Artist and a Magistrate Revive the Interest

Towards the end of the 18th century, both reflecting and refracting telescopes were increasing in availability, quality and manageability. Would-be Moon observers, armed with these much improved and more convenient (i.e. 'user-friendly', to use the current parlance) instruments, cannot have failed to notice that the commonly available maps, such as the degraded copies of the 1692 'Cassini' image acted as very poor guides to the topographical features. Even in the original Hevelius or Riccioli maps, if one were fortunate enough to have one available, the depictions of that topography – as already commented upon by Hooke – fell far short of reality, and a large amount of interesting intervening detail was totally missing.

Russell goes in one direction ...

John Russell (1745-1806), an English artist and Royal Academician of some note, was struck by the beauty and wealth of detail seen in a telescopic view of the Moon. Thus in a letter dated 9 Feb. 1789 to the Radcliffe Observatory in Oxford he writes: '... how much struck a young Man conversant with Light, and Shade, must be with the Moon in this (near first quarter) state; especially, as I was not taught to expect such clearness and expression, as is to be found near and upon the indented Edge ...'. Being conversant at that time with only the 'very inferior Prints to be met with in common Dictionarys, such unsatisfactory imitations, both as to incorrectness of Form and Effect led me to conclude I could produce a drawing in some measure corresponding to the feelings I had upon the first sight of the gibbous Moon through a telescope ...', he was somewhat taken aback on first 'meeting with' the colored copies, by Doppelmayer (cf. entry VIII.2.1), of Hevelius' and Riccioli's maps in the Homann atlas. He says he 'was again at a stand' after obtaining a copy of Hevelius' *Se-*

5. Image of the full Moon from 1692, apparently based on the drawings of Cassini and de La Hire. Reproduced in books for over a century.

6. Tobias Mayer, map drawn in 1749 but published only in 1775, after the death of its author. It is the first map based on measurement of the positions of the features on the Moon's surface.

lenographia, but that he thought he could produce results that were more artistic.

A little later he was shown a copy of the large Cassini map, which again impressed him, but he was fully aware of its shortcomings and was determined to press ahead and produce his own map. While making pencil sketches of all visible arreas of the Moon (cf. VIII.4.18), a program that he commenced as early as 1764 and continued for 40 years, he also measured the relative positions of 34 prominent features. The first product of this effort was not a flat map (planisphere) but a series of gores, engraved by Russell himself, to be pasted onto globes, each 12 inches in diameter. Of the few (about seven) globes that were made, five or six were mounted in a complicated brass mechanism by which the lunar librations, tilt of the lunar axis, and the sunrise or sunset line could be demonstrated. The globes, named 'Selenographias' (cf. entry VII.4.19) by Russell, are dated 1797. Nine years later, he published two lunar images, one of full Moon (fig.1) and the other with topographic details added, both about 36 cm diameter.

The former is clearly far more detailed than any of its predecessors, and the very complex interplay of delicate shadings reveals the hand of a master artist. Indeed, the highly detailed nature and general accuracy of this image were never surpassed artistically. Of course, the advent of photography later in the 19th century soon discouraged any further attempts at such an exacting and laborious task. Some of the surface topography portrayed in the second image is perhaps a little less reliable both in its positioning and reality.

Russell never placed a coordinate grid of lunar latitudes and longitudes on his images, nor were they accompanied by any form of nomenclature. Add to these disadvantages the fact that very few copies of the planispheres were printed, together with the restricted production of the globes, one can understand why Russell's work never had the impact in selenographical circles that its artistic and scientific contributions merited.

… and Schröter goes in another

In about 1787, well after Russell initiated his observational program, Johann Hieronymus Schröter (1745–1816), chief magistrate in Lilienthal near Bremen, Germany, and keen amateur astronomer, started up his own ambitious program – to observe and delineate lunar features under all conditions of illumination; to measure the heights and depths of the more important elevations and craters respectively; to look for evidence of a lunar atmosphere or changes on the lunar surface; and finally to make a map 46.5 ins. in diameter, based on Tobias Mayer's measures. He had observed the Moon on occasion over the previous three years, but mainly to note the appearance of the crater Aristarchus when not illuminated by the Sun, following William Herschel's announcement in 1783 that it was glowing like a volcano.

He obtained a 6.35 cm refractor by Dollond, and 12 and 15 cm reflectors by W. Herschel; later, he added a 24 cm reflector by Schräder, and finally constructed a 47 cm reflector, a large, clumsy and not very efficient monster. To aid in the drawing, he invented his 'Projections-Maschine', a simple contraption of somewhat doubtful efficacy whereby he viewed the image of the Moon's surface through the eyepiece using one eye, making a drawing on a board fixed to the telescope while using the other eye. A rotatable glass reticle with a grid of small squares was situated in the image plane, and the drawing paper was placed on the board, also rotatable. The paper was pre-marked with dots forming 13 mm squares. In use, the reticle was rotated until one set of lines paralleled the line between the Moon's horns, and the board then adjusted in angle and distance until the two grids were congruent – obviously not a very precise operation!

Schröter observed the Moon diligently, amassing numerous drawings of various areas of the disk, measuring mountain heights and crater depths from shadow lengths, searching for evidence of changes on the surface or the existence of an atmosphere, etc., so that by the end of 1790, he had enough material to publish in the form of a large volume. He gave this the title of *Selenographische Fragmente*, very apt in view of the fragmented nature of the subject matter and areas dealt with.

This book was published in 1791, and further similar observational work appeared as volume 2 in 1802. As a guide for readers he included a new engraving of Mayer's map, but with numbers placed on 89 craters, and letters on 18 of Riccioli's 21 'watery' designations. A list of these 107 identified features surrounds the map, with both Hevelius and Riccioli names given, but with Riccioli's first. The map and all of the drawings are oriented south up, as viewed in astronomical telescopes that used the wider field of view provided by positive eyepieces.

Schröter's quite detailed drawings necessitated an extended form of nomenclature, and he opted to once again give priority to that of Riccioli for the main features, but for the smaller details he used Roman and Greek letters, a scheme that has been in use ever since. His drawings, reproduced as engravings, use a rather quaint style in which crater rims are represented as aerial views of rings of trees!

Whatever criticisms may be leveled against Schröter's work, it can fairly be said that he pioneered the science of detailed and comprehensive selenography which, with Mayer's pioneering attention to positional accuracy, laid the ground for an unprecedented burst of lunar observation and cartography in Germany during the 19th century.

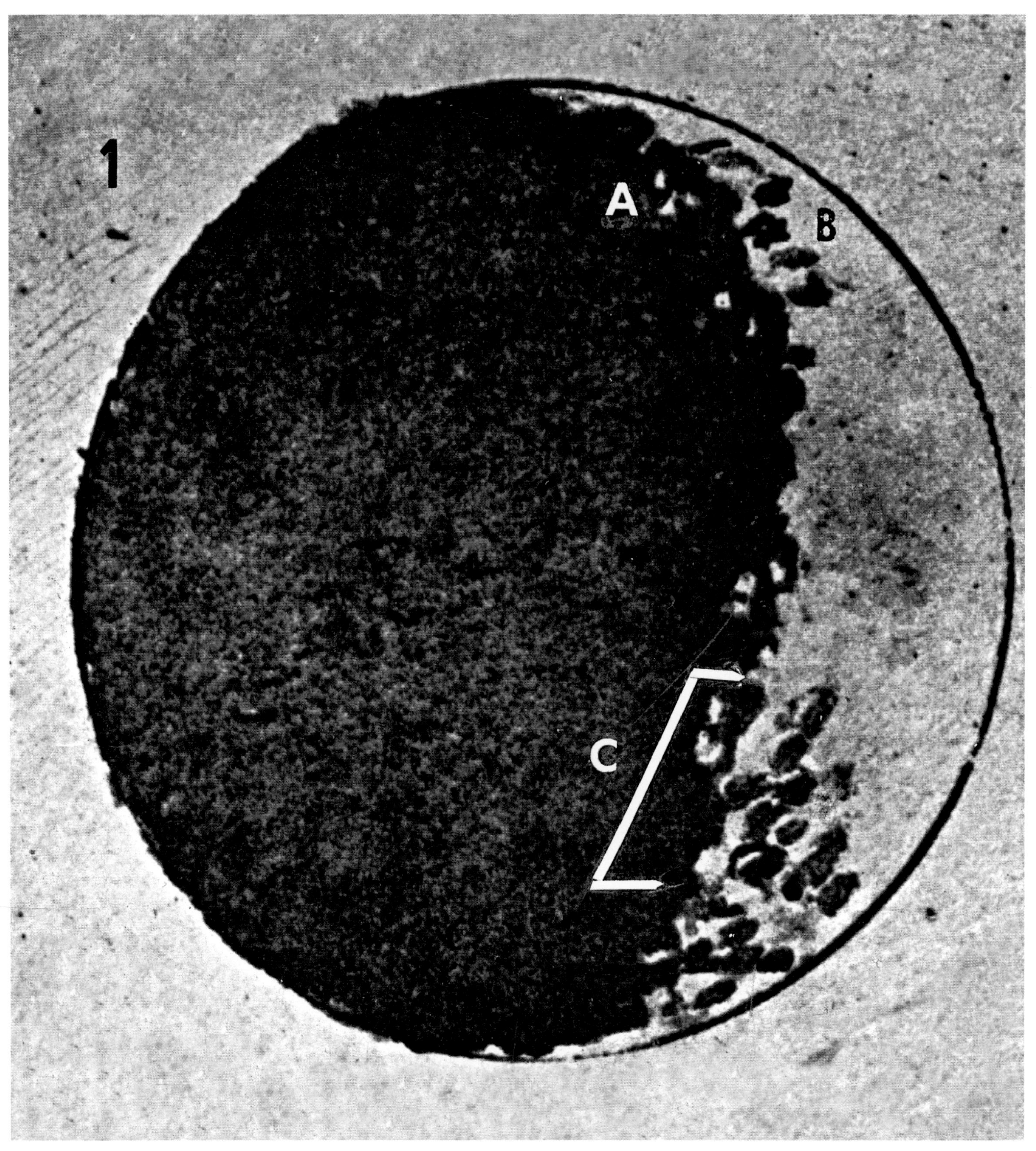
1
A
B
C

FROM RENAISSANCE TO THE SCIENTIFIC REVOLUTION

7| GALILEO: THE COSMOS THROUGH THE TELESCOPE

IDENTIFICATION AND DATING OF GALILEO'S OBSERVATIONS OF THE MOON

Ewen A. Whitaker

'A mere glance at one of Galileo's drawings of the Moon will convince us that he was not a great astronomical observer; or else that the excitement of so many telescopic discoveries made by him at that time had temporarily blurred his skill or critical sense; for none of the features recorded on this (and other) drawings of the Moon can be safely identified with any known markings of the lunar landscape.'

As an astronomer whose interest in the history of lunar cartography and related studies dates back to 1951, I considered that these bald statements by a well-known contemporary astronomer, when they appeared in the early 1960s, were a direct challenge that at least needed substantiating or refuting. Other astronomers also apparently felt the same, but papers by Profs. G. Righini, O. Gingerich and S. Drake on the subject in the mid-1970s revealed some disagreements between their findings.

I decided to attempt to find some common ground, and to research Galileo's lunar images as published in his *Sidereus Nuncius* as well as his seven manuscript ink-wash images. What follows is an abbreviated study based on my conclusions from that time, but with a few updates resulting from a renewed contact with Prof. Gingerich, who recently informed me about a copy of *Sidereus Nuncius* that has ink-wash drawings in place of the normal woodcut engravings!

For my research I used prints of the four pages of *Sidereus Nuncius* (cf. entry VII.2.1), that contain the five (one is repeated) engraved images of the Moon. This was the copy from the library of the Observatoire de Paris. For the seven ink-wash MS drawings (cf. entry VII.4.2) I used a black-and-white photo of the colour reproduction in Favaro's *Opere*, which increased the contrast of the rather weak details portrayed in that reproduction. Relevant correspondence between Galileo and other individuals was used, plus Stillman Drake's translation of *Sidereus Nuncius*, into English. I also had available a heterogeneous collection of Moon photographs at the Lunar and Planetary Laboratory, University of Arizona.

The Illustrations

Figures 1-11 arc reproductions of the four engravings from *Sidereus Nuncius*, plus black-and-white copies of the seven MS ink-wash images, arranged in order of the Moon's increasing 'age'. To the right in each illustration, except No. 1, is a photo of the Moon from the collection of the Lunar and Planetary Laboratory in Tucson, Arizona, that most closely matched the Galileo image. The photos were deliberately degraded to more closely match the lower resolution of Galileo's telescope. Figures 3, 6, 8, 10 are obviously the engraved images. All images except No. 1 have been deliberately mounted on a black background for better clarity.

Figure 1. Almost certainly his first attempt at drawing the crescent Moon. It is unnumbered in the top left corner of the MS page, and does not have an inked-in background.

Figure 2. Comparison with Fig. 1 suggests that this was made later in the evening; thus the three illuminated peaks at A are repeated, as is the curve of four shadowed crater floors at B. Also, the line of shadows at C is repeated, but with more finesse, and the terminator shape is much more natural. The original is surrounded by a square block of dark sky, so that the rest of the lunar disk displays the Earthshine. Galileo gave this number 1.

Figure 3. Poor resemblance to the last figure, but lettered points match photo reasonably well. The sequence of sunrise on the illuminated triangle and three peaks at G is described in some detail in the text.

Figure 4. Only a mediocre match between diagram and photo. Numbered both 2 and 8 by Galileo.

Figure 5. Good match here: L – sunlit; W – wall of Aristoteles; M – Mare Serenitatis with featureless floor and mountainous borders, exaggerated here to illustrate that point. Galileo No. 3.

Figure 6. Here he has once again exaggerated a feature (T – Albategnius) to illustrate an argument in the text, and has drawn the *maria* too far NW so as to include the Mare Serenitatis phenomena in a single engraving.

Figure 7. This drawing is complementary to Fig. 6 in that it now shows the western rim mountains of Mare Serenitatis casting shadows rather than catching sunlight before local sunrise as in Fig. 6. Galileo No. 5; anomalous on the MS page in that the north lunar pole is on the left.

Figure 8. Same phase as previous figure, but with better depiction of both the *mare* shadings and the topography near the terminator.

Figure 9. Galileo drawing No. 4. The W. rim mountains have now mysteriously vanished eastward into the night side, and have been replaced by the eastern rim mountains of Mare Imbrium!

Figure 10. The most accurate depiction of a phase. Apart from the deliberately exaggerated size of Albategnius (J), the *maria* and their brighter markings are well delineated, as are the craters in the lower area. Thus the formations Peurbach CP), Regiomontanus (R), Walter (WA), Orontius/Saussure (o), and Deslandres (D) are well shown in the engraving; below Orontius are Maginus (M), Longomontanus (L), Wilhelm (W), and even an indication of Clavius at the very bottom.

Figure 11. Another very good match here; K is the shadow of Montes Jura in Sinus Iridum, L is Prom. Laplace, M is Tobias Mayer and hills to the east, N is Montes Riphaeus, and R is Hainzel and A. From my calculations the star just emerged from occultation is Theta Librae.

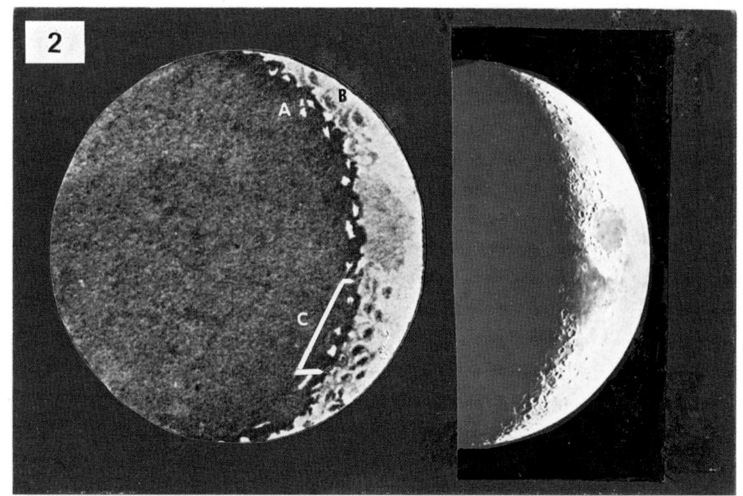

Dating the Images

Before attempting to ascertain the dates on which Galileo made his lunar observations and accompanying drawings, some limits had to be set on the time interval involved. Fortunately he provided a number of diverse clues in *Sidereus Nuncius* and his contemporary correspondence. From these I concluded that the limiting dates for those lunar observations that are recorded in *Sidereus Nuncius* are from about early November 1609 for the first observation to 7 January 1610 for the last. The next steps were to estimate the selenographic longitude of the sunrise/sunset line for each image, then compare these with actual longitudes calculated from available tables. The following table gives my estimates of the longitudes for the 11 figures. The probable error may vary from about half a degree for the best cases (the engravings) to about 2° for most of the ink-wash drawings. The sunrise and sunset terminators advance around the lunar globe at almost exactly 12° per day, or 1° every two hours. Thus for the quarter phases, the terminator can advance 2° during an observing session. Also, the terminator positions fall almost exactly halfway between the positions for the preceding and following lunations.

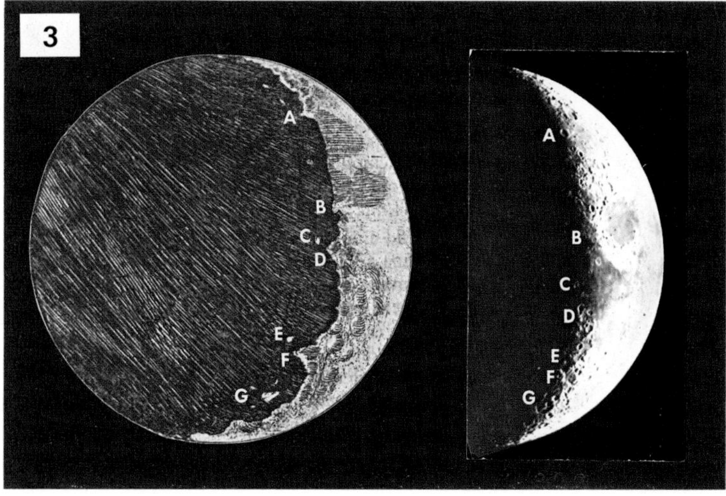

Figure number	Longitude of terminator	Date & time
1	about 37° E	Nov. 30, 8 pm
2	about 37° E	Nov. 30, 8 pm
3	about 37° E	Nov. 30, 8 pm

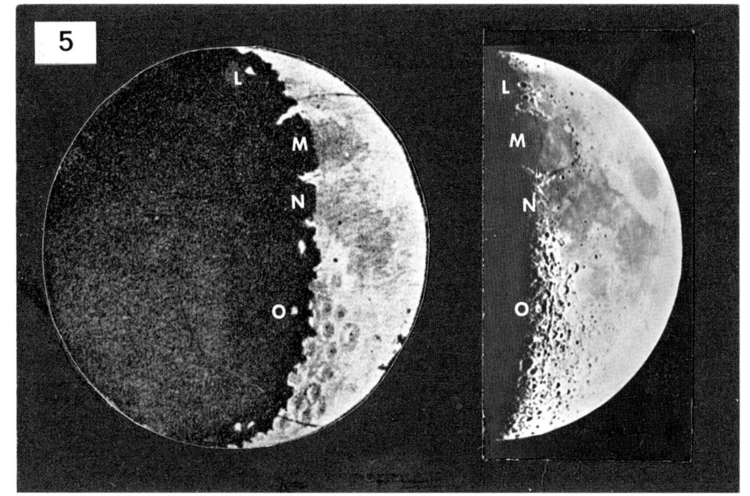
5
L
M
N
O
L
M
N
O

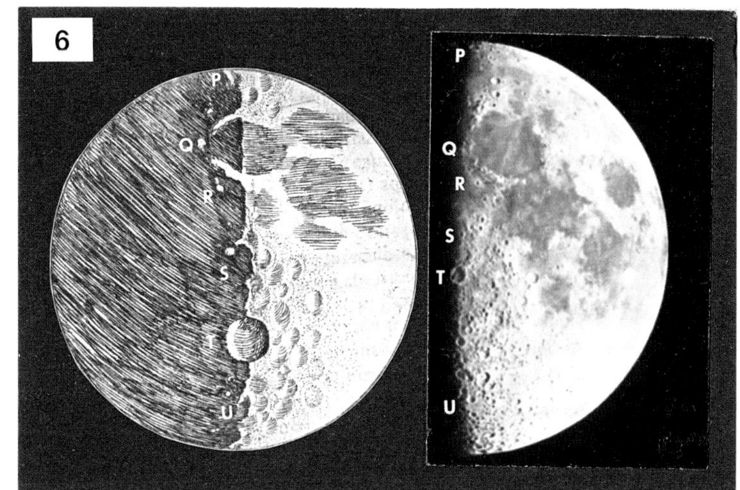
6
P
Q
R
S
T
U
P
Q
R
S
T
U

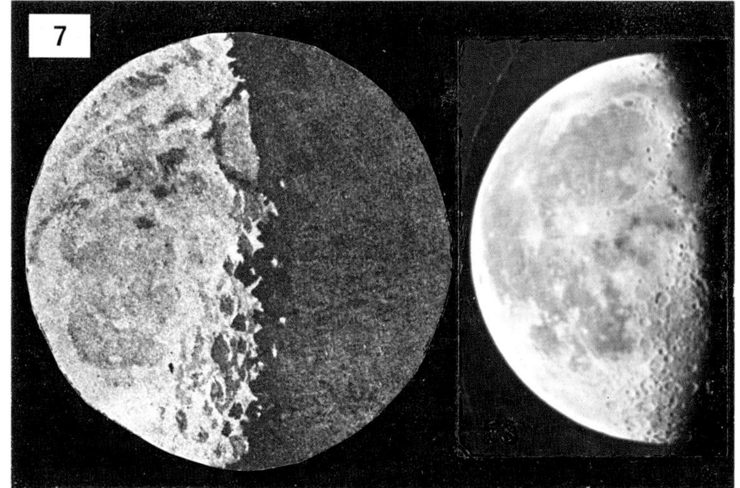
7

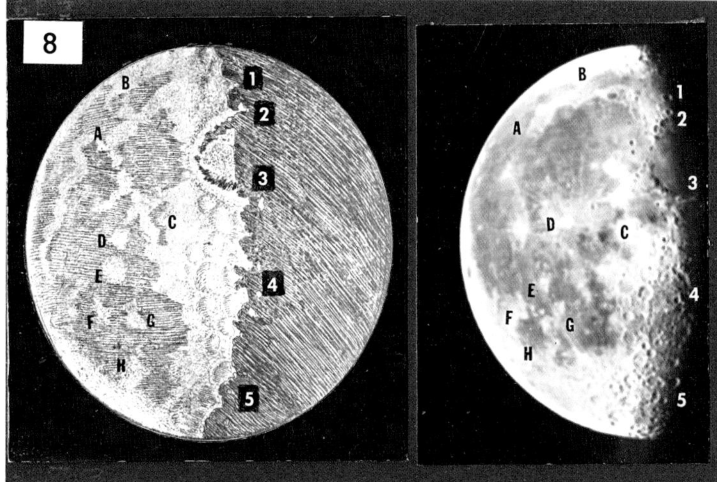
8
B
A
C
D
E
F
G
H
1
2
3
4
5
B
A
D
C
E
F
G
H
1
2
3
4
5

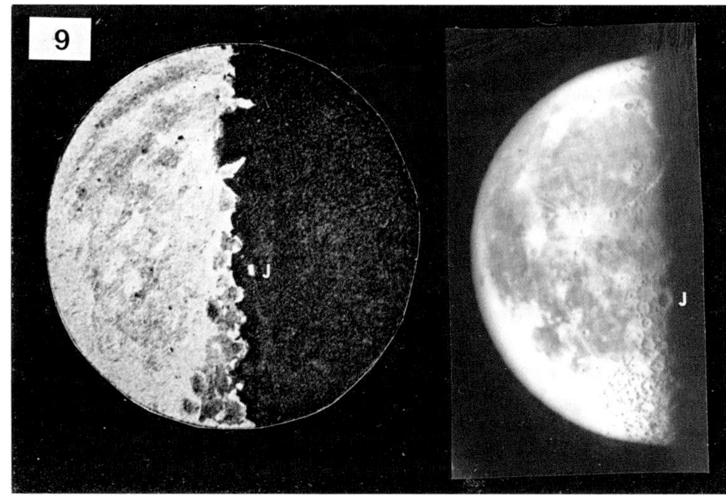
9
J
J

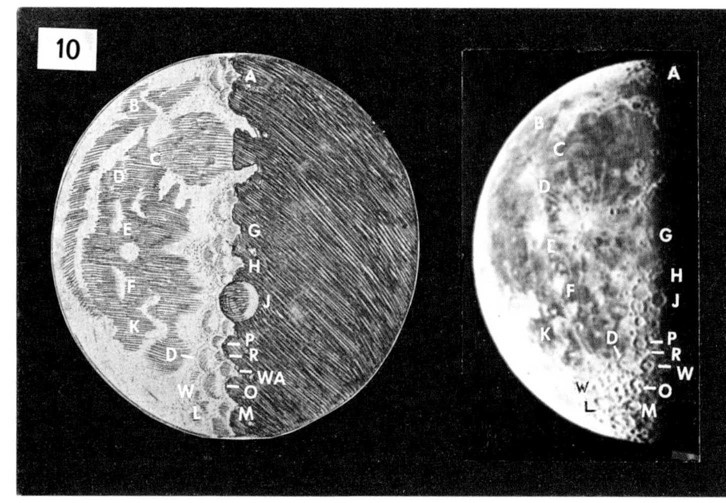
10
A
B
C
D
E
F
K
D
W
L
G
H
J
P
R
WA
O
M
A
B
C
D
E
F
K
D
W
L
G
H
J
P
R
W
O
M

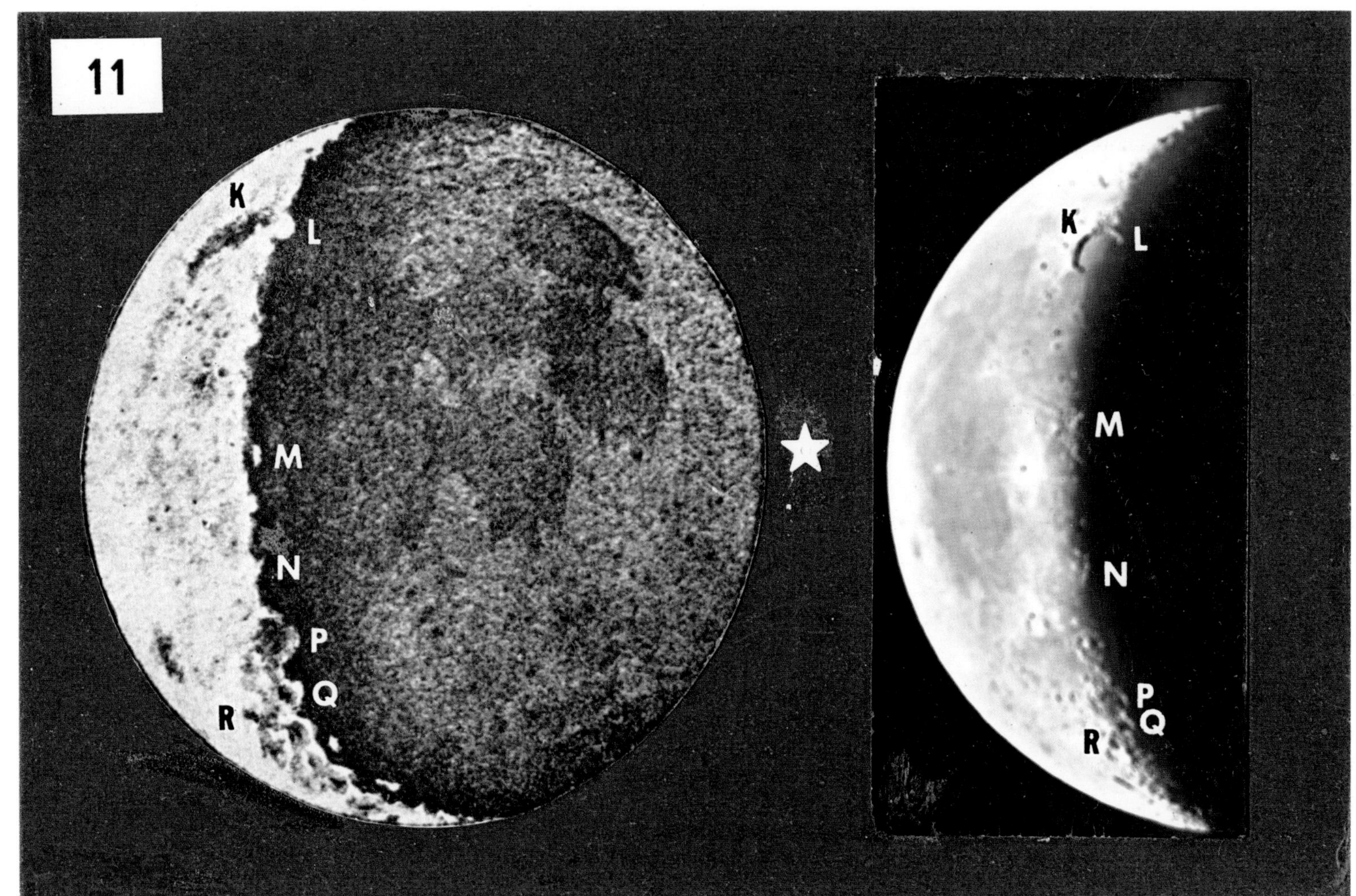
11
K
L
M
N
P
Q
R
K
L
M
N
P
Q
R

4	about 25° E	Dec. 1, 6 pm
5	about 14° E	Dec. 2, 5 pm
6	about 2° E	Dec. 3, 5 pm
7	about 18° E	Dec. 17, 5 am
8	about 18° E	Dec. 17, 5 am
9	about 5° E	Dec. 18, 6 am
10	about 6° E	Dec. 18, 5 am
11	about 24° W	Jan. 19, 6 am

The terminator positions for the period between the limiting observing dates were calculated from tables and a Nautical Almanac. It was soon obvious that on any dates in the November 1609 lunation that ended 27th of that month, the Moon was in the daytime sky for the estimated image longitudes.

However, the 37° longitude estimates for Figs. 1-3 agreed with the calculated date and Padua time of 1609 Nov. 30 at 8 p.m. The table shows the only correspondences between images and dates from Nov. 30 through 1610 Feb. 17.

The only permissible date for Fig. 11 within the time limits is 1610 Jan. 19 at around 6 a.m., give or take an hour or so. But here we have a good test of the result, because of the star close to the Moon's limb. Calculation showed that this star was Theta Librae, which emerged from central occultation at between 5.30 and 6 a.m. on that date. This unexpected confirmation of the date and time of the drawing adds confidence to the correctness of the other dates and times.

Comparing the Drawings with the Engravings

For the three cases in which an engraving has an MS drawing counterpart (Figs. 2-3, 7-8, 9-10), the engraving is a more accurate representation of the Moon at that phase. This means that the engraver had access to images that were superior to those on the MS page and which are presumably now lost. There is no drawing comparable to Fig. 6, which is an 'oddball' anyway. Galileo had observed this phase, since he describes a 'certain cavity larger than all others and of a perfectly round figure. I observed this near both quadratures ...' (T in Fig. 6 and J in Fig. 10). Also R (Manilius), the nearby sunrise line on Mare Vaporum, and the cape and prominent high ridges (S) west of Godin are depicted; these are visible at the terminator only at this phase.

Two other oddities about this engraving are the fact that (a) the lunar disk is about 3 mm smaller than the other three, and (b) it is printed upside down in the Paris copy of *Sidereus Nuncius*, an apparent rarity. One wonders whether the printer made this error because of a last-minute delivery of a hurriedly engraved printing block. This vitiated one of Galileo's arguments in the text, and I can imagine him ranting at printer Baglione, after receiving an early copy, to rotate this block immediately!

As a final note, I have recently received from Prof. Gingerich colour reproductions of the four pages of a copy of *Sidereus Nuncius* in which the spaces normally occupied by the five engravings contain ink-wash images, very reminiscent of the MS images, but obviously very similar in detail to the engraved versions! The terminators are just about identical, and the *maria* match reality better than in the MS versions. So the question is – is this the work of Galileo, or a copy made later, perhaps much later, by someone who had one of the known ten or so proof copies?

My guess is that this might be a proof copy given to Galileo before the square block engravings had been put in, so that he could draw in the images to indicate the correct order and orientation of the blocks for the printer. There is one other mystery – the image corresponding to Fig. 8 is oriented very closely to the way it is on the MS page – north to left! An excellent incentive for further research!

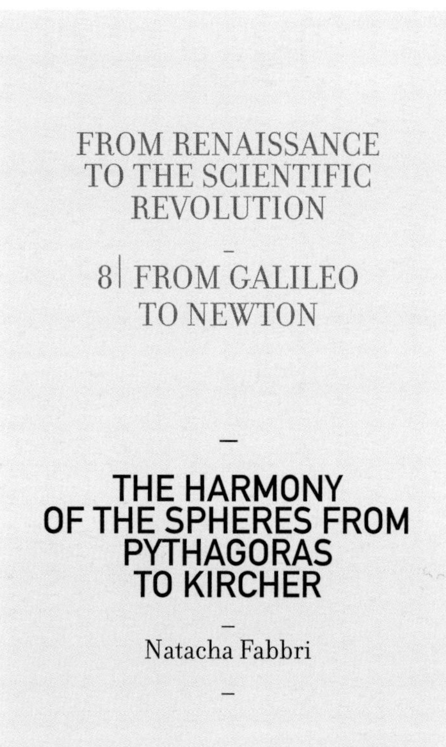

FROM RENAISSANCE TO THE SCIENTIFIC REVOLUTION
–
8| FROM GALILEO TO NEWTON
–
THE HARMONY OF THE SPHERES FROM PYTHAGORAS TO KIRCHER
–
Natacha Fabbri
–

The harmony of the spheres is the sonorous expression of the broader concept of *harmonia mundi*, which pervades philosophical and musical thought from Pythagoreans to the 17th century. The connection between harmony and *kosmos* is symbolically evoked by the figure of Pan: as a personification of nature, his horns suggest the correspondence between the celestial and the sublunary world, as well as the relations between the Macrocosm and the Microcosm, while the panpipes design the celestial harmony, of which Apollo is 'prince and governor'[1]. The world harmoniously resonates with the combinations of sounds produced by the motion of the elements, of the seasons, of the planets and of the universe: earthly music is an imperfect mirror, yet also one of the favoured ways to rise towards the intelligible. Musical proportions even become the *principium essendi* not only of the cosmos, but also of every one of its parts: 'the causes of music are inherent to the universal soul, which is indeed constituted by them; on its turn, the universal soul dispenses life to all living beings [...]. Therefore, it is logical for the living cosmos to be captivated by music, and the cause is that the celestial soul, from which the universe receives life, originated from music'[2].

The main foundation of the *harmonia mundi* doctrine can be pinpointed in Plato's works. We may recall at least three dialogues in which a definition of its characters, as well as of its application in a cosmologic dimension, is reached. In *Philebus* (25 C–26 B), harmony is a combination of opposites (high and low, dry and wet, cold and hot, etc.), by way of which, following the introduction of numbers, it is possible for a system of proportions to be created within a unit characterized by order, by measure and by limit. Indeed, imposing balance to opposites produces health for organisms and the soul, as well as music, seasons, beauty and strength. In *Timaeus* (35 A ss.), harmony appears not only as the archetype employed by the Demiurge, but also as the principle governing and conserving the cosmos, the visible body within the invisible World Soul. Specifically, it is the soul of the world that represents harmony: as a combination of opposites (Sameness and Difference) – and guaranteed by the combination of proportioned circular motions – it is composed of numerical relations that correspond to the musical scale and are structured starting from the two progressions of the square and cube of 2 and 3, forming the *lambda* (2-4-8, 3-9-27).

The relations of said pyramid occur both on a musical and on an astronomical level, just as several late antique and medieval commentators of the *Timaeus* demonstrated, by connecting the harmony of World Soul to the myth of Er in the *Republic*, and to the Pythagorean music of the spheres.

In the *Republic* (617 B), the Ananke-Necessity spindle is surrounded by eight concentric circles, which are matched by an equal number of Sirens who, through the emission of a single note each, generate harmony. Plato would have therefore assigned eight sounds of a continuous scale to the planets' movement, which would then be consistent with a Doric harmony composed of two disjunct tetrachords[3].

The reliance of *practica musica* on *mundana musica* derives from the legend according to which the celestial concert heard by Pythagoras – inaudible to any other man due to the inadequacy of human nature – served as model for the determination of consonant proportions. The discovery of said proportions resulted from recognition of the correspondence existing between the sounds produced by hammers on an anvil and those generated by the celestial spheres. As can be deduced from the celebrated depiction of *Theorica musicae* by Franchinus Gaffurius narrating the discovery of consonances, the primary importance of numbers coexists with an experimental dimension. This reading – dating back to Nichomacus of Gerasa, Boethius, Macrobius and still dominant throughout the Renaissance – was discontinued first by Vincenzo Galilei, and then by Marin Mersenne. They demonstrated the inexactness of the numerical proportions that had been assigned to weights, glasses and bells up till then, thus relegating the Pythagorean contribution to the aprioristic adoption of the supraparticular relations of the quaternary number: 1/2 for the interval of octave, 2/3 for the fifth, 3/4 for the fourth.

The basic requirement of Pythagorean musical theory is that the planetary concert be not only intelligible, but also perceptible. Aristotle rebuts this thesis by denying the sonority of orbital motion, given that the planets, as they are dragged by spheres and do not move by their own motion, do not generate the friction necessary to produce sound (*On the Heavens*, 291 a). The inaudible nature of the concert is thus due to its lack of sound, and not to a supposed inability of human hearing. Moreover, considering that sound is proportional to the body that produces it, celestial sound would be so thunderous it would pulverize stones. An attempt to conjugate the argument developed in *Timaeus* on celestial music with Aristotelian physics and the relevant denial of the production of planetary sounds was made in the 13th century. Drawing on Robert Grosseteste – who had linked sound to light motion in his comment to Aristotle's *Posterior Analytics* and in his *De Luce* – mundana, music is interpreted as a luminous phenomenon[4].

In the *Somnium Scipionis* Cicero is instead inspired by the Pythagorean doctrine. The Sun's collocation at the centre of the concentric spheres surrounding the Earth confers on it the imporantce of a *mens mundi* and *dux*, having a balancing function (*temperatio*), as the stability of all living beings depends upon its daily and seasonal cycles. Its role as a *princeps* – further developed in the solar theology illustrated by Macrobius in his *Saturnalia* – was often subsequently translated in the musical note called *mese* and identified with the connecting hinge represented by two conjunct tetrachords, which guaranteed the very existence of harmony.

In their comments to *Timaeus* instead, Calcidius (XCVI) and Macrobius (II, 3, 14) collocate the Sun beyond the Moon's sphere, according to what became known as 'Platonic system'. The rejection of cosmological centrality, however, does not determine an attenuation of its importance on the musical level: the interval of an octave (1/2) is in fact assigned to the Moon-Sun relation, and it is derived from the subdivision of the string at midpoint, which in the perfect Greek system corresponds to the *mese.*

The following diagram shows some of the theories developed in attempts to apply the different musical systems to the cosmological models, from Pythagoras' interpretation to the numerous sonorous variations of geocentrism. While keeping the planets' order unchanged, the authors adapt the planets' intervals (articulated in tones and semitones) to the selected tetrachord: in Boethius' reading of Cicero, in Gaffurius and in

	Spheres	Pythagoras from Pliny [and Theon]	Cicero from Boethius (*mus.*)	Nicomachus from Boethius***	Ptolemy *Harmonica*	Gaffurio *Theorica musice*	Fludd *Utriusque cosmi*
Elementary	Earth	*proslambanomenos*	–	–	–	–	*Γ*
		T					T
	air						*A*
							T
	water						*B*
							T
	fire						*C*
							s
Celestial	Moon	*hypate*	*proslambanomenos*	*nete syn.*	*hypate meson*	*proslambanomenos*	*D*
		s	T	T	2T+s	T	T
	Mercury	*parhypate*	*hypate hypaton*	*paranete sin.*	–	*hypate hypaton*	*E*
		s	s	T		s	T
	Venus	*lychanos*	*parhypate hip.*	*trite sin.*	*mese*	*parhypate hip.*	*F*
		T+s	T	s	T	T	T
	Sun	*mese*	*lychanos hip.*	*mese*	*paramese*	*lychanos hip.*	*G*
		T	T	T	T+s	T	s
	Mars	*paramese*	*hypate meson*	*lychanos mes.*	*nete synemmenon*	*hypate meson*	*a*
		s	s	T	T	s	T
	Jupiter	*trite*	*parhypate mes.*	*parhypate mes.*	*nete diezeugmenon*	*parhypate mes.*	*b*
		s	T	s	2T+s	T	T
	Saturn	*paranete*	*lychanos mes.*	*hypate mes.*	*nete hyperbolaion*	*lychanos mes.*	*c*
		T+s [o s]	T			T	T
	Fixed stars	*nete*	*mese*	–	–	*mese*	*d*
							T
Angelic	Ephiomae						*e*
							T
	Epiphonomiae						*f*
							T
	Epiphaniae						*gg*
		ascendant	ascendant	descendant	ascendant	ascendant	ascendant

T = tone s = semitone

* Pliny (*Historia naturalis* II 20) proposes T+s. Theo of Smirne *Expositio rerum mathematicarum*. . . .) proposes s.

** To comply with the seven notes (rather than eight) employed by Cicero, Macrobius (*Commentarii* II 4) attribues the same height to Mercury and Venus, defining them as 'satellites of the Sun'.

*** In the *Excerpta*, Nichomachus inverts the positions of Mercury and Venus.

1. Page 268, *Antifonario Mediceo*, Biblioteca Mediceo Laurenziana, Plut.29.1, c. 1v.

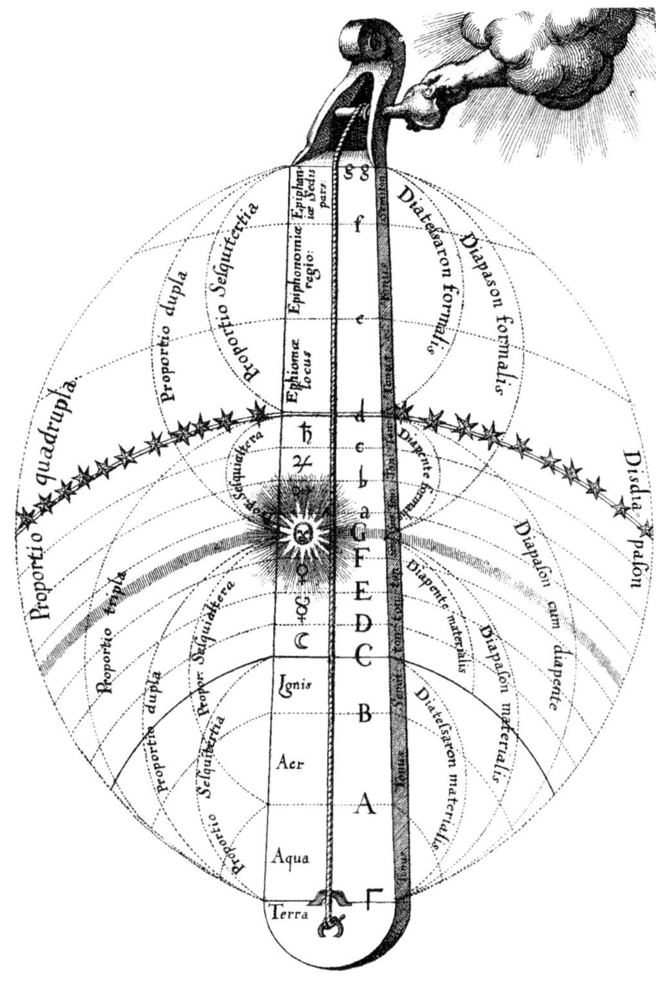

2. Fludd, *Utriusque cosmi...*, vol. I, p. 90.

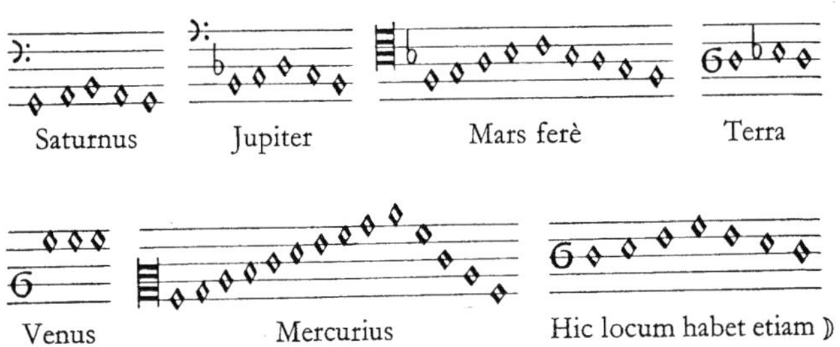

3. Kepler, *Harmonices Mundi Libri V...*, book V, chapt. VI.

Zarlino this choice determined the designation of the *proslambanomenos* (the fundamental sound in the Greek System) as starting note of the celestial harmony. In Nichomacus and in Pythagoras, as seen by Plinius and Theon of Smyrna, instead, this occurs in function of the Sun-*mese* correspondence. Said harmonies may be ascending or descending, and can also consider the spatial or temporal variable, that is, assign the lowest sound to Saturn, or the highest, depending on whether the criteria adopted is the distance from the centre, or the orbital speed. Conversely, Fludd employs the hexachordal system adopted at the time and revised by Guido of Arezzo: by assigning a role in the celestial concert to the four elements and the angelical hierarchies, his scale reaches an extension of two octaves – double those considered by most of his predecessors, yet still far from the four octaves, plus a fifth , contemplated by Macrobius and the *Timaeus*. Specifically, in said system, the Sun continues to play a central part, as it is always *mese* given it is diapason (1/2), and is also i an element of conjunction between the material octave (from the Sun to the Earth) and the spiritual octave (from the Sun to the divine triangle). The Ptolemaic model does not employ a scale, but rather, as previously done by Plato, adopts a regular succession of fourth intervals, constituting two conjunct tetrachords and one disjunct tetrachord (each composed of 2 T + s)[5].

Philosophical contemplation on the harmony of the spheres revolves around Boethius' *De institutione musica*, as well as Martianus Cappella's work[6]. In his *De nuptiis* (IX, 909-910), he suggests an original cosmic harmony, and introduces a personification of Harmony clearly inferred from both the Boethian tripartition and Neoplatonic tradition. *Musica mundana* is represented by the round shield inlaid with the cosmos' circles grasped by the young girl in her right hand, which emit perfectly matching sounds (that is, only musical consonances). *Musica instrumentalis* is evoked by the 'sweet dissonance' generated by the many theatrical instruments the young girl holds in her left hand, which, unable to reach celestial perfection, perform in the realm of *discordia concors*. An allusion to *musica humana* is made by depicting Harmony with her head and gown strewn with gold bells and by describing her solemn gait as 'regulated with measured composure'. *Musica humana* is the field in which this *extramundana intelligentia* plays its role of 'moderator': as the heavens' twin sister, it refers to a harmonic model of the celestial spheres and regulates all souls by imparting measure and limit to the body's limbs, as well as to the movements of reason and will.

During the Carolingian period, *musica humana* underwent a semantic rearrangement: the consequence of its identification with the *vox hominis* (no longer included in *musica instrumentalis*) and no longer with the Microcosm denotes the importance of liturgical singing, reflecting divine, planetary and angelical harmony as well as ascent towards the 'Father's House'.

4. A. Kircher, *Musurgia Universalis*, Rome 1650; Firenze Biblioteca Nazionale Centrale, Magl. 5._.92, vol. II, c. 366.

The Medicean Antiphonarius in the Medicea Laurenziana Library (fig. 1) depicts *musica humana* as a representation of four characters holding hands, as a symbol of concord – like the etymological pun that erroneously relates concord not to the heart (*cor*), but to the chord (*cordis*) indicated by one of said characters. Concord is also suggested by the presence of monks: a monastic community is the union of many individuals who, by sharing a common life, form a single man (*Monos*, hence 'monk'), that is, many bodies yet a single soul and heart[7].

Contemplation of the harmony of the celestial spheres is founded on some Scriptural passages, among them the famous 'Coeli enarrant gloriam Dei' (Ps. XVIII), and the verse from the Bible's Book of Wisdom (*Wisdom*. 11, 21), describing an episode in which creation occurred according to weight (music), number (arithmetic) and measure (geometry). 'It [the Logos] harmoniously ordered [...] the universe, and harmonized the disharmony of elements along the lines of an order of consonance, so that the entire creation would be in harmony with It. And this uninterrupted singing, support for the entire creation and harmony of the universe, stretched from the centre to the extremities, and from the extremities to the centre, thus harmonizing the entire creation'[8]. The correspondence between angelical singing and the harmony of the spheres – of which a worshippers' choir is only a pale reflection, capable however of exercising an edifying function – had been introduced by Ambrogius (*Hexaemeron Libri sex*, II, 2) and was then restated by other authors such as Dante (*Convivio* II, 6) and Giorgio Anselmi (*De musica* I, sec. 157-168)[9] .

The ascending impetus of vocal and instrumental music towards the harmony of the visible world – and also toward the invisible Creator's will, according to Christian mysticism – dominates the philosophical and musical thought of the Middle Ages, Renaissance and eary modern age. Along the lines of Porfirius (*Life of Pythagoras* XXXI), Franchinus Gaffurius correlates celestial spheres and musical intervals, by substituting the Muses for the Platonic Sirens (fig. 5). His model is based mainly on the work of Martianus Cappella (*De nuptiis*, I, 27-28) and accordingly, he suggests the same Muses-planets correspondence order. The summit of the ascetical journey, symbolized by the snakelike tail of the three-headed cerberus (placed on the Earth), is occupied by Apollo; at his side are the three Charites, Euphrosyne, Thalia and Aglaea – another result of the transposition of the three Moirae from the *Timaeus* – in keeping with Ausonius' verse, 'Mentis Apollineae vis has movet undique musas'.

This very same mystical and numerological tradition appears to relate even to Robert Fludd, a Rosecrucian doctor. In the light of Kepler and Mersenne's confutation of his work, their own cosmological models can be clearly identified[10]. Fludd devotes the third book of the first volume of *Utriusque Cosmi... historia* (1617-1624) to *musica mundana* (fig. 2). There are many references to Franciscan monk Francesco Giorgi who, in his *De Harmonia mundi* (1525), had linked the angelical and planetary spheres within a cosmos formed according to harmonic proportions. Similar to the Venetian monk, Fludd divides the universe in three parts (the realm of the angelical Hierarchies, that of Aether or of the Planets, that of the Elements) and between its two extremes, he places the *sphaera aequalitatis*, seat of the Sun and place where the opposite principles of Light and Darkness (represented by the opposite intersecting pyramids) are in perfect balance. The hermetic vision and Ficinian concept[11] that lie beneath said geocentric cosmological model develop a series of music-mediated relations between Macrocosm and Microcosm[12], that is, between astral influences, the concept of 'zodiac man' and the ethical and healing power of sound – a scheme reiterated later by the Jesuit Kircher.

As acknowledged by Mersenne[13], Kepler's harmonic conception differs from Fludd's mainly in the gathering of data, through accurate observations, and not based on analogies produced by an inordinate imagination. The five-polyhedra model included in the *Mysterium Cosmographicum* (1596) and the musical model proposed by the *Harmonice Mundi* (1619) – through which man is able to comprehend Creation – utilise geometrical shapes and proportions originating from comparison between dimensions obtained exclusively from the natural world (planetary distances from the Sun; speed of orbital motions), as well as from mathematical truths contained within the Word, used by God as archetypes of Creation and co-eternal and co-essential to It (fig. 3). Kepler embodies an attempt to interpret the great Pythagorean theme and the Platonic concepts based on the World Soul in light of modern astronomical discoveries, thus combining the exact observations of Tycho Brahe and the accurate mathematical calculations, with the musicological debates of the time and the theological inquiries at the core of Christian apologetics. The search for this 'priest-astronomer'[14] and the shift from static harmony, typical of the Copernican cosmos, to the dynamic harmony of celestial physics is possible thanks to faith in a Musician God, who has imparted form (as opposed to the ugliness of *deformitas*) to the cosmos, has enclosed it in the most perfect geometrical shape (the sphere) and has impressed upon it the image of his own essence. The geometrical shape performs a double function: it is not only the archetype of creation, but, being co-eternal and co-essential to God, it also reveals the relations of generation and spiration within the Trinity[15]. At a time of heated anti-Trinitarian debates pursued especially by the Socinians, Kepler, reinterpretating an image suggested by Cusanus and going well beyond mere analogy, identifies God with the Sun and the centre of the sphere, the Son with the Fixed Stars and the external surface, and the Holy Spirit with the in-between Aether in which planets move. But this does not authorize research carried out by acritically putting *a priori* models before astronomical observation and measurements: in the same year, 1604, Kepler decides to reject the notion of dogmatic perfection of the sphere in astronomy and in geometric and physiologic optics, as he delineates elliptical orbital motion, as well as conical lenses and the hyperbolic shape of the crystalline lens.

The diacronicity (the essential aspect of music) of the elliptical motions of planets and the variation of their angular speed (according to the law of areas) finds its culmination in the harmonic law, $T_1 : T_2 = (R_1 : R_2)^{3/2}$, which links the period of orbital revolution and the distance from the Sun in keeping with the consonance of fifth (3/2), expressed in the rule by the sesquialter proportion of the exponent. In this intellectual, non-vocal concert, each planet corresponds (with negligible approximation) not to a single note, but to an interval contained within the minimum angular velocity at the aphelium and the maximum speed at the perielium. Consequently, Saturn is characterized by major third (4/5), Jupiter by minor third (5/6), Mars by the fifth (2/3), Earth by the semitone (15/16, which corresponds to the modern 'diatonic semitone'), Venus by the sharp (24/25, that is, the difference between tone and semitone currently known as 'chromatic semitone') and Mercury by the union of the octave and minor third (5/12)[16]. The range of intervals relating to each single planet reflects the differences existing between their eccentricity, while the pitch of sounds produces an auditory transposition of their position within the cosmos, since it is directly proportional to their distance from the Sun. This celebrates the parallel progress of the 'sister sciences' (Plato, *Republic*, 530 D): Copernicanism and ellipticity of orbits in astronomy on the one side, broadening of consonances and polyphony in music on the other. In the 17th century, the harmony of the spheres reaches its full realization, as only thanks to Kepler said theme performs a heuristic function, by effectively interacting with astronomical research.

The geometricity of the divine archetype and of the universe's structure is not in any way renounced, but it is merely solved in musical harmony. Firstly, in a novel interpretation of the Quadrivium sciences, music is no longer subordinate to arithmetic, but to geometry: consonances now arise from the relations that exist between the sides of the five regular polygons and the circumference in which they are inscribed[17]. Furthermore, the additions made to the second edition of the *Mysterium Cosmographicum* (1621), albeit moving away from some of the symbolisms present in the 1596 version, make an attempt to conjugate the results reached in the *Harmonice Mundi* with the system of polyhedra described in his early writings, in so conferring 'form' to the 'material' appearance of the platonic solids[18].

Kepler assigns the role of expressing the rejection – albeit incom-

5. Franchino Gaffurio, *Practica musicae*, frontispiece, Venice 1512.

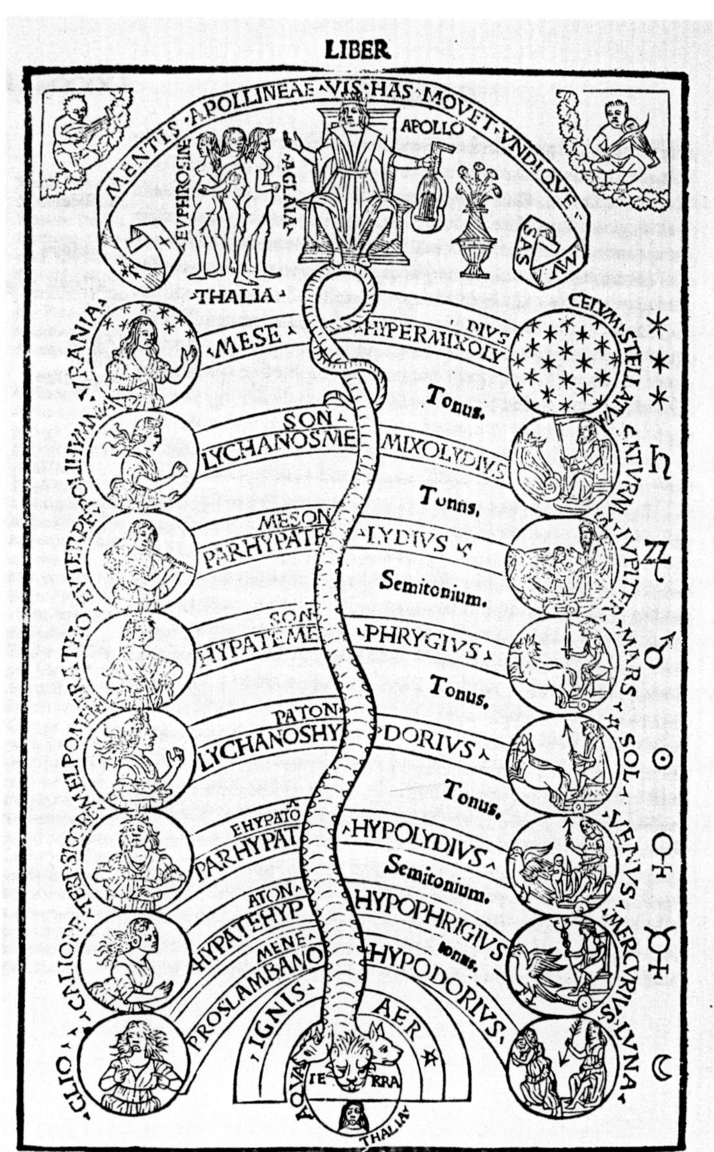

plete – of anthropocentrism and of the ontological differentiation of space to his conception of celestial music. In fact, decentralizing Earth implies the inability to hear the celestial concert: as a consequence, the planetary symphony would not result harmonic – neither from a visual, nor auditory perspective – to a listener or spectator positioned on the Earth, but it would be so only to one placed on the Sun, given that the angular speed of each single planet (which corresponds to the musical intervals) is calculated by assuming the solar body as point of reference.

The *Harmonice mundi* inspired the *Traité de l'harmonie universelle* (1627) by Mersenne, the only work tackling the topic of harmonic cosmos, as well as other pertinent metaphysical issues[19]: far from the criticism addressed to Kepler in his *Harmonie Universelle* of 1636-'37, in these more recent pages the Minimum moves away from the metaphysical and theological concepts presented by the German astronomer and onto the rebuttal of the concept of universal monochord put forward by Fludd, of the notions of alchemy and hermetic philosophy, as well as of the imaginative musical theories suggested by Plato, Plutarch, Cardanus and Ficinus.

The acoustics and organology studies in Mersenne's *Harmonie Universelle*, in his *Harmonicorum libri* (1636, 1648²) and in his *Cogitata physico-mathematica* (1644) play a decisive role in the development of the new image of cosmos proposed by the Jesuit Athanasius Kircher. As a scholar of automata and hydraulic organs – as confirmed by the many tables included in the *Musurgia Universalis* (1650) and by the organs placed in the Pontifical gardens at the Quirinale – in his *Harmonia nascentis Mundi*, Kircher does not present a monochord, but a more complex metaphor – an *organum* (fig.4). In the shift from a Platonic surveyor God to a more 'mechanic' God, the universe's organism is seen as a machine composed of numerous mutually and mechanically interacting parts (levers, bellows, valves, tie rods, rotating axles). Such an interpretation is in no way far off from the interest shown at the time by Alessandro Giorgi and the Lyncean Fabio Colonna in the *Spiritali* by Heron of Alexandria, as well as the works on organology by Cardanus (*De subtilitate*, *De proportionibus*), inspired by books V and X of Vitruvius' *De Architectura*. Just as creation occurs through divine voice and *Fiat lux*, and is given life by way of the *spiritus*, so the organ is a pneumatic instrument generating sound from air first introduced in the bellows and then expelled through pipes. The pipe structure of the organ is ultimately the evolution of the flute present in the myth of Pan, symbol of celestial harmony. It is this harmony that is celebrated with an angelical symphony on the frontispiece of the *Musurgia*: once abandoned all musical instruments, the ascent culminates in a 36-voice choir singing the *Sanctus* based on a canon by Romano Micheli, a composition that exerted such fascination on 17th and 18th century musicians as to be subsequently performed by Carl Philip Emanuel Bach[20].

Bibliography

Agostino 1956; Barker 1984-1989; Barker 2007; Boccaccio 1547; Clemente di Alessandria 2004; Elders 1994; Fabbri 2003; Fabbri 2007, pp. 287-308; Field 1988; Godwin 1987; Gouk 1999; Kepler 1941; Kepler 1945; Kepler 1963; Macrobio 1981; Melamed 1995, pp. 107-118; Mersenne 1627; Moutsopoulos 1959; Panti 2004, pp. 219-245; Palisca 1985; Ripa 1611; Spitzer 1963; Teeuwen 2002; Walker D.P. 2000.

[1] Boccaccio 1547, pp. 9*r-v*, 89v. Ripa 1611 entry *Mondo*.

[2] Macrobius 1981, II, 3, 11, p. 267.

[3] Moutsopoulos 1959; Barker 1984-1989, 2007. The Greek musical system is formed by tetrachords, that is, a succession of four sounds within the range of what shall here be called a perfect fourth. Depending on the range of the intervals included, these can be of three different genres: diatonic, chromatic and enharmonic. The semitone's position also marks the difference between the three modes of diatonic genre: doric (inferior semitone), phrygian (intermediate semitone) and lydian (superior semitone). In order to generate different harmonies, tetrachords may be disjunct (when they are juxtaposed) or conjunct (the last note of the first tetrachord corresponds to the first note of the second one).

[4] Panti 2004.

[5] Godwin 1987.

[6] Teeuwen 2002.

[7] Augustin 1956 Cxxxii, 6.

[8] Spitzer 1963. Clement of Alexandria 2004, pp. 52-53.

[9] Palisca 1985; Elders 1994.

[10] Fabbri 2003.

[11] Walker D.P. 2000.

[12] Gouk 1999.

[13] MERSENNE 1627, I, 16, p. 89; II, 12, p. 422.

[14] Kepler to Herwart von Hohenbur (26 March 1598), 1945, p. 193.

[15] Kepler 1963, p. 28.

[16] The musical system adopted by Kepler refers to the 'just intonation' by Gioseffo Zarlino, who subdivides the octave (1/2) in intervals of fifth (2/3), fourth (3/4), major third (4/5), minor third (5/6), major sixth (3/5), minor sixth (5/8), major tone (8/9), minor tone (9/10), diatonic semitone (15/16), chromatic semitone (24/25, resulting from the difference between the minor tone and the diatonic semitone), comma (80/81, resulting from the difference between the major tone and minor tone), considering as consonants the octave, fourth and fifth, thirds and sixths.

[17] Field 1988.

[18] Kepler 1940, v, 9, pp. 361-362.

[19] Fabbri 2003, 2007.

[20] Melamed 1995.

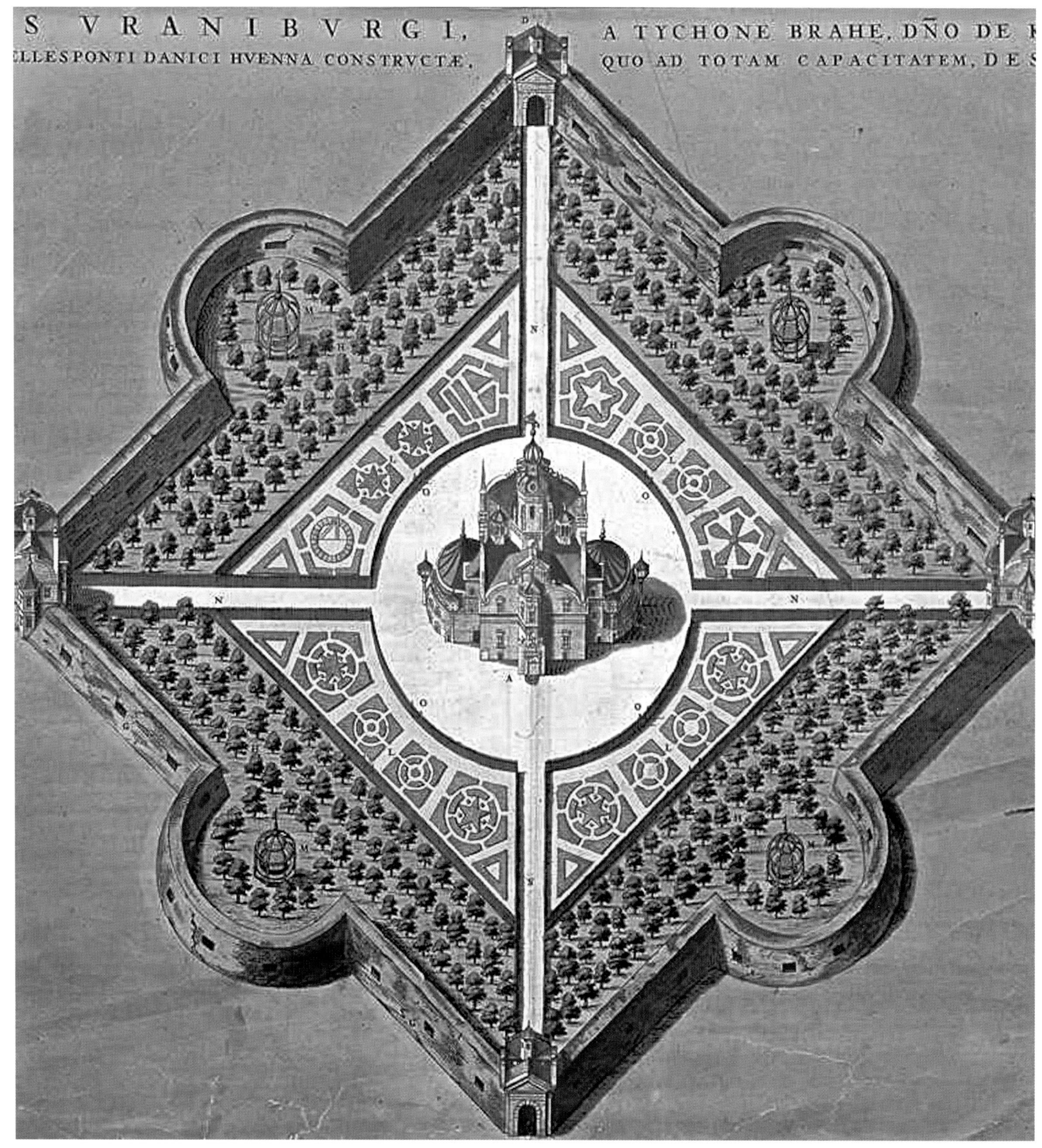
S VRANIBVRGI,
A TYCHONE BRAHE, DÑO DE
DANICI HVENNA CONSTRVCTÆ,
QUO AD TOTAM CAPACITATEM, DE

The passing of the torch

In 1577 the Imperial astronomer Taqî al-Dîn had the great satisfaction of observing the completion of an imposing astronomical observatory on the hills of Istanbul, called Dâr al-Rasad al-Jadîd (the new observatory). Built at the order of Murad III, Sultan of the Ottoman Empire, the observatory had an important library, excellent instruments for observation, armillary spheres and accurate clocks. When a spectacular comet appeared in November of that same year, the Sultan asked the astronomer what prophesies could be drawn from such an event. Although the predictions were highly favourable, the country was devastated by a deadly epidemic, which, along with the rise of religious factions and superstitions opposing the study of celestial objects, led the Sultan to have the Istanbul observatory totally destroyed on January 22, 1580.

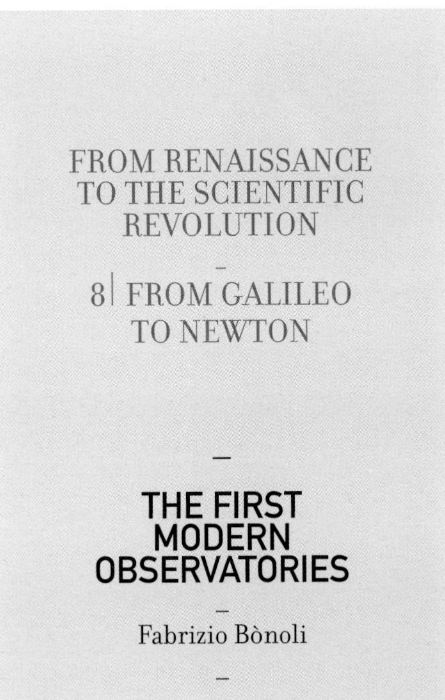

FROM RENAISSANCE
TO THE SCIENTIFIC
REVOLUTION
8| FROM GALILEO
TO NEWTON
THE FIRST
MODERN
OBSERVATORIES
Fabrizio Bònoli

Contemporaneously, this same comet was observed in Europe by many astronomers, among them the Danish scientist Tycho Brahe, who closely observed its motion and tried to estimate its distance. The comet did not appear to be a phenomenon caused by masses of heated air that reflected the light of the Sun, moving through our atmosphere, according to Aristotelian physics, but an object far beyond the Moon, moving through the incorruptible crystalline spheres.

Just one year before, on August 8, 1576, on the Danish (now Swedish) island of Hven, the first stone had been laid for what is considered the first European astronomical observatory (fig. 1), built at the initiative of Tycho and financed by King Frederick II of Denmark. Dedicated to Urania, the muse of astronomy, the observatory took the name of Uraniborg (the castle of Urania). A few years later Tycho moved there to superintend the final stages of construction and installation of the instruments; this was in 1580.

That year – 1580 – in which the Istanbul observatory was torn down and work on Uraniborg began, can thus be taken to symbolise the passing of the torch from Arab astronomy to that of Europe, marking the conclusion of a vast process that had begun over five centuries earlier: the confluence in Europe of Arab-Islamic culture with the Greek culture of the Classic and Hellenistic ages mediated and developed by Near Eastern scholars. These are, in fact, what may rightly be called the Greek and Arab roots of European science.

Why 'modern' observatories

As has been seen, Uraniborg, with its 'branch observational office' Stjerneborg (the castle of the stars) built in 1584, is deemed the first European observatory but, as is often the case, priorities are hard to establish. Some scholars, in fact, assign precedence to the observatory built around 1471 at Nuremberg, in his own home, by the wealthy merchant and humanist Bernard Walther, a pupil of Johannes Müller (Regiomontanus) and patron of the arts, one of the first to use a mechanical clock as aid to astronomical observations[1]; or to the tower built by Copernicus at his canonry in Frauenburg, in the early years of the 16th century, to house his instruments; or to the observatory built in 1561 on the tower of Kassel by the Landgrave William IV, containing numerous metal instruments and the first revolving dome, in which Christoph Rothmann and Joost Bürgi worked, and which was visited by Tycho in 1575.

It is thus important to define the subject of this article, that is, what is meant by the term 'modern observatories'. In this context, an observatory is not merely a collection of astronomical instruments – of larger or smaller size – installed on a terrace, a roof or the lawn of a residence, but rather a non-private institution, designed and built especially and exclusively for astronomical observation. And when we speak of 'modern' observatories, we mean those built after the invention of the telescope, at a time when the new instrument and the ensuing new observation techniques began to change the astronomers' conception of the cosmos as well as their working methods.

In effect, after Galileo's first observations in 1609 and the subsequent rapid dissemination of telescopes, scientists and men of culture all over Europe turned with great interest to observing the heavens, installing astronomical instruments in their own homes or those of their supporters, at their own expense or that of enlightened patrons. But the lesson taught by Tycho had shown that, to achieve the best results in observation, it was not enough to place good instruments on a roof and devote a few sleepless nights to them. The instruments had instead to be specially designed for the various types of observation and installed in suitable structures. Often differing in construction and operation, these instruments had to be utilised by expert astronomers to attain the most precise measurements possible and, above all, the observatory had to operate according to a logical programme of observation[2]. There had to be a 'research programme' such as the one behind the realisation of Uraniborg and Stjerneborg, which had led Tycho to make the most precise astronomical measurements prior to the age of the telescope and to propose a new World System to replace the ancient Aristotelian-Ptolemaic one, long grown old, and the modern one of Copernicus, the target of widespread criticism, if not actually suspected of heresy. And just because it was backed by a vast number of remarkable observations, Tycho's system survived the discoveries of Galileo and Kepler. Moreover, it remained almost to the end of the 17th century the system favoured by those who still refused to accept the fact that the Earth moved around the Sun. Most notable among these were the Jesuits, who embraced the system with the modifications introduced by Giovanni Battista Riccioli from the Collegio di Gesù in Bologna. Tycho was unable to complete the development of his observational and theoretical programme. In 1597 the death of his patron, Frederick II, and his fall from grace in the eyes of the court and the new sovereign, Christian IV, obliged him to abandon the observatory on Hven, which was then destroyed in 1601, the year of his death. Remaining from his vast body of work is his accurate description in the *Mechanica* of the instruments, their installation, the observation techniques practiced, and the personnel required for the observatory. Some years later Tycho found protection in Prague at the court of Rudolph II, Emperor of the Holy Roman Empire. Here he was joined by the young Johannes Kepler, who continued to carry out the programme for constructing a new vision of the cosmos, although not by confirming the great Danish astronomer's system but by formulating three laws and beginning to confer theoretical consistency on the Copernican system.

The research programmes

What kind of research programmes were carried out by the astronomers of the time? What instruments were used and, above all, what were their levels of precision? And why did such programmes require 'modern astronomical observatories' in the sense outlined above?

Galileo had already developed techniques for performing precision measurements with the telescope and had suggested their potential applications, but only since the 1730s had it been possible to improve the performance of the new instrument. Christoph Grienberger and Jean Baptiste Morin, the former in Rome at the *Collegio Romano*, the latter in Paris at the *Collège Royal*, mounted a telescope on an instrument with a graduated edge, such as an astronomical quadrant. Around the same time, instrument makers began to insert at the focal point of the telescope's eyepiece a reticle that served as precision sight or 'index line'; a small instrument originally made of 'two hairs, which form a Cross, and truly exert a beautiful effect, seeming to cut the objects, which can be seen distinctly', as wrote Eustachio Divini, who used the instrument in 1649 to make an accurate lunar map[3] (cf. entry VII.4.11).

In this first half of the 17th century, astronomers carried out research programmes linked to the question of the World System, and the related vicissitudes of Galileo. Observations were conducted on the Moon and the planets and their motions, to insert them in what was then called the 'theory of planets'. The 'fixed stars' were carefully observed, estimating their dimensions and distances, in the attempt to determine whether or not the universe was infinite in size, a question left open by Copernicus and discussed in dramatic terms by Giordano Bruno. This involved accurately measuring the positions of the stars and verifying the possible existence of a phenomenon, already discussed in the 3rd century B.C. by Aristarcus, which would have provided final proof that the Earth moved around the Sun: the 'annual parallax' of the stars, that is, the apparent annual minor displacement of a star observed from two opposite points of the terrestrial orbit.

Galileo, as has been mentioned, had already suggested a method of dealing with these questions. In observing the motion of the planets he had, in fact, seen the phases of Venus as they could not have existed in the Ptolemaic system[4]. He had attempted to measure the diameters of the stars and deduce their distances, through an original stratagem employing a 'little cord ... interposed between myself and the star', and had found them to be much smaller and thus much more distant than had hitherto been thought[5]. He had proposed verifying the existence of a stellar parallax, to serve as final proof of the heliocentric system: 'When we find with the telescope some very small star very close to one of the largest ones, which is however very high, it might happen that some perceptible change occurs between them... And if in this operation we should find some change, what and how much progress will result for astronomy? Because through that means, in addition to assuring us of its annual motion, we might come to know the size and distance of said star'[6]. In addition – and with life-long dedication – Galileo had tried to solve a problem of the utmost practical importance, one that was to play a major part in the development of the new observatories. It consisted of determining longitude at sea

1. Page 276, Map of Uraniborg, after W.J. Blaeu, Atlas Major, Amsterdam 1662. The castle of Urania built by Tycho Brahe in 1580 on the island of Hven, in a seventeenth-century elaboration by Blaeu taken from Tycho's *Astronomiae instauratae mechanica*. The observatory appears at the centre, surrounded by gardens and enclosed in high walls astronomically oriented.

2. Henri Testelin, *Colbert presents the members of the newly founded Académie des Sciences to Louis XIV*, 1667; Versailles, Musée national des châteaux de Versailles et de Trianon, MV 2074, inv. 2982, MR 2522. The painting is taken from a drawing by Charles Le Brun. Behind the King appears the Observatoire Royal still under construction. At the centre of the group of academicians, in the foreground, wearing a brown damasked mantle, is Gian Domenico Cassini.

by compiling accurate tables of the positions of Jupiter's satellites and observing them from aboard ship, using the Medicean stars as a sort of celestial clock[7]. Although Galileo's proposals turned out to be unfeasible for the times, they provided the idea on which many later developments were based.

Indubitably, the research programs outlined here were crucially important for knowledge of the structure of the cosmos and thus of man's position and role on Earth, and, as such were proper subjects for study by astronomers, mathematicians and philosophers. But it is also true that such research programmes – today we would call them 'basic' – could not attract financing sufficient to allow the scholars to build or purchase more precise, and thus more expensive, instruments and to devote themselves full-time to observation, measurement, consolidation and interpretation of data and theoretic study. Galileo's endless complaints over being distracted from his precious studies by the many activities he had to engage in to earn money – teaching, private lessons, building instruments – are well known. But it was just this problem of determining longitude now confronted by the Pisan scientist that was to provide astronomers with a solution to their difficulties and lead to the founding of the great modern observatories.

The Observatoire Royal in Paris

Navigation, geodesy and cartography – which is to say, improvement in routes across the little-known oceans, description of new places to be explored, perfecting the measurement and charting of territories already possessed – were (then as now) disciplines that could not do without astronomical techniques. Only with these was it possible to accurately determine latitude and longitude and thus to know and describe a territory for the purposes of control, of governmental and military utility – a relationship between science, power and productive activity that could not be clearer or more direct. And in this relationship astronomy played a privileged role, as an instrument, and no longer – or not merely – as an 'ornament' of authority. It was just for these immediate practical advantages, linked to vast campaigns of

3. The Royal Greenwich Observatory in a painting dating from around 1680, shortly after its completion. Within the walls of the observatory, to the right of Flamsteed House, can be seen the great flagstaff that supports the telescope having a focal length of 60 feet (around 20 m). National Maritime Museum, Greenwich, inv. BHC1812.

astronomical measurement conducted over extensive territories, that astronomy was the first of the experimental sciences obliged to abandon the 'craftsmanship' techniques of the individual astronomer peering by night through a telescope on the roof of his house, in favour of collective efforts requiring strong institutional backing. All of this drove astronomers to create a highly organised community, with practical problems shared and clearly defined and with ongoing cultural exchange – today we would call it 'a network' of researchers. As a result, the institutionalising of astronomy was on the one hand rather simple, on the other decidedly productive.

Obviously, the problem of determining longitude at sea was especially crucial to the nations involved in growing colonial expansion and maritime trade. Already since the 16th century the Spanish crown had offered rich rewards for a practical method of solving this problem, in 1567 with Philip II and in 1598 with Philip III (to the latter of whom Galileo had addressed his proposals); others were to follow. But the decisive change leading to the realisation of an institutional structure, exclusively dedicated to astronomical observation and to the 'useful arts' that could derive from it, took place in 1902, France. In 1655 some members of the scientific community, keenly interested in the practical and experimental aspects of research, began to plan a *Compagnie des Sciences et des Artes*. Through the astronomer Adrien Auzout they appealed to Louis XIV in these words: 'It is a question, Sire, of the Glory of Your Majesty, & of the reputation of France, & this is what allows us to hope that you will order some place in which to conduct in future all sorts of Celestial Observations...'. Well advised by the future Minister of the Royal House Jean-Baptiste Colbert, the Sun King replied to the scientists' request with two provisions: the creation of an academy modelled on the Roman Lyncei, the *Académie Royale des Sciences*, whose first meeting was held on December 22, 1666, and the purchase, on March 7 of the following year, of two and a half hectares of land on which to build the *Observatoire Royal*. Just two months later, on the day of the summer solstice, June 21, 1667, the mathematicians of the *Académie* determined, along what was to become the meridian of Paris, the astronomical orientation of the building designed by the architect Claude Perrault. Secretary of the *Académie* at that time was the Dutch scientist Christiaan Huygens, one of the outstanding figures of the time, inventor among other things of the pendulum clock, proponent of the light-wave theory and expert astronomer, discoverer of Titan, the first satellite di Saturn, of the separate stars that formed the Orion nebula, and the nature of the rings around Saturn. Unfortunately, the war waged by France against the Netherlands in 1672 obliged the Dutch scientist to leave Paris, preventing him from participating in the observatory's development.

While the work proceeded rapidly Colbert, assigned to procure top-level scientific personnel, convinced the Ligurian astronomer Giovanni Domenico Cassini to leave his post at the University of Bologna and supervise the conclusion of the work (fig. 2). In the twenty years spent in the western world's oldest university, Cassini had become famous for his expertise in conducting observations and his outstanding practical achievements[8]. In particular – and expressly linked to the project for an observatory dedicated mainly to geographic and cartographic research and to aiding navigation – he was known for having determined the periods and positions of Jupiter's satellites, the most accurate then available, utilised for many years (Galileo's proposals for their practical utilisation in determining longitude have already been mentioned[9]; as well as for his accurate construction of the great meridian line, the world's longest, in the Basilica of San Petronio. He was also renowned for having utilised a great number of measurements linked to observation of the motion of the Sun and, by reflection, to study of the Earth's motion, and for the first observational verification of Kepler's Second Law[10].

Cassini arrived in Paris on April 4, 1669, when the construction of the *Observatoire* was already well under way. He was thus able to contribute only in part by suggesting modifications based on his vast experience. From 1671, the year his observations commenced, to 1793, no less than four members of the Cassini family succeeded one another as directors of the *Observatoire*: a real dynasty of astronomers.

Many were the programmes carried out in Paris by Cassini, later continued and expanded by his successors, which made one of the greatest astronomers of the 17th century, if not of all time. In addition to conducting typically astronomical research he played a leading role in the cartographic, geographic and navigational activities for which the sovereign had decided to establish an astronomical institution of such importance. In addition to telescopes of great focal length, as long as 30-35 metres, built by the finest lens-makers such as Giuseppe Campani of Spoleto, who had furnished Cassini in Italy as well, for observing the planets and the Moon (in 1679 Cassini made a great *Carte de la Lune* that remained unrivalled up to the 19th century), the observatory was equipped with precision instruments such as mobile and wall-mounted quadrants furnished with micrometers, fabricated by Jean Picard and Adrien Auzout, and clocks that told time to the half-second, for measuring the positions of the celestial bodies, not only to study their motion but above all for topographical purposes. A great sundial, built by Cassini to determine the moment of noon, was used to verify the precision of the clock.

Here geodesy underwent modern development, in connection with projects for measuring the degree of meridian and preparing detailed maps of the region of Paris and the coasts. The *Carte de France corrigée par ordre du Roy*, completed between 1676 and 1681 by Cassini in collaboration with Picard and Philippe de La Hire, constituted the theoretical and methodological basis for the subsequent *Carte des Cassini*, the first map realised by means of arc triangulation, a project carried out throughout the second half of the 18th century under the direction of César-François Cassini (Cassini III) and Jean-Dominique Cassini (Cassini IV), the grandson and great-grandson of Cassini I. Significantly, de la Hire was sent in 1671 to Uraniborg (or what remained of the great Danish astronomer's observatory) to perform accurate measurements of longitude and compare them with Tycho's, returning from the journey accompanied by the young Ole Christensen Rømer. In Paris, under Cassini's guidance, Rømer performed the first valid measurement of the speed of light, utilising the tables of Jupiter's satellites and the differences in time observed between their appearance and disappearance on the planet's disc. Noteworthy also is the publication, begun in 1679 by Abbot Picard, of the *Connaissance des temps*, the famous astronomical and nautical almanac obtained from the ephemeris calculated at the *Observatoire*, still today published by the *Bureau des longitudes*.

All of these aspects involved in the foundation and early stages of construction of the first great European national astronomical observatory, briefly summarised here, ensured that, for the quantity and quality of activities carried out, the wealth of instrumentation, the organisation of work and the research programs conducted, the *Observatoire Royal* became an institutional model to be emulated by all of the later observatories.

The Greenwich Royal Observatory in Great Britain

The institution in France of an astronomical facility chiefly dedicated to solving the problems of navigation and cartography could not pass unnoticed by the other great nation engaged in oceanic navigation and maritime trade, which was of course Great Britain. Strangely enough, the incentive to founding a British national observatory came from a Frenchman, a certain Sieur de St Pierre[11]. Almost certainly a charlatan (a con man, we would say today), he appeared in 1674 at the court of Charles II claiming to know a method for determining longitude that called for a series of accurate measurements of the relative positions of the stars and the Moon, the so-called 'lunar distances method'. The English astronomers, among them Robert Hooke and the young but already expert John Flamsteed, soon realised how incompetent the Frenchman was, but understood that the method, which had been proposed already in the 16th century by Johann Werner and developed by Jean Baptiste Morin in 1634, could furnish acceptable results if the astronomical coordinates were to be greatly improved. Those available at the time, which still derived in part from Tycho Brahe's observations, led to errors in longitude as great as 110 nautical miles, more than 200 kilometres.

On March 4, 1675, through a royal decree, Flamsteed was appointed Astronomer Royal and, at the suggestion of the Royal Society, it was decided on June 22 to build a small observatory in the royal park at Greenwich, on the ruins of a castle situated on high ground. It was destined to become one of the world's most important astronomical institutions as well as the site of the fundamental meridian. The first stone of the building, later to be called Flamsteed House, was laid on August 10 of the same year. Work on the building, designed by the architect John Wren, was completed in less than a year, and on July 10, 1676, Flamsteed was able to move there and begin conducting observations (fig. 3). The clearly defined task of the astronomer was 'to apply himself with the most exact care and diligence to rectifying the tables of the motions of the heavens, and the places of the fixed stars, so as to find out the so-much-desired longitude of places for perfecting the art of navigation'. One again, an astronomical observatory found its reason for being not in the desire to improve *tout court* knowledge of the heavens, but in the 'practical fall-out' that such knowledge would bring.

For many years the personnel and financing of the Royal Greenwich Observatory remained modest as compared to the Paris observatory. A wall-mounted quadrant, an iron sextant, a wooden quadrant, a pair of small telescopes owned by Flamsteed, and two large clocks built by Thomas Tompion constituted the main instrumentation, housed in the Octagon Room, and the observatory even had to employ students to aid in the astronomical work. It was only thanks to an inheritance from his father that Flamsteed was later able to improve the instrumentation, purchasing it himself. The vast number of observations (around 50,000) of the stars, the Moon and the satellites of Jupiter took a great deal of time due to the complex reductions necessary for institutional purposes, and Newton, who became president of the Royal Society in 1703, strongly urged Flamsteed to have the results of over 25 years of observations published. From 1706 to 1712 the astronomer devoted himself to completing this work, but he found the published data, demanded of him by the Royal Society, so unsatisfactory that in 1715 he managed to track down and burn 300 unsold copies out of the 400 printed, setting to work again to compile a new and more accurate edition. Flamsteed died in 1719 and the work of his entire lifetime was published posthumously in 1725 in the *Historia Coelestis Britannica*. He was succeeded as Astronomer Royal by Edmond Halley, and after him, to remain within the limits of the observatory's first century of life, by

4. The observatory set up by Johannes Hevelius in 1641 on the roofs of his home in Danzig. The platform extends over the roofs of three buildings, and among the instruments, handled by various assistants, can be seen the telescope whith mount resembling the flagstaff of a ship; after J. Hevelius, *Machina celestis pars prior*, Gdansk 1673.

James Bradley, Nathaniel Bliss and Nevil Maskelyne, inaugurating a long line of astronomers who have made the history of this discipline. It was Maskelyne to begin, in 1767, publication of the *Nautical Almanac and Astronomical Ephemeris*, the collection of astronomical tables calculated at Greenwich, basically for maritime use. In 1818 it passed under the direction of Her Majesty's Nautical Almanac Office, which still today compiles an edition jointly with the US Naval Observatory. The astronomers of Greenwich were so massively engaged in these programs for measuring positions that John Herschel complained that, in the late 18th and early 19th centuries, 'the chilling torpor of routine had begun to spread itself over all the branches of science which wanted the excitement of experimental research'[12].

In the meantime, the Board of Longitude was instituted in 1714, for the scope of supervising the work of the observatory, and the name of this bureau itself reveals its ultimate purpose. The unsolved problem of longitude was still at issue, and, in fact, the British Parliament contemporaneously instituted the Longitude Prize, 'For such person or persons as shall discover the Longitude'; with this motivation: 'The Discovery of the Longitude is of such Consequence to Great Britain for the safety of the Navy and Merchant Ships as well as for the improvement of Trade that for want thereof many Ships have been retarded in their voyages, and many lost ...'.

But despite the efforts exerted by astronomers all over Europe to bring the precision of their observations up to a satisfactory level, the problem was solved only starting from 1735, when a self-taught carpenter, John Harrison, built the first of his marine timekeeper models, furnishing an instrument that in the following years was able to determine longitude at sea with an error of about half a minute, that is, less than 10 nautical miles; but this is another story, to be told at another time.

A 'mantle' of astronomical towers

In the second half of the 17th century, the astronomers' greatest concern was that of improving the precision of their measurements thanks to the possibilities offered by the telescope. A debatable point was whether it was better to use optical sights or telescopes. The famous catalogue of Johannes Hevelius, *Prodromus Astronomiae* dating from 1690, listed 1564 stars measured with optical sights, without a telescope, and was exceeded in precision, but by little, only in 1725 by the catalogue published by Flamsteed in the *Historia Caelestis Britannica*, with 2935 stars measured at Greenwich using telescopes applied to a sextant and a mural sector, both seven feet long (approx. 2 metres). From today's measurements it can be seen that that the mean precision for the positions of the bright stars achieved by Hevelius was

5. The tower of the observatory (today's Museo della Specola) built between 1712 and 1726 at the Istituto delle Scienze di Bologna (now the University headquarters). From the frontispiece to the first volume of the *De Bononiensi scientiarum et artium Instituto atque Academia Commentarii*, 1731-1791; Biblioteca 'Guido Horn d'Arturo', Department of Astronomy, Bologna).

50 seconds of arc, and by Flamsteed, 40"; not substantial differences. Parenthetically, a century and a half before, the measurements of the same stars performed by Tycho Brahe were precise to 1'40''[13].

In recalling the name of Hevelius we cannot fail to mention his observatory in Danzig (fig. 4), which, although pertaining to the category of private and not institutional observatories, played a significant part in the progress of astronomy and observation techniques. Hevelius had studied at Leiden and upon returning to Danzig had became a judge and consul. In 1641 he installed in his house some instruments of the highest quality that he had built himself, even grinding the lenses. Here, assisted by his wife, he devoted his whole life to observations, writing works of foremost importance for describing the cosmos: *Selenographia* in 1647, with the first accurate systematic representation of the Moon; *Cometographia* in 1688, with observations and discussions on the nature and motions of comets; *Machina coelestis*, whose first volume dates from 1673, while only some fifty copies of the second volume published in 1679 have survived. In that year, in fact, a fire destroyed his house and the observatory, the manuscripts and the remaining copies of the already printed volume, containing the results of thousands of observations starting from 1630. The astronomer set to work again, producing a new catalogue that was published posthumously by his wife in 1690, the previously mentioned *Prodromus Astronomiae*. Dating from the same year is the great atlas called *Uranographia* or *Firmamentum sobiescianum*, in honour of the Polish king, Jan III Sobieski, a man of culture and hero in the war against the Turks. The precision of Hevelius's measurements has already been noted; his commitment to perfecting to the maximum his instruments and the methods of using them made his observatory a refined example for astronomy.

Dating from only slightly before Hevelius' private observatory were two other observatories, in Holland and Denmark, and the astronomer from Danzig may have seen construction beginning on the former while a student in Leiden. In 1633, in fact, a university observatory was built in that city – probably the first university observatory in Europe – to house a great iron-and-brass mural quadrant, built years before by Willem Janszoon Blaeu for Willebrord Snell van Royen, who used it to determine the circumference of the Earth based on the difference in latitude measured between two Dutch cities. The other, also a university observatory, was built in Copenhagen at the initiative of King Christian IV, the same ruler who had obliged Tycho to abandon Uraniborg. It was a great circular tower called Rundetaarn, planned by the architect Hans Steenwinkel the Younger as the first step in a broader project that would include an astronomical observatory, a church for the students and a university library. The first stone was laid on July 7, 1637 and the work was finished five years later. The structure, recently restored, was over 38 m high, with a peculiar helical ramp winding inside it for over 200 m. One of Tycho's disciples, Christen Sorensen Longomontanus, was the first director of this observatory, which contained instruments similar to those of Uraniborg, many of them unfortunately destroyed by fire in 1728.

Although both had been built before the *Observatoire Royal*, these were, as has been said, university observatories, and thus dedicated to teaching and not exclusively to astronomical observations, as was instead the one – subsequent to both Paris and Greenwich, but smaller in size – built in Berlin by the *Societät der Wissenschaften*. In 1711 the Brandenburg scientific society, which had been founded by Gottfried Wilhelm Leibniz in 1700, set up an observatory in the royal stables, located in Dorothean Town, at the urging of one of its members, the astronomer Gottfried Kirch, who had long been conducting regular observations from a private observatory. Demonstrating the eminently practical purposes for which the Berliner Sternwarte had been founded is the fact that up to 1811 it managed to finance itself exclusively from income deriving from its monopoly on calculations for the calendar.

Just as Rudolph Glaber had written that, near the end of the first millennium, 'The land became covered with a white mantle of churches', it could be said that Europe was rapidly filled with a 'mantle' of astronomical towers. Now it was no longer a question of private observatories only, as had been the case in the late 16th-early 17th century, but every sovereign, every prince, every university and every big city wanted to have an observatory of its own[14]. The St. Petersburg Academy of Science, instituted in January 1724 by Tsar Peter the Great, erected a well-equipped observatory in the newly founded city on the banks of the Neva. In 1726 the astronomer and geographer Joseph-Nicolas Delisle, a disciple of Cassini II, was summoned to direct it. In 1839 the need to explore and map the vast unknown territories of the Russian Empire facilitated the construction, a few kilometres from the city and designed by Friedrich Georg Wilhelm von Struve, of the great observatory of Pulkovo, one of the 19th century's most important[15]. Then in less than a decade, from 1741 to 1748, no less than three new observatories were erected in Sweden, by the universities of Upsala and Lund and by the Royal Academy of Science at Stockholm. In Vienna, around the middle of the following decade, Empress Maria Theresa purchased the excellent instruments of the local private 'specola' of Giovanni Giacomo de' Marinoni to create the university observatory, not far from the 45-meter high tower erected in 1733 by the Jesuits to house their observatory. In those same years, at Vilnius in Lithuania, Thomas Zebrowski, architect, mathematician and astronomer, promoted the construction of an observatory on the university. This trend progressed so rapidly that a recent study has shown that the number of observatories built later increased exponentially[16].

The territory was covered by that previously mentioned 'network' of researchers, and the new institutions declared their presence and disseminated the results of their research in scientific publications sent to the other observatories. Reading and studying these memorandums and the correspondence between astronomers and institutions provides a priceless tool of knowledge for the astronomy of this period.

And in Italy?

And in Italy, what was happening? From the time of Galileo's first observations conducted at home, first in Padua and then in Florence, what changes had occurred in the situation of astronomers who spent the night observing the sky and the day making calculations on the data collected and attempting to interpret them in the light of the new theories and new models of the cosmos?

The fragmentation of the Italian territory into many states prevented the institution of a national astronomical centre, as had happened in the other European nations, and favoured the development of small 'specole', of greater or lesser importance. In addition to numerous private observatories, the various rulers and city governments wanted to create astronomical facilities, partly for reasons of prestige, since astronomy was deemed sovereign among the other disciplines also by public opinion; but above all because astronomers were for many years assigned other tasks of more practical purpose, if not actually political or military, as has been seen: measuring the territory, controlling watercourses, measuring time, and even conducting meteorological and seismic observations.

The first Italian public astronomical institution, contemporary with that of Berlin, was inaugurated in Bologna through the enlightened efforts of Count Luigi Ferdinando Marsili[17]. Marsili, after having studied mathematics with Giovanni Alfonso Borelli, astronomy with Geminiano Montanari and anatomy with Marcello Malpighi, had turned to the profession of warfare, engaging in military architecture and participating in the campaign that concluded with the rout of the Turks below Vienna. On this occasion he became convinced that only Europe's technical superiority, its military technology, had saved it from the Turks, and that this technical advantage was closely linked to the scientific and technological superiority of the European nations over those of the Turkish Empire. Upon returning to Bologna, where he had created in his home a sort of cenacle for all those interested in the natural sciences and had built an astronomical observatory under the guidance of the young Eustachio Manfredi, one of the founders of the local Accademia degli Inquieti, he decided to donate to the city the naturalist collections, physics apparatus, astronomical instruments and books he had collected for years. Accordingly, on December 12, 1711, the *Istituto delle Scienze di Bologna* was inaugurated, with an Academy of Science and one of Fine Arts, and it was planned to erect an imposing astronomical tower (fig. 5) on the building purchased by the Senate to house the institute. Marsili's program was partially inspired by the models of the *Académie* in Paris and the Royal Society in London. The *Istituto delle Scienze* was not to be merely a place in which to 'discuss' science, as was done in the regular meetings of the societies, but above all a place in which to 'make' science, by means of regular lessons and demonstrations of experiments conducted by the scientists of the Accademia, following the teaching path opened by Galileo when he decided to write his scientific works in the vulgar tongue rather than in Latin. For various reasons, financial above all, the astronomical tower was completed only in 1726, but already two years before Manfredi, who was its first director, had begun to conduct observations. Obviously, for astronomy too the original project was that of finding practical interests in the research carried out: what Manfredi himself called the 'fruits not to be disdained that civil society plucks from astronomy'. Thanks to Manfredi's qualities of acute observer and expert mathematician, the Bologna observatory became a point of excellence for astronomical research in the mid-eighteenth century. The *Ephemerides Bononienses*, a collection of everything useful for astronomical determination of the geographic coordinates of sites, compiled to make such work possible also for non-specialists, remained for decades the most extensive and complete of the many produced in Europe; published starting from 1715, the collection was then continued with the same commitment and high quality by Manfredi's successor, Eustachio Zanotti.

In Italy, inspired by the example of other nations and by the Bologna observatory, numerous other astronomical institutions were built in the second half of the 18th century, many of which are still active in research today. A brief list includes[18]: the observatory of Brera, founded in 1760 in Milan on the roofs of the Jesuit College and totally renovated by Ruggiero Boscovich; the Specola of Parma, erected in 1757 at the university by Jacopo Belgrado, mathematician to the ducal court; the Royal observatory of Turin, begun by Father Giovan Battista Beccaria in 1759 in an old tower, then moved to the Accademia delle Scienze and subsequently, first to Palazzo Madama and lastly to Pino Torinese; the Specola of Padua, planned in 1761 by the Senate of the Republic of Venice and completed in 1779 on the high tower of Castel Vecchio of Ezzelino da Romano; the observatory erected in 1787 at the initiative of Giuseppe Calandrelli in the Jesuit *Collegio Romano*, where Cristoforo Clavio and Christoph Scheiner had conducted observations; and then the last eighteenth-century observatory, that of Palermo, built in 1790 in the tower of Palazzo Reale, at the order of Ferdinand IV of Bourbon. Dating from the early 19th century instead is the Florence observatory, established in the Royal Museum in 1807 by the Queen of Etruria Maria Luisa and moved in 1872, at the initiative of Giovan Battista Donati, to Arcetri, on the hill where Galileo had been confined; the Naples observatory, completed in 1819 on the hill of Miradois at Capodimonte, splendidly constructed and equipped at the order of Ferdinand IV of Bourbon; the observatory of Modena, instituted in 1826 by Duke Francesco IV d'Este on Palazzo Estense; the observatory erected in 1849 in the eastern tower of the Campidoglio in Rome, as replacement for the previously existing private observatory of Feliciano Scarpellini. Other observatories were to be built later. Some of those mentioned here were suppressed or converted to other purposes, some were moved to other locations or opened observational branches far from the city lights. Today, the twelve Italian observatories are managed by the *Istituto Nazionale di Astrofisica*; but this too is another story.

A change of programme?

But what did the astronomers think of this change of programme? Did they have to adapt to devoting enormous amounts of time to the laborious work of geodesy, cartography, nautical tables, etc., to the detriment of their astronomical observations? After having spent centuries trying to describe the universe, were they now limited to 'measuring the Earth', only because this provided them with greater financing?

Obviously, the planning of vast geodetic projects made it possible to bring together groups of experts in the same field, to obtain new and better instrumentation, to develop common and more accurate techniques of observation, and to augment the number of researchers, thus laying the bases for that aforementioned network of scientific connections, which has led over the years to one of the prerogatives of today's international astronomical research, namely the projects for the great telescopes and for space research.

Just as obviously, the program for 'measuring the Earth' has allowed astronomers to determine the meridian arc length though extensive campaigns of triangulation, and to discover the imperfectly spherical shape of the Earth, based on variation in the period of oscillation of a pendulum at different latitudes; and thus to determine the real dimensions of our planet. From measurements performed by two observation stations not far from each other, at a known distance on the terrestrial surface, it was possible to determine the angular distance of Mars (the parallax); from this the distance between the Earth and the Sun could be deduced with precision of less than a second of arc, and then the distances of all of the other planets from Kepler's Third Law, their orbital periods being known, and finally, the real dimensions of our solar system. But these measurements, the size of the Earth and its distance from the Sun, determined between the 17th and 18th centuries, mainly by scientists operating in the big observatories, represent only the very first steps on the scale of astronomical distances. Astronomers call the Sun-Earth distance the Astronomical Unit, because it is on this unit of measurement that are based the distances of the nearby stars and then those of the distant ones, calculated through methods that are increasing refined and complex, but that must perforce be based on these first steps. Only in this way has it been possible to construct the modern image of the cosmos and to continue the work begun by Galileo on that night 400 years ago.

And so those astronomers, in devoting their efforts to 'measuring the Earth', had not really changed their research programme. They managed in fact to 'measure the Universe'; and those 'fruits not to be disdained that civil society plucks from astronomy', to gather which the first 'modern astronomical observatories' were built, have been transformed into 'fruits' that astronomy has plucked from 'civil society'.

–

Bibliography

Baiada-Bònoli-Braccesi 1995; Bònoli 2002, pp. 133-157; Bònoli-Foderà Serio-Poppi 2005, pp. 29-72; Bònoli-Parmeggiani-Poppi 2006; Cassini 1668; Cassini 1695; Chapman 1983, pp. 133-137; Débarbat-Grillot-Lévy 1990; Galilei 1610a, vol. X, letter n. 435, p. 483; Galilei 1612, vol. V, pp. 413-425 and ff.; Galilei 1616a, vol. XII, letter n. 1197, pp. 255-256; Galilei 1616b, vol. XII, letters n. 1201 and ff., pp. 260-261, 265 and ff.; Galilei 1618, vol. XII, letters n. 1324, pp. 389-392; Galilei 1630a, vol. VII, pp. 388-389; Galilei 1630b, vol. VII, pp. 409-416; Greenwich 1975; Hermann 1973, pp. 57-58; Howse 1986 and 1994, pp 207-218; Krisciunas 1988; North 1981, vol. 6, p. 364; Stroobant et al. 1931; Van Helden 1996, pp. 86-100.

[1] Krisciunas 1988.
[2] Ferguson K. 2003.
[3] Bònoli 2002.
[4] Galilei 1610a.
[5] Galilei 1630a.
[6] Galilei 1630b.
[7] Galilei 1612, 1616a, 1616b and 1618; Van Helden 1996
[8] Bònoli-Parmeggiani-Poppi 2006.
[9] Cassini 1668.
[10] Cassini 1695.
[11] Greenwich 1975.
[12] Greenwich 1975.
[13] North 1981, Chapman 1983.
[14] Hawse 1986 and 1994, Stroobant et al. 1931.
[15] Krisciunas 1988.
[16] Hermann 1973.
[17] Baiada-Bònoli-Braccesi 1995.
[18] Bònoli-Foderà Serio-Poppi 2005.

288

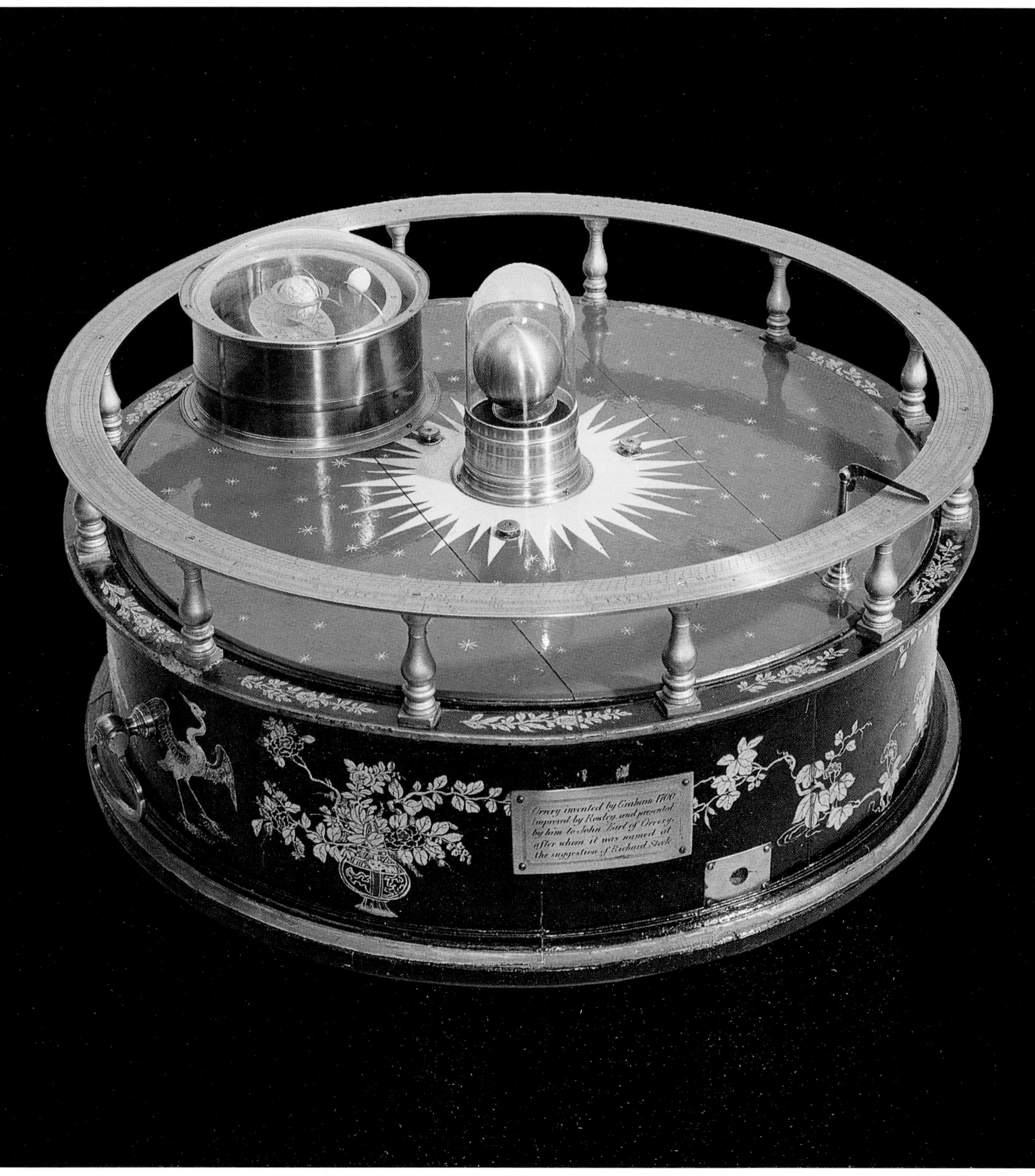
Orrery invented by Graham 1700
Improved by Rowley and presented
by him to John Earl of Orrery
after whom it was named at
the suggestion of Richard Steele

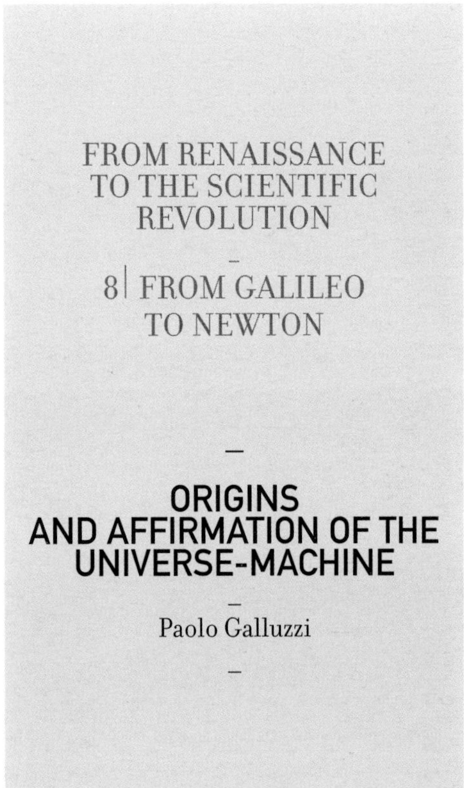

FROM RENAISSANCE TO THE SCIENTIFIC REVOLUTION

–

8| FROM GALILEO TO NEWTON

–

ORIGINS AND AFFIRMATION OF THE UNIVERSE-MACHINE

–

Paolo Galluzzi

–

It is frequently said that, although Galileo did not invent the telescope, he was the first to point it toward the celestial vault, urged on by the firm conviction that the phenomena revealed by the lenses were a true picture of reality.

Less frequently has the question been posed as to why, among all those in Europe who handled the first optical tubes from the Netherlands, the idea of using them to scrutinize the celestial bodies sprang into the mind of Galileo alone. Thomas Harriot had in reality preceded him by a few months, but without achieving the extraordinary results attained by Galileo (cf. entries VII.4.3-5).

The explanation is probably a simple one. Galileo was more prepared than other natural philosophers to seek through direct observation of the sky answers to the questions that thronged his mind. Since the beginning of his career, in fact, he had been intensely devoted to investigating the great world-machine, endeavouring to discover the laws that govern its operation.

Until a few years ago, one of the unanimously shared assumptions in the vast Galilean historiography was that of a sharp separation in his scientific interests between developing a rigorous science of natural and violent motions, on the one hand, and providing convincing proof of the Copernican vision of the universe on the other. Galileo was thought to have continuously pursued the latter objective only after he had used the telescope for astronomical observations (that is, during the second half of 1609), having been wholly absorbed in *de motu* studies during previous years. According to this scheme, only at the end of his life did Galileo, prevented from continuing his cosmological studies by the dramatic ecclesiastical condemnation of 1633, return to the long neglected research in mechanics, the results of which he finally published in the *Discorsi e dimostrazioni matematiche* [Discourses and mathematical demonstrations] (Leiden 1638).

One of the most penetrating works in all of Galilean historiography, the now somewhat outdated *Galilean Studies* by Alexander Koyré, published for the first time between 1935 and 1939, had in fact proposed a different reading of the relationship between mechanics and cosmology throughout the entire span of Galileo's intellectual biography. The great historian of science was the first to realise that Galileo's innovative research on motion had served an essential function in his drive to confirm the truth of the heliocentric system. Koyré, in fact, showed the intelligent use to which Galilco put the new concepts of motion (relativity, conservation, composition, circular inertia, etc.) to support the thesis of Copernicus (1473-1543) and, above all, to demolish the objections (all based on the incompatibility of the Earth's motion with the basic concepts of Aristotelian dynamics) that had been raised to the heliocentric system, declaring it to be absurd and the claims of its advocates ridiculous. Admittedly, the Copernican system could be used as a hypothesis for simplifying calculations, but its author's claim that it was physically true was to be staunchly rejected. Koyré's extraordinary contribution to the understanding of Galileo's project (grounding the reform of cosmology in a radical reformation in the concept of motion) depended mainly on his very perceptive reading of the *Dialogo sopra i due massimi sistemi del mondo* [Dialogue on the two chief world systems] (Florence 1632). Since the convergence between mechanics and cosmology first appeared in a late work, it remained possible to ascribe it to the final stage of Galileo's intellectual experience while retaining the traditional interpretation of a man of a dual nature: the brilliant investigator of motion and the convinced Copernican, alleged to have co-existed as total strangers almost all his life. Galileo himself contributed – albeit for reasons of *force majeure* – to accrediting this sharp juxtaposition. The condemnation inflicted on him by the Church in 1633 had in fact brutally silenced his passionate Copernican advocacy. So that his voice might still be heard, Galileo decided to make public his innovative conclusions on the nature of motion in the *Discorsi e dimostrazioni*. In his last work he had to omit the explicit references to the vital support to the Copernican hypothesis provided by the new science *de motu* that he had clearly stated in the *Dialogo*. Even today, often for apologetic reasons, there are those who acclaim the *Discorsi e dimostrazioni* - the result of painful self-censuring - as Galileo's real masterpiece, relegating the *Dialogo* – full of erroneous theories (the interpretations of the tides and comets) and of the residue of pre-scientific mentalities (circular orbits, the uniform velocity of the planets, etc.) – to the category of works that have not stood up to the severe test of progress in knowledge.

For Galileo, however, the *Dialogo* was the work of a lifetime, the culmination of his most ambitious project. The fact that, read from the perspective of today's state of scientific knowledge, this work appears less innovative than the *Discorsi*, should not blind us to the reasons for the crucial importance assigned it by its author: to demonstrate that it was possible to found on a new concept of motion an organic physical theory able to deliver the Copernican vision from the accusation of absurdity, thus freeing it from its narrow confinement within the realm of purely hypothetical concepts.

Several important works have contributed in recent years to revealing this essential motivation behind Galileo's research. The books of two scholars in particular must be mentioned. In the first place, Maurice Clavelin[1] has provided ample evidence not only of Galileo's constant interest in cosmology during his years in Padua (1592-1609), well before the advent of the telescope, but also of the direct relationship between some of Galileo's most painstaking studies on motion and the fundamental issues raised by Copernican cosmology. The most organic reconstruction of the programmatic alliance between mechanics and cosmology in Galileo is however Massimo Bucciantini's *Galileo e Keplero*[2]. This contribution is extraordinarily convincing. Evidence taken from documents and furnished by a penetrating analysis of the macro-context in which the Pisan scientist operated, with special attention to his relations with the German world, until now only marginally investigated, present us with a scenario totally different from that of the mechanics-cosmology dichotomy of historiographic tradition. There emerges the image of a natural philosopher, precociously Copernican, who resolutely undertakes the ambitious project of radically reforming the Aristotelian concept of motion to demonstrate the groundlessness of the objections moved by natural philosophers to the heliocentric theory. Raised already in antiquity against the Pythagorean doctrines, these objections had been revived and refined by the great Danish astronomer Tycho Brahe (1546-1601). Brahe had maintained that, based on principles of Aristotelian dynamics, the motion attributed to the Earth by Copernicus would have produced devastating consequences on the surface of our planet. Since these consequences did not occur, the heliocentric concept was proven groundless.

The new historiographic perspective allows us to attribute more precise significance to the explicit declarations of adhesion to Copernicus' ideas expressed by Galileo as early as 1597 in a letter to his old master in Pisa, Iacopo Mazzoni (1548-1598) and, above all, in his reply to Johannes Kepler (1571-1630) thanking him for having sent a copy of his *Mysterium Cosmographicum* (Tubing 1596). In this letter, Galileo informed his German colleague that the Copernican hypothesis allowed him to furnish convincing explanations of hitherto inexplicable natural phenomena. In all probability the Pisan scientist was referring to the tides, which some years later (in the letter to Cardinal Orsini dated January 1616 that circulated in manuscript form, and lastly in the *Giornata Quarta* [Fourth day] of the *Dialogo* of 1632) he was to interpret as due to the combined effect of the Earth's daily and annual motions.

The ensemble of evidence on the very strong connection, since the beginning of Galileo's research, between mechanics and cosmology helps to explain why he was the first to feel the need to aim the telescope at the sky, searching not only for unheard of novelties, but also for evidence that would definitively confirm his own Copernican beliefs. For Galileo, looking at the sky through the lenses of a telescope meant first of all verifying the grounds for his attempt to explain the motions of the celestial bodies according to the same principles that govern the motion of bodies on the Earth's surface. Galileo's working hypothesis was based in fact on the indispensable premise of the homogeneity of the universe. And it called for demonstrating the absurdity of Aristotle's sharp distinction between the elementary world (the terrestrial one), subject to change, and the celestial sphere, the realm of absolute perfection, where motion took place only at constant speed around circular orbits. The discoveries of the Moon's rough surface, of dark spots on the Sun and of satellites orbiting around Jupiter reinforced Galileo's belief that the celestial bodies did not differ physically from the Earth, increasing his conviction that the principles of the new mathematical science of the natural motion of falling bodies on Earth that he was then elaborating could also account for the dynamics of the heavens.

This was the operation that Galileo attempted to carry out in the *Dialogo* albeit with the masking and precautions imposed on him by the threatening admonitions issued by the ecclesiastical authorities at the conclusion of the so-called 'first trial' in 1616. It is significant that, had he not clashed with the adamant opposition of the ecclesiastical censors, Galileo would have given his masterpiece a different title – *Del flusso e reflusso del mare* [On the ebb and flow of the tides] – expressing much more clearly his real objective, that of grounding the truth of the Copernican hypothesis on the radical reform of the Aristotelian concept of motion. In the *Dialogo* Galileo did not present a new world system, limiting himself to proposing that of Copernicus just as it was. But he provided conceptual tools essential for demonstrating its reasonableness and clearing the field of the objections that

1. Page 288, John Rowley, *Orrery*, 1712-1713, Science Museum, London.

2. The zodiacal armillary of Tycho Brahe's observatory; *Astronomiae Instauratae Mechanica*, Wandesburg 1598.

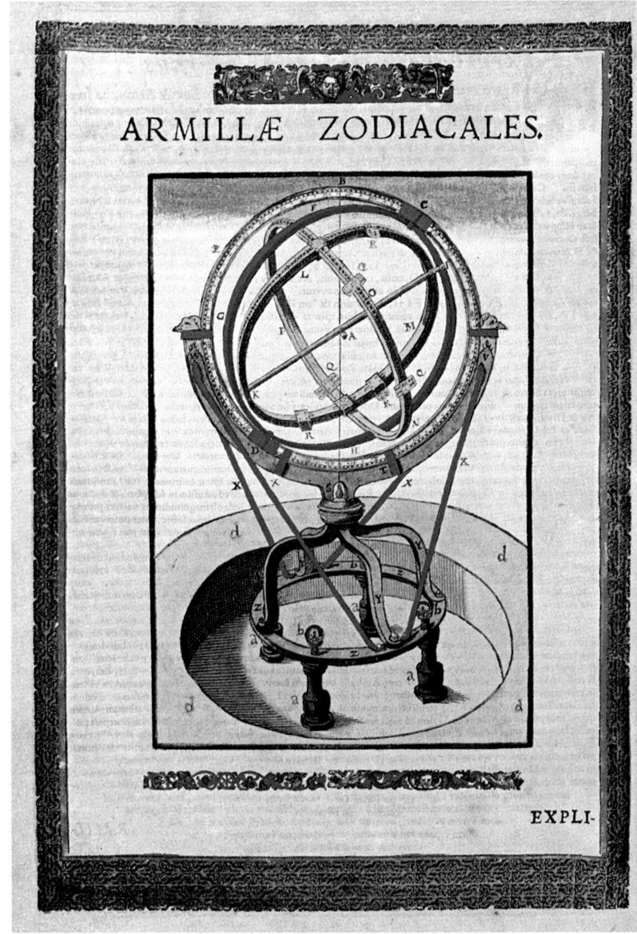

had hitherto prevented its affirmation. Through one of those singular coincidences that often occur in the history of the development of human knowledge, in those same months of 1609 when Galileo was beginning to scrutinize the sky with the telescope, there was published in Germany the *opus magnum* of an illustrious colleague, Johannes Kepler, with whom he had not been in touch since the brief exchange of letters in 1597. Kepler was no longer the young, almost unknown, mathematician, who had sent his colleague in Padua his first book, hoping to inaugurate profitable collaboration in the name of their common Copernican orientation. Having succeeded Tycho Brahe (fig. 3) in the prestigious position of Imperial Mathematician, already the author of mathematical and optical works of the highest quality, in 1609 Kepler was also famous as astronomer. The title of his new publication eloquently expressed his innovative programme: *Astronomia Nova, seu Physica Coelestis* [New Astronomy or Celestial Physics] (Prague 1609). The subtitle in particular clarified what the innovation consisted of: the celestial world was investigated by recurring to the principles of physics, and planetary motions were explained by the same laws employed to account for the motion of bodies on the surface of the Earth. Defining the 'new' astronomy as a 'physics of the skies' represented a revolutionary change. It meant manifesting full conviction of the structural homogeneity of the universe, and thus taking an unequivocal stance against the sharp distinction between the Earth and the celestial world posited by traditional natural philosophy.

It has been justly said that with Kepler's book, forces enter astronomy for the first time. The fragmentation of the solid orbs of the celestial sphere in the system of Tycho Brahe – who left as legacy to Kepler the immense treasure of astronomical data accumulated in twenty years of research using observation and measurement instruments of amazing precision (fig. 2) – and the evidence he had furnished of the superlunary course of comets, imposed acceptance of the hypothesis of fluid skies. The support provided by solids orbs having vanished, it became necessary to explain what caused the planets to remain stable in their orbits. While Galileo had explained the stability of planetary motions by the principle of 'circular inertia' (the natural tendency of all bodies moving in a circle at uniform speed to remain in that state), Kepler determined to find the physical cause. As he wrote to Longomontanus (1562-1642), who had been Tycho's chief assistant, he aimed to definitively break the barrier that had until then separated physics from astronomy: 'Both the sciences are so closely linked that neither of the two can reach perfection without the other'.

In pages that represent a crucial step in the great human adventure of exploring the cosmos, Kepler relates the exceedingly arduous process through which he managed to decipher the secret concealed in the great world-machine. The solid basis of departure consisted of Tycho Brahe's collection of data from observations, with which the general physical theory Kepler intended to formulate had to comply precisely. To the concreteness of the data – ineluctable term of comparison – was coupled the metaphysical assumption that the force compelling the planets to move in their orbits at their specific speeds originates from the Sun. Already formulated by Keplerin the *Mysterium Cosmographicum* of 1596, this thesis was based on the observation that the orbital velocities of the planets decrease constantly with their increasing distances from the Sun. While Mercury is the fastest planet, the slowest orbital motion is that of Saturn. Having identified the Sun as the seat of the force that moves the planets, Kepler supposed that this force decreases in proportion to distance (and not to the square of distance, like light, to which he explicitly compares it).

In the *Astronomia nova*, Kepler's design assumes a clearer configuration. If the Sun is the seat of motive force, it must necessarily be considered the real, physical centre of the cosmic system. Following an ancient tradition, Tycho had related the motions of the planets moving in circumsolar orbits to the 'mean' Sun, that is, to a point eccentric to its real position. This stratagem allowed the Danish astronomer to keep the planets moving in circular orbits at uniform speeds, thus obtaining an acceptable approximation between theory and data based on observations. Driven by the desire to establish a physically true system, Kepler was unable to accept this expedient (which in the geocentric tradition was applied to the 'mean' Earth). He thus undertook a new series of exhausting calculations to determine the distances of the planets (Earth included, since he was a convinced Copernican) from the 'true' Sun. Keeping the observational data of which he disposed as basic reference, Kepler was still unable to formulate a convincing theory, based on the hypothesis of motion at constant speed in circular orbits to predict the positions of the planetary bodies. He focussed his attention on Mars (Tycho had assigned him the task of determining its orbit when he summoned him to Prague in February 1600). Utilising the very precise data of which he disposed on the orbit of Mars, he engaged in a gigantic effort of calculation to define more precisely that of the Earth in relation to the 'true' Sun. This was a crucially important operation, since all astronomical measurements are made from the Earth. He thus discovered a non-negligible eccentricity of the Earth (unknown even to Copernicus) in relation to the 'true' Sun. Combining this fact with the principle of inverse proportion between the orbital velocity of planets and their distance from the Sun, Kepler was obliged to conclude that the Earth moves along its orbit (which at this point he still believed to be circular) at a continuously variable speed.

This powerful blow from Kepler thus shattered one of the fundamental paradigms of traditional cosmology (still accepted by Galileo): that which assigned uniform speed to all planetary motions.

A new challenge immediately faced the German mathematician; how could the point in its orbit that the Earth would occupy at a certain moment in the future be determined? To answer this question it was necessary to establish a precise relationship between the distances covered by the Earth along its orbit and the times employed to traverse them. Recurring to the method of exhaustion used by Archimedes to square the circle, Kepler divided the circumference described by the eccentric terrestrial orbit around the 'true' Sun into infinite segments of continuously variable length. He then considered each of the bands formed by the infinite contiguous segments as equivalent to the corresponding sector of the orbital circle. Applying the principle of inverse proportionality between distance from the Sun and orbital velocity, he was able to formulate the law universally known today as Kepler's 'second law' (or 'law of areas'): the radius vector (the line that connects the planet to the 'true' Sun) sweeps over equal areas during equal intervals of times. This means that the Earth moves at minimum speed up to the aphelion, having passed which it accelerates until reaching maximum speed at the perihelion. Geometry and physics thus appeared perfectly integrated. The calculations in fact, strictly accounted for the harmony of the cosmos, while the motive power of the Sun evidenced the forces that kept the world-machine cohesive and stable.

Success in determining the Earth's orbit allowed Kepler to face the problem of defining that of Mars with more satisfactory tools of analysis. But the assault on Mars was to prove much more arduous. The procedure that had been applied to the Earth failed to yield the expected results. Discrepancy with the observational data remained too great. Although Kepler gradually realised that the red planet does not move along a circular orbit, he encountered enormous difficulty in determining its true nature. Numerous chapters in the *Astronomia nova* reveal his tormented attempts to reconcile theory and data and bear witness to his tremendous labour of calculation. The firm conviction that the harmony governing the universe is intrinsically mathematical urged him to seek for a curve that, although alternative to the circumference, was regular. At last his superhuman efforts were repaid: the orbits of the planets are elliptical and the Sun occupies one of the two foci (the so-called 'first law', although formulated after the 'second'). Kepler verified that the 'law of areas' (the 'first law') remains equally valid in the case of elliptical orbits. The second fundamental paradigm of traditional astronomy – that celestial bodies moved only in perfectly circular orbits – accepted even by Copernicus and Galileo, was thus demolished. Kepler's enthusiasm was boundless. As he was to write in dedicating the *Astronomia nova* to his patron, Emperor Rudolph II (1552-1612), the hard-fought battle with Mars had concluded with the unconditional surrender of his belligerent adversary:

> I lead into the presence of Your Majesty a most noble prisoner [the planet Mars], captured by me in a hard, laborious war [...]. This is he who had triumphed over all human inventions, mocking all of the astronomer's campaigns [...]. The enemy, seeing me resolved to go to all lengths and feeling himself no longer secure at any point in his realm, resigned himself to peace; and with the intermediation of his mother, Nature, confessed to me his defeat, and surrendering on his word, passed over into my camp, escorted by arithmetic and geometry [...]. The war offers no more danger, since Mars is in our hands.[3]

The universe displayed a new countenance, revealing a perfectly harmonious interwoven fabric. The search for the harmonic structure of the cosmos – mathematical and musical harmony (in the *Harmonices Mundi* of 1619 he was to advance the hypothesis that the notes of true celestial music are emitted by continuous variations in the speed of the planets) – was from the outset a true obsession for Kepler, who devoted himself body and soul to astronomy for profoundly theological motivations. The rigorously harmonious project of creation now revealed itself clearly to him . The number of the planets depended on the selection of the five perfect solids as archetypal models (a concept already expressed in the *Mysterium Cosmographicum*). The Sun was not only the source of light, but also the seat of the motive force that drives with variations in intensity established by geometry the perfect world-machine, in which the planets proceed along elliptical orbits at speeds proportional to their distance from the Sun. Not even the positioning of the five planets in celestial space and their different velocities appeared random. The 'third law' published by Kepler in the *Harmonices Mundi* showed the exquisitely harmonic nature of these distinctive characteristics of the world-machine, evidencing the precise proportional relationship, valid for all of the planets, between the time employed to complete their orbits and the size of these orbits. Kepler's 'third law' states in fact that the squares of the orbital periods have the same relationship to one another as the cubes of the major semi-axes of the elliptical orbits.

While geometric models and analogy with musical harmony were tools that had always been used in efforts to decipher the secrets of the universe, extending physical investigation to the celestial world constituted a revolutionary innovation. In this Kepler followed, with original methods and with different motivations, the path first opened by Galileo. For both, the basic point of reference was the change of scenario introduced by Copernicus' *De revolutionibus*. As strongly convinced as Galileo of the mathematical structure of the universe, Kepler had put all his energy into discovcring the rules of cosmic harmony, venturing even further than his Italian colleague in the effort to formulate an organic physical theory capable of explaining the operation of the celestial machine. While in the *Mysterium* the motive force attributed to the Sun was still considered an 'animal' force, Kepler's subsequent reading of *De magnete* (London 1600) by Gilbert (1544-1603) – which had produced a striking impression on Galileo as well – urged him to seek a physical explanation of the fundamental energy that keeps the cosmos in ordered motion. In the *Astronomia nova* Kepler accepted the hypothesis advanced by Copernicus that the Sun rotates around its own axis (Galileo was to confirm its truth a little later, based on his telescopic observation of sunspots). According to Kepler, the rotation of the Sun constrains the planets to move in their orbits, like a whirlpool entraining the bodies immersed in it. In the *Astronomia nova* the elliptical nature of the orbits, as well as the accelerations and decelerations of celestial motions, are attributed to magnetic interactions between the Sun and the planets, considered to be magnets. Kepler states that magnetic power is proportional to the mass of a body. For this reason the attractive force of the Sun is enormously greater than that of the planets (which however do exert attraction on the Sun). The planets are drawn towards the Sun when the two opposing magnetic poles are close and they are repelled when the two equal poles are close. The periodic moving towards and away from the Sun caused by magnetic interaction explains why the orbits of the planets are elliptical (with the Sun in one of the foci, and the continuous variation in their speed, given that it is inversely proportional to the planet's distance from the Sun.

While the attraction and repulsion between the Sun and the planets appeared to many (almost certainly including Galileo) hypotheses too closely linked to animistic concepts, Kepler remained fully convinced of being able to transform the cosmos from an 'animal machine' into a clock or perfect organ, in which every motion was produced by harmonious mechanical actions.

Kepler died before the publication of Galileo's *Dialogo*. It is unlikely that this great text would have satisfied him, due to its fragmentary nature, to the frequent lengthy digressions and, above all, to the absence of any reference to the great methodological and 'philosophical' innovations he had introduced. The only physical proof of the Copernican system offered by Galileo in this text – the explanation of the tides as resulting from the combination of the Earth's diurnal and annual motions – would not have met with the approval of the German mathematician, who attributed the ebb and flow of the sea to the magnetic attraction exerted by the Moon. Moreover, the caution with which Galileo presented the arguments supporting the heliocentric concept would have appeared to Kepler – who had always refused to bend his thought to fit the prescriptions of the ecclesiastical authorities – as the expression of an inadmissible renunciation to peremptorily expressing his own ideas, and thus contributing to the search for truth and the discovery of the grandeur of the universe, the work of a perfect Being.

Although he had not read the *Dialogo*, Kepler had devoted great attention to Galileo's *Sidereus Nuncius* [Starry messenger], firmly contributing to quelling the opposition it had aroused and lending the decisive support of his scientific authority to the astronomical discoveries made by Galileo thanks to the telescope. Starting with the letter written to Galileo in 1597, Kepler had urged him to abandon all hesitation, and to fully commit himself to affirming the truth. He had addressed to his Italian colleague a number of heartfelt pleas, inviting him to speak out clearly on the great questions posed by the cosmos: the nature and the meaning of its structure, its purposes, the laws and reasons for its harmony, the role of man in creation, the existence of human beings on other celestial bodies, and whether the universe were finite or infinite. As we know, Galileo did not accept this challenge. Kepler's demands and the manner in which he formulated them already indicated the answers that the German scientist hoped to receive from Galileo. But Galileo had a different agenda. The confirmation he wished to confer on the Copernican hypothesis had to be based on experimentation and mathematical demonstrations. Through a patient process of observation and mathematical reasoning, Galileo intended to demonstrate that the universe is written in mathematical terms and that it is the theatre of strictly harmonic laws. Harmony, symmetry and mathematical order in the architecture of the universe would be revealed for Galileo at the conclusion of a process of research. They did not constitute – as for Kepler – the metaphysical and theological assumption that must necessarily be confirmed by the interpretative analysis of data from observations.

Kepler's cosmological commitment had rested on a predominant theological motivation that was to remain unchanged throughout his career. Although today, again for apologetic exigencies, there is a tendency to exalt Galileo's fundamental contribution to Biblical exegesis with his extraordinary 'Copernican letters', Galileo was not a theologian, nor would he ever have devoted his time to elaborating theological arguments and interpretations had he not been obliged to do so in self-defence. The Pisan scientist considered the endeavour to approach the truth an objective to be pursued exclusively through reason

3. Tycho Brahe (1546-1601).

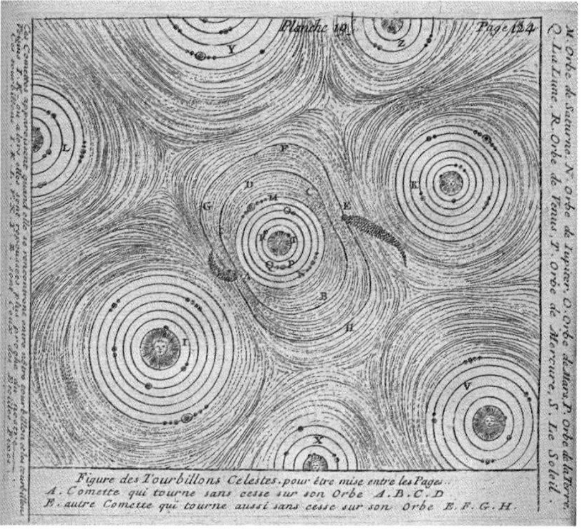

4. Descartes' universe of vortices; after Nicolas Bion, *L'usage des globes célestes et terrestres*, Paris 1699.

and attentive observation of natural phenomena, without recurring to any metaphysical principle to unveil the most recondite mysteries of the universe.

Engaged in combating common enemies, both promoters of a radical reform of the image of the cosmos, Galileo and Kepler were attuned to profoundly different wavelengths. This helps to explain why they did not join forces against the powerful bloc hostile to the new celestial physics, based on the alliance between traditional natural philosophy and ecclesiastical authority. Seen from the contemporary viewpoint, the telescope, the roughness of the Moon's surface, the sunspots and phases of Venus appear as acquisitions fully consonant with the discoveries of elliptical orbits, of variable speeds in planetary revolutions and of the existence of forces that hold the universe harmoniously together. But to their contemporaries and the leading figures of the following generations, Galileo and Kepler were not perceived in any way as companions in adventure. On the contrary, their contributions were interpreted as alternative models for bringing about a reformation in knowledge. The influence of Galileo was curtailed by his dramatic ecclesiastical condemnation and the prohibition of the *Dialogo* in 1633. Kepler's cosmological works had a limited number of readers (and even fewer admirers and followers) due to their intrinsic difficulty and to the combination, which appeared unacceptable to many, of precise observational data and rigorous mathematical demonstrations, on the one hand, with metaphysical assumptions and theological motivations on the other. Galileo's vision of the unity of terrestrial and celestial dynamics was to form the point of departure for the great figures who were to bring the revolution in astronomy to completion. Kepler's three laws were to remain, on the other hand, the obligatory term of reference in the following decades both for the advocates of astronomical observation, dedicated to collecting ever more precise data thanks to the progressive perfecting of observational instruments, and for the natural philosophers striving to understand nature and the operation of the forces that constrain celestial bodies to occupy certain positions and move along certain orbits at determined velocities.

During the third decade of the 17th century, which saw the death of Kepler (1630), the dramatic condemnation of Galileo under vehement suspicion of heresy (1633), the definitive banning of the Copernican theory, a young Frenchman, René Descartes (1596-1650) was engaged in writing a book presenting an original theory of the Universe, based on a strictly mechanistic view, on the assumption of the unity of terrestrial and celestial physics and on explicit adhesion to the Copernican concept. The work in question, *The World, or Treatise on Light*, was written in French and had already been drafted in 1630. Descartes planned to publish the book in 1633, although perfectly aware that it might appear too audacious to the censors. Accordingly, he decided to present his revolutionary ideas as a 'fable', not only as a precautionary measure but also to facilitate and lighten the path leading to the discovery of the truth:

> Let your thoughts then leave this world for a little while, and come to see another, very new one, that I will cause to be born before your eyes in imaginary space. [4]

As soon as Descartes received news of Galileo's condemnation he abandoned his plans for publication:

> I have heard that [...] Galileo's World System has been printed in Italy [and that] all of the copies have been burned and its author condemned [...]. I was so struck by this fact that I almost decided to burn all of my papers [...]. I recognise that if [this opinion] is false, then so are all of the bases of my philosophy.
>
> (Letter to Marin Mersenne, late November 1633)

Unlike that of Galileo and Kepler, Descartes' reasoning is entirely *a priori*. The French philosopher did not take into account observational data and limited recourse to mathematical demonstrations, entrusting the construction of his universe to the deduction of phenomena from clear, distinct principles. For Descartes, God is the author of the fundamental laws and the component elements from which, through purely mechanical processes, the world we know progressively takes shape. Having established the laws and created the materials, God withdraws from the world.

The elements of the Cartesian universe are homogeneous particles that differ only in form, size and motion. The first element consists of agitated particles, flexible, tiny and unstable in form (the element of fire). The second element is formed of round particles that move more slowly and are larger in size (the element of water). The third element consists of particles of great size, extremely slow and cubic in form. The space of the Cartesian world is full. The existence of a void is resolutely rejected as absurd. Through a penetrating demonstration of the purely subjective nature of the secondary qualities (odours, tastes, colours, hardness, etc.), Descartes reduces the matter that fills the space of his world to pure extension: a homogeneous space, like that of Euclidean geometry. In Descartes' universe, devoid of centre or boundaries, no distinction is made between the terrestrial and the celestial world. God has created matter-extension, has set it in motion destined to remain constant in quantity and has established the laws that have formed the world, and which confer on it perennial stability. The world is a clock, programmed by a craftsman so perfect as to require neither maintenance nor repair. The universal and necessary laws established by God in the act of creation define the basic properties of motion, the fundamental agent of the Cartesian universe. The first law states that each particle of matter always remains in the same state unless collision with other particles forces it to change. The second law states that the quantity of motion originally imparted by God to matter-extension remains constant: when one body pushes another it cannot give the other any motion except by losing as much of its own motion at the same time, nor can it remove motion from the other body without augmenting its own in the same measure[5]. Accordingly, motion does not 'exhaust itself'– as maintained by Aristotelian physics and the medieval *impetus* – but passes continuously from one body to another, without change in its overall quantity. The theory of conservation of the quantity of motion constitutes the basis for the third law, which presents the first organic formulation of the principle of inertia: when a body moves, even if it moves mainly along a curve, its parts always tend to continue their motion in a straight line[6].

Once the fundamental laws have been established, the homogeneous matter that fills space has been created and the necessary amount of motion imparted to it, the processes that lead to the formation of the world in which we live commence. The world assumes form through the purely mechanical action of matter in motion. On agitating matter-extension, motion causes it to fragment into three elements of different forms and dimensions (fire, water and earth). Since the world is full, the only motion possible for the three elements is circular. The particles are distributed at different distances from the centre, in respect to which they rotate according to their size and speed. Vortexes of matter are thus formed, at the edges of which cluster the largest and heaviest particles (the third element – earth – of which the planets and comets are made), entrained in their orbits at great speed. The particles of the second element form the skies, while at the centre of the vortexes converge the lighter, more mobile particles of the first element giving life to the Sun and the fixed stars. The vortexes are formed through strictly mechanical action. Matter and motion alone form a perfect cosmogony, compelling the bodies to distribute themselves according to precise rules in the spaces of the innumerable vortexes, one contiguous to another, that throng the universe. Light and gravity are also interpreted by Descartes as phenomena produced by purely mechanical action. Light loses its nature of substance, reduced to the sensation generated by pressure exerted by the moving particles on the organ of sight. Gravity, on the other hand, ceases to be an intrinsic property of bodies. Descartes was the first to explain that what we call gravity is the consequence of mechanical action exerted on bodies from the outside (the pressure toward the centre of particles in motion). Since for Descartes pressure is proportional to the surface on which it is exerted, the largest bodies are the heaviest.

Published for the first time in French in Paris in 1664 after the death of Descartes (1650), the 'fable' of *The World* remained unknown to his contemporaries. But his peculiar interpretation of the structure of the universe and the laws of motion that generated and govern it was divulged, with additions and explanations, in the *Principia philosophiae*, published in Amsterdam in 1644. The *Principia* was conceived as a manual of natural philosophy that, in the hopes of its author, would help to spread his ideas in schools, thus undermining the monopoly of the Jesuits. For this purpose he had divided the discussion into dense sequences of short paragraphs, systematically avoiding mathematical demonstrations. While Descartes' hopes for the success of the *Principia* as a teaching manual were disappointed, his physics of vortexes (fig. 4) – due to its radical mechanistic approach – exerted a powerful influence on researchers striving all over Europe to design an entirely new philosophy of nature, in which rational interpretation of the structure and dynamics of the cosmos was to be a fundamental chapter.

In France, Gassendi (1592-1655), who grasped more clearly than anyone else the new implications of the Galilean alliance between mechanics and cosmology, in Holland Huygens (1629-1695), and in England Hooke (1635-1702) were influenced to various degrees by Cartesian physics. And vast numbers of brilliant innovators viewed the body of organic knowledge (mathematics, medicine, metaphysics, logic, physics and religion) of the Cartesian system as an essential reference to be taken into account.

Vehemently opposed by the Jesuits (whom Descartes had mistakenly believed he could persuade to accept his ideas), by the Catholic hierarchies (the expulsion of God from the world, the concept of man and the universe as machines, the substantial atomism, although without the void, and the negation of miracles made him an enemy to be staunchly opposed) and by the followers of the Scholastic philosophy, Descartes' system was to be heatedly discussed by European scholars for many decades to come.

Among those who acknowledged the importance of Descartes' work was the young Isaac Newton (1642-1727), who was however progressively moving away from the physics of vortexes. Basing himself on Galileo's analysis of natural motion, on Descartes' revolutionary concept of motion (rectilinear inertia, impact laws, etc.) and on Huygens' discovery of the true nature of centrifugal force and its formula, Newton (who declared, not without reason, that he had been able to see far because he stood on the shoulders of giants) developed a new organic physics. The force that governs the complex dynamic phenomena of the entire universe is gravitational attraction, whose intensity is inversely proportional to the square of the distance and directly proportional to the quantity of matter (mass) of bodies. In his extraordinary work of synthesis, the *Philosophiae naturalis principia mathematica* (London 1687), Newton explained, through the action of this force, the structure of the entire universe as well as all the motions observed on the surface of our planet and in celestial space. From the motion of planets at variable speed along elliptical orbits, to the periodic motion of comets, from falling bodies to the ebb and flow of the sea on Earth, all phenomena could be explained by recurring to a very limited number of axioms and affirming the existence of a single force that exerts its power from the centre of the Earth to the furthest boundaries of the universe. Starting from these principles, through rigorous mathematical processes, Newton deduced the three laws that Kepler had formulated inductively on the basis of observation data. Newton's universe seemed a structure ordered according to infallible mathematical principles, whose image was perceived by many as that of a perfect machine. Nonetheless – unlike Descartes – the author of the *Principia* nourished the conviction that the great clock of the universe could not function without continuous divine intervention. After the act of creation, Newton's God had not abandoned the world. Ubiquitously and eternally present in absolute space and time, God guaranteed the stability of the universe. He constantly intervened to prevent gravitational interaction from producing imbalance that would cause the universe to collapse, with the masses of all the planets concentrating in a single body. Like Kepler, Newton deemed mathematics the essential tool for understanding and describing nature and the works of the divinity, who governs the world through universal attraction, a force that acts in a non-mechanical manner. In Newton's universe, in the spaces pervaded by the ambiguous substance of an ultra-fine aether, attraction exerts its force at a distance, with no physical contact between bodies. For the numerous and authoritative followers of Descartes on the Continent, action at a distance without contact was an unacceptable concept, a return to the 'occult qualities' of Aristotelian natural philosophy that had been definitively banned by Descartes.

Thus by a paradox of history, he who had devised a system able to furnish a transparent, rational explanation of the structure and workings of the universe based on mathematics, observation and experiments, appeared to the followers of systems, like that of Descartes, structurally dependent on metaphysical assumptions and founded on audacious hypotheses, as threatening to restore the ancient manner of philosophising.

While the debate between Cartesians and Newtonians, between resolute mechanists and advocates of 'experimental philosophy' continued to rage throughout the course of the 18th century, the concept of God as perfect clockmaker and the image of the universe as a machine had become universally accepted in the popular imagination. Eloquent proof is provided by the designing, in the early 18th century, and the large-scale production all over Europe for the rest of the century, of those highly refined and complex mechanical representations of the structure and motions of the universe, which from the name of Charles Boyle, Count of Orrery (promoter of the first example fabricated in 1722 by John Rowley) were called *orreries* (fig. 1): devices of evocative beauty, used to divulge even among non-initiates a new image of the universe-machine, fruit of the extraordinary intellectual revolution that had unfolded in the space of less than a century.

–

Bibliography

Bucciantini 2003; Camerota M. 2004; Clark 2006; Clavelin 1995, IV, pp. 149-166; Cohen-Smith 2002; Cartesio 1967; Cartesio 1969; Garber 2001; Koyré 1966; Koyré 1972; Koyré 1976; Kuhn 1966; Mamiani 1990; Newton 1983; Rodis Lewis 1995; Stephenson 1987; Voelkel 2001; Westfall 1984; Westfall 1989.

[1] Clavelin 1995.

[2] Bucciantini 2003.

[3] Koyré 1973, pp. 235-236.

[4] Cartesio 1969, p. 56.

[5] Cartesio 1969, pp. 64-65.

[6] *Ivi*, p. 67.

VI.1.1
Giuliano d'Arrigo also called 'Il Pesello'
Northern hemisphere
1442-1446
Fresco; diameter 400 cm
(reproduction in scale 1:1)
Florence, San Lorenzo, Old Sacristy

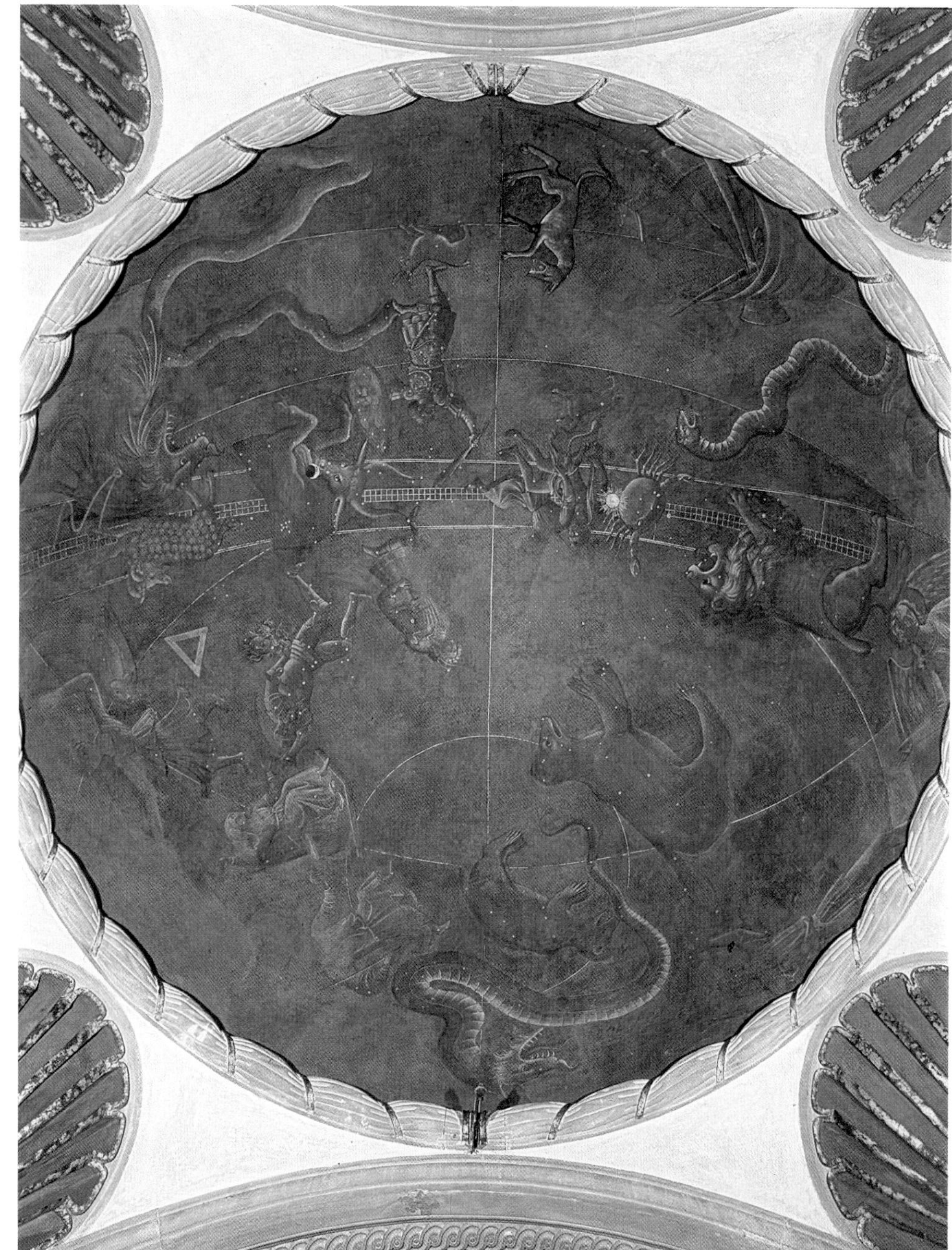

The *Hemisphere* in San Lorenzo is among the earliest evidence testifying to the Medici's patronage of science. Painted by Pesello (1367-1446) under the direction of an astronomer, perhaps Paolo dal Pozzo Toscanelli, the fresco is a portrait of the sky over Florence on the date of July 4, 1442 (Lapi Ballerini). The representation of the constellations is extremely detailed: many stars have a central point and an arrow that indicates its ray, others seem to be displaced a few centimetres in respect to their first positions, others are even numbered, and some are painted on the window-frame, hidden to the sight of viewers but represented just the same for the sake of astronomical completeness. A contemporary copy of this hemisphere in the Cappella dei Pazzi in Santa Croce might indicate the historical event connected to the date identified by critics: an event perhaps having to do with the arrival in Florence of Renato d'Angiò that the two Florentine families, the Medici and the Pazzi, wanted to immortalize in the form of a fortunate astral configuration.
(F.C.)

Bibliography: Brockhauss 1909, pp. 26 ff.; Warburg 1912-17; Parronchi 1979, 1984a 1984b; Fortini Brown 1981; Lapi Ballerini 1986, 1987, 1988, 1989, 2007; Forti et al. 1987; Lapi Ballerini 2007; Camerota F. 2008a, pp. 62-63.

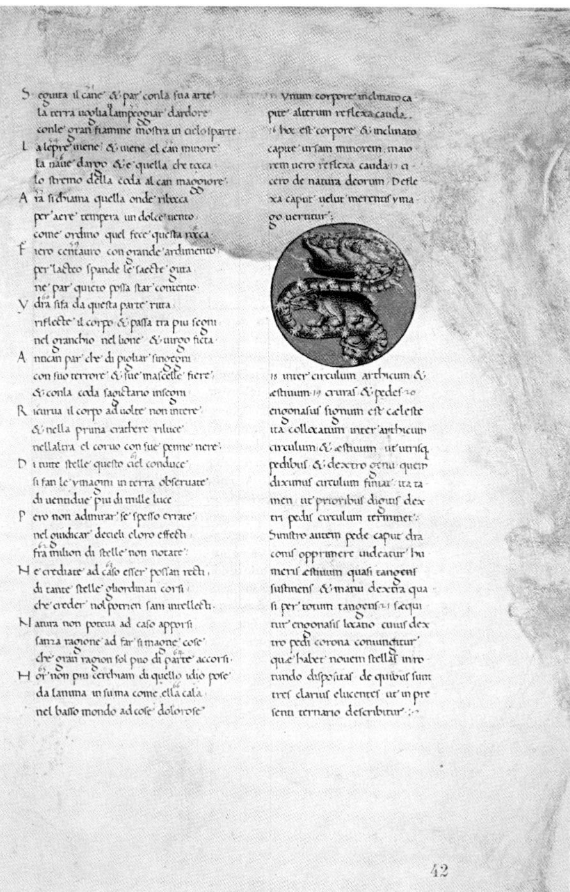

VI.1.2
Matteo Palmieri
Città di vita
15th century
Codex membranaceous, I, 303, I' fols.;
39 x 28.5 cm
Florence, Biblioteca Medicea Laurenziana,
Plut. 40,53, fols. 41v-42r

Matteo Palmieri, a Florentine humanist (1406-1475), conceived this poem in three books, inspired by Dante's works, as the voyage, from the sky to Earth, of souls towards incarnation. Even if his conception of the universe remains Aristotelian and Ptolemaic, his text echoes the strong spread of Platonism and Hermetism in the Florence of his times. As many as thirteen of the first book's thirty-three chapters are actually dedicated to the spheres of the planets, of the Moon and the Sun, and to the 'impressions' that they transmit to souls in transit. Tens of verses describe the solar myth as well.
Aware of the risks connected with adhering to rather unorthodox doctrines (such as the identification of the souls with the angels remaining neutral at the moment of Lucifer's rebellion), Palmieri entrusted the Laurentian Codex to the Arte dei Notai for safe-keeping until his death. The text, completed in 1473, was illuminated by Francesco Botticini.
The miniature in folios 41v-42r shows the constellations of the northern sky and the signs of the zodiac.
(S.B.)

Bibliography: *Catalogus codicum manuscriptorum BML* 1774-1778; Palmieri 1927; Rao 1994, p. 181, n. 65; Rao 2000, vol. I, pp. 84-85; Mita Ferraro 2005.

VI.1.3
Peter Bienewitz (Apianus)
Astronomicum Caesareum
Ingolstadii, in aedibus nostri ..., 1540
Florence, Biblioteca Nazionale Centrale,
Magl. 5._.41, pp. 27v-28r

Splendid volume, dedicated to Emperor Charles V, protector of Apianus (c. 1500-1552). It is truly a triumph of paper astronomical instruments, extremely colourful and functioning perfectly. These devices showed the principal characteristics of the Ptolemaic cosmos and permitted the prediction of celestial phenomena (eclipses and positions of planets), essential factor for the practice of astrology. Epicycles, deferents, equants, etc. are represented by the numerous 'volvelle' (discs of coloured paper rotating on discs) fixed to the pages of the book. The author dedicates particular attention to the observation of comets (among others, he describes the one that will later be named by Halley). On pages 27v-28r, 'volvella' of the motions of the planet Jupiter.
(P.G.)

Bibliography: Wattemburg 1967.

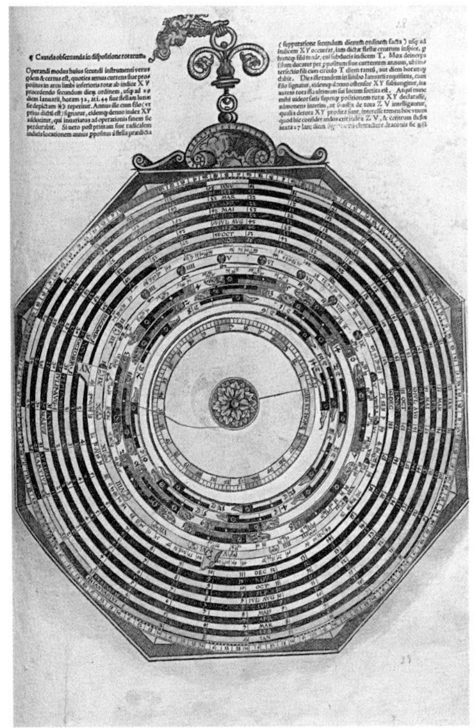

VI.1.4
Ottavio Pisani
Astrologia, seu motus et loca siderum
Antuerpiae, ex Officina Roberti Bruneau, 1613
Florence, Istituto e Museo di Storia della Scienza, MED GF 040, pls. on pp. XXX-XXXI

A work spectacular for its atlas format and, above all, for the large number of complex mobile tables, coloured by hand, that illustrate the structure of the celestial sphere and the motions of planets. For its artistic quality, this work rivals Apiano's *Astronomicum Caesareum* (cf. entry VI.1.3). The Neapolitan Ottavio Pisani (1575-post 1637) composed this work at Antwerp, from where he asked Galileo for help in obtaining Grand Duke Cosimo II's acceptance of its dedication. Galileo used his good offices to help Pisani obtain this goal.
Pisani's work introduces nothing new of scientific importance. But it shows his remarkable mastery as celestial cartographer and as inventor of complex paper astronomical instruments. It also shows that his information was well updated (he quotes Galileo, Kepler, Scheiner, etc.). Furthermore, in the table of the motions of Jupiter, in chart XXVII, he introduces a mobile circle to show the orbits of the Medicean planets. In addition to Galileo, Kepler and Rubens, he had excellent relations with Giovanbattista Della Porta. In the tables between pages XXX-XXXI, Earth-Moon system (XXX) with indications of lunar phases and eclipses (one of the two images of the Moon is derived from the engravings in the *Sidereus Nuncius*, while the other constitutes one of the oldest lunar maps) and planispherical representation of the world with spectacular figures of Atlantis and of the constellation of Aries (XXXI).
(P.G.)

Bibliography: Favaro 1896.

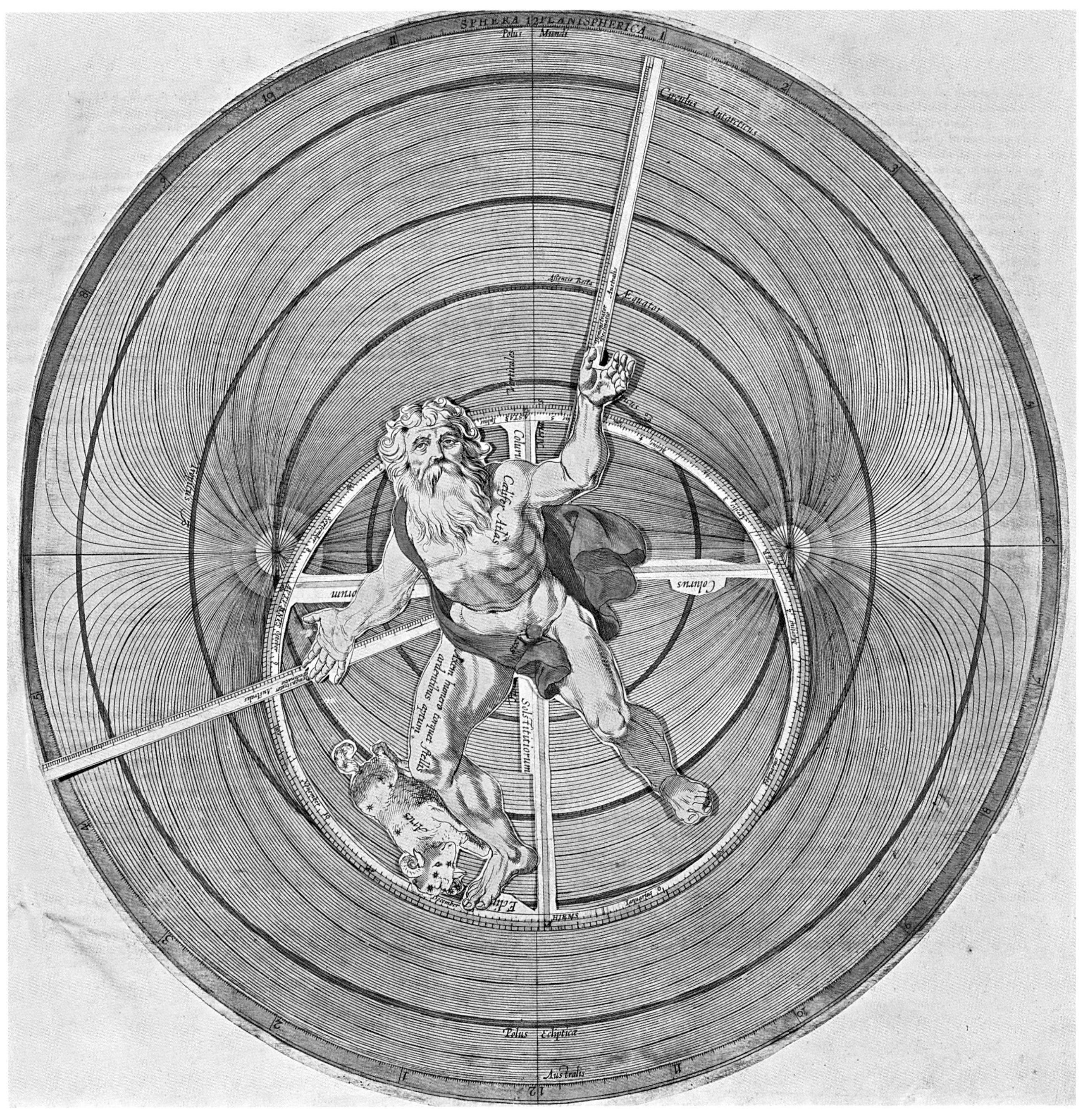
SPHERA PLANISPHERICA
Polus Mundi
Circulus Antarcticus
Æquator
Caelifer Atlas
Colurus
Solstitiorum
Aries
Polus Eclipticæ
Australis

VI.1.5
Franchino Gaffurio
Practica musicae utriusque cantus excellentis ... Quatuor libris modulatissima summaque diligentia nouissime impressa
Venetiis, multisque erroribus expurgata per Augustinum de Zannis de Portesio, 1512
Florence, Biblioteca Nazionale Centrale, Magl. 1.4.180, frontispiece

Gaffurio (1451-1522) presents the correlation between celestial spheres and musical intervals by substituting the Platonic Sirens for the Muses, according to the etymological origin of 'Camenae' found in the verb *canere*, 'to sing'. Such a model again proposes the order of correspondence between muses and planets found in Marziano Capella (*De nuptiis*, I 27-28) and places Apollo at the vertex of the ascetic path, with the three dancing Charites, Euphrosyne, Thalia and Aglaea at his side. Following the harmony impressed by Apollo's mind, everything turns around an ideal string, which, on one hand, alludes to the power of music, and on the other, to the different temporal dimensions of reality. The dragon's tail, in fact, refers to the victory of Apollo over the dragon Pyton; and Cerberus refers to Orpheus' charming music. The earthly condition (to which the three-headed dog is attributed) is scanned by the triple division into past, present and future, while the temporal dimension proper to God is the unity of eternity's absolute fullness.
(N.F.)

Bibliography: Wind 1958, pp. 323-327; Palisca 1985, pp. 191-225.

Practica musicae vtriusq3 cãtus excellẽtis Frã-
chini gaffori laudẽsis. Quattuor libris modula
tissima: Sũmaq3 diligẽtia nouissime ipressa.

VI.1.6
De sphaera
c. 1470
Un-signed and un-titled membrane codex; 24.5 x 17 cm
Modena, Biblioteca Estense, Ms. Lat. 209, fols. 9v-10r (facsimile)

Probably the most beautiful astrological codex of the entire Renaissance. The *De Sphaera* is of particular interest for its artistic quality rather than for the wealth and precision of the astronomical and astrological information, even if the author knows Sacrobosco e Peurbach. The codex is of Milanese origin and reflects the interest in astrology at the Visconti-Sforza court. At the end of the XV century it passed to the Biblioteca Estense.
Of spectacular beauty, the multicolour full-page miniatures, that represent the personifications of the planets (including the two luminaries), show the occupations towards which those who are subjected to their influence tend (the 'children of the planets').There is general agreement in considering these miniatures the direct work of the circle of the Milanese artist Cristoforo de Predis. On pages 9v-10r, representation of the Moon as a naked woman with a lighted torch in one hand and a golden horn in the other. Her feet rest on two wheels of fortune, while between her legs the sign of Cancer (in which the Moon exercises her maximum power) is seen. The occupations of the 'children' of the Moon are illustrated under her image and on page 10r. According to Ptolemy's statement in the *Tetrabiblos*, the Moon has a humidifying power. For this reason whoever comes under her influence tends towards water. In fact, the scenes portray the children of the Moon engaged in navigation and in fishing.
(P.G.)

Bibliography: *De sphaera* 1969; Washington 1991, p. 219.

LVNA

La luna al nauigar molto conforta
Et in peschare et ucellare et caccia
A tutti i suoy figliuoli apre la porta
Et anche al solazzare che ad altri piaccia :

VI.1.7
Baccio Baldini (attr.)
The seven planets
c. 1460
Engravings; 32 x 22 cm
Pavia, Museo Civico, inv. 1585-1591

One of the three known complete series of engravings of the Seven Planets, now generally ascribed to Baldini (1436?-1487), a Florentine artist of the circle of Maso Finiguerra. Based on preparatory drawings almost certainly by Finiguerra, they illustrate the nature and inclinations of the 'children' of the seven planets (Sun and Moon included), an astrological genre of northern European origin which was very widespread during the Renaissance. In the upper part of the sheet great prominence is given to the allegorical figure of the celestial body concerned, while beneath it, in detailed landscapes and architectural settings, we see human beings going about those tasks to which they are led by the influence of that celestial body. The bottom margin is always occupied with a copious explanation of the character, physical constitution, intellectual attitudes and practical orientations of the 'children' of the planet.
(P.G.)

Bibliography: Saxl 1985, pp. 275-277; Firenze 1980, pp. 329-331.

LALVNA EPIANETA FEMININO POSTO NEPRIMO CIELO FREDA HE VMIDA ET FLEMATICHA M
EZANA TRALMONDO ZVPERIORE ET LOINFERIORE AMA LAGEOMETRIA ET CIO CHEAEZZA
ZA PARTIENE DIFACCIA TONDA DIZTAA MEZANA METALLI ALARGIENTO DELLE CHONP
MPLEZZIONI LAFREA DETENPI ELVERNO DEGLIELEMENTI LAQVA ELDI ZVO EILVENERDI CH
ON LAHORA PRIMA 8 15 E Z Z ELAZVA NOTTE EQVELLA DELVENERDI AMICO ZVO E GIOVE IN
IMICO MARTE A VNA ZOLA ABITAZIONE E ELCHANCHCRO
CHEPARTENDOZI LALVNA DAZOLE
DI E 17 ORE EQVEZTO ZECONDO EMOVIMENTO DIMEZO

MARTE
MARTE E ZEGNO MARZCVLINO POZTO NEL QVINTO CIELO MOLTO CALDO FOCOZO EA QVEZTE P
ROPRIETA MILITIA BATTAGLIE ET VCCIZIONI MALIGNO DIZORDINATO DE METALLI HA IL
FERRO LACOLLERA DETEMPI LAZTATE ELDI ZVO E ILMARTEDI COLLAPRIMA HORA 8
15 ET Z Z ELAZVA NOTTE E ILZABATO ELZVO AMICO E ILZOLE EL NIMICO GIOVE A DVE
ITATIONI ELDI LARIETE E LANOTTE LOZCORPIONE LAVITA OVERO EZATAZIONE ZVA E
CARRICORNO LAZVA MORTE OVERO HVMILIAZIONE I ILCANCRO ET VA
E 12 ZENGNI IN 18 MEZI COMINCANDO NELLO ZCORPIONE IN VN
N MEZE E MEZO CIOE 45 DI IM ZENGNO 40 MINVTI PERDI ET PER ORA VN
MINVTO ET 4 ZECONDI

MERCVRIO E PIANETO MASCHVLINO POZTO NEL ZECONDO CIELO ET ZECHO MAPERCHE LA
ZVA ZICITA E MOLTO PAZZIVA LVI E FREDO CONQVEGLI ZENGNI CH ZONO FREDDI EVMIDO COG
LI VMIDI E LOQVENTE INGENGNIOZO AMA LE ZCIENTIE MATEMATICA EZTIVDIA NELLE DIVI
NAZIONE A ILCORPO GRACILE CO ZCHIETTO ZOTTILI IZTATVRA CHONPIVTA DE
METALLI A LARGIENTO VIVO ELDI ZVO E MERCOLEDI COLA PRIMA ORA 8 15 E Z Z
LANOTTE ZVA E DELDI DELLA DOMENICHA A PER AMICO ILZOLE PER NIMICO AVENE
RE LAZVA VITA OVERO EZALTATIONE E VIRGO LA ZV MORTE OVERO HVMILIAZIONE
E PIZCE HA HABITAZIONE GEMNI DI DI VIRGO DI NOTTE VA E 12 ZENGNI IN
DI COMINCIANDO DA VIRGO IN ZO DI E Z ORE VA VN ZENGNO

SATVRNO
CAPICORNO
AQVARIO
ZATVRNO E PIANETA MAZCVLINO POZTO NEZETTIMO CIELO FREDDO E ZECHO MA ACCIDE
TALMENTE VMIDO DINATVRA DITERRA MANICONICO DINATVRA DIPIONBO OZCVR
O AMA VEZTE NERE E TENACE RELIGIOZO DILETTAZI DELLA AGRITVLTVRA HA DEMETALLI
A PIOMBO DEGLIOMORI LAMANICONIA DILETTAZI DELLA AGRITVLTVRA DELETA LAVECHI
EZA DETENPI LAVTONO ELZVO DI E ZABATO CHOLORA PRIMA 8 ET 15 ET Z Z LANOTT
E DEMERCOLEDI E AMICO MARTE E NIMICO IZOLE A DVA ABITATIONE ILDI CAPICORNO LANO
TTE AQVARIO LAZVA VITTA OVERO EXALTIONE LIBRA MORTE OVERO HMILIATIONE ZVA E
ARIETE VA E 12 ZENGNI IN 30 ANNI E VN POPIV E QVAL POCO NON ZITIEN CVRA COMINCIAN
DO DACAPICORNO IN DVANNI E MEZO OVRO IN 30 LVNARI VA VN ZEGNO IN VMEZE VA
VN GRADO IN VNDI VA DVA MINVTI IN VN ORA E Z ZECONDI E POI RITORNA
O PRINCIPIO

AVE REGINA
ZOLE E PIANETA MAZCVLINO POZTO NEL QVARTO CIELO CALDO E ZECHO INFOCATO CHO
LERICO DI COLORE DORO CVPIDO DIREGNARE DRIBEROZO DORO AMA LANETEZA IL PARLARE E
GRAVE MAGNIFICO PIENO DI CARNE DI BELLA FACCIA DE METALLI A LORO EDI ZVO E LA DOMENICHA C
ON LA PRIMA HORA 8 15 ET Z Z LAZVA NOTTE E QVELLA DEL GIOVEDI ZVO AMICO E MARTE
NIMICO ZATVRNO HA VNA HABITAZIONE E QVEZTO E ILIONE ZVA VITA OVERO EXALTAT
IONE E ARIETE MORTE OVERO HVMILIATIONE E LIBRA VA 12 ZEGNI IN VNO
ANNO COMINCIANDO DARIETE IN VNO MEZE ET VA VN ZEGNIO IN VNO DI
VA VN GRADO ET IN VNA HORA VA Z MINVTI ET 30 ZECONDI

VENERE E ZEGNO FEMININO POZTO NEL TERZO CIELO E FREDDO E VMIDA TENPERATA
ALE A QVEZTE PROPIETA AMA BELLI VEZTIMENTI ORNATI DORO E DARGENTO E CHANZONE E G
ADII E GIVOCHI ET E LAZCIVA E A DOLCE PARLARE E BELLA NEGLIOCHI E NELLA FRONTE E DI CORPO LEGG
ERI DI CARNE E DI MEZANA ZTVRA DA A TVTTI OPERE
OZTO ALLEI LOTTONE ELZVO DI E VENERDI E LA PRIMA HORA 8 15 ET Z Z E LA NOTTE ZVA
E MARTEDI ELZVO AMICO E GIOVE EL NIMICO MERCVRIO ET A DVA ABITAZIONI EL TORO D
I GORNO E LIBRA DI NOTTE E PERCHONZIGLIERE EL ZOLE
E IL PEZCE E LA MORTE E VMILIAZIONE E VIRGO
GIORNI VA VNO ZENGHO E IN VN GIORNO VA VNO GRADO
E Z MINVTI E IN VNA ORA 30 MINVTI

VI.1.8
Albrecht Dürer
Melancolia I
1514
Burin engraving; 23.9 x 19 cm
Florence, Gabinetto Disegni e Stampe degli Uffizi, 4680 st. sc.

With an extraordinary capacity for figurative synthesis, Dürer (1471-1528) succeeds, in the limited space of this piece of paper, in providing a demonstration of astounding complexity even on a conceptual level. The etching was and is still the object of contrasting interpretations. According to Panofsky, it represents the personification of the melancholy humour, placed under the astrological influence of Saturn, whose 'children' incline towards intellectual activities (such as mathematics or geometry, to which the scene clearly alludes), but must bear the weight of a melancoly disposition. Besides being considered in the context of the four temperaments conferred by the 'aspects' of celestial bodies, the etching has been interpreted (Calvesi) as the alchemic representation of nature. Other scholars (Schuster) have identified the melancholy woman who dominates the scene with Astronomy, who elevates the mind of man towards God. The winged woman has a pair of compasses in her hand, while carpenters' tools can be seen at her feet. An hourglass, scales, a magic square and a semi-regular solid represent the more apparent symbols, together with a sleeping dog at her feet and the winged cherub sitting on a millstone.
(P.G.)

Bibliography: Panofsky 1948, II, pp. 156-171; Schuster 1991; Calvesi 1993; Parigi 2005; *Galleria degli Uffizi* 2007, pp. 127-129.

VI.2. ATLASES, ARMILLARY SPHERES AND GLOBES

VI.2.1-2
Albrecht Dürer
Northern and Southern celestial maps
1515
Woodcut; 42 x 42.7 cm (5069), 42.1 x 43.2 cm (5070)
Florence, Gabinetto Disegni e Stampe degli Uffizi, 5069-5070 st. sc.

The woodcuts were made by Dürer in 1515 for the astronomer Johannes Stabius, scholar at the court of Emperor Maxmillian. The design is based on that made in the first part of the century by the astronomer from Nuremberg, Konrad Heinfogel, and constitutes a reference model for many celestial maps in the 1500's. Among others, Pietro Apiano and Gemma Frisius used it, as well as several globe-makers as shown by, for example, the celestial globe displayed in the Museo Correr in Venice. (cf. entry VI.2.12). The constellations are inscribed within a graduated circle divided into twelve parts , 30° each.
At the four corners of the northern map there are the figures of the astronomers 'Aratus Cilix', 'Ptolemeus Aegyptus', 'M.Manlius Romanus' and 'Azophi Arabus', that is, Aratus of Soli, Claudius Ptolemy, Marco Manlio and Al-Sufi.
The southern map gives all the information relative to the making of both woodcuts, the person commissioning the work and the source of the observations.
High up on the map there is the coat of arms with a dedication to Cardinal Matthäus Lang von Wellenburg, lower, on the left, the cartouche regarding the three creators ('Ioann Stabius ordinavit / Conradus Heinfogel stellas posuit / Albertus Durer imaginibus circumscripsit'), on the right, the Imperial privilege with the date 1515.
(F.C.)

Bibliography: Bartsch 1808, VII, pp. 161-162; Weiss 1888, pp. 213 ff.; Panofsky 1948, II, p. 44, nn. 365-366; Rome 1971, p. 79, n. 11; Florence 1971, pp. 80-81, nn. 73-74; Washington 1971, pp. 190-191, nn. 198-199; Pizzorusso 1980, pp. 333-334; Strieder 1992, pp. 56-59; Fara 1996.

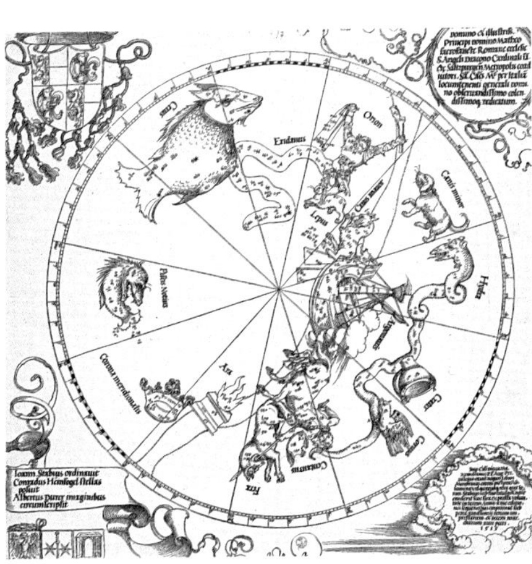

VI.2.3
Johann Bayer
Uranometria, omnium asterismorum continens schemata, nova methodo deliniata, aereis laminis expressa
Augsburg, Christophorus Mangus, 1603
Florence, Biblioteca Nazionale Centrale, Magl. 5._.54, pl. X

First modern atlas, the *Uranometria* includes 51 rectangular tables whose margins are graduated with one-degree notches. The belt eight degrees above and below the ecliptic (the belt in which the planets move) is highlighted in grey. The stars, in six magnitudes, are in trapezoidal concave projection and depicted for the year 1600.
Bayer's (1572-1625) work is based on Tycho Brahe's observations. In the table of the atlas depicting Cassiopea, he includes the *nova* star observed in 1572 by Tycho at Uranienborg (in spite of the fact that it was no longer visible). The last two tables present the northern and southern skies.
Bayer's atlas is full of beautiful engravings, true works of art realized by Alexander Mair.
(P.G.)

Bibliography: Stoppa 2006, pp. 38-41.

VI.2.5
Adrien Veen, Jodocus Hondius
Celestial globe
1613
Wood, papier mâché, chalk; 97 x 78 cm, diameter 53.5 cm
Florence, Istituto e Museo di Storia della Scienza, inv. 2696

The globe is dedicated to the Lords of the United Provinces of Belgium and shows the stars observed by Tycho Brahe as well as those Antarctic stars noted by Pieter Diercksz and Frederick de Houtman. The projection is convex and the names of the constellations are, for the most part, in Latin. Beneath the constellation of Cetus the portrait of Tycho is drawn.
(M.M.)

Bibliography: *Catalogo IMSS* 1954, p. 43; Righini Bonelli 1968a, p. 157; Miniati 1991, p. 96; *Istituto e Museo di storia della scienza (Firenze)* 2004, pp. 120-122.

VI.2.4
Johann Schöner
Celestial Globe
Nuremberg c. 1533
Papier maché, vellum, brass; 38 x 32 cm
London, Royal Astronomical Society, inv. 1910-249 (in deposito presso The Science Museum)

This is thought to be the oldest surviving printed celestial globe; the figures on the southern hemisphere are still well preserved although some on the northern hemisphere have been partly obliterated. The constellations shown are after Ptolemy, with names in Latin, while individual star names are mostly in Arabic.
The globe is marked with ecliptic, equatorial, tropic and arctic circles. The ecliptic circle is divided in degrees (10,20,30 for each sign of the Zodiac), while the equatorial circle is marked in ten-degree intervals. The brass meridian circle has a small hour circle at the North Pole, with an hour hand fixed to the globe's axis and rotating with it. The brass horizon circle is marked in four sectors of 90 degrees and carries the four compass points. The globe sits on an ornamental tripod base, with a plum bob to hang over a small compass in the recess of one of the legs. It was previously attributed to Peter Apianus and is very similar to the globe depicted in Hans Holbein's *The Ambassadors* of 1533.
(A.B.)

Bibliography: Zinner 1956a; Dekker-Lippincott 1999; Dekker 2007, pp. 144-145, fig. 6.6.

VI.2.6
Antonio Lupicini
Armillary spheres of the Planets
Florence, c. 1570-1574
Brass, bronze, wood; height c. 70 cm,
diameter min. 23 cm, max 32.5 cm
Florence, Biblioteca Medicea Laurenziana,
inv. beni art. 14-17

These are four spheres made in Florence under the guidance of the Florentine architect and astronomer Antonio Lupicini (c. 1530-c. 1598), probably commissioned by Cosimo I de' Medici and located in the library after his death. They are explanatory models of the movements: the first of the Sun, the Moon and the sphere of the fixed stars; the second of Mars, Jupiter and Saturn, the third of Mercury and the fourth that of Venus. They are supported by human figures or satyrs, the work of the sculptor Valerio Cioli (1529-1599). The manufacture of the spheres, directed by Lupicini himself, involved many talented craftsmen, including turners and gilders, braziers and engravers, whose names are recorded in the archives. Antonio Lupicini was an outstanding figure in the production of scientific instruments, and the author of texts on mathematical and topographical instruments.
(M.M.)

Bibliography: Casanova 1899, pp. 45-51; Fiorini 1899, pp. 226-227; *Istituto e Museo di storia della scienza (Firenze)* 2004, pp. 32-51; Camerota-Miniati 2008, pp. 164-165.

VI.2.7
Girolamo della Volpaia (attr.)
Geocentric armillary sphere
Florence, c. 1570-1580
Gilded bronze, wood, silver, translucent enamel; height 55 cm
Paris, Kugel Collection

The sphere is supported by a bronze Hercules on whose shoulders rest three quarters of a circle which in turn support the circle of the horizon, etched with a 360° scale (four times 90°) into which are punched indications of the directions of the winds. Within the meridian circle are three spheres revolving one above the other on different axes. The outer one, mounted on the axis of the ecliptic, is composed of seven rings for the colures, the polar circles, those of the tropics and of the ecliptic (the latter bears the signs of the zodiac). Within the third sphere are three rings. The outer two, which are mobile, indicate the orbits of the Sun (the larger one) and the Moon, represented by silver symbols. At the centre is a small blue-enamelled globe which, tilted at an angle, represents the Earth.
The attribution to Girolama della Volpaia (c. 1530-1614) is suggested by its similarity to other armillary spheres produced by this Florentine craftsman and by the triangular section of the polar circles, a detail typical of his work. The figure of Hercules supporting the sphere is probably an early 17th-century addition.
(P.G.)

Bibliography: Unpublished.

VI.2.8
Girolamo della Volpaia
Model of the Lunar Sphere
Florence, 1557
Gilded brass, wood; diameter 14.5 cm, height 23.6 cm
Florence, Istituto e Museo di Storia della Scienza, inv. 118

Girolamo della Volpaia was one of those instrument makers who set his hand to making models of the planetary spheres with concentric and eccentric partial spheres described by Georg von Peurbach (1423-1461) in his *Theoricae novae planetarum* (1472). He devoted himself in this case to the representation of the theory the Moon, one of the most complex, composed of an epicycle and three concentric partial spheres variously tilted with respect to each other. The model is composed of a number of thin gilded brass plates which exemplify two sections of the different partial spheres perpendicular to one another. The Moon has to be thought of as set on the equator of the epicycle, represented by a small metal ball inserted into the space between two eccentric partial spheres. These latter explained the noticeable variations in distance between the Moon and the Earth – not explicitly shown at the centre of the instrument – as according to Ptolemy's *Almagest*. Two concentric partial spheres moved the eccentric ones and explained the phenomenon of the progression of the lunar perigee. A fourth and final outer partial sphere, tilted in respect to the others, explained the retrograde motion of the lunar nodes (points of intersection) of the orbit of the Moon with respect to the ecliptic.
(G.S.)

Bibliography: Peurbach 1472, 'De Luna'; Righini Bonelli 1976, p. 160, no. 65; Miniati 1991, p. 50, no. 50; *Istituto e Museo di storia della scienza (Firenze)* 2004, pp. 70-72, no. 1.

VI.2.9
Girolamo della Volpaia
Armillary sphere
1564
Gilded brass, bronze, rock crystal; diameter 49 cm, height 77.5 cm
Florence, Istituto e Museo di Storia della Scienza, inv. 2711

Girolamo della Volpaia (c. 1530-1614), the last representative of a Tuscan family of skilful makers of scientific instruments, constructed nocturnal clocks and sundials as well as astronomic models fulfilling various functions. This armillary sphere was essentially an instrument for teaching. It served to illustrate the displacement of the chief celestial circumferences – the equator, the ecliptic, the tropics, the polar circles and the colures of the equinoxes and solstices – with respect to the particular place in which the observer stood. The whole sphere could be tilted on the horizon by rotating a vertical meridian ring marked with a graduated scale of the geographical latitudes. The Earth is represented by a rock crystal globe placed at the centre of the celestial sphere, while the large ring representing the ecliptic is marked with a calendar used for determining the position of the Sun along the Zodiac.
(G.S.)

Bibliography: Maccagni 1967, pp. 12-13; Righini Bonelli 1976, p. 161, no. 74; Miniati 1991, p. 50, no. 51; *Istituto e Museo di storia della scienza (Firenze)* 2004, pp. 72-76, no. 3.

VI.2.10
Vincenzo de' Rossi (attr.)
Hercules with celestial sphere
Florence, c. 1570
Gilded bronze, ebony; height 48 cm
Private collection

A superb bronze, very probably the work of Vincenzo de' Rossi (1527-1587), an artist of great quality, pupil of Baccio Bandinelli, and one who had felt the influence of Michelangelo. The sculpture bears the arms of the Putrella family, among whose members was Evangelista di Ranieri, an ally of Cosimo I de' Medici, who conferred on him the honorary citizenship of Florence. Given that Hercules was one of Cosimo's favourite symbols, it seems not unlikely that the globe was commissioned with a view to making a gift of it to the Duke of Florence.
The pierced constellations of the globe follow the model of François Demonget's engravings of the celestial gores (c. 1560).
(P.G.)

Bibliography: Parigi 2002a, pp. 30-31.

VI.2.11
Anonymous
Celestial globe
Milan and Prague, c. 1600
Rock crystal, steel; diameter 5.5 cm
Paris, Kugel Collection

This little globe is cut out of a block of rock crystal. It resembles the one made by Ottavio Miseroni (at that time in the service of Rudolph II), now part of the marvellous planetary clock made by Jost Bürgi, preserved in the Kunsthistorisches Museum in Vienna.
The globe comprises two hemispheres joined together at the equator and rotating about the polar axis, on which is mounted a meridian ring. The polar circles and the tropics are engraved on its surface. It is amazing how the engraver (perhaps Miseroni himself) succeeded in working on such a minute scale as this globe, conferring extraordinary definition on the 48 Ptolemaic constellations, (modelled on Dürer's map of the heavens, see entry VI.2.1-2), and on the stars within them shown in varying degrees of magnitude.
(P.G.)

Bibliography: Parigi 2002a, pp. 36-39.

VI.2.12
Anonymous
Celestial and terrestrial mechanical globe
France?, 16th century
Brass; diameter 25 cm, height 46.8 cm
Venice, Museo Correr, inv. Cl. XXIX, 31

The instrument is distinguished by the beautiful fretwork celestial sphere that faithfully copies the drawing of the northern and southern hemispheres published by Albrecht Dürer (1471-1528) in 1515 (cf. entry VI.2.1-2). Inside, there is a terrestrial globe with a clock-work mechanism that puts the celestial sphere in movement, indicating the time on the external band of the hour lines. A date of mid-sixteenth century for this instrument is suggested by the geographic representation, that seems to derive from the world map by Sebastian Münster (1544). A large part of Canada and all of Alaska are not yet included, whereas Japan (Zypangry) is situated near the west coast of America, summarily indicated without California, that was only discovered in 1565. The inscriptions are almost all in Latin, with the exception of a few names in French ('Lestroict de Magalian', 'La Terre des Geyan', 'La Terre du Bresil'), that would indicate France as the instrument's place of origin.
(F.C.)

Bibliography: Lazari 1859, p. 1103; Camerota F. 2008a, pp. 30-33.

VI.3.1
Gualterus Arsenius
Planispheric astrolabe
Louvain, 1572
Gilded brass; diameter 34.1 cm
Florence, Istituto e Museo di Storia della Scienza, inv. 1103

Gualterus Arsenius (d. c. 1580), belonged to a family of Flemish scientific instrument makers and worked in Louvain from 1555 to 1579. Nephew of the mathematician and cosmographer Reiner Gemma Frisius (1508-1555), he made astronomical instruments of fine workmanship and great precision: armillary spheres, astronomical rings and sundials. This planispheric astrolabe carries ten tympanums for different latitudes and is signed 'Gualterus Arsenius, nepos Gemma Frisij, Lovanii fecit anno 1572'. The fact that the suspension ring contains a tiny compass complete with magnetic needle shows that the instrument was intended also for topographical surveying work. It belonged to the Medici collections.
(G.S.)

Bibliography: Righini Bonelli 1976, p. 163, no. 92; Miniati 1991, p. 34, no. 69.

VI.3.2
Egnazio Danti (attr.)
Planispheric astrolabe called 'di Galileo'
Florence, c. 1570
Gilded brass, wood; diameter 80 cm, height 86 cm
Florence, Istituto e Museo di Storia della Scienza, inv. 3361

Unlike typical planispheric astrolabes, this large instrument has a single face equipped with a single tympanum marked for the latitude of Florence (43°40'). Complete with a rete and an alidade (revolving rod) carrying sights, it is set on an octagonal wooden table. The instrument can be placed upright and rotated with respect to the horizon when used for observations, or else arranged in a more convenient slanting or horizontal position for making astronomic calculations. Attributed on the basis of the punched in characters to Giovanni Battista Giusti (16th century), this astrolabe is more likely to be the work of Egnazio Danti (1536-1586), cosmographer to Cosimo I de' Medici. It was originally kept in the Uffizi and Galileo himself, on his return to Florence, requested the Grand Duke Cosimo II for the use of it in his calculations in the field of astronomy.

Bibliography: Righini Bonelli 1976, p. 163, no. 103; Felli 1983; Miniati 1991, p. 44, no. 27; Turner G. l'E. 1995, pp. 134-139, 157-160.

VI.3.3
Christoph Schissler
Planispheric astrolabe
Augsburg, 1560
Gilded brass; diameter 21.5 cm
Florence, Istituto e Museo di Storia
della Scienza, inv. 1114

The work of one of the finest craftsmen of the 17th century, this astrolabe is indicative of the tastes of the refined clientele of Chistoph Schissler (c. 1531-1608), composed of reigning heads, the nobility and the extremely wealthy. For example, Schissler furnished scientific instruments to the emperor Rudolph II, to the aristocratic Danish astronomer Tycho Brahe (1546-1601) and to several members of the famous banking family of Függer. The astrolabe on display carries a single tympanum for latitudes 45° and 48°. On the back is the maker's signature: 'Christophorus Schissler me faciebat Auguste Vindelicorum anno 1560'. It was brought to Tuscany by Prince Mattias de' Medici in the first half of the 17th century.
(G.S.)

Bibliography: Righini Bonelli 1976, p. 163, no. 102; Miniati 1991, p. 24, no. 1.

VI.3.4
Hans Christoph Schissler, jr.
Mathematial compendium
Second half of the 16th century
Gilt brass, silver; 19.8 x 20 x 9 cm
Florence, Istituto e Museo di Storia della
Scienza, inv: 2467

Designed to carry out many operations, on the front the instrument has an astrolabe and a geographical map complete with index, on which the maker's signature appears. A compass that can be positioned horizontally is located in the back. On the outside there is a calendar. At the top, a jointed rule with sights is used for calculating heights. A second folding rule is positioned below. The Compendium is completed by a leather case with gilt tooling.
(M.M.)

Bibliography: *Catalogo IMSS* 1954, p. 98, Righini Bonelli 1968a, p. 177; Miniati 1991, p.24.

VI.3.5
Christoph Schissler
Quadrant
1599
Gilt brass; side 38 cm
Florence, Istituto e Museo di Storia della Scienza, inv. 155, 156

The instrument bears two engraved horary quadrants, one with curved lines 'veterum more', drawn for the unequal hours, the other with straight hour lines, as in Stöffler's quadrant (German astronomer and map-maker, 1452-1531). The alidade is complete with sights and is graduated. Two other folding sights are on the two opposite sides. The shadow square and the appropriate graduations for making land surveys are also engraved. The instrument is set for the latitude of 48°, corresponding more or less to Augsburg, where Schissler's workshop was established. The quadrant is accompanied by a wooden stand, a ring of gilt brass, and a leather case with gilt tooling.
(M.M.)

Bibliography: *Catalogo IMSS* 1954, p. 77; Righini Bonelli 1968b, p. 169; Miniati 1991, p. 24; Turner A. 2007, p. 56.

VI.3.6
Josuah Habermel (attr.)
Quadrant
After 1582
Gilt brass; radius 15 cm
Florence, Istituto e Museo di Storia della Scienza, inv. 2518

A small instrument with a double graduation on the rim, to measure heights and distances. It bears, engraved, two open compasses. The sights are fixed, while the 'ostentor' is mobile, with a steel spring as a guide. On the back there is a table for finding the date of Easter with the indication *iuxta Kalendarii reformationem*, that is, according to the reformation of the calendar and therefore after 1582.
(M.M.)

Bibliography: *Catalogo IMSS* 1954, p. 81; Righini Bonelli 1968a, p. 170; Miniati 1991, p. 26; Turner A. 2007, p. 158.

VI.3.7
Tobias Volckmer
Quadrant
Braunschweig, 1608
Gilt copper, side 36 cm
Florence, Istituto e Museo di Storia della Scienza, inv. 2465, 1495

'Universal' quadrant, capable, that is, of carrying out various kinds of operations: mathematical, astronomical, astrological and military. The instrument consists of a quadrant engraved on both faces. The refinement of the decorations is joined by great precision in the drawing of the lines, making it possible to obtain reliable results within a restricted margin for error. The front is dominated by the network of sines, or reduction quarter, for the calculation of sines and cosines. The graduated arc has a vernier, that allows the division of each degree into five minutes. In the upper angle two graduated vanes are hinged together like compasses; one of these is equipped with sights. In the opposite angle there is a removable compass that indicates the difference between geographical North and magnetic North. The compass has an astrolabe tympanum on its back; its lid has, on one side, a sundial, and on the other, a nocturnal. Under the compass, on the plate of the instrument, a wind rose is engraved. The back of the instrument presents two Stöffler-type quadrants (so-called because created by Stöffler), a section for military use, another for astronomical use, the scale of degrees, a pendulum, and a disc with index, called 'Signore dell'hore ineguali', that constitutes the astrological calendar. Complete with a tripod, the instrument was acquired in Germany by Prince Mattias de' Medici in 1635.
(M.M.)

Bibliography: *Catalogo IMSS* 1954, pp. 78-80; Righini Bonelli 1968b, p. 170; Miniati-Rudan 1981, pp. 241-246; Miniati-Rudan 1982, pp. 83-111; Miniati 1991, p. 26; Camerota-Miniati 2008, p. 341.

VI.3.8
Egnazio Danti
Instrument of the Primum Mobile
Florence, 1568
Gilded brass; radius 27.9 cm
Florence, Istituto e Museo di Storia della Scienza, inv. 2643

Although the name evokes the eighth celestial sphere introduced by Islamic astronomers to explain the motion of the precession of the equinoxes ascribed to the sphere of the fixed stars, this 'instrument of the Primum Mobile' is basically a device to determine the sine and cosine of an angle. Peter Bienewitz, otherwise known as Apianus (1445/1501-1552), gave an account of it in his treatise *Instrumentum primi mobilis* (1524), in which he predicted a use for it in astronomy analogous to that of a portable quadrant. This exemplar, the only one known today, is signed 'F.E.D.P.F.', standing for 'Frater Egnatius Dantis Predicatorum Fecit'. The fact that it bears the arms of the Medici family shows that Danti (1536-1586) made it for the Grand Duke Cosimo I. It does in fact come from the Medici collections.
(G.S.)

Bibliography: Righini Bonelli 1976, p. 171, no. 149; Miniati 1991, p. 44, no. 28; Giusti 2004, p. 152.

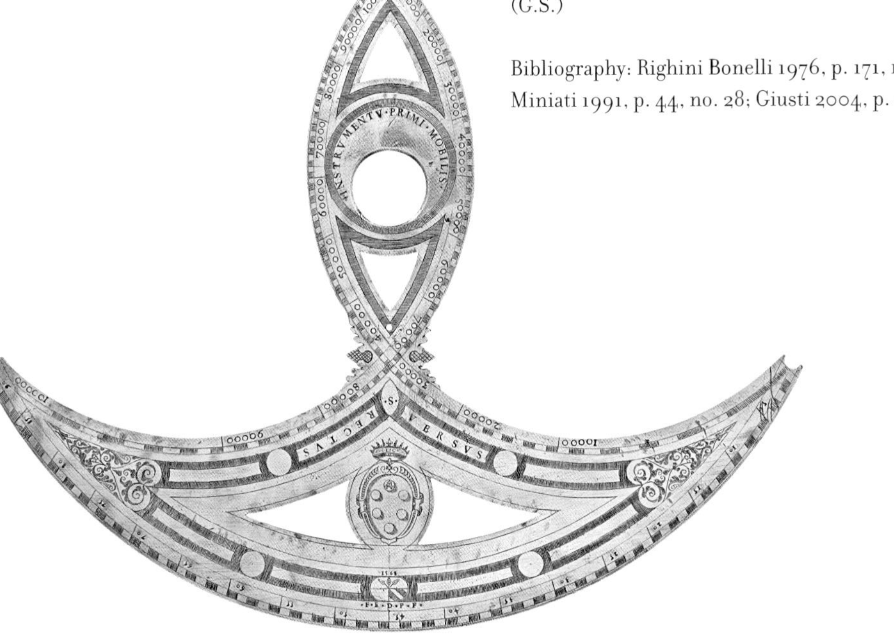

VI.3.9
Erasmus Habermel
Full Circle
End of the 16th century
Gilt copper; height 26.5 cm, diameter 26.8 cm
Paris, Observatoire de Paris, inv. 18

This instrument, which makes it possible to measure an angle and to find a direction, is signed by Erasmus Habermel (c.1538-1606). The author, perhaps a native of Nuremberg, was active in Prague from at least 1576, and his workshop produced hundreds of instruments, of which 150 still exist today. In 1594 he became the official instrument-maker of Emperor Rudolph II.
The full circle is placed on a vertical shaft and rests on a tripod. The plate, on which the alidade is missing, presents two fixed pinnule sights. Inscriptions on the inner circle specify the foot measure in Prague, Nuremberg, Vienna and Rome and, probably, the way to calculate the range of a projectile, whether of lead, iron, or stone.
(L.B.)

Bibliography: Zinner 1956b, pp. 329 ff.; Eckhard 1976.

VI.3.10
Anonymous
Nocturnal
17th century
Brass: diameter 10 cm, length 19 cm
Florence, Istituto e Museo di Storia della Scienza, inv. 2494

Probably Italian-made, the instrument presents two superimposed discs. The lower one is joined to the carved and modelled handle and is engraved with the calendar scale, the months and the symbols of the signs of the zodiac. The upper rotating disc has a third of its surface cut in a way making the disc underneath visible, and has a series of numbered teeth around the circumference. An index rotates around a centre sight hole.
(M.M.)

Bibliography: *Catalogo IMSS* 1954, p. 102; Righini Bonelli 1968a, p. 173; Miniati 1991, p. 10; Turner G. l'E. 2003, pp. 255-257, Turner A. 2007, p. 142.

VI.3.11
Girolamo della Volpaia
Nocturnal and horary quadrant
1568
Brass; diameter 14.7 cm
Florence, Istituto e Museo di Storia della Scienza, inv. 2503

The face of the instrument relative to the nocturnal is made up of three superimposed brass discs, held together by a central cylinder, around which the ring with the rotating index is fixed. The disc of days, underneath, presents a division in 360 degrees, the names of the signs of the zodiac in Latin, the months of the year and the days of each month (the beginning of Aries is placed on March 10th). The middle disc is divided into 24 hours and is provided with a small index with the indication 'MEDIA NOX'. The top disc is provided with 24 numbered teeth, one longer than the others having the function of index, and is divided into circles: the outer one bears the numbers 7, 6, 5, 4, repeated several times; the second, other numbers that, together with the previous ones represent the hours and the minutes occurring, in a certain period of the year, between sunset and midnight; the third, the abbreviated names of the months; the last, the inscription 'MEDIA NOX PER TOTUM ANNUM'. Around the hole in the centre, a ring bears the index with the inscription 'HOROLOGIUM NOCTURNUM' within an ornament. The back of the instrument presents the quadrant of height, with the hour lines for the sundial marked by curved lines and by dots. An inscription on the side states: 'LINEAE PVNCTOR: POST: MERIDIEM:' The abbreviated names of the months are marked on the sides of the quadrant. The quadrant of height is divided into 90 degrees. Under the division the indication 'AD LATITUDINEM GRADVVM. XXXXIII.ET.XXXXIIII' is engraved. The signature and the date: 'HIERONIMUS. VVLPARIAE. FLORENTIN. FECIT. MDLXVIII' are found near the top, along the circumference. Two pierced sights complete this face that also presents a disc divided into three circumferences: the first bears the letters of the alphabet relative to the zodiac signs, the second, those of the relative months of the year; the third, the numbers from 3 to 8, some of which are repeated several times. These numbers, in addition to the numerals written in the centre 'X.III', make it possible to know, for every day of the year, in which sign and in which degree the Sun is found.
(M.M.)

Bibliography: *Catalogo IMSS* 1954, p. 104, Righini Bonelli 1968b, p. 174; Righini Bonelli-Settle, pp. 94-95; Miniati 1991, p. 50; Turner A. 2007, pp. 136-140; Camerota-Miniati 2008, p. 129.

VI.3.12
Camillo della Volpaia (attr.)
Horizontal sundial
1542
Wood, 11.5 x 8 cm
Florence, Istituto e Museo di Storia della Scienza, inv. 2487

A rectangular tablet of wood with profiles of ebony is marked with the hour lines for the latitude of 43°44', corresponding, more or less, to Florence. A small vertical gnomon is inset so as to throw a shadow. A compass, complete with glass is set into the tablet: on the bottom there is a colourful map of Italy and, on the outside, above the compass, an angel-shaped folding brass weather-vane rotates. Along the edge of the tablet, a phrase suggests all the operations that can be done with the instrument.
(M.M.)

Bibliography: *Catalogo IMSS* 1954, p. 100, Righini Bonelli 1968a, p. 176, Miniati 1991, p. 50; Turner A. 2007, p.70.

VI.3.13
Anonymous
Book-shaped sundial
Germany, 16th century
Silverplated and gilt brass
Florence, Istituto e Museo di Storia della Scienza, inv. 2481

In the form of a mass-book, this astronomical compendium bears the insignia of the Company of Jesus ('IHS'). On the outer face of the cover there is a nocturnal that shows the phases of the Moon, while on the inner face the hour lines are engraved. There is a reclining gnomon inside, mounted on a compass (now missing), that ensured the correct orientation of the instrument and its use as a sundial. On the back of the book, the planetary hours are indicated.
(F.C.)

Bibliography: Righini Bonelli 1968a, p. 176; Miniati 1991, p: 10.

VI.3.14-15
Stefano Buonsignori
Sundials
16th century
Wood; height 20.3 cm (inv. 2458 and 17 cm inv. 2459)
Florence, Istituto e Museo di Storia della Scienza, inv. 2458 and 2459

Polyhedric sundials with hexagonal and square faces. On each of the faces a different kind of sundial is traced (horizontal, vertical or declining), complete with gnomon. In the upper part of each a compass is placed, used to orientate the instrument towards the local magnetic meridian (the magnetic needle of the sundial inv. 2459 is missing). The initials 'D.S.F.' found on the sundial inv. 2458 clearly attribute it to Stefano Buonsignori, while the other is not signed, even if the characteristics of its construction would attribute it to the same maker.
(M.M.)

Bibliography: *Catalogo IMSS* 1954, pp. 96-97; Righini Bonelli 1968a, p. 175; Righini Bonelli-Settle, pp. 86-87; Miniati 1991, p. 50; Turner A. 2004, pp. 118, 120; Camerota-Miniati 2008, p. 197.

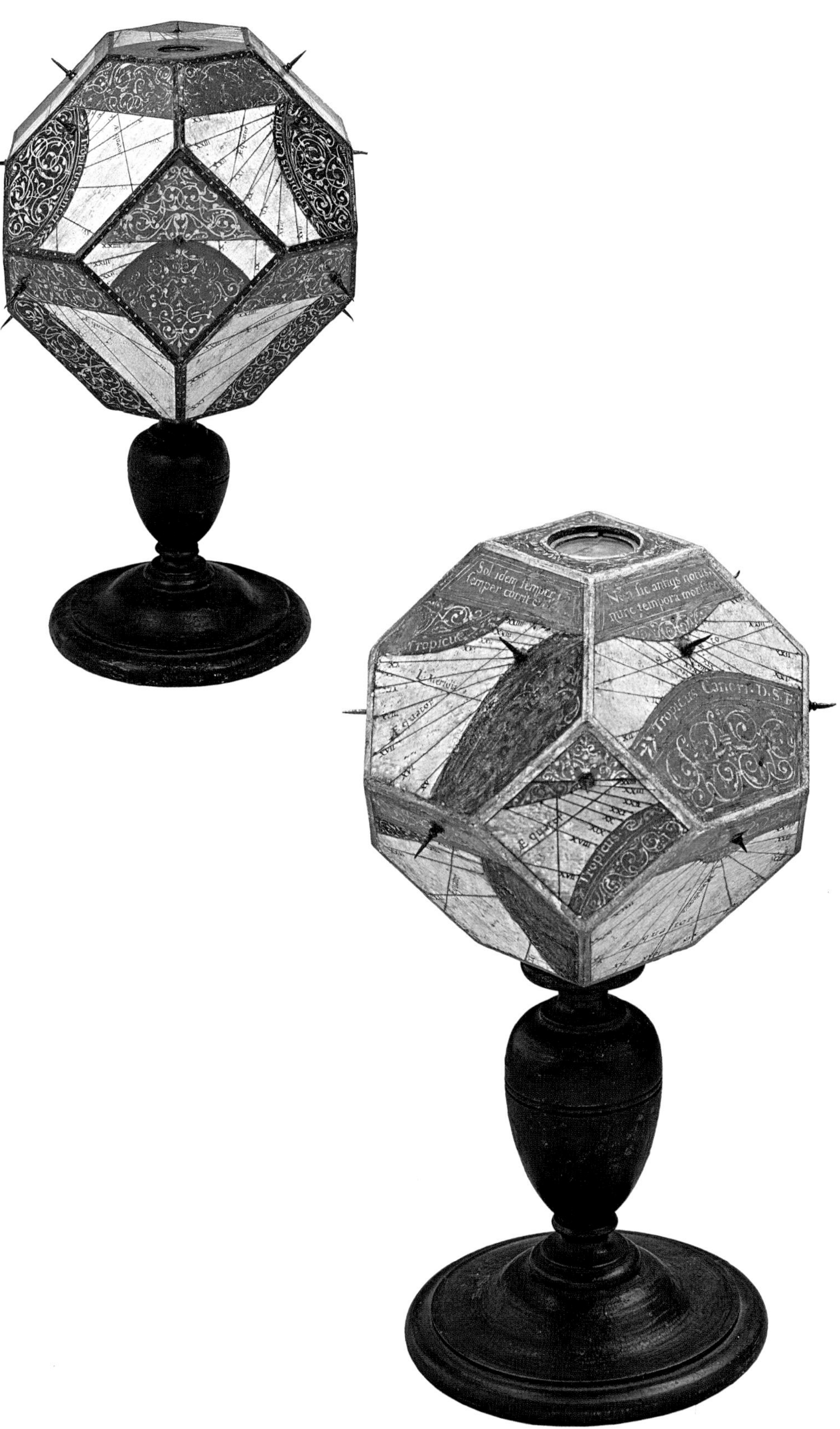

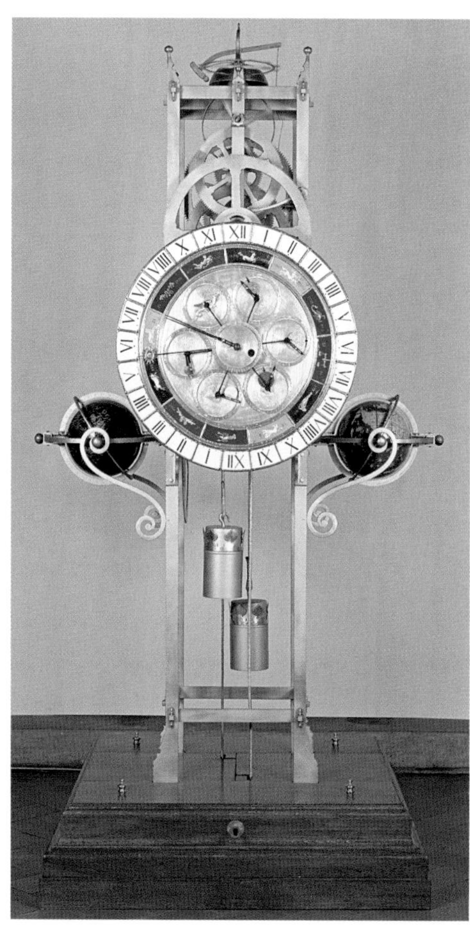

VI.4.1
Lorenzo della Volpaia
Planetary clock
1510
Replica (Alberto Gorla and Istituto Statale d'Arte, Florence, 1994)
Brass, enamelled iron; 235 x 117 x 75 cm
Florence, Istituto e Museo di Storia della Scienza, inv. 3817

This is a faithful reconstruction of the Planetary Clock designed and constructed in 1510 by Lorenzo della Volpaia (1446-1512) on commission from Lorenzo de' Medici, who wished to present it to Matthias Corvinus, King of Hungary.
The very precise details recorded in the manuscripts by Lorenzo and his heirs have made it possible to make a perfect replica of this extraordinary instrument, much lauded by contemporaries but already lost by the middle of the 17th century. The clock has an innovative type of dial which permits the motion of all the planets to be viewed simultaneously (unlike Dondi's *Astrarium*, see entry V.1.1b). It shows the motions of Mercury, Venus, Mars, Jupiter, Saturn, the phases and age of the Moon and the mean motion and true position of the Sun. In addition, it shows the hour, the day and the month. The driving trains of the dial are arranged vertically on parallel planes and are of such extraordinary complexity as to be without precedent. The clock is accompanied by two globes, one terrestrial and the other celestial, the latter being worked by the mechanism of the clock itself. The numerous movements of the planetary clock (including a sophisticated chime system) are driven by a single weight-powered motor.
(P.G.)

Bibliography: Brusa 1994.

VI.4.2
Philipp Immser (alias Ymbser)
Astronomical clock
Strasbourg, 1555-1557
Gilt brass; height 88 cm, base 55 x 55 cm
Vienna, Technisches Museum für Industrie und Gewerbe, inv. 11939

This spectacular astronomical clock is a work by Philipp Immser, professor of mathematics in Tübingen, but originally from Strasbourg. The clock belonged to Archiduke Ferdinand, the future Emperor Ferdinand II.
The clock presents a quadrangular base on which an octagonal structure rests, surmounted by a celestial sphere. The complex astronomical quadrant on the front depicts the zodiac, which has a division in degrees. On the quadrant there are the indexes of the irregular motions of the planets according to the Ptolemaic hypothesis, of the Sun and of the phases of the Moon. On the large quadrant on the right side, an angel indicates the calendar, the lengths of day and night, with the determination of sunrise and sunset, the current time (divided into 12), the day of the week and the Dominical letter. The quadrant on the left side indicates the latitudes of Jupiter, Saturn, Venus and Mars. The quadrant on the back (on which the map of central Europe is engraved) opens to give access to the extremely complex mechanism that controls the clock's many functions. Indicating the scale of minutes with her left hand, the Virgin Mary moves along the perimeter of the octagonal structure, making a complete revolution every hour. Every 15 minutes, the Virgin reaches one of the four doors at the base of the octagonal structure, that open to show small sculptures, in sequence, that represent the four ages of man (adolescence, maturity, old-age, death). At the stroke of the hour, the centre door opens showing the figure of Christ. The celestial sphere makes a full rotation on its axis once every 24 hours.
(P.G.)

Bibliography: King H.C. 1978a, pp. 68-72; Linz 1990, vol. II, pp. 69-70.

VI.4.3
Copy from Hans Holbein the younger
Portrait of Nikolaus Kratzer
20th century
Oil on canvas; 156 x 124 cm
Florence, Istituto e Museo di Storia
della Scienza, inv. 3566

The craftsman and mathematician Kratzer (Munich 1487 – London 1550) was astronomer and clock-maker to Henry VIII of England. He taught at Oxford and constructed beautiful sundials. Holbein the Younger (Augsburg 1497 or 1498 – London 1543) portrays him in his laboratory, together with his instruments.
(M.M.)

Bibliography: King H.C. 1978a, p.50; Miniati 1991, p. 36.

VI.4.4
Pierre de Fobis
Mechanical celestial sphere
Lyons, 1540-1550
Gilded bronze, silver, glass: height 54 cm, diameter of the terrestrial globe 8 cm, diameter of the celestial sphere 17 cm
Paris, Kugel Collection

One of the finest astronomical clocks of the Renaissance period, this was formerly part of the Rothschild collection in Vienna and was for half a century on show at the Kunsthistorisches Museum in that city. Pierre de Fobis (c. 1507-c. 1580) worked as a clockmaker in Lyons, where in all probability he made this clock for some important client.

The celestial sphere in the centre makes a complete rotation in 23 hours, 56 minutes and 4 seconds. Within it the Sun proceeds at the rate of one degree a day along the ecliptic, completing a whole orbit in a year. Another hoop, now missing, formerly recorded the orbit of the Moon around the Earth in 29½ days. On the sphere of the coordinates the lines marking the hours are, quite exceptionally, unequal. This system measures the day in 12 daylight hours and 12 night hours, their length varying with the seasons (the daylight hours are longer in summer and shorter in winter). The sphere functions by means of an extraordinarily complicated mechanism (complete with chime system) visible through the glass walls of the cylindrical column beneath the sphere. The engravings on the sphere itself are of the highest artistic quality. The Earth shows the most up-to-date cartographical results of the time according to the cordiform projection of Oronce Finé.
(P.G.)

Bibliography: Parigi 2002a, pp. 144-150.

VI.4.5
Eberhard Baldewein
Mechanical celestial globe
Kassel, 1574
Gilded and silver plated brass, wood;
height 32 cm, diameter 14 cm
Paris, Kugel Collection

Made in Kassel for Wilhelm IV, landgrave of Hesse-Kassel, a passionate promoter of astronomical studies (he supported Tycho Brahe, among others), this precious instrument by the most gifted clockmaker of the time, Eberhard Baldewein (c. 1525-1593), is the oldest mobile celestial sphere ever made in Germany. Wilhelm IV presented it as a gift to the Emperor Maximilian II in 1575.
Fixed to the circle of the meridian graduated to 360°, the globe consists of two brass hemispheres joined at the ecliptic. Also marked are the polar circles and the ecliptic (with 360° graduation). Starting from the poles of the ecliptic are six engraved circles dividing the sphere into twelve sections. The stars are represented in five different magnitudes. Part of the original mechanism which drove the sphere is missing, due to its being subjected to a 19th-century 'modernization' the results of which were recently removed in order to restore the instrument to its original appearance and function.
(P.G.)

Bibliography: Leupold 1986, pp. 88-92; Parigi 2002a, pp. 152-157.

VI.4.6
Johann Reinhold
Mechanical celestial sphere
Augsburg, 1588
Brass, wood, glass; height 49 cm, diameter of globe 31 cm
Paris, Musée des Arts et Métiers, inv. 07491

One of the five surviving and substantially similar astronomical clocks constructed by the Augsburg clockmaker Johann Reinhold (1550-1596) with the collaboration of his colleague and fellow townsman Georg Roll.
On the exterior of the globe are two cursors which rotate around the polar axis. The smaller cursor closer to the globe makes a complete rotation in 24 hours, causing the symbol representing the Sun to move along the ecliptic. The larger of the two cursors guides the hemisphere representing the Moon along a path beneath the ecliptic. All the functions are worked by a complex mechanism concealed within the globe. The globe itself makes an entire revolution in 23 hours, 56 minutes and 95 seconds, which corresponds to 365 days on the calendar ring. The two concentric dials fixed at the North Pole have hands showing the average solar time. Beneath the celestial globe is a small terrestrial globe on which are traced the continents and a system of coordinates.
(P.G.)

Bibliography: Hayward 1950; Bertele 1961, p. 17; King H.C. 1978a, pp. 83-85.

VI.4.7
Hans Christoph Schissler the Younger
Mobile celestial globe
Augsburg, c. 1600
Silver plated copper, gilded bronze; height 46 cm, diameter 16 cm
Private collection

This is the only known mechanical celestial globe by Hans Christoph (1561-1652), son of the famous German constructor of scientific instruments Christoph Schissler, and himself a craftsman of repute. The globe rests on the shoulders of a bronze Atlas of German workmanship. Three quarters of a circle support the horizon which bears a double graduated scale, on the outside a calendar, on the inner side the signs of the zodiac. Ptolemy's 48 constellations, with stars divided into six different magnitudes, are engraved on the sphere and given their Latin names. They are delineated in keeping with the model of the gores on the celestial map by François Demonget (c. 1560). The globe is silver plated and composed of two hemispheres joined together along the ecliptic, graduated in 360°. The constructor's name is shown on a scroll. The original verge escapement controlled by a circular foliot was replaced in about 1700 by a twin-armed balance-wheel.
(P.G.)

Bibliography: Parigi 2002a, pp. 166-171.

VI.4.8
Caspar Rauber (attr.)
Table astronomical clock
Southern Germany, c. 1575
Gilded brass, silver; 21.4 x 15.1 x 32.5 cm
Florence, Istituto e Museo di Storia
della Scienza, inv. 3370

Punched into the instrument is the maker's mark, 'CR', perhaps identifiable with that of Caspar Rauber of Degersee, a member of the clockmakers' guild of Augsburg. It is a mechanical compendium of everything known in the late 16th century about the measurement of time, the calendar and the movement of the stars, and evidently intended for very rich clients. Scrutiny of the Medici inventories tells us that the clock was one of the 'gems brought from France' by Maria Christina of Lorraine, or else with some measure of contradiction, that it was a present from her husband Ferdinando I de' Medici some time after 1589. The main dial of the clock – later altered by the addition of a pendulum – shows a mechanical astrolabe. Whereas in the Middle Ages the astrolabe enabled one to tell the time according to the height of the stars above the horizon, the extreme mastery of the mechanical devices achieved by German clockmakers led to an inversion of their function, so that they merely demonstrated the positions of the principal celestial bodies.
(G.S.)

Bibliography: Righini Bonelli 1976, p. 178, no. 244; Brusa 1978, p. 410, nos. 114-116; Miniati 1991, pp. 198-200, no. 1; *Istituto e Museo di storia della scienza (Firenze)* 2004, p. 78, no. 5; Caneva-Solinas 2005, p. 133.

VI.5.1
Nicolaus Copernicus
De revolutionibus orbium coelestium Libri Sex
Norimbergae, apud Joh. Petreium, 1543
Florence, Biblioteca Nazionale Centrale,
Magl. 5.2.132, title page

One of the strongest reasons for which, in history of science manuals, the year 1543 is considered as marking the clear break between the Middle Ages and the Modern Era, is the publication of the masterpiece by Copernicus (1473-1543), destined to have a profound influence on following generations. Bruno, Digges, Galilei and Kepler considered the text with admiration, drawing important stimulus from it.
Already conceived by Copernicus in its essential lines at the beginning of the second decade of the 1500's, the heliocentric hypothesis was explained in *De revolutionibus* by turning to both metaphysical and analogical reasoning, as well as by subjecting the results of observations to refined mathematical elaborations. Copernicus introduced the concept of a plurality of centres in the universe and advanced the hypothesis that at the centre of the world the Sun rotates on its own axis.
The anonymous preface (that readers were led to believe was by Copernicus himself) written by the editor of the work, Andreas Osiander, invited the reader to confer a purely hypothetical meaning on the explicit heliocentric formulations in the text. It was probably for this reason that the work did not meet with censure until the moment of the clash between Galileo and the ecclesiastical authorities more than 60 years after its publication (cf. entry 0.0.0). *De revolutionibus* was suspended *donec corrigatur* in 1616, at the conclusion of Galileo's first trial. With the decree of May 1620 the Tribunal of the Inquisition made public the censured passages that were to be erased from the copies already printed.
(P.G.)

Bibliography: Koyré 1966; Kuhn 1972; Lerner 1997, II, pp. 67-100.

VI.5.2
Vincenzo Coronelli
Epitome cosmografica o compendiosa introduttione all'astronomia, geografia e idrografia ...
Colonia [Venezia], ad istanza di Andrea Poletti in Venetia, 1693
Florence, Istituto e Museo di Storia della Scienza, MED 0391, pp. 28-29

The *Epitome* by the great globe-maker Coronelli (1650-1718) is a compendium that provides information on the principal systems of the world, of which he schematically outlines the structure. On pages 28 and 29, illustration of the yearly motion of the Earth's revolution around the Sun according to Copernicus' hypothesis.
(P.G.)

Bibliography: Domini-Milanesi 1998, pp. 39-40; Venezia 2007, pp. 49-56.

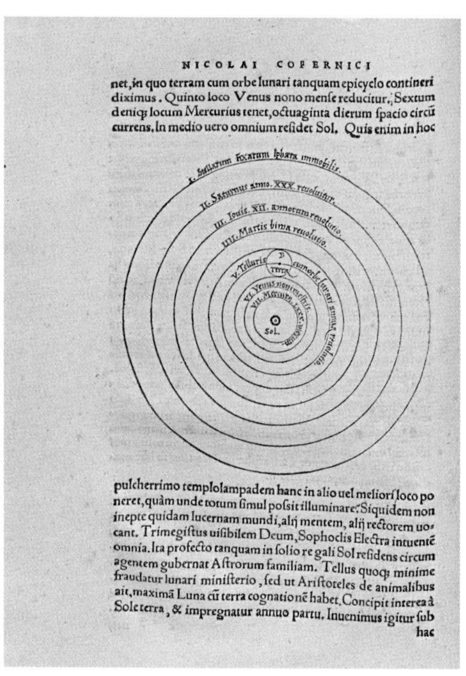
NICOLAI COPERNICI

net, in quo terram cum orbe lunari tanquam epicyclo contineri diximus. Quinto loco Venus nono menſe reducitur, Sextum deniq; locum Mercurius tenet, octuaginta dierum ſpacio circũ currens. In medio uero omnium reſidet Sol. Quis enim in hoc

pulcherrimo templo lampadem hanc in alio uel meliori loco poneret, quàm unde totum ſimul poſsit illuminare? Siquidem non inepte quidam lucernam mundi, alij mentem, alij rectorem uocant. Trimegiſtus uiſibilem Deum, Sophoclis Electra intuentẽ omnia. Ita profecto tanquam in ſolio regali Sol reſidens circum agentem gubernat Aſtrorum familiam. Tellus quoq; minime fraudatur lunari miniſterio, ſed ut Ariſtoteles de animalibus ait, maximã Luna cũ terra cognationẽ habet. Concipit interea à Sole terra, & impregnatur annuo partu. Inuenimus igitur ſub hac

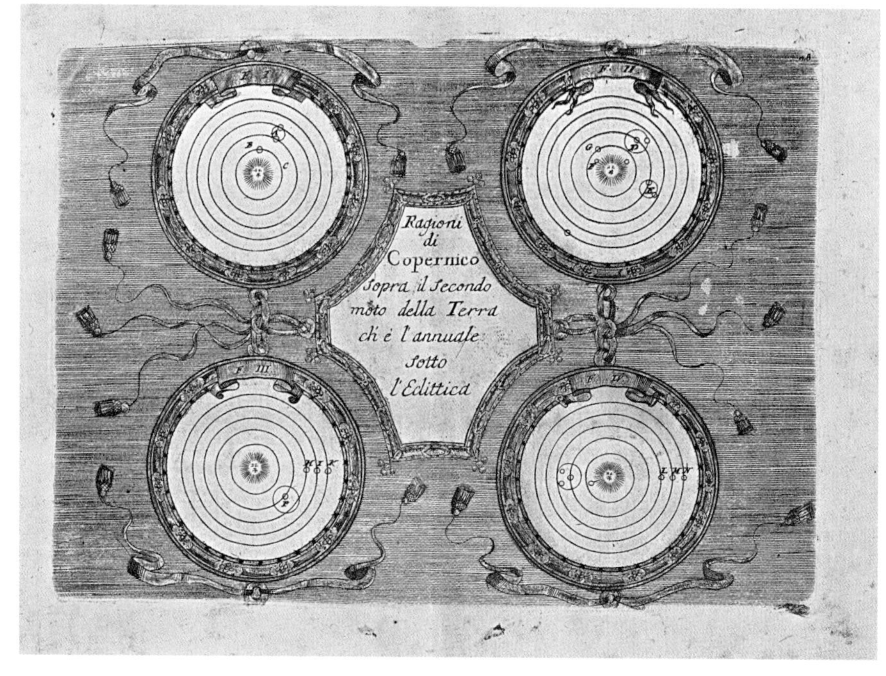

VI.5.3
Andreas Cellarius
Atlas coelestis seu Harmonia Macrocosmica
Amsterdam, Johannes Janssonius, 1660
Florence, Biblioteca Nazionale Centrale,
Magl. 5._.81, pl. 5 (*Planisphaerium Copernicanum*)

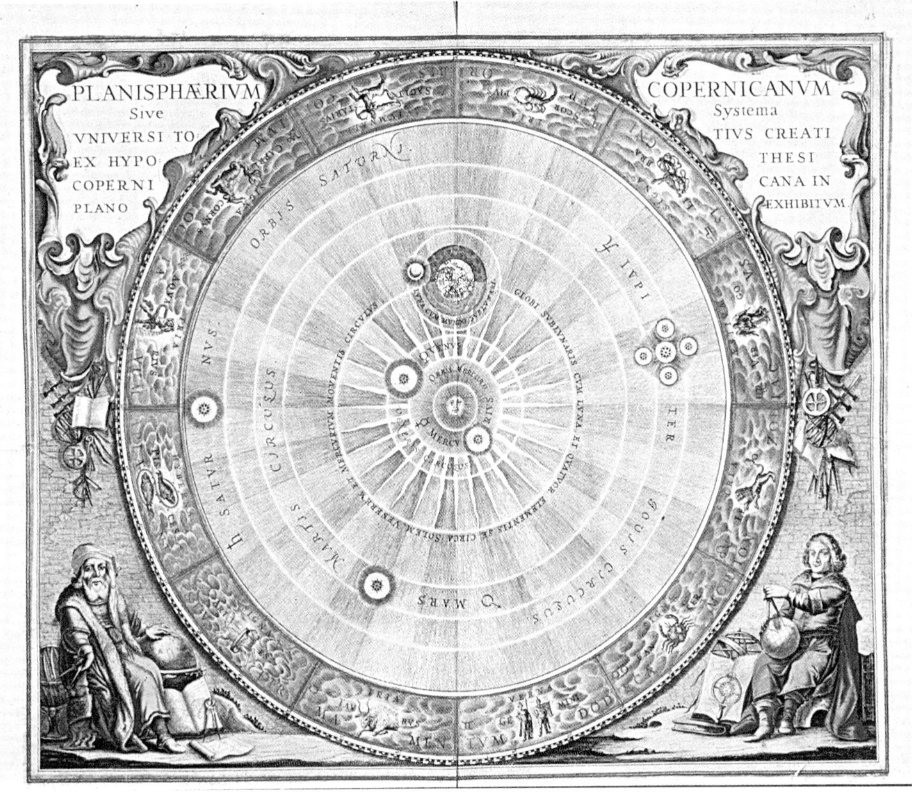

Cf. entry III.5.2.
The shining Sun dominates from the centre of this splendid table that represents Copernicus' system updated with the addition, around Jupiter, of the four satellites discovered by Galileo. In the lower right-hand corner Copernicus is portrayed with astronomical and measuring instruments, while the figure in the opposite margin can probably be recognized as Aristarchus of Samos, the ancient prophet of heliocentrism.
(P.G.)

Bibliography: Cellarius 2006, pp. 47-51.

VI.5.4
Andreas Cellarius
Atlas coelestis seu Harmonia Macrocosmica
Amsterdam, Johannes Janssonius, 1660
Florence, Biblioteca Nazionale Centrale,
Magl. 5._.81, pl. 6 (*Scenographia Systematis Copernicani*)

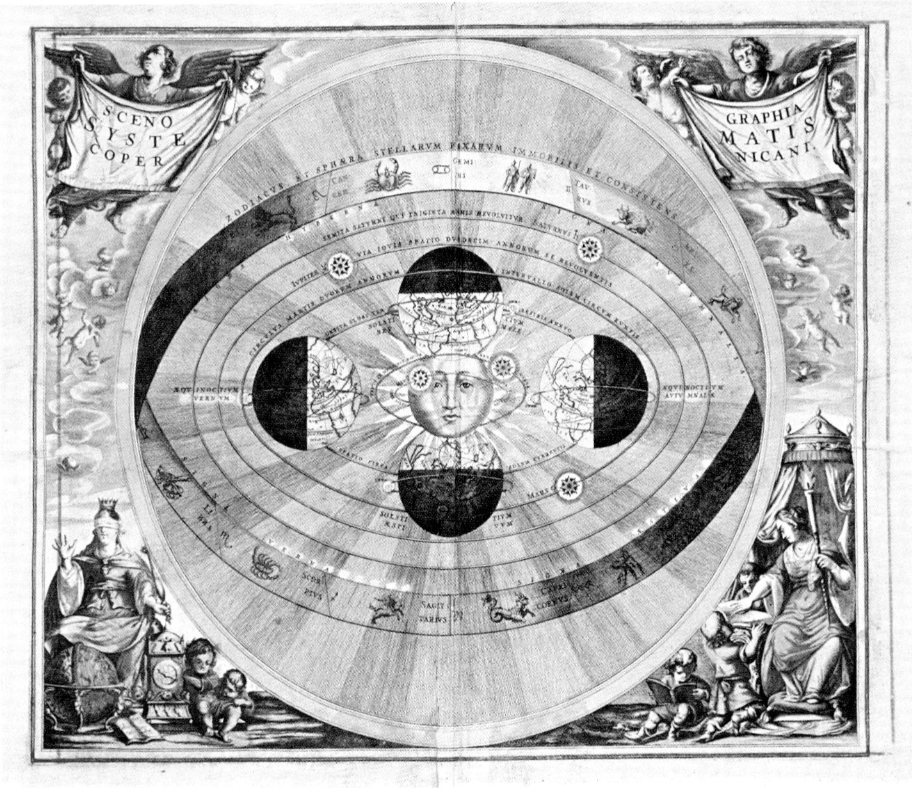

Cf. entry III.5.2.
A scenographic view of the heliocentric system. The four images of the Earth indicate the positions of our planet corresponding to the four seasons. In the lower left-hand margin, the blind-folded goddess portrays Astrea (blind because representing justice); while, lower to the right, Calliope is seen.
(P.G.)

Bibliography: Cellarius 2006, pp. 53-57.

VI.5.5
Richard Glynne
Copernican Armillary Orrery
c. 1720
Brass, silvered brass, steel, ivory, wood;
diameter 73 cm, height 101 cm
Oxford, Museum of the History of Science,
inv. 57605

Richard Glynne was a maker of mathematical instruments, such as sundials and armillary spheres, who also sold maps at his shop in London, identified by the sign of 'Atlas & Hercules'. He advertised 'all Kinds of Dials, Spheres and Globes of all Sizes.' The armillary orrery must have been at the top of his range: an impressive and expensive purchase by one of his most wealthy customers. It is an attempt to combine one of the oldest forms of astronomical instrument, the armillary sphere, with what was then one of the most recent, the orrery or planetarium. The armillary sphere in the enclosing outer part of the instrument, composed of rings representing the circles of the celestial sphere, such as the equator, tropics (Capricorn is missing) and the zodiac: it was best suited to illustrating the traditional Ptolemaic system with the Earth stationary at the centre of the cosmos and the heavens rotating around it. The celestial sphere rotates on an axis in this instrument but – somewhat inconsistently – at the centre is a planetarium based on the Copernican system, where the Sun is central and the Earth both rotates on its axis daily and moves in an annual orbit. The Earth and Moon, Mercury and Venus are moved by wheelwork activated by a hand-crank, while Mars, Jupiter and Saturn are pushed round by hand. The drum at the north celestial pole has wheelwork moving the celestial sphere and a dial and hands for displaying the time.
(J.B.)

Bibliography: Taylor 1966, p. 119; King H.C. 1978b, pp. 157-159; Clifton 1995, p. 114.

VI.5.6
Anonymous
The commission for the calendar reform
Biccherna tablet
Siena, July 1582-June 1583
Tempera and gold on wood; 52.4 x 67.8 cm
Siena, Archivio di Stato, n. 72

It belongs to the series of Sienese painted tablets that annually commemorated particularly important events occurring during the year. The one displayed here celebrates the approval of the Gregorian calendar that from October 4th, 1582 substituted the ancient Julian calendar in Catholic countries. The reform was carried out by moving the date ahead from October 4th to October 15th. The scene depicted in the tablet shows Pope Gregory XIII who, sitting enthroned, presides the calendar commission. Around the table, on the right, various eminent members of the clergy and an Oriental scholar (identifiable by his turban) are portrayed while engaged in a lively discussion. The person standing uses a rod to indicate the notches on a zodiacal calendar corresponding to the days from the 4th through the 15th of October, symbolized by the sign of the Scorpion. This figure might represent Antonio Lilio, the brother of Luigi, author of the project for the reform of the Julian calendar, who never saw it realized since he passed away before its completion.
(P.G.)

Bibliography: Roma 2001, pp. 161-163; *Biccherne* 1984, pp. 274-275.

VI.5.7
Anonymous
Portrait of Wilhelm Schickart
1632
Oil on canvas; 60.5 x 49 cm
Tübingen, Bildnissammlung im Senatsaal
Universität Tübingen

Professor of Hebrew and later, as successor of Mästlin (Kepler's teacher), of Mathematics and Astronomy at Tübingen, Wilhelm Schickart (1592-1635) was an admirer of Copernicus and Kepler. He is here shown holding a small Copernican planetarium the hand-worked mechanism of which shows the annual orbit of the Earth around a Sun with a human face and its daily motion. Around the Earth orbits the Moon, depicted in two waxing phases. This is the oldest known painting showing a heliocentric planetarium.
(P.G.)

Bibliography: King H.C. 1978a, pp. 93-94.

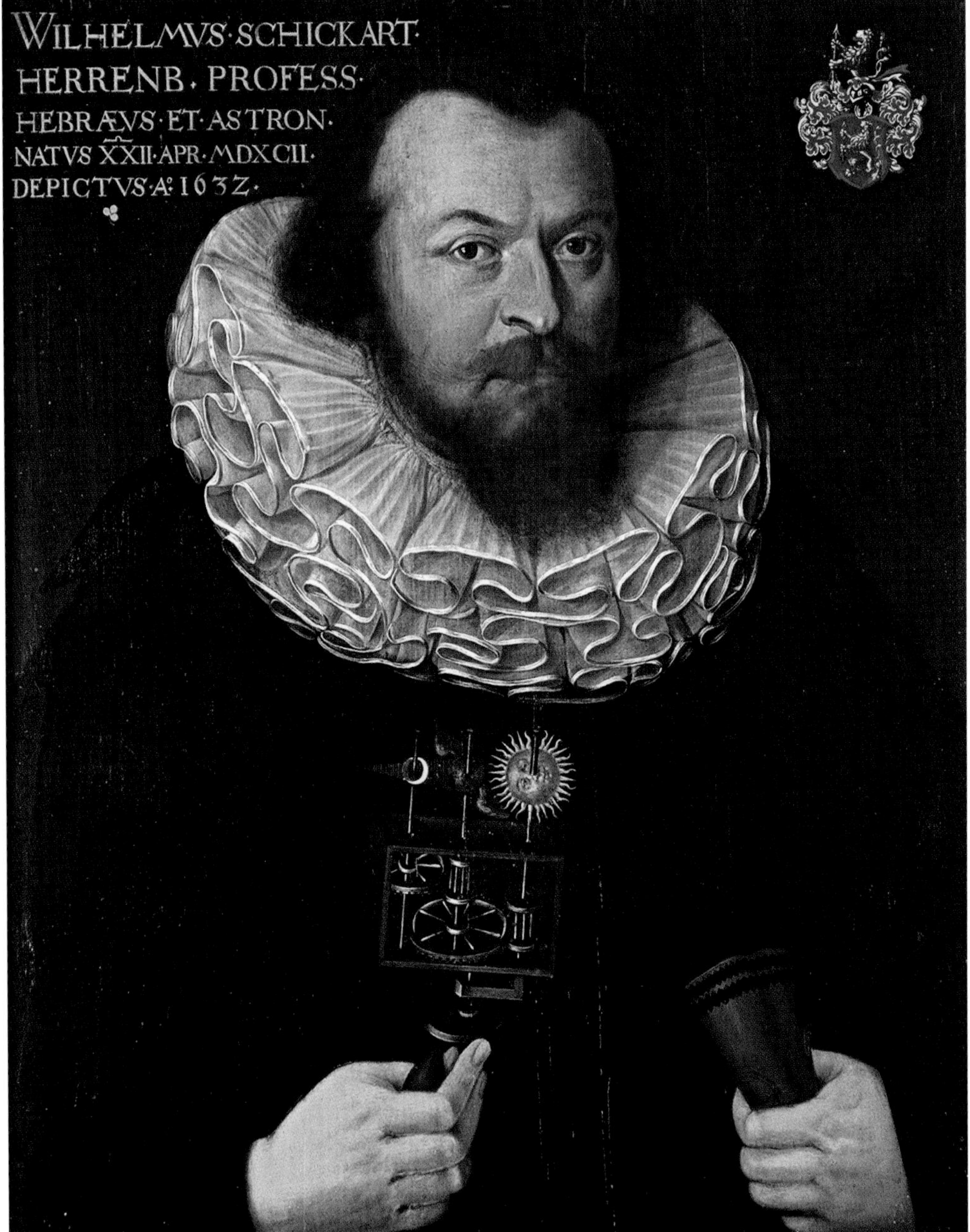

WILHELMVS·SCHICKART·
HERRENB· PROFESS·
HEBRÆVS·ET·ASTRON·
NATVS XXII·APR·MDXCII·
DEPICTVS·A° 1632·

VI.5.8
Tycho Brahe
De mundi aetherei recentioribus phaenomenis
Francofurti, apud Godefridum Tampachium, 1610 (Colophon ed. 1588)
Florence, Istituto e Museo di Storia della Scienza, MED 1246, p. 189

After the case of the extraordinary celestial phenomenon that was the subject of his *De nova stella* (1573), Tycho Brahe (1546-1601) applied himself to the task of determining the distance from the Earth of the comet which appeared in 1577. This was no easy matter, and Tycho was only able to expound his results a decade after his observations, which he did in *De mundi aetherei recentioribus phaenomenis* (1588). Together with the conclusion that the comet was a celestial body orbiting the Sun, the work also contains a preview of the geo-heliocentric system of the cosmos which Tycho had been working on since 1584. The incompleteness of this account is due to his anxiety about losing the credit for the new system, in view of the claims of the plagiarists Nicolai Reymers Bär (1551-1600), known as Ursus, e Duncan Liddel (1561-1613).
On page 189, Tycho's geo-heliocentric system.
(G.S.)

Bibliography: Thoren 1990, pp. 236-264; Strano 2005, pp. 19-21.

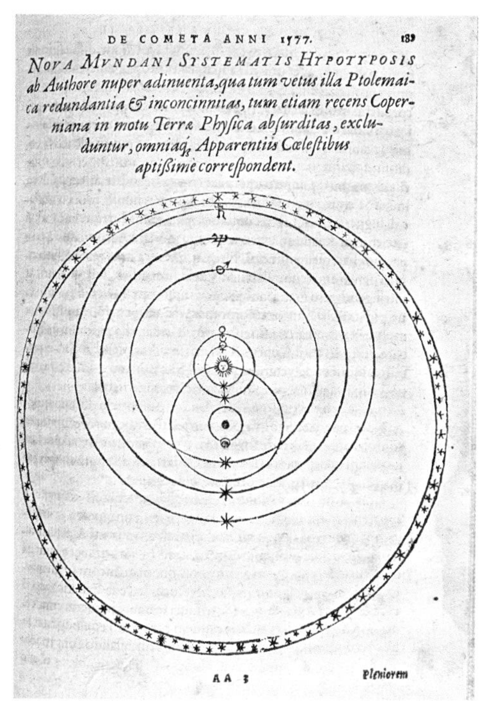

VI.5.9
Tycho Brahe
Astronomiae instauratae progymnasmata ...
Francofurti, apud Godefridum Tampachium, 1610
Florence, Istituto e Museo di Storia della Scienza, MED 1247, tav. f.t. fra le pp. 8-9

Printed posthumously and edited by Johann Kepler (1571-1630), the *Astronomiae instauratae progymnasmata* (1602) of Tycho Brahe (1546-1601) put forward all the arguments that were indispensable to the foundation of a new astronomy. The *Progymnasmata* in fact provided not only the methods to follow in order to measure the celestial coordinates but also the tables needed to correct certain anomalies in observation (for example, atmospheric refraction, a phenomenon which alters the apparent position of the stars). The work also contains the geo-heliocentric planetary models which Tycho had already obtained for the Sun, the Moon and Saturn, a catalogue of 777 stars and their related coordinates, in addition to a new scrutiny of the celestial nature of the *nova* of 1572. The engraving forming the frontispiece of the first reprinting of the *Progymnasmata* (1610) is a portrait of Tycho conspicuously displaying the coats of arms of the families with which the Brahes were connected, the medal of the Order of the Elephant conferred on the Danish astronomer by King Frederick II, and the famous prosthesis which Tycho wore on his nasal septum.
(G.S.)

Bibliography: Strano 2005, pp. 23-25.

STELLÆBURGUM five OBSERVATORIUM SUBTERRANEVM, A TYCHONE BRAHE NOBILI DANO
IN INSULA HVÆNA, EXTRA ARCEM URANIAM, EXTRVCTVM CIRCA ANNVM M D LXXXIIII.

VI.5.10
Willem Jansz Blaeu
Le grand atlas, ou, Cosmographie Blaviane ...
Amsterdam, chez Jean Blaeu, 1667
Florence, Istituto e Museo di Storia della Scienza, MED GF 034, tav. f.t. fra le pp. 89-90

The observatories of Uraniborg and Stjerneborg, established by Tycho Brahe (1546-1601) on the island of Hveen, soon became exemplary models. Their own founder publicized their merits by sending detailed descriptions to eminent astronomers such as Wilhelm IV (1532-1592), landgrave of Hesse-Kassel, and the Italian Giovanni Antonio Magini (1555-1617). Willem Jansz Blaeu (1571-1638), a Dutch instrument maker who had also been Tycho's assistant in 1595-96, included a description of the two observatories in his *Atlas Maior, sive Cosmographia Blaviana*, which was translated into several languages. This work also contains tinted engravings most of which are based on Tycho's *Astronomiae instauratae mechanica* (1598).
In the engraving showing the Stjerneborg observatory may be seen the roofs of the five crypts which housed the most advanced astronomical instruments.
(G.S.)

Bibliography: Brahe 1598, pp. Hr-H4r; Christianson 2001, pp. 254-256.

VI.5.11
Andreas Cellarius
Atlas coelestis seu Harmonia Macrocosmica
Amsterdam, Johannes Janssonius, 1660
Florence, Biblioteca Nazionale Centrale,
Magl. 5._.81, pl. 7 (*Planisphaerium Braheum*)

Cf. entry III.5.2.
Visualization of the geo-heliocentric system conceived by Tycho Brahe. The Earth is immobile in a central position. The Moon and the Sun rotate around it, while the other planets move around the Sun. In the lower right-hand corner, the Danish astronomer is portrayed, surrounded by students, while in the opposite margin, an unidentified person lectures on cosmography and geography to a group of young men.
(P.G.)

Bibliography: Cellarius 2006, pp. 59-64.

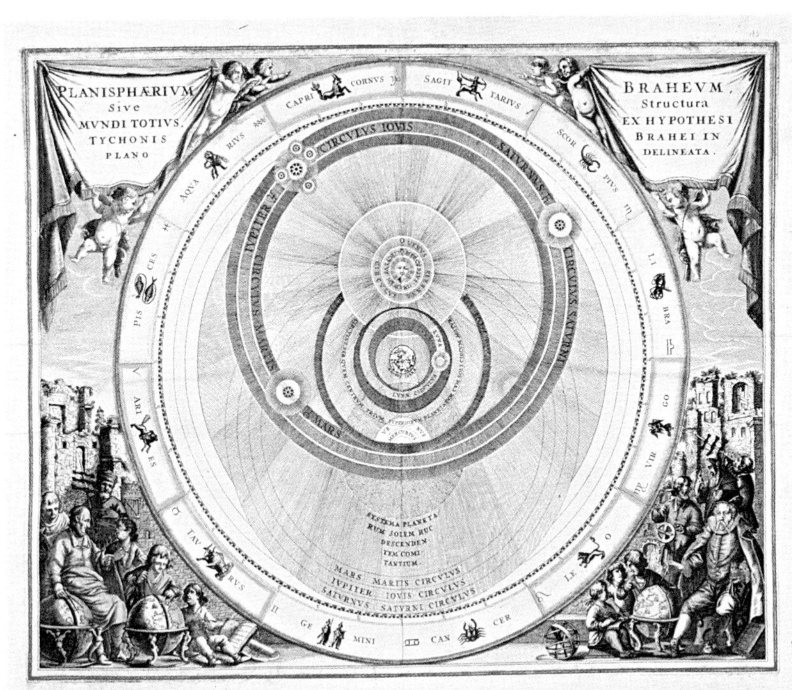

VI.5.12
Andreas Cellarius
Atlas coelestis seu Harmonia Macrocosmica
Amsterdam, Johannes Janssonius, 1660
Florence, Biblioteca Nazionale Centrale,
Magl. 5._.81, pl. 8 (*Scenographiae compagis mundanae Brahea*)

Cf. entry III.5.2.
With *Scenographia* Cellarius indicates, here and in other cases, a view, seen in transparence, of the system of the world observed from an external position. The table offers a splendid view of the mixed system conceived by Tycho Brahe. In the lower left-hand margin, an allegoric representation of Wisdom, in the opposite margin, Urania.
(P.G.)

Bibliography: Cellarius 2006, pp. 65-70.

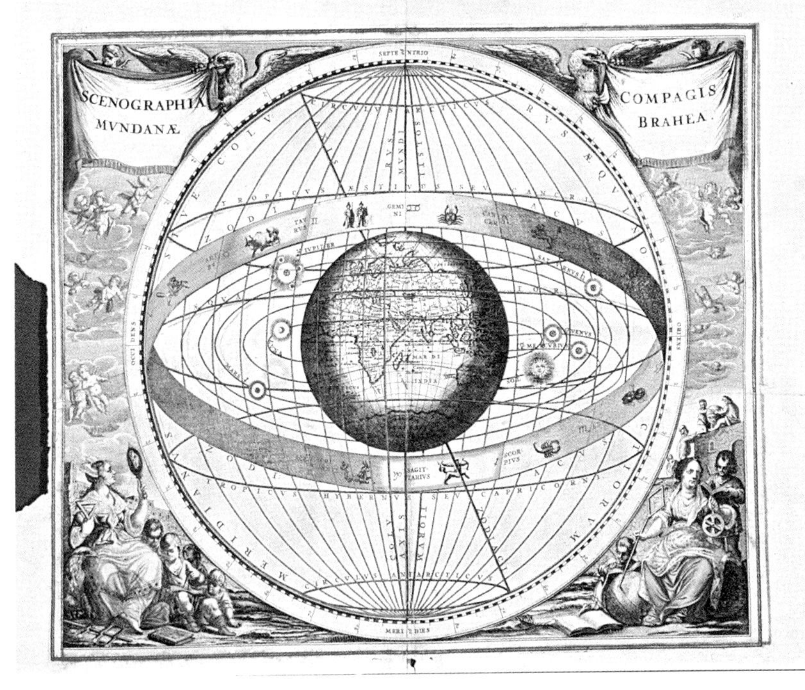

VI.5.13
Jansz Willem Blaeu
Celestial globe
After 1630
Wood, paper, 111 x 92 cm, diameter 68 cm
Florence, Istituto e Museo di Storia
della Scienza, inv. 2697

The globe belongs to the undated editions and was perhaps printed by Joan Blaeu (son of Jansz Willem Blaeu) after 1630. It bears the production serial number 11. The names of the finely portrayed constellations are in Latin, Greek and Arabic. There is a portrait drawn of Tycho Brahe, of whom Blaeu was a disciple.
(M.M.)

Bibliography: *Catalogo IMSS* 1954, p. 40, Righini Bonelli 1968a, p. 156, Miniati 1991, p. 100; *Istituto e Museo di storia della scienza (Firenze)* 2004, p. 132.

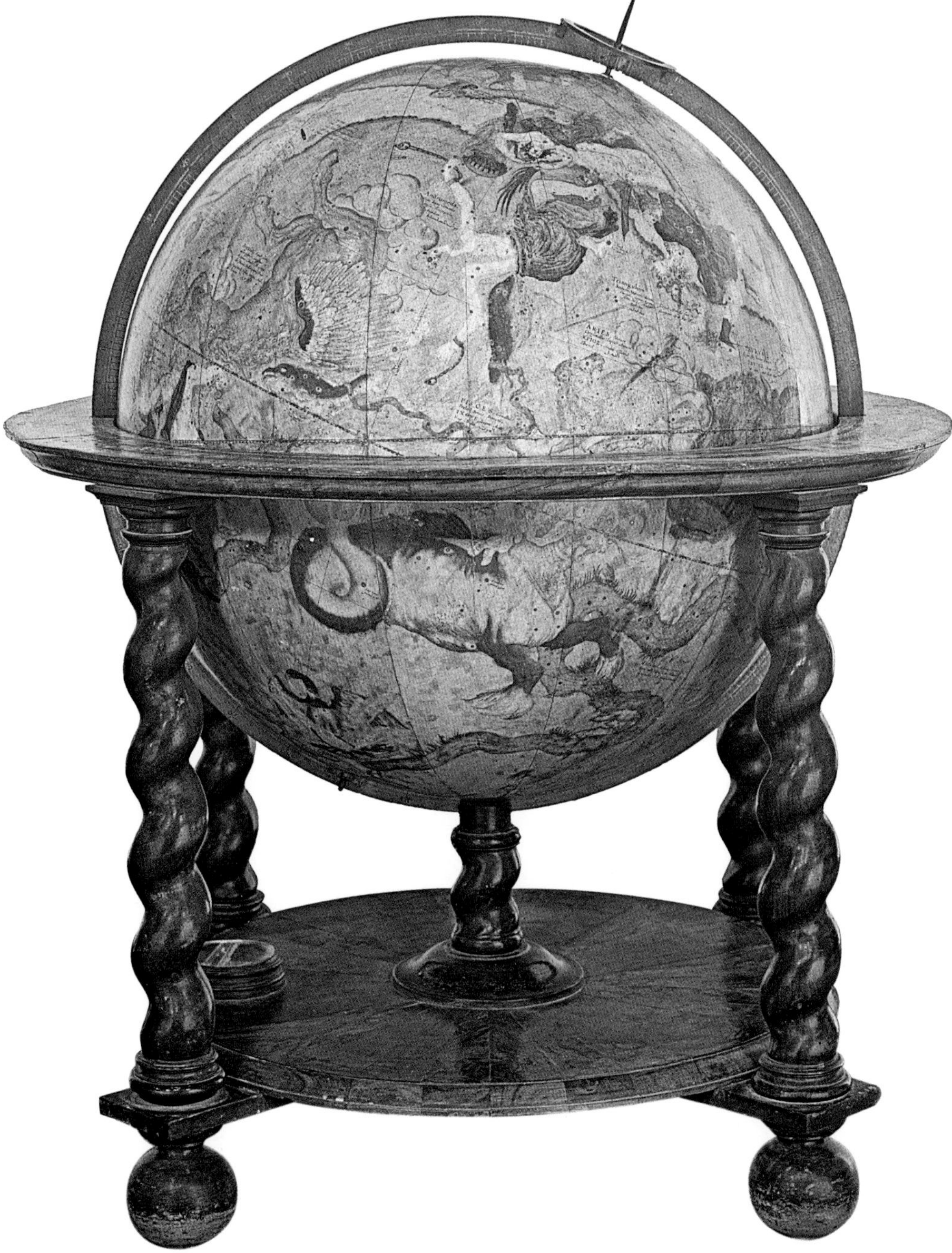

VI.5.14
Joost Bürgi
Sextant
c. 1600
Steel, brass, wrought iron, wood; radius 112.2 cm, height c. 170 cm
Prague, Národní Technické Muzeum, inv. 17195

Joost Bürgi (1552-1632) worked from 1579 as clockmaker and constructor of astronomical and mathematical instruments to Wilhelm IV (1532-1592), landgrave of Hesse-Kassel. Here he got word of a new type of steel sextant for a single observer which Tycho Brahe (1546-1601) had constructed in 1575. The great repute Bürgi acquired for himself at Kassel brought him to Prague, where he took up residence in about 1603 to become clockmaker to the emperor Rudolf II. Because some parts of it are missing, it is not altogether clear whether this instrument, made by Bürgi in about 1600, is still of that type of steel sextant or else of the more advanced type of triangular astronomical sextant for two observers described by Tycho in his *Astronomiae instauratae mechanica* (1598).
(G.S.)

Bibliography: Brahe 1598, pp. Dv-D3r; Horský-Škopová 1968, p. 163; Janoušek 1997, p. 36.

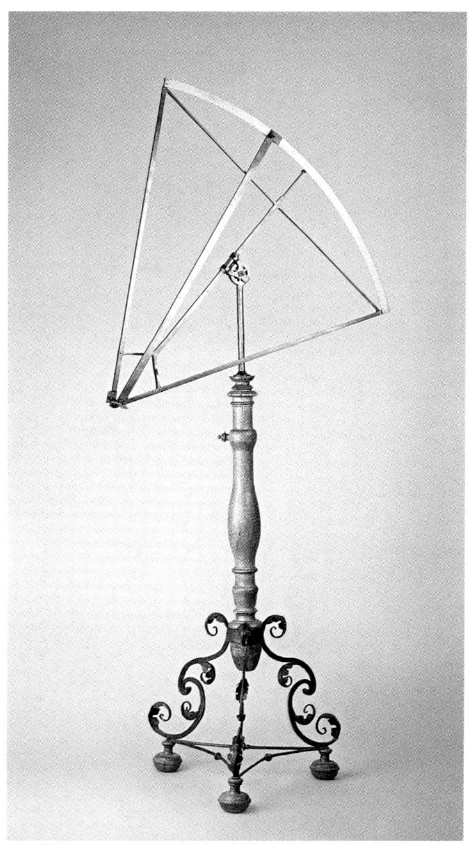

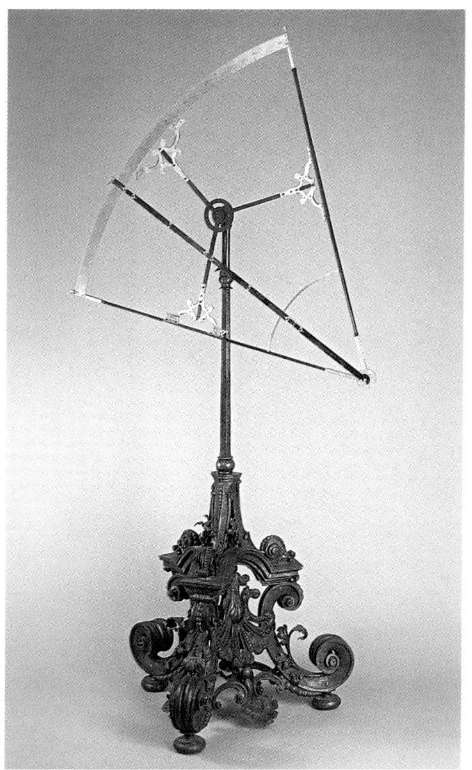

VI.5.15
Erasmus Habermel
Sextant
1600
Steel, brass, wrought iron; radius 131.7 cm, height c. 170 cm
Praga, Národní Technické Muzeum, inv. 24551

Erasmus Habermel (c. 1538-1606), an engraver and craftsman of German origin, took up residence in Prague in about 1585 in the service of the emperor Rudolf II. His acquaintanceship with Tycho Brahe (1546-1601), who himself was in Prague as Imperial Mathematician from 1599 on, clearly appears from this instrument which, although missing some parts, is a reinterpretation on a smaller scale of the triangular astronomical sextant for two observers the definitive form of which Tycho built in 1582 and thereafter described in *Astronomiae instauratae mechanica* (1598). The sextant is signed 'Pragae Fecit Erasmus Habermel 1600'.
(G.S.)

Bibliography: Brahe 1598, pp. Dv-D2r; Horský-Škopová 1968, p. 162; Janoušek 1997, p. 37.

VII.1.1
Carlo Marcellini
Bust of Galileo Galilei with compasses and telescope
1674-1677
Marble; height 78 cm
Florence, Istituto e Museo di Storia della Scienza

The commission for this work on the part of Cosimo III dates from 1674 and was assigned to Carlo Marcellini (1644-1713) who was working at the Academy of Sculpture in Palazzo Madama in Rome. For use as a model the artist was sent the *Portrait of Galileo* from the Gioviana Series in the Uffizi, as indicated in a note in the *Giornaletto di Galleria* (Library of the Uffizi, MS. 62, fols. 110, 111). Marcellini took a long time about it, but the end result was very fine. The sculptor portrays Galileo with his head slightly turned to the left with respect to the central axis of the bust. In his right hand, beneath the folds of the cloak, he holds two of the instruments which had most contributed to his renown, the compasses and the telescope.
(F.T.)

Bibliography: Favaro 1913, p. 1037; Fahie 1929, p. 124; Lankeit 1962, pp. 162, 254, nos. 117, 120; Büttner 1976, pp. 105-108; Visonà 1990, pp. 36-38; Freddolini 2007, p. 92.

VII.1.2
Florentine painter of the 17th century
Portrait of Galileo Galilei with telescope and ring of the Accademia dei Lincei
1640-1645
Oil on canvas; 78 x 64 cm
Florence, Uffizi, inv. 1890, no. 5432
(on deposit at the Domus Galilaeana, Pisa)

The painting presents a front view of Galileo, seated and holding a telescope and wearing the ring of the Accademia dei Lincei. It is one of the few such paintings to correspond to the descriptions given in 17th century inventories recording the presence of a "portrait of Galileo dressed in black with an old-fashioned collar and holding in his right hand a telescope and a ring on the finger of his left hand". Worthy of note is the form of the telescope, very similar to the one belonging to Galileo now preserved at the Institute and Museum of the History of Science in Florence (cf. entry VII.2.8).
Sent by the Uffizi in 1942 for deposit at the Domus Galilaeana in Pisa, the picture is a replica of the iconic portrait of Galileo painted in about 1640 by Justus Sutterman on commission from Ferdinand II for his own gallery of famous men.
(F.T.)

Bibliography: Goldenberg Stoppato in Florence 1986, I, p. 324, n. 1.167; Tognoni in Geneva 2004, pp. 88, 92; Goldenberg Stoppato in Florence 2006, pp. 50-51, n. 14 (with bibliography); Tognoni 2007, pp. 143-144.

VII.1.3
Ottavio Leoni
Portrait of Galileo Galilei
1624
Black stone, white lead and red ochre on turquoise blue paper; 23.7 x 16.5 cm
Florence, Biblioteca Marucelliana,
Vol. H drawings

This portrait is part of an album preserved in the Biblioteca Marucelliana in Florence and containing 27 portraits of famous men immortalized by Ottavio Leoni (1578-1630). Galileo appears dressed in doctoral robes, his face distinguished by a thick beard and wrinkled brows which emphasize his expression of deep thought, just as he had appeared on the flyleaf of the *Istoria e dimostrazione intorno alle macchie solari* (cf. entry VII.2.6), thereafter reinserted in *Il Saggiatore* (cf. entry VII.2.4).
The success which Galileo attained with these works persuaded Leoni to include him in the collection of prints of which he is the author.
(F.T.)

Bibliography: Favaro 1913, pp. 1005-1006; Fahie 1929, pp. 19-24; Roma 1964, pp. 80-81, no. 50; Luigi Ficacci in Roma 1989, p. 150, no. 11 (with bibliography); Tognoni 1999, p. 362; Sani 2005, p. 178.

VII.1.4
Richard Rowley (attr.)
Pair of planetaria, Ptolemaic and Copernican
c. 1700
Brass, silvered brass, brass wire, ivory, wooden stands; diameters 40 cm, 39 cm
Oxford, Christ Church, (On loan from the Museum of the History of Science, inv. 68353, 19978)

This is an unusual – perhaps unique – solution to the problem of representing the cosmos by an instrument and accommodating both the traditional Ptolemaic arrangement, with the Earth at the centre, and the Copernican, where the Earth is in orbit around the Sun, accompanied by the Moon and rotating on its axis once a day. The two systems are treated in a pair of matching instruments, which follow diagrams in J.C. Sturm's *Scientia Cosmica* of 1670. Each planetarium has an outer ring for the zodiac and concentric rings for the planets, each carrying a planetary symbol. Since the zodiac is horizontal, the Earth – whether at the centre in the Ptolemaic system or in orbit in the Copernican – is inclined. The orbital rings, each carried by four curved supports rising from the centre, can be rotated to represent movements and configurations of the planets; the exception is that in the Copernican instrument the Earth is carried by a train of three wheels, so that it rotates as it is moved around in its orbit. In the Ptolemaic instrument the symbols for Mercury and Venus, and for Saturn and Jupiter, are erroneously reversed, perhaps as the result of some subsequent repair.
(J.B.)

Bibliography: King H.C. 1978a, p. 157; Turner A. 1987, p. 232.

VII.1.5-6
Matthäus Greuter
Celestial and terrestrial globes
Rome, 1632 and 1636
Paper, wood; 152 x 83 cm, diameter 49 cm
Florence, Istituto e Museo di Storia della Scienza, inv. 2702 and 2701

The globes form a pair with the same characteristics: the wooden sphere, closed within the brass meridian ring, that runs in grooves made in the horizon ring, rests on an elegant structure with curved feet. The globes are covered with 24 printed paper half-gores and protected by a cover made of painted canvas with figures of the constellations.
In the celestial globe, the stars, whose names are in Latin and Arabic, are those reported by Pieter Dircksz Keyser (Nauclero), who with Houtman observed, for the first time, twelve southern constellations, in the Dutch expedition organized between 1595 and 1597. The cartographic images are for the most part borrowed from the globes by the Dutchman Willem Jansz Blaeu, published in 1622.
In the terrestrial globe – dedicated to Prince

Jacopo Boncompagni, a descendent of Pope Gregory XIII, author of the reformation of the calendar – there is the new addition of the name "Nieun Nederland" on the coast of the present United States.
Matthäus Greuter (1566-1638), worked in Rome (especially for the Accademia dei Lincei), where he gained fame as an engraver and draftsman.
(M.M.)

Bibliography: *Catalogo IMSS* 1954, pp. 43-44; Righini Bonelli 1968a, p. 157; Miniati 1991, p. 96; Miniati *et. al.* 1995; *Istituto e Museo di storia della scienza (Firenze)* 2004, pp. 134, 136, 138; Camerota-Miniati 2008, pp. 162-163.

VII.1.7
Middle finger of Galileo's right hand
Reliquary c. 1737
Marble, glass (reliquary); 44.5 x 15 cm
Florence, Istituto e Museo di Storia della Scienza, inv. 2432

Characteristic example of the celebration of Galileo as a symbol to venerate as well as an author to study and to comprehend. The finger was detached from Galileo's mortal remains by the provost Anton Francesco Gori on the occasion (12 March 1737) of the belated transfer of his body from the little room under the bell-tower of the Basilica di Santa Croce, near the Capella dei Santi Cosma e Damiano, to the monumental tomb built in the left nave of the Basilica. The finger came into the possession of Angelo M. Bandini, librarian of the Biblioteca Laurenziana, from where it was transferred to the Tribuna di Galileo (1841) and then to the Museo di Storia della Scienza di Firenze. In the circular alabaster base, an inscription that exalts the scientific and moral virtues of Galileo, by Tommaso Perelli, astronomer of the University of Pisa.
(P.G.)

Bibliography: Galluzzi 1993.

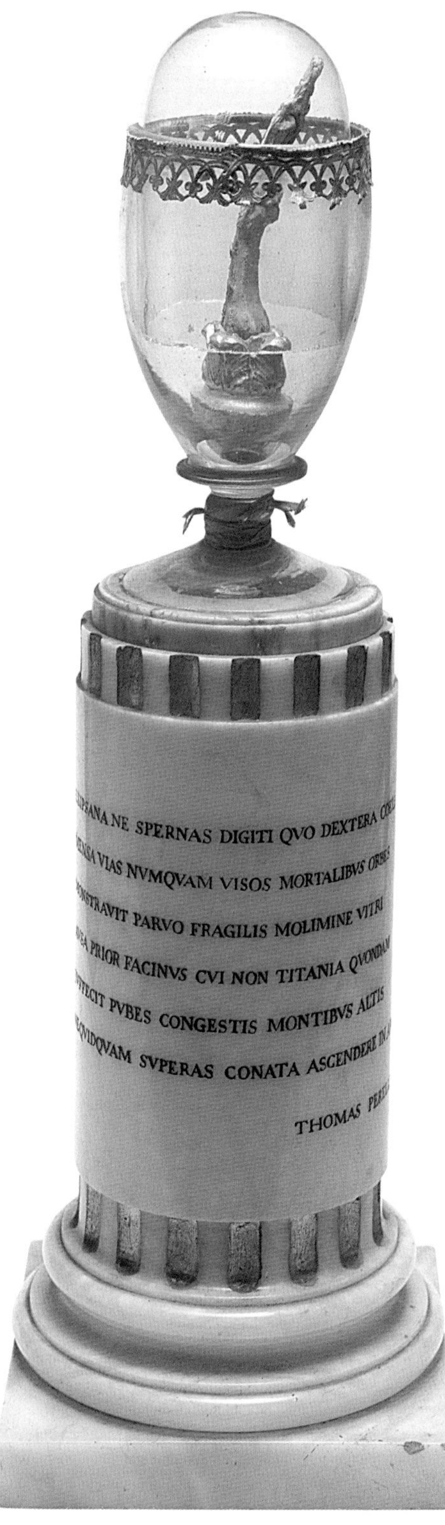

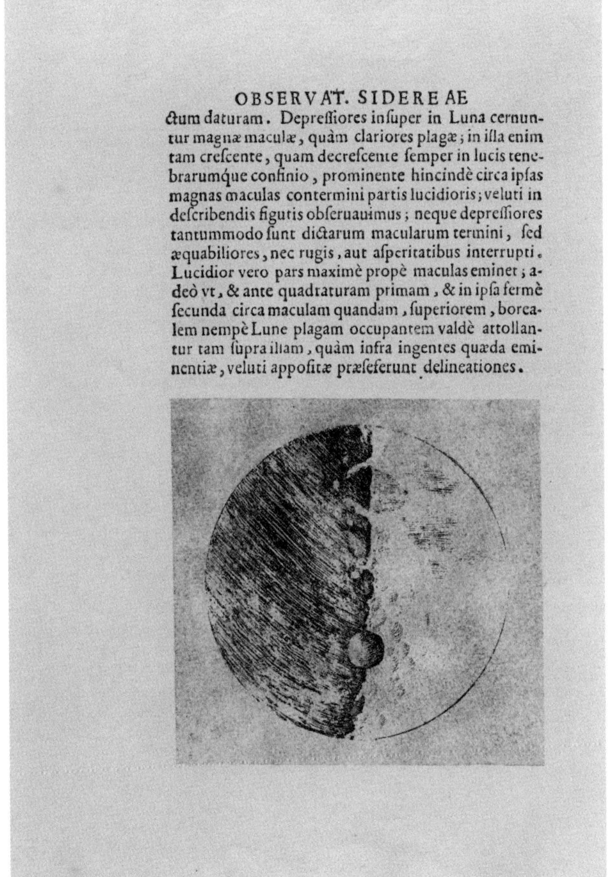

OBSERVAT. SIDEREAE

ctum daturam. Depreſſiores inſuper in Luna cernuntur magnæ maculæ, quàm clariores plagæ; in illa enim tam creſcente, quam decreſcente ſemper in lucis tenebrarumque confinio, prominente hincindè circa ipſas magnas maculas contermini partis lucidioris; veluti in deſcribendis figuris obſeruauimus; neque depreſſiores tantummodo ſunt dictarum macularum termini, ſed æquabiliores, nec rugis, aut aſperitatibus interrupti. Lucidior vero pars maximè propè maculas eminet; adeò vt, & ante quadraturam primam, & in ipſa fermè ſecunda circa maculam quandam, ſuperiorem, borealem nempè Lunę plagam occupantem valdè attollantur tam ſupra illam, quàm infra ingentes quædam eminentiæ, veluti appoſitæ præſeferunt delineationes.

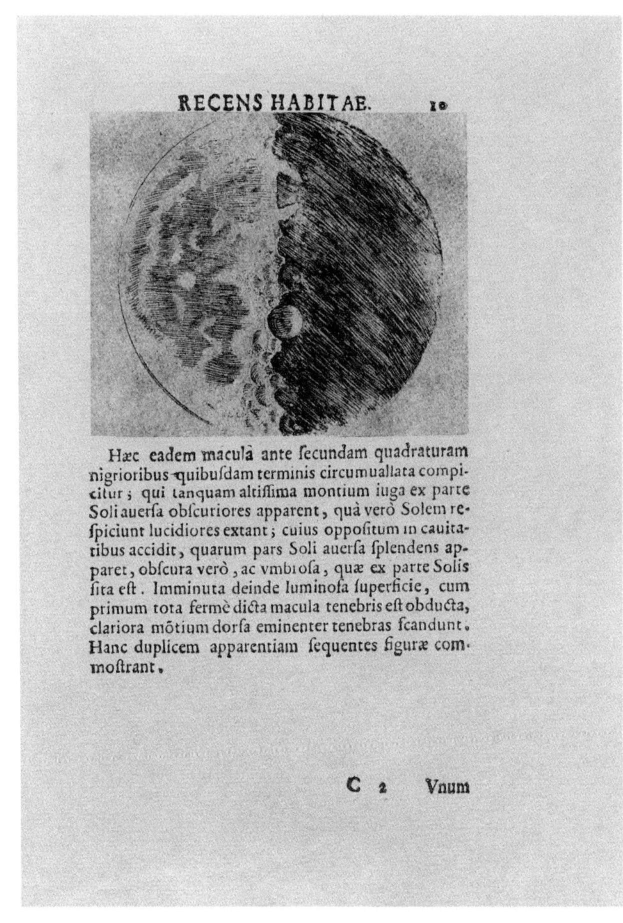

RECENS HABITAE. 10

Hæc eadem macula ante ſecundam quadraturam nigrioribus quibuſdam terminis circumuallata compicitur; qui tanquam altiſſima montium iuga ex parte Soli auerſa obſcuriores apparent, quà verò Solem reſpiciunt lucidiores extant; cuius oppoſitum in cauitatibus accidit, quarum pars Soli auerſa ſplendens apparet, obſcura verò, ac vmbroſa, quæ ex parte Solis ſita eſt. Imminuta deinde luminoſa ſuperficie, cum primum tota fermè dicta macula tenebris eſt obducta, clariora mõtium dorſa eminenter tenebras ſcandunt. Hanc duplicem apparentiam ſequentes figuræ commoſtrant.

C 2 Vnum

VII.2.1
Galileo Galilei
Sidereus Nuncius, magna longeque admirabilia spectacula pandens ...
Venetiis, apud Thomam Baglionum, 1610
Florence, Biblioteca Nazionale Centrale, Postillati 110, fols. 9v-10r

The work, published very hastily in a modest-style edition in the Spring of 1610, announced to the world the series of extraordinary celestial discoveries made by Galileo in just a few weeks, thanks to the astronomical use of the telescope, that he had greatly perfected. In a pressing sequence, Galileo referred to the face, full of mountains and valleys, of the Moon (that was, therefore, not a perfect body, as the followers of Aristotle claimed), of the discovery of four satellites around Jupiter and of the mass of stars that form the Milky Way. In the final pages the author emphasized how his discoveries contributed to bearing out the Copernican hypothesis.
Galileo dedicated his work to Grand Duke Cosimo II de' Medici, naming the four satellites of Jupiter, that he entitled "Medicean stars" (*Medicea Siderea*), after the Tuscan family.
On folios 9v and 10r, engravings of the Moon observed with a telescope (cf. entry VII.2.8).
(P.G.)

Bibliography: Gingerich-Van Helden 2003; Bucciantini 2003, pp. 162-193; Camerota M. 2004, pp. 150-198.

VII.2.2
Galileo Galilei
Autograph diary of the observations of Jupiter
1619
Florence, Biblioteca Nazionale Centrale,
Ms. Gal. 48, f. 30r

Precious manuscript that documents the enormous energy which Galileo dedicated, from the beginning of the year 1610, to telescopic observations of Jupiter and its four satellites. The manuscript contains observations and calculations made between 1610 and 1619, for the precise tabulation of the four satellites' periods in order to use Jupiter's system like a perfect clock, to resolve the dramatic problem of determining longitude at sea.
In chart 30r Galileo records his first telescopic observation of Jupiter, on the evening of January 7th, 1610. At first he thinks that the bodies next to the planet are stars fixed on the back of the firmament. Having noted during successive evenings that they do not move more than a modest distance away from Jupiter, he comes to the conclusion that they are satellites. The concise daily annotations are dated and indicate the time of observation. Jupiter is drawn like a small wheel with spokes, while the satellites are indicated by three crossed strokes.
(P.G.)

Bibliografia: Drake 1976; Righini 1978, pp. 45-75.

VII.2.3
Galileo Galilei
Letter to Belisario Vinta
Padua, July 1610
Florence, Biblioteca Nazionale Centrale,
Ms. Gal. 86, f. 42r

From Padua, Galileo announces to the Secretary of State of Tuscany, for referral to the Grand Duke, his discovery with a telescope of another new celestial body "that no one has observed before me": the planet Saturn is not a single "star... but is composed of three, which almost touch each other, nor do they ever move or change...". Galileo traces a schematic drawing on paper of three-bodied Saturn. He is convinced that satellites orbit around even the most distant planet – exactly as he had observed with Jupiter. It will be Huygens, almost forty years later, to definitively establish that the bulge observed by Galileo was the ring that encircles the planet.
(P.G.)

Bibliography: Camerota M. 2004, pp. 194-195; Van Helden 1974.

altri l'incontrasse, sappino che niuno l'ha osservata
avanti di me, se ben tengo per fermo che niuno la
vedrà se non dopo che ne l'haverò fatto avvertito:
questo è che la Stella di Saturno non è una sola
ma un composto di 3. le quali quasi si tocca:
no, ne mai tra di loro si muovono, o mutano; et
son poste in fila secondo la lunghezza del Zodiaco,
essendo quella di mezzo circa 3. volte maggiore
delle altre 2. laterali, et stanno situate in
questa forma. oOo. si come quanto prima
farò vedere a loro AA. essendo in questo autunno
per haver bellissima comodità di osservare le cose
celesti co i pianeti tutti sopra l'orizzonte.
Non occuperò più V. S. Ill.ma et baciandoli con ogni
reverenza le mani, la supplico ad inchinarsi humil:
mente in mio nome a loro AA. Ser.me N. S. la feliciti.
Di Padova li 30. di Luglio 1610.
Di V. S. Ill.ma
Ser.re Oblig.mo
Galileo Galilei

VII.2.4
Galileo Galilei
Il Saggiatore
In Roma, appresso Giacomo Mascardi, 1623
Florence, Biblioteca Nazionale Centrale,
Magl. 3.2.406, p. 217

Published under the auspices of the Accademia dei Lincei, *Il Saggiatore* is rightfully appreciated for its extraordinary literary quality, that makes it one of the absolute masterpieces of Italian literature. In it Galileo advanced, in controversy with the Jesuit Orazio Grassi, the interpretation of comets as vapours given off by the Earth and condensed in cosmic space. He also proposed the famous distinction between primary qualities (objective) and secondary qualities (subjective), demonstrating his inclination for atomistic concepts. For this reason, the work was denounced to the Holy Office, that did not, in any case, consider that there were grounds for censure. The engraving on page 217 shows the planet Saturn, no longer triple (cf. entry VII.2.3), but surrounded by a kind of ring, Jupiter, Mercury and (below) the phases of Venus, that displays also a remarkable variation in size during its cycle.
(P.G.)

Bibliography: Redondi 1983; Galilei 2005.

DEL SIG. GALILEI. 217

ducete ſino à dannar con lunghi diſcorſi chi prende il termine vſitatiſſimo d'infinito per grandiſſimo. Quando noi abbiamo detto, che il Teleſcopio ſpoglia le Stelle di quello irraggiamento, abbiamo voluto dire, ch'egli opera intorno à loro in modo, che ci fà vedere i lor corpi terminati, e figurati, come ſe fuſſero nudi, e ſenza quello oſtacolo, che all'occhio ſemplice aſconde la lor figura. E egli vero Sig. Sarſi, che Saturno, Gioue, Venere, e Marte all'occhio libero non moſtrano trà di loro vna minima differenza di figura, e non molto di grandezza ſeco medeſimi in diuerſi tempi? e che coll' occhiale ſi veggono Saturno, come appare nella preſente figura, e Gioue, e Marte, in quel modo ſempre; e Venere in tutte queſte forme diuerſe? e quel, ch'è più merauiglioſo con ſimile diuerſità di grandezza? ſi che cornicolata moſtra il ſuo diſco 40. volte maggiore, che rotonda, e Marte 60.

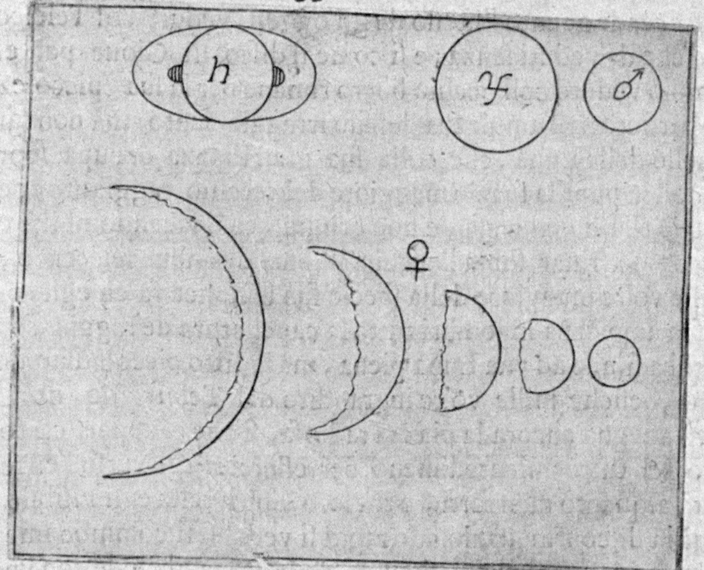

volte, quando è perigeo, che quando è a pogeo, ancorche all'occhio libero non ſi moſtri più che 4. ò 5.? Biſogna, che riſpondiate di ſi, perche queſte ſon coſe ſenſate, ed eterne, ſi che non ſi può ſperare di poter per via di ſillogiſmi dare ad

E e inten-

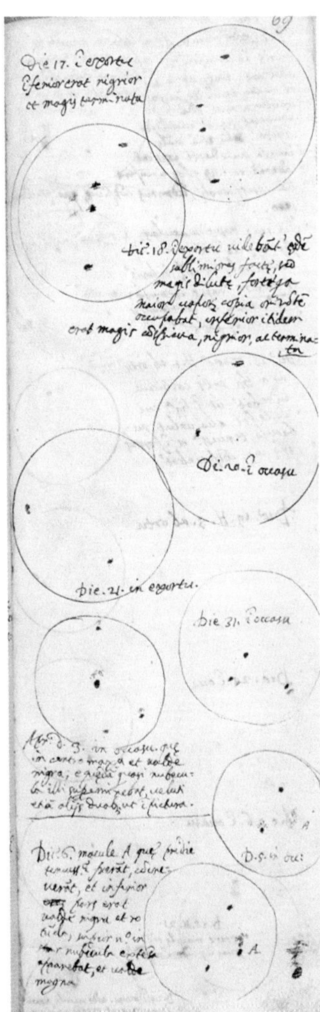

VII.2.5
Galileo Galilei
Drawings of sunspots
c. 1612
Florence, Biblioteca Nazionale Centrale,
Ms. Gal. 57, f. 69r.

One of the numerous drawings of the spots Galileo observed on the Sun between 1611 and 1612. Using a projection instrument, the helioscope, the Pisan scientist succeeded in making drawings of near-photographic precision of the sunspots, without risking his sight. Many of his drawings were transferred into engravings and included in the *Istoria e dimostrazioni* (cf. entry VII.2.6). (P.G.)

Bibliography: Camerota M. 2004, pp. 238-59; Bredekamp 2007, pp. 217-82, 363-478.

VII.2.6
Galileo Galilei
Istoria e dimostrazioni intorno alle macchie solari e loro accidenti: comprese in tre lettere scritte all'illustrissimo Marco Velseri
In Roma, appresso Giacomo Mascardi, 1613
Florence, Biblioteca Nazionale Centrale,
Postillati 155, pp. 94-95

The letters announce the discovery of dark spots on the surface of the Sun, that Galileo could observe, projecting the image of the Sun by means of a helioscope. The work was printed by the Accademia dei Lincei, to which Galileo was enrolled in 1611 on his first visit to Rome, during which he had shown the sunspots to many important members of the clergy and of the nobility. The *Istoria* contains explicit declarations supporting the Copernican hypothesis. On the base of prolonged observations of the spots, Galileo advances the hypothesis that the Sun rotates on its own axis. For this reason and for the renewed affirmation of the corruptibility of the heavens (Galileo was convinced that the sunspots were located on the surface of the Sun), the work encountered difficulty in obtaining a licence to print. In the *Istoria* Galileo claims priority of the discovery of sunspots over the Jesuit Christoph Scheiner, who had taken the merit for the discovery in a work published in Augsburg in 1612 with the pseudonym of *Apelles post tabulam latens*. The letters to Velser are accompanied by a great number of engravings that depict the positions of the spots on the solar surface noted in a series of continuous observations during the summer of 1612.
On pages 94 and 95 engravings of the sunspots observed on the 19th and the 20th of August 1612. (P.G.)

Bibliography: Camerota M. 2004, pp. 238-59; Firenze 2008, pp. 82-83; Bredekamp 2007, pp. 217-82, 363-478.

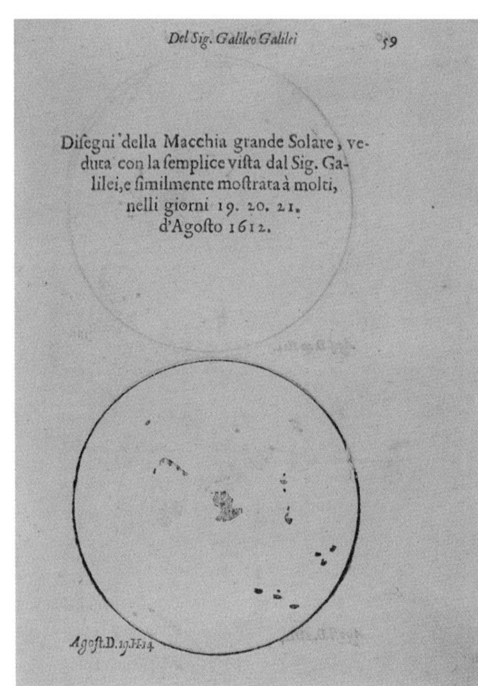
Del Sig. Galileo Galilei 59

Diſegni della Macchia grande Solare, veduta con la ſemplice viſta dal Sig. Galilei, e ſimilmente moſtrata à molti, nelli giorni 19. 20. 21. d'Agoſto 1612.

Agoſt.D.19.H14

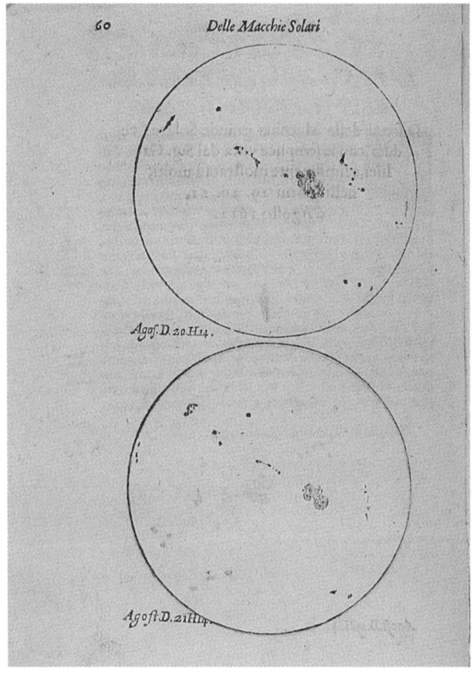
60 *Delle Macchie Solari*

Agoſt.D.20.H14.

Agoſt.D.21.H14

VII.2.7
Jean Chalette
Astra medicea
1611
Pen with Indian ink; 31 x 21.5 cm
Carpentras, Bibliothèque Inguimbertine, Ms. 803, f. 285 (facsimile)

As soon as he received *Sidereus Nuncius*, Peiresc tried to verify, with a telescope, the discoveries of the Pisan scientist. The observations were done with such care that Peiresc believed that he could take the merit for being the first to have distinguished the four satellites of Jupiter, for which he even proposed precise denominations: Cosmus mayor, Franciscus, Ferdinandus, Cosmus minor. Peiresc thought of publishing the results of the observations that, in his opinion, improved, in some aspects, on those of Galileo. The work was to be dedicated to Maria de' Medici and Malherbe offered to revise the text. Jean Chalette designed the title page, in which above the zodiac the four Medicean planets (depicted as the four Grand Dukes) are represented allegorically with Jupiter at the centre, on which Maria de' Medici and the Medicean coat-of-arms dominate.
(P.G.)

Bibliography: Rizza 1965, pp. 190-203; *Catalogue général des manuscripts BPF* 1899, p. 444; Abbé 1912-1914, pp. 185-187, table XIV.

VII.2.8
Galileo Galilei
Telescope
Florence, c. 1610
Glass, wood, leather; diameter 6 cm, length 92.7 cm
Florence, Istituto e Museo di Storia della Scienza, inv. 2428

In the letter dated 19 March 1610 with which he sent Cosimo II the *Sidereus nuncius* (cf. entry VII.2.1) and his own most highly developed telescope, Galileo assured the Grand Duke that he would have every opportunity of providing him with astronomical instruments first-rate from both the optical and the aesthetic point of view. As soon as he was nominated "first mathematician" at the University of Pisa and "chief mathematician and philosopher" to the Grand Duke, Galileo had to make good his promise, as we see from this telescope which is part of the Medici collections.

The instrument is constructed using an unusual technique, revealed in the course of restoration in 1996, with the tube made of thin strips of wood glued together, then covered with red leather to which narrower strips of brown leather were applied. Elaborate decorations in gold leaf are impressed on the whole length of the tube and the two lens barrels make this an extremely precious object in itself. Only some of the optical features have been preserved: the lens is original, but the eyepiece was replaced with a biconvex lens at the turn of the 19th-20th centuries. The present magnifying power of the instrument is of about 20 times.
(G.S.)

Bibliography: Galilei 1890-1909, v. X, pp. 297-298; Righini Bonelli 1976, p. 151, no. 2; Miniati 1991, p. 72, no. 2; Van Helden 1999, pp. 30-31, no. 1; Firenze 2008b, p. 136.

VII.2.9
Exploded replica of Galileo's telescope
Jim and Rhoda Morris

External examination of the telescope donated by Galileo to the Grand Duke of Tuscany (cf. entry VII.2.8) gives only a vague idea of its beauty, and none at all of its technical complexity. But during the restoration conducted in 1996 it was possible to inspect the internal structure of the instrument and identify its various diverse components. This exploded replica, with and without the leather covering, shows with the utmost clarity the conformation and composition of all of the various parts of Galileo's telescope: from the tube made of wooden strips held together by glue and black cloth, to the lens housings and the diaphragms.
(G.S.)

VII.2.10
Galileo Galilei
Objective lens
Padua, end of 1609
Glass; 5.8 cm (frame: ebony, ivory, gilded brass; 41 x 30 cm)
Florence, Istituto e Museo di Storia della Scienza, inv. 2429

To create increasingly close relations with the Medici court and facilitate his return to Tuscany, Galileo sent an as yet unbound copy of the *Sidereus nuncius* (cf. entry VII.2.1) to Cosimo II de' Medici together with the telescope he used for his discoveries during the winter of 1609-1610, including that of the four satellites of Jupiter. As Galileo told the Grand Duke in a letter of 19 March 1610, this telescope was completely devoid of aesthetic value, other than the beauty of the many hours spent observing the stars through it. And it must have been only for its aesthetic value that it was kept in the Grand Duke's collection of scientific instruments, seeing that in only a few years it fell to pieces. The objective lens, now unattached to the barrel of the instrument, fell on the ground and broke even during Galileo's lifetime. In 1677, when the great Pisan scientist was beginning to become a myth, the lens was rescued, reassembled and placed in a frame evocative of Galileo's discoveries created in ebony and ivory by Vittorio Crosten, an engraver of Dutch origin. Optical analyses performed in recent years have shown that the lens, plane convex in form, was extremely well made.
(G.S.)

Bibliography: Galilei 1890-1909, v. X, pp. 297-298; Righini Bonelli 1976, p. 151, no. 3; Miniati 1991, p. 72, no. 3; Van Helden 1999, pp. 32-33, no. 3; Firenze 2008b, p. 135.

VII.2.11
Evangelista Torricelli
Telescope
Florence, 1647 (objective lens), second half of the 18th century (tube)
Brass, cardboard, glass; length 111.5 cm
Florence, Istituto e Museo di Storia della Scienza, inv. 2554

A number of historical circumstances bear witness to the high technical level achieved by Torricelli (1608-1647) in the production of lenses. One of them is that as late as the end of the 18th century one of his objective lenses was used in the building of a new telescope with a brass tube. This objective is a biconvex lens mounted in a cardboard ring bearing the signature: "V. Torr. in Fior. 1647. Br. 1 3/4", which means "Vangelista Torricelli in Fiorenza 1647. Braccia 1 ¾" (about 1 metre in focal length). Along with the excellent quality of the grinding and polishing, the yellowish lens also shows some of the bubbles and imperfections typical of the glass produced in the 17th century.
(G.S.)

Bibliography: Righini Bonelli 1976, p. 188, no. 422; Miniati 1991, p. 74, no. 26; Van Helden 1999, pp. 54-55, no. 5.

VII.2.12
Evangelista Torricelli
Objective lens
Florence, 1646
Glass, cardboard, leather; diameter 11.5 cm
Florence, Istituto e Museo di Storia della Scienza, inv. 2571

Proof of Torricelli's great skill in optics is provided by the special investigations carried out by wish of the Grand Duke of Tuscany after the former's sudden, early death. Witnesses were called on to reveal the various phases in Torricelli's working method which enabled him to obtain especially polished and transparent lenses. But their reports failed to indicate anything very different from the procedures followed by other telescope makers of the time. It is clear that Torricelli's real secret was his outstanding manual skill. In common with many lens makers he signed his own most important products, especially the objective lenses. In this particular objective, which was exceptionally large for its time, the signature reads "Vangelista Torricelli. Fiorenza. 1646. Braccia 10 1/4", corresponding to a focal length of about 6 metres.
(G.S.)

Bibliography: Righini Bonelli 1976, p. 189, no. 434; Galluzzi 1976, pp. 84-95; Miniati 1991, p. 72, no. 5; Van Helden 1999, pp. 36-37, no. 8; Firenze 2008b, p. 143.

VII.2.13
Eustachio Divini
Octagonal telescope with seven extensions
Rome, 1674
Wood, cardboard, glass; length (fully open) 565 cm
Florence, Istituto e Museo di Storia della Scienza, inv. 2557

Trained as a clockmaker, Eustachio Divini (1610-1685) became a leading light in telescope making as early as 1649. In his work he shows a continuous tendency towards experimentation, as shown by his frequent use of variable optical combinations, to the point of combining seven different lenses in a single instrument. In this telescope with an octagonal section and seven extensions the optical system was originally composed of four lenses (one of which is now missing). The objective lens, plane convex in section, is signed on the edge "Eustachio Divini in Roma 1674". Its magnification was about 55 times.
(G.S.)

Bibliography: Righini Bonelli 1976, p. 189, no. 425; Miniati 1991, pp. 76-77, no. 54; Van Helden 1999, pp. 42-16, no. 17.

VII.2.14
Eustachio Divini
Eyepiece with biconcave lens
Cardboard, glass; diameter 6.3 cm, length 10.7 cm
Florence, Istituto e Museo di Storia della Scienza, inv. 2574

This eyepiece, signed "Eustachio Divini in Roma 1666 acuto per palmi 26" (that is, for a telescope with an objective of about 5.8 metres in focal length) is composed of a biconcave lens. It shows that as early as 1666 Divini was making instruments with a basic structure of the Galilean type. This does not mean that Divini did not also adopt the basic structure of the Keplerian telescope, characterized by an eyepiece with a biconvex lens. This structure is in fact seen in many of the instruments of his preserved today. Divini's leadership in the field of optics had, however, been seriously threatened ever since 1660 by the emergence on the European scene of two very different and mutually antagonistic figures: the Dutch natural philosopher Christian Huygens (1629-1694), the inventor of a new type of eyepiece with two convex lenses, and Giuseppe Campani (1635-1715).
(G.S.)

Bibliography: Righini Bonelli 1976, p. 189, no. 437; Miniati 1991, pp. 72-73, no. 9; Van Helden 1999, pp. 46-47, no. 19; Firenze 2008b, p. 144.

VII.2.15
Giuseppe Campani
Telescope with four extensions
Rome, 1666
Cardboard, leather, wood, glass; length (fully open) 343 cm
Florence, Istituto e Museo di Storia della Scienza, inv. 2556

Like Divini, Giuseppe Campani (1635-1715) made his name as a clockmaker and only later (in about 1659) devoted himself to optics. All the same, unlike his rival, Campani very soon turned to the construction of a specific model of telescope of the "terrestrial" type, that is, one capable of providing direct images. Campani in fact discovered that the limitation of the Keplerian telescope, giving a broad visual field but producing upside-down images, could be got over by inserting a group of two equal convex lenses between the objective lens and the eyepiece. This pair – known also as the "erector" – produced a second reversal of the image which, combined with the first, turned it right way up again. In this telescope, signed on the edge of the objective lens "Giuseppe Campani in Roma anno 1666", the erector group is lodged in a small cardboard cylinder inserted in the last extension of the telescope, opposite the eyepiece lens.
(G.S.)

Bibliography: Righini Bonelli 1976, p. 188, no. 424; Miniati 1991, p. 76, no. 52; Van Helden 1999, pp. 52-53, no. 22.

VII.2.16
Giuseppe Campani
Objective lens
Rome, 1665
Glass, cardboard; diameter 13.7 cm
Florence, Istituto e Museo di Storia della Scienza, inv. 2587

Like many opticians of the 17th century, Campani considered the lenses he made to be genuine masterpieces worthy of signature and dedication. The edge of this particular lens is engraved with "Joseph Campanus faciebat Romae anno 1665" and "Ferdinando II Serenissimo Magno Etrurie [sic] Duci". It was indeed made for a telescope of ten extensions which, when fully open, reached a length of some 11 metres. Presented by Campani to the Grand Duke of Tuscany, on the largest segment of its tube this telescope bore the arms of the Medici family.
(G.S.)

Bibliography: Righini Bonelli 1976, p. 189, no. 439 and 447; Miniati 1991, p. 72, no. 6 and p. 76, no. 51; Van Helden 1999, pp. 50-52, no. 21.

VII.2.17
Giuseppe Campani
Metal forms for telescopes and microscopes
17th century
Brass, wood; diameter min. 3.5 cm, max 16 cm
Bologna, Museo di Fisica, Università di Bologna, inv. 593, 594, 595, 596/1956

Concave or convex metal plates with handles, in metal or wood, used for making lenses on a lathe or by hand. Giuseppe Campani (1635-1715) had constructed, for his optics workshop in Rome, a great number of these forms, diversifying them in size and curvature (convex or concave), so as to adapt them to all the phases of the production of optical lenses (roughing, polishing, cleaning, etc.) to make lenses (nearly achromatic) of all kinds, whether for telescopes or for microscopes. The original seventeenth-century lathe with which Campani realized, in part with secret techniques, his famous lenses and eyepieces was dismantled at the end of the 1700's.
A large part of the metal forms, just as several series of shims and measures, are conserved by the University Museum of Physics in Bologna.
In the illustration, a typical metal form.
(G.D.)

Bibliography: Bedini 1961; Dragoni 2006.

VII.2.18
Giuseppe Campani
Measures
17th century
Metal; length min. 6 cm, max 37.5 cm
Bologna, Museo di Fisica, Università di Bologna, inv. 393/1956

A series of twenty-two metal parts with varying dimensions (length, curvature, thickness, etc.) used by G. Campani and, after his death (1715) and until 1747, by his daughters for the construction of precise optical instruments, ordered by the most important persons from all Europe. These small metal plates (gauges) were used to size the lenses, the openings of the diaphragms, the distances between eye, ocular and lens.
(G.D.)

Bibliography: Bedini 1961; Dragoni 2006.

VII.2.19
Chérubin d'Orléans (Michel Lasséré)
Binocular telescope
Wood, leather, glass; length (open) c. 105 cm
Florence, Istituto e Museo di Storia della Scienza, inv. 2563

Since the first appearance of such instruments in the Low Countries, clients in search of telescopes demanded binocular devices, considering it just too awkward to peer one-eyed through an optical instrument while keeping the other eye closed. And in effect the difficulty of making two telescopes with identical magnification prevented the first "binoculars" from being anything but a curiosity of negligible use in astronomy. In this instrument two identical telescopes of 15 magnifications are enclosed in a rectangular tube with three extensions. The eyepieces, each consisting of three lenses, are placed at the tip of the broadest section, which is covered with black leather, while the objective lens is in the narrowest part. The gilt decorative motifs, including the arms of the Medici family and the figures of cherubim, show that the instrument was made for the Grand Duke Cosimo III by the Capucin friar Chérubin d'Orléans (1613-1697), author of *La dioptrique oculaire* (1671), in which this type of telescope is minutely described.
(G.S.)

Bibliography: Righini Bonelli 1976, p. 189, no. 431; Miniati 1991, p. 76, no. 43; Van Helden 1999, pp. 76-77, no. 42.

VII.3.1
Peter Paul Rubens
Saturn devours one of his sons
1637-1638
Oil on canvas; 180 x 87 cm
Madrid, Museo del Prado, inv. PO1678

Saturn devours one of his sons – of which a sketch is known, but not accepted by everyone as a work by Rubens (1577-1640), with even darker and more terrible tones (Jaffé 1989, p. 363, nn. 1323-1324) – is part of a nucleus of works done between 1636 and 1638 for the Torre de la Parada, the hunting pavilion built by Phillip IV of Spain near Madrid and decorated with paintings by the artist and his assistants on mythological subjects inspired for the most part by Ovidian themes.
If in the pitiless representation of the melancholy drama interest returns for the Classical statues studied in the years spent in Rome (1600-1608), with remembrances of the *Laocoonte* – as in the *Rape of Ganymede*, companion to the *Saturn* and mentioned together with it in the 1700 inventory of Torre de la Parada as "de mano de Rubens" (Padova 1990, p. 142) – and even more than the idea today generally held of the painting, which passes through the startling transformation made by Goya, what is surprising is the detail of the three stars that act as cusp to the scene. An unknown astronomical vision that anticipates the observations by Christiaan Huygens in the *Systema Saturnium* (1659) and offers the first pictorial representation of "three-bodied" Saturn that Galileo had observed, with "great admiration", since 1610 – "that is, an aggregate of three stars arranged in a straight line parallel to the equinoctial, of which the middle one is much larger than the side ones", as he wrote again in the *Istoria e dimostrazioni intorno alle macchie solari* (Letters on the Solar Spots) in 1613. The network of relations that ties Rubens (1577-1640) to the spread of Galileo's discoveries, recomposed in relation to the *Saturn* (Baudouin 1995), are scanned by episodes such as the *Self-portrait with friends in Mantua* (1605-1606; Cologne, Wallraf Richartz Museum), in which the portrait of Galileo has been identified (Huemer 1983; Reeves 1997, pp. 68-76), but also by interest in optics and by the frequentation in Antwerp of François Aguilon, for whom Rubens made the tables of the work *Opticorum libri sex* (1613), or, again, by the common friendship with Nicolas-Claude Fabri de Peiresc, who, in a letter of April 1, 1635 (therefore, the year before the commission for Phillip IV) wrote to Galileo in Arcetri presenting the painter as a "great admirer of Your genius" (*Opere*, XVI, pp. 245-248).
(A.T.)

Bibliography: Alpers 1971, pp. 259-260; Jaffé 1989, p. 363; Baudouin 1995; Rome 1990.

VII.3.2-5
Maria Clara Eimmart
Lunar phase
Phases of Venus
Aspect of Jupiter
Aspect of Saturn
Late 17th century
Pastel on blue cardboard; 64 x 52 cm
Bologna, Museo della Specola, Università di Bologna, inv. MdS 124e, MdS 124g, MdS 124i, MdS 124l

These illustrations of celestial phenomena are part of a gift from Georg Friedrich Eimmart to count Luigi Ferdinando Marsili, who founded in Bologna the Istituto delle Scienze. Painter, sculptor as well as keen amateur astronomer, Eimmart had built a private observatory in Nuremberg, where he was director of the Malerakademie (academy of painting).

His daughter, Maria Clara, cultivated drawing, painting, sculpture and engraving under the guidance of the father. She did a large number of drawings of flowers and birds and, to help her father with his observations, of astronomical subjects too. From 1693 to 1698 she did drawings for about 350 lunar phases observed by telescope. Only ten of the twelve tables donated by her father to Marsili remain at the Museo della Specola, bearing witness to the drawing and keen observational skills of Maria Clara.

The *lunar phase* represents the waning Moon as it appeared to the telescope on August 29, 1697, with a fine description of lunar surface. The image has a particular detail, probably because of the painter desire to put the Moon in a symmetric and central position. In fact, one can see the Moon lying on the horizon like a ship only at tropical and equatorial latitudes, and not in Nuremberg.

The *phases of Venus* illustrate as the planet appeared to the telescope in its different phases. Galileo was the first to observe them in 1610, giving an observational support to the critics moved to the Ptolemaic system, which was not able to explain the sequence of the phases.

In the *aspect of Jupiter* we can see the planet with the satellites discovered by Galileo (above) and the bands on the surface of Jupiter (below), as they were observed by Riccioli and Grimaldi in Bologna, Huygens in France and Hooke in England.

The *aspects of Saturn* present the rings surrounding the planet as they appeared to Huygens, who was the first to realize that they were composed by many bodies rotating around Saturn.

(A.G.)

Bibliografia: Baiada-Bònoli-Braccesi 1995, pp. 162-163.

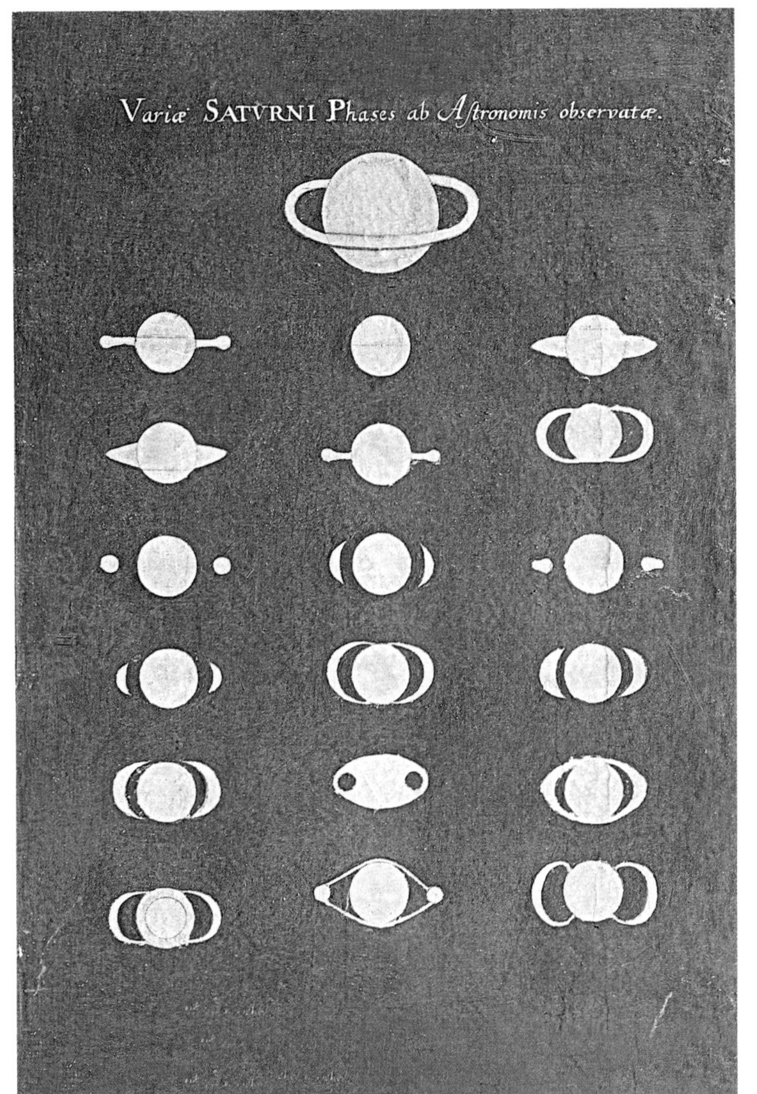
Variæ SATVRNI Phases ab Astronomis observatæ.

PHASIS LVNÆ POST □ VLT. DECR:
Anno Chr: 1697. Die 29. Aug: st: v.
ad Archetyp: depinxit. M.C.Eimarta Norimb:

VII.3.6-7
Donato Creti
Moon and Jupiter
1711
Oil on canvas; 51 x 35 cm
Rome, Pinacoteca Vaticana, inv. 40433
and 40437

These two paintings form part of the co-called *Osservazioni astronomiche*, a series of small canvasses depicting stars and planets set in animated landscapes: the Sun, the Moon, Mercury, Venus, Mars, Jupiter, Saturn and one comet, in other words the system of the planets as then known, since Uranus was discovered only in 1781. The history of the *Osservazioni astronomiche* was already known to Giovanni Fantuzzi, who in the *Memorie* of Luigi Ferdinando Marsili tells us how that Bolognese count "had all the planets painted in so many little pictures by the Painter Donato Creti", in order to present them to Pope Clement XI with a view to persuading him to finance the building of an astronomical observatory as part of the Institute of Sciences then under construction in Bologna.
Although the overall project is to be attributed to Donato Creti (1671-1749), the painter – born in Cremona but Bolognese by adoption – was assisted by the miniaturist Raimondo Manzini (1668-

1774), who was responsible for the representation of the planets.

In each painting, as well as showing young men in the course of astronomic explorations, Creti included the chief scientific instruments in the possession of the Institute. Specifically, "For the observation of the Moon are shown one or two Astronomers looking at it through a medium-sized telescope. For Jupiter are shown the same using a longer telescope [...]. In such a manner all the chief instruments of Your Excellency's Observatory will be shown in the pictures, and the Painter will have scope to show off his talent in the various postures of the observers".

The painting representing the Moon shows two young men, one of whom, seated on the ground, seems to be discussing the data just collected by an astronomer looking through a telescope at the full moon low on the horizon and marked with seas and craters in Galilean fashion. In the canvas devoted to Jupiter, Manzini is very exact in his depiction of the great red blotch which had been observed for the first time in 1664 by Giovanni Domenico Cassini.

(F.T.)

Bibliography: Fantuzzi 1770, p. 319; Bedini 1980; Roli 1988; Johns 1992; Crema 1999, pp. 152-154 (with bibliography); Biagi Maino 2005, pp. 55-57.

VII.4.1
Galileo's Moons
Demonstration models
S. Battaglia e G. Miglietta

These three-dimensional models permit the observation of the rough and wrinkled face of the Moon, as evidenced by Galileo's autograph drawings (cf. entry VII.4.2), from which they draw inspiration. The models have been realized with the contribution of the Fondazione Sistema Toscana and the Regione Toscana, on the occasion of the Florence Festival of Creativity 2008.

VII.4.2
Galileo Galilei
Drawings of the Moon
November-December 1609
Autograph watercolour
Florence, Biblioteca Nazionale Centrale,
Ms. Gal. 48, f. 28r

Famous series of six water-colours of the Moon in different phases realized "live" by Galileo, engaged in telescopic observation of the Earth's satellite in the autumn of 1609. To appreciate the importance of this exceptional document, see the essay by E. Whitaker published in this volume. The first realistic representations of the Moon, they were destined to produce a veritable earthquake not only in natural philosophy but also in art. The engravings published in the *Sidereus Nuncius* (cf. entry VII.2.1) were derived from these autograph drawings by Galileo.
(P.G.)

Bibliography Whitaker 1978; Reeves 1997, pp. 138-183; Bredekamp 2008, pp. 101-121, 346-362.

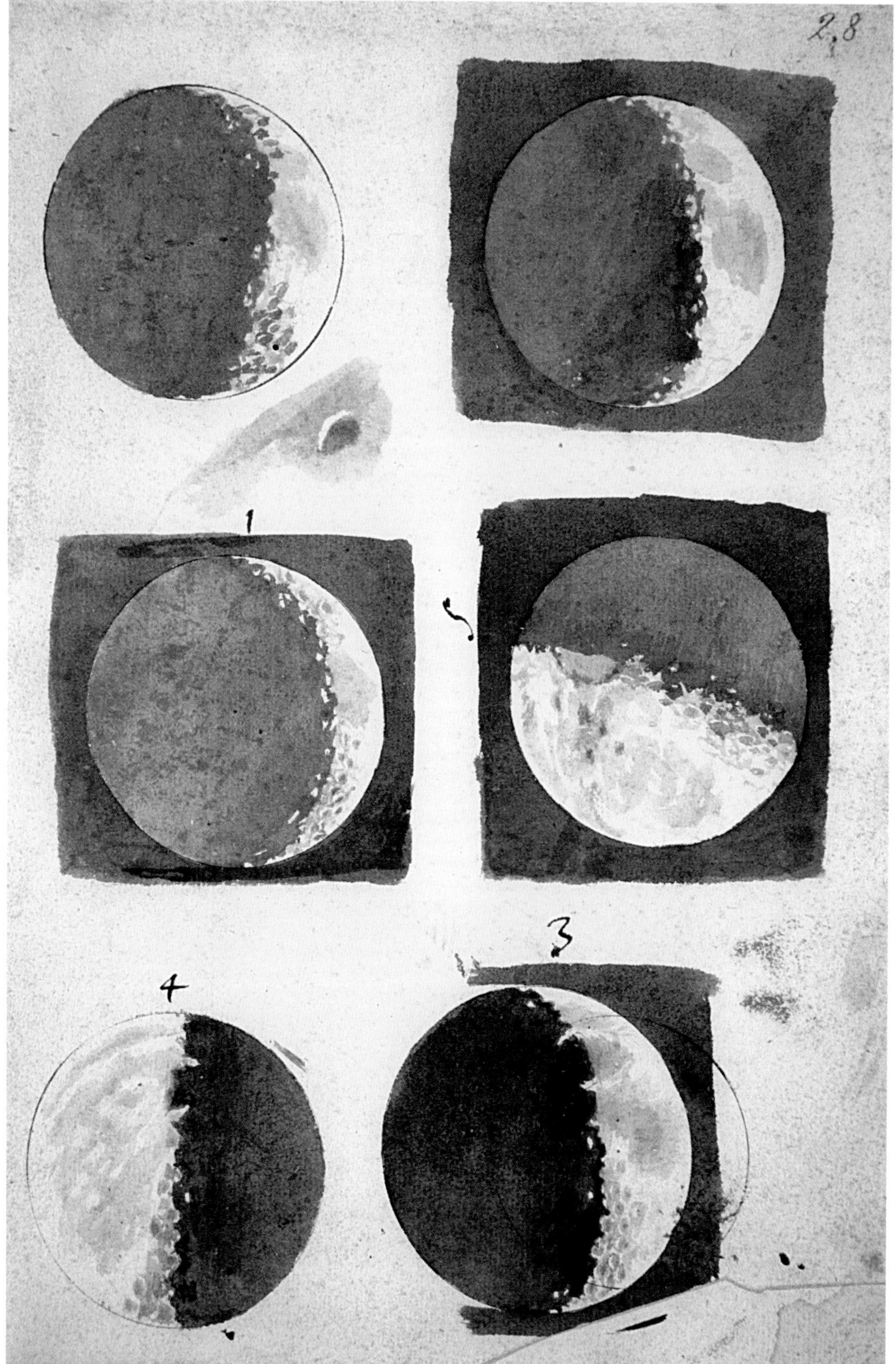

VII.4.3-5
Thomas Harriot
Three drawings of the Moon
1609-1611
Pen on paper; 30.5 x 20 cm (each drawing)
Petworth, Lord Egremont's Collection

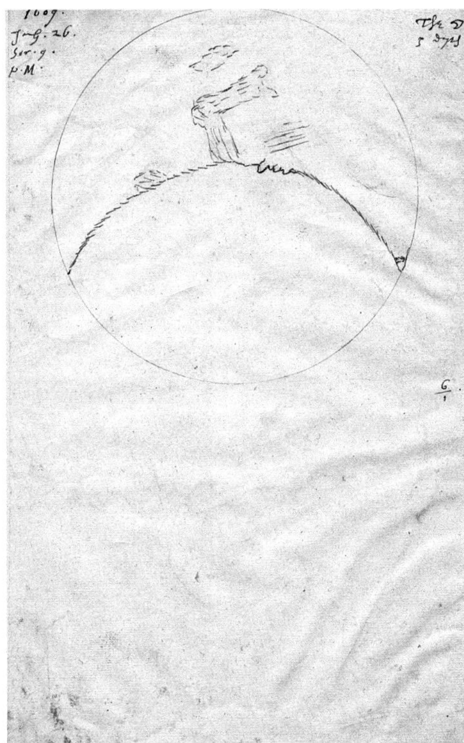

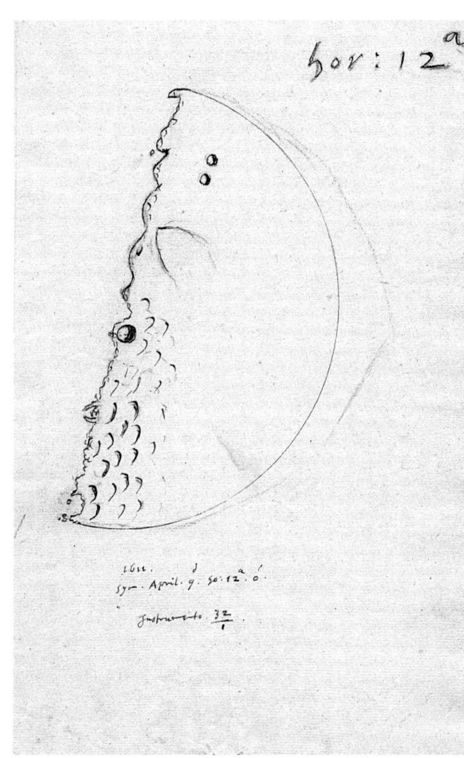

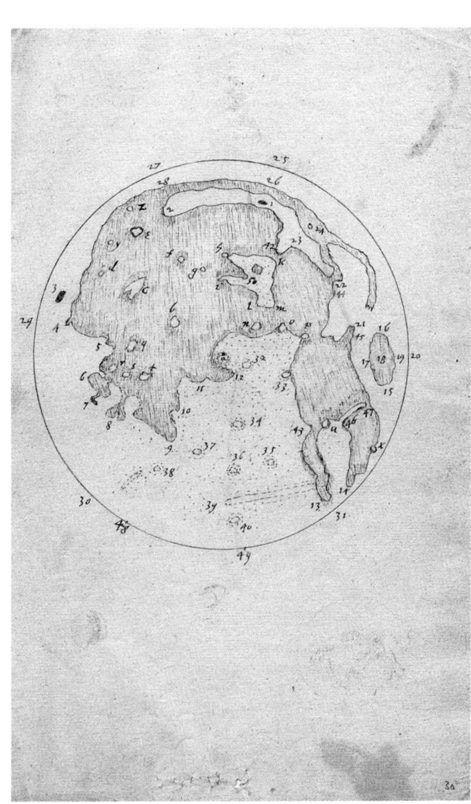

Four months before Galileo first aimed his telescope at the Moon (cf. entry VII.2.8), a remarkable English mathematician using a telescope with a magnifying power x 6 made the first known observations of the Earth's satellite. Of the drawings which have come down to us, the first displayed here, which records the first observation made by Harriot ((1560-1621), is in fact dated at nine in the evening of 26 July 1609 (which corresponds to August 5 in the Gregorian calendar). It shows a five-days-old moon on the surface of which are vague and sketchy drawings which with a bit of imaginative effort we may recognize as the outlines of the Mare Crisium, the Mare Serenitatis and the Mare Tranquillitatis.
The second drawing, dated 9-10 April 1611, shows the moon in quadrature and reveals the influence of Galileo's engravings on Harriot, who at this point had read the *Sidereus Nuncius*; cf. entry VII.2.1).
The third drawing, probably also dating from 1611, is the earliest known attempt to make a map of the full Moon. Harriot uses letters of the alphabet and numbers to mark the chief reliefs on the face of the Moon.
(P.G.)

Bibliography; Whitaker 1999, pp. 17-19; Schirley 1978.

VII.4.6
Francesco Fontana
Novae coelestium terrestriumq[ue] rerum observationes et fortasse hactenus non vulgatae
Neapoli, apud Gaffarum, 1646
Milan, Biblioteca del Dipartimento di Astronomia, XVII.75, pp. 82-83

Most of the treatise is dedicated to the description of the Moon, observed through lenses of the telescope made by Fontana (1580-1656) himself, who proposes as many as 28 engravings relative to the same number of observations of the Earth's satellite, carried out between the 5th of October 1645 and January 1646. Two of these engravings (pp. 81 and 83) refer to observations done many years before the publication of the volume, respectively, 31 October 1629 and 20 June 1630 (the latter erroneously entitled *De Lunae deliquii observationibus*, while the one depicted is a waxing Moon). These two representations were included in works by other authors printed before the publication of Fontana's text.

A common characteristic of all Fontana's images, that do not introduce any appreciable innovation to the description of the Moon's face, is that they appear upside-down. That depends on the fact that he used a telescope with a positive lens, whereas Galileo and previous observers used concave lenses.
(P.G.)

Bibliography: Vyver 1971, p. 75; Whitaker 1999, p. 25.

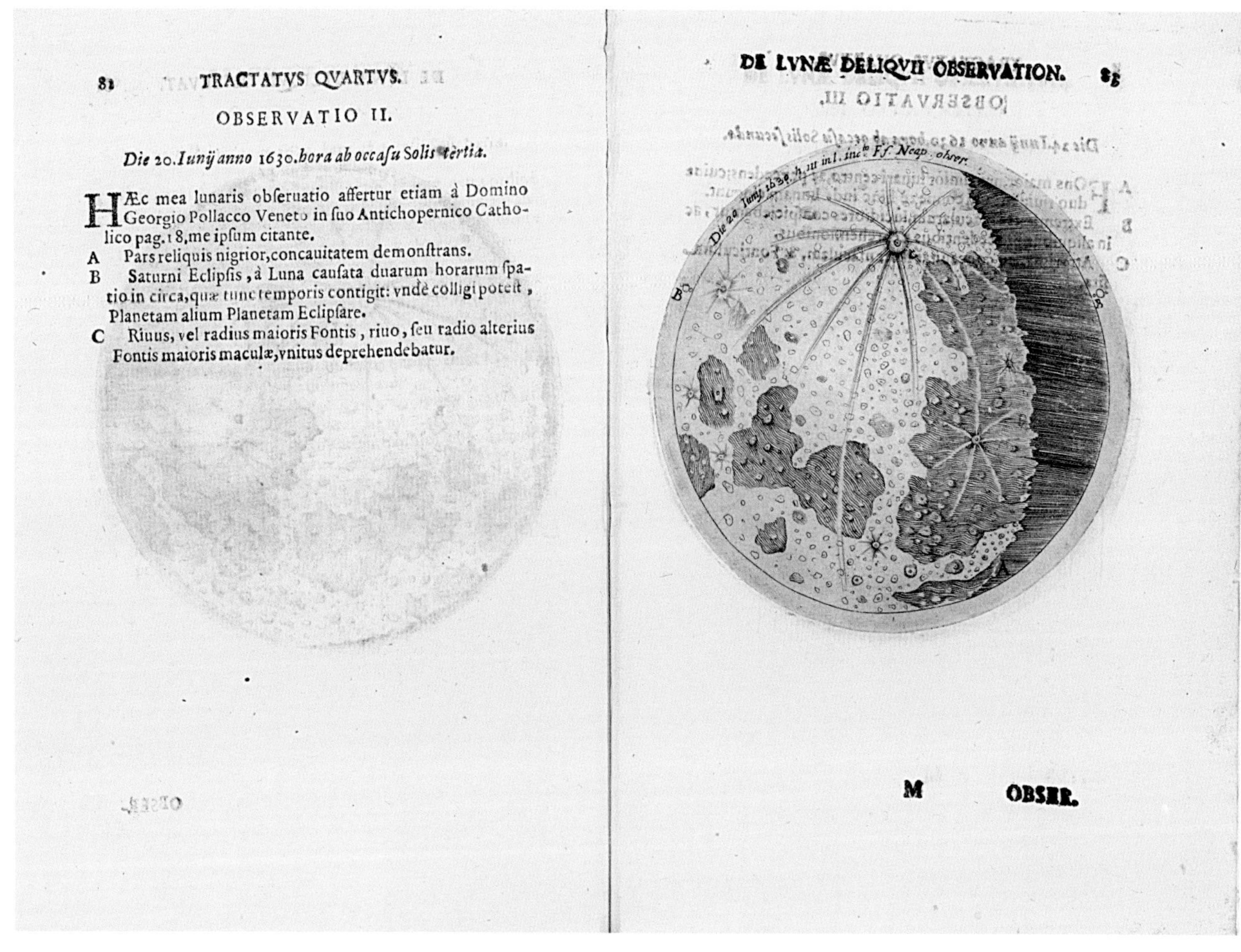
82 TRACTATVS QVARTVS.

OBSERVATIO II.

Die 20. Iunij anno 1630. hora ab occasu Solis tertia.

HÆc mea lunaris obseruatio affertur etiam à Domino Georgio Pollacco Veneto in suo Antichopernico Catholico pag. 18, me ipsum citante.
A Pars reliquis nigrior, concauitatem demonstrans.
B Saturni Eclipsis, à Luna causata duarum horarum spatio in circa, quæ tunc temporis contigit: vndè colligi potest, Planetam alium Planetam Eclipsare.
C Riuus, vel radius maioris Fontis, riuo, seu radio alterius Fontis maioris maculæ, vnitus deprehendebatur.

DE LVNÆ DELIQVII OBSERVATION. 83

M OBSER.

VII.4.7
Claude Mellan, Pierre Gassendi
Three charts of the Moon
1637
Engravings on paper; 20.8 x 23.3 cm; 22.3 x 16.8 cm; 224 x 13.1 cm
Abbeville, Musée Boucher de Perthes

Pierre Gassendi (1591-1655) was persuaded to undertake a campaign of systematic observations of the Moon by the need to perfect reliable moon charts for the determination of longitudes on Earth (it would have been sufficient to record, from two different places, the exact moment that the Earth's shadow passed on a minute morphological detail of the Moon, during a total eclipse). To draw the charts, Gassendi employed a talented French artist, Claude Mellan (1598-1688), who had met Galileo in Rome. Mellan made the engravings of three lunar phases.
Gassendi was the first to devise a project of nomenclature of the lunar sites, that was, however, not successful. For an evaluation of the importance of Mellan's engravings and of Gassendi's project, see Whitaker's essay in this volume.
(P.G.)

Bibliography: Vyver 1971, pp. 71-72; Whitaker 1999, pp. 25-35.

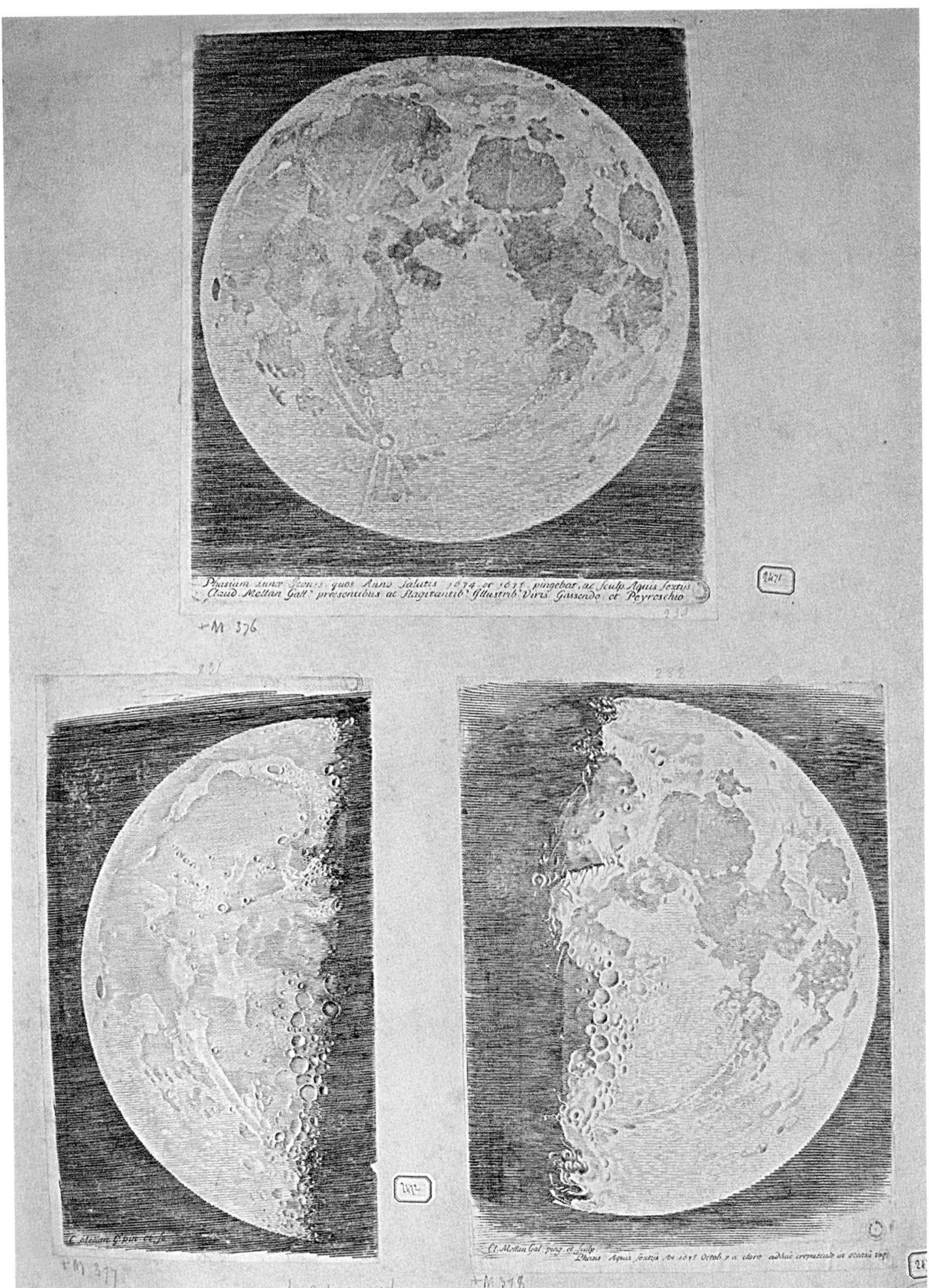

VII.4.8
Michel Florent Van Langren
Plenilunii Lumina Austriaca Philippica
1645
Engraving on paper; diameter 35 cm
Edinburgh, Crawford Library

The lunar map by the Belgian Van Langren (1600-1675), cosmographer to the king of Spain, is the result of the programme conceived by its author for solving the problem of the determination of longitude by resorting to the apparition and the disappearance of certain characteristics of the lunar surface, not during the rare eclipses, but for the entire length of lunation. The term *lumina* in the title indicates the particularly luminous places useful for the determination of longitude. In the Archives du Royaume de Belgique in Brussels, there is an autograph draft of Van Langren's moon chart made in 1644.

Van Langren's chart, dedicated to Philip IV of Spain, is the oldest moon chart existing on which the names proposed by the author for identifying the most outstanding sites of the Earth's satellite have been recorded. For the crucial importance of this document, that marks the beginnings of scientific lunar topography, and for the criteria adopted by Van Langren for the nomenclature of the lunar sites, see the contribution, in this volume, by E. Whitaker.
(P.G.)

Bibliography: Vyver 1971, pp. 71-74; Whitaker 1999, pp. 37-46.

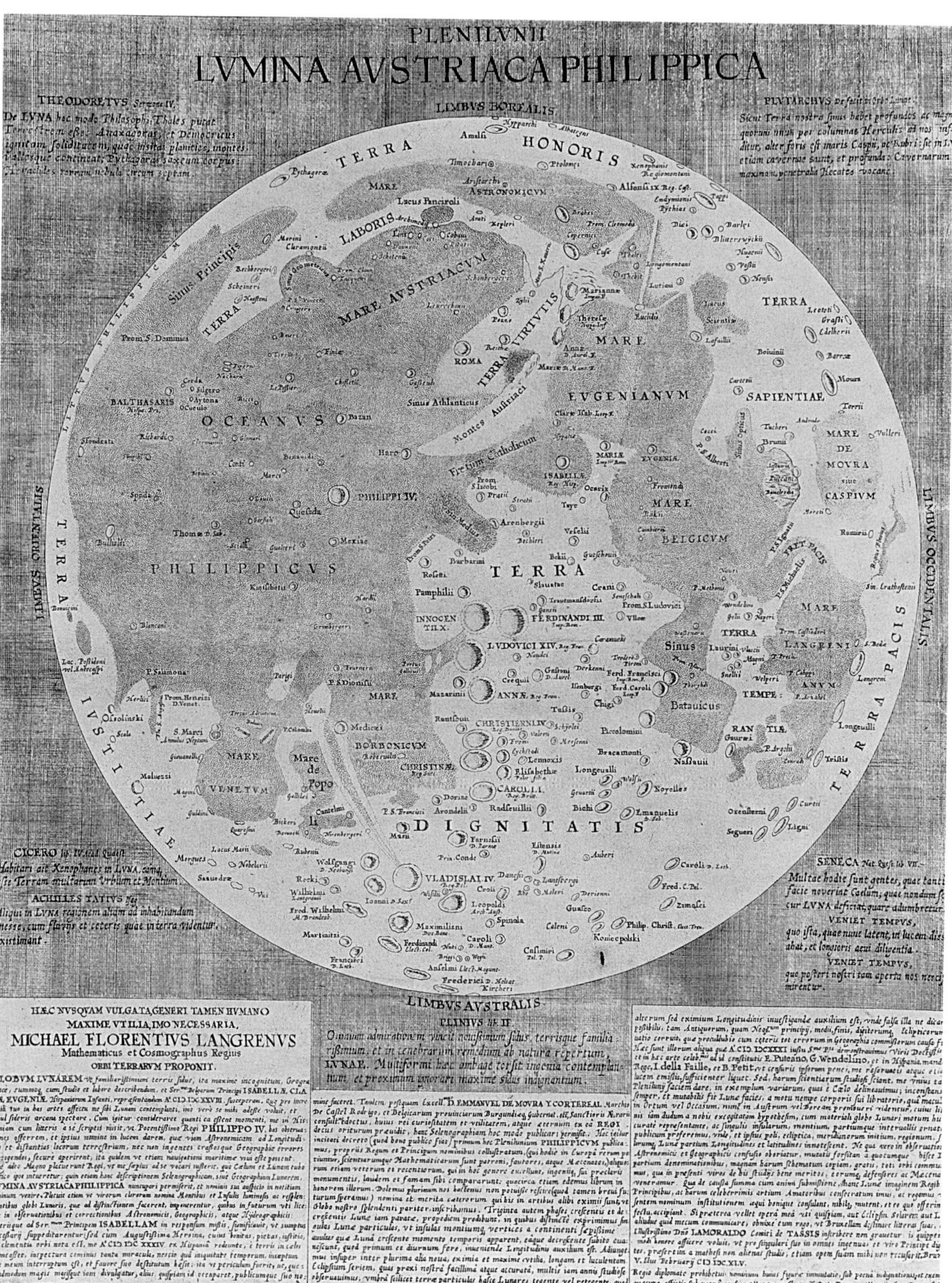

VII.4.9
Antonius Maria Schyrleus de Rheita
Oculus Enoch et Eliae sive Radius sidereomysticus ...
Antuerpiae, ex Officina typographica H. Verdussii, 1645
Florence, Istituto e Museo di Storia della Scienza, MED 2070, pl. after p. 356

The Bohemian Capuchin friar Schyrleus de Rheita (1597-1660), competent student of optics, published in Belgium, where he had moved , a large-size map of the full Moon. In spite of the fact that Rheita is considered the inventor of the erector lens (which turned subjects shown upside-down by the astronomic or Keplerian telescope), his lunar chart, without nomenclature, shows the Moon's South Pole in the place of its North Pole. Rheita's engraving must be appreciated for the proper delineation of the lunar seas and for the clear contrast that he establishes between the luminous parts and the dark parts of the lunar surface. Nevertheless the proportions between the sizes of the different craters are not respected. (P.G.)

Bibliography: Vyver 1971, pp. 73-74; Kansas City 1989, p. 3; Whitaker 1999, p. 47.

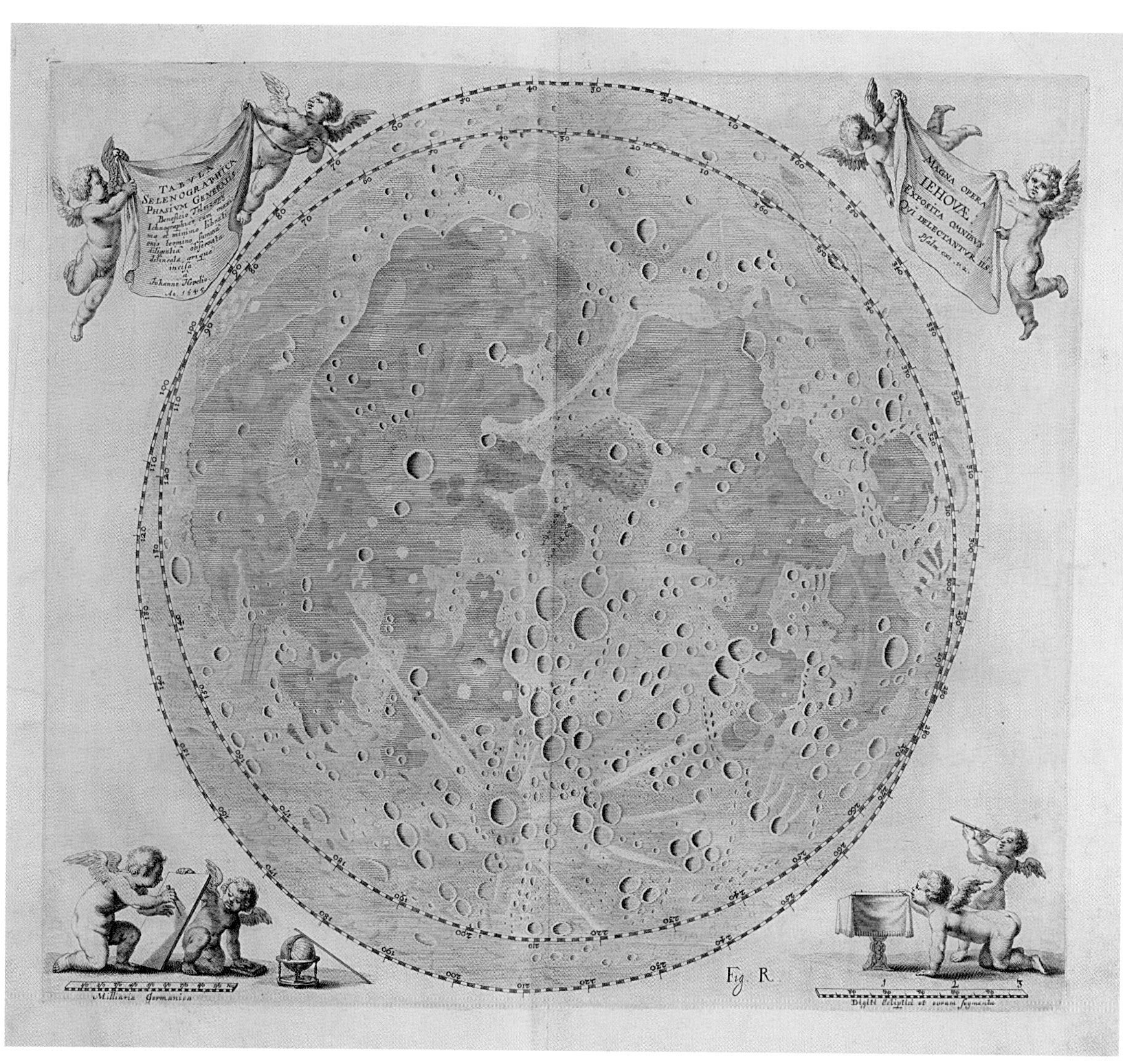

VII.4.10

Johannes Hevelius (Hoewel)
Selenographia, sive, Lunae descriptio atque accurata ... delineatio
Gedani, Typis Hünefeldianis, 1647
Florence, Istituto e Museo di Storia della Scienza, MED 2149, fig. R

The volume, completed by a great number of splendid engravings, presents the results of the careful campaign of telescopic observations of the Moon and of other celestial bodies carried out by the Polish astronomer, over a period of more than one and a half years. Hevelius (1611-1687) provides a detailed description and precise illustrations of the telescopes used. More than forty beautiful engravings of the Moon with its different phases and three large lunar maps can be admired. The latter present the face of the Moon in unprecedented detail. In two of the lunar maps, Hevelius illustrates the libration of the Earth's satellite. Finally, he provides instructions for building a lunar globe capable of mechanically simulating the phenomenon of libration.
Hevelius assigned ancient geographical names to the main morphological characteristics of the Moon's surface. Only a few of Hevelius' denominations are still used. For more information on Hevelius' contribution see Whitaker's essay in this volume.
In table R, an image of the full Moon, that presents its morphology with admirable precision. The double circumference drawn there shows the areas of the Moon affected by the phenomenon of libration.
(P.G.)

Bibliography: Vyver 1971, p. 76; Whitaker 1999, pp. 50-57.

VII.4.11
Eustachio Divini
Chart of the Moon
1649 (re-printed at the end of the 19th century from the original copper)
Engraving on paper; 44 x 37 cm
Osimo, Biblioteca Comunale

Note-worthy maker of telescopes and microscopes, considered, together with those by Giuseppe Campani, his main rival, as among the best in Europe, Eustachio Divini (1610-1685), a native of the Marches in Central Italy, dedicated his chart of the Moon to the Grand Duke of Tuscany, Ferdinand II de' Medici. In spite of declaring in the dedication to have realized this work after intense campaigns of observation with telescopes of which he describes the characteristics, many details suggest that Divini drew inspiration from Hevelius' lunar cartography (cf. entry VII.4.10). On the four margins of the chart are delineated Jupiter (with the satellites), Saturn (with the ring), Venus and the Moon as they appear when seen with Divini's telescope.
No examples of the seventeenth-century printing of the chart are known. The one often published is a re-print done in 1883 in Rome from Divini's original copperplate, that I was able to identify in the Biblioteca Comunale of Osimo, where it is conserved together with another two of Divini's copperplates that illustrate Mars (unknown up to now) and the portrait of the author. I would like to express my thanks to Ivana Lorenzini, in charge of the Biblioteca Comunale of Osimo, for her invaluable collaboration.
(P.G.)

Bibliography: Govi 1887; Vyver 1971, pp. 76-77; Whitaker 1999, pp. 57-58.

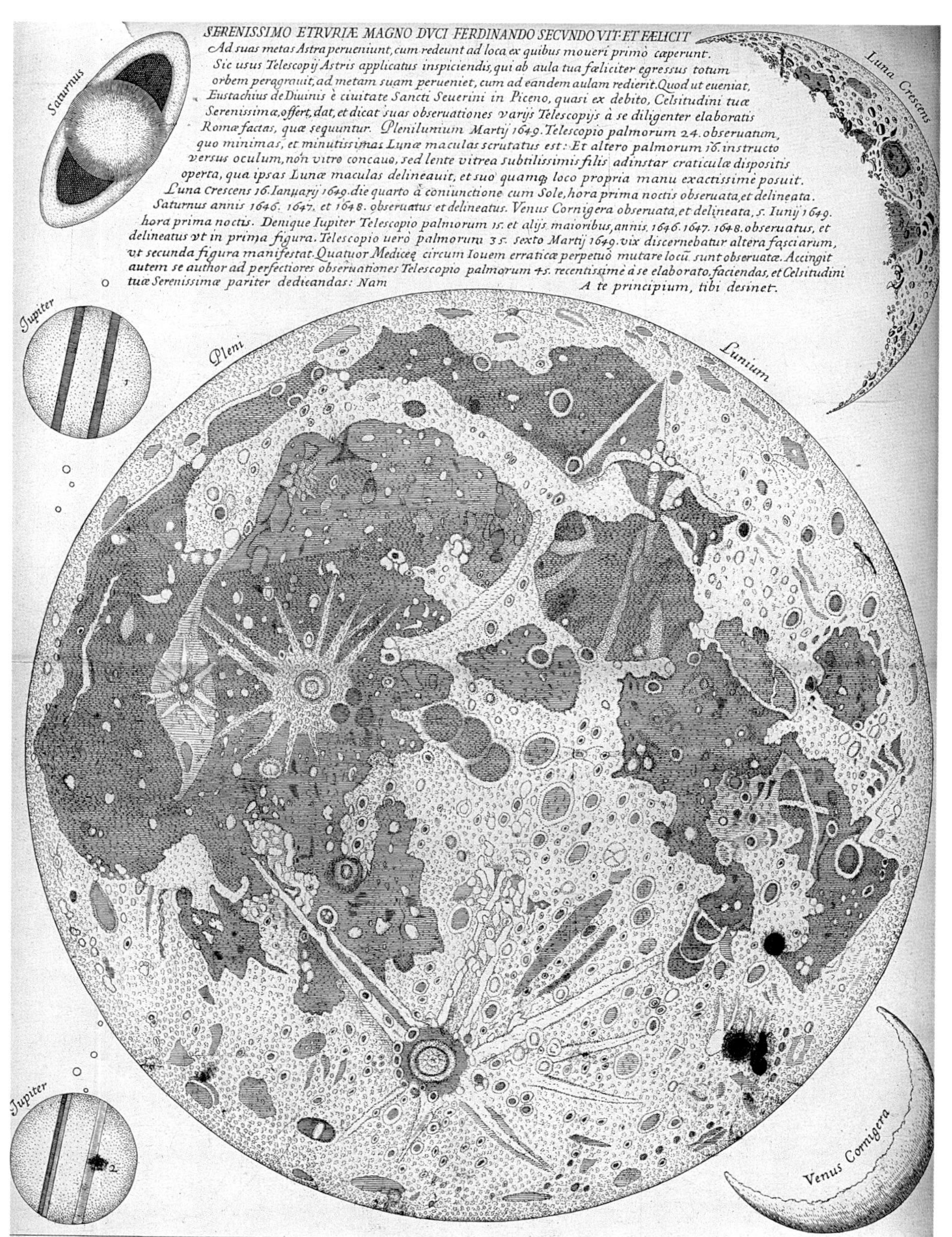

VII.4.12
Giovanni Battista Riccioli S.J.
Almagestum novum astronomiam veterem novamque complectens ... in tres tomos distributam
Bononiae, ex typographia haeredis Victorii Benatii, 1651
Florence, Istituto e Museo di Storia della Scienza, MED 2165, figs. I and VI, p. 204

The Almagestum novum by Riccioli (1598-1671) represented the most significant attempt made by the Company of Jesus to assimilate some of the most outstanding new evidence that had emerged from astronomical research after the invention of the telescope, although the doctrine on the centrality and immobility of the Earth was always firmly maintained.
In the fourth book of the *Almagestum novum* Riccioli included two large-size maps of the Moon (figures I and IV, p. 204) drawn by his brother Francesco Maria Grimaldi (1613-1663). The first offers a panoramic view of the Moon and its phases, two of which show the Moon in quadratures highlighting the limits of libration. The second map, besides highlighting the areas interested by libration, presents the results of the systematic work of nomenclature carried out by Riccioli, who assigned 248 names of ancient and contemporary astronomers, grouped according to their different schools of thought, to as many sites. Regarding the success of Riccioli's nomenclature, see, in this volume, the contribution by E. Whitaker.
(P.G.)

Bibliography: Vyver 1971, pp. 77-78; Whitaker 1999, pp. 60-68, 210-217.

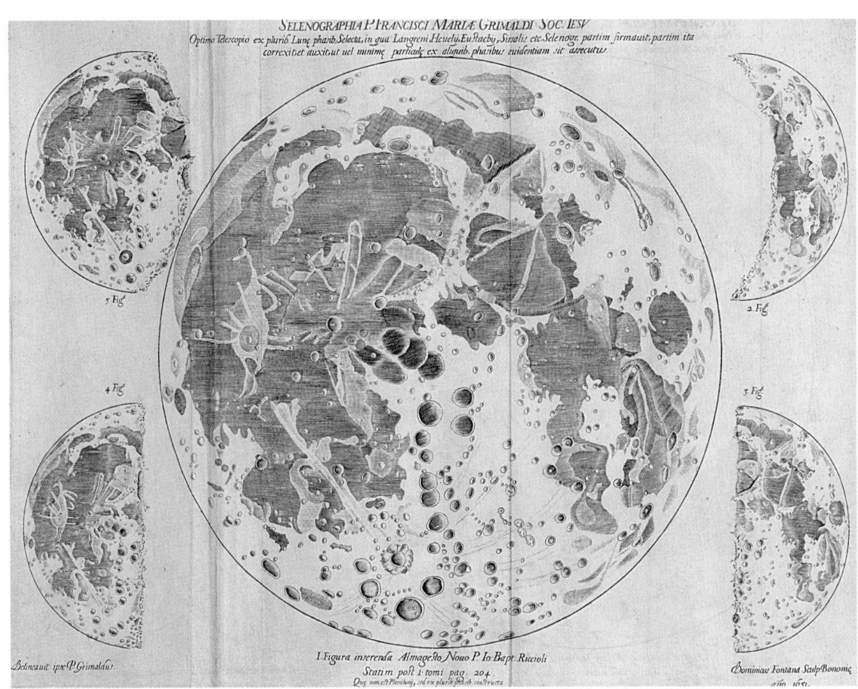

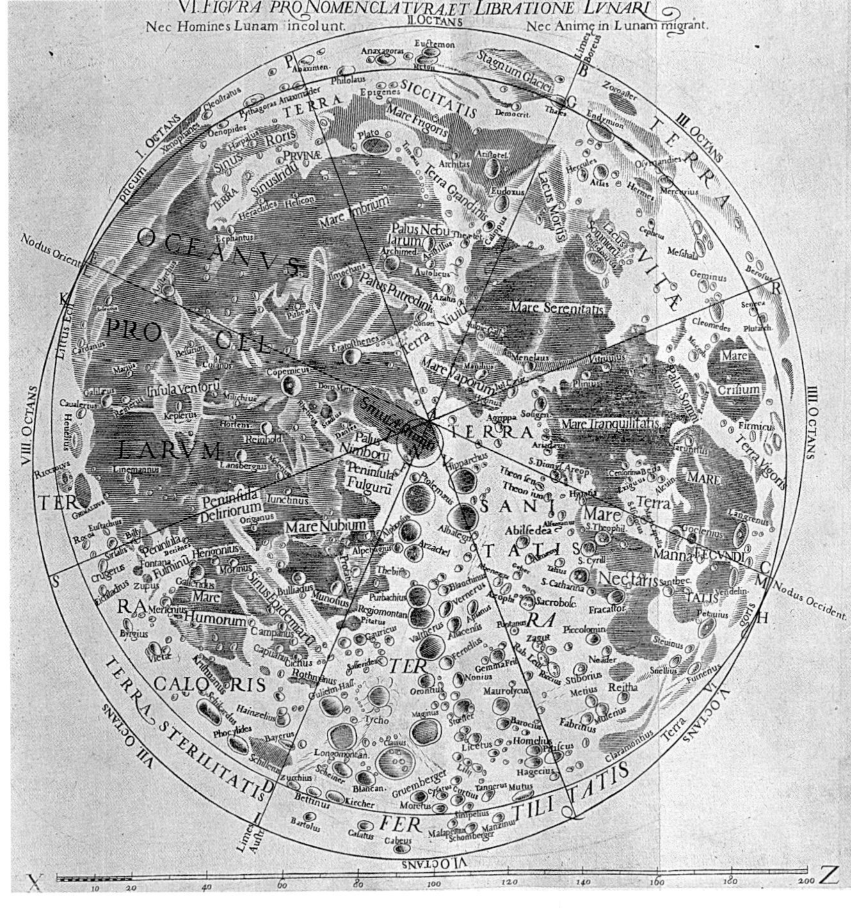

VII.4.13
Geminiano Montanari
Moon chart
In Cornelio Malvasia, *Ephemerides novissime motuum coelestium*
Mutinae, ex typographia Andreae Cassiani, 1662
Modena, Biblioteca dell'Osservatorio Astronomico, (facsimile)

The chart, extremely rare, is the result of the intense campaign of telescopic observations of the Moon carried out by Geminiano Montanari (1633-1687) in Modena in 1662. Montanari observed, night after night, an entire cycle of phases, drawing them one by one. He then "mounted" the single drawings into a map of the full Moon that he transferred into an engraving (the broken lines that cross it indicate the seams between the single phases observed). Montanari's results seem disappointing with regard to the delineation of the seas, while they are satisfactory in rendering the morphology of the terrains.
(P.G.)

Bibliography: Vyver 1971, p. 79; Whitaker 1999, p. 73.

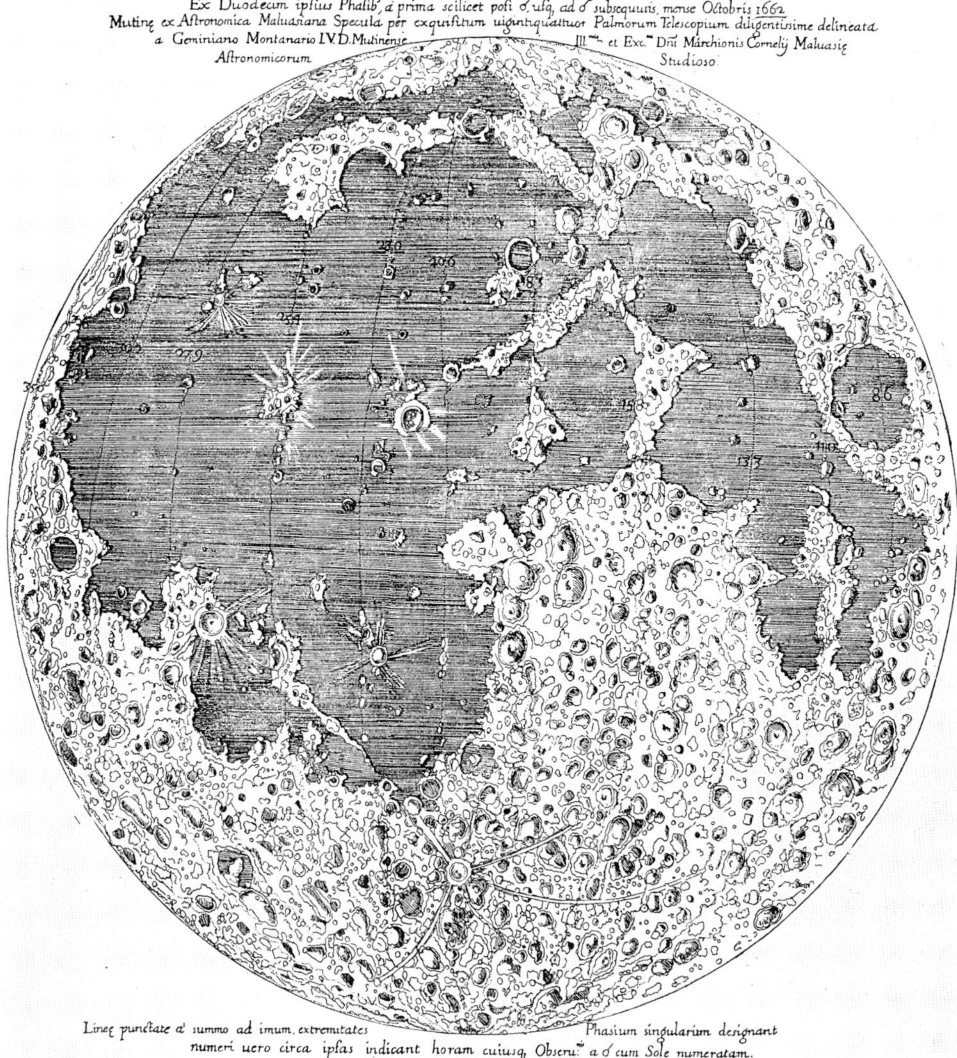

VII.4.14
Robert Hooke
Micrographia, or some physiological descriptions of minute bodies made by magnifying glasses
London, printed by J. Martin and J. Allestry, 1665
Florence, Biblioteca Nazionale Centrale, Magl. 1.5.187, fig. 2, p. 241

In his *Micrographia*, one of the fundamental texts of optics and of modern measurement, the great English experimenter Robert Hooke (1635-1703) – one of Newton's main interlocutors – published the results of the observation of the Moon in its first quarter with a 30-foot telescope. Hooke concentrated his attention on a few limited areas of the lunar surface to show how the previously published charts lacked the necessary precision of detail required for an appropriate knowledge of the Moon's surface. He delineated the crater Hipparchus in an admirably realistic manner, thus giving eloquent proof of the limits of earlier cartography. Regarding Hooke's chart, see, in this catalogue, the contribution by E. Whitaker.
(P.G.)

Bibliography: Kansas City 1989, p. 8; Whitaker 1999, pp. 73-75.

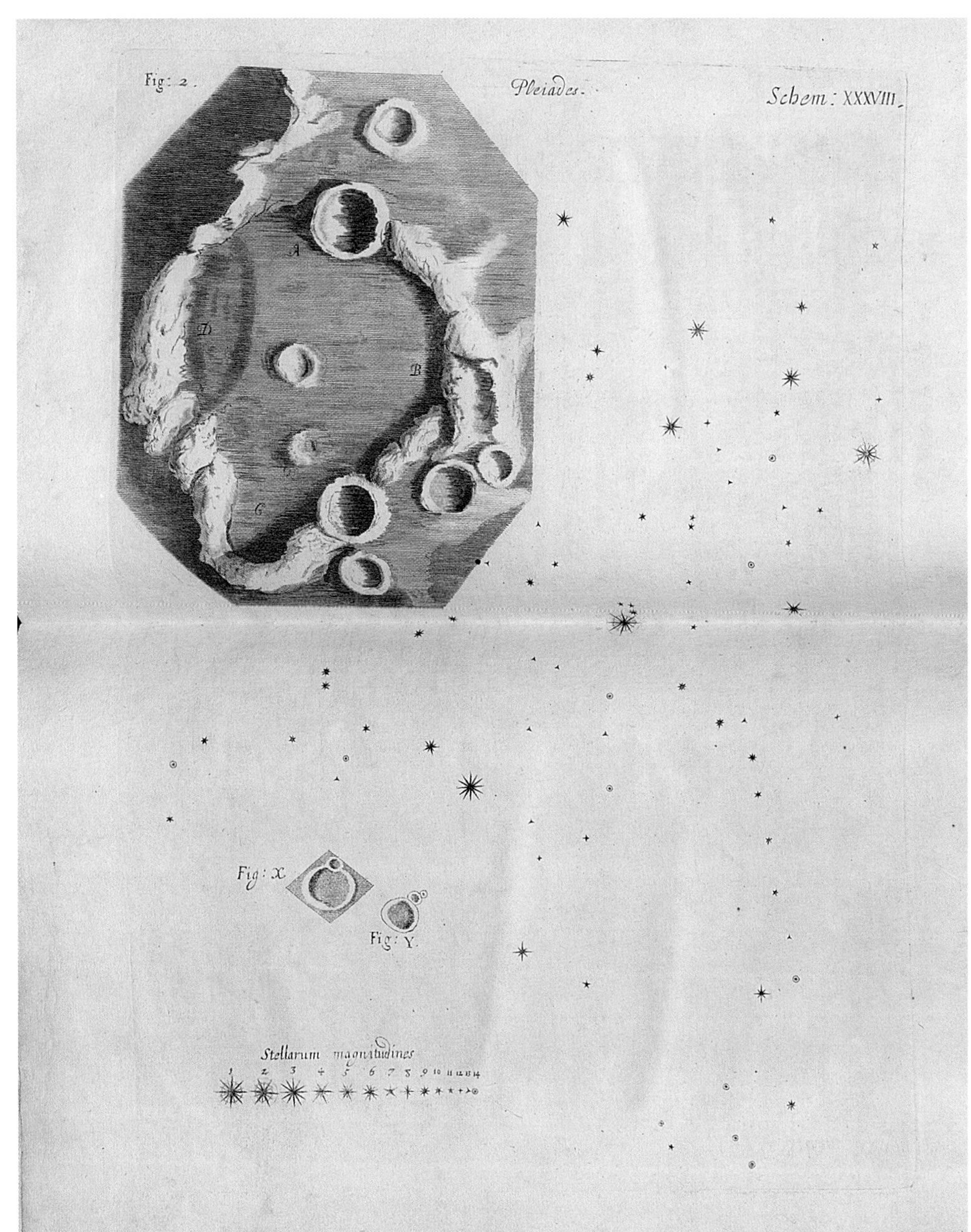

OBSERVATION DV DISQVE DE LA LVNE, EN SON OPPOSITION AV SOLEIL.
37
Faite par le Pere Cherubin d'Orleans Capucin.
nouuellement inuenté, pour Contretirer
exquise, toutes sortes d'Objects soit du
sont Veus par l'Oculaire
Au moyen de l'Instrument qu'il a
proportionellement dans l'exactitude
Ciel, soit de la Terre, comme ils
Dioptrique

VII.4.15
Chérubin d'Orléans (Michel Lasséré)
La Dioptrique Oculaire, ou la Théorique, la positive, et la méchanique de l'oculaire dioptrique en toutes ses espèces
Paris, chez Thomas Jolly et Simon Benard, 1671
Florence, Istituto e Museo di Storia della Scienza, MED 2162, pl. 37

In his vast treatise on optics, the Capuchin friar Cherubino d'Orléans (1613-1697) included two charts of the full Moon to be used in the observation of lunar eclipses. In the *Dioptrique Oculaire* Cherubino describes his invention of a pantograph to attach to a telescope for easily making enlarged drawings of far-away objects. In the text opposite the first Moon chart (table 37, displayed here), the Capuchin friar claims to have produced it using the new instrument. The pantograph is shown operated by cherubs in the two lower margins. In actual fact, his moon chart, as well as the one pictured in table 38, is derived from tables P and R of Hevelius' *Selenographia* (cf. entry VII.4.10), who in fact accused the friar of plagiary. Cherubino's charts do not display nomenclature.
(P.G.)

Bibliography: Vyver 1971, pp. 78-80; Whitaker 1999, pp. 75-78.

VII.4.16
Giandomenico Cassini
Original drawings of the Moon
1671-1679
Sanguine and black pencil on prepared blue paper; 63.5 x 47.5 cm
Paris, Observatoire de Paris, inv. Ms D-VI-40, fols. 52 and 56

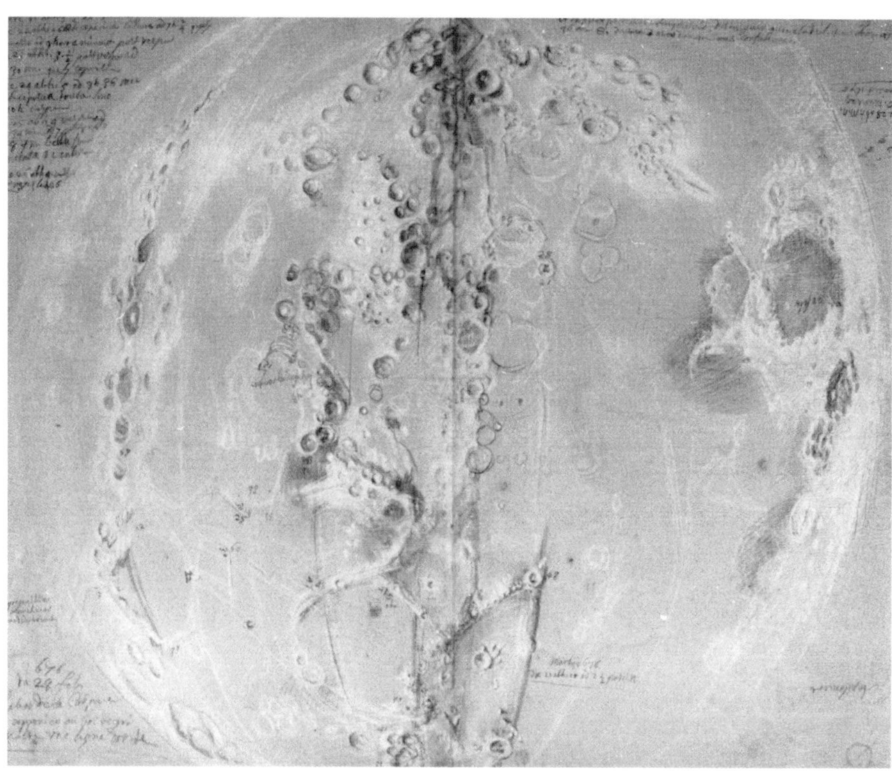

Cassini (1625-1712) dedicated nine years of intense research to the Moon, from his arrival at the Paris Observatory in 1671, until 1679. His observations will give rise to a large lunar atlas made up of drawings by two artists, Sébastien Leclerc and Jean Patigny. The original drawings form a whole of 60 plates. On most of the drawings, Cassini wrote in black pencil, recording the date, the time, and the circumstances in which the observations took place. Kept in the archives of the Cassini family, this precious collection was given to the Bureau des Longitudes by Cassini IV, grand nephew of Giandomenico, in 1823.
(L.B.)

Bibliography: Wolf 1902; Vyver 1971, p. 80; Whitaker 1999, pp. 78-80.

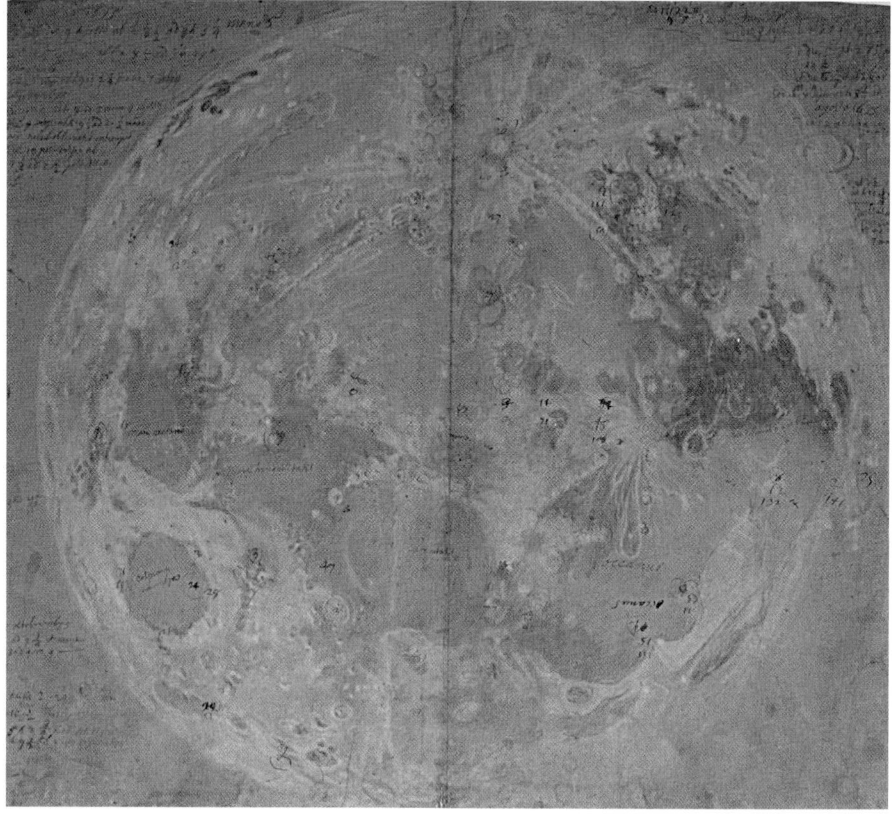

VII.4.17
Giandomenico Cassini
Large map of the Moon
1679
Engraving on paper; diameter 53 cm
Paris, Observatoire de Paris, inv. I.1576

This extraordinary document, realized on the basis of the original drawings of the lunar morphology (cf. VII.4.16), was presented on 18 February 1679 by Cassini to the Académie des Sciences. Even if the map is not signed, it was undoubtedly engraved by Jean Patigny, charged by the King "to draw or engrave the figures of the constellations and the spots of the Moon". At the height of the Heraclides Promontory, there is the head of a woman with ruffled hair, believed to be a portrait of Cassini's wife. In 1787, since it had become extremely rare, Cassini IV, the great grand-son of Giandomenico, had a new printing of the map done from the original copper plate that had been found in the royal print workshop. A year later he had a reduced version printed (the diameter of the Moon is only 17.6 cm.), to which he added a long historical and descriptive commentary.
Cassini's large map that, like his autograph drawings, was realized using telescopes made by Giuseppe Campani, marks a fundamental stage in the process of definition of the true face of the Moon.
(L.B.)

Bibliography: Wolf 1902; Vyver 1971, p. 80; Whitaker 1999, pp. 78-80.

VII.4.18
John Russell, London
Printed gores and polar caps for the Selenographia
1797
Paper; gore length 36.5 cm, cap diameter 10.3 cm
Oxford, Museum of the History of Science, inv. 11665

Terrestrial and celestial globes are generally formed of a plaster sphere to which are pasted printed sheets known as 'gores', shaped to lie on the spherical surface. Once applied, they can be coloured and varnished. The ends are covered with circular caps. These sheets come from a rare set of unused and uncut gores and caps for John Russell's lunar globe (cf. entry VII.4.19).
(J.B.)

Bibliography: Ryan 1966.

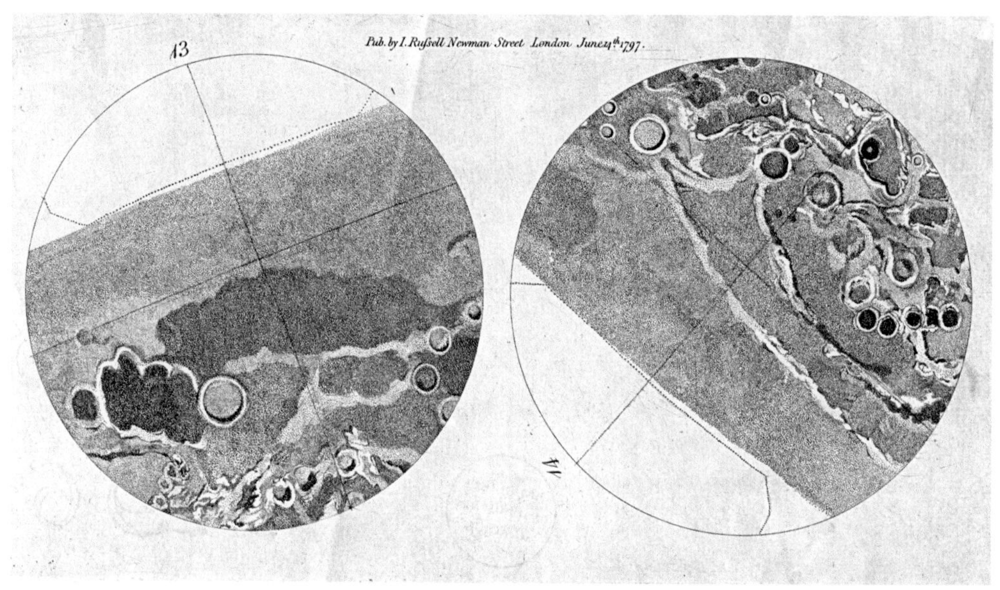

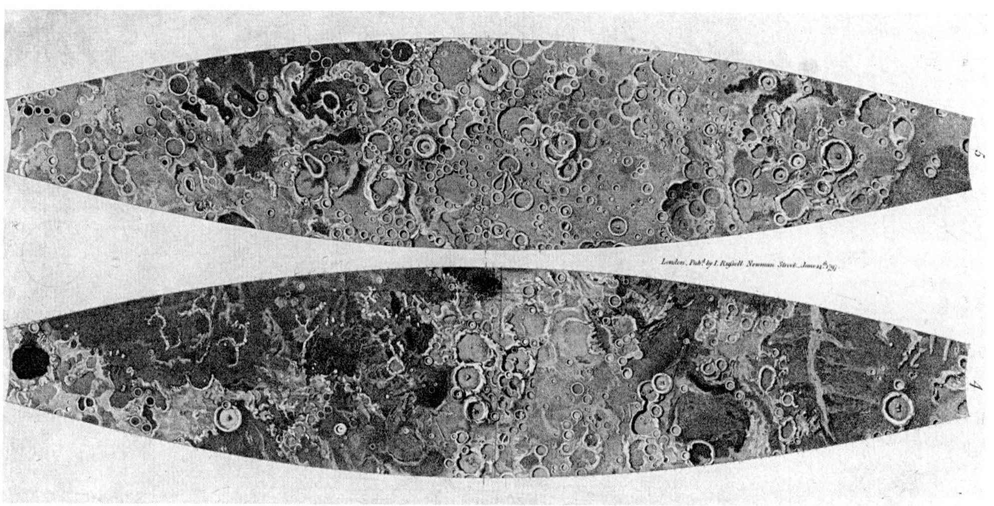

VII.4.19
John Russell
Lunar globe (Selenographia)
London, 1797-1805
Paper, wood, plaster, brass, steel; 50 x 45 cm
London, Science Museum, inv. 1949-117

Russell's *Selenographia* is an assembly of a lunar globe with a small terrestrial globe on a mechanical stand and is designed to demonstrate the libration of the Moon.

The back of the globe is mounted within what Russell describes as a brass hemisphere. Rather than being solid, this is comprised of parts which serve to operate the different motions and provide scales. The globe is attached to a curved plate which sits at the pole of a vertical great circle. Four arcs run from the curved plate to the circle and along these arcs brass squares clamp the globe in place. The great circle is numbered with latitudes marked in degrees. Attached to the great circle are two semicircles, an ecliptic and a moveable terminator, also with degree marks.

The small terrestrial globe sits on a quarter circle attached to the ecliptic; its small size allows the demonstration of parallax at the greatly-reduced Earth-Moon distance of the model. The Earth is mounted on a polar axis inclined to the ecliptic; the orientation of this axis can be adjusted to demonstrate diurnal libration. A geared disc at the lunar pole and the 'polar guide', a quarter-circle running from the lunar pole to a bar at the pole of the vertical circle, allows the demonstration of latitudinal libration.

The globe itself, which shows the Moon's visible area, was based on Russell's own telescopic observations. Financed through private subscription, only small numbers of Selenographia were ever produced. This example was presented to the Science Museum by King George VI.
(A.B.)

Bibliography: Russell 1797; Ryan 1966; Dekker 2000.

VII.5.1

Decree of the Congregation of the Index of Forbidden Books

Rome, Typographia Camerae Apostolicae, 5 March 1616

Rome, Biblioteca Casanatense, Per. Est. 18/4

A printed sheet making public the decisions arrived at by the Congregation of the Index at the conclusion of Galileo's so-called "first trial". It took place in 1615, as the result of a denunciation to the Congregation of the Inquisition by the Dominican friar Tommaso Caccini concerning certain statements in Galileo's *Lettera a Madama Cristina di Lorena*. Following the inquiry the ecclesiastical court confined itself to giving Galileo (who had been the root cause of the scandal) a formal injunction not to uphold or teach the doctrine of Copernicus. This warning was to assume great importance in the second dramatic trial of Galileo in 1633. In the decree of March 5th the heliocentric concept is declared contrary to Holy Writ and therefore false and pernicious. Padre Antonio Foscarini's book, *Lettera sopra l'opinione de' Pitagorici* (Naples 1615) was banned for having maintained that doctrine. Different treatment was reserved for the commentary on the Book of Job by Diego de Zunica and Copernicus' *De revolutionibus*, which were suspended while awaiting correction (*donec corrigantur*).

(P.G.)

Bibliography: Pagano 1984, pp. 102-103; Bucciantini 1985.

DECRETVM

Sacræ Congregationis Illustrissimorum S. R. E. Cardinalium, à S. D. N. PAVLO Papa V. Sanctàq. Sede Apostolica ad Indicem Librorum, eorumdemq; permissionem, prohibitionem, expurgationem, & impressionem, in vniuersa Republica Christiana specialiter deputatorum, vbiquè publicandum.

CVM ab aliquo tempore citra, prodierint in lucem inter alios nonnulli Libri, varias hæreses, atq; errores continentes, Ideo Sacra Congregatio Illustrissimorum S. R. E. Cardinalium ad Indicem deputatorum, nè ex eorum lectione grauiora in dies damna in tota Republica Christiana oriantur, eos omninò damnandos, atque prohibendos esse voluit; Sicuti præsenti Decreto pœnitus damnat, & prohibet vbicumq; & quouis idiomate impressos, aut imprimendos. Mandans, vt nullus deinceps cuiuscumque gradus, & conditionis, sub pœnis in Sacro Concilio Tridentino, & in Indice Librorum prohibitorum contentis, eos audeat imprimere, aut imprimi curare, vel quomodocumque apud se detinere, aut legere; Et sub ijsdem pœnis quicumque nunc illos habent, vel habuerint in futurum, locorum Ordinarijs, seù Inquisitoribus, statim à præsentis Decreti notitia exhibere teneantur, Libri autem sunt infrascripti, videlicet.

Theologiæ Caluinistarũ Libri tres, auctore Conrado Schlusserburgio.

Scotanus Rediuiuus, siue Comentarius Erotematicus in tres priores libros, codicis, &c.

Grauissimæ quæstionis Christianarum Ecclesiarum in Occidentis, præsertim partibus ab Apostolicis temporibus ad nostram vsque ætatem continua successione, & statu, historica explicatio, Auctore Jacobo Vsserio Sacræ Theologiæ in Dulbiniensi Academia apud Hybernos professore.

Friderici Achillis Ducis Vvertemberg. Consultatio de Principatu inter Prouincias Europæ habita Tubingæ in Illustri Collegio Anno Christi 1613.

Donelli Enucleati siue Commentariorum Hugonis Donelli, de Iure Ciuili in compendium ita redactorum &c.

Et quia etiam ad notitiam præfatæ Sacræ Congregationis peruenit, falsam illam doctrinam Pithagoricam, diuinæq; scripturæ omnino aduersantem, de mobilitate Terræ, & immobilitate Solis, quam Nicolaus Copernicus de reuolutionibus orbium cœlestium, & Didacus Astunica in Iob etiam docent, iam diuulgari & à multis recipi; sicuti videre est ex quadam epistola impressa cuiusdam Patris Carmelitæ, cui titulus, Lettera del R. Padre Maestro Paolo Antonio Foscarini Carmelitano, sopra l'opinione de Pittagorici, e del Copernico, della mobilità della Terra, e stabilità del Sole, & il nuouo Pittagorico Sistema del Mondo, in Napoli per Lazzaro Scoriggio 1615. in qua dictus Pater ostendere conatur, præfatam doctrinam de immobilitate Solis in centro Mundi, & mobilitate Terræ, consonam esse veritati, & non aduersari Sacræ Scripturæ: Ideo nè vlteriùs huiusmodi opinio in perniciem Catholicæ veritatis serpat, censuit dictos Nicolaum Copernicum de reuolutionibus orbium, & Didacum Astunica in Iob, suspendendos esse donec corrigantur. Librum verò Patris Pauli Antonij Foscarini Carmelitæ omninò prohibendum, atque damnandum; aliosq; omnes Libros pariter idem docentes prohibendos, Prout præsenti Decreto omnes respectiuè prohibet, damnat, atque suspendit. In quorum fidem præsens Decretum manu, & sigillo Illustrissimi & Reuerendissimi D. Cardinalis S. Cæciliæ Epi Albaneñ signatum, & munitum fuit die 5. Martij 1616.

P. Episc. Albanen. Card. S. Cæciliæ.

Registr. fol. 90.

Locus ✝ sigilli.

F. Franciscus Magdalenus Capiferreus Ord. Prædic. Secret:

ROMÆ, Ex Typographia Cameræ Apostolicæ. M. D C X V I.

VII.5.2
Galileo Galilei
Dialogo sopra i due massimi sistemi del mondo
In Fiorenza, per Giovan Battista Landini, 1632
Florence, Biblioteca Nazionale Centrale, B.R. 171, frontispiece

Galileo's scientific and literary masterpiece, conceived in the form of a dialogue and articulated in four Days. To the reader, the discussions between the three interlocutors suggest the clear superiority of the Copernican vision, in respect to which the traditional hypotheses (including Tycho Brahe's recent one) evidence insuperable limits. In the last day Galileo advances a physical interpretation of the phenomena of tides based on the combination of the yearly and daily motions of the Earth.
The *Dialogo* was denounced to the Tribunal of the Inquisition shortly after its publication. After the condemnation of its author for "vehement suspicion of heresy" (the Copernican doctrine was judged incompatible with the affirmations contained in the Sacred Texts) and of his abjuration, the work was banned.
This exemplar presents Galileo's autograph dedication to Giovanni Ronconi. The frontispiece, a work by Stefano della Bella, shows the imaginary dialogue on the constitution of the universe between (from left to right) Aristotle, Ptolemy and Copernicus.
(P.G.)

Bibliography: Galilei 1999.

VII.5.3
Cristiano Banti
Galileo before the Inquisition
1857
Oil on canvas; 106 x 140.5 cm
Milan, Private collection

The painting, that gave sudden success to the Tuscan artist, was awarded the silver medal at the 1857 Exposition of the Società Promotrice di Belle Arti in Florence. In particular, there was appreciation for the philological precision with which Banti (1824-1904) reconstructed the scene of the trial, based on the version of the facts attested by the trial records made known by Eugenio Alberi in the edition of the *Opere* by Galileo Galilei.
The drama took place in a bare room, where a young and proud Galileo is placed centre-front before the Tribunal of the Holy Office. The Commissioner of the Holy Office, Father Vincenzo Maculano, can be recognized between two Dominican friars, while engaged in confuting the heliocentric theories set forth by the Tuscan scientist in the *Dialogo*, leaning on the table where the unsealed foolscap is also visible: the warning given to Galileo by Cardinal Roberto Bellarmino in February of 1616, made known for the first time in 1850, by Monsignor Marino Marini in his text dedicated to the Pisan scientist's trial.
(F.T.)

Bibliografia: Favaro 1913, p. 1032; Fahie 1929, pp. 68-69; Matteucci 1982, pp. 49-51, 188, 343; Milano 1982, pp. 9-10, 11, 22, 30; Spalletti 1985, pp. 131-132, 256, n. 106; Redondi 1994, p. 83.

VII.5.4
Jacques Courtois, known as il Borgognone
Joshua commands the Sun to stand still
c. 1650
Oil on canvas; 53 x 69.4 cm
Rome, Galleria Spada

Rendered with notable dramatic intensity, this scene depicts the incident related in the Old Testament, particularly in the *Book of Joshua* (10, 6-15), concerning Joshua's victory over the king of the Amorites. The moment chosen is that in which by divine intervention Joshua orders the Sun to stand still so as to prolong the day and enable his people to revenge themselves upon their enemies.
The painting employs the same compositional layout as the one on a comparable subject painted by Guillaume Courtois, the younger brother of il Borgognone (1621-1666), recorded in 1717 in the inventory of the collection of Cardinal Fabrizio Spada, and bears witness to the interest shown by the Spada family in the relationship between Holy Writ and the new discoveries of science. The passage in the Book of Joshua had in December 1613 been invoked by Christina of Lorraine in the presence of Benedetto Castelli, a disciple of Galileo, as an argument against the motion of the Earth as maintained by him. The occasion gave the great Pisan an opportunity to enunciate in the form of a letter to Castelli (OG, xi, p. 606) his opinion on the specific Biblical passage and also on the words of the Scriptures in the scientific questions involved, which were to find their most complete expression in the famous *Letter to Christina of Lorraine* (1615).
(F.T.)

Bibliography: Cannatà 1992, p. 129; Camerota M. 2004, pp. 265-272; Sperindei in Forte di Bard 2007, pp. 201-202, n. 28.

VII.6.1
Anonymous
Galileo's Jovilabe
17th century
Brass; 19.5 x 40 cm
Florence, Istituto e Museo di Storia
della Scienza, inv. 3178

This brass Jovilabe unites two of the calculating instruments invented by Galileo in late 1611 and early 1612 in order to finish the "titanic labour" of determining the periods of revolution of the four satellites of Jupiter. The larger disk of the instrument shows a diagram of the system of Jupiter with the four circular orbits of the satellites and a series of segments parallel to the line of sight of the observer on the Earth. The arm, the pointer and the smaller disk on the other hand show the so-called "diagram of prosthaphaeresis", also worked out by Galileo in about 1611. After setting on the smaller disk the position of the Earth (the small knob) with respect to the Sun (the centre of the small disk), on the upper rim of the brass Jovilabe may be read the amount of correction to be made in the apparent position of each satellite in order to obtain its position with respect to the heliocentric system. These tables permit the use of the instrument for calculating the apparent positions of the satellite of Jupiter, as used in the method devised by Galileo for determining longitude at sea.
(G.S.)

Bibliography: Galilei 1890-1909, v. III-2, pp. 477-487 and 521; Righini Bonelli 1976, pp. 171-172, no. 151; Righini 1978, pp. 50-75; Bedini 1986, pp. 25-46; Miniati 1991, p. 60, no. 3; Acidini Luchinat-Capretti 2002, p. 304; Del Santo-Strano 2004, p. 101; Firenze 2008b, p. 141.

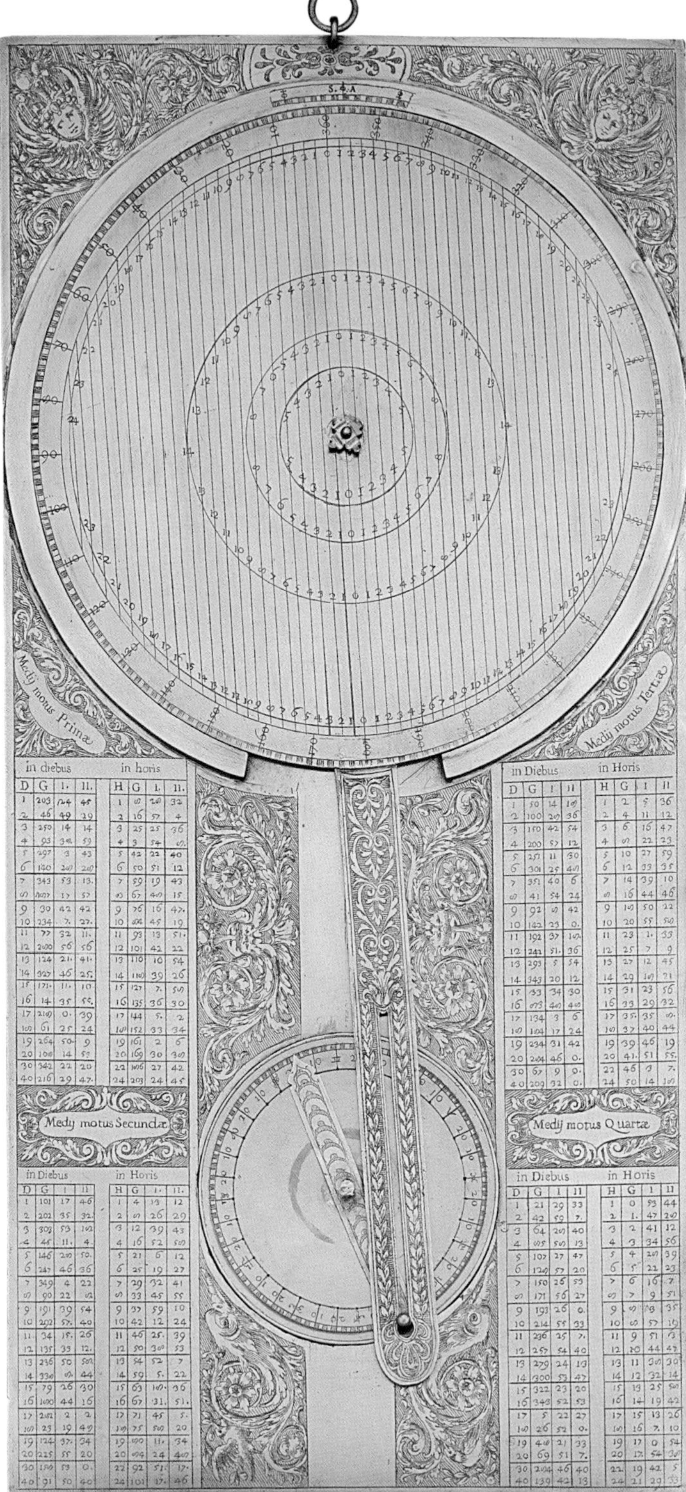

VII.6.2
Eustachio Porcellotti
Galileo's time-keeper
Florence, 1879
Iron, brass, lead; 16 x 35 cm
Florence, Istituto e Museo di Storia della Scienza, inv. 3450

In order to refine the method of determining longitude at sea which he had expounded to the States General of Holland, in 1697 Galileo set his mind to making a time-keeping machine with a pendulum to ensure its regularity. As a young man Galileo had discovered that the oscillations of a pendulum are isochronous, meaning that they always occur in the same space of time. Even so, in 1637 he had to design a device called an escapement to prevent the spring from unwinding all at once and to keep the pendulum in motion for long periods. To demonstrate the correctness of this solution, the Florentine clockmaker Eustachio Porcellotti constructed an instrument based on the drawing of Galileo's time-keeper made by Vincenzo Viviani (1622-1703). In a first version (1877) Porcellotti transformed the basic idea into a complete clock, including a face; in a second version (1879) he stuck more closely to the original scheme, adding only a driving spring contained in a small brass barrel.
(G.S.)

Bibliography: Galilei 1890-1909, Vol. XIX, pp. 648-659; Miniati 1991, p. 60, no. 5 and p. 204, no. 6; Firenze 2003, pp. 107-108.

VII.6.3
Anonymous
Model of the cycloidal pendulum by Christiaan Huygens
18th century
Steel, wood, ivory, brass, fabric; 200 x 160 cm
Paris, Musée des Arts et Métiers, inv. 01434

One of Christiaan Huygens' most important discoveries is that of the tautochronism of the cycloidal pendulum. The Dutch scientist demonstrated that the circular pendulum used by Galileo, isochronal only with small oscillations (cf. entry VII.6.2), could not guarantee to mechanical clocks the constant level of precision necessary for the determination of longitude. The model displayed here comes from the laboratory of experimental physics of Jacques Alexandre Charles (1746-1823), known for his contribution to the development of aerostatic flight (he substituted hydrogen for air) after the Montgolfier brothers' famous experiment. The model was presumably made in the last decades of the 1700's for demonstration purposes.
The shaft supports a rhomboidal steel frame with two metal arms shaped like cycloidal arcs attached to one extreme. The pendulum, hung from the vertex of the frame, once made to swing, is forced to describe trajectories that correspond to a cycloidal arc. In this way its oscillations result perfectly isochronic.
(P.G.)

Bibliography: *Catalogue CNAM* 1955, pp. 33-35.

VII.6.4
Johannes van Ceulen
Haagsche Klokje, early pendulum clock
The Hague, c. 1675
Copper alloy, steel, glass, wood; 42 x 26 x 12.4 cm (closed)
London, Science Museum, inv. 1954-580

This clock was made by the Dutch Johannes van Ceulen of the Hague, who made clocks for Christiaan Huygens. Van Ceulen also made Huygens' planetarium which is now in the Museum Boerhaave, Leiden.
A single spring drives the running and striking mechanisms, with control by a verge escapement. The pendulum is suspended between curved 'cheeks', as recommended by Huygens, to make the time of swing independent of the arc. However as with many clocks of this type, the cheeks are too sharply curved to provide adequate compensation. The wooden carcass has thin wooden which have been painted (possibly to mimic a darker wood). Glass panels at the front and sides allow the inner workings to be seen.
The front glass panel discover the velvet mount on which is placed with dial; this opens with a catch to show the internal workings. The maker's name appears below the cherub spandrel and on the inner workings.
(A.B.)

Bibliography: King H.C. 1978a, pp. 113-117.

VII.6.5
John Harrison
Marine timekeeper
Replica (Leonard Salzer)
c. 1975
Wood, brass, steel; 90 x 75 x 60 cm
Greenwich, National Maritime Museum, inv. no. ZAA0276

In 1714 the British Government offered huge prizes (the largest £ 20,000) for any solution to the problem of finding longitude when at sea. It was the greatest scientific problem of the age. One solution was the creation of an accurate sea-going timekeeper for use on board ship, but owing to the motion of the ship and the big changes in temperature on voyages, no such clock had ever been made. In 1726, the clockmaker John Harrison (1693-1776) heard of the great longitude prize offered by Act of Parliament and decided to try and create a marine timekeeper. In 1735 he produced an extraordinary timekeeper, based on revolutionary design. It is generally labelled "H1" in order to distinguish it from the timekeepers that Harrison developed later (H2, H3 and H4).The last one finally solved the longitude problem and won the great prize.
Made in the early 1970s by model engineer, Leonard Salzer, this is a close replica of Harrison's first marine timekeeper (H1). H1 has three principal design features. Instead of a pendulum, the timekeeper has two linked balances which swing in 'anti-phase', by which means Harrison intended the timekeeper to be unaffected by the motion of the ship. The timekeeper is compensated for temperature changes. Normally all clocks and watches will run slow when the temperature gets hotter, but H1 automatically adjusts the timekeeping whatever the temperature.

For his third timekeeper Harrison invented the temperature-sensitive 'bimetal', a design still in use today for thermostats and many other applications. H1 (and H2 and H3) is designed to work with no lubrication. Harrison later developed his rolling contact bearing designs into what became known as the caged roller bearing, the 'father' of the ball-bearing and still much in use in modern machinery. But it was his fourth timekeeper, H4, with its high frequency, high energy oscillator, which solved the longitude problem.
(J.Be.)

Bibliography: Gould 1923; Quill 1966; Andrewes 1996; Betts 2007.

VII.6.6
Paul Philip Barraud
Marine chronometer
c. 1850
Silver and brass, double case in mahogany;
20.5 x 19.5 x 19.5 cm
Bologna, Museo della Specola, Università di Bologna, inv. MdS 75

Developed from the models devised by John Harrison in the first half of 18th century, marine chronometers became irreplaceable instruments for time keeping and longitude measuring, and necessary on every ship and in any observatory. The movement of this chronometer is contained in a brass case, fixed to a mahogany case by a gimbal suspension in order to give stability to the instrument. It is possible to charge to the chronometer with a brass key inserted behind the case. On the little dial above we read the seconds, in the other below the wound up, that can last for eight days.
The writing on the quadrant reads the maker's name: «Barraud / Maker to the Royal Navy / 41, Cornhill / London / n. 2365». Paul Philip Barraud made more than 1000 very fine chronometers between the end of the 17th century and the first two decades of the 18th.
(A.G.)

Bibliografia: Baiada-Bònoli-Braccesi 1995, p. 182.

VIII.1.1a
Johannes Kepler
Tabulae Rudolphinae, quibus astronomicae scientiae, temporum longinquitate collapsae restauratio continetur
Ulmae, Typis J. Saurii, 1627
Florence, Biblioteca Nazionale Centrale,
Magl. 5.1.118, frontispiece

The temple of Urania, with the diagram of Tycho's system on the ceiling, places in the foreground the discussion between Tycho and Copernicus, at whose side Ptolemy and Hipparchus stand in silence. On the vault, surmounted by the Imperial eagle of Rudolf II, Matthias and Ferdinand II, the dispenser of wealth and honour, there are the muses of the mathematical disciplines that lead to the definition of Kepler's (1571-1630) celestial physics and to the interpretation of the Book of Nature: magnetism, statics (cosmic scales whose fire is occupied by the Sun, that alludes to the laws of equal areas), geometry (the ellipse of the orbital motion), the logarithmic art, dioptrics (applied to telescopes) and optics. On the panels of the twelve-sided base are depicted the island of Hven – on which Brahe conducted his own observations – and the titles of Kepler's works determinant for the creation of the tables: *Mysterium Cosmographicum* (1596), *Astronomiae pars optica* (1604), *Astronomia nova* (1609), *Epitome Astronomiae Copernicanae* (1618).
(N.F.)

Bibliography: Gingerich 1971; Pantin 1993, pp. 71-94; Bucciantini 2003, pp. 291-293.

VIII.1.1b
The Keplerian motion of a planet
Demonstration model
Opera Laboratori Fiorentini

In his *Astronomia nova* (1609), Johann Kepler (1571-1630) expounded the first two laws of planetary motion, which he had determined by studying the motions of Mars. The first law (though the second to be discovered) states that the orbit of each planet is an "ellipse" – one of those curves, known as "conics", obtainable by intersecting a right circular cone with an oblique plane – of which the Sun occupies one of the focal points. The second law states that the segment uniting the planet to the Sun sweeps out equal areas in equal intervals of time. This mechanical model combines both laws, and in particular exemplifies the second law by exploiting the so-called "simplified Keplerian equation". In the model the planet moves at uniform angular speed with respect to the "empty" focus of the ellipse.
(G.S.)

Bibliography: Dreyer 1970, p. 354-361; Hoskin 1999, pp. 106-109; North 2008, pp. 355-360; Del Santo-Strano 2004, pp. 72-75, 105.

VIII.1.2
Robert Fludd
Utriusque Cosmi maioris scilicet et minoris metaphysica ... historia
Oppenhemii, aere Johan-Theodori de Bry; typis Hieronymi Galleri, 1617-1621
Florence, Biblioteca Nazionale Centrale, Pal. 1.8.3.5/I, vol. I, p. 90

Fludd's (1574-1637) universe is a monochord tuned by the divine hand, and along which there are, disposed hierarchically, the spheres of the Elements, the Ether (planets) and the Empyreal (angelic hierarchies). The two octaves (1/2) in which it is divided – one material, from the Earth to the Sun, and the other formal, from the Sun to the peak – are in turn scanned by the consonant proportions of the Pythagorean musical system: the fifth (2/3) and the fourth (3/4).
This bipartition reflects the following cosmological model: the spheres of the universe are characterized by the permeation of two opposing pyramids of Light (Form) and Darkness (Matter) – the first with its base in the divine triangle and its vertex in the Earth, and the second, its opposite – that reach perfect equilibrium in the Sun, *sphaera aequalitatis*. The musical intervals reproduce the degrees of the descent of the formal principle in Matter: by the harmony of the formal octave, God gives light to the Sun and, through the material octave, diffuses its influences on the Earth.
(N.F.)

Bibliography: Hutin 1972, pp. 125-134, 148-152; Godwin 1979, pp. 44-45; Field 1988, pp. 179-187; Fabbri 2003, pp. 175-185.

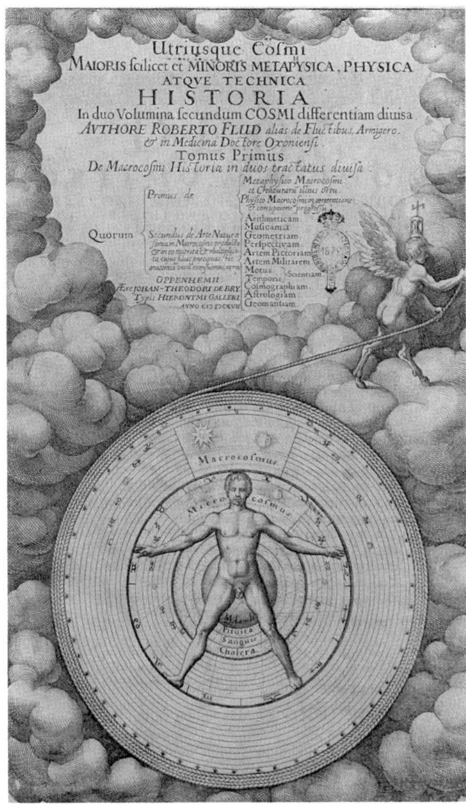

VIII.1.3
The monochord man
Demonstration model realized by S. Battaglia, G. Miglietta and S. Rubini
Metal, fibreglass; diameter 150 cm

Blending the teachings of Ficino, Agrippa and Dürer, Fludd completes the passage from "zodiac man" to "monochord man", where to the correspondences and relative influences with the Ptolemaic universe are added those between musical consonances, anatomical proportions (outer microcosm) and human faculties (inner microcosm).
Like the *Monochordum Mundi*, the microcosm is divided into the Empyrean, Ethereal and Elementary spheres, relatively corresponding to head and neck, shoulders and chest, abdomen and reproductive organs. Furthermore, it is articulated in two octaves: the *spiritualis* between reason and the heart (Sun) and the *corporalis* between the heart and the genitals (Earth). Regarding the faculties, the relationship of spiritual octave that is realized between intellect and imagination is divided in those of fourth (intellect-reason) and fifth (reason-imagination); the corporeal octave, that arises from the imagination-body proportion, is divided into imagination-sense (fourth) and sense-body (fifth).
(N.F.)

Bibliography: Hutin 1972, pp. 134-138, 152-156; Godwin 1979, pp. 46-47; Gouk 1999, pp. 98-99, 146-148.

VIII.1.4
Athanasius Kircher
Musurgia universalis sive ars magna consoni et dissoni in X. libros digesta
Romae, Ex typographia haeredum Francisci Corbelletti, 1650
Florence, Biblioteca Nazionale Centrale, Magl. 5._.92, vol. I, frontispiece

Kircher (1602-1680) conceives the frontispiece as a visual compendium of the philosophical concepts connected to the subject of *harmonia mundi*. More than the Boethian tripartition of music in *mundana* (sphere of the zodiac), *humana* (here intended as the dimension of *concordia* evoked by the circular dances of satyres and sirens), *instrumentalis* (musical instruments at the feet of Pythagorus and of the Muse), Kircher adds acoustics (the echo in the reflection of the shepherd's words) and *coelestis*, a reflection of divine music. In fact, the angels are entrusted with the execution of a canon in thirty-six voices, a form of composition that presents the same characteristics as planetary motion and angelic song. First of all, it has a circular structure, and therefore can, potentially, be performed endlessly. Furthermore, it is the highest form of *concordia discors*: the unity of the melodic theme is articulated in the diversity of the vocal registers, while perfect unison is realized only in the Trinity. The contemplation of mundane and celestial music accompanies the ascension of souls towards God, symbolized by the stairs with Pegasus at the top. In one of the illustrations within the work (vol. II, Iconismus XXIII), Kircher depicts the universe as a pipe organ. Eternal divine wisdom sets the six stops that correspond to the days of the Creation represented in the spheres. The structure of the organ is specular to that of the musical canon in the frontispiece: here again the parts enter in succession, executing in their various registers the harmony that the breath of the Holy Spirit sounds from the first day.
(N.F.)

Bibliography: Scharlau 1969; Lowinsky 1977, pp. 169-173; Godwin 1979, pp. 68-71.

VIII.1.5
George Starkey
Musaeum Hermeticum reformatum et ampliatum ...
Francofurti, apud Hermannum a Sande, 1678
Florence, Biblioteca Nazionale Centrale, Magl. 15.1.146/a, fig. IV

Second edition of a collection of German Hermetic and alchemical texts, published, translated into Latin, for the first time, in Frankfurt in 1625. The volume displayed here belongs to the second edition, that presents numerous additions, one of which (at the end of the volume) is made up of a series of four engravings that illustrate the principles of Mosaic-Hermetic science (*Janitor Pansophus ... superiorum ac inferiorum scientiam Mosaico-Hermeticam analytice exhibens*). Figure IV illustrates the very close hermetic relationship between man and the universe. The name of God is written in Hebrew, at the top, next to the Christian symbols of the dove (Holy Spirit) and the sacrificial lamb. Beneath, the horn, the swan, the dragon and the phoenix represent the alchemical symbols of the five planets. Next to the Moon, the man-deer indicates the hermetic initiation. Beneath the sphere, the man with a star-covered garment is the wise-man who distils spiritual truth from the material appearances of the world. On his right, the man-microcosm (with the cosmic symbols of the Moon and of the Sun), and then the lion and the phoenix, solar animals that symbolize the male principle that brings life to the universe. (P.G.)

Bibliography: Battistini 2004, pp. 110-111.

VIII.1.6
Studio of Jan Brueghel the Elder
Linder Gallery Interior
c. 1622-1629
Oil on copper; 56.5 x 82.2 cm
New York, Private Collection

In the second and third decades of the seventeenth century a completely new genre of painting emerged from the city of Antwerp: the gallery interior. The early examples of the genre, associated with a group of Flemish painters including Jan Brueghel the Elder and Frans Francken the Younger, represented highly idealized collections. Depicting fictitious architectural spaces (palatial in scale in relation to the relatively low-ceilinged dwellings of Antwerp) overlooking impossible views and overflowing with encyclopedic collections of paintings, antique sculptures, books and musical and astronomical instruments, these gallery settings were often inhabited by allegorical figures in classical garb or conversing connoisseurs (including celebrated scholars of the past) along with assorted monkeys, parrots and dogs. The Rubens-Brueghel series of allegories of the five senses in the Prado painted in 1618 is possibly the most famous example of the genre. It was only in mid-century that gallery interiors began to be portraits of actual collections, notably with David Teniers the Younger's paintings of the collection of Archduke Leopold Wilhelm.

Gallery interiors were generally collaborative creations and were designed for a new breed of intellectual art collector, generally wealthy Antwerp merchants who would compete with each other to identify the styles of the different artists represented, and tease out the allegorical significance of the works. The *Linder Gallery Interior* presented here is one of the most remarkable examples of this genre, both for the extraordinary quality of the painting, executed in minute detail on copper, and for its engagement with the astronomical discussions of the early the seventeenth century through a rich and complex intellectual programme.
The painting shows the interior of a vaulted gallery in perspective, with an open portico looking out over an Italianate garden containing a fountain and an obelisk. The walls of the room are hung with paintings in the styles of Flemish and Italian artists. Sculptural works, including both copies of classical sculptures and recent works such as Giambologna's Bull, books and musical instruments are also present in the gallery. Three tables bear an impressive array of mathematical instruments, drawings and diagrams.
The central octagonal table includes a celestial globe, a large Arsenius astrolabe, a Jacob's Staff, a Galilean Geometric and Military Compass (with an alidade not found in Galileo's original instrument), and a perspective-drawing instrument. This table also displays a variety of compasses, pens, an inkwell, lenses, an hourglass, a book of drawings and an engraving that can be identified as the *Martyrdom of St. Catherine* by the Master MZ, possibly in reference to the persecution of heterodox beliefs. The three books to the right of the celestial globe can be identified as the *Rudolphine Tables* (1627) and *Harmonies of the World* (1619) both by German astronomer Johannes Kepler (1571-1630) and, on top, the *Description of the Wonderful Canon of Logarithms* (1614) of John Napier (1550-1617), a work used extensively by Kepler in deriving his Third Law of planetary motion.[1]
At the front of the table is a diagram depicting three competing cosmic systems: the Ptolemaic system, the Copernican system and the "compromise" Tychonic system in which the inner planets orbit the sun and remaining planets orbit the earth. Beneath the three systems is the enigmatic inscription "ALY ET ALIA VIDENT", "different people see it differently" or "others see it yet otherwise". This inscription appears to advocate an agnostic approach to the cosmic debate, not dissimilar to the position advocated by Jesuit authors such as Cardinal Bellarmine, rather than the polemical pro-Copernican position adopted by Galileo. The prominent inclusion of the Tychonic system (ignored almost completely by Galileo) is reminiscent of the illustrated frontispiece of Kepler's *Rudolphine Tables*. Partially hidden behind the diagram of the cosmic systems is an astrological geniture, alluding to the intimate relationship between astronomy and astrology. Also prominently displayed on the table are identifiable portrait medals of Muzio Oddi (1569-1639), Girolamo Cardano (1501-1576), Andrea Alciati (1492-1550), Albrecht Dürer (1471-1528), Michelangelo Buonarroti (1475-1564), and Donato Bramante (1444-1514).
The allegorical figures in the *Linder Gallery Interior* are of particular interest. The bearded male figure can probably be identified as *Disegno* or Drawing, and may be intended as a likeness of astronomer Johannes Kepler whose books are represented prominently on the octagonal table. The reclining female figure in classical dress, with paintbrushes, mallet, maulstick, and a book, and wearing a laurel wreath and a sun pendant, may be identified as a personification of *Pictura* (Painting), or perhaps more broadly "the Arts". The laurel wreath and sun pendant are the attributes of Virtue, according to Cesare Ripa's *Iconologia*, so the allegory can maybe be read as "the arts and virtue rest on design" (punning on the double meaning of *disegno* as "drawing" and also as "purpose").
The identity of the patron of the painting may be deduced from the coat of arms in the upper left-hand window showing three leaves in a diagonal band, the arms of the Linder family. A letter sent to Urbino mathematician and architect Muzio Oddi from his friend and pupil Giambattista Caravaggio described seeing this painting in 1629 during a visit to the house of German merchant Peter Linder in Milan. According to Caravaggio, Oddi was himself largely responsible for the "invention" of the painting, further supported by the presence of a portrait medal of Oddi on the central octagonal table. A small double portrait on the right hand red-table depicts the patron, identified as Linder, pointing at a drawing. On close inspection the drawing may be seen to be a perspective scheme for the whole painting. Another figure, presumably the artist, is looking at the perspective drawing and painting from it. A preparatory drawing for the *Linder Gallery Interior* has been discovered in Windsor Castle, with a group of conversing connoisseurs replacing the allegorical figures. Surprisingly an identification of the artist of this remarkable painting remains challenging. Jan Brueghel the Younger visited Milan in the early 1620s, when the painting is likely to have been commissioned, but stylistically the painting appears more consistent with the collaborations between Jan Brueghel the Elder (who died in 1625 before the painting was completed) and Hendrick van Balen.
(Michael John Gorman and Alexander Marr)

Bibliography: Gorman-Marr 2007; Härting 1993; Honig 1995; New York 1998; Speth-Holterhoff 1957; Winner 1957.

VIII.2.1
Johann Gabriel Doppelmayr
Atlas novus coelestis
Norimberga, Sumptibus Haeredum Homannianorum, 1742
Milan, Biblioteca del Dipartimento di Astronomia, 18ORI.3.B, pl. XIX

A student of astronomy and geography, an excellent map-maker and constructor of mathematical instruments and of celestial and terrestrial globes, Doppelmayr (1677-1750) published this spectacular atlas in Johann Baptist Homan's print workshop, that specialized in the production of geographical charts. A lunar crater was named after him for his contribution to celestial cartography. The atlas consists of 30 large-size tables that illustrate the most recent astronomic hypotheses, with, however, the curious exception of Kepler's. For the first time, any reference to the Ptolemaic system is lacking. Doppelmayr conceived his atlas as an introduction to the study of astronomy.
In table XIX, constellations of the southern hemisphere for the year 1731. The astronomical observatories of Greenwich (founded in 1666), Copenhagen (1642), Kassel (1714) and Berlin (1711) are represented in the four margins.
(P.G.)

Bibliography: Wilson 1971.

VIII.2.2
Sébastien Leclerc
Visit of Louis XIV to the Académie des Sciences
1671
Engraving on paper; 44 x 32.5 cm
Paris, Observatoire de Paris, inv. I.110

Famous illustration that appeared in one of the first collections of scientific memoirs placed under the responsibility of the young Academy. The location of the scene's setting is unknown. In that period the academicians often met at the Bibliothèque du Roi, in Rue Vivienne, using the garden for conducting observations. At other times, they met in the galleries and in the gardens of the Louvre. The hypothesis has also been advanced that the scene's setting is a hall of the Jardin du Roi. Among the instruments used, Giandomenico Cassini mentions a quarter-circle similar to that depicted by Leclerc, who includes other astronomical instruments in the scene. Given that in the background the characteristic aspect is seen of the Paris Observatory (whose construction began in 1667), not visible from any of the previously mentioned spots, it is likely that Leclerc had created an imaginary place in order to show the Observatory, visited by the Sun King for the first time in 1682.
(L.B.)

Bibliography: Wolf 1902.

VIII.2.3
Antoine Cocquart
The Paris Observatory
1705
Engraving on paper; 25.2 x 35 cm
Paris, Observatoire de Paris, inv. I.123

This engraving, that includes three views of the Observatory, was realized for Nicolas de Fer's *Atlas curieux*. It shows the south and the north façades of the Observatory and presents the activities that were carried out there. The Marly Tower (seen on the right), previously used to lift water for the Versailles fountains, was moved between 1685 and 1688 into the structure which was, at the time, located in the countryside. To observe the stars, the astronomers in the foreground use large lenses without tubes, that is, an eyepiece and a simple lens placed at the end of a long rod. In the case of shorter focal lengths, a tube was used, like that seen between the Observatory building and the Marly Tower.
(L.B.)

Bibliography: Wolf 1902.

VIII.2.4
Sante Menini
Movable astronomical quadrant
1710
Iron, brass; radius c. 100 cm
Bologna, Museo della Specola, Università di Bologna, inv. MdS 118

Movable quadrants, equipped with telescopes, became part of the basic instrumentation of observatories in the last decades of 17th century. We know, from the 1727 inventory of the *specola* of the Istituto delle Scienze in Bologna, that this movable quadrant had been donated by cardinal Antonio Davia. On the central brass escutcheon we can read the maker's name and the date: «Sante Menini orologiere (clock maker) / in Bologna 1710».
The craftman's dexterity consisted in the hand-engraving, on the graduated scale, the divisions ideated by Tycho Brahe at the end of 16th century. One of the telescopes is missing together with the object lenses of the second, which apparently was the movable one. The connection to the limb could give any orientation to the telescope for taking topographic and astronomic measures.
(A.G.)

Bibliografia: Baiada-Bònoli-Braccesi 1995, pp. 102-104.

VIII.2.5
Comparative dimensions of the planets
Patinated wood and fibreglass; length 200 cm
S. Battaglia and G. Miglietta

The exhibit compares the relative dimensions of the planets, of the Sun and of the Moon in relation to the Earth, according to the estimates formulated by Tycho Brahe in 1601 and by Christiaan Huygens in the *Cosmotheoros* (The Hague 1699) to the dimensions assigned to them today.
The large semicircle represents the Sun, next to which, arranged on three parallel lines, are the planets according to the sizes estimated by Tycho, by Huygens and of the present day.
(P.G.)

VIII.3.1
Andreas Cellarius
Atlas coelestis seu Harmonia Macrocosmica
Amsterdam, Johannes Janssonius, 1660
Florence, Biblioteca Nazionale Centrale, Magl. 5._.81, pl. 27 (*Hemisphaeri borealis coeli et terrae sphaerica scenographia*)

Cf. entry III.5.2.
Perhaps the most spectacular table of the *Atlas*, that shows, in a single vision, the globe of the Earth and the celestial sphere outside of which the eye of the observer is placed.
(P.G.)

Bibliography: Cellarius 2006, pp. 173-177.

VIII.3.2
Johannes Hevelius (Hoewel)
Prodromus astronomiae et novae tabb. Solares quibus additus uterque catalogus stellarum fixarum nec non tabula motus Lunae libratorii ad duo secula proxume ventura ...
Gedani, typis Joh. Zach. Stollii, 1690
Florence, Biblioteca Nazionale Centrale, Pal. 8.9.7.21, plate 16

Published after his death by his wife Elisabeth, who had long assisted him in his observations, the *Prodromus astronomiae* (1690) of Jan Hövel (1611-1687) is an accurate catalogue of 1,564 stars, listed according to their constellations. Each star is accompanied by the celestial coordinates (ecliptic latitude and longitude) required to locate it correctly and determined by the use of highly accurate graduated instruments. A series of 56 plates, also published in 1690 and probably drawn by Hövel, shows the stars in the context of the various constellations.
Plate 16 in particular exemplifies three characteristics of the work: the representation is "convex" (that is, it shows the sphere of the fixed stars as if viewed from the outside), it includes traditional constellations (Antinous) suppressed by later astronomers, and it includes new constellations outlined by Hövel to fill the gaps between the traditional constellations (*Scutum Sobiescianum*).
(G.S.)

Bibliography: Hevelius 1968, p. 56.

VIII.3.3
Johannes Hevelius (Hoewel)
Machina Coelestis, pars prior
Gedani, Auctoris typis et sumptibus,
imprimebat S. Reiniger, 1673
Florence, Biblioteca Nazionale Centrale,
Pal. 8.9.7.20, fig. AA

The scientific activities of Jan Hövel (1611-1687) took place on the boundaries of traditional astronomy, characterized by the use of large graduated instruments, and the new telescopic astronomy inaugurated by Galileo. In his *Machina Coelestis, pars prior* (1673) Hövel gave a detailed description of all his own observational instruments. After a long section devoted to graduated instruments, based on further development of those described by Tycho Brahe (1546-1601) in his *Astronomiae instauratae mechanica* (1598), Hövel went on to display his own telescopic devices and the mountings with which he intended to make them functional.
The large plate containing Fig. AA shows the telescope of 150 foot in length which Hövel built in Danzig. This telescope has no real tube, but a complex system of extensions which keep the lenses aligned at any inclination.
(G.S.)

Bibliography: Hoskin, 1999, pp. 125-126; Firenze 2008b, p. 154.

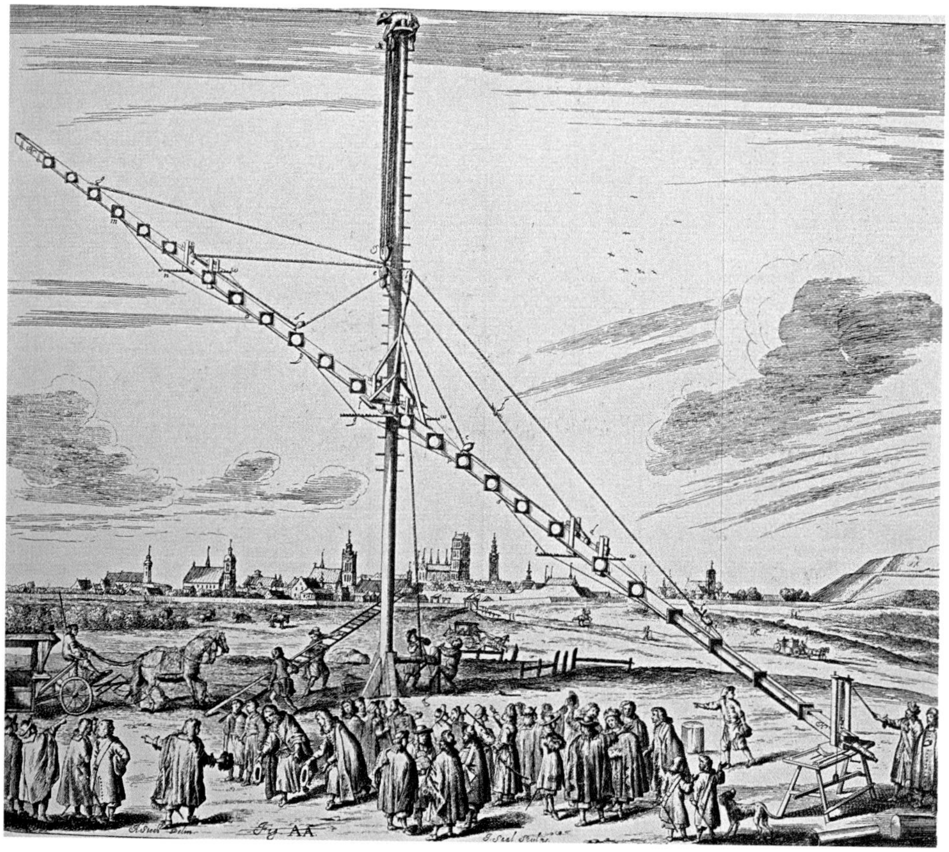

VIII.3.4
Vincenzo Coronelli
Idea of the Universe
Laboratory of P. Coronelli in Venice, 1683-1685
Engraving on copper; 39 x 53 cm
Florence, Istituto e Museo di Storia
della Scienza, MED 2233, pl. 63

This exemplar is dedicated to Abbot Sebastiano Venier; there are others, later than this, dedicated to Cardinals Albani and Azzolini. The work, recorded in the sales catalogues of Coronelli (1650-1715) from as early as 1688, is inserted into some copies of the first volume of the *Atlante Veneto* (post-1690) and also in the *Libro dei Globi* in the British Library (1710) and in the *Cronologia universale* of 1709. It consists of a cosmographical synopsis, for mainly astrological use, connected with the *Calendario perpetuo sacro-profano* published by Coronelli in his youth and with his activity as publisher of almanacs. Recognizable in the various wheels are the themes, taken up later in his *Epitome cosmographica* (1693; cf. entry VI.5.2), devoted to "matter and fabric of the world according to the Ancients and according to the Moderns", and the depiction of a "celestial Figure", which is to say a horoscope such as the one in the centre of the plate. The *Epitome*, however, places a lot less emphasis on the astrological aspects (wheels of planetary influences on the signs of the zodiac and on human organs, of famine and abundance etc.) and on those of religion (the wheel at the top, which represents the universe from the fires of hell to the sphere of the Primum Mobile, and the calendars of moveable feasts at the bottom, linked to the Lunar or Metonic cycle). This plate is one of the few surviving records of Coronelli's activity as an astrologer.
(M.Mi.)

Bibliography: Armao 1944; Domini-Milanesi 1998; Tavoni 1999.

VIII.3.5
Vincenzo Coronelli
Celestial Globe
1692
Wood and papier mâché; diameter 108 cm, height 150 cm, width 150 cm
Florence, Istituto e Museo di Storia della Scienza, inv. 2366

The celestial globe is a re-print of the Venetian edition of 1688. Forming a pair with a terrestrial globe, it was dedicated by Vincenzo Coronelli (1650-1718) to the Most Serene Republic of Venice and to the doge Francesco Morosini in thanks for the financing received for the printing of the *Atlante Veneto*, published in 1690-91. The globe is a smaller-scale version of the one, nearly four metres in diameter, constructed for Louis XIV. It is made up of 24 half-gores and two polar caps that contain 3 northern, 12 zodiacal and 33 southern constellations, indicated with names in Italian, Latin, Greek and Arabic. The stars indicated by Coronelli are 1902, whereas Ptolemy reported 1022. It comes from the Medici collections and in 1753 became part of the collections of the Osservatorio Ximeniano. It was later displayed during the first History of Science Exposition held in Florence in 1929.
(F.C.)

Bibliography: Righini Bonelli 1968a, p. 157; Miniati 1991, p. 100; *Istituto e Museo di storia della scienza (Firenze)* 2004, pp. 144-148.

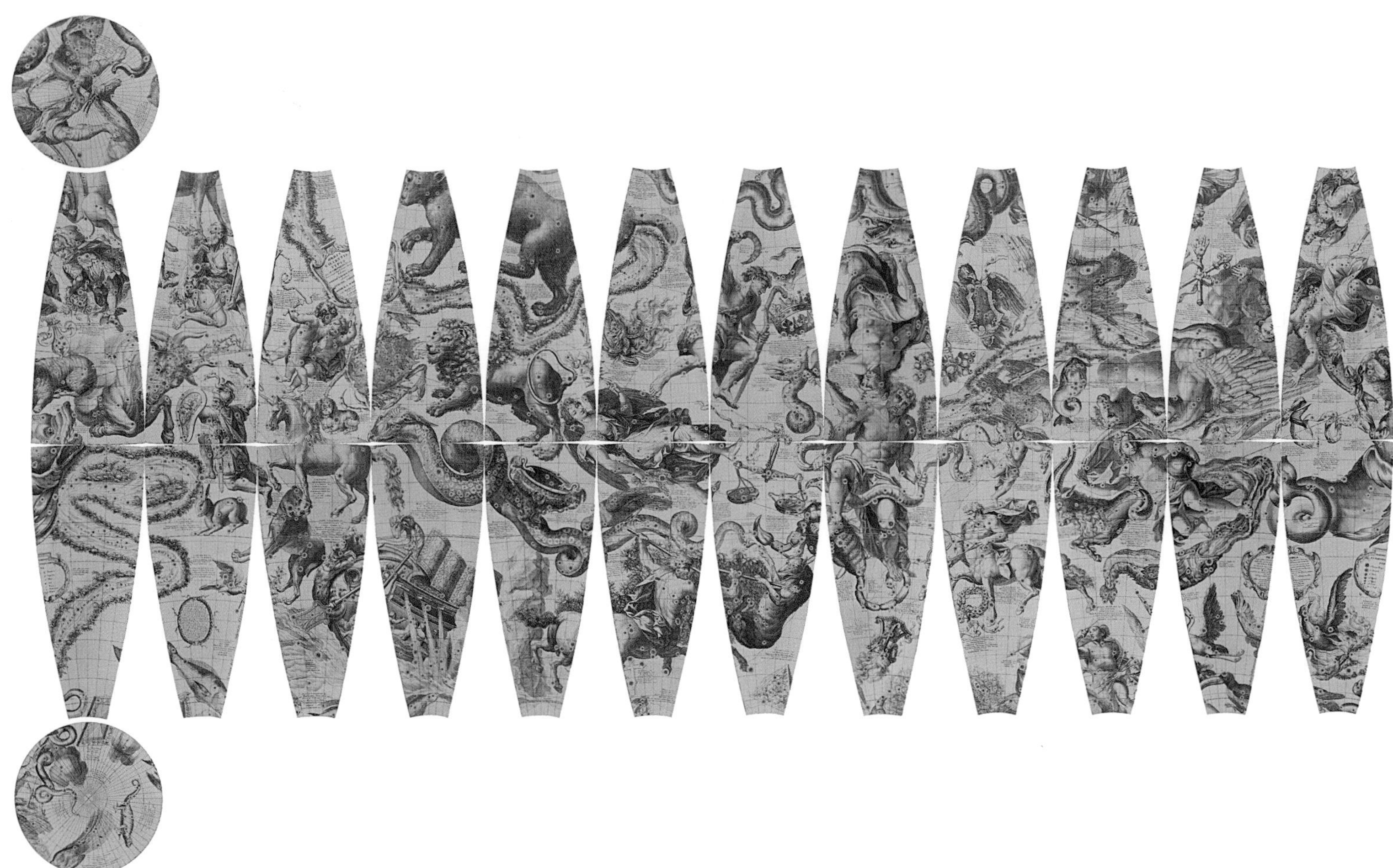

VIII.3.6
Vincenzo Coronelli and Jean-Baptiste Nolin
Celestial globe gores
1693 (20th century printing)
Copper engraving, 72 x 54 cm
Florence, Istituto e Museo di Storia della Scienza

The 26 sheets, printed in the last century from the original copper plates preserved in the Biblioteque Nationale in Paris (24 half-gores and 2 polar caps), belong to the second version of the celestial globe by Coronelli (1650-1718) printed in Paris by Jean-Baptiste Nolin (1657-1725) in 1693. The engraving of the plates began in 1686, but was interrupted by a controversy between the French engraver and the Venetian cosmographer. Having already finished the terrestrial globe that formed a pair together with the celestial globe, Coronelli had all the gores engraved anew by a Venetian engraver, obtaining the series finished in 1692. The next year, Nolin finished his work as well, having the celestial globe printed at the expense of a "Societas Gallica". The gores make a globe with a diameter of 108 cm (cf. entry VIII.3.5).
(F.C.)

Bibliography: Righini Bonelli 1968a, p. 157; Miniati 1991, p. 100; *Istituto e Museo di storia della scienza (Firenze)* 2004, pp. 152-156.

VIII.3.7
John Flamsteed
Atlas Coelestis
London, s.n., 1753
Turin, Biblioteca Nazionale Universitaria,
Ris. 105.27, pl. 2

A work by one of the greatest astronomers of the second half of the seventeenth century, founder and, for many years, director of the Astronomical Observatory of Greenwich, the atlas by Flamsteed (1646-1719) inaugurates a new season for this kind of publication for the precision and abundance of information. The atlas appeared for the first time in London in 1729, after the death of its author. The 25 large-size tables that it consists of, embellished by beautiful representations of the constellations, present more than 3,300 stars for the year 1690 (double the number indicated in the *Uranographia* by Hevelius). For the first time, the stars are divided into seven magnitudes with the indication of their equatorial coordinates. The use of the pendulum clock and of large-size telescopes permitted Flamsteed to reduce margins for error very significantly. The work enjoyed remarkable success and was reprinted many times. In table 2, a representation of the constellation of Taurus. Above the ecliptic, at the height of the bull's shoulder, Flamsteed indicated, as a small star, the planet Uranus, that he had observed without understanding its true nature.
(P.G.)

Bibliography: Flamsteed 1997; Stoppa 2006, pp. 50-51.

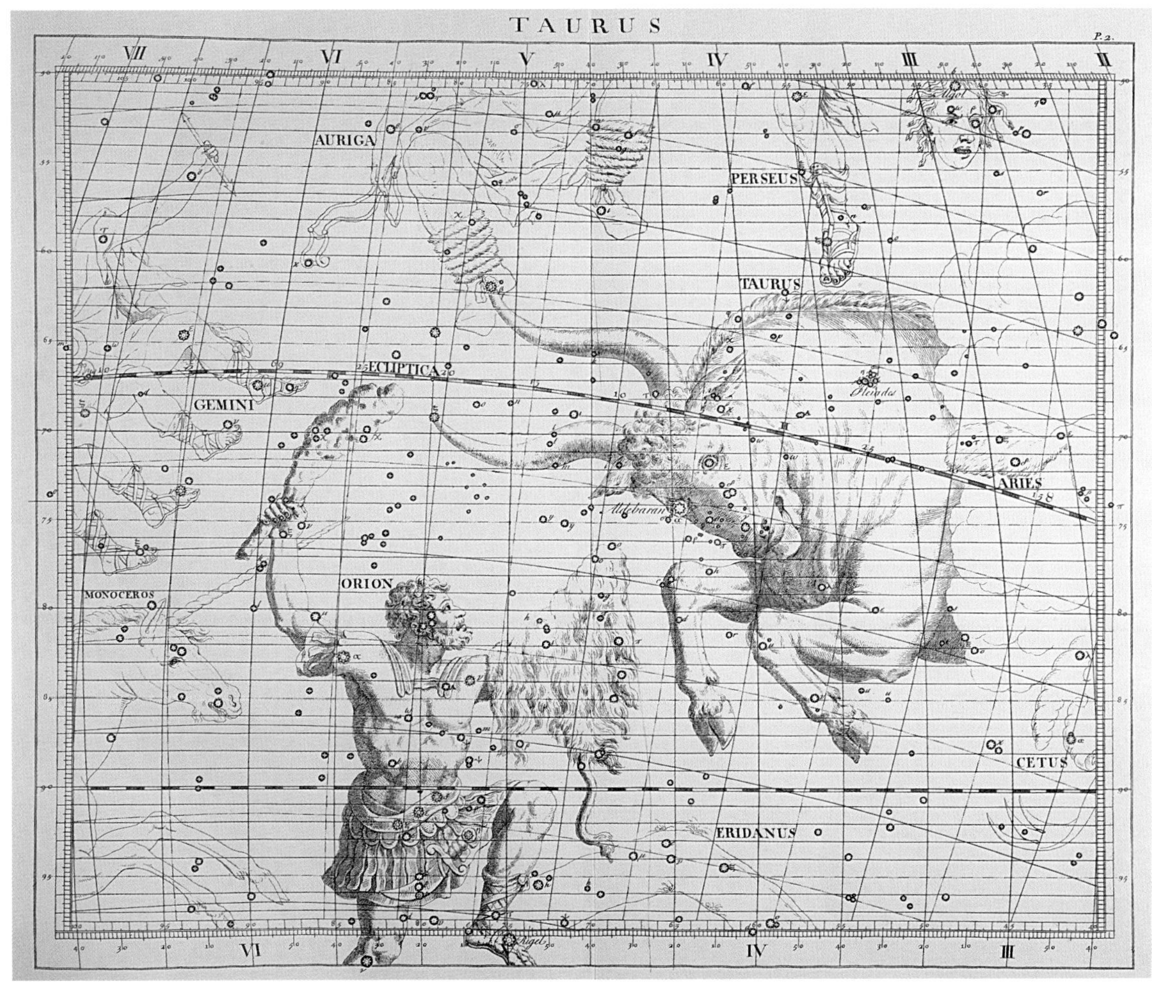

VIII.3.8
Johann Gabriel Doppelmayr
Six star charts in gnomonic projection
1742
Coloured engraving; 54.5 x 62 cm (each sheet)
Vienna, Private collection

The sheets, numbered from 20 to 25, were part of the *Atlas Coelestis* (see entry VIII.2.1) by Doppelmayr (Nuremberg 1742). Four show the equatorial constellations, the other two show the northern and southern circumpolar constellations, up to a declination of 45°. The stars are indicated with the traditional magnitudes from the first to the sixth. On both sides of the charts the positions of the stars belonging to the represented constellations are listed.
The gnomonic star charts published in 1674 by Father Ignace-Gaston Pardies, a Jesuit and professor of mathematics at the Collège de Louis-le-Grand in Paris, served as a model for Doppelmayr. The latter, like Pardies, also included the orbits of numerous comets in the star charts. The representation of the constellations is "concave"; once a chart is orientated coherently with the cardinal points of the place of observation, the stars are seen represented just as they appear in the sky. Usually, the ancient celestial globes instead give a "convex" representation, that is, a specular image of the constellations. In ancient times it was, in fact, thought that the stars were all found at the same distance from the Earth, fixed to a crystalline sphere. It was therefore natural to represent the constellations as they could have been observed from outside such a sphere.
Johann Gabriel Doppelmayr was one of the most important globe-makers of his times. Besides law, he studied mathematics and physics, but he also acquired knowledge in the fields of geography, cartography and astronomy. He was a member of important scientific societies, in London and St. Petersburg. Doppelmayr's globes had wide-spread distribution throughout central Europe and were republished, updated, in the following decades. (H.W.)

Bibliography: Warner 1979.

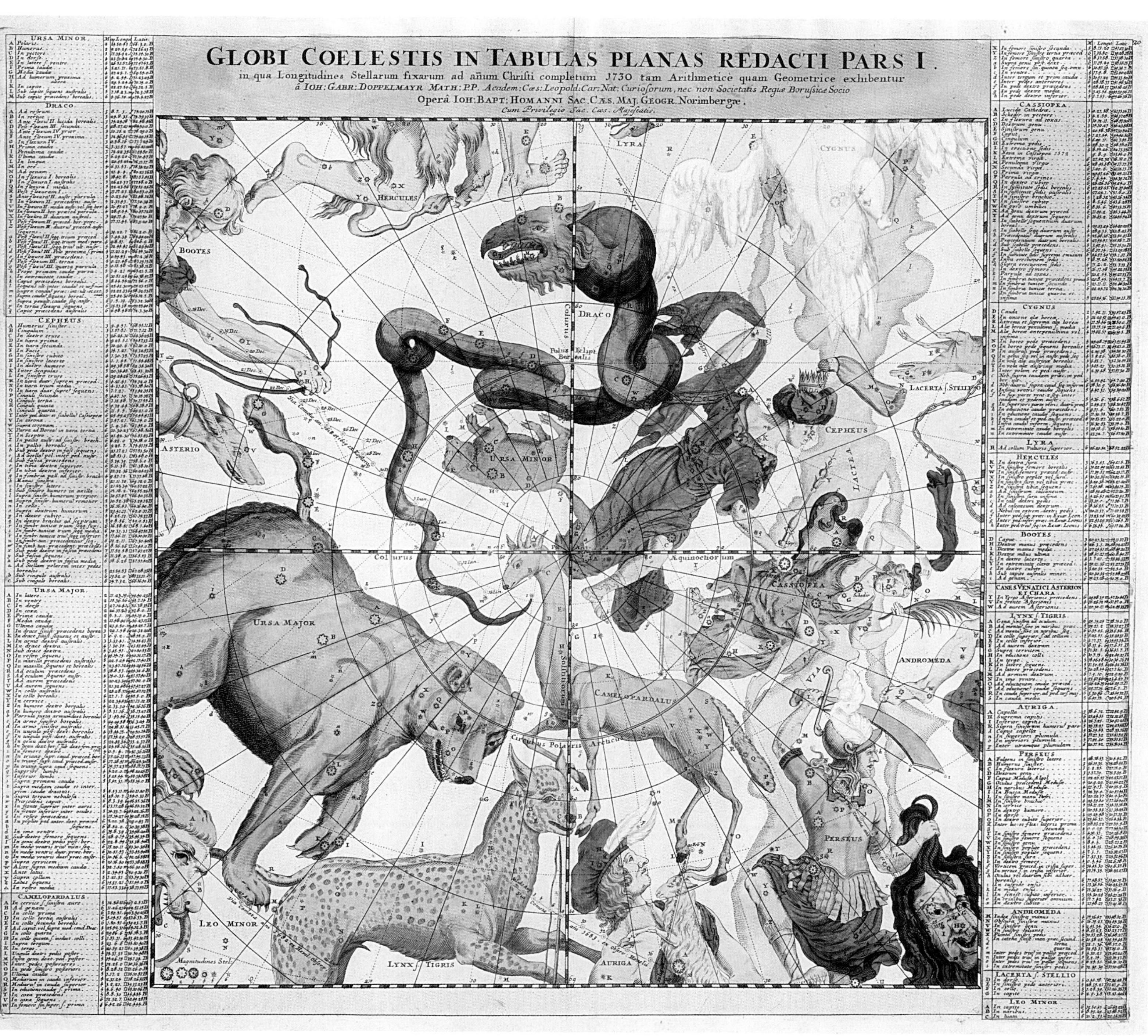
GLOBI COELESTIS IN TABULAS PLANAS REDACTI PARS I.
in qua Longitudines Stellarum fixarum ad aňum Christi completum 1730 tam Arithmeticè quam Geometricè exhibentur
à IOH: GABR: DOPPELMAYR MATH: P.P. Academ: Cæs: Leopold: Car: Nat: Curiosorum, nec non Societatis Regiæ Borussicæ Socio
Operâ IOH: BAPT: HOMANNI SAC. CÆS. MAJ. GEOGR. Norimbergæ.
Cum Privilegio Sac. Cæs. Majestatis.
URSA MINOR.
DRACO.
CEPHEUS.
URSA MAJOR.
CAMELOPARDALUS.
CASSIOPEA.
CYGNUS.
LYRA.
HERCULES.
BOOTES.
CANES VENATICI ASTERION ET CHARA.
LYNX f. TIGRIS.
AURIGA.
PERSEUS.
ANDROMEDA.
LACERTA f. STELLIO.
LEO MINOR.
HERCULES
BOOTES
LYRA
CYGNUS
DRACO
Polus Eclipt. Borealis
Colurus
URSA MINOR
ASTERIO
CEPHEUS
LACERTA f. STELLIO
LACTEA
Æquinoctiorum
CASSIOPEA
URSA MAJOR
ANDROMEDA
VIA
Solstitiorum
CAMELOPARDALUS
Circulus Polaris Arcticus
PERSEUS
LEO MINOR
LYNX f. TIGRIS
AURIGA
Magnitudines Stel.

VIII.3.9
Erhard Weigel
Astroscopium Orbi Europaeo Sacrum
Jena, 1688
(facsimile)

Sky chart produced by Weigel (1625-1699), astronomer and professor of mathematics in Jena (he was one of Leibniz's teachers), with celebratory purposes. Above the images of the constellations, the author has impressed the coats-of-arms and the emblems of many reigning houses and religious orders in Europe at that time. Predominance is clearly given to the three eagles (n. 1), symbol of the German Empire (*Coelum sedes mea*), explicitly compared to the symbol of the Trinity, but many other coats-of-arms can be recognized: the fleurs-de-lis of France (n. 2), the three crowns of the Kingdom of Sweden (n. 3), the emblem of the Company of Jesus (n. 4), the crest of the Duchy of Savoy (n. 5), the Lion of Saint Mark (n. 6), the Golden Fleece of the Kingdom of Spain (n. 7).
(A.S.)

Bibliography: Siebmacher 1989.

VIII.4.1
Ole Rømer
Planetarium
1680
Wood, glided bronze, steel, precious stones;
70 x 49 cm
Paris, Bibliothèque Nationale de France,
inv. GA 280

An octagonal instrument designed by Rømer (1644-1710) at the request of Colbert and constructed by the great clockmaker Isaac Thuret in 1680. It is a twin of the *Eclipsareon* (see entry VIII.4.2). A second exemplar of this Copernican planetarium was made for Christian V of Denmark and is now in the Rosenborg Castle in Copenhagen. The brass face is surrounded by a fixed zodiacal circle and contains six circular tracks representing the orbits of the planets. Those of Venus, the Earth (with a disk for the moon attached) and Saturn have as their centre the Sun, which is off-centre with respect to the other planets. The mechanism shows rods with conical gears (a novel feature due to Rømer). It controls the mechanism of the individual planets and it is concealed inside the body of the planetarium. The planets move at varying speeds, with a maximum at the perihelion and minimum at the aphelion, as laid down by Kepler. It was the first time this effect was successfully achieved by mechanical means. Four pairs of metal bridges ensure the connection of the individual tracks to the body of the structure. The fixed rear quadrant shows a calendar with months and days and also registers the stars and form of the constellations, with pointers for calculating which stars are on the horizon at a given moment. It is wound up with a key which engages the square-headed central shaft. Each complete revolution represents a solar year. The instrument was considered at the time to be a marvel of mechanics, and in 1680 was given a solemn presentation at the Paris Académie des Sciences. The elaborate decoration, the lilies of France and the emblem of the regal Sun which dominates the planetarium allude to the patron of the enterprise, Louis XIV, the "Roi Soleil".
(P.G.)

Bibliography: King H.C. 1978a, pp. 107-110; Sarazin 2003.

VIII.4.2
Ole Rømer
Eclipsareon
[1680-1681]
Wood, gilded bronze, steel, precious stones;
70 x 49 cm
Paris, Bibliothèque Nationale de France,
inv. GA 281

With respect to size, form and decoration, a twin of Rømer's Copernican planetarium (see entry VIII.4.1). This instrument, which repeats the mechanisms of the planetarium though assembling them differently, permits the prediction of the eclipses of the Sun and Moon. This is obtained by winding the key on the rear quadrant until the moving hand approaches the disks of the Sun and Moon. At this point the year and day are indicated by means of two mobile indexes on the rear quadrant, in which a tiny mobile hand points a finger at the month. Each complete turn of the key corresponds to a tropical year.
(P.G.)

Bibliography: King H.C. 1978a, p. 111; Sarazin 2003.

VIII.4.3
Anonymous (Copy from Joseph Wright of Derby)
A Philosopher giving that Lecture on the Orrery, in which a lamp is put in place of the Sun
c. 1766
Oil on canvas; 65 x 77.5 cm
Vienna, Private collection

The painter Joseph Wright (1734-1797) showed a constant interest in mechanics. The *Orrery*, painted in 1766, shows a 'natural philosopher' giving a lecture around a large planetarium.
John Rowley (c. 1665-1728) was the first to construct a mechanical planetarium, following a suggestion by Charles Boyle, fourth Count of Orrery (1676-1731). For this reason, the numerous similar instruments, often of considerable size and remarkable mechanical complexity, that were constructed afterwards, mainly in England, took on the name of *orreries*.
The copy is contemporary to the original painting, conserved in the Derby Museum and Art Gallery.
(R.S.)

Bibliography: King H.C. 1978a, pp. 165 ff.

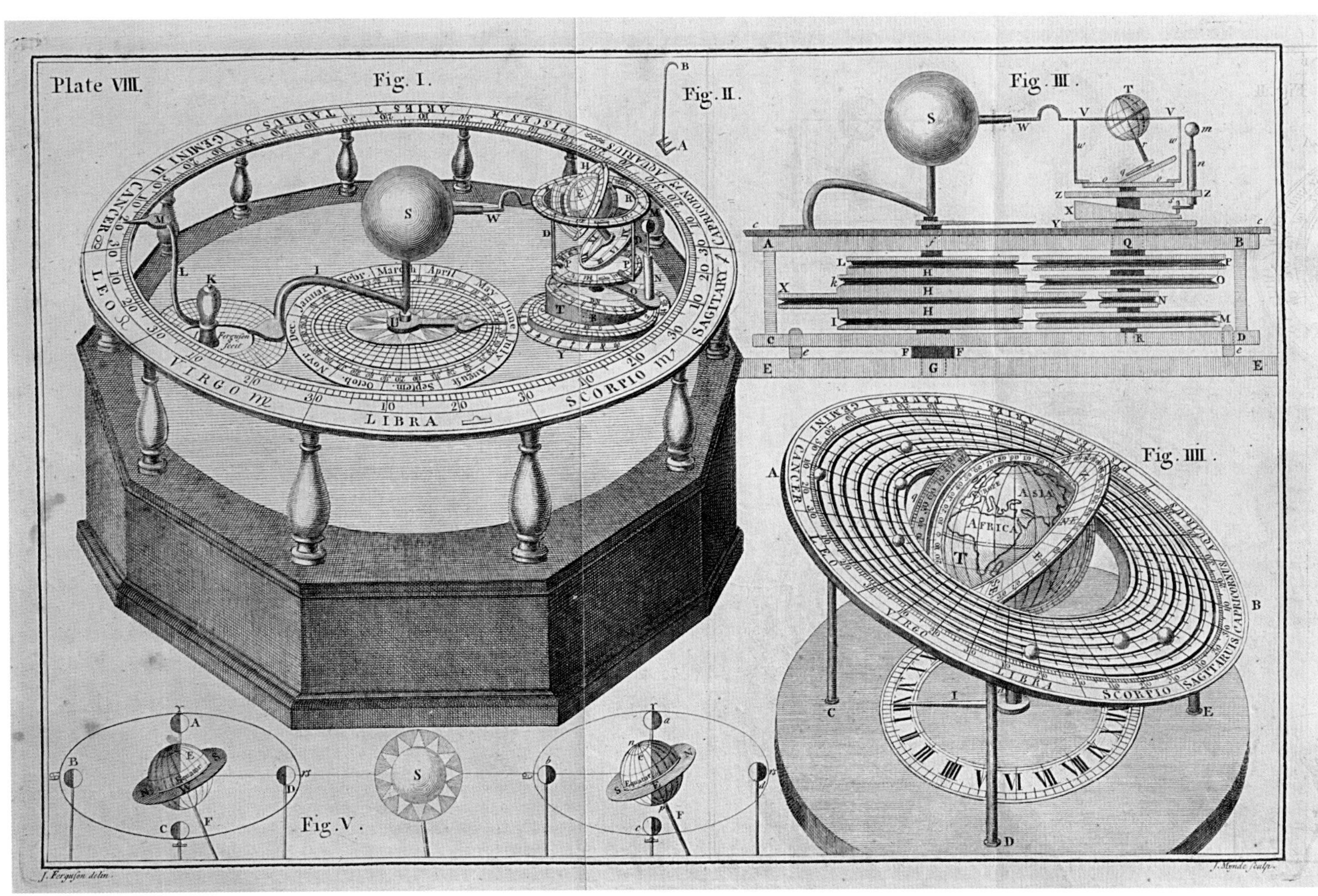

VIII.4.4
James Ferguson
Astronomy explained upon Sir Isaac Newton's Principles ...
London, Printed for A. Millar, 1764
Florence, Istituto e Museo di Storia della Scienza, MED 1961, pl. VIII

Third edition (the first is of 1756) of the popular treatise for the divulgation of Newtonian astrophysics by the Scotsman James Ferguson (1710-1776), talented in mechanics, inventor of renowned clocks and *orreries* and a successful lecturer. Planche VIII illustrates the aspect and constructive details of his *orrery* (cf. entries VIII.4.5 and VIII.4.6).
(P.G.)

Bibliography: Laudan 1972.

VIII.4.5
James Ferguson
Planetarium-Orrery
c. 1760
Mahogany, paper, hemp; 27 x 36 cm
London, Science Museum, inv. 1934-134

This simple planetarium-orrery, by the self-taught Scottish astronomer, instrument-maker and lecturer James Ferguson, is made almost entirely of wood. It is driven by string belts passing around pulleys, as described by Ferguson in 1747. The orrery demonstrates the annual revolution of the earth around the sun, the rotation of the moon's orbit, the approximate phase of the moon (shown by a pointer on the spindle which carries the sun) and the motion of the Moon's apogee. The circles around the Earth are calibrated to show the signs of the Zodiac and the position of the Moon's ascending and descending nodes. The main calendar scale on the base shows the Sun's position in the sky as seen from the Earth. The lunar scale shows the Moon's angular orbital position and inclination with respect to the ecliptic. A table shows 'the time of the mean new moon in January, and of the conjunction of the sun with the Moon's ascending node' for the years 1760-1800.
(A.B.)

Bibliography: Ferguson J. 1747; Ferguson J. 1764a; Milburn-King 1988; Rothman 2000.

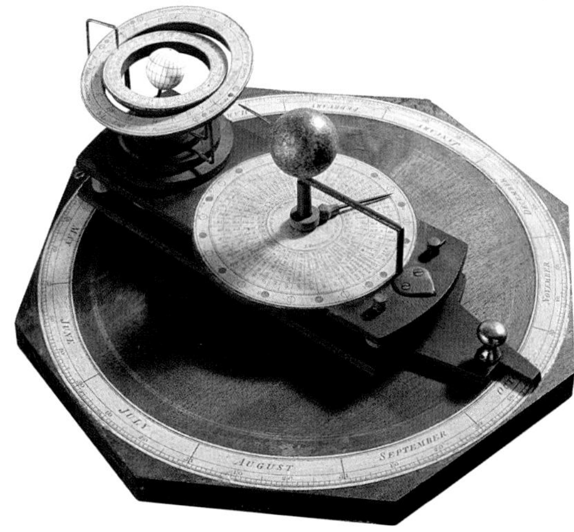

VIII.4.6
Anonymous
Orrery of Venus
Florence, 1775-1776
Brass, steel, glass, wood; 46 x 46 x 28.5 cm
Florence, Istituto e Museo di Storia della Scienza, inv. 581

James Ferguson (1710-1776) was very active in spreading knowledge of Newtonian astronomy. In his widely read *Astronomy Explained upon Sir Isaac Newton's Principles* (1756; cf. entry VIII.4.4) he suggested the idea of building planetariums, known by the name of *orreries*, which clearly explained the concept of the " celestial mechanism", for by the accurate use of gears it was possible to reproduce the motions of the heavens. The London scientific instrument manufacturer John Rowley (c. 1665-1728) had called this type of planetarium an *orrery*, in honour of Charles Boyle, 4th Earl of Orrery (1676-1731). A product of the workshops of the Imperiale e Reale Museo di Fisica e Storia Naturale in Florence, and following the example set by Ferguson, this *orrery* of Venus, worked by winding a cranck, exactly reproduced the heliocentric motions of Mercury, Venus and the Earth, as well as that of the Moon around the Earth.
(G.S.)

Bibliography: Ferguson J. 1764a, pp. 278-283; Ferguson J. 1773, pp. 72-87; Righini-Bonelli 1976, p. 161, no. 82; King H.C. 1978a, pp. 178-194; Miniati 1991, p. 104, no. 39; *Istituto e Museo di storia della scienza (Firenze)* 2004, pp. 98-100, no. 18.

VIII.4.7
Heath & Wing, London
Grand planetarium-orrery
c. 1765
Brass, silvered brass, steel, mahogany, glass; diameter 90 cm, height 175 cm
Oxford, All Souls College (On loan from Oxford, the Museum of the History of Science, inv. 39896)

The partnership between Thomas Heath and his former apprentice Tycho Wing lasted from 1751 to 1773, with premises at various addresses in the Strand, London, and this is one of their most ambitious creations – a complete 'grand orrery' with all the known planets and satellites fully driven by clockwork. The pendulum-regulated clockwork movement is beneath the base plate and it drives the planets out to Saturn with their respective periods, as well as the Moon, four satellites of Jupiter (discovered by Galileo) and five of Saturn. The Earth moved over a calendar scale giving the date. The glazed mahogany case is designed both to be appropriate to an elegant room and to reveal the wheelwork in addition to the planetary system – a clear sign that the mechanism was meant to impress the viewer as well as the motions of the planets.
(J.B.)

Bibliography: Taylor 1966, pp. 129, 208; King H.C. 1978a, p. 164; Clifton 1995, p. 131.

VIII.4.8
Jesse Ramsden
Orrery
Date unknown
Brass, steel, wood, glass; 16 x 50 cm
London, Science Museum, inv. 1936-645

This is the only known orrery by the celebrated instrument maker Jesse Ramsden. It appears to be unfinished, allowing the wheelwork to be clearly seen.
The orrery was discovered in the 1930s in the disused observatory of the School of Military Engineering in Chatham and it seems to have been the private property of an officer. It was presented to the Science Museum, London, by the War Office.
(A.B.)

Bibliography: McConnell 2007.

VIII.4.9
Charles-François Delamarche (attr.)
Tellurium
Painted wood, brass; width 29 cm, height 33 cm
Florence, Istituto e Museo di Storia della Scienza, inv. CSBASF04

With beginnings in the second half of the 18th century, the so-called Tellurium was one of the most commonly used mechanical devices for teaching astronomy. James Ferguson, in his *Select Mechanical Exercises* (1773), presented it as a "mechanical paradox" invented by him about 18 years previously. The paradox lay in the fact that whatever movement the Earth made around the Sun the three main gears kept the terrestrial axis constantly parallel to itself. In an extremely simplified version, and what is more not in scale, the device also showed the motion of the Earth round the Sun and that of the Moon round the Earth. This particular Tellurium was probably constructed by Charles-François Delamarche (1740-1817), to whom we owe for certain the cartography of the small terrestrial globe in it. Delamarche himself described this type of instrument in his *Usage de la Sphère, et des Globes Céleste et Terrestre* (1791), calling it a *machine geo-cyclique*.
(G.S.)

Bibliography: Ferguson J. 1773, pp. 44-71; Delamarche 1798, pp. 164-188; King H.C. 1978a, p. 186; *Istituto e Museo di storia della scienza (Firenze)* 2004, pp. 102-106, no. 20.

VIII.5.1
Giovanni Battista Pittoni
Homage to Newton
1732
Oil on canvas; 155 x 219 cm
Valdagno (VC), Marzotto Collection

Coming from the Fiévez sale in Brussels in 1928, this painting has been associated with the large arched vertical canvas representing the *Allegory of Newton* (Cambridge, Fitzwilliam, inv. PD.52-1973), executed by Giovanni Battista Pittoni (1687-1767) with the assistance of Domenico and Giuseppe Valeriani (that is, one of the 24 canvasses intended to illustrate English history commissioned by the impresario of Irish origin Owen McSwiny on behalf of the Duke of Richmond). In particular it seems possible to identify the canvas displayed here with the version requested by John Conduitt, husband of Newton's niece and his successor as director of the Royal Mint. In a letter to McSwiny dated 4 June 1729, John Conduitt requested that the monument should be shown as in the open air, and that "it should in some way resemble the School of Athens" in Raphael's painting. This version differs from that in Cambridge in that it lacks the famous experiment conducted with the prism.

Bibliography: Jaffé in Cambridge 1973, pp. 4-11; Zava Boccazzi 1979, pp. 164-165; Haskell 1989, pp. 14, 17-21; Mazza in Crema 1999, pp. 96-97 (with bibliography); Cottino in Forte di Bard 2007, pp. 205-206, n. 32.

VIII.5.2
Luigi Mussini
The Triumph of Truth
1847
Oil on canvas, 143.5 x 213 cm
Milan, Accademia di Belle Arti di Brera,
inv. 1980, n. 358

Commissioned by Marquis Filippo Ala Ponzi, the painting reveals a wide-ranging meditation of style in which the work of Raphael is of central importance. Exhibited in Florence in 1848, the *Triumph* was awarded a prize at the Paris Salon of 1849. It represents Truth Triumphant personified by a unveiled girl holding aloft a torch. Around her are the great men who have contributed to the search for truth, whether religious, moral, philosophical, scientific or artistic. On her right is St Philip baptizing the eunuch, Plato, Socrates, Aristotle, Confucius, Aeschylus, Alexander, Alcibiades, Demosthenes, Phidias and Giotto, and, at the edge of the picture, Savonarola as in the famous portrait by Fra Bartolomeo. On her left, together with Dante, Cuvier, Pascal, Giordano Bruno, Christopher Columbus and Herodotus, is the group of the astronomers, gathered round the central figure of Galileo as if in conversation. In a narrative crescendo, Ptolemy, depicted kneeling and from behind, is turned not towards Truth but towards Copernicus, who is holding a volume (evidently his *De revolutionibus orbium coelestium*, 1543) to which Galileo points while directing his gaze at Truth. Lower down is Kepler showing Truth his *Astronomia nova* (1609), while just behind stands Isaac Newton.painting depicting *The Reign of Error*, which would for example have used the Baroque to exemplify art and astrology for the sciences.
(P.S.)

Bibliography: *Explication des ouvrages* 1849, p. 134; Pinto 1982, p. 1056; Spalletti in *Pinacoteca di Brera* 1994, pp. 510-513; Lombardi in Siena 2007, pp. 116, 120-122.

REFERENCES

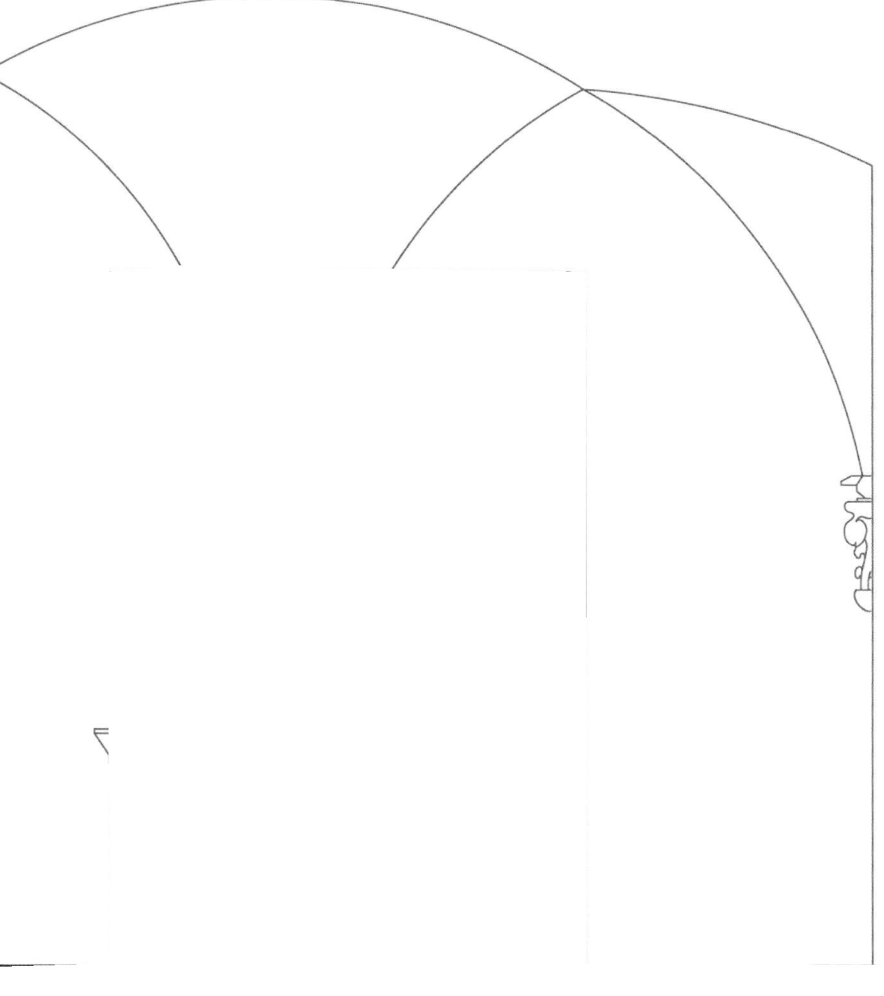

Installation project
Studio Gris
Stefano Gris with Stefania Ingoglia,
Federica Bassi, Laura Bello,
Graphics project: Stefano Rovai
Executive Planning and Work Supervision:
Luigi Cupellini

The installation involves making a covering that completely lines all the rooms; in at least two focal points in each room, where important objects will be placed, there will be very deep and large openings up to the ceiling, which lead the visitor to look up.
These alternating heights, one on a human scale and the other surprisingly marked in some points, will give the space a connotation of sacredness that will emphasize some situations, also due to the effect of surprise and discovery.
The walls of these 'overturned wells', covered with graphics and quotations, will accompany the visitor's glance toward the ceiling, where images of ancient constellations and pictures of the universe will be projected.

BIBLIOGRAPHY

Aaboe 2001
A. Aaboe, *Episodes from the Early History of Astronomy*, New York 2001.

Abbé 1912-1914
A. Abbé, *Un dessin inédit de Chalette*, "Bulletin de la Société d'Archéologie", 1912-1914, pp. 185-187, tav. XIV.

Acidini Luchinat-Capretti 2002
C. Acidini Luchinat, E. Capretti, *Il mito di Europa: Da fanciulla rapita a continente*, Firenze 2002.

Acidini Luchinat-Morolli 2006
C. Acidini Luchinat, G. Morolli, *L'uomo del Rinascimento: Leon Battista Alberti e le arti a Firenze tra ragione e bellezza*, Firenze 2006.

Agostino 1956
A. Agostino, *Enarrationes in Psalmos*, Turnholti 1956.

Albumasar 1995
Albumasar, *Introductorium maius in astronomiam*, Augsburg 1485; edited by R. Lemay, vols. 9, Napoli 1995.

Alfonso X Di Castiglia 1981
Alfonso X Di Castiglia, *Lapidario*, edited by S. Rodriguez-Montalvo, Madrid 1981.

Alfonso X Di Castiglia 1982
Alfonso El Sabio, *Astromagia* (Ms. Reg. lat. 1283a), edited by A. D'Agostino, Napoli 1982.

Allen 1899
R.H. Allen, *Star-Names and their Meanings*, New York 1899.

Allen 1963
R.H. Allen, *Star names: their lore and meaning*, Dover 1963.

al-Magriti 1986
Maslamah ibn Ahmad al-Magriti, *Picatrix, the Latin version of the Ghayat al-hakim*, edited by D. Pingree, London 1986.

Allmayer-Beck 1997
P.E. Allmayer-Beck, (edited by), *Modelle der Welt. Erd- und Himmelsgloben. Kulturerbe aus österreichschen Sammlungen*, Wien 1997.

Alpers 1971
S. Alpers, *The Decoration of the Torre de la Parada*, London-New York 1971.

Alvino 1887
F. Alvino, *Calendari*, Firenze 1887.

Andrewes 1996
W. Andrewes (edited by), *The Quest for Longitude*, Harvard 1996.

Appenzeller *et al.* 2003
I. Appenzeller, T. Rivinius, H. Mandel, C. Scorza de Appl, *Vorstellung der Gestirne auf XXXIV Taffeln von J. E. Bode, 1782*, Heidelberg 2003.

Armao 1944
E. Armao, *Vincenzo Coronelli. Cenni sull'uomo e la sua vita. Catalogo ragionato delle sue opere*, Firenze 1944.

Aubourg 1995
E. Aubourg, *La date de conception du zodiaque du Temple d'Hathor à Dendera*, "BIFAO", 95, 1995, pp. 1-10.

Aujac 1994
G. Aujac, *La géographie grecque durant le Quattrocento: l'example de Strabon*, "Geographia antiqua", 2, 1993-1994, pp. 147-169.

Azzarita 1987
F. Azzarita, *Il Globo di Matelica*, "Atti del 1° Seminario Nazionale di Gnomonica", december 1987.

Babicz 1987
J. Babicz, *The celestial and terrestrial globes of the Vatican Library, dating from 1477, and their maker Donus Nicolaus Germanus (ca. 1420-ca. 1490)*, in "Der Globusfreund", 35-37, 1987, pp. 155-168.

Bagnani 1934
G. Bagnani, *Il Primo Intendente del Palazzo, Imenhotpe, detto Huy*, "Aegyptus", 14, 1934, pp. 33-48.

Baiada-Bònoli-Braccesi 1995
E. Baiada, F. Bònoli, A. Braccesi, *Museo della Specola*, Bologna 1995.

Baldini-Carusi 1989
D. Baldini, A. Carusi, *Gli enigmi del globo di Matelica*, "L'Astronomia", 92, (1989).

Baldini-Carusi 1991
D. Baldini, A. Carusi, *Una sfera misteriosa*, "Archeo", 80, (october 1991).

Barale 2000
P. Barale, *La costellazione di Orione nella tradizione popolare delle Alpi sud-occidentali*, in *Atti del XIX Congresso Nazionale di Storia della Fisica e dell'Astronomia*, Milano 2000, pp. 147-155.

Barbanera-Venafro 1993
I Musei dell'Università "La Sapienza", edited by M. Barbanera and I. Venafro, Roma 1993.

Barker 1984-1989
A. Barker, *Greek Musical Writings*, 2 vols., Cambridge 1984-1989.

Barker 2007
A. Barker, *The Science of harmonics in classical Greece*, Cambridge 2007.

Barnett-Wiseman 1960
R.D. Barnett, D.J. Wiseman, *Fifty Masterpieces of Ancient Near Eastern Art in the Department of Western Asiatic Antiquities British Museum* (1ª ed.), London 1960.

Bartsch 1808
A. Bartsch, *Le Peintre-Graveur*, 21 vols., Wien 1802-1821.

Barzon 1924
A. Barzon, *I cieli e la loro influenza negli affreschi del Salone di Padova*, Padova 1924.

Bastianelli Moscati 2008
G. Bastianelli Moscati, *L'universo in una grotta. Il rilievo mitraico di Terni e la sua simbologia*, "Automata", 3, 2008, (now printing).

Battistini 2004
M. Battistini, *Astrologia, magia, alchimia*, Milano 2004.

Baudouin 1995
F. Baudouin, *Peter Paul Rubens en Galileo Galilei: een minder bekende bladzijde uit de Europese cultuurgeschiedenis*, "Studia Europaea", I (1995), pp. 69-96.

Bayer 2000
I. Bayer, *Uranometria (Augusta 1603)*, Milano 2000.

BEA 2007
BEA (Biographical Encyclopedia of Astronomers), 2 vols., New York 2007.
Bedini 1961
S. Bedini, *The Optical Workshop Equipment of Giuseppe Campani*, "Journal of the History of Medicine and Allied Sciences", 16, 1 (1961), pp. 18-38.

Bedini 1980
S.A. Bedini *The Vatican's astronomical paintings and Institute of the sciences of Bologna*, in *Proceendings of the eleventh lunar and planetary science conference*, New York 1980, pp. XIII-XXXIII.

Bedini 1986
S.A. Bedini, *The Galilean Jovilabe*, "Nuncius", I-1 (1986), pp. 25-46.

418

Bennett 1987
J. Bennett, *The Divided Circle: a history of instruments for astronomy, navigation and surveying*, Oxford 1987.

Beretta-Di Pasquale 2004
M. Beretta, G. Di Pasquale, *Vitrum. Il vetro fra arte e scienza nel mondo romano*, Firenze 2004.

Berggren 1986
J.L. Berggren, *Episodes in the Mathematics of Medieval Islam*, New York 1986.

Bertele 1961
H. von Bertele, *Globes and spheres; Globen und Sphären. Globes et Sphères*, Lausanne 1961.

Betts 2007
J. Betts, *Harrison*, NMM, London 1993-2007.

Bevis 1987
J. Bevis, *Atlas Celeste: a reproduction of the copy in the British library together with a reproduction of the text in the Library of the American philosophical society*, a cura di O. Gingerich, Alburgh 1987.

Biagi Maino 2005
D. Biagi Maino, *I pittori per l'Istituto. La cultura d'Arcadia e le scienze*, in *L'immagine del Settecento: da Luigi Ferdinando Marsili a Benedetto XIV*, edited by D. Biagi Maino, Torino 2005, pp. 51-64.

Biagioli 1993
M. Biagioli, *Galileo Courtier: The Practice of Science in the Cultural of Absolutism*, Chicago 1993.

Biagioli 2006
M. Biagioli, *Galileo's Instruments of Credit: Telescopes, Images, Secrecy*, Chicago 2006.

Bianchini 1752
F. Bianchini, *Globus Farnesianus et in eo Rudimenta Astronomiae, Chronologiae, et Historia Aetatis Aeroicae, a Grecis, ad nos transmissa*, Roma 1752.

Biblioteca medicea 1986
Biblioteca medicea laurenziana, texts by A. Morandini, G. De Angelis d'Ossat, M. Tesi, Firenze 1986.

Bickerman 1980
E.J. Bickerman, *Chronology of the Ancient World*, London 1980.

Biga 2001
M.G. Biga, *Il computo del tempo*, in M. Liverani (edited by), *Il Vicino Oriente antico. Storia della Scienza*, vol. I, chapt. XII, Roma 2001, pp. 409-416.

Biga-Capomacchia 2008
M.G. Biga, A.M.G. Capomacchia, *Il politeismo vicino-orientale*, Roma 2008.

Bion 1728
N. Bion, *L'usage des globes celeste et terrestre et des spheres suivant les differens systemes du monde*, Paris 1728[5].

Björnbo 1976
A.A. Björnbo, *Die matematischen S. Marcohandschriften in Florenz*, edited by G.C. Garfagnini, Pisa 1976.

Boccaccio 1547
G. Boccaccio, *Geneologia degli Dei*, edited by G. Betussi da Bassano, Venezia 1547.

Boccuto 1985
G. Boccuto, *Il 'Liber de astronomia' di Marziano Capella e i 'Disciplinarum libri' di Varrone Reatino*, in "Rivista di cultura classica e medioevale", XXVII, 1985, no. 3, pp. 135-151.

Boeselager 1983
D. von Boeselager, *Antike Mosaiken in Sizilien. Hellenismus und römische Kaiserzeit 3. jahrhundert a.C. – 3. Jahrhundert d.C.*, Roma 1983.

Boll 1903
F. Boll, *Sphaera, Neue griechische Texte und*

Untersuchungen zu Geschichte der Sternbilder, Leipzig 1903.

Boll-Bezold-Gundel 1979
F. Boll, C. Bezold, W. Gundel, *Storia dell'Astrologia*, Bari 1979.

Bologna 1991
Giovanni Francesco Barbieri Il Guercino 1591-1666, edited by D. Mahon, catalogue of the exhibition (Bologna, september-november 1991), Bologna 1991.

Bommas 1999
M. Bommas, *Die Mythologisierung der Zeit. Die beiden Bücher über die altägyptischen Schalttage des magischen P. Leiden I 346* (Göttinger Orientforschungen, IV Reihe, Ägypten, 37), Wiesbaden 1999.

Bonifacio-Sodo 2001
G. Bonifacio, A.M. Sodo, *Stabiae. Guida Archeologica alle Ville*, Castellammare di Stabia 2001.

Bònoli 2002
F. Bònoli, *Riccioli e gli strumenti dell'astronomia*, in *Giambattista Riccioli e il merito scientifico dei Gesuiti nell'età barocca*, edited by M.T. Borgato, "Biblioteca di Nuncius. Studi e testi", Firenze 2002, no. 44, pp. 133-157.

Bònoli-Foderà Serio-Poppi 2005
F. Bònoli, G. Foderà Serio, F. Poppi, *La ricerca astronomica in Italia al momento dell'Unità: uomini e strutture*, in *Cento anni di astronomia in Italia 1860-1960*, "Atti dei Convegni Lincei", no. 217, Roma 2005, pp. 29-72.

Bònoli-Parmeggiani-Poppi 2006
F. Bònoli, G. Parmeggiani, F. Poppi (edited by), Atti del Convegno *"Il Sole nella Chiesa: Cassini e la grandi meridiane come strumenti di indagine scientifica"*, in "Giornale di Astronomia", 32 (1), 2006.

Borchardt 1899
L. Borchardt, *Ein altägyptisches astronomisches Instrument*, "Zeitschrift für Ägyptische Sprache und Altertumskunde", 37, 1899, pp. 10-17.

Borchardt 1920
L. Borchardt, *Altägyptische Zeitmessung*, Leipzig 1920.

Borelli 1666
G.A. Borelli, *Theoricae Mediceorum planetarum ex causis physicis deductae*, Florentiae 1666.

Bosticco 1957
S. Bosticco, *Due frammenti di orologi solari egiziani*, in *Studi in onore di Aristide Calderoni e Roberto Paribeni*, vol. II, Milano-Varese 1957, pp. 33-49.

Bosticco 1972
S. Bosticco, *Museo Archeologico di Firenze. Le stele egiziane di Epoca Tarda*, Roma 1972.

Bottéro-Kramer 1992
J. Bottéro, S.N. Kramer, *Uomini e dei della Mesopotamia*, Torino 1992.

Boyer 1976
C. B. Boyer, *Storia della matematica*, Milano 1976.

Bradley 1748
J. Bradley, *A Letter to the Right honorable George Earl of Macclesfield concerning an apparent Motion observed in some of the fixed Stars*, "Philosophical Transactions", 45 (1748), pp. 1-43.

Bragantini 1995
I. Bragantini, *Problemi di pittura romana*, "Annali di Archeologia e Storia Antica", 2, 1995, pp. 175-197.

Brahe 1598
T. Brahe, *Astronomiae instauratae mechanica*, Hamburgum 1598.

Brahe 1913-1929
J.L.E. Dreyer (edited by), *Tychonis Brahe opera omnia*, Copenhagen 1913-1929.

Brecht 1955
B. Brecht, *Leben das Galilei*, Berlin 1955.

Bredekamp 2007
H. Bredekamp, *Galilei der Künstler*, Berlin 2007.

Brescia 1981
Aspetti della società bresciana nel Settecento, catalogue of the exhibition (Brescia, 1981), Brescia 1981.

Brockhaus 1909
H. Brockhaus, *Michelangelo und die Medici-Kapelle*, Leipzig 1909.

Brown B.J.W. 1932
B.J.W. Brown, *Astronomical Atlases, Maps & Charts: An Historical & General Guide*, London 1932.

Brown D. 2000
D. Brown, *Mesopotamian Planetary Astronomy-Astrology*, Groningen 2000.

Brugsch 1856
H. Brugsch, *Nouvelles recherches sur la division de l'année des anciens égyptiens*, Berlin 1856.

Brunner 1973
H. Brunner, *Zeichendeutung aus Sternen und Winden in Ägypten*, in *Wort und Geschichte* (Fs. Elliger), Neukirchen 1973, pp. 25-30.

Brusa 1978
G. Brusa, *L'arte dell'orologeria in Europa: Sette secoli di orologi meccanici*, Busto Arsizio 1978.

Brusa 1994
G. Brusa, *L'orologio dei pianeti di Lorenzo della Volpaia*, "Nuncius. Annali di Storia della Scienza", IX, 1994, 2, pp. 645-669.

Brusa 2004
G. Brusa, *Huygens e lo storico evento dell'invenzione*

dell'orologio a pendolo, "Voce di Hora", 17 (2004), pp. 3-35.

Bucciantini 1995
M. Bucciantini, *Contro Galileo. Alle origini dell'*affaire, Firenze 1995.

Bucciantini 2003
M. Bucciantini, *Galileo e Keplero. Filosofia, cosmologia e teologia nell'età della Controriforma*, Torino 2003.

Budge 1989
E.A.W. Budge, *The Rosetta stone*, Dover 1989.

Burnett 1994
C. Burnett, *Michael Scoto and the Trasmission of Scientific Culture from Toledo in Bologna Via the Court of Frederick II Hohenstaufen*, in *Nature, Science and Medieval Society*, II, *Le scienze alla Corte di Federico II*, Micrologus II, Turnhout, 1994.

Büttner 1976
F. Büttner, *Die ältesten Monumente für Galileo Galilei in Florenz*, in *Kunst des Barock in der Toskana. Studien zur Kunst unter den letzten Medici*, Münich 1976, pp. 103-117.

C.I.L. 2007
Corpus inscriptionum Latinarum, Berlin 2007.

Caiazzo 2003
A. Caiazzo, *Image d'Orient au Moyen âge*, Paris 2003.

Calderoni Masetti-Dalli Regoli 1973
A.R. Calderoni Masetti, G. Dalli Regoli, *Sanctae Hildegardis Revelationes. Manoscritto 1942*, Lucca 1973.

Calisi 1991
M. Calisi, *Guida alla visita del Museo Astronomico e Copernicano di Roma*, Roma 1991.

Calisi 2000
M. Calisi, *Storia e strumenti del Museo Astronomico e Copernicano di Roma*, Roma 2000.

Calvesi 1993
M. Calvesi, *La melanconia di Albrecht Dürer*, Torino 1993.

Cambridge 1973
The European fame of Isaac Newton. An exhibition in the Fitzwilliam Museum, catalogue (Cambridge, november 1973-january 1974), Cambridge 1973.

Camerota F. 2008
F. Camerota, *Catalogo delle opere in collezione*, in *Gli strumenti scientifici delle collezioni dei Musei Civici Veneziani*, "Bollettino dei Musei Civici Veneziani", III serie, Venezia 2008, pp. 29-79.

Camerota M. 2004
M. Camerota, *Galileo Galilei e la cultura scientifica nell'età della controriforma*, Roma 2004.

Caneva-Solinas 2005
C. Caneva, F. Solinas, *Maria de' Medici (1573-1642): Una Principessa fiorentina sul trono di Francia*, Livorno 2005.

Cannatà 1992
R. Cannatà, *Il collezionismo del cardinale Fabrizio Spada (1643-1717)*, in *La galleria di Palazzo Spada. Genesi e storia di una collezione*, Roma 1992, pp. 121-153.

Capella 2001
M. Capella, *Le nozze di Filologia e Mercurio*, edited by I. Ramelli, Milano 2001.

Cartesio 1967
R. Descartes, *Opere scientifiche*, edited by G. Micheli, Torino 1967.

Cartesio 1969
R. Descartes, *Il Mondo, Trattato della luce, L'Uomo*, Bari 1969.

Cassini 1668
G.D. Cassini, *Ephemerides Bononienses mediceorum syderum ex hypothesibus, et tabulis Io: Dominici Cassini*, Bologna 1668.

Cassini 1695
G.D. Cassini, *La Meridiana del Tempio di S. Petronio Tirata e preparata per le Osservazioni Astronomiche l'Anno 1655*, Bologna 1695.

Castellammare 2000
In Stabiano. Cultura e archeologia da Stabiae, catalogue of the exhibition (Castellammare di Stabia, november 2000-january 2001), Castellammare di Stabia 2001.

Castellino 1972
G.R. Castellino, *Two Shulgi Hymns (BC)*, Roma 1972.

Castellino 1977
G.R. Castellino, *Testi sumerici e accadici*, Torino 1977.

Catalogo IMSS 1954
Catalogo degli strumenti del Museo di Storia della Scienza, Firenze 1954.

Catalogo M.C.R. 1982
Catalogo del Museo della Civiltà Romana, Roma 1982.

Catalogue CNAM 1955
Conservatoire national des arts et métiers. Catalogue du musée, Section GA: Physique mécanique, Paris 1955, pp. 33-35.

Catalogue général des manuscripts BPF 1899
Catalogue Général des Manuscrits des Bibliothèques Publiques de France. Carpentras, Paris 1899.

Catalogus codicum manuscriptorum BML 1764-1770
Catalogus codicum manuscriptorum Bibliothecae Mediceae Laurentianae varia continens opera Graecorum patrum, ...Angelus Maria Bandini ... recensuit, illustravit, edidit, Firenze 1764-1770.

Catalogus codicum manuscriptorum BML 1774-1778

Catalogus codicum Latinorum Bibliothecae Mediceae Laurentianae, ... Angelus Maria Bandini ... recensuit, illustravit, edidit, Firenze, 1774-1778.

Cattaneo 2008
A. Cattaneo, in *I Medici e le scienze. Strumenti e macchine delle collezioni medicee*, edited by F. Camerota and M. Miniati, catalogue of the exhibition (Firenze, 15 may 2008-11 january 2009), Firenze 2008, p. 79.

Cauville 1997
S. Cauville, *Le Zodiaque d'Osiris*, Leuven 1997.

Cellario 2000
A. Cellario, *Atlas Coelestis seu Harmonia macrocosmica, (Amsterdam 1661)*, edited by F. Stoppa, Milano 2000.

Cellarius 2006
A. Cellarius, *The finest Atlas of the Heavens*, edited by R.H. van Gent, Köln 2006.

Cernuti 2002
S. Cernuti, *La Patera di Parebiago e i calendari romani*, in "L'Astronomia", 237, december 2002, pp. 44-52.

Chapman 1983
A. Chapman, *The accuracy of angular measuring instruments used in Astronomy between 1500 and 1800*, in "Journal for the History of Astronomy", XIV, 1983, p. 133-137.

Charvet 1998
P. Charvet, *Le Ciel. Mythes et histoire des constellations*, Paris 1998.

Christianson 2000
J.R. Christianson, *On Tycho's Island: Tycho Brahe and His Assistants, 1570-1601*, Cambridge 2000.

Christie's (New York) 1998
Christie's (New York), *Important Old Master Paintings from the Thomas Mellon Evans Collection*, New York, 22 may 1998.

Ciarallo-De Carolis 1998
A. Ciarallo, E. De Carolis, *La data dell' eruzione*, in "Riv. St. Pomp.", 1998, pp. 63-73.

Il Cielo 1994
Il Cielo: intorno alla cosmologia di Plinio: capolavori delle rappresentazioni miniate nei codici delle principali biblioteche del mondo, Torino 1994.

Cipriani 2003
C. Cipriani (edited by), *Il Tempo della Natura: Ciclicità e irreversibilità dei fenomeni naturali*, Firenze 2003.

Clagett 1995
M. Clagett, *Ancient Egyptian Science*, II, *Calendars, Clocks and Astronomy*, American Philosophical Society, Philadelphia 1995.

Clark 2006
M. Desmond Clark, *Descartes. A Biography*, Cambridge (UK) 2006.

Clavelin 1995
M. Clavelin, *Le Copernicanism padouan de Galilée*, in *Galileo a Padova 1592-1610*, 5 vols., Trieste 1995, IV, pp. 149-166.

Clemente di Alessandria 2004
Clemente di Alessandria, *Protrettico ai Greci*, edited by F. Migliore, Roma 2004.

Clifton 1995
G. Clifton, *Directory of British Scientific Instrument Makers 1550-1851*, London 1995.

Cohen-Smith 2002
The Cambridge Companion to Newton, edited by I.B. Cohen and G.E. Smith, Cambridge (UK) 2002.

Collezioni MANN 1986
Le collezioni del Museo archeologico nazionale di Napoli, vols. I-II, Roma 1986.

Colli 1992
G. Colli, *La Sapienza greca*, II, Milano 1992.

Columella 1977
Columella, *L' arte dell'agricoltura*, Torino 1977.

Condos 1997
T. Condos, *Star Myths of the Greeks and Romans: A Sourcebook containing 'The Constellations' of Pseudo-Eratosthenes and the 'Poetic Astronomy' of Hyginus*, Grand Rapids 1997.

Copenhaver 1991
B.P. Copenhaver, *"Hermetica"*, Cambridge 1991.

Copernico 1975
Opere di Nicola Copernico, edited by F. Barone, Torino 1975.

Copernico 1995
Nicolaus Copernicus, *On the Revolutions of the Heavenly Spheres*, Chicago 1995.

Coralini 2001
A. Coralini, *Hercules Domesticus. Immagini di Ercole nelle case della regione vesuviana (I secolo a.C.-79 d.C.)*, Napoli 2001.

Coronelli 1693
V. Coronelli, *Epitome cosmografica*, Köln 1693.

Crema 1999
La ragione e il metodo. Immagini della scienza nell'arte italiana dal XVI al XIX secolo, edited by M. Bona Castellotti, E. Gamba; F. Mazzocca, catalogue of the exhibition (Crema, march-june 1999), Milano 1999.

Cumont 1909
F. Cumont, *Le mysticisme astral dans l'antiquité*, "Bulletin de la Classe des Lettres et des Sciences morales et politiques et de la Classe des Beaux-Arts", 1, 1909, pp. 256-286.

Cumont 1913
F. Cumont, *Les mystères de Mitra*, Bruxelles 1913.

Cumont 1919a
F. Cumont, *Sol*, in C. Daremberg, E. Saglio (edited by), *Dictionnaire des Antiquités grecques et romaines*, vol. IV, Paris 1919.

Cumont 1919b
F. Cumont, *Zodiacus*, in C. Daremberg, E. Saglio, *Dictionnaire des Antiquités grecques et romaines*, vol. V, Paris 1919, p. 1054.

Cumont 1997
F. Cumont, *Astrologia e religione presso i greci e i romani. Il culto degli astri nel mondo antico*, edited by A. Panaino, Milano 1997.

Cuvigny 2002
H. Cuvigny, *Silver celestial globe from Antiquity*, in J. Kugel, *Spheres. The Art of Celestial Mechanics*, Paris 2002, pp. 22-27.

Cuvigny 2004
H. Cuvigny, *Une sphère céleste antique en argent ciselé*, in H. Harrauer-R. Pintaudi (eds.), *Gedenkschrift Ulrike Horak*, Firenze 2004, pp. 345-377.

D'Amicone-Fontanella 2005
E. d'Amicone, E. Fontanella, *Nefer. La donna nell'antico Egitto*, Milano 2005.

D'Ancona 1954
P. D'Ancona, *Les mois de Schifanoia à Ferrara*, Milano 1954.

Dalen 1993
B. van Dalen, *Ancient and Mediaeval Astronomical Tables - Mathematical Structure and Parameter Values*, Utrecht 1993.

Dalton 1926
O.M. Dalton. *The Byzantine astrolabe of Brescia*, "Proceedings of the British Academy", 1926, pp. 133 ff.

Daumas 1953
M. Daumas, *Les instruments scientifiques aux XVII e XVIII siècles*, Paris 1953.

Dawson 1965
C.M. Dawson, *Romano-Campanian Mythological Landscape Painting*, New Haven 1944 (reprinted 1965).

De Caro 1994
S. De Caro (edited by), *Il Museo Archeologico Nazionale di Napoli*, Napoli 1994.

De Carolis-Esposito-Ferrara 2007
E. De Carolis, F. Esposito, D. Ferrara, *Domus Sirici in Pompei (VII, 1, 25.47): appunti sulla tecnica di esecuzione degli apparati decorativi*, in "Ocnus. Quaderni della Scuola di Specializzazione in Archeologia", 15, 2007, pp. 117-141.

De Santillana-von Dechend 2006
G. de Santillana, H. von Dechend, *Il mulino di Amleto. Saggio sul mito e sulla struttura del tempo*, Milano 2006.

Débarbat-Grillot-Lévy 2002
S. Débarbat, S. Grillot, J. Lévy, *Observatoire de Paris : Son histoire (1667-1963)*, Paris 1990.

Dekker 1995
E. Dekker, *Conspicuous features on sixteenth century celestial globes*, in "Der Globusfreund", 43/44, Wien 1995, p. 79.

Dekker 1999
E. Dekker, *Globes at Greenwich. A Catalogue of Globes and Armillary Spheres in the National Maritime Museum*, Oxford 1999.

Dekker 2007
E. Dekker, *Globes in Renaissance Europe*, in *The History of Cartography*, vol. 3: *Cartography in the European Renaissance*, edited by D. Woodward, Chicago 2007, pp. 135-173.

Dekker-Lippincott 1999
E. Dekker, K. Lippincott, *The Scientific Instruments in Holbein's Ambassadors: A Re-Examination*, in "Journal of the Warburg and Courtauld Institutes", 62, (1999), pp. 93-125.

Del Santo-Strano 2004
P. Del Santo, G. Strano, *Machina Mundi: Images and Measures of the Cosmos from Copernicus to Newton*, Firenze 2004.

Delamarche 1798
C.-F. Delamarche, *Les usages de la sphère et des globes céleste et terrestre*, Paris 1798[2].

Demichelis 2002
S. Demichelis, *La divination par l'huile à l'époque ramesside*, in *La magie égyptienne: à la recherche d'une définition*, Paris 2002, pp. 151-165.

Denza 1894
F. Denza, *Globi celesti della Specola Vaticana*, Torino 1894, vol. IV.

Der Globusfreund 1952
Der Globusfreund / Globe Studies, Wissenschaftliche Zeitschrift für Globenkunde, in "The Journal of the International Coronelli Society", 54 vols., Wien 1952.

Derchain 1989
P. Derchain, *Harkhébis, le Psylle-Astrologue*, in "Chronique d'Egypte", 64 (1989), pp. 74-89.

Di Bono 1990
M. Di Bono, *Le sfere omocentriche di Giovanni Battista Amico nell'astronomica del Cinquecento*, Genova CNR 1990.

Domenicucci 1996
P. Domenicucci, *Astra Caesarum, Astronomia, astrologia e catasterismo da Cesare a Domiziano*, Pisa 1996.

Dominguez Rodriguez 1982
A. Dominguez Rodriguez, *Lapidario de Alfonso X el Sabio*, Madrid 1982.

Domini-Milanesi 1998
D. Domini, M. Milanesi (edited by), *Vincenzo Coronelli e l'imago mundi*, Ravenna 1998.

Dondi dall'Orologio 2003
G. Dondi dall'Orologio, *Tractatus astrarii*, edited by A. Bullo, Conselve 2003.

Dosi-Schnell 1992
A. Dosi, F. Schnell, *Spazio e tempo*, in *Vita e Costumi dei Romani Antichi*, edited by G. Pisani Sartorio and A.M. Liberati Silverio, vol. 14, Roma 1992.

I dossografi greci 1961
I dossografi greci, Padova 1961.

Drake 1976
S. Drake, *Galileo's first telescopic observations*, "Journal of the History of Astronomy", 7 (1976), pp. 153-168.

Dreyer 1953
J.L.E. Dreyer, *A History of Astronomy from Thales to Kepler*, New York 1953.

Dreyer 1970
J.L.E. Dreyer, *Storia dell'astronomia da Talete a Keplero*, Milano 1970.

DSB 1970-1980
DSB (Dictionary of Scientific Biography), edited by C.C. Gillispie, 16 vols., New York 1970-1980.

Duhem 1913-1959
P. Duhem, *Le système du monde. Histoire des doctrines cosmologiques de Platon à Copernic*, Paris 1913-1959.

Dupré 2005
S. Dupré, *Ausonio's mirrors and Galileo's lenses: the telescope and sixteenth-century practical optical knowledge*, in "Galilæana", vol. 2 (2005), pp. 145-180.

Dupuis 1765
C. Dupuis, *L'Origine de tous les cultes ou religion universelle*, Paris 1765.

Durand 1988
J.-M. Durand, *Archives Royales de Mari*, XXVI/1, Paris 1988.

Dürer 1525
A. Dürer, *Underweysung der Messung ...*, Nurnberg 1525.

Eckhard 1976
W. Eckhard, *Erasmus Habermeli zur Biographie des Instrumentenmachers Kaiser Rudolfs II*, "Jahrbuch der Hamburger Kunstsammlungen", 21 (1976), pp. 55-92.

Edwards 1985
G.M. Edwards, *The two redactions of Michael Scoto'* Liber introductorius, "Traditio", 41 (1985), pp. 329-340.

Elders 1994
W. Elders, *Symbolic scores: Studies in the Music of the Renaissance*, Leiden 1994.

Elia 1957
O. Elia, *Pitture di Stabia*, Napoli 1957.

Enciclopedia Islam 1960-2004
Encyclopaedia of Islam, 12 vols., Leiden 1960-2004.

Engel 1488
G. Engel, *Astrolabium planum*, Augusta 1488.

Esiodo 1997
Esiodo, *Le opere e i giorni*, Milano 1997.

Explication des ouvrages 1849
Explication des ouvrages de Peinture, Sculpture, Architecture, Gravure et Lithographie des Artistes vivants, exposés au Palais des Tuileries le 15 juin 1849, Paris 1849.

Fabbri 2003
N. Fabbri, *Cosmologia e armonia in Kepler e Mersenne. Contrappunto a due voci sul tema dell'*Harmonice Mundi, Firenze 2003.

Fabbri 2007
N. Fabbri, *Genesis of Mersenne's Harmonie universelle: the manuscript Livre de la nature des sons*, *Nuncius* XXII (2007), pp. 287-308.

Fabretti-Rossi-Lanzone 1882
A. Fabretti, F. Rossi, R.V. Lanzone, *Regio Museo di Torino. Antichità egizie*, vol. I, Torino 1882.

Fabretti-Rossi-Lanzone 1888
A. Fabretti, F. Rossi, R.V. Lanzone, *Regio Museo di Torino. Antichità Egizie*, vol. II, Torino 1888.

Fahie 1929
J.J. Fahie, *Memorials of Galileo Galilei 1564 - 1642, portraits and painting, medals and medallions, busts and statues, monument and mural inscriptions*, London 1929.

Fales 1974
F.M. Fales, "L'«ideologo» Adad-shumu-usur", *Accademia Nazionale dei Lincei. Rendiconti*, 29 (1974), pp. 453-496.

Fales 2001
F.M. Fales, *L'impero assiro*, Roma-Bari 2001.

Fantoni 1990
G. Fantoni, *Orologi solari dell'antica Grecia: i globi di Prosymna e di Matelica (Differenze ed analogie)*, "Archeologia e Astronomia", may 1990.

Fantuzzi 1770
G. Fantuzzi, *Memorie della vita del generale co. Luigi Ferdinando Marsigli*, Bologna 1770.

Favaro 1896
A. Favaro, *Amici e Corrispondenti di Galileo Galilei*, II: *Ottavio Pisani*, Atti del Real Istituto veneto di Scienze, Lettere ed Arti, t. VII, s. VII, 1895-1896, pp. 411-440, reprinted in *Amici e Corrispondenti di Galileo*, edited by P. Galluzzi, 3 vols., Firenze 1983, I, pp. 33-57.

Favaro 1913
A. Favaro, *Studi e ricerche per una iconografia galileiana*, "Atti del Real Istituto Veneto di Scienze Lettere ed Arti", 72, 1913, pp. 995-1051.

Federici Vescovini 1986
G. Federici Vescovini, *Pietro d'Abano e gli affreschi astrologici del Palazzo della Ragione di Padova*, in "Labyrinthos", 9 (1986).

Federici Vescovini 1991
G. Federici Vescovini, *Su un trattatello anonimo di fisiognomica astrologica*, in W. Prinz, *Uomo e natura nella letteratura e nell'arte italiana del Tre-Quattrocento*, (Quaderni dell'Accademia del Disegno di Firenze 3) Firenze 1991.

Federici Vescovini 1996
G. Federici Vescovini, *L'espressività del cielo e Marsilio Ficino*, in "Bochumer Philosophisches Handbuch für Antike und Mittelalter", I, 1996.

Federici Vescovini 2002
G. Federici Vescovini, *Gli affreschi astrologici del Palazzo Schifanoia e l'astrologia alla corte dei Duchi d'Este tra Medioevo e Rinascimento*, in *L'art de la Renaissance entre science et magie*, edited by P. Morel, Roma, Académie de France à Rome, 2002.

Federici Vescovini 2008a
G. Federici Vescovini, *Medioevo magico: la magia tra religione e scienza (secoli XIII e XIV)*, Torino 2008.

Federici Vescovini 2008b
G. Federici Vescovini, *Michele Scoto*, in G. Federici Vescovini, *Medioevo magico: la magia tra religione e scienza (secoli XIII-XIV)*, Torino 2008, pp. 47-70.

Felli 1983
M. Felli, *L'astrolabio di Galileo*, Firenze 1983.

Feraboli 1984
S. Feraboli (edited by), *Claudio Tolomeo: Le previsioni astrologiche (Tetrabiblos)*, Milano 1984.

Ferguson J. 1747
J. Ferguson, *The description and use of a new four wheel'd orrery*, London 1747.

Ferguson J. 1764a
J. Ferguson, *Astronomy explained upon sir Isaac Newton's Principles and made easy to those who have not studied mathematics*, London 1764[3].

Ferguson 1764b
J. Ferguson, *The description and use of a new machine called the Mechanical Paradox*, 1764.

Ferguson J. 1773
J. Ferguson, *Select mechanical exercises: showing how to construct different clocks, orreries and sun-dials on plain and easy principles*, London 1773.

Ferguson K. 2003
K. Ferguson, *L'uomo dal naso d'oro. Tycho Brahe e Giovanni Keplero: la strana coppia che rivoluzionò la scienza*, Milano 2003.

Ferrara 1996
Pompei. Abitare sotto il Vesuvio, catalogue of the exhibition (Ferrara, september 1996-january 1997), edited by M. Borriello, A. d'Ambrosio, S. De Caro, P.G. Guzzo, Ferrara 1996.

Ferraro 2005
A.M. Ferraro, *Matteo Palmieri: una biografia intellettuale*, Genova 2005.

Field 1988
J.V. Field, *Kepler's geometrical cosmology*, London 1988.

Field 1990
J.V. Field, *Some Roman and Byzantine Portable Sundials and the London Sundial-Calendar*, "History of Technology", 12 (1990), pp. 103-135.

Field-Wright 1985a
J.V. Field, M.T. Wright, *The Early History of Mathematical Gearing*, in "Endeavour", 9 (4), 1985, pp. 198-203.

Field-Wright 1985b
J.V. Field, M.T. Wright, *Gears from the Byzantines: a Portable Sundial with Calendrical Gearing*, "Annals of Science", 42 (1985), pp. 87-138.

Finocchiaro 2008
M. A. Finocchiaro, *The Essential Galileo*, New York 2008.

Fiorini 1899
M. Fiorini, *Sfere Terrestri e Celesti di Autore Italiano oppure fatte o conservate in Italia*, Roma 1899.

Firenze 1955
Mostra del Poliziano nella Biblioteca medicea laurenziana: manoscritti, libri rari, autografi e documenti, edited by A. Perosa, catalogue of the exhibition (Firenze, september-november 1954), Firenze 1955.

Firenze 1971
Omaggio a Dürer, edited by A.M. Petrioli Tofani, catalogue of the exhibition (Firenze, 1971), Firenze 1971.

Firenze 1977
Rubens e la pittura fiamminga del Seicento nelle collezioni pubbliche fiorentine, edited by D. Bodart, catalogue of the exhibition (Firenze, july-october 1977), Firenze 1977.

Firenze 1980
Astrologia, magia e alchimia nel Rinascimento fiorentino ed europeo, in *Firenze e la Toscana dei Medici nell'Europa del Cinquecento*, edited by P. Zambelli, catalogue of the exhibition, (Firenze, 1980), Milano 1980, pp. 309-435.

Firenze 1986
Il Seicento Fiorentino. Arte a Firenze da Ferdinando I a Cosimo III, catalogue of the exhibition (Firenze, december 1986-may 1987), Firenze 1986.

Firenze 1992
Firenze e la scoperta dell'America: umanesimo e geografia nel '400 fiorentino, edited by S. Gentile, catalogue of the exhibition (Firenze, 1992), Firenze 1992.

Firenze 2001
Scienziati a Corte: l'arte della sperimentazione nell'Accademia Galileiana del Cimento (1657-1667), edited by P. Galluzzi, catalogue of the exhibition (Firenze, march-june 2001), Livorno 2001.

Firenze 2003
Il tempo della natura: ciclicità e irreversibilità dei fenomeni naturali, edited by C. Cipriani, catalogue of the exhibition (Firenze, october 2003-march 2004), Firenze 2003.

Firenze 2004a
Botticelli e Filippino. L'inquietudine e la grazia nella pittura fiorentina del Quattrocento, edited by P. De Vecchi, D. Arasse, J.K. Nelson, catalogue of the exhibition (Firenze, march-july 2004), Milano 2004.

Firenze 2004b
Vitrum: il vetro tra arte e scienza nel mondo romano, edited by M. Beretta, G. di Pasquale, catalogue of the exhibition (Firenze, march-october 2004), Firenze 2004.

Firenze 2005
Il numero e le sue forme. Storie di poliedri da Platone a Poinsot passando per Luca Pacioli, edited by R. Folicaldi, catalogue of the exhibition (Firenze, march-october 2005), Firenze 2005, pp. 42-43.

Firenze 2006
Un granduca e il suo ritrattista. Cosimo III de' Medici e la "stanza de' quadri" di Giusto Suttermans, edited by L. Goldenberg Stoppato, catalogue of the exhibition, Livorno 2006.

Firenze 2007a
Animali fantastici: la biblioteca in mostra, catalogue of the exhibition (Firenze, april-july 2007), Firenze 2007.

Firenze 2007b
Il giardino antico da Babilonia a Roma: scienza, arte e natura, edited by G. di Pasquale, F. Paolucci, catalogue of the exhibition (Firenze, may-october 2007), Livorno 2007.

Firenze 2008a
Galileo e l'universo dei suoi libri, edited by E. Benucci, P. Scapecchi, R. Setti, I. Truci, catalogue of the exhibition (Firenze, december 2008-february 2009), Firenze 2008.

Firenze 2008b
Galileo's Telescope: the Instrument that Changed the World, edited by G. Strano, catalogue of the exhibition (Firenze, march-december 2008), Firenze 2008.

Firenze 2008c
I Medici e le scienze: strumenti e macchine delle collezioni medicee, edited by F. Camerota e M. Miniati, catalogue of the exhibition (Firenze may 2008-january 2009), Firenze 2008, entry II.I.4, p. 112.

Flamsteed 1987
J. Flamsteed, *Atlas coelestis*, edited by F. Stoppa, Milano 1987.

Folicaldi 2001
R. Folicaldi, Scheda VI.2.4, in *Nel segno di Masaccio: l'invenzione della prospettiva*, edited by F. Camerota, catalogue of the exhibition (Firenze, october 2001-january 2002), Firenze 2001, p. 130.

Forte di Bard 2007
In cima alle stelle: l'universo tra arte, archeologia e scienza, edited by L. di Corato, catalogue of the exhibition (Forte di Bard, april-september 2007), Cinisello Balsamo (MI) 2007.

Forti *et al.* 1987
G. Forti *et al.*, *Un planetario del XV secolo*, "L'astronomia", IX, (1987), pp. 5 ff.

Fortini Brown 1981
P. Fortini Brown, *Laetentur caeli: the Council of Florence and the astronomical fresco in the Old Sacristy*, "Journal of the Warburg and Courtauld Institutes", XLIV, (1981), pp. 176 ff.

Foster 1993
B. Foster, *Before the Muses*, vols. I-II, Bethesda 1993.

Frankfort 1948
H.A. Frankfort, *Kingship and the Gods*, Chicago 1948.

Freddolini 2007
F. Freddolini, *Effigi d'insigne e singolare virtù. Monumenti funebri dei professori dello Studio tra Sei e Settecento*, in *Scultura a Pisa nell'età moderna. Le sepolture dei docenti dello Studio*, edited by C.M. Sicca, Pisa 2007, pp. 91-108.

Freeth *et al.* 2006
T. Freeth *et al.*, *Decoding the ancient Greek astronomical calculator known as the Antikythera Mechanism*, "Nature", 444 (30 november 2006), pp. 587-591.

Freeth *et al.* 2008
T. Freeth *et al.*, *Calendars with Olympiad display and eclipse prediction on the Antikythera Mechanism*, "Nature", 454 (31 july 2008), pp. 614-617.

Fresa 1959
A. Fresa, *Su un'iscrizione pompeiana allusiva al tramonto eliaco di Deneb*, in "Atti Accademia Pontaniana", n.s. 7, Napoli 1959, pp. 249-255.

Fresa 1970
A. Fresa, *L'astrologia nel corso dei secoli*, in "Atti dell'Accademie Pontaniana", n.s. 17, (1970), pp. 253-265.

Fresa 1973
A. Fresa, *Le Pleiadi nel poemetto di Esiodo "Le opere e i giorni"*, in "Atti Accademia Pontaniana", n.s. 20, (1973), pp. 7-15.

Frosini 2005
F. Frosini edited by, *Leonardo e Pico. Analogie, contatti, confronti* (Atti del Convegno di Mirandola, 10 may 2003), Firenze 2005.

Fryde 1996
E.B. Fryde, *Greek manuscripts in the private library of the Medici: 1469-1510*, Aberystwyth 1996.

Galilei 1610a
G. Galilei a Giuliano de' Medici, 11 dicembre 1610, in *Le opere di Galileo Galilei, national edition*, edited by A. Favaro [and I. Del Lungo], Firenze 1890-1909, vol. X, letter n. 435, p. 483.

Galilei 1610b
G. Galilei, *Sidereus Nuncius*, Venezia 1610.

Galilei 1612
G. Galilei, *Proposta della longitudine*, [1612], in *Le opere di Galileo Galilei, national edition*, edited by A. Favaro [and I. Del Lungo], Firenze 1890-1909, vol. V, pp. 413-425 ff.

Galilei 1613
G. Galilei, *Istoria e dimostrazioni intorno alle macchie solari e loro accidenti, comprese in tre lettere scritte all'illustrissimo ... Marco Velseri*, Roma 1613.

Galilei 1616a
G. Galilei to [Curzio Picchena], 23 april 1616, in *Le opere di Galileo Galilei, national edition*, edited by A. Favaro [and I. Del Lungo], Firenze 1890-1909, vol. XII, letter n. 1197, pp. 255-256.

Galilei 1616b
G. Galilei to Bartolomeo Leonardi d'Argensola, 16 may 1616, in *Le opere di Galileo Galilei, national edition*, edited by A. Favaro [and I. Del Lungo], Firenze 1890-1909, vol. XII, letter n. 1201 ff., pp. 260-261, 265 ff.

Galilei 1618
G. Galilei to Leopoldo of Austria, 23 may 1618, in *Le opere di Galileo Galilei, national edition*, edited by A. Favaro [and I. Del Lungo], Firenze 1890-1909, vol. XII, letter n. 1324, pp. 389-392.

Galilei 1623
G. Galilei, *Il saggiatore: nel quale con bilancia esquisita e giusta si ponderano le cose contenute nella Libra astronomica e filosofica di Lotario Sarsi*, Roma 1623.

Galilei 1630a
G. Galilei, *Dialogo sui due massimi sistemi*, 1630, in *Le opere di Galileo Galilei, national edition*, edited by A. Favaro [and I. Del Lungo], Firenze 1890-1909, vol. VII, pp. 388-389.

Galilei 1630b
G. Galilei, *Dialogo sui due massimi sistemi*, 1630, in *Le opere di Galileo Galilei, national edition*, edited by A. Favaro [and I. Del Lungo], Firenze 1890-1909, vol. VII, pp. 409-416.

Galilei 1632
G. Galilei, *Dialogo ... dove ne i congressi di quattro giornate si discorre sopra i due massimi sistemi del mondo tolemaico e copernicano*, Firenze 1632.

Galilei 1890-1909
Le opere di Galileo Galilei, national edition, edited by A. Favaro [and I. Del Lungo], Firenze 1890-1909.

Galilei 1989
G. Galilei, *Sidereus Nuncius or the Sidereal Messenger*, edited by A. Van Helden, Chicago 1989.

Galilei 1993
G. Galilei, *Sidereus Nuncius*, edited by A. Battistini, Venezia 1993.

Galilei 1999
G. Galilei, *Dialogo sopra i due massimi sistemi del mondo tolemaico e copernicano*, edited by O. Besomi, M. Helbing, Padova 1998.

Galilei 2005
G. Galilei, *Il saggiatore*, edited by O. Besomi, M. Helbing, Padova 2005.

Galleria degli Uffizi 2007
Gabinetto disegni e stampe degli Uffizi, *Dürer: originali, copie, derivazioni*, edited by G.M. Fara, Firenze 2007.

Galluzzi 1976
P. Galluzzi, *Evangelista Torricelli : concezione della matematica e segreto degli occhiali*, "Annali dell'Istituto e Museo di storia della scienza di Firenze", 1, fasc. 1 (1976), pp. 71-95.

Galluzzi 1991
P. Galluzzi, (edited by), *Storia delle Scienze, Gli strumenti*,Torino 1991.

Galluzzi 1992
P. Galluzzi, (edited by), *Storia delle Scienze. Le scienze fisiche e astronomiche*, Torino 1992.

Galluzzi 1993
P. Galluzzi, *I sepolcri di Galileo: le spoglie vive di un eroe della scienza*, in *Il pantheon di Santa Croce a Firenze*, edited by L. Berti, Firenze 1993.

Garber 2001
D. Garber, *Descartes Embodied: Reading Cartesian Philosophy through Cartesian Science*, Cambridge (UK) 2001.

Gasse 1996
A. Gasse, *Les sarcophages de la Troisième Période*

intermédiaire du Museo Gregoriano Egizio, Città del Vaticano 1996.

Gautier Dalché 2007
P. Gautier Dalché, *The reception of Ptolemy's Geography (end of the fourteenth to beginning of the sixteenth century)*, in *The history of cartography*, III, *Cartography in the European Renaissance*, edited by D. Woodward, Chicago 2007, pp. 285-364.

Gelb-Steinkeller-Whiting 1991
I.J. Gelb, P. Steinkeller, R.M. Whiting, *Earliest Land Tenure Systems in the Ancient Near East: ancient Kudurrus*, Chicago 1991.

Gentile 1992
S. Gentile, *Firenze e la scoperta della America. Umanesimo e geografia nel '400 fiorentino*, Firenze 1992.

Ghedini 1997
E.F. Ghedini, *Trasmissione delle iconografie*, in *Enciclopedia dell'Arte Antica, Classica ed Orientale*, II suppl., V, 1997, pp. 825-828.

Ginevra 2004
Galileo e Pisa, edited by R. Vergara Caffarelli, catalogue of the exhibition (Genève, october 2004-february 2005) Pisa 2004.

Gingerich 1971
O. Gingerich, *Kepler and the Ruldolphine Tables*, "Sky and Telescope", XLII, (1971), pp. 1-8.

Gingerich-Van Helden 2003
O. Gingerich, A. Van Helden, *From* occhiale *to printed pages: the making of Galileo's* Sidereus Nuncius, "Journal of the History of Astronomy", 34 (2003), pp. 251-267.

Gingerich-Voelkel 1998
O. Gingerich, J.R. Voelkel, *Tycho Brahe's Copernican Campaign*, in "Journal for the History of Astronomy", 29 (1998), pp. 1-34.

Giusti 2004
A. Giusti, *Masters of Florence: Glory and Genius at the Court of the Medici*, Memphis 2004.

Glareanus 1527
H. Glareanus, *De geographia liber unus*, cap. XIX, *De inducemda papyro in globus*, Basel 1527.

Godwin 1979
J. Godwin, *Robert Fludd: Hermetic Philosopher and Surveyor of two Worlds*, London 1979.

Godwin 1987
J. Godwin, *Harmonies of heaven and earth: the spiritual dimension of music from antiquity to the avant-garde*, London 1987.

Goldstein 1985
B.R. Goldstein, *Theory and Observation in Ancient and Medieval Astronomy*, London 1985.

Gorman-Marr 2007
M.J. Gorman, A. Marr, *"Others see it yet otherwise":* disegno *and* pictura *in a Flemish gallery interior*, "The Burlington Magazine", CXLIX (february 2007), pp. 85-91.

Gouk 1999
P.M. Gouk, *Music, Science and Natural Magic in seventeenth-century England*, New Haven 1999.

Gould 1923
R.T. Gould, *The Marine Chronometer*, London 1923.

Govi 1887
G. Govi, *Della invenzione del micrometro per gli strumenti astronomici*, "Bullettino di Bibliografia di Storia delle Scienze Matematiche e Fisiche", XX, 1887, pp. 607-622.

Graefe 1984
E. Graefe, *Sonnenuhr*, in *Lexikon der Ägyptologie*, vol. V, coll. 1105-1106, Wiesbaden 1984.

Graefe 2001
E. Graefe, *Sat-Sobek und Peti-Imen-menu. Zwei ägyptische Särge aus Assiut und Theben*, Stadt Hamm 2001.

Grant 1994
E. Grant, *Planets, Stars, and Orbs. The Medieval Cosmos, 1200-1687*, Cambridge 1994.

Grant 1996
E. Grant, *The Foundations of Modern Science in the Middle Ages. Their Religious, Institutional, and Intellectual Contexts*, Cambridge 1996.

Grasshoff 1990
G. Grasshoff, *The history of Ptolemy's star catalogue*, New York 1990.

Graves 1955
R. Graves, *I miti greci*, Milano 1955, p. 24.

Greenwich 1975
Greenwich Observatory. One of three volumes by different authors telling the story of Britain's oldest scientific institution. The Royal Observatory at Greenwich and Herstmonceux. 1675-1975. Volume 1: Origins and early history (1675-1835), edited by E.G. Forbes; *Volume 2: Recent history (1836-1975)*, edited by A.J. Meadows; *Volume 3: Buildings and instruments*, edited by D. Howse, London 1975.

Gregory 1992
T. Gregory, *Mundana Sapientia. Forme di conoscenza nella cultura medievale*, Roma 1992.

Gregory 2007
T. Gregory, *Natura e «qualitas planetarum»*, in *Speculum naturale. Percorsi del pensiero medievale*, Roma 2007.

Grötzsch 1963
H. Grötzsch, *Veröffentlichungen des Staatlichen mathematisch-physikalischen Salons*, 2 vols., Berlin 1963.

Gunther 1932
R.T. Gunther, *The Astrolabes of the World*, 2 vols., Oxford 1932, reprint I vol., London 1976.

Hamel 2002
J. Hamel, *Geschichte der Astronomie*, Stuttgart 2002.

Härting 1993
U. Härting, *Doctrina et Pietas: über frühe Galeriebilder*, "Jaarboek Koninklijk museum voor Schone Kunsten Antwerpen", 1993, pp. 95-133.

Haskell 1989
F. Haskell, *L'apoteosi di Newton nell'arte*, in *Le metamorfosi del gusto. Studi su arte e pubblico nel XVIII e XIX secolo*, Torino 1989, pp. 3-28.

Haskins 1927
C.H. Haskins, *The Renaissance of the Twelfth Century*, Cambridge (MA) 1927.

Haskins 1960
C.H. Haskins, *Studies in the History of Medieval Science*, New York 1960, p. 75.

Hayes 1938
W.C. Hayes, *A writing-palette of the Chief Steward Amenhotpe and some notes on its owner*, "Journal of Egyptian Archaeology", 24, 1938, pp. 9-24.

Hayward 1950
J.F. Hayward, *The celestial globes of George Roll and Johannes Reinhold*, "Connoisseurs", 126, pp. 167-172.

Hermann 1973
D.B. Hermann, *An exponential law for the establishment of observatories in the nineteenth century*, in "Journal for the History of Astronomy", IV, 1973, pp. 57-58.

Hevelius 1968
J. Hevelius, *The Star Atlas*, edited by V.P. Sheglov, Tashkent 1968.

Hill 1985
D.R. Hill, *Al-B r n 's Mechanical Calendar*, "Annals of Science", 42 (1985), pp. 139-163.

Hissette 1977
R. Hissette, *Enquête sur les 219 articles condamnés à Paris le 7 mars 1277*, Louvain-Paris 1977, p. 64.

Histoire de l'Academie Royale 1708
Histoire de l'Academie Royale des Sciences, Paris 1708.

Hoffmann 2007
K.F.V. Hoffmann, *Himmelsatlas fur freunde und Liebaber der Sternkunde su zeichen, Stuttgart 1835*, edited by F. Stoppa, Milano 2007.

Honig 1995
E. Honig, *The beholder as work of art: A study in the location of value in seventeenth-century Flemish painting*, "Nederlands Kunsthistorisch Jaarboek", 1995, pp. 253-297.

Hornung 1982
E. Hornung, *Der Mythos von der Himmelskuh. Eine Ätiologie des Unvollkommenen* (Orbis Biblicus et Orientalis 46), Freiburg-Göttingen 1982.

Horowitz 1988
W. Horowitz, *The Babylonian Map of the World*, "Iraq", 50 (1988), pp. 147-165.

Horowitz 1998
W. Horowitz, *Mesopotamian Cosmic Geography*, Winona Lake 1998.

Horowitz 2000
W. Horowitz, *The Sun-Disk Tablet of Nabû-Apla-Iddina*, in W.W. Hallo (edited by), *The Context of Scripture*, Leiden 2000, vol. II, pp. 364-368.

Horowitz 2006
W. Horowitz, *A Late Babylonian Tablet with Concentric Circles from the University Museum (CBS 1766)*, "Journal of Ancient Near Eastern Studies", 30 (2006), pp. 37-53.

Horsky-Škopová 1968
Z. Horský, O. Škopová, *Astronomy Gnomonics: A Catalogue of the Instruments of the 15th to the 19th Centuries in the Collections of the National Technical Museum, Prague*, Prague 1968.

Hoskin 1997
M. Hoskin, *The Cambridge Illustrated History of Astronomy*, Cambridge 1997.

Hoskin 1999
M. Hoskin (edited by), *The Cambridge Concise History of Astronomy*, Cambridge 1999.

Howse 1986 e 1994
D. Howse, *The Greenwich list of Observatories: a world list of astronomical Observatories, instrument and clocks, 1670 - 1850*, in "Journal for the History of Astronomy", XVII (4), 1986; *Amendment list no. 1*, 25 (3), 1994, pp 207-218.

Hugues D'Hancarville 1766
P.F. Hugues D'Hancarville, *The Collection of Antiquities from the Cabinet of Sir William Hamilton*, Napoli 1766, III, 94.

Hunger 1992
H. Hunger, *Astrological Reports to Assyrian Kings*, *State Archives of Assyria*, VIII, Helsinki 1992.

Hunger 2001
H. Hunger, *I primi cataloghi stellari. Le osservazioni astronomiche. L'astronomia matematica nel periodo tardobabilonese*, in M. Liverani (edited by), *Il Vicino Oriente antico. Storia della Scienza*, vol. I, chapt. XIII, *Astronomia e astrologia*, pp. 419-426.

Hunger-Pingree 1989
H. Hunger, D. Pingree, *Mul.Apin. An Astronomical Compendium in Cuneiform*, Horn (A) 1989.

Hunger-Pingree 1999
H. Hunger, D. Pingree, *Astral Sciences in*

Mesopotamia, Leiden 1999.

Hutin 1972
S. Hutin, *Robert Fludd. Alchimiste et philosophe rosicrucien*, Paris 1972.

Huygens 1659
C. Huygens, *Systema Saturnium, sive, de causis mirandorum Saturni phaenomenon, et comite ejius planeta novo*, Den Haag 1659.

Huygens 1963
C. Huygens, *Horologium oscillatorium e Traité de la lumière*, edited by C. Pighetti, Firenze 1963.

Ideler 1809
L. Ideler, *Untersuchungen über den Ursprung und die Bedeutung der Sternnamen: Ein Beytrag zur Geschichte des gestirnten Himmels*, Berlin 1809.

Igino 1983
Hygin, *L'Astronomie*, edited by A. Le Boeuffle, Paris 1983.

Ildegarda di Bingen 1996
Hildegardis Bingensis, *Liber divinorum operum*, edited by A. Derolez, P. Dronke, Turnhout 1996.

Ildegarda di Bingen 2003
Ildegarda di Bingen, *Il Libro delle opere divine*, edited by M. Cristiani, M. Pereira, Milano 2003.

Indicopleustes 1968
C. Indicopleustes, *Topographie Chrétienne*, edited by W. Wolska-Connu, Paris 1968.

Indicopleustes 1992
C. Indicopleustes, *Topographia Christiana libri I-IV*, edited by A. Garzya, Napoli 1992.

Invernizzi 1994
A. Invernizzi, *Il Calendario*, in *Vita e Costumi dei Romani Antichi*, edited by G. Pisani Sartorio and A.M. Liberati Silverio, vol. 16, Roma 1994.

Iori 2002
A. Iori, (edited by), *Il Cielo*, 284a, Milano 2002, p. 19 ff.

Istituto e Museo di storia della scienza (Firenze) 2004
Istituto e Museo di storia della scienza (Firenze), *Catalogue of orbs, spheres and globes*, edited by E. Dekker, Firenze 2004.

Jackson 1998
D.F. Jackson, *Fabio Vigili's inventory of Medici Greek manuscripts*, "Scriptorium", 52 (1998), pp. 199-204.

Jaffé 1989
M. Jaffé, *Rubens. Catalogo completo*, Milano 1989.

Jamieson 2004
A. Jamieson, *Celestial Atlas series of thirty maps, (London 1822)*, edited by F. Stoppa, Milano 2004.

Jasnow-Zauzich 2005
R. Jasnow, K.-Th. Zauzich, *The Ancient Egyptian Book of Thot*, Wiesbaden 2005.

Joannès 2000
F. Joannès, *La Mésopotamie au 1er millénaire avant J.-C.*, Paris 2000.

Johns 1992
C.M.S. Johns, *Art and science in eighteenth-century Bologna: Donato Creti's astronomical landscape paintings*, "Zeitschrift für Kunstgeschichte", 55, 1992, pp. 578-589.

Kanas 2007
N. Kanas, *Star Maps, History, Artistry and Cartography*, Chichester 2007.

Kansas City 1989
The face of the Moon. Galileo to Apollo, edited by W.B. Ashworth Jr., catalogue of the exhibition (Kansas City, october 1989-february 1990), Kansas City 1989.

Kennedy 1956
E.S. Kennedy, *A Survey of Islamic Astronomical Tables*, in "Transactions of the American Philosophical Society", N.S., 46 (1956), reprinted about 1990.

Kennedy 1983
E.S. Kennedy, *Studies in the Islamic Exact Sciences*, Beirut 1983.

Kennedy 1998
E.S. Kennedy, *Astronomy and Astrology in the Medieval Islamic World*, Ashgate 1998.

Kennedy-Pingree 1971
E.S. Kennedy, D. Pingree (edited by), *The Astrological History of Masha-Allah*, Cambridge (MA) 1971.

Kepler 1611
J. Kepler, *Dioptrice, seu Demonstratio eorum quae visui et visibilibus propter conspicilla non ita pridem inventa accidunt*, Augustae Vindelicorum 1611.

Kepler 1941
J. Kepler, *Harmonice Mundi*, in *Gesammelte Werke* VI, edited by M. Caspar, München 1941.

Kepler 1945
J. Kepler, *Briefe 1590-1599*, in *Gesammelte Werke* XIII, edited by M. Caspar, München 1945.

Kepler 1963
J. Kepler, *Mysterium Cosmographicum. Editio altera cum notis*, in *Gesammelte Werke* VI, edited by M. Caspar, München 1963.

Kepler 1995
J. Kepler, *Epitome of Copernican Astronomy & Harmonies of the World*, Amherst 1995.

Kier-Reinert 1995
J. Kier, F. Reinert, *Homère et les neuf muses à Vichten. Sensationelle découverte d'une mosaïque*, in "Dossiers d'Archeologie", fuori serie no. 5, 1995, pp.71-73.

King D.A. 1986
D.A. King, *Islamic Mathematical Astronomy*, London 1986, Aldershot 1993.

King D.A. 1987
D.A. King, *Islamic Astronomical Instruments*, London 1987.

King D.A. 1993
D.A. King, *Astronomy in the Service of Islam*, Aldershot 1993.

King D.A. 1996
D.A. King, *Islamic Astronomy*, in *Astronomy before the Telescope*, edited by C. Walker, London 1996, pp. 143-174.

King D.A. 2001
D.A. King, *The ciphers of the monks: a forgotten number-notation of the Middle Ages*, Stuttgart 2001.

King D.A. 2004-2005
D.A. King, *In Synchrony with the Heavens: studies in Astronomical Timekeeping and Instrumentation in Medieval Islamic Civilization*, Leiden 2004-2005.

King D.A. 2007a
D.A. King, *Astrolabes and Angels, Epigrams and Enigmas. From Regiomontanus' Acrostic for Cardinal Bessarione to Piero della Francesca's Flagellation of Christ*, Stuttgart 2007, pp. 27-31, 220-233.

King 2007b
D.A. King, *Die Astrolabiensammlung in Nürnberg*, in *Focus Behaim Globus*, edited by G. Bott, Nuremberg 1991, II, pp. 581-586.

King H.C.1978a
H.C. King (with J.R. Millburn), *Geared to the Stars. The Evolution of Planetaríums, Orreries, and Astronomical Clocks*, Bristol 1978.

King H.C.1978b
H.C. King (with J. R. Millburn), *Geared to the Stars. The Evolution of Planetaríums, Orreries, and Astronomical Clocks*, Toronto 1978.

King L.W. 1912a
L.W. King, *Babylonian Boundary-stones and Memorial Tablets in the British Museum*, London 1912.

King L.W. 1912b
L.W. King, *Cuneiform Texts from Babylonian Tablets in the British Museum*, vol. 33, London, 1912.

King-Saliba 1986
D.A. King, G. Saliba, (edited by), *Kennedy Festschrift*, in *From Deferent to Equant: Studies in the History of Science in the Ancient and Medieval Near East in Honor of E.S. Kennedy*, *Annals of the New York Academy of Sciences* (500), 1986.

Koch J. 1989
J. Koch, *Neue Untersuchungen zur Topographie des babylonischen Fixsternhimmels*, Wiesbaden 1989.

Koch U.S. 2005
U.S. Koch, *Secrets of extispicy*, Münster 2005.

Koch Westenholz 1995
U. Koch Westenholz, *Mesopotamian Astrology. An Introduction to Babylonian and Assyrian Celestial Divination*, Copenhagen 1995.

Kohbach *et al.* 2007
M. Kohbach *et al.* (edited by), *Festschrift für Hermann Hunger zum 65. Geburtstag gewidmet von seinen Freunden, Kollegen und Schülern*, Wien 2007.

Konecˇnyˊ 2005
L. Konecˇnyˊ, *Peter Paul Rubens, Galileo Galilei und die Schlacht am Weissen Berg* "Artibus et Historiae", 26, 52, (2005), pp. 85-91.

Koyré 1957
A. Koyré, *From the closed world to the infinite Universe*, Baltimore, 1957.

Koyré 1966
A. Koyré, *La rivoluzione astronomica: Copernico, Keplero, Borelli*, Milano 1966.

Koyré 1972
A. Koyré, *Studi newtoniani*, Torino 1972.

Koyré 1976
A. Koyré, *Studi galileiani*, Torino 1976.

Kramer 1956
S.N. Kramer, *Sumerian Theology and Ethics*, in "Harvard Theological Review", 49 (1956), pp. 45-62.

Kramer 1964
S.N. Kramer, *«Vox Populi» and the Sumerian Literary Documents*, "Revue d'Assyriologie", 58 (1964), pp. 149-152.

Kriech Ritner 1993
R. Kriech Ritner, *The Mechanics of Ancient Egyptian Magical Practice*, Chicago 1993.

Krier *et al.* 2002
J. Krier *et al.*, *Peintures Romaines de Vichten, Fouille: étude et restauration*, "Archéologia", 395, december 2002, pp. 44-47.

Krisciunas 1988
K. Krisciunas, *Astronomical centers of the world*, Cambridge 1988.

Krogt 1993
P. van der Krogt, *Globi Neerlandici. The production of globes in the Low Countries*, Utrecht 1993.

KSB II 2004
Koptisches Sammelbuch, vol. II, edited by M.R.M. Hasitzka, Wien 2004.

Kuhn 1972
T. Kuhn, *La rivoluzione copernicana*, Torino 1972.

Kunitzsch 1961
P. Kunitzsch, *Untersuchungen zur Sternnomenklatur*

der Araber, Wiesbaden 1961.

Kunitzsch 1989
P. Kunitzsch, *The Arabs and the Stars*, Northampton (UK) 1989.

Kunitzsch-Smart 1986
P. Kunitzsch, T. Smart, *Short Guide to Modern Star Names and their Derivation*, Wiesbaden 1986.

Künzl 1997-1998
H. Künzl, *Der globus im Römisch-Germanischen Zentralmuseum Mainz: der bisher einzige komplette himmelsglobus aus dem griechisch-römischen altertum*, "Der Globusfreund", 45-46, 1997-1998.

Künzl 2003
E. Künzl, *Ein römischer Himmelsglobus der mittleren Kaiserzeit* (extraordinary edition of the Roman-Germanic Museum year-book of Mainz), 47, Mainz 2003.

La Rocca 2008
E. La Rocca, *Lo spazio negato. La pittura di paesaggio nella cultura artistica greca e romana*, Milano 2008.

Lachièze Rey-Luminet 1998
M. Lachièze Rey, J.-P. Luminet, *Figures du ciel: De l'harmonie des sphères à la conquête spatiale*, Paris 1998.

Lafitte 2001
R. Lafitte, *Héritages Arabes: Des noms arabes pour les étoiles*, Paris 2001.

Lambert 1975a
W.G. Lambert, *The Historical Development of the Mesopotamian Pantheon: A Study in Sophisticated Polytheism*, in H. Goedicke e J.J. Roberts (edited by), *Unity and Diversity: Essays in the History, Literature and Religion of the Ancient Near East*, Baltimore-London 1975, pp. 191-200.

Lambert 1975b
W.G. Lambert, *The Cosmology of Sumer and Babylon*, in C. Blacker, M. Loewe (edited by), *Ancient Cosmologies*, London 1975, pp. 42-65.

Lankheit 1962
K. Lankheit, *Florentinische Barokplastik*, München 1962.

Lapi Ballerini 1986
I. Lapi Ballerini, *L'emisfero celeste della Sagrestia Vecchia: rendiconti da un giornale di restauro, in Donatello e la Sagrestia Vecchia di San Lorenzo. Temi, studi, proposte di un cantiere di restauro*, catalogue of the exhibition, (Firenze june-september 1986), Firenze 1986, pp. 75 ff.

Lapi Ballerini 1987
I. Lapi Ballerini, *The celestial hemisphere of the Old Sacristy and its restoration*, in *Donatello at Close Range*, "The Burlington Magazine", CXXIX, (1987), pp. 51 ff.

Lapi Ballerini 1988
I. Lapi Ballerini, *Gli emisferi celesti della Sagrestia Vecchia e della Cappella Pazzi*, "Rinascimento", XXVIII, (1988), pp. 321 ff.

Lapi Ballerini 1989
I. Lapi Ballerini, *Considerazioni a margine del restauro della 'cupolina' dipinta nella Sagrestia Vecchia*, in *Donatello-Studien*, edited by M. Cammerer, Munchen 1989, pp. 102 ff.

Lapi Ballerini 2007
I. Lapi Ballerini, *Il "cielo" di San Lorenzo*, in *La linea del Sole. Le grandi meridiane fiorentine*, edited by F. Camerota, catalogue of the exhibition (Firenze, march- september 2007), Firenze 2007, pp. 29-39.

Laudan 1972
L. Laudan, *James Ferguson*, in *DSB*, IV, 1972, pp. 565-566.

Lazari 1859
V. Lazari, *Notizia delle opere d'arte e d'antichità della raccolta Correr*, Venezia 1859.

Le Boeuffle 1977
A. Le Boeuffle, *Les nomes latines d'astres et des constellations*, Paris 1977.

Le Boeuffle 1989
A. Le Boeuffle, *Le ciel des Romains*, Paris 1989.

Le Boeuffle 1996
A. Le Boeuffle, *Astronymie : les noms des étoiles*, Paris 1996.

Leitz 1991a
C. Leitz, *Dekane und Dekansternbilder*, Wiesbaden 1991.

Leitz 1991b
C. Leitz, *Studien zur ägyptischen Astronomie*, Wiesbaden 1991.

Leitz 1995
C. Leitz, *Altägyptische Sternuhren*, Leuven 1995.

Leonardi 1960
C. Leonardi, *I codici di Marziano Capella*, in "Aevum", XXXIV, (1960), pp. 47-48, no. 60.

Leopold 1986
Astronomen, Sterne, Geräte - Landgraf Wilhelm IV. und seine sich selbst bewegenden Globen, Luzern 1986.

Lepsius 1865
R. Lepsius, *Die alt-aegyptische Elle und ihre Eintheilung*, Berlin 1865.

Lerner 1997
M.P. Lerner, *Le Monde des Spheres : genèse et triomphe d'une représentation cosmique*, Paris 1997.

Lerner 2000
M.P. Lerner, *Il mondo delle sfere. Genesi e trionfo di una rappresentazione del cosmo*, Milano 2000, p. 16.

Lieven 1999
A. von Lieven, *Divination in Ägypten*, "Altorientalische Forschungen", 26 (1999), pp. 77-126.

Lieven 2000
A. von Lieven, *Der Himmel über Esna. Eine Fallstudie zur Religiösen Astronomie in Ägypten*, Wiesbaden 2000.

Lieven 2007
A. von Lieven, *Grundriss des Laufes der Sterne. Das sogenannte Nutbuch, The Carlsberg Papyri 8* (CNI 31), København 2007.

LIMC
Lexicon Iconographicum Mythologiae Classicae, Zurich 1981.

Lindberg 1978
D.C. Lindberg (edited by), *Science in the Middle Ages*, Chicago 1978.

Lindberg 1992
D.C. Lindberg, *The Beginning of Western Science. The European Scientific Tradition in Philosophical, Religious, and Institutional Context 600 B.C. to A.D. 1450*, Chicago 1992.

Linton 2004
C. M. Linton, *From Eudoxus to Einstein: A History of Mathematical Astronomy*, Cambridge 2004.

Linz 1990
Mensch und Kosmos: OÖ Landesausstellung Linz 1990, edited by W.Seipel, catalogue of the exhibition (Linz, may-november 1990), Linz 1990.

Lippincott 1999
K. Lippincott, *The story of time*, London 1999.

Londra 1985
Early gearing: geared mechanism in the ancient and mediaeval world, edited by J.V. Field, M.T. Wright, catalogue of the exhibition (London, march-september 1985), London 1985.

Lovi-Tirion 1989
G. Lovi, W. Tirion, *Men, monsters and the moderne universe*, Richmond 1989.

Lowinsky 1977
E. Lowinsky, *Ockeghem's Canon for Thirty-six Voices: An Essay in Musical Iconography*, in *Essay in Musicology in honor of Dragan Plamena on his 70th Birthday*, New York 1977, pp. 155-180.

Lucchetta 2001
G. Lucchetta, *La filosofia della natura tra VI e V secolo*, in *Storia della Scienza*, vol. 1, Roma 2001.

Maccagni 1967
C. Maccagni, *Notizie sugli artigiani della famiglia della Volpaia*, "Rassegna periodica di informazioni del Comune di Pisa", 3-8 (1967), pp. 3-13.

Macrobio 1981
Macrobio, *Commentarii in Ciceronis somnium Scipionis*, Padova 1981.

Maddison 1962
F. Maddison, *A Fifteenth Century Spherical Astrolabe*, "Physis", 4 (1962), pp. 101-109.

Mahoney 2000
M.S. Mahoney, *Huygens and the pendulum: from device to mathematical relation*, in *Growth of mathematical knowledge*, Dordrecht 2000, pp. 17-39.

Maiuri 1932
A. Maiuri, *La Casa del Menandro e il suo tesoro di argenteria*, Roma 1932.

Maiuri 1958
A. Maiuri, *Ercolano. I nuovi scavi (1927-1958)*, Roma 1958.

Mamiani 1990
M. Mamiani, *Introduzione a Newton*, Roma 1990.

Mancioli 1984
D. Mancioli, *Un calendario astrologico al Museo della civiltà romana*, "Bollettino dei Musei Comunali di Roma", (1984), vols. 28-30, pp. 18-22.

Mansuelli 1961
G. Mansuelli, *Galleria degli Uffizi. Le sculture*, Roma 1961.

Maqbul Ahmad 1975
S. Maqbul Ahmad, *Al-Qazw n* , in *DSB*, edited by C.C. Gillispie, XI, New York 1975, pp. 230-233.

Marengo 1998
S.M. Marengo, *Orologio solare sferico da Matelica*, "Epigrafia romana in area adriatica", 1998.

Matteucci 1982
G. Matteucci, *Cristiano Banti*, Firenze 1982.

Matthiae 1985
P. Matthiae, *I tesori di Ebla*, Roma 1985.

Matthiae 1992
P. Matthiae, *Henri Frankfort. Il dio che muore: mito e cultura nel mondo preclassico*, Firenze 1992.

Matthiae 1994
P. Matthiae, *Il sovrano e l'opera: arte e potere nella Mesopotamia antica*, Roma 1994.

Matthiae 1995
P. Matthiae, *Ebla, un impero ritrovato. Dai primi scavi alle ultime scoperte*, Torino 1995.

Mayer 1956
L.A. Mayer, *Islamic Astrolabists and their Works*, Geneva 1956.

Mazza 1992
B. Mazza, *Il trionfo della scienza ovvero "la luce dell'intelligenza vince le tenebre dell'ignoranza": ideologie dell'illuminismo e questioni iconologiche nella decorazione delle ville venete tra Seicento e Settecento*, "Studi veneziani", n.s. 23, (1992), pp. 163-181.

McConnell 2007
A. McConnell, *Jesse Ramsden (1735-1800): London's leading scientific instrument maker*, Aldershot 2007.

Melamed 1995
D. Melamed, *A thirty-six voice canon in the hand of C.P.E. Bach*, in *Bach Studies* 2, edited by D.R. Melamed, Cambridge 1995, pp. 107-118.

Mendillo *et al.* 2005
M. Mendillo, P.M. Burnham, D.J. Warner, S.Y. Edgerton, *Celestial Images. Antiquarian astronomical charts and maps from the Mendillo Collection*, Boston 2005.

Mengoli 1986
P. Mengoli, *La clessidra egizia del Museo Barracco*, "Vicino Oriente", 6, (1986), pp. 193-218.

Mersenne 1627
M. Mersenne, *Traité de l'harmonie universelle*, Paris 1627.

Meucci 1878
F. Meucci, *Il globo celeste arabico del secolo XI esistente nel Gabinetto degli strumenti antichi di astronomia, di fisica e di matematica del R. Istituto di studi superiori*, Firenze 1878.

Meyer 1988
F. Meucci, *Untersuchungen zu den Tonlebermodellen aus dem Alten Orient*, Münster 1988.

Milano 1982
Cristiano Banti un macchiaiolo nel suo tempo 1824-1904, edited by G. Matteucci, catalogue of the exhibition (Milano, june-july 1982), Firenze 1982.

Milburn-King 1988
J.R. Milburn, H.C. King, *Wheelwright of the Heavens: the life and works of James Ferguson FRS*, London 1988.

Miniati 1989
M. Miniati, *Les Cistae Mathematicae et l'organisation des connaissances au XVIIe siècle*, in *Studies in the History of Scientific Instruments. Papers presented at the 7th Symposium of the Scientific Instruments Commission of the Union Internationale d'Histoire et de Philosophie des Sciences. Paris 15-19 September 1987*, edited by C. Blondel *et al.*, London 1989.

Miniati 1991
M. Miniati (edited by), *Museo di storia della scienza: catalogo*, Firenze 1991.

Miniati 1992
M. Miniati, *Un nuovo orologio notturno*, "Nuncius", VII, 2, (1992), pp. 115-117.

Miniati 1999
M. Miniati, *'Organum mathematicum' e organizzazione del sapere*, in *Giacomo Leopardi Viaggio nella Memoria*, edited by F. Cacciapuoti, Milano 1999.

Miniati 2003
Misurare cielo e terra. Strumenti scientifici tra Medioevo e Rinascimento, edited by M. Miniati, Brescia 2003.

Miniati *et.al.* 1995
M. Miniati *et al.*, *Sul restauro di due globi di Matthäus Greuter*, "Nuncius", X, 1, (1995), pp. 173-178.

Miniati-Rudan 1981
M. Miniati, M. Rudan, *Il Quadrante universale di Tobias Volckmer di Brunswick, I*, "Annali dell'Istituto e Museo di Storia della Scienza di Firenze", VI, 1, (1981), pp. 241-246.

Miniati-Rudan 1982
M. Miniati, M. Rudan, *Il Quadrante universale di Tobias Volckmer di Brunswick, II*, "Annali dell'Istituto e Museo di Storia della Scienza di Firenze", VII, 1, (1982), pp. 83-111.

Mondolfo 1982
R. Mondolfo, *Polis, lavoro e tecnica*, Milano, Feltrinelli, 1982.

Moutsopoulos 1959
E. Moutsopoulos, *La Musique dans l'oeuvre de Platon*, Paris 1959.

Müller 1884
K.K. Müller, *Neue Mittheilungen über Janos Lascaris und die Mediceische Bibliothek*, "Centralblatt für Bibliothekwesen", 1 (1884), p. 376.

Murdoch 1984
J. Murdoch, *Album of Science. Antiquity and the Middle Ages*, New York 1984.

Museo della civiltà romana 1982
Museo della civiltà romana: catalogo, Roma 1982.

Napoli 1999
Homo Faber. Natura, scienza e tecnica nell'antica Pompei, catalogue of the exhibition (Napoli, march-july 1999), edited by A. Ciarallo, E. De Carolis, Milano 1999.

Napoli 2006
Argenti: Pompei, Napoli, Torino, edited by G. Guzzo, catalogue of the exhibition (Napoli, april-september 2006), Milano 2006.

Nava-Paris-Friggeri 2007
M.L. Nava, R. Paris, R. Friggeri (edited by), *Rosso Pompeiano. La decorazione pittorica nelle Collezioni del Museo di Napoli e a Pompei*, Milano 2007.

Naval Observatory 1987
U.S. Naval Observatory, *The Almanac for Computers 1987*, Washington 1987.

Neugebauer 1955
O. Neugebauer, *The Egyptian 'Decans'*, "Vistas in Astronomy", 1, 1955, pp. 47-51.

Neugebauer 1975a
O. Neugebauer, *A History of Ancient Mathematical Astronomy*, Berlin 1975.

Neugebauer 1975b
O. Neugebauer, *A History of Ancient Mathematical Astronomy*, New York 1975.

Neugebauer-Parker 1960-1969
O. Neugebauer, R.A. Parker, *Egyptian Astronomical Texts*, London 1960-1969.

Newton 1687
I. Newton, *Philosophiae naturalis principia mathematica*, London 1687.

Newton 1983
I. Newton, *Il Sistema del Mondo e gli scolii classici*, Roma 1983.

Niwinski 1989
A. Niwinski, *Studies on the Illustrated Theban Funerary Papyri of the 11th and 10th centuries B.C.*, Freiburg 1989.

North 1981
J.D. North, *Hevelius Johannes*, in C.C. Gillispie (edited by), *Dictionary of Scientific Biography*, New York 1981, vol. VI, p. 364.

North 1986
J. North, *Horoscopes and History*, London 1986.

North 1989a
J.D. North, *The Universal Frame. Historical Essays in Astronomy, Natural Philosophy and Scientific Method*, London-Ronceverte 1989.

North 1989b
J.D. North, *The Universal Frame. Essays in Ancient and Medieval Cosmology*, London 1989.

North 2008
J. North, *Cosmos: An Illustrated History of Astronomy and Cosmology*, Chicago 2008.

Olcott 2004
W.T. Olcott, *Star Lore, Myths, Legends, and Facts*, Mineola, New York 2004.

Oresme 1968
N. Oresme, *Le Livre du ciel et du monde*, edited by A.D. Menut, A.J. Denomy, Madison 1968, pp. 167-171.

Il p. Vincenzo Coronelli 1951
Il p. V. Coronelli dei frati minori conventuali (1650-1718) nel III centenario della nascita, Roma 1951.

Padova 1990
Pietro Paolo Rubens (1577-1640), edited by D. Bodart, catalogue of the exhibition (Padova, march-may 1990, Roma 1990.

Pagano 1984
I documenti del processo di Galileo Galilei, edited by S.M. Pagano, Città del Vaticano 1984.

Pagano-Prisciandaro 2006
M. Pagano, R. Prisciandaro, *Studio sulle provenienze degli oggetti rinvenuti negli scavi borbonici del Regno di Napoli*, I-II, Castellammare di Stabia 2006.

Palisca 1985
C.V. Palisca, *Humanism in Italian Renaissance musical thought*, New Haven 1985.

Palmieri 1927
M. Palmieri, *Libro del Poema chiamato 'Città di vita'*, 2 vols., Northampton (MA) 1927.

Panaino 1987
A. Panaino, *Sirio stella-freccia nell'Oriente antico*, in *Atti della 4ª giornata di Studi camito-semitici e indoeuropei*, edited by G. Bernini e V. Brugnatelli, Milano 1987, pp. 139-155.

Panaino 2001
A. Panaino, *I calendari dell'Iran antico*, in M. Liverani (edited by), *Il Vicino Oriente antico. Storia della Scienza*, vol. I, chapt. XII, pp. 416-418.

Panofski 1948
E. Panofski, *Albrecht Dürer*, 2 vols., Princeton (N.J.) 1948.

Panti 2004
C. Panti, *Suono interiore e musica umana fra tradizione boeziana e aristotelismo: le glosse pseudo-grossatestiane al "De institutione musica"*, in *Parva naturalia: saperi medievali, natura e vita*, edited by C. Crisciani, R. Lambertini, R. Martorelli Vico, Pisa 2004, pp. 219-245.

Pantin 1993
I. Pantin, *Une "Ecole d'Athènes" des astronomes?: la représentation de l'astronome antique dans les frontispices de la Renaissance*, in *Images de l'antiquité dans la littérature française: le texte et son illustration : actes du colloque tenu à l'Université Paris XII les 11 et 12 avril 1991*, edited by E. Baumgartner, L. Harf-Lancner, Paris 1993, pp. 87-95.

Parigi 1998
Figures du ciel, de l'harmonie des sphères à la conquête spatiale, edited by M. Lachièze-Rey, J.P. Luminet, catalogue of the exhibition (Parigi, october 1998-january 1999), Paris 1999.

Parigi 2002a
Spheres. L'art des mécaniques célestes, edited by A. Kugel, catalogue of the exhibition (Paris, september-november 2002), Paris 2002.

Parigi 2002b
Spheres. The Art of the Celestial Mechanics, edited by A. Kugel, catalogue of the exhibition (Paris, september-november 2002), Paris 2002.

Parigi 2005
Mélancolie, génie et folie en Occident, edited by J. Clair, catalogue of the exhibition (Parigi, october 2005-january 2006), Paris 2005.

Parpola 1993
S. Parpola, *Letters from Assyrian and Babylonian Scholars*, Helsinki 1993.

Parrish 1984
D. Parrish, *Season Mosaics of Roman North Africa*, Roma 1984.

Parronchi 1979
A. Parronchi, *Il cielo notturno della Sagrestia Vecchia di San Lorenzo*, Firenze 1979, pp. 3 ff.

Parronchi 1984a
A. Parronchi, *L'emisfero settentrionale della Sagrestia Vecchia*, in *San Lorenzo. La Basilica, la Sagrestia, le Cappelle, la Biblioteca*, edited by U. Baldini e B. Nardini, Firenze 1984, pp. 73 ff.

Parronchi 1984b
A. Parronchi, *L'emisfero della Sacrestia Vecchia: Giuliano Pesello?*, in *Scritti di storia dell'arte in onore di Federico Zeri*, Milano 1984, I, pp. 134 ff.

Pasquinelli 1958
A. Pasquinelli, *I Presocratici. Frammenti e testimonianze*, Torino 1958, p. 10.

Passeri 1750
G.B. Passeri, *Atlas Faresianus marmoreus insigne vetustatis monumentum commentario*, Firenze 1750.

Pattie 1980
T.S. Pattie, *Astrology as illustrated in the collections of the British Library and the British Museum*, London 1980.

Paviot 1995
J. Paviot, *Ung Mapmonde rond, en guise de pom(m)e: Ein Erdglobus von 1440-44, hergestellt für Philipp den Guten, Herzog von Burgund*, in "Der Globusfreund", 43/44, (1995), pp. 19-29.

Pedersen 1993
O. Pedersen, *Early Physics and Astronomy: a Historical Introduction*, Cambridge 1993.

Pelling 2008
N. Pelling, *Who invented the Telescope?*, in "History Today", 58, n. 10 (2008), pp. 26-31.

Pepe 1996
L. Pepe (edited by), *Copernico e la questione copernicana in Italia dal XVII al XIX secolo*, Firenze 1996.

Pettinato 1992
G. Pettinato, *La saga di Gilgamesh*, Milano 1992.

Pettinato 1998
G. Pettinato, *La scrittura celeste*, Milano 1998.

Peurbach 1472
G. Peurbach, *Theoricae Novae Planetarum*, (Venezia), c. 1472.

Pietro D'Abano 2008
Pietro D'Abano, *I trattati di astronomia*, (*Lucidator dubitabilium astronomiae, De motu octavae sphaere*) e *altre opere*, edited by G. Federici Vescovini, Padova 2008.

Pinacoteca di Brera 1994
Pinacoteca di Brera. Dipinti dell'Ottocento e del Novecento: collezioni dell'Accademia e della Pinacoteca, coordination of F. Zeri, Milano 1994, vol. II.

Pingree 1973
D. Pingree, *The Greek Influences on Early Islamic Mathematical Astronomy*, in "Journal of the American Oriental Society" 93 (1973), pp. 32-43.

Pinto 1982
S. Pinto, *La promozione delle arti negli Stati italiani dall'età delle riforme all'Unità*, in *Storia dell'arte italiana*, Torino 1982, part II, vol. II (*Settecento e Ottocento*), pp. 791-1097.

Pizzorusso 1980
C. Pizzorusso, *Records*, in *Astrologia, magia e alchimia nel Rinascimento fiorentino ed europeo*, in *Firenze e la Toscana dei medici nell'Europa del Cinquecento*, catalogue of the exhibitions (Firenze, 1980), edited by P. Zambelli, Milano 1980, pp. 327-348.

Platone 1977
Platone, *Timaeus and Critias*, 22-23, London 1977.

Platone 1992
Platon, *Timée, Critias*, edited by L. Brisson, Paris 1992.

Plinio 1977
Plinio, *Storia Naturale*, Torino 1977.

Pompei 1990-2003
Pompei. Pitture e Mosaici, vols. I-X, 1990-2003.

Poulle 1984
E. Poulle, *Les Tables Alphonsines avec les Canons de Jean de Saxe*, Paris 1984.

Poulle 2003
Tractatus Astrarii. Giovanni Dondi dall'Orologio, edited by E. Poulle, Genève 2003.

I Presocratici 1969
I presocratici: testimonianze e frammenti, Bari 1969, vol. I, p. 276.

Puliatti 1969
P. Puliatti, *Il 'De Sphaera estense'*, Bergamo 1969.

Quill 1966
H. Quill, *John Harrison*, London 1966.

Ragep 1993
F.J. Ragep, *Medieval Islamic Cosmology: The Tadhkira of Nasîr al-Dîn al-Tûsî (text, translation and commentary)*, New York 1993.

Rao 1994
I.G. Rao, *Matteo Palmieri, "Città di vita" (col commento di Leonardo Dati)*, in *I luoghi della memoria scritta: manoscritti, incunaboli, libri a stampa di biblioteche statali italiane*, edited by G. Cavallo, catalogue of the exhibition (Roma, march-may 1994), Roma 1994.

Rao 2000
I.G. Rao, *Matteo Palmieri. La "Città di vita"*, in

Sandro Botticelli: pittore della Divina Commedia, edited by S. Gentile, Milano 2000.

Redondi 1983
P. Redondi, *Galileo eretico*, Torino 1983.

Redondi 1994
P. Redondi, *Dietro l'immagine: rappresentazioni di Galileo nella cultura positivistica*, "Nuncius", IX, 1, (1994), pp. 65-116.

Reeves 1997
H. Reeves, *Painting the Heavens: art and science in the Age of Galileo*, Princeton (N.J.) 1997.

Reeves 2008
E. Reeves, *Galileo's Glassworks: the Telescope and the Mirror*, Cambridge (MA) 2008.

Reeves-Van Helden 2009
E. Reeves, A. Van Helden, *Galileo and Scheiner on Sunspots*, Chicago 2009.

Regiomontano 1496
J. Regiomontano, *Epytoma ... in Almagestum Ptolomei*, Venezia 1496.

Regiomontano 1544
J. Regiomontano, *Scripta ... de Torqueto, Astrolabio armillari ...*, Norimbergae 1544.

Regiomontano 1949
Joannis Regiomontani Opera collectanea, edited by F. Schmeidler, Osnabrück 1949.

Reiner 2005
E. Reiner, *Babylonian Planetary Omens*, Leiden 2005.

Reiner-Pingree 1975
E. Reiner, D. Pingree, *The Venus Tablet of Ammis aduqa*, Malibu 1975.

Richter 1965
G.M.A. Richter, *The Portraits of the Greeks*, London 1965.

Ridpath 1988
I. Ridpath, *Star Tales*, Cambridge 1988.

Riedweg 2007
C. Riedweg, *Pitagora. Vita, dottrina, influenza*, Milano 2007, p. 150.

Righini 1978
G. Righini, *Contributo all'interpretazione scientifica dell'opera astronomica di Galileo*, in "Annali dell'Istituto e Museo di storia della scienza", 2, (1978).

Righini Bonelli 1960
M.L. Righini Bonelli, *Catalogo dei globi antichi conservati in Italia. I Globi di Vincenzo Coronelli*, 2, Firenze 1960.

Righini Bonelli 1968a
M.L. Righini Bonelli (edited by), *Il Museo di storia della scienza a Firenze*, Firenze 1968.

Righini Bonelli 1968b
M.L. Righini Bonelli (edited by), *Il Museo di storia della scienza a Firenze*, Milano 1968.

Righini Bonelli 1976
M.L. Righini Bonelli (edited by), *Il Museo di storia della scienza a Firenze*, Milano 1976.

Righini Bonelli-Settle 1978
M.L. Righini Bonelli, T.B. Settle (edited by), *The Antique Instruments of the Museum of history of science in Florence*, Firenze 1978.

Ripa 1611
C. Ripa, *Iconologia*, Padova 1611.

Rizza 1965
C. Rizza, *Peiresc e l'Italia*, Torino 1965, pp. 190-203.

Roccati 1980
A. Roccati, *Aspetti di Dio nella civiltà egizia*, in *Dio nella Bibbia e nelle culture ad essa contemporanee e connesse*, Torino 1980, pp. 218-231.

Roccati 1989
A. Roccati, *Libro magico-religioso*, in *Dal museo al museo. Passato e futuro del Museo egizio di Torino*, edited by A.M. Donadoni Roveri, Torino 1989, pp. 125-127.

Roccati 1994
A. Roccati, *Smw sxnw*, in *Hommages à Jean Leclant*, Il Cairo 1994, pp. 493-497.

Rochberg 1988
F. Rochberg, *Aspects of Babylonian Celestial Divination*, Horn (A) 1988.

Rochberg 1998
F. Rochberg, *Babylonian Horoscopes*, Philadelphia 1998.

Rochberg 2001
F. Rochberg, *La diffusione dell'astronomia babilonese. L'astrologia tardobabilonese: gli oroscopi*, in *Storia della Scienza, sez. III: Il Vicino Oriente antico*, edited by M. Liverani,. Roma 2001, vol. I, chapt. XIII, (*Astronomia e astrologia*), pp. 426-433.

Rochberg 2004
F. Rochberg, *The Heavenly Writing. Divination, Horoscopy and Astronomy in Mesopotamian Culture*, Cambridge (MA) 2004.

Rodis Lewis 1995
G. Rodis Lewis, *Descartes : biographie*, Paris 1995.

Roli 1988
R. Roli, *Le scene astronomiche di Donato Creti*, in *Palazzo Poggi: da dimora aristocratica a sede dell'Università di Bologna*, edited by A. Ottani Cavina, Bologna 1988, pp. 151-159.

Roma 1964
Documenti lincei e cimeli galileiani: mostra per il IV centenario della nascita di Galileo Galilei, edited by A. Alessandrini, catalogue of the exhibition (Roma april-december 1964), Roma 1965.

Roma 1971
Albrecht Dürer. Opere grafiche, edited by H. Mielke, catalogue of the exhibition (Roma, january-february 1971), Roma 1971.

Roma 1981
5 miliardi di anni: ipotesi per un museo della scienza, catalogue of the exhibition (Roma, may-july 1981), Roma 1981.

Roma 1989
Claude Mellan, gli anni romani: un incisore tra Vouet e Bernini, edited by L. Ficacci, catalogue of the exhibition (Roma, october 1989-january 1990), Roma 1989.

Roma 2000
Aurea Roma. Dalla città pagana alla città cristiana, catalogue of the exhibition (Roma, december 2000-april 2001), edited by S. Ensoli, E. La Rocca, Roma 2000.

Roma 2001
I Giustiniani e l'antico, edited by G. Fusconi, catalogue of the exhibition (Roma october 2001-january 2002), Roma 2001.

Rossi 1894-1895
F. Rossi, *Di alcuni cocci copti del Museo egizio di Torino*, "Atti della R. Accademia delle Scienze di Torino", 30, (1894-95), p. 801 ssg.

Rothman 2000
P. Rothman, *By the light of his own mind: the story of James Ferguson, astronomer*, in "Notes and Records of the Royal Society", 54, 1 (Jan. 2000), pp. 33-45.

Rotondò 1960
A. Rotondò, *Pellegrino Prisciani*, in "Rinascimento", IX, (1960), pp. 69-110.

Rullini 1949
G. Rullini, *La statua di Aristotele*, "Archeologia classica", vol. 1, 2, (1949), pp. 130-147.

Russell 1797
J. Russell, *A Description of the Selenographia: an apparatus for exhibiting the phenomena of the moon*, London 1797.

Russo 1996
L. Russo, *La rivoluzione dimenticata*, Milano 1996, p. 107.

Ruysschaert 1985
J. Ruysschaert, *Du globe terrestre attribué à Giulio Romano aux globes et au planisphère oubliés de Nicolaus Germanus*, in "Bollettino dei monumenti, musei e gallerie pontificie", 6 (1985), pp. 93-104.

Ryan 1966
W.F. Ryan, *John Russell, R.A., and Early Lunar Mapping*, "Smithsonian Journal of History", 1 (1966), pp. 27-48.

Sachs-Hunger 1988
A. Sachs, H. Hunger, *Astronomical Diaries and Related Texts from Babylonia*, Wien 1988.

Sadan 2000
Sadan, *I Segreti astrologici di Albumasar*, edited by G. Federici Vescovini, Torino 2000.

Salerno 1988
L. Salerno, *I dipinti del Guercino*, Roma 1988.

Saliba 1995
G. Saliba, *History of Arabic Astronomy: Planetary Theories During the Golden Age of Islam*, New York 1995.

Saliba 2007
G. Saliba, *Islamic Science and the Making of the European Renaissance*, Cambridge (MA) 2007.

Samek Ludovici 1962
S. Samek Ludovici, *Il 'De sphaera estense' e l'iconografia astrologica*, Milano 1962.

Samsó 1992
J. Samsó, *Las ciencias de los antiguos en al-Andalus*, Madrid 1992.

Samsó 1994
J. Samsó, *Islamic Astronomy and Medieval Spain*, Aldershot 1994.

Samsó 2007
J. Samsó, *Astronomy and Astrology in al-Andalus and the Maghrib*, Ashgate 2007.

Sani 2005
B. Sani, *Ottavio Leoni: la fatica virtuosa*, Torino 2005.

Sarazin 2003
J.Y. Sarazin, *Belles et obsolètes: deux "machines" astronomiques*, "Revue de la Bibliothèque nationale de France", 14 (2003), pp. 46-47.

Sauron 2007
G. Sauron, *La pittura allegorica a Pompei: lo sguardo di Cicerone*, Barcelona 2007.

Savage Smith 1984
E. Savage Smith, *Islamicate celestial globes*, Washington 1984.

Savage Smith 1985
E. Savage Smith, *Islamicate Celestial Globes: their History, Construction and Use*, Washington (D.C.) 1985.

Saxl 1985
F. Saxl, *La fede negli astri: dall'Antichità al Rinascimento*, edited by S. Settis, Torino 1985.

Sayılı 1960
A. Sayılı, *The Observatory in Islam*: and its place in the general history of the observatory, Ankara 1960.

Schaaf 1988
J.D.W. Schaaf, *The New Patterns in the Sky: myths and legends of the Stars*, Blacksburg 1988.

Schaffer 2005
B.E. Schaffer, *The epoch of the constellations on the Farnese Atlas and their origin in Hipparchus's lost catalogue*, "Journal of the History of Astronomy", 36 (2005), pp. 167-196.

Scharlau 1969
U. Scharlau, *Athanasius Kircher (1601-1680) als Musikscrifisteller*, Marburg 1969.

Scheiner 1630
C. Scheiner, *Rosa Ursina, sive Sol ex admirando facularum et macularum suarum phoenomenon varius ...* , Bracciani 1630.

Schiaparelli 1997
G. V. Schiaparelli, *Scritti sulla storia della astronomia antica*, Milano 1997.

Schmidt 2003
R. Schmidt in Internationalen Coronelli-Gesellschaft für Globenkunde, *News 2003*, pp. 21-22.

Schuster 1991
P.K. Schuster, *Melanconia I. Dürers Denkbild*, Berlin 1991.

Sedley 1976
D. Sedley, *Epicurus and the mathematicians of Cyzicus*, in "Cronache Ercolanesi", (1976), pp. 23-54.

Seidl 1989
U. Seidl, *Die babylonischen Kudurru-Reliefs: Symbole mesopotamischer Gottheiten*, Freiburg 1989.

Seidl 2001
U. Seidl, *Das Ringen um das richtige Bild des Šamaš von Sippar*, "Zeitschrift für Archäologie", 91 (2001), pp. 121-132.

Sergeant Snyder 1984
G. Sergeant Snyder, *Maps of the Heavens*, London 1984.

Sesti 1987
G. M. Sesti, *Le dimore del cielo: archeologia e mito delle costellazioni*, Palermo 1987.

Settle 2006
T. B. Settle, *Danti, Gualterotti, Galileo: their telescopes?*, in "Atti della Fondazione Giorgio Ronchi", vol. 61, no. 5 (2006), pp. 625-638.

Sezgin 1974-1979
F. Sezgin, *Geschichte des arabischen Schrifttums*, vol. V: Mathematik, VI: Astronomie, VII: Astrologie - Meteorologie und Verwandtes, Leiden 1974, 1978-1979.

Shaltout-Fekri-Belmonte 2006
M. Shaltout, M. Fekri, J.A. Belmonte, *The ancient Egyptian monuments and their relation to the position of the sun, stars and planets. Report on the first phase, Upper Egypt and Lower Nubia*, (february 2003), in *The world of ancient Egypt. Essays in honor of Ahmed Abd el-Qader el-Sawi*, Le Caire 2006, pp. 93-112.

Shank 1998
M. H. Shank, *Regiomontanus and Homocentric Astronomy*, in "Journal for the History of Astronomy", 29 (1998), pp. 157-166.

Shea 2001
W. Shea, *Copernico: un rivoluzionario prudente*, "I grandi della Scienza", 20, 2001.

Shirley 1978
J.W. Shirley, *Thomas Harriot's lunar observations*, in *Science and history. Studies in honor of Edward Rosen*, edited by E. Hilfstein, P. Czartoryzski, F.D. Grande, Wroclaw 1978, pp. 283-308.

Siebmacher 1989
J. Siebmacher, *Wappenbuch von 1605*, herausgegeben von H. Appuhn, Dortmund 1989.

Siena 2007
Nel segno di Ingres. Luigi Mussini e l'Accademia in Europa nell'Ottocento edited by C. Sisi, E. Spalletti, catalogue of the exhibition (Siena, october 2007-january 2008), Milano 2007.

Sist 1996
L. Sist, *Museo Barracco: arte egizia*, Roma 1996.

Slansky 2000
K. Slansky, *Classification, Historiography, and Monumental Authority. The Babylonian Entitlement Narûs (Kudurrus)*, "Journal of Cuneiform Studies", 52 (2000), pp. 95-114.

Sloley 1931
R.W. Sloley, *Primitive methods of measuring time*, "Journal of Egyptian Archaeology", 17, (1931), pp.166-178.

Spalletti 1985
E. Spalletti, *Gli anni del Caffè Michelangelo (1848-1861)*, Roma 1985.

Speth-Holterhoff 1957
S. Speth-Holterhoff, *Les Peintres flamands de cabinets d'amateurs au XVIIe siècle*, Bruxelles 1957.

Spitzer 1963
L. Spitzer, *Classical and Christian Ideas of World Harmony*, Baltimore 1963.

Star 1990
I. Starr, *Queries to the Sun God. Divination and Politics in Sargonic Assyria*, Helsinki 1990.

Steele-Imhausen 2002
J.M. Steele, A. Imhausen (edited by.), *Under One Sky: Astronomy and Mathematics in the Ancient Near East*, Münster 2002.

Stephenson 1987
B. Stephenson, *Kepler's physical astronomy*, New York 1987.

Stern 1878
L. Stern, *Sahidische Inschriften*, "Zeitschrift für Ägyptische Sprache und Altertumskunde", 16, (1878), 9 ff.

Stevenson 1921
E. L. Stevenson, *Terrestrial and Celestial Globes. Their History and Construction including a consideration of their value as aids in the study of Geography and Astronomy*, New Haven 1921.

Stoppa 2006
F. Stoppa, *Atlas Coelestis. Il cielo stellato nella scienza e nell'arte*, Milano 2006.

Storey 1958
C.A. Storey, *Persian Literature: A Bio-Bibliographical Survey*, Vol. II, Pt. 1, London 1958.

Storia della Scienza 2001
Storia della Scienza, Istituto dell'Enciclopedia Italiana, vol. IV, Roma 2001.

Stott 1991
C. Stott, *Celestial Charts: antique Maps of the Heavens*, London 1991.

Strano 2005
G. Strano, *Tycho Brahe*, "La nuova informazione bibliografica", 1 (2005), pp. 7-47.

Strano 2007a
G. Strano, *L'osservatorio essenziale: fortuna e ricezione degli strumenti astronomici di Tycho Brahe dall'Europa alla Cina*, "Giornale di Astronomia", 2007, pp. 8-15.

Strano 2007b
G. Strano, *Strumenti alessandrini per l'osservazione astronomica: Tolomeo e la Mathematiké yntaxis*, "Automata" 2 (2007), pp. 79-92.

Strohmaier 1984
G. Strohmaier, *Die Sterne des Abd ar-Rahman as-Suf*, Leipzig 1984.

Stroobant *et al.* 1931
P. Stroobant *et al.*, *Les Observatoires Astronomiques et les astronomes*, Tournai 1931.

Stuart Jones 1912
H. Stuart Jones, *Catalogue of the Ancient Sculptures Preserved in the Municipal Collections of Rome*, vol. I: *The Sculptures of the Museo Capitolino*, Oxford 1912.

Suter 1900
H. Suter, *Die Mathematiker und Astronomen der Araber und ihre Werke*, Leipzig 1900, pp. 157-185.

Swerdlow 1999
N.M. Swerdlow, *Regiomontanus's Concentric-Sphere Models for the Sun and Moon*, in "Journal for the History of Astronomy", 30 (1999), pp. 1-23.

Tabarroni 1955
G. Tabarroni, *Sfere celesti sulle monete romane*, Bologna 1955.

Tanara 1651
L'economia del cittadino in villa del sig. Vincenzo Tanara Libri VII, Bologna 1651.

Tardieu 1986
M. Tardieu, *Sabiens coranique et Sabien de Harran*, "Journal asiatique", 274 (1986) p. 1-44.

Tavoni 1999
M.G. Tavoni (edited by), *Un intellettuale europeo e il suo universo: Vincenzo Coronelli (1650-1718)*, Bologna 1999.

Taylor 1966
E.G.R. Taylor, *The Mathematical Practitioners of Hanoverian England 1714-1840*, Cambridge 1966.

Teeuwen 2002
M. Teeuwen, *Harmony and the Music of the Spheres*, Leiden 2002.

Teodorico di Chartres, Guglielmo di Conches, Bernardo Silvestre 1980
Teodorico di Chartres, Guglielmo di Conches, Bernardo Silvestre, *Il Divino e il megacosmo. Testi filosofici e scientifici della scuola di Chartres*, edited by E. Maccagnolo, Milano 1980, p. 234.

Thoren 1990
V.E. Thoren, *The Lord of Uraniborg: A Biography of Tycho Brahe*, Cambridge 1990.

Thorndike 1923-1958
L. Thorndike, *A History of Magic and Experimental Science*, New York 1923-1958.

Thorndike 1949
L. Thorndike, *The "Sphere" of Sacrobosco and its Commentators*, Chicago 1949.

Till 1962
W.C. Till, *Datierung und Prosopographie der koptischen Urkunden aus Theben*, Wien 1962.

Tiradritti 1999
F. Tiradritti, *Il cammino di Harwa*, Milano 1999.

Tognoni 1999
F. Tognoni, *I ritratti di Galileo: la celebrazione del genio*, in *Principio di secol novo: saggi su Galileo*, edited by L.A. Radicati di Brozolo, Pisa 1999, pp. 359-367.

Tognoni 2007
Tognoni F. *«È fatto più giorni sono, similissimo, da mano eccellente»: il ritratto-icona di Galileo*, "Galilaeana", 4, (2007), pp. 127-155.

Tolomeo 1927
Ptolomaeus, *Almagestum*, (*Venetiis 1515*), edited by Halma, Paris 1927.

Tolomeo 1932
Claudii Ptolemaei Geographiae: Codex Urbinas Graecus 82, edited by J. Fischer, Lugduni Batavorum 1932.

Tolomeo 1984a
C. Tolomeo, *Le previsioni astrologiche (Tetrabiblos)*, edited by S. Feraboli, Milano 1984.

Tolomeo 1984b
Ptolemy's Almagest, edited by G.J. Toomer, New York 1984.

Tolomeo 1985
Ptolomaeus, *Quadripartitum cum glosis Haly Rodoan*, Venetiis, per Bonetum Locatellum, Ottaviano Scoto, 1493; edited by S. Feraboli, Milano 1985.

Tolomeo 1998a
C. Ptolemaeus, *Opera quae exstant omnia*, vol. III, 1: *Apotelesmatika*, Leipzig-Stuttgart 1998.

Tolomeo 1998b
Ptolemy's Almagest, edited by G.J. Toomer, Princeton 1998.

Tolomeo 2000
Ptolemy's Geografy: an annotated translation of the theoretical chapters, edited by J. Berggren, A. L. Jones, Princeton 2000.

Torino 1997
Pompeii: picta fragmenta. Decorazioni parietali dalle città sepolte, edited by P.G. Guzzo, catalogue of the exhibition (Torino september 1997-january 1998), Torino 1997.

440

Trevisan 1997
C. Trevisan, *La rappresentazione delle costellazioni nello zodiaco circolare di Dendera*.

Turner A. 1987
A. Turner, *Early Scientific Instruments. Europe 1400-1800*, London 1987.

Turner A. 1994
A. Turner, *Mathematical Instruments in Antiquity and the Middle Ages: an introduction*, London 1994.

Turner A. 2007
A. Turner, *Catalogue of Sun-dials, Nocturnals and Related Instruments*, Firenze 2007.

Turner G.L'E. 1995
G.L'E. Turner, *The Florentine workshop of Giovan Battista Giusti, 1556 - c.1575*, "Nuncius", 10, fasc. 1 (1995), pp. 131-172.

Turner G.L'E. 2000
G. L'E. Turner, *Elizabethan Instrument Makers. The Origin of the London Trade in Precision Instrument Making*, Oxford 2000.

Turner G.L'E. 2003
G. L'E. Turner, *The Italian Hour Nocturnal*, "Annals of Science", LX, 2003, pp. 249-268.

Valerio 1987
V. Valerio, *Historiographic and numerical notes on the Atlante Farnese and ist celestial sphere*, "Der Globusfreund", 35-37, (1987), pp. 97-114.

Valerio 1995
V. Valerio, *Sui planisferi tolemaici: alcune questioni interpretative e prospettiche*, in *Esplorazioni geografiche e immagini del mondo nei secoli XV e XVI: atti Convegno, Messina, 14-15 ottobre 1993*, edited by S. Ballo Alagna, Messina 1995, pp. 63-82.

Valerio 2005
V. Valerio, *L'Atlante Farnese e la rappresentazione delle costellazioni*, in *Eureka! Il genio degli antichi*, edited by E. Lo Sardo, catalogue of the exhibition (Napoli, july 2005-january 2006), Napoli 2005.

Van Helden 1973
A. Van Helden, *The Accademia del Cimento and Saturn's rings*, "Physis", XV, (1973), pp. 237-259.

Van Helden 1974
A. Van Helden, *Saturn and his anses*, "Journal of the History of Astronomy", 5 (1974), pp. 105-121.

Van Helden 1977
A. Van Helden, *The Invention of the Telescope*, in "American philosophical society transactions", vol. 67, pt. 4 (1977).

Van Helden 1996
A. Van Helden, *Longitude and the Satellites of Jupiter*, in *The Quest for Longitude*, edited by W.J. Andrewes, Harvard 1996, pp. 86-100.

Van Helden 1999
A.Van Helden, *Catalogue of Early Telescopes*, Firenze 1999.

Van Helden 2004
A. Van Helden, *Huygens's ring, Cassini's division and Saturn's children*, Washington 2004.

Varisco 1993
D.M. Varisco, *Medieval Agriculture and Islamic Science: the Almanac of a Yemeni Sultan*, Seattle (WA) 1993.

Varrone 1930
Varrone, *La vita dei campi*, Villasanta (MI) 1930.

Venezia 2007
Sfere del Cielo, sfere della Terra: globi celesti e terrestri dal XVI al XX secolo, catalogue of the exhibition, (Venezia, september 2007-april 2008), edited by M. Milanesi and R. Schmidt, Milano 2007.

Venturi-d'Arcais 1917
A. Venturi, F. d'Arcais, *La fonte di una composizione del Guariento*, "L'Arte", XVII, (1917).

Venturi-d'Arcais 1965
A. Venturi, F. d'Arcais, *Guariento*, Venezia 1965.

Verdet 1992
J.P. Verdet, *L'astronomia dalle origini a Copernico*, in *Storia delle Scienze. Le scienze fisiche e astronomiche*, edited by W.R. Shea, Torino 1992, pp. 38-109.

Vernant 2001
J.P. Vernant, *Mito e pensiero presso i Greci: studi di psicologia storica*, Torino 2001, p. 205.

Vernet 1978
J. Vernet, *La cultura hispanoárabe en Oriente y Occidente*, Barcelona 1978.

Visconti 1835
P.E. Visconti, *Nota intorno un antico globo celeste scolpito in marmo porino conservato presso Monsignor G. de' Marchesi Zacchia, uditore della S. Rota Romana*, Roma 1835.

Visonà 1990
M. Visonà, *Carlo Marcellini Accademico "spiantato" nella cultura fiorentina tardo-barocca*, Pisa 1990.

Voelkel 2001
R. Voelkel, *The composition of Kepler's Astronomia Nova*, Princeton 2001.

Vyver 1971
O. Van de Vyver S.J., *Lunar maps of the 17th century*, Città del Vaticano 1971.

Wagman 2003
M. Wagman, *Lost Stars: Lost, Missing, and Troublesome Stars from the Catalogues of Johannes Bayer, Nicholas-Louis de Lacaille, John Flamsteed, and Sundry Others*, Granville 2003.

Wagner 1983
D.L. Wagner (edited by), *The Seven Liberal Arts in the Middle Ages*, Bloomington 1983.

Walker C. 1997
C. Walker (edited by), *L'astronomia prima del telescopio*, Bari 1997.

Walker D.P. 2000
D.P. Walker, *Spiritual and demonic magic from Ficino to Campanella*, Stroud 2000.

Warburg 1912-1917
A. Warburg, *Die astronomische Himmelsdarstellung im Gewölbe der alten Sakristei von San Lorenzo in Florenz*, "Mitteilungen des Kunsthistorischen Institutes in Florenz", II, (1912), pp. 34-36.

Ward Perkins-Claridge 1978
J. Ward Perkins, A. Claridge, *Pompeii AD 79*, New York 1978.

Warner 1979
D. J. Warner, *The Sky Explored: Celestial Cartography 1500-1800*, New York 1979.

Washington 1971
Dürer in America. His Graphic Work, edited by C.W. Talbot, G.F. Ravenel, J.A. Levenson, catalogue of the exhibition (Washington, april-july 1971), Washington 1971.

Washington 1991
Circa 1492. Art in the Age of Exploration, edited by J.A. Levenson, catalogue of the exhibition (Washington, october 1991-january 1992), New Haven 1992.

Wattemberg 1967
D. Wattemberg, *Peter Apianus und sein Astronomicum Caesareum*, Leipzig 1967.

Weill-Parot 2002
N. Weill-Parot, *Les images astrologiques au Moyen âge et à la Renaissance*, Paris 2002.

Weiss 1888
E. Weiss, *Albrecht Dürer's Geographische Astronomische und Astrologische Tafeln*, "Jahrbuch des Kunst Sammlungen", VII (1888), pp. 207-220.

Wellesz 1965
E. Wellesz, *An Islamic Book of Constellations*, Oxford 1965.

Werner-Schmeidler 1986
H. Werner, F. Schmeidler, *Synopsis der Nomenklatur der Fixsterne/Synopsis of the Nomenclature of the Fixed Stars*, Stuttgart 1986.

Westfall 1984
R.S. Westfall, *La rivoluzione scientifica nel XVII secolo*, Bologna 1984.

Westfall 1989
R.S. Westfall, *Newton*, edited by A. Serafini, Torino 1989.

Whitaker 1978
E. Whitaker, *Galileo's Lunar observations and the dating of the composition of Sidereus Nuncius*, "Journal of the History of Astronomy", 9 (1978), pp. 155-169.

Whitaker 1999
E. Withaker, *Mapping and naming the Moon. A history of Lunar cartography and nomenclature*, Cambridge (UK) 1999.

Whitfield 1995
P. Whitfield, *The Mapping of the Heavens*, London 1995.

Wiggerman 1992
F. Wiggerman, *Mythological Foundation of Nature*, in *Natural Phenomena. Their Meaning, Depiction and Description in the Ancient Near East*, edited by D.J.W. Meijer, Amsterdam 1992, pp. 279-304.

Willach 2008
R. Willach, *The Long Route to the Invention of the Telescope*, in "American philosophical society transactions", vol. 98 pt. 5 (2008).

Willemsen 1980
C.A. Willemsen, *L'enigma di Otranto*, Lecce 1980.

Willmoth 1997
Flamsteed Stars. New Perspective on the Life and Work of the First Astronomer Royal, 1646-1719, edited by F. Willmoth, Woodbridge 1997.

Wilson 1971
C. Wilson, *Doppelmayr, Johann Gabriel*, in *DSB*, edited by C.C. Gillispie, New York 1971, vol. IV, pp. 166-167.

Wind 1958
E. Wind, *I misteri pagani nel Rinascimento*, Milano 1971.

Winner 1957
M. Winner, *Die Quellen der Pictura-Allegorien in gemalten Bildergalerie des 17 Jahrhunderts zu Antwerpen*, Köln 1957.

Winter 2002
I.J. Winter, *Defining 'aesthetics' for Non-western Studies: the Case of Ancient Mesopotamia*, in *Art History, Aesthetics, Visual Studies, Clark Studies in the Visual Arts*, edited by M.A. Holly e K. Moxey, New Haven 2002, pp. 3-28.

Wolf 1902
C. Wolf, *Histoire de l'Observatoire de Paris, de sa fondation à 1793*, Paris 1902.

Woods 2004
C.E. Woods, *The Sun-God Tablet of Nabû-apla-iddina Revisited*, "Journal of Cuneiform Studies", 56 (2004), pp. 23-103.

Wright M.T. 1990
M.T. Wright, *Rational and Irrational Reconstruction: the London Sundial-Calendar and the Early History of Geared Mechanisms*, "History of Technology", 12 (1990), pp. 65-102.

Wright M.T. 2003
M.T. Wright, *In the Steps of the Master Mechanic*, in *Ancient Greece and the Modern World: 2nd World Congress, Ancient Olympia, 12-17 July 2002*, pp. 86-97.

Wright M.T. 2007
M.T. Wright, *The Antikythera Mechanism reconsidered*, "Interdisciplinary Science Reviews", 2007, vol. 32, no. 1 (2007), pp. 27-43.

Wright R.R. 1934
R.R. Wright, *The Book of Instruction in the Elements of Astrology by... al-Bîrûnî*, London 1934.

Yates 2006
F. Yates, *Giordano Bruno e la tradizione ermetica*, Bari 2006.

Yavetz 1998
I. Yavetz, "On the Homocentric Spheres of Eudoxus", *Archive for History of Exact Sciences*, 52 (1998), pp. 221-278.

Zava Boccazzi 1979
F. Zava Boccazzi, *Pittoni*, Venezia 1979.

Zinner 1956a
E. Zinner, *Deutsche und niederlandische astronomische Instrumente des 11.-18. Jahrhunderts*, Beck 1956.

Zinner 1956b
E. Zinner, *Deutsche und Niederländische astronomische Instrumente des 11.-18. Jahrhunderts*, München 1956.

Zucker 2008
A. Zucker, *La function de l'image dans l'astronomie grecque in Eratosthène. Un atlète du savoir*, Saint-Étienne 2008.